Python Programming on Win32

Python Programming on Win32

Mark Hammond and Andy Robinson

O'REILLY®

Beijing · Cambridge · Farnham · Köln · Paris · Sebastopol · Taipei · Tokyo

Python Programming on Win32
by Mark Hammond and Andy Robinson

Published by O'Reilly & Associates, Inc., 101 Morris Street, Sebastopol, CA 95472.

Editor: Robert Denn

Production Editor: Mary Anne Weeks Mayo

Cover Designer: Edie Freedman

Printing History:

> January 2000: First Edition.

Library of Congress Cataloging-in-Publication Data

Hammond, Mark (Mark J.)
    Python programming on Win 32/Mark Hammond and Andy Robinson.--1st ed.
      p. cm.
    ISBN 1-56592-621-8 (alk. paper)
      1. Python (Computer program language) 2. Microsoft Win 32. I. Robinson, Andy,
    1967- II. Title.

    QA76.73.P98 H36 2000
    005.265--dc21

                                                              99-085714

ISBN: 1-56592-621-8   [6/00]
[M]

Table of Contents

Preface

About This Book

This book is about using Python to get jobs done on Windows.

We hope by now you have heard of Python, the exciting object-oriented scripting language that is rapidly entering the programming mainstream. Although Python is perhaps better known on the Unix platform, it offers a superb degree of integration with the Windows environment. One of us, Mark Hammond, is responsible for many of Python's Windows extensions and has coauthored the Python COM support, both of which are major topics of this book. This book can thus be considered the definitive reference to date for Python on the Windows platform.

This is intended to be a practical book focused on tasks. It doesn't aim to teach Python programming, although we do provide a brief tutorial. Instead, it aims to cover:

- How Python works on Windows

- The key integration technologies supported by Python on Windows, such as the Win32 extensions, which let you call the Windows API, and the support for COM

- Examples in many topic areas showing what Python can do and how to put it to work

In the end, we hope you will have a clear idea of what Python can do and how to put it to work on real-world tasks.

Who Is This Book for?

We expect this book to be of interest to two groups of people:

Windows developers, administrators, and IT managers
You may be an experienced Windows developer using C++, Visual Basic, Delphi or other development tools, or you may be involved in managing information technology (IT) and need to make decisions as to the right tools for large projects. No doubt you hear about several new languages every year and meet zealots who insist that each is the ultimate development tool. You've perhaps heard a colleague talking about Python or read a few articles about it and are curious why people rave about it. By the end of this book, you should know!

Python converts from Unix
Python is one of the major products of the Open Source revolution (*http://opensource.org/*) and has a large following on Unix platforms. There are a large number of Python users within the Unix tradition who are forced, with varying degrees of resistance, to work in a Windows environment. We hope to open your eyes. Most of the things you do on Unix can be done on Windows, and Windows offers exciting programming possibilities.

Readers may vary considerably in their programming experience. We don't aim to teach the language systematically and assume you are familiar with other programming languages. Someone familiar with Visual Basic, for example, should be able to follow most of the book. However, some sections regarding Windows internals or C integration assume C or C++ familiarity.

We assume a fairly typical business-computing platform with Windows NT 4.0, Microsoft Office, access to the Internet or an internal TCP/IP network, and adequate memory to run smoothly. Python is equally happy on Windows 95 and 98, and we have tried to comment on the differences as they occur.

How the Book Is Organized

The book is broken into three parts. The first part is mainly introductory in nature and sets the framework for the other two sections. The second section focuses on building an advanced Windows application using Python. The main purpose of this application is to show some possibilities for your applications. The third section provides a Python on Windows cookbook.

Part I, *Introduction to Python*

This part covers the basics about the language and the platform and should be read by everyone not familiar with using Python on Windows.

Chapter 1, *What Is Python?*

This is a Python primer: what it's good for, who's using it for what, and where to get hold of it. If you want to brief your manager on Python, show her this chapter!

Chapter 2, *Python Language Review*

This chapter is a high-speed minitutorial; it should at least enable you to follow the code examples. We don't aim to teach Python from scratch, but instead point you to the right places for more detailed tutorials.

Chapter 3, *Python on Windows*

Here we cover how Python is set up on Windows and review some of the Windows-specific packages and extensions.

Chapter 4, *Integrated Development Environments for Python*

Chapter 4 covers PythonWin and IDLE, two integrated development environments for Python, each complete with syntax coloring, object browsers, and debuggers.

Chapter 5, *Introduction to COM*

Here we introduce Python's support for COM, Microsoft's key integration technology.

Part II, *Building an Advanced Python Application*

This part is an in-depth exploration of what you can do with a Python application on Windows. "Advanced" refers to the capabilities Python gives to your programs, not to the level of programming difficulty. Although the focus is on COM, it brings many features of the language together. In some cases, we use features not fully explained until later chapters; we want to make you say "Wow, so you *can* do that," rather than "Wow, so *that's* how you do it": we save that revelation for the last section. The project is to develop an extensible accounting toolkit in Python. Part II, like Part I, is intended to be read straight through.

Chapter 6, *A Financial Modeling Toolkit in Python*

This chapter explains the business requirements of our application and develops a Python class library that encapsulates the basic rules followed by accounting systems. For people new to Python, this provides a more in-depth set of examples of object-oriented programming with Python.

Chapter 7, *Building a GUI with COM*

Here we show how to build a COM server that exposes our Python "engine" to other applications, building a fairly standard user interface in Visual Basic on top of our application. In the process, we cover how to move data of all types back and forth between Python and other languages using COM.

Chapter 8, *Adding a Macro Language*

Next we show how to expose the Python interpreter to end users. Our application allows users to work with a command prompt, write scripts, and even define new event handlers and graphical views, thereby making the application extensible. Python makes this capability, normally found only in large commercial applications, child's play.

Chapter 9, *Integration with Excel*

This chapter shows the other side of the coin: using Python as a COM object to acquire data from and send data to Excel.

Chapter 10, *Printed Output*

Here we cover a range of techniques for printing and for producing reports in general, including direct printer control, automating Microsoft Word, and direct generation of financial reports in PDF format.

Chapter 11, *Distributing Our Application*

Finally, we show how COM makes it extremely easy to run the Python engine on one machine and the client interface on another.

Part III, *Python on Windows Cookbook*

Each chapter in this section may be taken in isolation and covers one particular area of interest in detail. The focus is task-based, and we look at various technologies and libraries in each section, concentrating on how to get jobs done with Python. These chapters naturally vary in their technical depth and appeal, but we hope that there will be plenty of interest for everyone.

Chapter 12, *Advanced Python and COM*

This is the definitive reference on Python's support for COM.

Chapter 13, *Databases*

This chapter shows how to connect to databases from Python and illustrates how to manipulate data.

Chapter 14, *Working with Email*

Here we take a look at some common techniques for dealing with email on Windows.

Chapter 15, *Using the Basic Internet Protocols*

This is a brief discussion on how to use common Internet protocols from Python on Windows.

Chapter 16, *Windows NT Administration*

In this chapter, we discuss the language extensions for working with users, groups, drives, shares, servers, and so forth.

Chapter 17, *Processes and Files*
> This chapter presents Python's facilities for working with processes and files, both in a portable and a Windows-specific way.

Chapter 18, *Windows NT Services*
> Here we explore Python's thorough support for Windows NT services.

Chapter 19, *Communications*
> This chapter discusses serial I/O, remote access services, and TCP/IP sockets.

Chapter 20, *GUI Development*
> Here we present three toolkits: PythonWin, Tkinter, and wxPython.

Chapter 21, *Active Scripting*
> This chapter presents a complete guide to Python's extensions to support Microsoft's Active Scripting technology.

Chapter 22, *Extending and Embedding with Visual C++ and Delphi*
> As the name implies, this chapter explains how you can extend Python's capabilities using other languages.

Part IV, *Appendixes*

Appendix A, *Key Python Modules and Functions*
> This appendix is a short reference to the most important modules and functions in Python.

Appendix B, *Win32 Extensions Reference*
> This appendix is a brief reference to the SDK functions and objects presented in this book.

Appendix C, *The Python Database API Version 2.0*
> This appendix is a reproduction of the specification.

Appendix D, *Threads*
> This appendix is limited to Windows-specific threading issues.

About the Examples

All examples in this book have been tested with Python 1.5.2, but should work as later versions of Python are released.

Many examples are so small they can be typed interactively into the Python interpreter. In these cases, the examples always show the Python prompts and responses:

```
>>> print "This is interactive source code"
This is interactive source code
>>>
```

All example code presented as source files are available for download from the authors' web page, *http://starship.python.net/crew/mhammond/ppw32/*. The source code is available as a ZIP file organized by chapter. See the web page and the *README.TXT* file in the ZIP file for more details.

Font Conventions Used in This Book

This book uses the following typographical conventions:

Italic

    Introduces new terms and indicates URLS, variables or user-defined files and directories, programs, file extensions, filenames, hostnames, directory or folder names, and UNC pathnames.

`Constant width`

    Indicates Python language elements, command-line computer output, code examples, commands, keywords, functions, modules, classes, interfaces, instances, collections, objects, properties, methods, packages, and constants.

`Constant width italic`

    Indicates placeholder names in syntax specifications and registry keys.

 The owl icon designates a note, which is an important aside to the nearby text.

 The turkey icon designates a warning relating to the nearby text.

How to Contact Us

Please address comments and questions concerning this book to the publisher:

O'Reilly & Associates
101 Morris Street
Sebastopol, CA 95472
1-800-998-9938 (in United States or Canada)
1-707-829-0515 (international or local)
1-707-829-0104 (fax)

You can also send us messages electronically. To be put on the mailing list or request a catalog, send email to *info@oreilly.com.*

To ask technical questions or comment on the book, send email to *bookques-tions@oreilly.com.*

We have a web site for the book, where we list errata and any plans for future editions. You can find it at *http://www.oreilly.com/catalog/pythonwin32/.*

For more information about this book and others, see the O'Reilly web site *http://www.oreilly.com.*

Acknowledgments

Although we were warned about what it takes to write a book like this, we were still not prepared! Many people contributed to this book and assisted with the enormous workload it involved.

The support of Guido van Rossum, the author of the Python language, for the Windows version of Python has enabled it to develop into a serious contender for most Windows development work. Guido somehow manages to balance the opposing forces of maintaining platform independence and allowing Python to take advantage of the platform's unique features.

The wonderful Python community also has itself to thank for allowing this book to come to fruition. The Python newsgroup seems to be one of the final bastions of Usenet where spams are ignored, newbies are treated kindly, and trolls are either ignored or quickly turned into a serious and on-topic discussion. Many smart and friendly people hang out on the newsgroup, and it's one of the more esoteric reasons many people find using the language enjoyable.

The following people have provided invaluable help, whether with full reviews, in-depth knowledge of particular areas, or informal feedback: Guido van Rossum, Gordon McMillan, Greg Stein, Marc-André Lemburg, Christian Tismer, Gary Herron, Robin Dunn, Mike Da Silva, Richard Kennedy, and Damien Watkins. Many others too numerous to mention, have played a part in shaping the book, whether in direct correspondence with us or in developing and working with the packages in this book.

At O'Reilly, we'd like to thank Robert Denn, Steven Abrams, and probably a whole bunch of other people we have never heard of.

Most important of all, Mark and Andy both wish to thank their families for their support and incredible patience, and they promise not to do this again any time soon.

I

Introduction to Python

I

1

What Is Python?

Python is an interpreted, interactive, object-oriented programming language, first developed in 1990 by Guido van Rossum. By the end of 1998, it had grown to an estimated user base of 300,000, and it's beginning to attract wide attention in the industry.

Python doesn't offer revolutionary new features. Rather, it combines many of the best design principles and ideas from many different programming languages. It's simple and powerful. More than any other language, it gets out of the way so that you can think about the problem, not the language. Programming in Python just feels right.

Language Features

Here are some of Python's distinctive features:

Interpreted to bytecodes

> Python code lives in text files ending in *.py*. The program compiles the text files to a machine-independent set of *bytecodes* in a way similar to Java, which are usually saved in files ending in *.pyc*; these can then later be imported and run quickly. The source is recompiled only when necessary. Python's speed is of a similar order of magnitude to Java or Perl.

Very high level

> All languages support basic types such as strings, integers, and floating-point numbers. Python has higher-level built-in types such as lists and dictionaries, and high-level operations to work on them. For example, you can load a file into a string with one line and split it into chunks based on a delimiter with another line. This means writing less code. It also means that the speed is better than you might suppose: the built-in functions have been written in C and

extensively optimized by a lot of smart people, and are faster than C or C++ code you might write yourself.

Interactive mode

You can use Python interactively, entering expressions one line at a time. This mode allows you to try ideas quickly and cheaply, testing each function or method as you write it. This style of programming encourages experimentation and ideas. As with Smalltalk (with which it has much in common), the interactive mode is perhaps the major reason your productivity will increase with Python.

The interpreter is always available

Every Python program has the ability to compile and execute text files while running; there is no distinction between the runtime and development environments. This makes it a great macro language for other programs.

Clean syntax

The syntax is straightforward and obvious, and there are no cryptic special characters to learn. Indentation delimits blocks, so the visual structure of a chunk of code mirrors its logical structure; it's easy to read and learn. Eric Raymond, one of the leaders of the Open Source movement, now recommends Python as the ideal first language to learn. (See his essay, "How to Become a Hacker," located at *http://www.tuxedo.org/~esr/faqs/hacker-howto.html*.)

Advanced language features

Python offers all the features expected in a modern programming language: object-oriented programming with multiple inheritance, exception handling, overloading of common operators, default arguments, namespaces, and packages.

Introspection

Python can introspect to an uncanny degree. You can ask an object what attributes it has at runtime and give it new ones. Hooks are provided to let you control how functions are applied and what to, and when attributes are set and fetched. Magic Methods let you define the meaning of operators, so that you can define the + operation for a matrix class or trap what happens when someone accesses an item in a list. Features from other languages can often be easily implemented in Python itself.

Platform independence

Python is written in ANSI C and is available for a wide range of platforms including Windows, Unix, and Macintosh. The core language and standard libraries are identical on all platforms, although each platform offers its own dedicated extensions.

Extensible

> Python is written in C in a modular architecture. It can be extended easily to add new features or APIs. If you want a new feature, you can add it and find plenty of help to do so.

Extensive libraries

> The Python library, included in the standard installation, includes over 200 modules, covering everything from operating-system functions and data structures to full-blown web servers. The main Python web site provides a comprehensive index to the many Python projects and third-party libraries. Whatever your problem domain, you will probably find someone else working on it and a good base of code to start with.

Support

> Python has a large and enthusiastic user community; it's currently doubling in size every two years. So far, there are four books by O'Reilly alone and several by other publishers, eight annual Python conferences have been held, the *comp.lang.python* newsgroup on Usenet attracts well over 100 posts a day, and there are a growing number of consultants and small firms offering commercial support.

Python as an Integration Tool

Python can integrate a variety of disparate systems; you may hear it referred to as a *glue language,* because it's a powerful way to glue systems together. We have broken the basic integration technologies available on Windows into five groups: files, DLLs, COM, networking, and distributed objects. We'll take a quick look at the Python features that support each one.

Working with Files

The most fundamental technique for making systems talk is working with files. They are at the foundation of every operating system, and huge and reliable systems can be built and maintained by batch-processing files. Every programming language can work with files, but some make it easier than others. Here are some key features:

- Python can read a file into a string (or read a multiline text file into a list of strings) in one line. Strings have no limitations on what they can hold: null bytes and non-ASCII encodings are fine.

- Python can capture and redirect its own standard input and output; subroutines that print to standard output can thus be diverted to different destinations.

- It provides a platform-independent API for working with filenames and paths, selecting multiple files, and even recursing through directory trees.

- For binary files, Python can read and write arrays of uniform types.

- A variety of text-parsing tools are available, ranging from string splitting and joining operations and a pattern-matching language, up to complete data-driven parsers. The key parts of these are written in C, allowing Python text-processing programs to run as fast as fully compiled languages.

- When generating output, Python allows you to create multiline templates with formatting codes and perform text substitutions to them from a set of keys and values. In essence, you can do a mailmerge in one line at incredibly high speeds.

Chapter 17, *Processes and Files*, provides a comprehensive introduction to these features.

Working with DLLs and C Programs

Windows uses dynamic link libraries extensively. DLLs allow collections of functions, usually written in C or C++, to be stored in one file and loaded dynamically by many different programs. DLLs influence everything that happens on Windows; indeed, the Windows API is a collection of such DLLs.

Python is written in ANSI C, and one of its original design goals was to be easy to extend and embed at the C level. Most of its functionality lives in a DLL, so that other programs can import Python at runtime and start using it to execute and evaluate expressions. Python extension modules can also be written in C, C++, or Delphi to add new capabilities to the language that can be imported at runtime.

The Win32 extensions for Python, which we cover throughout this book, are a collection of such libraries that expose much of the Windows API to Python.

The basic Python distribution includes a manual called *Extending and Embedding the Python Interpreter*, which describes the process in detail. Chapter 22, *Extending and Embedding with Visual C++ and Delphi*, shows you how to work with Python at this level on Windows.

COM

The Component Object Model (COM) is Microsoft's newest integration technology and pervades Windows 95, 98, NT, and 2000. The DLL lets you call functions someone else has written; COM lets you talk to objects someone else has written. They don't even have to be on the same computer!

Windows provides a host of API calls to get things done, but using the calls generally requires C programming expertise, and they have a tortuous syntax. COM provides alternative, easier-to-use interfaces to a wide range of operating-system services, and it lets applications expose and share their functionality as well. COM is now mature, stable, and as fast as using DLLs, but much easier to use, and so opens up many new possibilities. Want a spreadsheet and chart within your application? Borrow the ones in Excel. To a programmer with a COM-enabled language (and most of them are by now), Windows feels like a sea of objects, each with its own capabilities, standing by and waiting to help you get your job done.

Python's support for COM is superb and is the thrust for a large portion of this book.

Networking

The fourth integration technology we'll talk about is the network. Most of the world's networks now run on TCP/IP, the Internet protocol. There is a standard programming API to TCP/IP, the *sockets* interface, which is available at the C level on Windows and almost every other operating system. Python exposes the sockets API and allows you to directly write network applications and protocols. We cover sockets in Chapter 19, *Communications*.

You may not want to work with sockets directly, but you will certainly have use for the higher-level protocols built on top of it, such as Telnet, FTP, and HTTP. Python's standard library provides modules that implement these protocols, allowing you to automate FTP sessions or retrieval of data from email servers and the Web. It even includes ready-made web servers for you to customize. Chapter 14, *Working with Email*, and Chapter 15, *Using the Basic Internet Protocols*, cover these standard library features.

Distributed Objects

The most sophisticated level of integration yet seen in computing is the field of *distributed objects*: essentially, letting objects on different machines (and written in different languages) talk to each other. Many large corporations are moving from two-tier applications with databases and GUIs to three-tier applications that have a layer of *business objects* in the middle. These objects offer a higher level of abstraction than the database row and can represent tangible things in the business such as a customer or an invoice. The two main contenders in this arena are COM, which is a Windows-only solution and Common Object Request Broker Architecture (CORBA), which is multiplatform. Python is used extensively with both. Our focus is on COM, and we show how to build a distributed Python application in Chapter 11, *Distributing Our Application*. Building a distributed application is absurdly easy; COM does all the work, and it's a matter of configuring the machine correctly.

Python's support for all five technologies and the fact that it runs on many different operating systems are what makes it a superb integration tool. We believe that Python can be used to acquire data easily from anything, anywhere.

Where Python Fits in the Development Picture

You are of course free to fall in love with Python, switch over to it for all your development needs, and hang out extolling its virtues on Usenet in the small hours of the morning: you'll find good company, possibly including the authors. However, if you have so far escaped conversion, we have tried to identify the areas where Python fits into a corporate computing environment. Home users are a more varied bunch, but what follows should give you an idea of what the language is good for.

A standard corporate computing environment these days involves Windows NT 4.0 and Microsoft Office on the desktop; networks using TCP/IP; developers building systems tools and business objects in C and C++; GUI development in Visual Basic; and relational databases such as Oracle, Sybase, and SQL Server. It may involve legacy systems predating relational databases and Unix boxes in the back office running databases and network services. It undoubtedly involves a dozen applications bought or developed over time that need to be kept talking to each other as things evolve. More sophisticated environments are moving from two- to three-tier architectures and building distributed object systems with COM and CORBA, with libraries of C++ business objects in between the database and the GUI.

Maintaining the diversity of skills necessary to support such an environment is a challenge, and IT managers won't allow a new development tool unless it offers clear business benefits. Arguments that Language X is twice as productive as Language Y just don't suffice and are impossible to prove. The following areas are ones in which you may not be well served at present, and in which Python can supply a missing piece of the puzzle:

A macro language

If we had to pick one killer feature, this would be it. You can use Python to add a macro language or scripting capability to existing applications, and it's simple enough for user-level scripting with a minimum of training. If a useful application starts growing more and more features, needing larger and larger configuration files and more options screens and GUIs to do its job, it may be time to add a macro language. All those configuration screens can be replaced with short scripts that do exactly what they say and can be adapted easily. The problem is that most people don't have a clue where to start. Developing a new language is often thought of as a task for the big boys in Redmond and no one else. You might be vaguely aware that Visio Corporation licensed Visual Basic for Applications, but this choice is undoubtedly going to (a) be expensive, and (b) require enormous resources and levels of skill in making your applications work just like Microsoft Office. Python is an off-the-shelf macro language you can plug in to your existing tools at a variety of levels. In Part II we'll show you how easy it is and how far it can take you.

A rapid prototyping tool for object models and algorithms

Designing software in C++ is expensive and time-consuming, although superb results can be achieved. As a consequence, many companies try to design object models using data-modeling languages and graphical tools, or at least by writing and criticizing design documents before allowing their developers to start writing code. But these tools don't run, and they can't tell you much. You can create objects in Python with fewer lines of code and fewer hours than any other language we know, and there is full support for inheritance (single and multiple), encapsulation, and polymorphism. A popular approach is to prototype a program in Python until you're sure the design is right, and only then move to C++. An even more popular approach is to profile the Python application and rewrite just the speed-critical parts in C++. There is, however, a risk that the prototype will work so well you may end up using Python in a production environment!

A testing tool

New programs and code libraries need testing. Experienced developers know that building a test suite for a new function or program saves them time and grief. These test suites are often regarded as disposable and thus a low-risk place to introduce and start learning about Python. If a program works with files as its input and output, Python scripts can generate input, execute the program, look at the output, and analyze it. If the data is the issue, you can write disposable scripts to check identities in the data. If you are building a general-purpose C++ component or library, it's quite likely that only a small proportion of its functionality will be used in its early days, and bugs could lurk for a long time. By exposing the component or library to Python, you can quickly write test scripts to exercise functionality and prove it works correctly, then rerun the scripts every time the C++ source changes. We'll show you how later on.

Data cleaning and transformation

You may need to move data from an old to a new database, refreshing daily for months during a changeover, or build interfaces to let data flow between incompatible systems. This can be a tedious and error-prone process when done by hand, and you always miss something and have to redo it later.

Python's native support for lists and dictionaries makes complex data transformations easy, and the interactive mode lets programmers view the data at each stage in the process. Scripts can be written to transform data from source to destination and run as often as needed until they do the job right.

Python as glue

Incompatible systems often need to be tied together, and processes need to be automated. Python supports all the key technologies for integration; it's equally happy working with files, network protocols, DLLs, and COM objects, and it offers extensive libraries to help you get at almost any kind of data. It's well suited to controlling other packages, doing system-administration tasks, and controlling the flow of data between other systems.

Case Studies of Python Deployment

Throughout this book we will talk about cases where Python has solved problems in the real world. Both of us use Python in our daily work, and we will present a couple of examples of how we are personally using Python to solve real-world problems.

A Japanese Python?

Andy is currently working for a global investment company that is internationalizing its core applications to work with Far Eastern markets. The company's client platform is Windows, and core data is stored on Sybase servers and AS400 mini-computers; data flows back and forth among all three platforms continually. All these systems represent Japanese characters in totally different ways and work with different character sets. It was necessary not only to develop a library to convert between these encodings, but also to prove that it worked with 100% effectiveness for all the data that might be encountered in future years. This was not an easy task, as the size of the character set varied from one platform to another.

The first stage was to code the conversions in Python, based on published algorithms and lookup tables. The interactive prompt lets you look at the input and output strings early on and get all the details right working with single, short strings. I then developed classes to represent character sets and character maps and fed in the published government character sets—easy to do with Python's lists and dictionaries. I found subtle holes in published information and was able to correct for them. Having done this, I was able to prove that round-trip conversion was possible in many cases and to identify the characters that would not survive a round trip in others.

The company's cross-platform C++ guru then wrote a DLL to carry out string translations at high speed. Having a Python prototype allowed me to test the output early and compare it with the prototype. Python also generated and inspected test data sets with every valid character, something that would have taken months by hand. A Python wrapper was written around the DLL, and I wrote scripts to perform heavy-duty tests on it, feeding large customer databases through all possible conversions and back to the start. Naturally the tests uncovered bugs, but I found them in two days rather than in months.

The DLL was then put to work converting large amounts of report data from mainframe to PC formats. A Python program called the DLL to perform translations of individual strings; it scanned for files, decided what to do with them based on the names, broke them up, converted them a field at a time, and managed FTP sessions to send the data on to a destination database server. It also generated a web page for each file translated, displaying its contents in an easy-to-read table along with the results of basic integrity checks. This enabled users on two continents to test the data daily. When the data and algorithms were fully tested and known to be in their final shape, a fairly junior developer with six month's experience wrote the eventual C++ program in less than a week.

There's a Python on the Scoreboard!

A number of large sports stadiums in Australia (including the two largest, with 100,000-person capacities) run custom scoreboard-control software during all matches. The software keeps and displays the score for the games (including personal player information) and displays other messages and advertising during matches. The information is relayed to huge video scoreboards, as well as smaller strip scoreboards located around the ground and locally to the scorers' PC using HTML.

The system runs on Windows NT computers and needs to talk to a variety of custom software and hardware, including a custom input device for score keeping and custom hardware to control the video and strip scoreboards. The system also needs to read data during the game from an external database that provides detailed game statistics for each player.

The scoreboard software is written in C++ and Python. The C++ components of the system are responsible for keeping the match score and maintaining the key score database. All scoreboard output functionality is written in Python and exposes Python as a macro language.

Each output device (e.g., the video screen, strip scoreboard, or HTML file) has a particular "language" that controls the output. HTML, for example, uses <TAGS>, while the video scoreboard uses a formatting language somewhat similar to PostScript. A common thread is that all output formats are text-based.

A scheme has been devised that allows the scoreboard operator to embed Python code in the various layout formats. As the format is displayed, the Python code is executed to substitute the actual score. For example, the scoreboard operator may design a HTML page with code similar to:

```
<P>The player name is <I><%= player.Name %></I>
```

Anything within the `<% ...%>` tag is considered Python code, and the value substituted at runtime. Thus, this single HTML layout can display the information for any player in the game.

The nature of Python has allowed it to provide features that would not be possible using other languages. One such feature is that the scoreboard operator is free to create new database fields for a player using Microsoft Access and use them in the scoreboard layouts immediately using `player.FieldName` syntax; thus the object model exposed to the user is actually partially controlled by the user. The use of Python also allows arbitrary code to be executed to control the formatting. For example, the scoreboard operator may use the following HTML to display the list of players in the home team:

```
<P>Team <% = home.Name %>
<% for player in home.Players: %>
<P><%= player.Name %>
<% #end %>
```

These options have resulted in a situation programmers strive for, but see all too rarely: a system with enough flexibility to let users do things with your software you'd never have dreamt of.

Other Python Sightings in the Wild

To further dispel any impressions that Python is new, immature, or unsuited to critical applications, we've included a small selection of projects and organizations using Python in the real world. These have been culled from a much longer list on the main Python web site, *http://www.python.org/*:

- NASA's Johnson Space Center uses Python as the scripting language for its Integrated Planning System.

- UltraSeek Server, Infoseek's commercial web search engine, is implemented as a Python application, with some C extensions to provide primitive operations for fast indexing and searching. The core product involves 11,000 lines of Python, and the user interface consists of 17,000 lines of Python-scripted HTML templates.

- The Red Hat Commercial Linux distributions use Python for their installation procedures.

- Caligari Corporation's 3D modeling and animation package, trueSpace 4, uses Python as a scripting language. Users can create custom modeling and animation effects, write interactive applications, and develop game prototypes entirely inside trueSpace 4. We'll show you how to do something similar for your own applications in Part II.

- IBM's East Fishkill factory uses Python to control material entry, exit, and data collection for an entire semiconductor plant.

- Scientists in the Theoretical Physics department of Los Alamos National Laboratory are using Python to control large-scale physics computations on massively parallel supercomputers, high-end servers, and clusters. Python plays a central role in controlling simulations, performing data analysis, and visualization.

- SMHI, the Swedish civilian weather, hydrological, and oceanographic organization, uses Python extensively to acquire data, analyze it, and present it to outside interests such as the media. They are developing a Python-based Radar Analysis and Visualization Environment to use with the national network of weather radars.

The Python Community

Let's take a quick tour around the Python community and view some of the available support resources. The home page for the language is at *www.python.org*. The site is hosted by the Corporation for National Research Initiatives (CNRI) of Reston, Virginia, USA. CNRI employs Guido van Rossum, the inventor of Python, and a number of other Python figures. As shown in Figure 1-1, everything is a click or two away.

The Python newsgroup on Usenet, *comp.lang.python*, is another good place to start. It attracts over 100 posts per day, with most of the world's Python experts listening in, and has a high signal-to-noise ratio. People are generally helpful towards newcomers, although as with all newsgroups, you are expected to make at least a token effort to find your own answers before asking for help.

The Python Software Activity (*http://www.python.org/psa/*) is a nonprofit organization that helps to coordinate and promote Python. The PSA operates web, FTP, and email services, organizes conferences, and engages in other activities that benefit the Python user community. Membership costs $50 per year for individuals, $25 for students, and $500 for organizations. Benefits include a mailing list for members, early previews of new releases, and conference discounts.

PSA members also get an account on Starship. *http://starship.python.net* is a web site devoted to promoting Python; there are currently over 200 members, many of

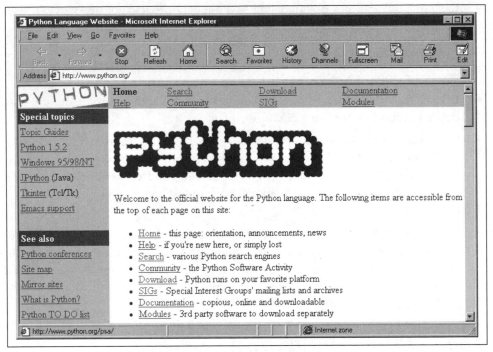

Figure 1-1. Python's home page at www.python.org

whom keep Python packages they have written on the site (including one of the authors).

The Python web site hosts a number of special interest groups (SIGs) devoted to particular topics such as databases or image processing. These are created with a fixed lifetime and charter, such as the creation of a standard Database API. They each have a home page with useful links, a mailing list, and an archive to which anyone can subscribe. Current SIGs include Development of a C++ binding, Databases, Distribution Utilities, Distributed Objects, Documentation, Image Processing, Matrix Manipulation, Plotting and Graphing, Apple Macintosh, String Processing, the Python Type System, and XML Processing.

There is also a specific page covering Windows-related resources at *http://www. python.org/windows/*.

Installation and Setup

Now it's time to download and install Python, if you have not already done so. Point your web browser at *http://www.python.org/* and click on the links to Download, then to Windows 95/98/NT, shown in Figure 1-2 (or follow the link from the

Windows resources page). At the time of writing, the full URL of the download page for Windows is *http://www.python.org/download/download_windows.html*.

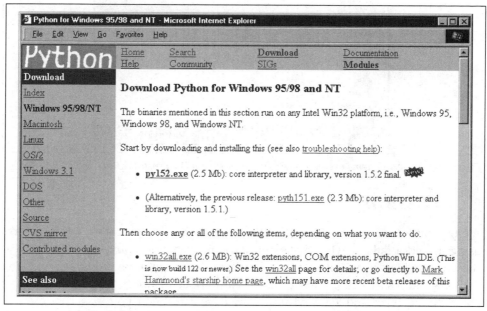

Figure 1-2. Windows download page

You need to download and install two files, both of which are standard Windows installation programs. First download and install the latest stable build of Python, *py152.exe* in Figure 1-2, then download and install the Python for Windows Extensions package, *win32all.exe* in the figure.

That's all there is to it. On your Start menu, there should now be a program group named *Python 1.X*, containing a number of items. Figure 1-3 shows the present program group, though more may be added in the future.

To verify the installation, click on the PythonWin icon. A Windows application should start up and display an input prompt. Enter 2 + 2 and press Enter; you should be rewarded by a 4. Python and PythonWin are now successfully installed. In the next few chapters, we'll show you what to do with them.

At this point, it's well worth clicking on Python Manuals and browsing around. The manuals are stored in HTML format and are now installed on your hard disk. They include a tutorial and a complete library reference.

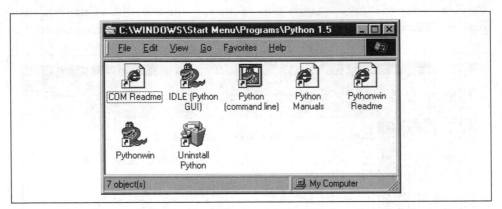

Figure 1-3. Program items created by Python and PythonWin installation

Conclusion

We have attempted a whistle-stop tour of what Python is, what it's good for, who's using it, and a little of what makes up the online Python community. We've also shown you how to install it with the standard configuration. Although we sing Python's praises, the best way to really learn about Python is to install and try it out. Sit back, relax, and learn what this language can do for you.

2

Python Language Review

This book isn't a Python tutorial. We feel that Python is a straightforward language, and if you have any programming experience, you should be able to follow the examples in the book and understand them. For readers new to Python, this chapter provides a brief introduction; others can safely skip it.

A Crash Course

Python offers an interactive mode that lets you evaluate an expression at a time. This is an excellent way to learn the language. We will step rapidly through the main features of the language in interactive mode. We won't provide detailed explanations, since most features are remarkably clear and obvious anyway.

Either go to an MS-DOS prompt, or (if you've already installed it) start PythonWin. You should see something like this:

```
Pythonwin 1.5.2b2 (#0, Feb 16 1999, 17:09:09) [MSC 32 bit (Intel)] on win32
Copyright 1991-1995 Stichting Mathematisch Centrum, Amsterdam
Portions Copyright 1994-1998 Mark Hammond (MHammond@skippinet.com.au)
>>>
```

You can type in simple expressions, which are evaluated for you:

```
>>> 2+2
4
```

Numbers, Strings, and Variables

You can assign to variables with =. There is no separate declaration required before you assign a variable:

```
>>> x=3
>>> x
```

```
3
>>> y=x*2
>>> y
6
>>>
```

Python supports all standard arithmetic operators. Note that the division operator (
/) yields different results on integer and floating-point types:

```
>>> 22 / 7
3
>>> 22.0 / 7.0
3.14285714286
>>>
```

Scientists and mathematicians will be pleased to hear that complex numbers are
fully supported using the letter *j*:

```
>>> (3 + 1j) * (3 - 1j)
(10+0j)
>>>
```

Strings can be wrapped in either double or single quotes. They can be concate-
nated with the + operator and repeated with the * operator. You can also access
individual characters by their position:

```
>>> greeting = 'hello'
>>> epithet = 'stranger'
>>> greeting + ", " + epithet
'hello, stranger'
>>> "spam" * 10
'spamspamspamspamspamspamspamspamspamspam'
>>>
```

Lists and Tuples

Much of Python's power comes from its support for lists and its compact syntax
for manipulating them. Lists are wrapped in square brackets and can contain any
Python objects. You can also insert and delete items in a list and even use negative positions to access the end of the list without knowing its length:

```
>>> mylunch = ['spam','eggs', 'guinness','raspberries','wafer-thin mint']
>>> mylunch[0]
'spam'
>>> mylunch[1:3], mylunch[-1]
(['eggs', 'guinness'], 'wafer-thin mint')
>>>
```

When you enter two results separated by a comma on the same line, you get two
expressions, but enclosed in parentheses. Parentheses indicate a *tuple*, which is
similar to a list but can't be modified once created:

```
>>> mylunch[2] = 'tea'
>>> mylunch
```

```
['spam', 'eggs', 'tea', 'raspberries', 'wafer-thin mint']
>>> meal_deal = ('burger','fries','coke')    # a tuple
>>> meal_deal[1] = 'onion rings'
Traceback (innermost last):
  File "<interactive input>", line 1, in ?
TypeError: object doesn't support item assignment
>>>
```

The last example also shows our first error message. When errors occur, you see a *traceback* stating which functions were active and the line of the source file that caused the error, as well as the error type and message on the last line. In this case, you type commands interactively rather than running a source file, so you don't see a helpful filename or line number.

Control Structures

The for loop actually operates over lists, not numbers:

```
>>> for item in mylunch:
...     print item
...
spam
eggs
tea
raspberries
wafer-thin mint
>>>
```

There are several things to note at this point. First, after typing the colon and pressing the Return key, Python indents the next line, and you don't have to type anything to end the for loop. Python actually uses indentation for syntax, saving typing and making the language highly readable: the layout of code on the page indicates its structure. A second point is that the >>> prompt changes to ... for subsequent lines. This indicates that Python knows you are entering a multiline statement at the command prompt.

Another common structure is the while loop:

```
>>> x = 2
>>> while x < 50:
...     x = x * 2
...     print x
...
4
8
16
32
64
>>>
```

The `if` structure is also present; the `else` clause is optional:

```
>>> if 'chocolate' in mylunch:
...     print "that's not allowed"
... else:
...     print "enjoy your meal"
...
enjoy your meal
>>>
```

You can also have a number of intermediate `elif` clauses, short for else-if. These allow something like the `switch` or `case` statements in other languages:

```
>>> salary = 20000
>>> if salary < 4000:
...     tax_rate = 0
... elif salary < 29000:
...     tax_rate = 0.25
... elif salary < 100000:
...     tax_rate = 0.4
... else:
...     emigrate()      # that's a function call
...
>>>
```

Functions

Functions are defined by the `def` statement and use `return` to exit immediately from the function and return a value. You can return more than one value by using a tuple or return no value at all:

```
>>> def double(x):
...     return x * 2
...
>>> double(2)
4
>>> def first_and_last(aList):
...     return (aList[0], aList[-1])
...
>>> first_and_last(range(5))
(0, 4)
>>> def sayHello():
...     print 'hello'
...
>>> sayHello()
hello
>>>
```

Functions may have default arguments that allow them to be called in certain ways or allow you to initialize variables:

```
>>> def makeCoffee(size, milk=None, sugar=None):
...     order = 'one ' + size + ' coffee'
...     if milk and sugar:
```

```
...                 order = order + ' with milk and sugar'
...         elif milk:
...                 order = order + ' with milk'
...         elif sugar:
...                 order = order + ' with sugar'
...         else:
...                 pass  # pass means 'do nothing'
...         return order
...
>>> makeCoffee('large')
'one large coffee'
>>> makeCoffee('large', 1)
'one large coffee with milk'
>>> makeCoffee('large', milk=0, sugar=1)
'one large coffee with sugar'
>>>
```

Note that you can name the arguments and that both 0 and the special variable **None** are treated as false.

Dictionaries

Python also offers a dictionary type. This is based on a hash table, and the lookup time is almost constant, irrespective of size. Dictionaries are enclosed in braces ({}), and the keys and values are displayed separated by a colon. You can access and set their elements with a notation similar to list indexes:

```
>>> fur_colors = {}
>>> fur_colors['Tinky-Winky'] = 'purple'
>>> fur_colors['Dipsy'] = 'green'
>>> fur_colors['LaLa'] = 'yellow'
>>> fur_colors
{'Tinky-Winky': 'purple', 'Dipsy': 'green', 'LaLa': 'yellow'}
>>> fur_colors['LaLa']
'yellow'
>>>
```

Dictionaries have no natural order. They support some useful methods of searching, e.g., by keys, values, and whether or not a certain key is present:

```
>>> fur_colors.keys()
['Tinky-Winky', 'Dipsy', 'LaLa']
>>> fur_colors.values()
['purple', 'green', 'yellow']
>>> fur_colors.items()     # converts to a list of tuples
[('Tinky-Winky', 'purple'), ('Dipsy', 'green'), ('LaLa', 'yellow')]
>>> len(fur_colors)
3
>>> fur_colors.has_key('Po')
0
>>>
```

Lists and dictionaries together allow you to build more powerful data structures, such as sets or even database indexes, in few lines of code. The values in a dictionary can be anything, while the keys can be strings, numbers, or tuples of other values. In Chapter 6, *A Financial Modeling Toolkit in Python,* we show how to construct some extremely useful utilities from dictionaries.

Modules

Python code is organized into *modules.* A module must be loaded into memory using the `import` statement. Some modules are built into Python and always available; others are stored in external files. Modules can also be written either in C (in which case they are compiled as a special kind of DLL) or in Python (in which case they are saved in text files ending in *.py*). As far as the user is concerned, they are all used the same way:

```
>>> import math
>>> math.sin(math.pi/2)
1.0
>>>
```

We used both a function and a constant from the `math` module. Note that the module's name must be prefixed. This prevents namespace collisions: imagine how many different programs might wish to define a function called `read()` or `save()`. It's also possible to import a function explicitly into the present namespace:

```
>>> from string import split, join
>>> split('We are the knights who say Ni')
['We', 'are', 'the', 'knights', 'who', 'say', 'Ni']
>>>
```

This procedure can be used for brevity but increases the risk of a collision, and, more important, of losing track of what your code means a few months later. It should be used sparingly.

Classes

Python makes object-oriented programming easy. The `class` statement begins the definition of a class. Classes can use a special constructor called `__init__()` to initialize their data. Because Python doesn't declare variables, this constructor is a common place to initialize any variables the class may require:

```
>>> class Car:
...     def __init__(self):
...         self.milespergallon = 25.0
...         self.travelled = 0
...         self.color = 'blue'
...         self.gas = 20
```

```
...      def drive(self, miles):
...          self.travelled = self.travelled + miles
...          self.gas = self.gas - (miles / self.milespergallon)
...
>>> c = Car()
>>> c.drive(100)
>>> c.travelled
100
>>> c.gas
16.0
>>>
```

Note that you have to use the keyword **self** each time you access an attribute.

As with other languages, classes may inherit from a base class and be initialized with arguments supplied by the constructor. We won't give any further examples at this point; you can see many classes throughout this book, and the syntax is self-evident if you are used to object-oriented programming.

Exception Handling

When errors occur, Python throws an exception and prints an informative trace-back to standard output. If the error occurred in a source file and not a console session, you get the filename and line number. Here's a simple error, nested three functions deep, and its traceback:

```
>>> def func1(arg):
...      func2(arg)
...
>>> def func2(arg):
...      func3(arg)
...
>>> def func3(arg):
...      # this should cause an error
...      return arg / 0
...
>>> func1(17)
Traceback (innermost last):
  File "<interactive input>", line 0, in ?
  File "<interactive input>", line 2, in func1
  File "<interactive input>", line 2, in func2
  File "<interactive input>", line 3, in func3
ZeroDivisionError: integer division or modulo
>>>
```

The traceback tells us where the error happened and the enclosing functions that called the functions that caused the error.

Exceptions can be handled using the **try...except** and **try...finally** structure. If you aren't used to exception handling, these offer two benefits over Visual Basic-style error-handling. First, you can write a decent-sized chunk of code and put the error handlers at the end; the intent of the programmer is clearer than with a lot of `on error goto` and `on error resume next` statements. Second, exception handlers don't work on just the present chunk of code, but also on any subroutines within it, however deeply nested.

The `except` clause can optionally specify particular error types to look for or handle all errors:

```
>>> try:
...     y_scale_factor = plotHeight / (dataMax - dataMin)
... except ZeroDivisionError:
...     y_scale_factor = 0
...
>>>
```

The `try...finally` clause always executes the `finally` section whether an error occurs or not. This ensures that resources such as files are freed up:

```
>>> f = open('somefile.dat', 'wb')
>>> try:
...     #fetch some data
...     #store it in the file
... finally:
...     f.close()  # make sure the file is closed,
...                # even if errors occurred
...
>>>
```

Conclusion

This concludes our brief introduction. We have left out many features, but hopefully have given you a feel for how straightforward Python is.

We urge you to look at the Python tutorial or one of the books noted in the next section, but if you want to survey what Python can do, you should now be able to follow the code examples in the next few chapters.

References

Python comes with a comprehensive tutorial in HTML format written by Guido van Rossum. This can be completed in two to three hours and is worth reading at this point. If you've installed Python, the master documentation index can be found on your hard disk at *C:\Program Files\Python\Doc\index.html*. We also recommend O'Reilly's books *Learning Python* by Mark Lutz and David Ascher and *Programming Python* by Mark Lutz.

3

Python on Windows

This chapter introduces using Python on Windows. Rather than describe how to use Python on Windows, we discuss the architecture and briefly cover some of the extension modules available.

When you install the Python binaries for Windows, you install a fully functional version of Python that runs under Windows. This version of Python is similar to what you would find on any installation of Python, regardless of the platform, and we begin by briefly discussing how to take full advantage of the standard Python on Windows.

Although this standard version of Python is fully functional, you don't obtain much Windows-specific functionality. To fill the gap, there is a standard set of extensions for Python known collectively as the Python for Windows extensions. These extensions provide access to many Windows-specific features, such as a GUI and IDE environment, Microsoft's COM, the raw Win32 API, Windows NT-specific features, and so forth. We assume you have already installed the Python for Windows extensions, so these extensions are covered in detail. As discussed in Chapter 1, *What Is Python?*, you can find the latest official version of these extensions at *http://www.python.org/windows* (look for the Windows 95/NT-specific extensions entry).

To complete the picture, we also discuss some other extension modules available for Python on Windows. Many of these are not Windows-specific, but do support Windows, so they are worthy of discussion. Extensions falling into this category include OpenGL, mxTools, Zope, PIL, and others.

The Python Core on Windows

Python is an Open Source tool, and on many platforms, the standard way to install Python is to download the Python sources and run an automated procedure for compiling Python on the machine, resulting in Python binaries that are installed and ready to use. The key advantage of this process is that it can be customized for a particular installation; if you have a specific requirement, it can normally be accommodated.

Under Microsoft Windows, however, this strategy doesn't work. Most people don't have C compilers, and probably would not be happy with the arrangements even if they did. Therefore, Python provides an installation package that contains a version of Python built with useful default options. The installation allows you to choose which components are installed from the following:

- The Python core implemented in a Windows DLL named *Python1x.dll* (e.g., *Python15.dll* for the Python 1.5 family). This DLL is installed into your PC's Windows system directory.

- The standard Python executable, *Python.exe*. This provides the default interactive prompt and allows you to run Python programs. Additionally, *Pythonw.exe* is also installed, which allows you to write GUI applications using Python. Only advanced users should employ *Pythonw.exe*, because Python errors aren't printed; this means that *Pythonw.exe* usually appears to do nothing, and this is intentional. You should avoid using *Pythonw.exe* until you are proficient with Python itself.

- A few useful Python extension modules providing an interface to such things as *.zip* compatible compression, the Tkinter GUI library, and so forth. Python extension modules are implemented as Windows DLLs, but are typically provided as *.pyd* files. For example, the interface to the zlib compression tool is a DLL named *zlib.pyd*.

- The Python library as Python source files (*.py*). The Python library contains many useful cross-platform modules for working with Python. These include the basic Python library (such as the **string** and **os** modules), as well as advanced modules, such as web servers or modules for inspecting and decoding various audio format files.

- The Python test suite. This is a set of Python source files that test the Python installation. In general, you don't need to run these tests: they are designed primarily to test ports of Python to new architectures, or by the creators of Python to test major changes to Python itself. If you really feel a need to run this, you can start the Python interpreter and execute the command:

```
>>> import test.autotest
```

Python responds with:

```
test_grammar
test_opcodes
test_operations
test_builtin
test_exceptions
test_types
test_al
test test_al skipped -- an optional feature could not be imported
...
```

A hundred or so lines will print over the next few minutes; it takes some time to complete. Note the last message printed; you will see many of these warnings, and they can be safely ignored.

- The Python documentation in HTML format, accessible from the Windows Start Menu.

- Headers (*.h* files) and libraries (*.lib* files) for the C components needed to build your own extension modules. This is covered in Chapter 22, *Extending and Embedding with Visual C++ and Delphi*.

- The portable GUI environment Tkinter and a Python IDE known as IDLE. Tkinter is discussed in more detail in Chapter 20, *GUI Development*, while IDLE is discussed in Chapter 4, *Integrated Development Environments for Python*.

- Various Python scripts and utility programs. Browse the *\tools* subdirectory of your Python installation.

You should browse the supplied Python documentation. You will find a reference guide for most of the standard library, as well as the language tutorial and reference. Additionally, you should check for later documentation at *http://www.python.org/doc/*; it's quite common for new documentation to be written between major Python releases, and the latest documentation is always available for online browsing or download in both HTML and printable (PostScript/PDF) formats.

The Windows Registry

When Python is installed, a number of configuration options are stored in the Windows registry. The Windows registry provides a central location where programs can store their preferences and settings and provides more features than traditional techniques of saving configuration information. The Windows registry also has some limitations, and many people would dearly like to see it suffer a slow and painful death! Whatever your views, good Windows applications, and therefore Python, store their information in the Windows registry.

In general, it isn't necessary for you to understand or edit the registry; Python and any extensions you install normally manages this for you. Indeed, if you are unfamiliar with the Windows registry, you should avoid it completely: it's all too easy to do serious damage to your PC's configuration. However, if you are experienced with the Windows registry or are curious to see how everything works, read on.

The most important configuration option stored in the registry is the PythonPath, the list of directories where Python looks to find modules, which can be viewed at runtime via *sys.path*. Under Unix, the common way of storing this option is by setting a PYTHONPATH environment variable. Under Windows, this information is stored in the registry rather than in the environment.*

Python also stores other configuration data in the registry, including the location where Python was installed, a list of Python help files, and so forth. For full details on Python's use of the registry, please see the Python documentation.

Let's take a quick look at the Python registry information using the standard Windows Registry Editor. Start the Registry Editor by executing the program *regedit.exe* (or possibly *regedt32.exe* on Windows 95, depending on the configuration). You should see a window that looks similar to the Windows Explorer: a list of folders on the left, and data on the right.

Locate the folder named HKEY_LOCAL_MACHINE, and expand it. Locate the subfolder named Software, and expand it, then continue down through the Python, PythonCore, 1.5, and PythonPath subfolders. Your screen should look something like Figure 3-1, which shows the default PythonPath (i.e., the path used by the Python core) has been installed in *E:\Program Files\Python*, and the three existing path subkeys: PythonWin, win32, and win32com. These entries have been added by the Python for Windows extensions and contain the additional PythonPath entries required by the respective packages.

If you need to add your own PythonPath entry, you can create a subkey under the PythonPath key and add your new path entries to the key. The names of the keys are for documentation purposes only; they are the name of the package that requires the path entry. Only the key values are actually used by Python itself.

 The registry is a system-level tool that allows you freedom to do irreparable damage to your operating system, requiring complete reinstallation. Be careful with any changes you make to the registry and make no changes unless you are certain of their impact.

---

* It should be noted that Python on Windows can also use the PYTHONPATH environment variable, but by default the value is stored in the registry.

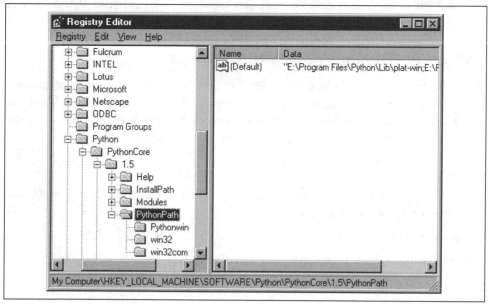

Figure 3-1. The Windows Registry Editor

Windows Explorer Integration

If you open the Windows Explorer after installing Python, you might notice that all *.py* and *.pyc* files have their own cute Python icon! If you right-click on a *.py* file, notice the default menu entry is Run; you can select this entry from the menu or double-click on the *.py* file to run the program using the standard *Python.exe*. It's possible that other Python extensions will install new items in this menu; for example, PythonWin (discussed later in this chapter) adds an Edit item, allowing you to open the Python source file for editing.

In addition, you can drag these *.py* files to your favorite text editor (including PythonWin) for editing. This can be any editor of your choice, or even the standard Windows *notepad* tool.*

Running Python programs from the Windows Explorer has one major problem: a new window is created for the Python program, and when it terminates, the window closes immediately. This means that any messages displayed by the program (either informational or error messages) usually vanish just as you are trying to read them. For this reason, most Windows users don't execute their Python programs in this manner; they do so either from the Windows command prompt or

---

* Many standard Python library files are supplied with Unix-style line terminators. *notepad* is still one of the few Windows editors unable to cope with files of this format. For this and other reasons, you shouldn't use *notepad* to edit Python source.

from a Python integrated development environment (IDE), such as PythonWin or
IDLE.

Using the Windows Command Prompt

Both the Windows 95/98 and NT/2000 families come with a command prompt
allowing users to run programs from a command-line interface. The Windows
command prompt has a long and not-so-glorious history; it has grown from the
first versions of MS-DOS and still uses the same basic syntax.

Running Python programs

For these discussions, let's assume you have a file named *C:\Scripts\hello.py*, and
this file consists of the single line:

```
print "Hello from Python"
```

A first attempt to run this program may surprise you:

```
C:\Scripts>python.exe hello.py
The name specified is not recognized as an
internal or external command, operable program or batch file.

C:\Scripts>
```

Although *Python.exe* has been installed, it hasn't modified the system environment variable PATH: Windows doesn't know how to find *Python.exe*. Windows
NT does, however, know how to run *.py* files directly. Thus, if you ask the command prompt to execute *hello.py*, it will:

```
C:\Scripts>hello.py
Hello from Python

C:\Scripts>
```

Take this one step further and avoid the use of the *.py* extension, making a Python
program appear like a *.exe*, *.com*, or *.bat* file. Windows NT supports this using the
PATHEXT environment variable. You can view the current settings of this variable
by entering the command:

```
C:\Scripts>echo %PATHEXT%
.exe;.bat;.cmd

C:\Scripts>
```

This is a list of the default extensions Windows searches for when a command is
executed. You can add Python files to this list (and check the change was successful) by executing:

```
C:\Scripts>set PATHEXT=%PATHEXT%;.py

C:\Scripts>echo %PATHEXT%
.exe;.bat;.cmd;.py

C:\Scripts>
```

Now execute your Python programs by specifying the base name of the file:

```
C:\Scripts>hello
Hello from Python

C:\Scripts>
```

For more information, please see the Windows NT documentation.

Unfortunately, none of this applies to Windows 95 or 98, only to Windows NT and 2000. Users of Windows 95 or 98 often take one of the following actions:

- Add the Python directory to the system environment variable PATH by modifying their *autoexec.bat* file.

- Copy *Python.exe* to the Windows system directory. The biggest problems with this are that it's one more file in an already overused directory, and when Python is upgraded, this file may cause some conflicts.

The facilities we described that are available under Windows NT usually make these changes unnecessary.

Finally, both operating systems support using the **start** command to start Python in a separate window. For example, you could use the command **start python. exe** to start an interactive *Python.exe* in a new window or the command **start hello.py** to run your script in a new window. However, just as with Windows Explorer, this window closes as the program exits, meaning you don't get a chance to read the message printed by your script.

Command-line editing

All versions of Windows have some capability for command-line editing: that is, recalling previous commands that have been entered, so they can be reexecuted without retyping them.

Windows NT supports command-line editing by default, but Windows 95 and 98 require you to execute a program named *doskey* before this functionality is available. Windows 95 and 98 users often configure their environment so that *doskey* is automatically executed whenever a command prompt is started.

To operate the command-line editing tools, use the arrow keys on the keyboard. The up and down arrows scroll between the commands you executed recently, while the left and right arrow keys allow you to edit the current command. In addition, Windows NT also provides command-line editing for *Python.exe*; once you start Python, you can recall previous commands in the same way you can at the command prompt. Unfortunately, Windows 95 or 98 doesn't offer this feature.

The *doskey* program can also provide command macros. A *command macro* is a shortcut you assign to a program, so when the shortcut is executed the command prompt, the program is executed.

You can use this to your advantage when working with Python. For example, Windows 95 users who can't take advantage of the Windows NT command prompt can use the following command to assign the shortcut p to execute Python:

```
C:\Scripts> doskey p="C:\Program Files\Python\Python.exe" $*
```

The $* at the end of the command indicates that any command-line parameters should be passed to the program, in this case, Python. Thus, you could execute:

```
C:\Scripts>p hello.py
Hello from Python

C:\Scripts>
```

Users of Windows NT and Windows 95 may also like to use these shortcuts to execute their favorite editor. For example, if you execute the following commands:

```
C:\Scripts>doskey n=start notepad.exe $*
C:\Scripts>doskey pw=start pythonwin.exe $*
```

you could use:

```
C:\Scripts>n hello.py
```

to edit the file using *notepad*, or:

```
C:\Scripts>pw hello.py
```

to edit the file using PythonWin.

To take advantage of these *doskey* macros, you can place them all in a single batch file that can be configured to be run whenever a command prompt is opened. There are many techniques, but a simple one is to place all the commands in a batch file, then modify the shortcut you use to execute the command prompt to include the parameter /k *your_batchfile.bat*. This forces the command prompt to execute your batch file, but remains open, allowing you to continue entering commands.

Copy and Paste from the command prompt

Although fairly minor, there are a couple of other features that can help you work with Python.

The first is Copy and Paste. Both Windows 95 and NT support an option that allows you to copy text from the command prompt using the mouse. Windows NT also allows you to paste information into your command prompt with a simple right-click of the mouse. This can be handy when you need to paste a string or sample code into your Python prompt. You can enable this by selecting the Quick Edit option from the command prompt's properties.

Another nice feature for all versions is that you can drag a file from Windows Explorer and drop it into a command prompt, pasting the full filename to the prompt. This can be a handy way to execute Python programs from Windows Explorer without losing the output when the program completes: simply drop the filename onto an existing command prompt and press Enter.

Windows Gotchas

As we have stressed a number of times, Python is cross-platform. Although the sheer market penetration of Windows makes it one of Python's most popular platforms, it's still only one of the many operating systems Python has to work with.

Accordingly, there are some features available on other platforms that don't exist on Windows. To make matters worse, there are a number of features that do work on both platforms, but not in exactly the same way.

Most people who use Python only on Windows never need to worry about these features; they have probably never heard of these functions anyway, and they won't find further comment on them in this book. But for people moving to Windows from the Unix and Linux worlds, seemingly trivial things can cause much aggravation. Although far from exhaustive, some of the more common gotchas are detailed here.

Text-mode versus binary-mode files

Since the early days of computing (well before Unix), lines in text files were terminated with *carriage-return* and *line-feed* characters. This is directly attributable to the early teletype devices that required a command to move the printhead (or carriage) back to the left, and another to eject a new line. The creators of Unix decided the convention was pointless and terminated all lines in text files by the line-feed character, which by then had become known as the *newline* character. Then the C language came up with a new technique for opening files, such that regardless of the local line-ending conventions, your program would always see a consistent single newline character at the end of each line. A differentiation was made between binary- and text-mode files, which was specified when opening the file.

Unfortunately, over time many Unix programmers became somewhat lazy. As Unix uses a single newline character to terminate lines anyway, there was no difference on that operating system between text- and binary-mode files; the program always worked identically on Unix, regardless of the mode used to open the file. Over time, it became common practice for programmers to omit the binary- or text-mode specifiers completely. To add to the confusion, we also have the Apple Macintosh, which uses a single carriage return.

Windows traces its roots right back to the old teletype days. Every version of Windows, including the most recent, has had to retain some level of compatibility with early versions of MS-DOS, and MS-DOS itself strove to retain some compatibility with CP/M. As a direct result of this history, the common default-line terminator on Windows is a carriage-return character followed by a newline character. This is the file format editors such as *notepad* use. Most modern editors (including most you are likely to use with Python) support either line convention.

The end result of all this discussion comes down to two points:

- If you open a file and wish to see a single newline character terminating each line (regardless of what really terminates the lines), the file should be opened in text mode. You should open in text mode on all operating systems, including Unix where it will have no effect; you never know when some poor soul will try to run your code on a different operating system!

- If you open a file and need to see the raw, binary data, you should specify binary mode.

If you open a file in text mode, but it contains binary data, the data often appears corrupt due to the newline and carriage-return mapping. If you open a file in binary mode but you process it as if it contained text data, each line may have additional (or missing) carriage returns at the end of each line.

To open a file in binary mode, append a b to the mode in the open() call. The default is text mode, but on Windows, you can also specify this by appending a t. Thus, to open a file for reading in text mode, use this:

```
file = open(filename, "r")
```

Or to open a file for writing in binary mode, use this:

```
file = open(filename, "wb")
```

Fork

Unix provides a function called fork() to spawn subprocesses. fork() is often used in situations where Windows programmers would consider using threads. Until recently, some of the more popular Unix systems didn't have support for threads, and those that did frequently had their own proprietary API, making it difficult to write portable, threaded code for Unix. `fork()` has a number of subtleties and features that make it particularly useful in this context, and thus `fork()` is widespread in the Unix world.

Windows doesn't support `fork()` and, unfortunately, doesn't support anything that comes close. If you have a Unix program that uses `fork()`, then porting it to run under Windows is likely to be significant work and requires fairly intimate understanding of the program.

In many cases, the best solution is to rebuild this part of the application for Windows. On a typical Unix machine, creating new processes (as `fork()` does) is a relatively cheap operation. On Windows, however, the overhead of creating a new process is significant, so solutions using this architecture on Windows won't often scale or perform as you would hope. Rewriting this portion of the application to use multiple threads instead of multiple processes is often the best solution for Windows.

Python exposes the `fork()` function in the `os` module (i.e., `os.fork()`) on platforms that support it. As Windows isn't one of these supporting platforms, using `os.fork()` yields an `AttributeError` exception.

Select

Another common Unixism that causes problems on Windows is the use of the `select()` function. Under Unix, the `select()` function determines when more input is available from a file. When your program is reading a file on a disk, you won't have much use for this function. However, it's common for programs to be reading from files that are not on disk: for example, reading the output of another process (i.e., a pipe) or reading data from a network connection. By being notified when a particular file has more data available to read, using `select()` allows a program to read from multiple files concurrently.

Windows does provide the `select()` function, but it can be used only with sockets (see Chapter 19, *Communications*). Attempting to use `select()` with a regular Python file object will fail.

The most common technique on Windows for simple asynchronous input/output is to use threads; and indeed threads are the only portable technique to perform this style of I/O in Python. A simple thread-based solution doesn't scale well once the number of threads becomes large, so Windows provides other native techniques for performing asynchronous I/O. Although these techniques are beyond the scope of this book, they are all fully supported by Python on Windows.

Pipes

This issue is similar to the one outlined previously for `os.fork()`: a feature for working with subprocesses that doesn't work as you may hope on Windows.

Quite often, Unix programs use a function called `os.popen()` to create a child process and establish a pipe between your process and the new child. Depending on the direction of the pipe, you can read the output from the process or supply input to the process. The most common use of `os.popen()` is to execute a program and capture its output. When you read from the pipe, you are actually reading the output of the child process.

Although provided under Windows, the `os.popen()` function is practically useless. Due to various bugs in Windows, `os.popen()` works only on Windows NT from a console (i.e., DOS prompt) program. Windows 95, 98, and Windows NT GUI programs all fail when attempting to use `os.popen()`.

Bill Tutt has come to the rescue with his various `popen()` replacement functions for Windows. These functions are exposed in the `win32pipe` module and documented in the standard Win32 Extensions Help file.

The Python for Windows Extensions

To supplement the standard Python distribution, there is a set of extensions specific to Microsoft Win32 platforms (currently Windows NT/2000, Windows 95/98, and Windows CE).

These extensions actually consist of three discrete Python extensions: access to the native Win32 API, interfaces to COM, and the PythonWin GUI extensions. These are currently released as a single unit, in an installation package named *win32all*. Each specific release is given a build number that is incorporated into the installation name; at time of printing, the current build number is 128, so the installation package is named *win32all-128.exe*. By the time you read this, the build number is likely to have advanced, so install the version recommended by the web page when you connect. For obvious reasons, this package is also known as the "win32all package."

The Python for Windows extensions can be found at *http://www.python.org/windows* and also at *http://starship.python.net/crew/mhammond*.

Win32 Extensions

The most fundamental interface to Windows features is provided by the Win32 extensions. In most cases, these modules provide access similar to the Win32 API that C or C++ programmers would have, such as access to Windows handles and other low-level concepts.

Table 3-1 displays the Win32 extension modules.

Table 3-1. Win32 Extension Modules

Module	Description
mmapfile	Interfaces to Windows memory-mapped files, a mechanism that allows data to be shared among multiple processes.
odbc	An interface to the Open DataBase Connectivity API, a portable API for connecting to multiple databases. We discuss ODBC and other database techniques in Chapter 13, *Databases*.
win32api	Accesses many of the common and simple Windows APIs; a general-purpose module with a cross section of API support.
win32event	Accesses the Windows event and signaling API. This module allows you to manipulate and wait for Windows events, semaphores, mutexes, etc.
win32evtlog win32evtlogutil	An interface to the Windows NT Event Log. The win32evtlog module provides a raw interface to the Windows NT API, while the win32evtlogutil module provides utilities to simplify working with the module. This is discussed in Chapter 18, *Windows NT Services*.
win32pdh	An interface to the Windows NT Performance Monitor. This module uses a helper DLL provided by Microsoft known as the Performance Data Helper or PDH. We discuss the Windows NT Performance Monitor in Chapter 18.
win32pipe	Accesses the pipe-related Win32 functions, such as functions for creating and using pipes, including named pipes. We discuss pipes briefly in Chapter 17, *Processes and Files*, and use a pipe from the win32pipe module in Chapter 18.
win32file	Accesses the file-related Win32 functions. This module exposes a low-level, raw interface to files on Windows and is used only when the standard Python file object isn't suitable. Python files and the win32file module are discussed in Chapter 17.
win32lz	An interface to the Windows LZ compression library. Note that since this module was created, Python now ships with support for the *gzip* compression format, so in most cases win32lz is no longer used.
win32net win32wnet	Interface to the Windows networking API. win32net provides an interface to Windows NT-specific server networking, while win32wnet provides client-networking functions available to all versions. We discuss the Windows networking functions in Chapter 16, *Windows NT Administration*.
win32print	Interface to the printer-related Windows APIs.
win32process	Interface to the process-related Windows APIs. This module is discussed in detail in Chapter 17.

Table 3-1. Win32 Extension Modules (continued)

Module	Description
win32ras	Interface to the Windows Remote Access Service (RAS). Used for establishing remote connections to Windows NT servers, typically using a modem. The RAS interface is discussed in Chapter 19.
win32security	Accesses the Windows NT security-related functions. Although beyond the scope of this book, we present a brief example in Chapter 16.
win32service win32serviceutil	Accesses the Windows NT Services-related API. This module is discussed in detail in Chapter 18.
win32trace win32traceutil	Debugging related modules. These modules allow you to collect the output of a Python process in a separate process. This is most useful when debugging server-style applications, where Python error and other messages are not available.

When the extensions are installed, a Reference Manual (a Windows Help file) is installed detailing each of the methods and their parameters.

You will notice that some modules have a "helper" companion; for example, the win32evtlog module has a helper named win32evtlogutil. In all cases, the core module exposes the native Windows API, and the "helper" provides more convenient access to that API.

PythonWin

When you install the Python for Windows extensions, an environment known as PythonWin is also installed. One of the most noticeable changes that occurs when you install the extensions is that a shortcut to PythonWin is installed into the Python group on the Windows Start menu.

PythonWin is a GUI environment and IDE for Python. When you start PythonWin, you are presented with an interactive window (a window where you can enter and execute arbitrary Python commands, similar to *Python.exe*). You can also edit and execute *.py* files within the environment, using a graphical debugger if necessary. Finally, you can also use the PythonWin framework to create your own GUI-based programs.

Technically, PythonWin consists of two discrete parts:

- A large Python extension that exposes the Microsoft Foundation Classes (MFC) to Python. MFC is a C++ library provided by Microsoft to create Windows programs. Similar to MFC itself, this extension can be considered a toolkit; it contains all the elements you need to build GUI applications, but it isn't an application itself.

- A set of Python modules that use these MFC facilities to create the IDE environment you see when you start PythonWin. These modules can almost be considered sample code for the MFC extensions.

As you run PythonWin, it's worth noting that almost all the functionality you are using is written in Python. Everything from handling the menu commands to updating the line and character positions on the status bar is implemented in the supplied *.py* Python source files.

PythonWin is discussed in more detail in Chapter 4.

PythonCOM

The Python for Windows extensions also include excellent support for the Microsoft Component Object Model (COM). COM is a technology that allows you to use "objects" from your favorite language, even if the object isn't implemented in your language.

Microsoft has invested heavily in COM, and it should be familiar to any Visual Basic programmer. Many applications for Windows (including Microsoft Office) can be controlled using COM, making it particularly suitable for scripting-related tasks; for example, a Python program to open an Excel spreadsheet and populate the sheet is quite simple, as we shall see later in the book.

COM and PythonCOM are discussed in Chapter 5, *Introduction to COM*, and in more detail in Chapter 12, *Advanced Python and COM*.

The Python Imaging Library (PIL)

The Python Imaging Library (PIL) is a set of modules that can perform all sorts of image manipulation and processing in Python. PIL is designed to be cross-platform, so it can be used on almost any platform with Python support. But it does support some Windows-specific extensions, allowing PIL to display images using the Windows API.

PIL is suitable for many image-related tasks. You can use it to create thumbnails automatically from a collection of images, to convert between graphical formats, or even as the basis of a graphical image-manipulation tool.

PIL comes with extensive documentation and can be found on the Internet at *http://www.pythonware.com*.

PyOpenGL

OpenGL is a high-performance, portable 2D and 3D rendering library. OpenGL was created in 1992 by Silicon Graphics and quickly became the industry standard for 2D and 3D graphics. It's currently maintained by an independent industry consortium, the OpenGL Architecture Review Board. More information on OpenGL can be found at *http://www.opengl.org*.

Most versions of Microsoft Windows support the OpenGL standard. Windows NT and 98 both come with OpenGL support installed by default, while Windows 95 has an add-on available to obtain OpenGL support.

David Ascher, a well-known Python luminary and O'Reilly author, currently maintains a set of Python extensions that allow interface to the OpenGL libraries known as PyOpenGL. OpenGL and PyOpenGL are both cross-platform libraries, and both are also supported on Windows.

OpenGL is a complex API, and a good book on OpenGL is highly recommended before you attempt to use the library. The PyOpenGL pages recommend the following books:

- Woo, Neider & Davis, *OpenGL Programming Guide, Second Edition: The Official Guide to Learning OpenGL, Version 1.1*, Addison Wesley Developers Press. ISBN: 0-201-46138-2.

- Kemp & Frasier, *OpenGL Reference Guide, Second Edition: The Official Reference Document to OpenGL, Version 1.1*, Addison Wesley Developers Press. ISBN: 0-201-46140-4.

PyOpenGL itself comes with a number of demos that use the Tkinter graphics library, and PythonWin comes with a single sample that demonstrates how to use OpenGL in the PythonWin environment.

Information on PyOpenGL can be found at *http://starship.python.net/crew/da/ PyOpenGL*.

Web Publishing Tools

There are a number of Internet publishing tools available for Python. Python itself comes with its own HTTP server (web server), which is discussed in some detail in Chapter 15, *Using the Basic Internet Protocols*.

A number of packages have extended Python's capability in this area; these include the Medusa Suite and Zope.

Medusa

Medusa is a platform for building high-performance, long-running servers using Python, written by Sam Rushing of Nightmare Software. Medusa uses an asynchronous model for supporting high-performance, single-threaded servers, particularly suitable for HTTP or FTP servers. Although Medusa comes with HTTP and FTP servers, the library is suitable for almost any high-performance/high-load socket-based communication; in fact, the core Medusa engine was recently adopted as part of the standard Python library and can be found on any standard Python 1.5.2 or later distribution.

Medusa is currently used by a number of mission-critical systems around the world. It's free for personal use, although it requires a license for commercial use.

Information on Medusa can be found at *http://www.nightmare.com/medusa*.

Zope

Zope is an Open Source application server and portal toolkit supplied and supported by Digital Creations. While a quick look at Zope may give you the impression it's yet another web server, it's actually far more.

Most web servers earn their living by serving static HTML text, or possibly executing code using the CGI interface. Instead of serving HTML pages, Zope publishes "objects" stored in the integrated object database, a relational database, or other content systems such as LDAP servers. Zope maps these requests to Python objects, which are retrieved from the object database and queried. Whenever you display a page using Zope, you are actually calling some Python object. You can easily create new types of publishable objects and use any Python facilities including Windows-specific Python extensions. At the time of this writing a Zope extension to facilitate the use of COM objects is in development.

This provides a natural way of developing content for the Web. You design your web page as a combination of HTML templates and a set of objects. The templates can reference your objects to obtain the final HTML sent to the user.

While Zope's HTML templates may resemble IIS ASP files, they operate quite differently. Rather than being bound to web pages like ASP files, Zope templates are associated with Python objects. A Zope template builds a web representation of an object by calling the object's methods and/or calling other objects and their templates. In this way web pages are built out of assemblages of objects and their templates.

Unlike ASP, Zope can operate with almost any web server and can run on almost any platform that supports Python. Zope comes with its own web server, but it can also operate hand in hand with other web servers such as IIS. When you use Zope with IIS, Zope runs as an NT service, and IIS forwards web requests to Zope for processing.

As Zope is released as Open Source, it's free, including for commercial use. In addition to customizing Zope for your own purposes, you can participate in

Zope's development by following changes in Concurrent Versioning System (CVS), proposing features, submitting patches, and contributing extensions.

Further information can be found at *http://www.zope.org*; the site also provides a handy demo.

The mx Extensions

Not necessarily written for Windows platforms, but nevertheless worth a look, are the extensions written for Python by Marc-André Lemburg. Most extensions come with a Python-style license and can be freely used for your own projects (although some do require a license for commercial use: see the license for details). Many of them even include precompiled binaries for direct use on Windows; installation is then a matter of unzipping the package archive.

You can download the most recent versions from the Starship server, where many other Pythoneers also keep their gems. The documentation, license information, and download instructions are all just a few clicks away from *http://starship. python.net/crew/lemburg/*.

mxDateTime

`mxDateTime` provides three new object types, `DateTime`, `DateTimeDelta`, and `RelativeDateTime`, which let you store and handle date/time values in a more natural way than by using Unix ticks (seconds since 1.1.70 0:00 UTC, the encoding used by the standard Python time module). We'll see this used in Chapter 13, *Databases*.

You can add, subtract, and even multiply instances, or use the standard Python `pickle` module to copy them and convert the results to strings, COM dates, ticks, and some other more esoteric values. In addition, there are several convenient constructors, formatters, and parsers to greatly simplify dealing with dates and times in real-world applications.

Besides providing an easy-to-use Python interface, the package also exports a comfortable C API interface for other extensions to build on. This is especially interesting for database applications that often have to deal with date/time values; the mxODBC package is one example of an extension using this interface.

mxTextTools

`mxTextTools` includes several useful functions and types that implement high-performance text-manipulation and searching algorithms.

For experts, `mxTextTools` also includes a flexible and extensible state machine, the Tagging Engine, that allows scanning and processing text based on low-level bytecode "programs" written using Python tuples. It gives you access to the speed of C without having to compile and link steps every time you change the parsing description.

Applications include parsing structured text, finding and extracting text (either exact or using translation tables), and recombining strings to form new text.

mxODBC

`mxODBC` is an extension package that provides a Python Database API-compliant interface to ODBC 2.0-capable database drivers and managers.

Apart from implementing the standard Database API interface, it also gives access to a rich set of catalog methods that allow you to scan the database for tables, procedures, and so forth. Furthermore, it uses the `mxDateTime` package for date/time value interfacing eliminating most of the problems these types normally introduce (other I/O formats are available too).

The latest versions of the package allow you to interface to more than one database from one process. It includes a variety of preconfigured setups for many commonly used databases such as MySQL, Oracle, Informix, Solid, and many more. A precompiled version of the extension for the Windows ODBC manager is also included.

Chapter 13 covers `mxODBC` in considerable detail.

mxStack

This is one of the smaller offerings: `mxStack` implements a new object type called `Stack`. It works much as you would expect from such a type, having `.push()` and `.pop()` methods and focusing on obtaining maximum speed at low memory costs.

mxTools

The `mxTools` package is collection of handy functions and objects extending Python's functionality in many useful ways. You'll find many goodies you've often missed in this package, such as `dict()` for constructing dictionaries from item lists or a replacement for `range(len(object))` called `indices()`. There are more than 25 new functions provided by this package; too many to detail here, and listing only a few runs the risk of skipping the one you might find most useful. The online documentation provides an excellent reference.

mxCrypto

mxCrypto is an extension package that provides object-oriented-style access to the cipher algorithms and hash functions included in SSLeay, a sophisticated cryptographic library written by Eric Young, now maintained by the OpenSSL (*http://www.openssl.org*) team.

SSLeay/OpenSSL isn't subject to the U.S. government's International Traffic in Arms Regulations (ITAR) export restrictions on cryptographic software, so it's available worldwide.

mxProxy

This small package gives you complete control of how an object may be accessed and by whom. It's suitable to implement bastion-like features without the need to run in restricted execution environments.

The package features secure data encapsulation (the hidden objects are not accessible from Python since they are stored in internal C structures), customizable attribute lookup methods, and a cleanup protocol that helps to break circular references prior to object deletion.

Scientific Tools

Python is popular in scientific circles. One of the first major packages to come from this environment is Numeric Python. Numeric Python supports efficient multidimensional arrays and can perform complex number-crunching chores normally reserved for packages such as MATLAB or IDL. Also included in Numeric Python are tools for working with linear algebra, Fast Fourier Transforms, and so forth.

Apart from Numeric Python, other scientific tools include support for managing huge sets of data, extensions for plotting and other data analysis, and others.

All these tools are released under a license similar to that of Python and can be found at the Python web site, *http://www.python.org/topics/scicomp/*.

XML

Python provides excellent support for the Extensible Markup Language (XML), one of the recent hot topics in the computer science world. XML is a format for structured data interchange and is being widely adopted by many influential corporations, including Microsoft. Python has a number of validating and nonvalidating parsers available and a number of tools for working with the Document Object Model (DOM). There is extensive sample code and an active SIG mailing list.

Releases of the XML toolkit usually come with a prebuilt Python binary for Windows. The package is distributed under a license similar to that of Python, so the latest source code is always available.

Information on Python support for XML and links to general XML resources can all be found at the Python web site, *http://www.python.org/topics/xml/*.

Conclusion

In this chapter, we have attempted to discuss Python on Windows without showing any Python code! We focused on using Python in the Windows environment and how Python integrates with the standard Windows tools.

We discussed some extensions you may find useful on Windows. By talking about only a few, we run the risk of giving the impression that these are the only Python modules available for Windows, and this would be unfair. There are many other useful Python extensions, either designed for Windows or that work perfectly on Windows.

To find the particular module you are after, you should use the facilities provided at *http://www.python.org/search/* to search the main Python web site, other Python-related web sites, and the main Python newsgroup.

4

Integrated Development Environments for Python

In this chapter we look at two integrated development environments (IDEs) for Python on Windows:

- PythonWin provides IDE capabilities for Python on Windows. It has a number of features in its environment that make editing and debugging Python code more pleasant and productive than standard text editors. Because the IDE features are part of the PythonWin package, you can take advantage of them if you develop your GUI application using PythonWin or if you extend your existing C++ MFC application by embedding PythonWin. More detail on the PythonWin framework can be found in Chapter 20, *GUI Development*.

- IDLE is an IDE developed by Python author, Guido van Rossum. IDLE uses the Tkinter GUI framework and is portable to all Python platforms with Tkinter support. IDLE is a standalone IDE for Python; it doesn't attempt to provide a GUI or application framework. IDLE would be particularly suitable if you develop your GUI applications using Tkinter or regularly use Python on operating systems other than Windows. Guido has kindly assisted in the section of this chapter devoted to IDLE.

The PythonWin IDE

PythonWin is many things. As we discuss in Chapter 20, one of PythonWin's major roles is to be a Python interface to the Microsoft Foundation Classes, allowing an application to take advantage of some of the more esoteric user interface features available on Windows.

PythonWin is almost a sample application for these MFC extensions. Over time, it has slowly developed features that make it useful as an IDE. As time goes on, we can expect these features to improve.

The PythonWin Environment

When PythonWin starts, it automatically opens its Interactive Window, where you see the Python copyright message and the standard Python prompt:

```
>>>
```

If you are familiar with Python on any other operating system or have used the standard *Python.exe* included with the Python distribution, you can immediately start entering Python commands to be executed interactively. Chapter 2, *Python Language Review*, and the Python tutorial (optionally installed with the Python distribution), describes using Python interactively, and we discuss some additional PythonWin features later in this chapter.

As much as possible, PythonWin conforms to the standard user-interface features of Windows. Thus, you will notice a Windows toolbar with familiar File → Open and File → New icons, and a fairly standard set of menus at the top of the application. Most of the items on the menus are obvious, so we won't describe the exact operation of the File → Open and File → New operations. Instead, we will focus on the features specific to PythonWin.

Now would be a good time to create a new Python source file to demonstrate some of the features of PythonWin. To create a new file, select the blank document toolbar item, then select File → New or press Ctrl-N. A dialog box appears that asks which type of document to create. Select Python Script.

A blank source file is created. Type the following code:

```python
def hello(msg):
    print "Hello, " + msg

def main():
    import sys
    print "Script name is", sys.argv[0]
    if len(sys.argv)>=2:
        hello(sys.argv[1])
    else:
        hello("Please say something next time")

if __name__=='__main__':
    main()
```

As you type, notice the first feature: Python syntax coloring. If you don't like the particular styles, they can be changed via the View → Options menu. Now save the file as *pywindemo.py* in a convenient directory, and you're ready to begin.

Running scripts

PythonWin allows you to run arbitrary scripts from within its environment. Changes to the file are saved before the script is run. You can execute a script by selecting the "running man" toolbar button, and then select File → Run, or press Ctrl-R.

Let's run the script we just created. When you select this option, the PythonWin environment should look something like Figure 4-1.

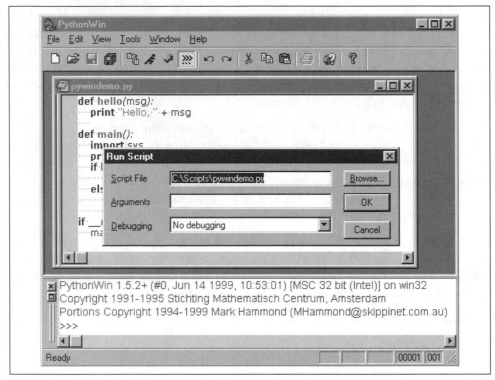

Figure 4-1. PythonWin's Run Script dialog

For now, ignore the debugger, so you can leave everything with its default values and select OK.

You should see the following message output to the interactive window:

```
Script name is c:\scripts\pywindemo.py
Hello, Please say something next time
```

Notice that the script is run the same way you executed **python.exe pywindemo. py**. The **if __name__=='__main__':** block is entered, and **sys.argv** is used to obtain the command-line parameters. If you perform this procedure again, you can experiment with adding command-line arguments in the Run dialog.

A handy feature to note is that if you hold down the Shift key while running the module (i.e., while clicking the toolbar or by pressing Ctrl-Shift-R), the code runs without displaying the dialog. This is handy for repeatedly running the same script with the same arguments.

Import modules

Importing modules in the PythonWin environment is similar to running Python scripts; they both execute Python code. However, there is an important distinction between importing modules and running scripts.

Importing the module *pywindemo.py* operates almost identically to typing the Python statement:

```
>>> import pywindemo
```

When a module is imported this way, the `if __name__=='__main__':` block isn't entered, but the name of the script is entered into the Python namespace.

There are two important differences between the PythonWin import functionality and simply typing `import pywindemo`. First, the file is saved; and second, PythonWin automatically performs a `reload()` of the module if necessary. These features combine to ensure the latest version of the code is made available.

You can import a module in PythonWin by selecting the Import toolbar icon, and selecting File → Import or pressing Ctrl-I. If an editor window has the focus, that module is imported; otherwise, a dialog is opened allowing you to select the Python module to be imported.

Let's import the test module. Make sure it's the foreground window and press Ctrl-I. The status bar displays the message `Successfully imported the module 'pywindemo'`, and no message is printed to the interactive window. So although the module is imported, the `if __name__=='__main__':` block isn't executed.

Now that you've imported the module, you can use it as you would any Python module. Go to the Interactive Window and type:

```
>>> pywindemo.hello("how are you")
Hello, how are you
>>>
```

Importing modules is primarily useful when developing or debugging a fairly large application under PythonWin. For example, let's assume you have the following code structure:

```
# module spam1
import spamutil
...
    spamutil.MakeEggs()
```

And another similar module:

```
# module spam2
import spamutil
...
    spamutil.MakeEggs()
```

If you find a bug in the **spamutil** module, you can edit it in PythonWin, then import the module. The **spam1** and **spam2** modules will then also be working with the new version of **spamutil**.

Checking modules

PythonWin includes a function that allows you to check a Python source file without executing it. The syntax of the source code is checked using Python itself, while the Python *tabnanny* tool checks the source-code whitespace. Any syntax or whitespace errors are reported in the PythonWin status bar.

You can check a module by selecting the Check Module toolbar item, then selecting File → Check or pressing Ctrl-Shift-C.

Locating source files

To assist in locating your Python source files, PythonWin can look down the Python **sys.path** for a file.

To locate a Python file, select File → Locate or press Ctrl-L. A dialog is displayed asking for the name of a module to locate.

If you enter **string** into this dialog, PythonWin searches the path for a module named *string.py*. PythonWin should locate and open the standard Python string module.

This feature is aware of Python packages. You could enter a module name of **pywin.framework.app** to locate the PythonWin application module in the file *pywin\framework\app.py*.

Command-Line Parameters

PythonWin supports a number of command-line parameters as shown in this table.

Command Line	Description
/edit *filename*	Starts PythonWin and opens the named file for editing.
/run *filename*	Starts PythonWin and runs the specified script.
/nodde	Must be the first parameter. Starts PythonWin without DDE support, allowing for multiple PythonWin instances.
/app *appmodule*	Treats the named file as a PythonWin application. This is for advanced users only and is discussed in Chapter 20.

By default, PythonWin allows only one instance to be open. If you attempt to start a new instance of PythonWin, the existing instance is reused, primarily to support better integration with Windows Explorer, as described later in this chapter. PythonWin uses Dynamic Data Exchange (DDE) to communicate between instances, so the /nodde parameter can disable this behavior and allow as many PythonWin instances as you care to start.

To demonstrate these command lines, close the source file *pywindemo.py* (leave PythonWin running) and start a command prompt window. Enter the command:

```
C:\Somewhere> start pythonwin.exe /edit C:\Scripts\pywindemo.py
```

You should see your existing PythonWin application come to the foreground, and see *pywindemo.py* opened for editing. Switch back to the command prompt and enter the command:

```
C:\Somewhere> start pythonwin.exe /run c:\Scripts\pywindemo.py
```

You should see the same messages printed as when you ran the script directly from PythonWin. Finally, from the command prompt enter:

```
C:\Somewhere> start pythonwin.exe /nodde /edit c:\scripts\pywindemo.py
```

And a new instance of PythonWin starts, with its own copy of *pywindemo.py* open for editing.

The Interactive Window

At the most obvious level, the PythonWin interactive window simulates the built-in Python interpreter in interactive mode. Almost anything you type in the standard Python shell can be used in PythonWin.

To reexecute blocks of code you previously executed, scroll the cursor to the old block and press Enter. The block is copied to the end of the interactive window, allowing you to make any changes before finally reexecuting the code. Alternatively, the Ctrl-Up and Ctrl-Down keys allow you to scroll through the previously executed commands.

PythonWin can also help you locate the source of errors in standard Python tracebacks. All Python tracebacks are printed to the interactive window, and you can double-click (or press Enter) on any line in a traceback to open the offending line in the editor.

As an example, let's force an error in our test script. Open the same *pywindemo.py* created earlier and select File → Import. Now close the source file. In the interactive window, type:

```
>>> pywindemo.hello(0)
```

PythonWin responds with:

```
Traceback (innermost last):
  File "<interactive input>", line 0, in ?
  File "c:\scripts\pywindemo.py", line 2, in hello
    print "Hello, " + msg
TypeError: illegal argument type for built-in operation
>>>
```

If you double-click on the third or fourth lines of this traceback, the test script is opened, and you are at line 2, the line with the indicated error.

The Python Editor

The PythonWin editor has many features especially designed for Python programs. In many cases these features are shared between IDLE and PythonWin; both IDEs use exactly the same (Python!) code to implement the same features.[*] The most important features with a brief description are provided here:

Unlimited undo and redo capabilities
Enough said!

Smart indentation
The editor examines existing source files to determine their indentation. If configured, the editor can override your tab preferences to match the existing file. When indenting an incomplete expression (such as a multiline list definition or function call), the correct indentation is applied to line up elements in the list or the call parameters. Entire blocks can be indented or not to allow easy program restructuring.

Block commenting
You can select a block of text and have it all commented or not with a single command.

Comment and multiline string formatting
Comment blocks and multiline strings can be reformatted. This command correctly reformats paragraphs to a 70-character width.

Attribute expansion
If you type the name of a module and certain other objects, then press the period key, a list box is displayed with a selection of attributes. The arrow keys allow you to change the selection, and the Tab key selects it. You can see this by typing **string.** in an editor or interactive window. As this book goes to press, this feature had not yet been ported to IDLE.

---

[*] And truth be told, PythonWin stole most of these features after IDLE had already implemented them. No point reinventing the wheel!

Call tips

As you type the name of a Python function and open the parenthesis, a pop-up window with information about the function may be displayed. The easiest way to see this in action is to type `string.split(`, and the Call Tip window should display.

Auto completion

This is a handy feature that means you need never mistype a variable name again. You can type the start of any word and press the ALT-/ key to complete the word. The current file is searched for words, and all words that match are selected. For example, let's assume you have an editor window with the code:

```
import string
strval = string.join(["hi", "there"])
```

If you type `st` and press ALT-/, `string` is substituted. If you press it again, `strval` is substituted, and so forth.

View whitespace

As whitespace is significant in Python, there is an option in PythonWin that allows you to view the whitespace in your file. Space characters are shown as a soft dot; tab characters are shown as an arrow. IDLE doesn't support this feature.

Fixed and proportional fonts

Many people prefer to use proportional fonts to edit source code, but proportional fonts often make it hard to see if your source code is correctly aligned. PythonWin allows you to choose your preferred fixed and proportional font and quickly toggle between the two.

Integrated object browser

Each editor window in PythonWin has an integrated browser window. This window is initially closed, but can be shown by selecting the splitter bar on the left side of the window. This browser allows you to see all the classes and functions defined in the current source file and quickly move between them.

Bookmarks

The Ctrl-F2 key allows you to set a bookmark at any line in a source file. Pressing F2 moves you between bookmarks defined in the current file. A bookmark is indicated in the margin of the editor window. Bookmarks are not available in IDLE.

Automatic file backup

PythonWin can be configured to save backup copies of your source files. These backups can be saved either in the same directory as the original but with the file extensions changed to *.bak*, or with the same name into a *bak* subdirectory in your Windows *temp* directory.

Python Path Browser

Available from the Tools menu, the Python path browser is really a bit of a misnomer. When you open the browser, it does indeed display each directory on your PythonPath and each module in that directory. However, the browser also allows you to delve into the modules, examining the functions and classes defined within.

Object Browser

PythonWin supports a fairly simple object browser. This allows you to peer deep inside any Python object, allowing you to discover various details about the object.

In contrast with the Python path browser, the object browser doesn't browse Python source code: only Python objects. This means that objects you wish to browse must actually exist in the Python environment. For example, the only way to browse a Python module in this browser is to import the module.

The object browser can be found by selecting Tools → Browser or by pressing Ctrl-B. A dialog is presented asking for the object to browse; to browse the sample Python module, enter **pywindemo** and select OK.

If you expand the **hello()** function in the browser, you should have a window similar to that shown in Figure 4-2.

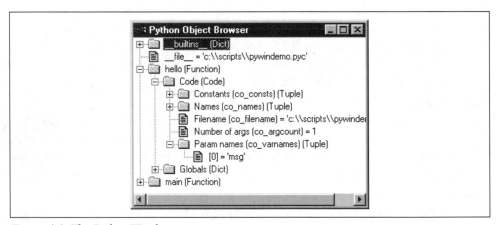

Figure 4-2. The PythonWin browser

Because the browser digs deeply into Python's internals, some of the information presented is quite esoteric. However, it can often provide useful information about your objects.

Windows Explorer Integration

PythonWin provides basic integration with the Windows Explorer. All *.py* and *.pyw* files shown in the Windows Explorer have an Edit option on their context (i.e., right-click) menu. Selecting this option starts PythonWin if it isn't already running, and opens the file for editing.

You can also drag and drop files from the Windows Explorer into PythonWin. These files are also open for editing.

PythonWin has also been registered with Windows in such a way that it can be run without knowing its specific location and without having it on your system path. If you select Start → Run from the Windows taskbar and enter `pythonwin`, it's correctly located and started. From a command prompt, you can also execute the command `start pythonwin` from any directory, and PythonWin starts. See the previous section, "Command-Line Parameters."

The Debugger

PythonWin also has a built-in Python debugger to help you develop your scripts. The PythonWin debugger includes all the features you expect in debuggers, including:

- Breakpoints that can be set at any location. Optionally, these breakpoints may have a condition that must evaluate to `true` before the breakpoint stops.

- A watch window allowing easy tracking of changes to key variables.

- Commands allowing you to step into, over, or out of functions.

If you are familiar with other Windows IDE debugging environments (such as Visual C++, Visual Basic, or Delphi) you should find the debugger easy to work with.

For a language as flexible as Python, there is one huge limitation in the debugger that is worth noting. It isn't possible to modify the code while it's being debugged. If you spot a bug while debugging, code changes you make aren't applied until you reload the module. Further, any source-code changes are likely to disrupt the debugging session, as the debugger will still be stepping though the original line positions even though they are likely to have changed.

The simplest way to use the debugger is to run scripts using the same technique described earlier, but this time select one of the debugging options. The Run Script dialog provides the following debugging options:

No debugging
   This means that the script runs normally without any debugging; it doesn't stop at breakpoints.

Step through in the debugger

Steps through each line in the debugger. Selecting this option invokes the debugger at the first line in our script. The default PythonWin configuration binds the F11 (step in) or F10 (step over) keys to this function.

Run in the debugger

Runs the script under the debugger, stopping only at breakpoints. If you select this option when no breakpoints are set, PythonWin warns you that the debugger is unlikely to be invoked. Of course, PythonWin can't determine if your breakpoints are on lines that are actually executed. If none of your breakpoints are actually hit, this command appears to run without the debugger at all; the script starts and completes normally (albeit slightly slower due to the debugger overhead). The default PythonWin configuration binds the F5 key (Go) to this function.

Postmortem of unhandled exceptions

The script isn't run under the debugger, but if an unhandled exception occurs, the debugger is invoked to perform postmortem analysis. This can be handy, as it can show you the complete state of your Python program, including all variable values, at the point where the exception was raised. If your script runs successfully (i.e., doesn't generate a traceback while running), this option has no effect.

The following discussion demonstrates the debugger using the same script developed earlier in this chapter. For the example, set a breakpoint at the first line of the `main()` function. You can set a breakpoint by moving to the line where the breakpoint should be applied and either display the debugging toolbar (View → Toolbars → Debugging) and selecting the appropriate button or press the F9 key. PythonWin should respond by placing a breakpoint indicator in the margin of the editor window. The breakpoint is simply a black outline as shown in Figure 4-3, to indicate the breakpoint is currently disabled (the debugger isn't yet running).

Select the OK button, and if all goes well, the PythonWin debugger kicks in, and you will be stopped at your breakpoint. Notice a number of changes to the PythonWin environment, as shown in Figure 4-4. The most obvious are:

- A new Debugging toolbar appears, giving access to debugger-related features (this toolbar can always be displayed using View → Toolbars → Debugging).

- A few new debugging windows appear. These windows can be docked in the PythonWin frame or left floating. Figure 4-4 shows the Stack window docked on the left side of PythonWin, and the Breakpoints and Watch windows floating.

- The debugger breakpoint turns red, indicating the debugger is active.

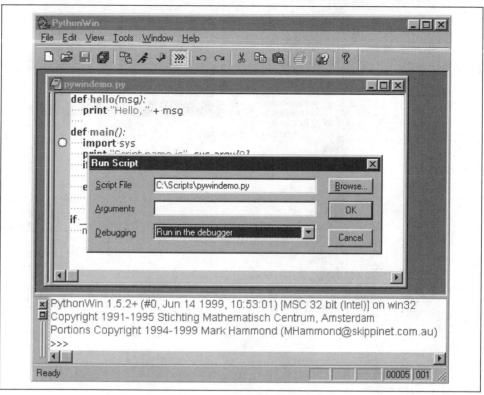

Figure 4-3. PythonWin about to debug our sample script

- The Interactive Window shows a [Dbg] indicator before the standard >>> and ... prompts, indicating that expressions you enter will be evaluated under the debugger's current context rather than in the global context used by default. This means you can view or change any local or global variables in the debugger's current function.

At this point, you can experiment with some of the debugger windows and use the debugger toolbar (or the keyboard shortcuts) to step through the program. Figure 4-4 shows the debugger after stopping at the breakpoint and selecting the Step command once.

Hard breakpoints

The term *hard breakpoint* refers to the process of changing your source code to explicitly invoke the debugger. You add a line of code that invokes the debugger directly, regardless of how you are running the script. These breakpoints are called hard because they can't be removed by the debugger: they are embedded in your code, and there is no way to reset them other than again changing the code!

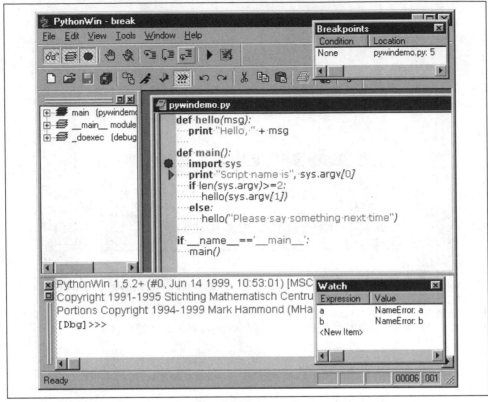

Figure 4-4. PythonWin debugging our sample script

Hard breakpoints are particularly useful when you are unable or would find it difficult to run your scripts under PythonWin. You can add a hard breakpoint to almost any Python program, be it a PythonWin program or even a Python COM object running under Active Server Pages or Internet Explorer. In almost all cases, the PythonWin debugger environment will start up, and you can debug to your heart's content.

You can set a hard breakpoint by calling the function `pywin.debugger.brk()`. It's likely that you will need to import the `pywin.debugger` module before making the call, so the code to invoke the debugger typically looks like:

```
import pywin.debugger
pywin.debugger.brk()
```

The PythonWin debugger is installed with thorough documentation, including a tutorial and sample code that demonstrates these techniques. You should familiarize yourself with this documentation to discover other debugger features.

IDLE

IDLE is an alternative Integrated Development Environment for Python. By default, the Python 1.5.2 and later installations install IDLE and a shortcut to start IDLE on your Start menu.

"IDLE" is a twist on the standard IDE acronym and is also named after Eric Idle, one of the sillier members of the Monty Python comedy troupe, but don't tell him.

As we have discussed, many IDE functions are shared between PythonWin and IDLE (or more correctly, stolen from IDLE by PythonWin, with Guido's blessing). So the differences between PythonWin and IDLE have less to do with features and more to do with platforms.

IDLE runs on almost all platforms that support Python. Although the user interface it provides isn't quite as slick as PythonWin's, you do have an IDE that runs places other than Windows. For many people, this is the single killer feature!

Of course, your choice of environment is up to you, but it appears that people who use Python on multiple platforms prefer IDLE because their environment can follow them. People who use Python only on Windows typically prefer PythonWin and its interface. As IDLE evolves further and the Tkinter GUI framework offers more features on Windows, we may find this simple distinction blurring. We recommend you spend time with both IDE environments and choose for yourself.

Platforms and Versions

IDLE is itself written in Python, using Tkinter, Python's de facto cross-platform GUI package based on Tcl/Tk. Because Python and Tcl/Tk are cross platform, so is IDLE; it works as well on Windows (95, 98, NT) as on Unix (including Linux), with minor, unavoidable differences because of inherent differences between the platforms. It also works on Macintosh (although occasionally you may experience a slight problem, because this platform gets less testing).

This section describes IDLE Version 0.5, which hasn't been released at the time of writing. The Python 1.5.2 distribution comes with IDLE Version 0.4, which differs in a number of details, so these will be detailed where appropriate. In any case, IDLE requires Python 1.5.2 or later to run. Tcl/Tk 8.0 or later (optionally installed with Python 1.5.2) is needed.

As the version number should imply, IDLE is still a young application, and features are developing at a great rate. Check the online documentation regularly to keep up with the current feature set.

Shell Window

When IDLE starts, it presents its shell window. This window is equivalent to PythonWin's Interactive Window or the interactive Python session, and it's where you enter arbitrary Python commands.

By now, you should be completely familiar with Python's own interactive (command-line) mode. We first discussed this in Chapter 2, and also previously in this chapter, so you already know how to use IDLE's Python shell window! Figure 4-5 shows the Python shell window with a few interactive commands.

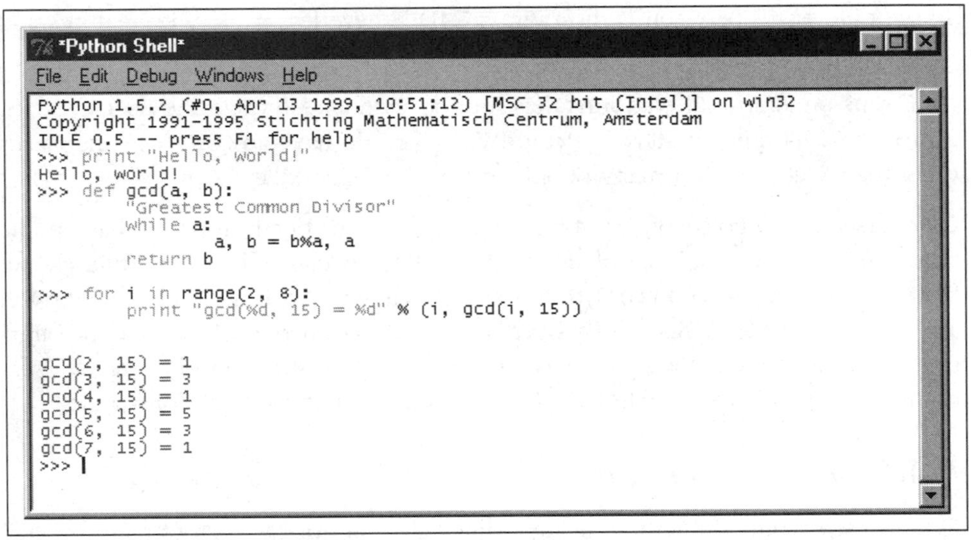

Figure 4-5. IDLE's shell window on Windows

Since we made a big song-and-dance about the cross-platform capabilities of IDLE, Figure 4-6 shows the Python shell window running on a Unix system. You will probably notice some subtle differences between the two windows; the fonts are different, hence the slightly different window sizes: the default is 80×24 character cells on all platforms. You may also notice that on Windows the Help menu is placed next to the other menus, while on Unix it's placed to the far right of the menu bar.

One of the first things the astute reader might query is the lack of the ... prompt in multiline statements. Using the "official" interactive Python mode or PythonWin, multiline statements normally look like:

```
>>> while x < 10:
...     x = x + 1
...     print x, x**3
...
>>>
```

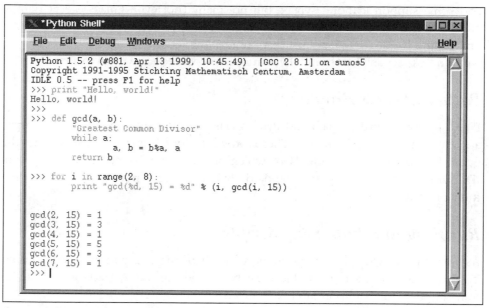

Figure 4-6. IDLE's shell window on Unix

IDLE takes a different approach. Instead of showing secondary prompts, Python automatically indents these lines with whitespace, just like the regular editor. This is one feature not provided by PythonWin; although the interactive window does perform some smart indentation, it doesn't offer the full-blown smart indentation used by IDLE and the PythonWin editor.

Just like PythonWin, you can move to a previous command and press Enter to copy the command to the end of the buffer, ready for subsequent editing and execution. The shell window also provides history capabilities, allowing you to quickly recall next and previous commands, activated by the ALT-N and ALT-P keys, respectively.

The Python Editor

You can use IDLE as an ordinary text editor to write Python programs. As discussed previously in this chapter, PythonWin recently adopted many of IDLE's best editor features, so the same, rich, Python-aware editing environment is available in IDLE. It's worth noting that IDLE and PythonWin have different default keyboard bindings, so the same features may be accessed in different ways; check the IDLE menus for the shortcut keys.

IDLE also colors the text of your program according to syntactic categories. For example, strings are displayed in green, so when you forget a string quote, you will probably notice before you run the program. Other editors have this feature, and some support Python's syntax, but not many (not even Emacs) get it right at all times. The inaccuracy can be annoying, especially when you are editing multi-line string literals. IDLE boasts that it gets the coloring 100% right, but you wouldn't expect any less from a Python source-code editor written in Python!

Path and Class Browsers

IDLE supports a Python path and Python class browser by selecting the appropriate entry from the File menu. These browsers look remarkably similar to the equivalent browsers in PythonWin, which should come as no surprise, as both IDLE and PythonWin use the standard Python module `pyclbr` to obtain their functionality.

Running and Importing Scripts

As with PythonWin, IDLE supports the concept of running and importing scripts. To run or import a script, the file must be opened in the text editor and Edit → Run Script or Edit → Import Module selected.

These features work the same as under PythonWin. Since we have experimented with these functions using PythonWin, we won't bore you with a repeat for IDLE. However, you may still want to open the same sample script used for PythonWin and test the features using IDLE.

If a traceback is printed to the Python shell window, you can move the cursor to one of the error lines and select the Go to file/line option (from the Debug or right-click menus) to open the file.

The Debugger

As you expect of an IDE, IDLE contains a built-in debugger. To use the debugger, it must first be enabled via the Debug → Debugger command from the Python shell window. The debugger dialog appears, and the shell window responds with:

```
[DEBUG ON]
>>>
```

IDLE is now ready to debug. To start the debugger, open the script to debug and run (or import) it. For the purposes of this example, let's debug the same script you used for PythonWin (*C:\Scripts\pywindemo.py* in the example). Once the file is open, select Edit → Run script (or press Ctrl-F5). The debugger dialog becomes active, and the debugging session begins. Figure 4-7 shows you stopped inside your main function.

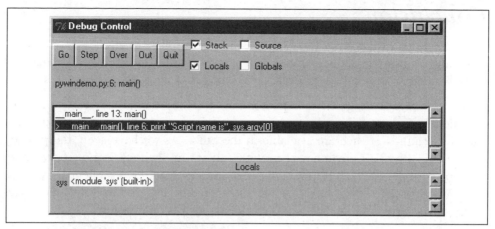

Figure 4-7. IDLE's debugger

The stack leading to the current call is shown. Selecting an entry displays the local and global variables and the source code for the stack entry, depending on the options selected at the top of the dialog.

At the time of writing, there are a few limitations in the IDLE debugger worth mentioning:

- When debugging the top-level of a module, the Go and Over commands function like the Step command. Go and Over don't function correctly until the top-level script calls a function.

- The Python shell window is effectively disabled during the debugging session. You can't use normal Python commands to view and change variables while the debugger is active.

It's quite possible that these and other limitations will be removed by the time you install IDLE.

Postmortem debugging

IDLE supports postmortem debugging, which allows you to capture the state of a Python program after an exception. Unlike PythonWin, where postmortem debugging must be explicitly enabled when running a script, IDLE allows you to perform this analysis at any time directly after an unhandled exception has occurred. To perform postmortem debugging, select Debug → Stack Viewer after the traceback has been printed. The debugger dialog is then activated, allowing you to view the state of each stack entry in the traceback.

Conclusion

This chapter provided a look at two IDEs available for Python on Windows. Both IDLE and PythonWin allow you to develop, run, and debug Python programs, and provide unique Python-based features you won't find in other environments.

PythonWin and IDLE are not competitors; in fact, they can be viewed as partners. The developers of both packages have gone to considerable effort to ensure that the best features of each are available in the other. As we have seen, the primary difference is the GUI environment in which they run. PythonWin runs only under Windows, and it takes full advantage of Windows features: excellent if you use only Windows. IDLE provides the one key feature PythonWin will almost certainly never have: its runs on all popular, modern operating systems.

Hopefully this chapter has allowed you to see how each development environment operates and encouraged you to try both. Although most examples in this book use PythonWin to run sample programs, they all work perfectly under IDLE, so feel free to use the environment of your choice.

5

Introduction to COM

In this chapter, we provide an introduction to using the Microsoft Component Object Model (COM) from Python. We will present enough introductory material so you can understand the key concepts and some simple examples that use Python and COM.

COM is a technique for using or publishing objects, regardless of the language they were implemented in. Any COM-aware environment uses a COM object in a consistent and reliable way; you need to know nothing about how the object is implemented.

COM has grown from humble beginnings. Its lineage can be traced through the Object Linking and Embedding (OLE) technology that first appeared in the Microsoft Windows 3.x family. The first version of Visual Basic included a technology known as Visual Basic Extensions, or VBXs. Microsoft started merging these technologies into OLE2, which was soon renamed COM. Since then, the Microsoft marketing machine has begun to refer to the technology as ActiveX, although COM remains the mnemonic of choice in the Windows development world. Recently, COM has been extended with the ability to distribute objects across a network, and these extensions are known as Distributed COM, or DCOM. Over time, the term DCOM will slowly vanish as the capabilities it offers are considered a standard part of COM. Microsoft is already hard at work on the next major revision of COM, currently known as COM+. Although COM+ isn't discussed in this book, all the existing COM concepts will remain for the foreseeable future.

Throughout the rest of the book, we present a number of examples that use Python and COM, so the intent of this chapter is to give you the groundwork to follow the samples. In Chapter 12, *Advanced Python and COM*, we expand on all these concepts, explaining the Python COM support in greater detail.

What It Is

COM is a technology from Microsoft that allows objects to communicate without the need for either object to know any details about the other, even the language it's implemented in.

At the lowest level, COM deals with interfaces and objects and makes a clear distinction between an object's interface and its implementation. The interface defines how an object is used, but the implementation of the interface is up to the object.

COM defines many interfaces but doesn't provide implementations for many of these interfaces. One commonly used interface, IDispatch, allows COM objects to be used from a scripting environment, such as Visual Basic or Python. Although COM has defined the interface for IDispatch, it's the responsibility of the COM objects themselves to implement this interface, and exactly how they implement it depends on the object model or functionality the COM object is trying to expose.

Objects that implement the IDispatch interface are known as automation objects. The rest of this chapter shows how to use automation objects from Python, and then we show how to create a COM object in Python and call from Visual Basic. Chapter 12 covers all these details in greater depth.

Using COM Objects from Python

When people discuss COM, they are often talking about only one side of COM—using automation objects. Automation objects are objects that expose a programmable interface that can be used by another program or environment. Examples of automation objects are Microsoft Office, the Netscape browser, or programs you write yourself in any language, such as Visual Basic, Python, Delphi, C++, and so forth.

Information about COM objects is stored in the Windows registry. Details about the object's class are stored, so that when that particular object needs to be created, the correct class is located and used. Although the term "class" doesn't refer to a Python (or C++) class, the concept is identical: the class defines the implementation, and the object is an instance of the class. Classes are registered with a unique (but complex) class ID (CLSID) and a friendly (but not guaranteed unique) program ID (ProgID). The CLSID is a globally unique identifier (GUID), as discussed later in this chapter, while the ProgID for an object is a short string that names the object and typically creates an instance of the object. For example, Microsoft Excel defines its ProgID as Excel.Application, Microsoft Word defines Word.Application, and so forth.

Python programs use the `win32com.client.Dispatch()` method to create COM objects from a ProgID or CLSID. For example, you could use this code to create an Excel object:

```
>>> import win32com.client
>>> xl = win32com.client.Dispatch("Excel.Application")
>>>
```

or to create a Microsoft Word object:

```
>>> import win32com.client
>>> wd = win32com.client.Dispatch("Word.Application")
>>>
```

So what to do with these objects? One of COM's greatest strengths is also one of its greatest weaknesses. Each COM object can define its own object model, that is, the methods and properties the object exposes to allow it to perform its task. The problem with this approach is that many COM objects present a unique object model, and if you learn how to use Microsoft Office using COM, the next COM object you need to use could define a different model. Microsoft is addressing this issue in its own products by attempting to define a similar object model across applications: the interface to Microsoft Excel is similar to the interface for Microsoft Word. However, the COM objects you need may present a completely different interface. The only solution to this problem is documentation; you must locate and read the documentation on the object model for the COM object you wish to use.

When you install Microsoft Office, the documentation for the COM object model isn't installed by default During the installation process, you should select each product from the Installation Options and check the Help options for that product. If you have already installed Microsoft Office, you can run the setup program again and add these Help components to your installation.

If you view the documentation for Microsoft Office, notice that both `Excel.Application` and `Word.Application` have a `Visible` property. Let's look at this property for Microsoft Excel:

```
>>> xl.Visible
0
>>>
```

Excel isn't visible, explaining why you can't see an instance of Excel running on your PC. (It's there, though!)

Let's set the `Visible` property to `true`:

```
>>> xl.Visible = 1
>>>
```

Excel now appears on the display. If you try the same thing with the Microsoft Word object, you get the same results:

```
>>> wd.Visible
>>> 0
>>> wd.Visible = 1
>>>
```

Python manages COM lifetimes automatically for you; when your **xl** variable is no longer used, Excel automatically closes. In Python, the simplest way to remove this variable is to assign it to another value. If you use the following code, notice that Excel vanishes from the screen; it knows there are no longer any programs referring to it:

```
>>> xl = None
>>>
```

For more information on using COM objects from Python, please see Chapter 12.

Implementing COM Objects with Python

In this section, we discuss how to implement COM objects using Python and a small sample of such an object. We also present some Visual Basic code that uses our Python implemented object.

For this demonstration, you'll write a simple COM object that supports a number of string operations. As Visual Basic is somewhat lacking in the string-processing department where Python excels, it's a good candidate. The sample provides a COM object with a single method, **SplitString()**. This method has semantics identical to the standard Python function **string.split()**; the first argument is a string to split, and the second optional argument is a string holding the character to use to make the split. As you have no doubt guessed, the method won't do much more than call the Python **string.split()** function.

There are two steps to implement COM objects in Python:

- Define a Python class with the methods and properties you wish to expose.

- Annotate the Python class with special attributes required by the PythonCOM framework to expose the Python class as a COM object. These annotations include information such as the objects ProgID, CLSID, and so forth.

The following code shows a small COM server written in Python:

```
# SimpleCOMServer.py - A sample COM server - almost as small as they come!
#
# We expose a single method in a Python COM object.
class PythonUtilities:
    _public_methods_ = [ 'SplitString' ]
    _reg_progid_ = "PythonDemos.Utilities"
    # NEVER copy the following ID
```

```
# Use "print pythoncom.CreateGuid()" to make a new one.
_reg_clsid_ = "{41E24E95-D45A-11D2-852C-204C4F4F5020}"

def SplitString(self, val, item=None):
    import string
    if item != None: item = str(item)
    return string.split(str(val), item)

# Add code so that when this script is run by
# Python.exe, it self-registers.
if __name__=='__main__':
    print "Registering COM server..."
    import win32com.server.register
    win32com.server.register.UseCommandLine(PythonUtilities)
```

The bulk of the class definition is taken up by the special attributes:

_public_methods_

A list of all methods in the object that are to be exposed via COM; the sample exposes only one method, SplitString.

_reg_progid_

The ProgID for the new object, that is, the name that the users of this object must use to create the object.

_reg_clsid_

The unique CLSID for the object. As noted in the source code, you must never copy these IDs, but create new ones using pythoncom.CreateGuid().

Full details of these and other possible attributes can be found in Chapter 12.

The SplitString() method is quite simple: it mirrors the behavior of the Python string.split() function. A complication is that COM passes all strings as Unicode characters, so you must convert them to Python strings using the str() function. Note that in Python 1.6, it's expected that the string and Unicode types will be unified allowing the explicit conversions to be removed.

The only thing remaining is to register the object with COM. As the comments in the code imply, you can do this by executing the code as a normal Python script. The easiest way to do this is to open the source file in PythonWin and use the Run command from the File menu. After running the script, the PythonWin interactive window should display:

```
Registering COM server...
Registered: PythonDemos.Utilities
```

Finally, let's test the COM object. Use Visual Basic for Applications, which ships with both Microsoft Office and Microsoft Excel, and perform the following steps:

1. Start Microsoft Word or Microsoft Excel.

2. Press ALT-F8 to display the macros dialog.

3. Enter a name for the macro (e.g., `TestPython`) and select Create.

4. The Visual Basic editor is displayed. In the editor, enter the following code:

```
Set PythonUtils = CreateObject("PythonDemos.Utilities")
response = PythonUtils.SplitString("Hello from VB")
for each Item in response
  MsgBox Item
next
```

Your display should look something like Figure 5-1.

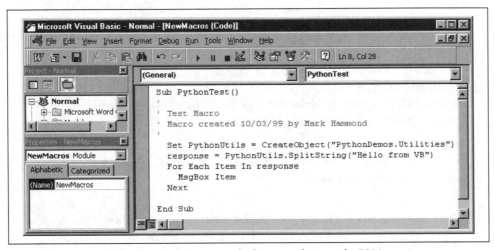

Figure 5-1. Visual Basic for Applications code that uses the sample COM server

Now run this code by pressing the F5 key. If all goes well, you should see three message boxes. The first one is shown in Figure 5-2.

Figure 5-2. First of three message boxes displayed by the VB code

Just to be complete and help keep your registry clean, unregister your sample COM server. You do this by following the same process that registered the server, except specify --**unregister** as an argument to your script. A message is printed saying the object is unregistered.

Globally Unique Identifiers

As mentioned earlier in the chapter, a COM object registers itself with a unique identifier. Whenever COM needs a truly unique identifier, it uses a globally unique identifier or GUID. A GUID is a 128-bit number, generated using a complex algorithm and the unique ID burnt into a computer's network interface card, which makes it statistically improbable the same number will ever be generated twice.

New GUIDs can be created from Python code using the following code:

```
>>> import pythoncom
>>> print pythoncom.CreateGuid()
{FA21CDC1-381F-11D3-8559-204C4F4F5020}
```

Python prints the GUID using the standard hexadecimal representation inside braces, and this same format is used everywhere an ASCII representation of a GUID is required.

GUIDs are used for a variety of purposes in COM; we have already discussed how they function as CLSIDs to uniquely identify object implementations, and in later chapters you'll see them put to use in a variety of different ways.

Conclusion

In this chapter, we presented a quick introduction to using Python and COM. We covered:

- Some key fundamental COM concepts to provide a context for the Python discussions.

- Using COM objects from Python and a quick example using Microsoft Excel or Microsoft Word.

- Implementation of COM objects in Python so they can be used by other COM-aware environments or languages. We demonstrated a COM object using Visual Basic for Applications.

- The concept of the COM GUID to help you understand how those strange looking strings are used.

We use the concepts introduced here throughout the book. In Chapter 12 these concepts are described in far greater detail.

II

Building an Advanced Python Application

6

A Financial Modeling Toolkit in Python

Welcome to Part II. By now you should have a good idea what Python is and the general techniques for integrating Python into a Windows environment. Part II focuses on developing an advanced Windows application using Python and COM. Over the next few chapters, we'll build the core of an application, put an industry-standard Visual Basic GUI up front, demonstrate how to access it from other Office applications, show how to give the users a macro language and their own scripting capabilities, and introduce distributed processing.

In this chapter, there won't be any Windows specifics. Instead, we'll design and build a Python engine that is sophisticated enough to do some interesting and useful work; we'll then develop and integrate this further into Windows over the next few chapters. If you are new to Python, this chapter should also strengthen your understanding of object-oriented programming in Python and of manipulating basic data structures such as lists and dictionaries. Although this is just an example application, we'll touch on how you would optimize for both performance and robustness in a commercial environment.

Doubletalk

The example application is a slimmed-down version of a set of tools developed by one of the authors over the last few years. The toolkit is intended to be a language for *double-entry bookkeeping*, hence the name *DoubleTalk*. The original intention, many years ago, was to develop a language for dealing with financial objects, in which users could express and solve a variety of financial problems. An absolute requirement is for end users to be able to work interactively and compile and run their own scripts. Python took away the need to create a whole new language; all that is needed is a class library.

We believe this general approach has great benefits in other fields. If you can build a class library to capture the essence of some problem domain and expose those classes to users in an easy-to-use environment like Python, you give them the ability to create new applications for themselves.

 Since this is an example in a book and not a commercial product, let's clearly state our "quality objective." We want a simple class library that lets a careful user write scripts to manipulate financial data. We aren't creating a production-quality application that checks everything and saves the user from all possible mistakes, and there will be a number of shortcuts and hacks a production application would not take; we'll point these out as we go.

The core of the library is a pair of classes, **Transaction** and **BookSet**, which aim to capture the essence of a set of accounts. They enforce the rules of accounting that must be obeyed, but allow the user to perform a wide range of high-level manipulations.

Applications for the toolkit might include:

Doing real accounts

Although the class library could do this, it probably shouldn't; the place for a small company's accounts is in a commercial accounting package, and the place for a large company's accounts is in a well-managed and secure database. Nevertheless, the toolkit could be used as a layer on top of a more-secure form of storage.

Doing forecast accounts

You can write a Python simulation program to generate streams of future transactions. Such a simulation starts off with some sort of real accounts to date and adds expected future transactions. This builds a seamless picture for a business in which past and future results are evaluated on the same basis.

Matching up sets of accounts

Accountants and financial analysts often need to compare accounts. The comparison could be for different companies, different periods with varying accounting standards, or several subsidiaries needing to consolidate accounts into one coherent set of books. To do this you need interactive tools to spot gaps, close them with the right entries, establish the transformations, and write cleanup scripts.

Data laundering

You can acquire data from various databases and manual sources and write scripts to convert the data into transactions, integrating them into one overall picture of a business.

Market models

In the securities business people frequently model the behavior of financial instruments under various conditions. These instruments can be created as objects that generate transactions in response to chronology or changing economic variables. A Python simulation won't be as fast as C++, but you can have it today instead of next month. The model output includes detailed portfolio breakdowns (the balance sheet) at each point, as well as a profit-and-loss picture.

Reporting

Financial reports can be complex; they involve a lot of tables with numbers. But there are also things that must add up and rules the numbers must obey. These constraints derive from the double-entry accounting model, and reports are far easier to design if you start with a coherent data model.

Why use Python? Quite simply, because all these tasks vary slightly from company to company and from situation to situation. Rather than a monolithic application, what you need is a basic set of tools for dealing with financial objects that ensure the rules are respected and a macro language to let you customize their behavior.

A Crash Course in Accounting

We'll make this as quick as possible. There are two concepts to grasp: transactions and the chart of accounts.

Transactions

The *double-entry* system of accounting dates back over 400 years, to an Italian named Fra. Luca Pacioli (who recently had a PC accounting package named after him). The key idea was to keep track of where money comes from and where it goes. Double-entry must rate as one of the most powerful notations ever, the business equivalent of Newton's achievements in physics. What follows is a formal notation and set of rules to encapsulate double-entry. As with physics, it's best just to work through a few examples rather than analyze the concepts too early.

A *transaction* is a financial event. It occurs at a certain point in time, affects two or more accounts, and the effect of those accounts sums to zero. The use of the term transaction in the database world was borrowed from accountants, who got there first by a few centuries. The key concept is that the whole thing has to happen at once or not at all; if only part of a transaction takes place, your system goes out of whack. Conceptually you can lay one out on the page like the following table.

Date:	01/01/1998
Comment:	Start the company
Cash	+10 000
Share Capital	-10 000

A set of accounts (or BookSet) is basically a list of such transactions. An account is a way of categorizing money, but it has no precise economic meaning; fortunately, it soon becomes obvious what an account means in practice.

Here's what happens when you go out and buy something for cash.

Date:	07/03/1998
Comment:	Buy computer manuals
Cash	-27.95
Expenditure (Publications)	+27.95

By convention, increases in cash are positive, and decreases are negative. Thus, accounts for tracking expenditure like the previous one for Publications, are usually positive, and Share Capital (from the first example) has to be negative. The nonintuitive part is that accounts for classifying income have to be negative, and so does profit, which is income minus expenditure. It could as easily have been the other way around, but the decision was made centuries ago.

Cleaning this process up for the shareholders and managers should be a function of the *reporting layer* of the system, which aims to hide the complexity of these negative numbers. Only the programmer or database designer really needs to grasp them.

The ancients were not so happy with negative numbers and used the left and right sides of a sheet of paper, naming them *debit* and *credit*, which are *plus* and *minus* in our system. Accountants just knew that cash went on the left and income went on the right, and nobody saw a minus sign. Most people expect it to be the other way around, but the banks have been fooling you by using their viewpoint on statements and not the customer's; when your bank statement says "CR" in small letters, it means the bank is in credit: they owe you money. We programmers should be perfectly happy with a minus sign and a list of numbers, so we'll use the raw data.

It's worth noting that the phrase double-entry bookkeeping itself is slightly out of date. The old paper procedures involved two entries, but with the addition of sales taxes, many real-world transactions have three entries, and others have many entries. So *multiple-entry* would be a better name. If a business sells three items in the United Kingdom you want to classify separately and where sales tax is 17.5%, the sales transaction needs five entries that look like the following table.

Date:	10/03/1999
Comment:	Sell Widgets
Cash	+117.50
Sales Category 1	-50.00
Sales Category 2	-30.00
Sales Category 3	-20.00
Sales tax on all three (owed to Customs & Excise)	-17.50

Unfortunately, accountants generally are not database designers, and arguments rage in theoretical texts over the proper way to deconstruct this into pairs of entries. We won't worry about it; we've got a simple master-detail view and a constraint that the right column sums to zero, and that's all there is to it.

The Chart of Accounts

The second concept to grasp is that of the *chart of accounts*, or as we call it, the *tree of accounts*. There is an almost universal consensus on what standard accounts should be called and how they relate to each other. This is a large part of what is known as Generally Accepted Accounting Practice or GAAP. If you have ever struggled with rules such as *assets = liabilities + capital*, relax: we deal with that in the next few minutes. Every company's balance sheet is just a tree, and (with the arrival of Windows 95) almost everyone in the world knows what tree views look like, as shown in Figure 6-1..

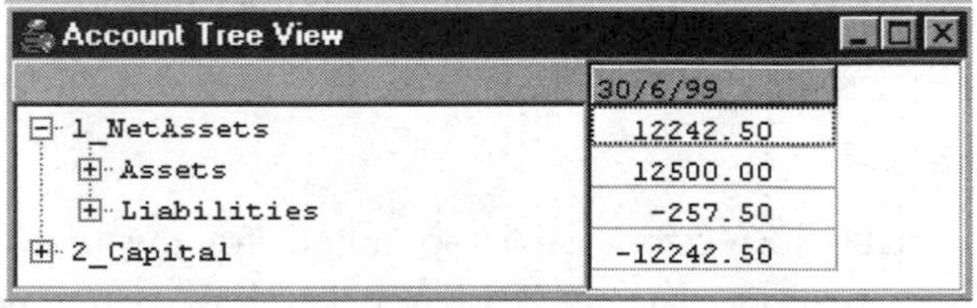

Figure 6-1. The outermost layers of a balance sheet, as a tree

Figure 6-1 shows a tree view of a company's account structure. The balance sheet has two sections, Net Assets and Capital, both of which necessarily have equal size and opposite signs.* Net Assets are what the company is worth on paper and include Assets, which have a plus sign, and Liabilities, which have a negative sign.

---

* Some companies cut the cake differently, displaying Assets as the top half of the balance sheet, and Liabilities and Capital together on the bottom half. If you are interested in the book value of the company, the way we have done it brings the right numbers to the top. It won't affect our data structures either way.

The totals on the right are inclusive balances showing everything in the tree below that point; ignore them for now.

If you investigate further (see Figure 6-2), you'll see that Assets are made up of cash, tangible assets a company owns (like computers), and money owed by others. Similarly, Liabilities includes overdrafts, money owed to creditors, and long-term loans. Capital, which has to match Net Assets, is made up of what you started with (your capital) and what you have made or lost since (Profit/Loss). Profit/Loss is simply income minus expenditure.

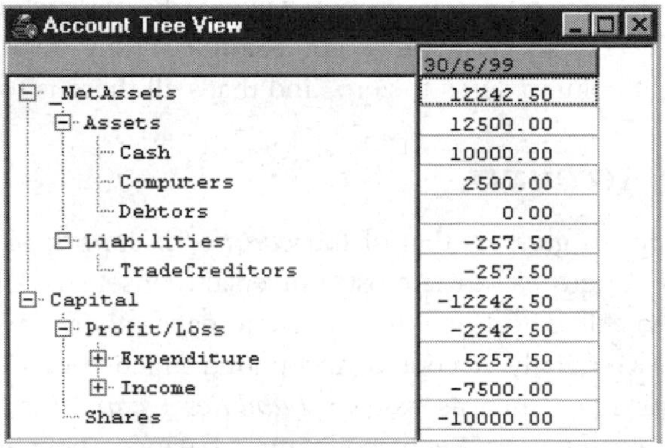

Account Tree View	30/6/99
⊟ _NetAssets	12242.50
⊟ Assets	12500.00
Cash	10000.00
Computers	2500.00
Debtors	0.00
⊟ Liabilities	-257.50
TradeCreditors	-257.50
⊟ Capital	-12242.50
⊟ Profit/Loss	-2242.50
⊞ Expenditure	5257.50
⊞ Income	-7500.00
Shares	-10000.00

Figure 6-2. A simple tree of accounts

Naturally, Income and Expenditure can be divided into further specific categories, as can just about any of the accounts. But this is the simplest, reasonably complete picture of an accounting system.

Timing considerations

Figure 6-2 is essentially correct but a bit too simple for the real world. What follows presents more realistic data, so feel free to skip to the next section if it doesn't interest you.

One of the main reasons companies have to publish accounts is to tell the world how safe they are to do business with. There are two definitions of insolvency. If a company's net assets go below zero, it's insolvent. However, an important consideration for managers, suppliers, and shareholders is whether the company has enough cash to meet its short-term obligations. If a company doesn't appear able to meet its short-term obligations, it can also be ruled insolvent. In the United Kingdom, there are titled aristocrats who own huge, historic estates they are not allowed to sell or modify for heritage reasons, and they can't possibly meet the running costs. These people have positive net assets, but they are insolvent by the second criterion. Company accounts have to handle these possibilities. We therefore introduce a distinction between current assets (cash, or things that should turn into cash within a year, like stock and debtors) and fixed assets (things with longer term value, like your factory). We then regroup things to get a single total of net current assets (NCA), a key indication of the short-term health of a business.

Figure 6-3 shows a simple business from two viewpoints. The left side displays six transactions occurring in date order; the right, a tree view at a point in time following the six transactions, with inclusive totals at each level. This is the tree structure we will use in examples from now on. You may find it interesting to trace how the totals were worked out.

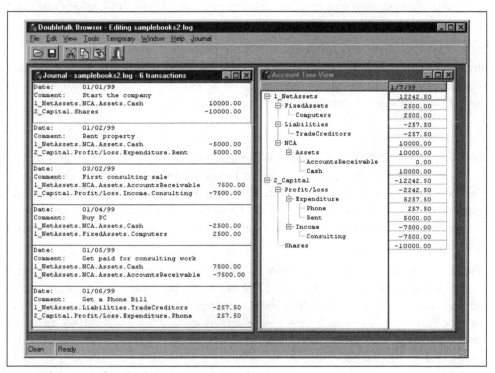

Figure 6-3. A set of books showing Journal and Tree Views

In the real world, category names differ from country to country, and there are many more sublevels and exceptions to deal with. But the chart of accounts is still a tree and broadly follows that pattern.

A large number of accounting systems don't actually use a tree structure. They have a flat list of numbered accounts with hardcoded rules defining which numeric ranges are assets, liabilities, income, and expenditure. This can lead to complex reporting problems, when the accounts system doesn't quite match the desired grouping for a particular kind of report. We're going to sidestep all that.

The data structures we need, then, must capture the following features:

- A transaction affects a number of accounts, but must sum to zero.

- The accounts must be arranged in a tree.

Back to Python

Our design goal is a general-purpose toolkit that allows you to formulate and solve financial problems in Python. To create the toolkit, we will build classes to represent common financial objects. All the code is available for downloading, so we show only selected excerpts; we do, however, list the main functions our class library makes available, for use in later chapters.

First of all, let's look at a few utilities. If you are fluent in Python, the code will be straightforward and not particularly interesting; but please skim through it anyway to grasp the business logic. If you are new to Python, this chapter should help consolidate your understanding of the language.

Dates and times

Python uses the Unix time system, which measures seconds since midnight on January 1, 1970 (which is when urban legend says the first Unix system booted up). The latest time possible in the system is sometime on January 19, 2038. We don't want to be tied to this system forever and will therefore express input and output in calendar units, hiding the actual implementation. The *dates.py* module defines a few helper constants and functions.

EARLY is defined as the earliest date possible on your system or at least earlier than any transactions you will enter. LATE is an arbitrary date later than any transaction you will enter. The functions asc2sec(aDateString) and sec2asc (aTime) convert between a string representation such as 31-Dec-1998 and seconds. Be aware that the Python time module exposes functions to do the same thing, in a slightly wordy manner, but with more options. There is also a package available called mxDateTime that offers a wider range of date utilities and functions and is worth considering for a commercial application.

The function later() works with the constants YEARS, MONTHS, WEEKS, DAYS, HOURS, MINUTES, and SECONDS to let you do calendar math easily. The following console session should clarify these:

```
>>> from dates import *
>>> sec2asc(EARLY), sec2asc(LATE)
('1-Jan-1970', '19-Jan-2038')
>>> endAugust = asc2sec('31-Aug-1999')
>>> billingDate = later(endAugust, 5, DAYS)
>>> sec2asc(billingDate)
'5-Sep-1999'
```

```
>>> paymentDate = later(billingDate, 2, MONTHS)
>>> sec2asc(paymentDate)
'5-Nov-1999'
>>>
```

Now we examine a couple of helper data structures that will come in handy later. These can be found in the module *datastruct.py*. A `Set` holds only one copy of each item; we'll use it to find the unique elements in a big list quickly. A `NumDict` categorizes numbers. Here's the usage:

```
>>> import datastruct
>>> myset = datastruct.Set()
>>> myset.add('Spam')
>>> myset.add('Eggs')
>>> myset.add('Spam')
>>> myset.contains('beer')
0
>>> myset.elements()          # returned in alpha order
['Eggs', 'Spam']
>>> sales = datastruct.NumDict()
>>> sales['North'] = 100      # direct assignment, like a dictionary
>>> sales.inc('North',50)     # increment it
>>> sales.inc('East', 130)
>>> sales['East']
130
>>> sales.items()
[('East', 130), ('North', 150)]
>>> sales['South']            # returned in alpha order
0
>>>
```

Both structures are built on top of Python dictionaries and are extremely efficient with large amounts of data. `NumDict` is particularly useful as we will spend a lot of time categorizing numeric data.

Now to see how these are defined. Here is the module *datastruct.py*:

```
# datastruct.py - some generic data structures
# see the Language Reference under 3.3, Special Method Names

class Set:
    "minimal implementation to help clarity of code elsewhere"
    def __init__(self):
        self.data = {}
    def contains(self, element):
        return self.data.has_key(element)
    def add(self, element):
        self.data[element] = 1
    def elements(self):
        keys = self.data.keys()
        keys.sort()
        return keys

class NumDict:
    "Dictionary to categorize numbers."
```

```
def __init__(self, input = None):
    self.data = {}
    if input is not None:
        for item in input:
            (category, value) = item
            self.inc(category, value)


def __getitem__(self, key):
    return self.data.get(key, 0)

def __setitem__(self, key, value):
    self.data[key] = value

def inc(self, key, value):
    self.data[key] = self.data.get(key, 0) + value

def items(self):
    it = self.data.items()
    it.sort()
    return it

def clear(self):
    self.data.clear()
```

These data structures introduce some of Python's Magic Methods such as
_ _getitem_ _(self, key). Magic Methods allow user-defined classes to respond
to just about every operator Python provides. You can think of the most compact
syntax you want for users of your class, and then implement it with Magic Methods. They are fully documented in the Python reference manual, Section 3.3,
which is part of the standard distribution.

Coding Transactions

Now it's time to design a core object model. The module *transac.py* defines a
Transaction class that captures the key notions we covered earlier. It also goes
somewhat further; we've used Magic Methods to define a basic algebra of accounting. The class construction is straightforward. However, first we need to mention
three design issues. Since this is a contrived application, we've gone for simple
solutions that are good enough for our needs; for a proper accounting system, the
solutions would be different.

- The first issue is how to represent the tree structure behind a company's
  accounts. After several years of experimenting with different designs, it's clear
  that simple strings do the job nicely. Thus a cash account can be represented
  with a string like *MyCo.Assets.NCA.CurAss.Cash.MyWallet.* This reduces lots of
  complex tree operations to simple string functions; finding the sum of all cash
  accounts becomes trivial. It should of course be hidden in the user interface to
  save end users from typing, but it clarifies the data structure.

- The second issue is how to keep the balance sheet in the right order as shown in Figure 6-3. You'll see that the accounts were named in alphabetical order at every level; we cheated and used 1_NetAssets and 2_Capital at the top level to force an alphabetical order. This hack keeps our tree in the conventional balance sheet order without needing any extra sort fields. The display account names used in reports (or indeed a GUI) could easily be looked up in a dictionary.

- The final design issue is whether to have a separate class instance for every single transaction, or to go for a lower-level (and faster) implementation involving nested lists and tuples, since indexing into a list is faster than accessing a class attribute. For this book we've opted for a slower but more readable implementation, and a recent upgrade from 75 to 266 MHz largely covers up the loss. We discuss options for optimizing later on.

Let's take a quick tour of how to construct and work with transactions:

```
>>> import transac
>>> T1 = transac.Transaction()
>>> T1.date = asc2sec('1/1/1999')
>>> T1.comment = 'Start the company'
>>> T1.addLine('MyCo.Assets.NCA.CurAss.Cash', 10000)
>>> T1.addLine('MyCo.Capital.Shares', -10000)
>>> T1.validate()
>>> T1.display()                                    # print to standard output
Date:          1-Jan-1999
Comment:       Start the company
MyCo.Assets.NCA.CurAss.Cash             10000.000000
MyCo.Capital.Shares                     -10000.000000

>>> T2 = transac.Transaction()
>>> T2.date = asc2sec('5-Jan-1999')                 # four days later...
>>> T2.comment = 'Loan from Grandma'
>>> T2.addLine('MyCo.Assets.NCA.CurAss.Cash', 15000)
>>> T2.addLastLine('MyCo.Assets.OtherLia.Loans')    # addLastLine rounds\
>>>                                                 # off the final line for you
>>> T2.display()
Date:          5-Jan-1999
Comment:       Loan from Grandma
MyCo.Assets.NCA.CurAss.Cash             15000.000000
MyCo.Assets.OtherLia.Loans              -15000.000000
```

The **validate()** method checks if a transaction balances and raises an error if it doesn't. Later on we'll show how to ensure this is called.

Transaction objects are atomic packets of data; they don't do a lot by themselves and get interesting only in large numbers. However, they can display themselves, convert themselves to and from other formats such as blocks of text, and most important, they support some mathematical operations:

```
>>> T3 = T1 + T2     # we can add them together
>>> T3.display()
Date:          5-Jan-1999
Comment:       <derived transaction>
MyCo.Assets.NCA.CurAss.Cash              25000.000000
MyCo.Assets.OtherLia.Loans              -15000.000000
MyCo.Capital.Shares                     -10000.000000

>>> T4 = T1 * 1.2
>>> T4.display()
Date:          1-Jan-1999
Comment:     <New Transaction>
MyCo.Assets.NCA.CurAss.Cash              12000.000000
MyCo.Capital.Shares                     -12000.000000

>>>
```

These operations make it simple to express, for example, the combined effects of a complex multistage deal or to model sales growing by 10% per month. The full API supported by **Transaction** objects is as follows:

def __init__(self):
Creates **Transactions** with the current time and no lines.

__cmp__(self, other)
Sorts **Transactions** according to date.

__str__(self)
Returns a printable description suitable for inclusion in, e.g., a list box.

getDateString(self)
Returns its date as a string formatted as "12-Aug-1999 18:55:42."

setDateString(self, aDateString)
Allows date to be set from a text string as well as directly.

isEqual(self, other)
Returns **true** if the **Transactions** agree to the nearest second and 1/100 of a currency unit (even if comments differ).

addLine(self, account, amount, dict=None)
Lets you build transactions up a line at a time.

addLastLine(self, account, dict=None)
Saves you doing the math. The amount for the last line is worked out for you to ensure the transaction balances.

validate(self, autocorrect=0)
By default, raises an exception if the transaction isn't zero. If **autocorrect** is set to zero, it silently adds an entry for the magic account (**uncategorized**) to round it off. This might be useful in a huge import, and the extra account shows up on all your reports.

renameAccount(self, oldAcct, newAcct)

> Renames accounts, or the first part of any accounts, within the transaction, thereby allowing you to restructure the tree of accounts.

compact(self)

> If there are several lines, e.g., for Cash, compacts them into one total.

effectOn(self, targetAccount)

> Tells you the effect the transaction has on the target account.

__add__(self, other), __neg__(self), __mul__(self, scalar), __div__ (self, scalar)

> Implements basic transaction algebra.

flows(self, fromAccount)

> For analyzing financial flows: tells you how much money flowed into (or out of, if negative) the transaction from the given account.

display(self)

> Prints a readable representation containing all the lines on standard output.

asTuple(self)

> Returns a compact representation as a Python tuple, useful sometimes for portability and speed, as we will see later on. The module defines a function tranFromTuple*(aTuple)* that converts these back to **Transaction** class instances.

asString(self)

> Returns a multiline string for use in displaying or saving to text files. The module defines a function tranFromString*(aChunk)* to help parse transactions in text files, although slight rounding errors can become a problem with text storage and prevent perfect round trips.

asDicts(self)

> Returns a set of dictionaries holding data for multidimensional analysis.

magnitude(self)

> Returns a number indicating the rough size of the transaction, for display in graphical views to help users find transactions. The meaning is somewhat undefined for complex multiline transactions!

Finally, the **transac** module defines a function transfer*(date, comment, debitAccount, creditAccount, amount)* that lets you create a transaction rapidly with just two lines.

BookSets

The next step is to represent a set of books. Many accounting systems grew up with programmers and analysts trying to model the paper processes of old accounting systems, with complex posting and validation rules. Our representation turns out to be nothing more than a list of transactions in date order. Many of the common financial reports can be extracted with some simple loops through this list. In database parlance, we have normalized our design, and will now define lots of *views* on top of it to get the data the users want. By storing transactions and only transactions, rather than allowing the line items to exist separately in some other kind of database, it's easy to ensure that the whole system obeys the fundamental rule of summing to zero as we manipulate the data.

The `BookSet` class now captures the logical structure of a general set of books. We also give it the ability to load and save its data, add, edit, and delete transactions, and display common views of the data.

The examples at the web site *http://starship.python.net/crew/mhammond/ppw32/* include a script, *demodata1.py*, that generates a `BookSet` with 1,000 transactions and saves it to a file for future use. This test set of data is constant and can be used for volume testing and optimization. It shows a two-year forecast business model for a small consulting company called Pythonics Ltd. which, after a shaky start, achieves superior productivity and wealth through Python.

As before, we kick off with a quick demo of some of `BookSet`'s capabilities. We adopt the convention that methods beginning with `get` retrieve data, usually in the form of a list of strings or tuples, and methods beginning with `list` print that data to the console:

```
>>> bs = demodata1.getData()
>>> bs[0].display()
Date:       1-Jan-1999
Comment:    Initial investment
MyCo.Assets.NCA.CurAss.Cash           10000.000000
MyCo.Capital.Shares                  -10000.000000

>>> bs.listAccountDetails('MyCo.Assets.OtherLia.BankLoan')
Details of account MyCo.Assets.OtherLia.BankLoan
------------------ ---------------------------
    37 1-Feb-1999    Loan drawdown           -10000.00  -10000.00
    72 1-Mar-1999    Loan repayment             378.12   -9621.88
   113 1-Apr-1999    Loan repayment             381.27   -9240.61
   149 1-May-1999    Loan repayment             384.45   -8856.16
<<lines omitted>>
   993 1-Jan-2001    Loan repayment             453.86    -457.50
   998 1-Feb-2001    Final loan repayment       457.50       0.00

>>> endOfYear2 = asc2sec('31-Dec-2000')
>>> bs.getAccountBalance('MyCo.Capital.PL', endOfYear2)  # are we in profit yet?
-258416.088
>>> # Yes, rolling in it  (remember, cash is positive, profits and income are
>>> # negative)
>>> Q1, Q2 = asc2sec('31-Mar-2000'), asc2sec('30-Jun-2000')
```

```
>>> bs.getAccountActivity('MyCo.Capital.PL.Expenses', Q1, Q2)
69961.19
>>>
```

All these queries are implemented as simple loops over the transactions in the BookSet. For example, to get the previous account details, we implement an internal function called `getAccountDetails()` as follows:

```
def getAccountDetails(self, match):
    from string import find  # import into local namespace, a bit faster
    runtot = 0
    tranNo = 0
    results = []
    for tran in self.__journal:
        dateStr = sec2asc(tran.date)
        comment = tran.comment
        for (account, delta, etc) in tran.lines:
            if find(account,match) <> -1:
                runtot = runtot + delta
                results.append((tranNo, dateStr, comment, delta, runtot))
        tranNo = tranNo + 1
    return results

def listAccountDetails(self, match):
    print 'Details of account',match
    print '------------------ ' + ('-' * len(match))
    for row in self.getAccountDetails(match):
        print '%5d %-12s %-40s %10.2f %10.2f' % row
    print
```

Note line 6, `for tran in self.__journal`. The `__` convention provides private attributes; these attributes can be referenced by name only inside the class, not by external users of the class. This is a good way to hide information.

It's worth noting the way transactions are added. They must be stored internally in date order. To ensure this, use a modified binary insertion routine lifted from the Python library module *insort.py*. You first validate the transaction, and then do a quick check to see if it's the first transaction in the BookSet or if it's dated the same or later than the last one, and put it at the end. Loading from a file that's already in date order is fast and saves searching. Otherwise, you should do a binary search. Inserting a transaction in a 1000-transaction journal takes no more than eight comparisons:

```
def add(self, tran):
    # this could be optimized by putting the
    # length=0 case in an exception handler
    tran.validate()
    if len(self.__journal) == 0:
        self.__journal.append(tran)
    else:
        # quick check if it's the last - might happen
        # very often when loading from a file
```

```
                if cmp(tran, self.__journal[-1]) >= 0:
                    self.__journal.append(tran)
                else:
                    self._insertInOrder(tran)

        def _insertInOrder(self, tran):
            # copied from Python library - binary
            # insertion routine
            lo = 0
            hi = len(self.__journal)
            while lo < hi:
                mid = (lo + hi) / 2
                if tran < self.__journal[mid]:
                    hi = mid
                else:
                    lo = mid + 1
            self.__journal.insert(lo, tran)
```

Adding persistence: Pickles last forever

In most languages you would have to write a lot of code to save and load your data. In Python you don't.

BookSet uses one of Python's persistence tools, the **cPickle** module. Python has three modules that can save almost any structure to disk for you. **Marshal** is written in C and is the fastest, but is limited to numbers, strings, lists, dictionaries, and tuples. **Pickle** was written in Python and allows arbitrary objects to be stored to disk. **cPickle** is a recent rewrite of **pickle** in C, which allows high-speed storage approaching that of **Marshal**. Here are the **BookSet** methods to save and load the data:

```
        def save(self, filename):
            f = open(filename,'wb')
            cPickle.dump(self.__journal,f)
            f.close()

        def load(self, filename):
            f = open(filename, 'r')
            data = cPickle.load(f)
            for tran in data:
                self.add(tran)
            f.close()
```

We did a little preparation by opening a file, but it takes only one line to save and reload all of our data. If you subsequently redesign your **Transaction** class, you don't need to rewrite the persistence code. Persistence is one of Python's most powerful features.

Summary of the BookSet API

BookSet offers a lot of methods. We won't list them exhaustively—you'll see plenty later on—but here are the main families:

Editing methods

add(*self, tran*), remove(*self, index*), edit(*self, index, newTran*), renameAccount(*seDates 1f, oldAcct, newAcct*, compact=1). These allow modification. edit() breaks down into a remove() followed by an add(), since the date and thus the location in the array might have changed. renameAccount() loops over the whole bookset; like the DOS rename command, it can also move things to a different part of the tree.

Storage methods

save(*self, filename*), saveAsText(*self, filename*), load(*self, filename*), loadFromText(*self, filename*) allow storage in files in either a fast native format or human-readable text. The native format is that produced by the cPickle utility discussed previously.

Query methods

getAccountDetails(*self, account*) gets the full history of entries in an account. getAccountList(*self*) returns a list of all the unique accounts in a BookSet. getAccountBalance(*self, acct, date=LATE*) tells you the balance of an account on a date, and getAccountActivity(*self, acct, startDate=EARLY, endDate=LATE*) gives the change in the account between two dates. getAllBalancesOn(*self, date=LATE*) returns the balances of all accounts on the given date or the closing balances if no date is given. We'll see how to extend the BookSet to let the user create custom queries in Chapter 8, *Adding a Macro Language*.

Storing Extra Information in Transactions

We've defined some basic classes that represent what is commonly known as the general ledger or nominal ledger, the core of any accounting system. Accounting systems generally build layers and modules around the general ledger to handle things like sales and purchases, cash management, payroll, and job and project tracking. In a conventional architecture, these might each be extra modules (sold separately) that add tables, editing screens, and reports. When new items are added, these modules might post entries to the general ledger as well as keep their own records. Unfortunately, this is the point at which businesses start to vary from each other: it's hard to predict in advance what facts companies need to keep track of.

Our transactions so far deal with the two dimensions of time and account. However, you may wish to store extra information in the future, such as the name of a customer or supplier, a check number for a payment, or a tax code for an invoice line; and you don't want to be limited to a predefined set of attributes.

Python has an unusual and extremely flexible (but potentially dangerous) feature that enables you to minimize the number of these extensions: any class instance can be given any attribute, regardless of its class definition. Let's look at how a transaction is initialized:

```
class Transaction:
    def __init__(self):
        "By default, you get a zero transaction with time = now"
        import time
        self.date = int(time.time())
        self.comment = '<New Transaction>'
        self.lines = []
```

It has three attributes, `date`, `comment`, and `lines`. In most other object-oriented languages you would be limited to these. In Python there is absolutely nothing to stop you from doing the following:

```
>>> import doubletalk.transac
>>> t = doubletalk.transac.Transaction()
>>> t.Customer = 'HugeCo'
>>> t.InvoiceNo = 199904007
>>>
```

You don't need to define the attributes `Customer` and `InvoiceNo` in the class definition, which means you aren't limited. Your transactions can store any extra facts you wish. Furthermore, the `cPickle` module that provides the persistence capabilities will still save and load the objects.

In general, adding attributes on the fly like this is a bad design, because there is a strong chance users will overwrite attributes that are important to the functioning of the program. We can get away with it here since `Transaction` is essentially just a packet of data to be manipulated, and we want to keep the code short. In Chapter 13, *Databases*, you will see a much safer technique for doing the same thing, which preserves the friendly user-level syntax.

By adding these two facts to sales invoices and records of payments, you can generate reports showing who owes what or breaking down sales by customer. The converse also applies to invoices received and payments to suppliers. You can also imagine end users finding interesting new applications for this; you could tag transactions with the person who entered them, add cross references to check stubs, or anything else you want.

However, there are occasions when an attribute doesn't apply to the whole transaction but just to one line. Imagine you are billing a large customer for consulting work done by four of your staff, all working in different departments, and you want to track the income by department or team internally. You have only one

Introspection in Python

Python objects can examine their own insides and trap access to them, a feature rarely found in compiled languages. This enables modules such as `pickle` and `cPickle` to be written. `dir(`*object*`)` lists the attributes of any object; the magic attribute `__dict__` returns a dictionary of keys and values. `getattr(`*object, key*`)` and `setattr(`*object, key, value*`)` let you create and access attributes dynamically at runtime. Let's explore the transaction object previously created:

```
>>> dir(t)    # lists an object's attributes
['Customer', 'InvoiceNo', 'comment', 'date', 'lines']
>>> from pprint import pprint # displays nicely over several lines
>>> pprint(t.__dict__)
{'Customer': 'HugeCo',
 'InvoiceNo': 199904007,
 'comment': '<New Transaction>',
 'date': 925245509,
 'lines': []}
>>> getattr(t, 'Customer')
'HugeCo'
>>> setattr(t, 'InputBy', 'A.Anorak')
>>> t.InputBy
'A.Anorak'
```

It's also possible for objects to trap attempts to set and get attributes and react in special ways using the Magic Methods `__getattr__(`*self, name*`)` and `__setattr__(`*self, name, value*`)`. We've defined a class that lets you set attributes unless they are named "spam":

```
class HateSpam:
    def __setattr__(self, name, value):
        if name == 'spam':
            print "Keep that stuff away from me"
        else:
            self.__dict__[name] = value

    def __getattr__(self, name):
        if name == 'spam':
            print "you won't find any of that here"
        else:
            return self.__dict__[name]
```

Having defined this, we can do the following:

```
>>> h = HateSpam()
>>> h.eggs = 12
>>> h.spam = 3
```

—Continued—

```
    Keep that stuff away from me
    >>> h.spam
    you won't find any of that here
    >>> h.eggs
    12
```

You can even grab a function and attach it to an object at runtime:

```
    >>> def sing(food):
    ...      print '%s, %s, %s, %s, everybody loves %s' %
    (food,food,food,food,food)
    ...
    >>> sing('eggs')
    eggs, eggs, eggs, eggs, everybody loves eggs
    >>> h.shout = sing
    >>> h.shout('beer')
    beer, beer, beer, beer, everybody loves beer
    >>> dir(h)
    ['eggs', 'shout']
    >>>
```

transaction, but different attributes per line. To cope with this, the lines inside transactions are three-element tuples. Element three is usually **None**, but can be a dictionary. Later we will write queries that can loop over a **BookSet** and query based on these attributes. In the next example, we create a transaction with extra attributes at both the transaction and line level and split the income from a sale between two internal projects:

```
    >>> INCOME='MyCo.Capital.PL.Income.Consulting'  # save typing
    >>> t = doubletalk.transac.Transaction()
    >>> t.Customer = 'HugeCo'
    >>> t.InvoiceNo = 199904007
    >>> t.addLine(INCOME, 15000, {'Project':'P1'} )
    >>> t.addLine(INCOME, 10000, {'Project':'P2'} )
    >>> t.addLine('MyCo.NCA.CurrentAssets.Creditors', 25000)
    >>> t.display()    # shows the basics
    Date:      27-Apr-1999 21:17:52
    Comment:   <New Transaction>
    MyCo.Capital.PL.Income.Consulting        10000.000000
    MyCo.Capital.PL.Income.Consulting        15000.000000
    MyCo.NCA.CurrentAssets.Creditors         25000.000000
    >>> from pprint import pprint
    >>> pprint(t.__dict__)    # look inside the object
    {'Customer': 'HugeCo',
     'InvoiceNo': 199904007,
     'comment': '<New Transaction>',
     'date': 925247872,
     'lines': [('MyCo.Capital.PL.Income.Consulting', 10000, {'Project': 'P2'}),
               ('MyCo.Capital.PL.Income.Consulting', 15000, {'Project': 'P1'}),
               ('MyCo.NCA.CurrentAssets.Creditors', 25000, None)]}
    >>>
```

Our data model still obeys all the fundamental rules of double-entry accounting but is now much more extensible: users can add their own attributes at will. This is the basis of a highly open, extensible system

The Doubletalk Toolkit at Work

In the next few chapters we'll see some examples of the class library at work. At the beginning of the chapter, we listed some application areas. Now we'll run briefly through how the toolkit supports some of these to give a feel for how it might be useful.

Comparing, Combining, and Contrasting Accounts

Imagine that you had one accounting system until the end of 1997. You switched in 1998, and there were some slight differences in the new chart of accounts that grouped things differently at a high level, in addition to merging one or two existing accounts. Not being administratively perfect, you didn't get it all set up on the first of January, and there is an annoying discrepancy at the changeover point you can't figure out. Export scripts can be written to get the data into BookSets. A dictionary can be prepared that maps account names in the old system to account names in the new one, and then both sets of data can be merged. Ad hoc queries using an interactive prompt also make it easy to see where data doesn't match.

Building Business Models

One of the main uses of Doubletalk is building detailed cash-flow forecasts. Most cash-flow forecasts are done in Excel, but they tend to focus only on cash; building and maintaining a spreadsheet to correctly handle a full balance sheet and profit and loss is hard work in Excel, and anything less is ultimately not useful for long-term planning. It's also important to lay out your forecast using the same headings and tree structure as the actual data and to take care not to leave black holes where the past data meets the future. Large corporations have often invested a great deal in building such models of their businesses. The combination of object-oriented programming and our class library makes it easy.

The general concept is to create a hierarchy of business model objects that represent things in the business; these generate a stream of future transactions at the right time. The module *demodata.py* uses crude examples of this to generate a file of 1000 transactions. Here's a simple base class for this hierarchy:

```
class BusinessObject:
    def getTransactions(self):
        return []
```

There are a limited number of common business objects that can be modeled quite accurately. For example, a simple loan can be described by just four attributes: amount, date drawn, interest rate, and number of periods. A `Loan` object is initialized with these attributes and generates a stream of transactions covering the drawdown and the subsequent repayments. An `IncomeItem` gives rise to an invoice and a payment transaction, with a time lag. An `IncomeStream` creates a series of `IncomeItems`, perhaps with a given annual growth rate. The model usually needs changing only a little each month and represents cash flows accurately.

A more sophisticated model uses a discrete-event simulation approach, sending ticks of the clock to the business objects and allowing objects to make decisions based on the state of the accounts and to interact with each other. For example, a `CorporationTax` object could wake up once a year, look at the profits, and schedule in a few payments a few months ahead.

This approach is also important in the securities industry, where quantitative analysts (*quants*) build models of portfolios of financial instruments and see how they behave under different economic scenarios. A financial instrument can be seen as a business model object that gives rise to transactions at various points in its lifetime.

Multidimensional Analysis of Financial Data

Our `BookSet` and `Transaction` classes can be thought of as classifying amounts of money by time and by account—a 2D classification. In fact, many standard financial reports follow a format of months across the top, and accounts (drawn from some level of the tree) down the left. Previously, we saw how to extend the system to add any attributes we wish. This effectively makes it a multidimensional model. Analyzing multidimensional data is a big business currently using the buzzword OLAP (online analytical processing). Furthermore, a common problem is to ensure the integrity of the double-entry while querying and selecting subsets of data. There is almost have a data warehouse in our `BookSet`; however, it's currently optimized for adding, editing, and deleting transactions, not for querying.

To query the `BookSet`, flatten the transactions into a separate list of facts per line. Taking the sales transaction earlier, you might extract something like what's in Table 6-1.

Table 6-1. Multidimensional Analysis of Accounts

Date	Account	Customer	Project	Amount
27-Apr-1999	...Income.Consulting	HugeCo	P1	-15000
27-Apr-1999	...Income.Consulting	HugeCo	P2	-10000
27-Apr-1999	...Creditors	HugeCo	(none)	25000

This kind of fact-table structure is as easy to analyze in Python as it is in SQL. However, Python has a big advantage over the database world in that it's not tied to particular sets of facts, or column headings, beforehand. Transactions have the following method, which converts a three-line transaction to a list of three dictionaries, each with all the facts about transaction and line:

```
class Transaction:
    # (one method of many)
    def asDicts(self):
        dicts = []
        i = 0
        for line in self.lines:
            rowdict = self.__dict__.copy()
            del rowdict['lines']
            rowdict['account'] = line[0]
            rowdict['amount'] = line[1]
            if line[2]:
                rowdict.update(line[2])
            i = i + 1
            dicts.append(rowdict)
        return dicts
```

Running this on the example transaction gives everything you need to know:

```
>>> pprint(t.asDicts())
[{'Customer': 'HugeCo',
  'InvoiceNo': 199904007,
  'Project': 'P2',
  'account': 'MyCo.Capital.PL.Income.Consulting',
  'amount': 10000,
  'comment': '<New Transaction>',
  'date': 925247872},
 {'Customer': 'HugeCo',
  'InvoiceNo': 199904007,
  'Project': 'P1',
  'account': 'MyCo.Capital.PL.Income.Consulting',
  'amount': 15000,
  'comment': '<New Transaction>',
  'date': 925247872},
 {'Customer': 'HugeCo',
  'InvoiceNo': 199904007,
  'account': 'MyCo.NCA.CurrentAssets.Creditors',
  'amount': 25000,
  'comment': '<New Transaction>',
  'date': 925247872}]
>>>
```

This is just a few lines away from an SQL-like query language that can pull out arbitrary queries from a BookSet, tabulating the keys it's interested in from the previous lists of dictionaries. You also have the ability to drill down from higher-level summaries of the data to the individual transactions that gave rise to them.

Cash-Flow Analysis

Many accounting systems can't do a cash-flow report. This sounds shocking, but it's true. The reason is they store the individual transaction lines, often in a separate table for each account and have lost the transaction itself. The cash flow report records where all the cash came from and where it went to, and is an important tool for managers.

To get a basic cash-flow report, you need to look at the other lines in all the transactions affecting the cash account. If you buy all your supplies with cash, this report breaks down how you spent your money. But if most sales and purchases are on account, the system produces the earth-shattering observation that most of your cash comes from other people paying your bills, and it goes to pay other peoples' bills. We'll call this the Brain-Dead Cash-Flow Analysis (BDCFA). A general ledger doesn't formally store the information needed to trace through the system and see what the bill you just paid was actually for.

This analysis is easy to do, if you tag the transactions with a customer and invoice number. Write a script to find all transactions with a given invoice number, add together the invoice and payment using the magic addition methods, and then perform a BDCFA on that. This lets you trace where cash went through a series of transactions.

Putting It Together

In the context of a business, our toolkit could easily be (and has been) used to:

- Hold data exported from an accounts system
- Generate future data from a financial model
- Put the past and future together on the same basis
- Analyze this stream in various ways to produce the data for reports
- Dig down to extract more detail from totals in reports
- Compare this month's actual/forecast data against what we thought we would achieve at the beginning of the year

Conclusion

This part of the book showed how Python can easily build extensible applications that capture the essence of a business problem and leave users free to build their own solutions around the core.

As an example, we built a small class library which, while quick and dirty, is applicable to a wide range of financial problems. We hope that this has demonstrated the ease with which Python can capture abstractions and manipulate data.

We don't yet have an application program to use these classes or a way to look at the data. Over the next few chapters, we will build one around this class library.

7

Building a GUI with COM

In the last chapter we built a number of Python classes that let us do some useful work in the financial domain, assuming we were happy to work at a command prompt and write our own scripts. Now we'll embed this in a traditional GUI by exposing the Python classes as COM servers that provide an engine.

You can imagine a whole family of applications based on our classes, each specialized for a specific task such as viewing and editing data, comparing BookSets, generating forecasts and laying out reports. What you need first is a browser for your sets of accounts that can show the same types of views as the command-line version: lists of accounts, details of any account, and a date-ordered "journal." It should also allow you to edit existing transactions and add new ones.

Our example browser is written in Visual Basic (VB) 6. We cover only a small selection of the features and code, but the full application is available with the code examples at *http://starship.python.net/crew/mhammond/ppw32/*. We have also built a cut-down version of the browser in Delphi; a small section at the end of the chapter explains the differences when using Delphi as a client language. Most mainstream development environments support COM, so you should be able to easily adapt what follows to your favorite development environment.

Designing COM Servers

We want to expose the Transaction and BookSet classes as COM servers. In Chapter 5, *Introduction to COM*, we saw an example of how a few simple additions can turn any Python class into a COM server. Now that our classes are larger and more complex, this isn't always the best solution, and it's worth thinking about alternatives. The basic problem is that COM-exposed methods sometimes need to handle their arguments in a different way than ordinary Python methods.

For example, if a COM client such as Visual Basic calls the **save** method of our **BookSet**, it passes in a Unicode string, which needs to be converted to a Python string:

```
# our ordinary save method for use from Python
def save(self, filename):
    f = open(filename,'wb')
    cPickle.dump(self.__journal,f)
    f.close()

# what we would need for use from COM
def save(self, unicode_filename):
    # convert it to a python string:
    python_filename = str(unicode_filename)

    f = open(python_filename,'wb')
    cPickle.dump(self.__journal,f)
    f.close()
```

Furthermore, the whole philosophy of COM is about defining a fixed interface and sticking to it. This strongly suggests building a separate class for the COM interface and hooking it to our native Python classes, which can be far more dynamic. Here are several design patterns to do this:

COM base class, pure Python subclass

> Here you define a base class and expose it as a COM server, initially doing nothing with the arguments to the methods, which defines your COM interface neatly in one place. Then implement a subclass (which is much longer) to do the actual work. This pattern is most appropriate when designing a class whose main function is to be used from COM and not from Python.

Pure Python base class, COM subclass

> Here you inherit from the existing Python **BookSet** class and rewrite the relevant methods to handle string and object arguments differently.

COM interface, Python delegate

> Here you define a COM class to define your interface. Rather than using inheritance, this has an internal variable pointing to a pure Python counterpart, the *delegate*. Its methods translate their arguments, return values as needed, and forward them to the delegate.

Since we designed our Python classes first and want to be able to use them independently from COM, we'll go for the delegate pattern.

We've made a separate Python source file within the Doubletalk package called *comservers.py*. You'll add to this later, but let's start off with an absolutely trivial COM server:

```
# comservers.py - to be expanded
class COMBookSet:
```

```
        _reg_clsid_ = '{38CB8241-D698-11D2-B806-0060974AB8A9}'
        _reg_progid_ = 'Doubletalk.BookServer'
        _public_methods_ = ['double']

        def __init__(self):
            self.__BookSet = doubletalk.bookset.BookSet()

        def double(self, arg):
            # trivial test function to check it's alive
            return arg * 2

if __name__ == '__main__':
    win32com.server.register.UseCommandLine(COMBookSet)
```

When this is created, it creates a pure Python `BookSet` and stores it in `self.__BookSet`. For now we've just exposed a single public method that doubles a number. The module needs to be registered, which can be done from File → Run in PythonWin or a double-click in Explorer. It would be a good idea at this point to register it in debug mode, which provides extra information for developers; this is covered later on in Chapter 12, *Advanced Python and COM*.

A VB Client

Next, we've created a VB application with a multiple document interface. You can do this by hand and add the forms and modules you need, or use VB's Application Wizard and strip out the stuff you don't need. We've defined a public variable called `BookServer` and three public methods in the form, `InitCOMServer`, `CloseCOMServer`, and `TestCOMServer`, and hooked them up so that `InitCOMServer` is called when the form loads:

```
Public BookServer As Object

Private Sub MDIForm_Load()
    InitCOMServer
    frmJournal.Show
End Sub

Private Sub MDIForm_Unload(Cancel As Integer)
    CloseCOMServer
End Sub

Sub InitCOMServer()
    'called when the program starts
    On Error GoTo InitCOMServer_error
    Set BookServer = CreateObject("Doubletalk.BookServer")
    Exit Sub

InitCOMServer_error:
    Dim msg As String
    msg = "There was an error trying to initialize the BookServer." + _
```

```
                    "Please check that it is properly registered and try the Python " + _
                    "test functions first.  The program will now abort."
            MsgBox msg
            End

    End Sub

    Sub CloseCOMServer()
        Set BookServer = Nothing
    End Sub

    Sub TestCOMServer()
        'just to check it is alive
        Dim hopefully_four As Integer
        hopefully_four = BookServer.Double(2)
        MsgBox "2 x 2 = " & hopefully_four & ", so your server is alive"
    End Sub


    Private Sub mnuToolsTestServer_Click()
        'this helps establish if the COM server is alive
        'using a minimal diagnostic function in the modMain module
        TestCOMServer
    End Sub
```

That the COM server isn't registered is a common error, so you need to handle this error and close the program immediately if it occurs.

It's not necessary to explicitly unload the **BookServer**; it's freed automatically when the VB program closes down. However, it's good programming practice to free variables explicitly to show that you know when it's happening, and it provides the right hook in case you want to do some extra processing at this point (such as committing changes to a file or database).

We've also added a menu item on the Tools menu to call our test function. Hit Run, and the application should start up. If you get as far as the main screen, it should have a live Python COM server inside it. To prove it, click on Tools → Test Server, and you should see Figure 7-1.

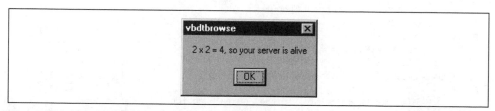

Figure 7-1. Not much of a GUI yet!

Now we've got this running, we can start to expand the capabilities of the COM server and add the code to call it on the VB side. We've added a number of public methods, declaring them in the `_public_methods_` attribute as we implement them.

Building the First View

Adding the following methods to your `COMBookSet` allows you to load a data file, see how many transactions the `BookSet` contains, and then build a view that displays a Journal, a listing of all the transactions in date order:

```
# more methods for COMBookSet - must be named in _public_methods_
    def load(self, filename):
        self.__BookSet.load(str(filename))

    def count(self):
        # return number of transactions
        return len(self.__BookSet)


    def getTransactionString(self, index):
        return self.__BookSet[index].asString()
```

In `load`, you perform a `str(filename)` operation to convert the Unicode filename from COM into an ordinary Python string. Then pass the request to the delegate Python `BookSet` instance. Most methods follow this pattern, doing any necessary transformations of arguments on the way in and out and passing the real work onto the delegate.

Now you need to open files. This is the VB code for the File → Open menu option (generated by one of VB's Wizards and so is somewhat verbose):

```
    Private Sub mnuFileOpen_Click()
        Dim sFile As String
        With dlgCommonDialog
            .DialogTitle = "Open"
            .CancelError = False
            'ToDo: set the flags and attributes of the common dialog control
            .Filter = "Doubletalk Journal Files (*.dtj)|*.dtj"
            .ShowOpen
            If Len(.FileName) = 0 Then
                Exit Sub
            End If
            sFile = .FileName
        End With
        BookServer.Load sFile

        'display something helpful in the Journal caption
        frmJournal.Caption = sFile & ", " & BookServer.count & " Transactions"
    End Sub
```

The only line of interest here is in `BookServer.Load sFile`, where Python is asked to do the work. Then, clicking on File → Open lets you open a `BookSet` stored on disk. The Doubletalk package includes one file created by the *demodata1.py* script with a thousand transactions; it takes about one second to load on a Pentium 120. The various other loading and saving methods in your COMBookSet class can be hooked up to menu items in a similar manner.

Next, build a Journal view, an MDI child window to display a list of transactions in date order. This has a list box filling its client area and some code to resize it smoothly. It also has a method called UpdateView as follows:

```
Public Sub UpdateView()
    'make a list with a string describing each transaction

    Dim count, i As Integer
    Dim trantext As String
    Dim tran As Object

    Screen.MousePointer = vbHourglass
    lstJournal.Clear

    For i = 0 To frmMain.BookServer.count - 1
        trantext = frmMain.BookServer.getOneLineDescription(i)
        lstJournal.AddItem trantext
    Next i

    Screen.MousePointer = vbDefault
    Caption = "Journal view - " & lstJournal.ListCount & " transactions"

End Sub
```

The implementation of this UpdateView method is simple: first ask the Book-Server for the number of transactions, then for the text representation of each one in turn. These are added to the list one at a time. When run, you see a view like Figure 7-2.

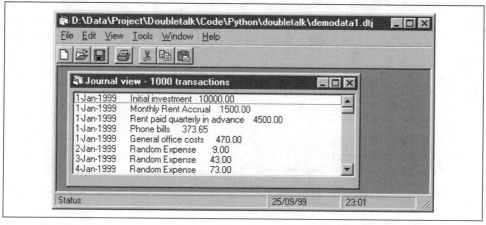

Figure 7-2. The first view

We'll define a range of views in the next few pages, all with an `UpdateView` public method. You can then ask them all to redraw themselves whenever the data changes. Later on we will see some other techniques that remove the need to do the looping in VB; the Python COM framework can return a list of strings or allow VB to iterate over the `BookSet` directly.

At this point, it's worth it to pause and reflect. We have built the engine of an application in Python, but delivered it inside an industry-standard, 100% Windows user interface of the kind users expect.

More About Transactions

You'll want to add and edit individual transactions. This leads to more fundamental design considerations. You need to expose `Transaction` class as a COM server. You also need to think about how to create these transactions and manage their lifecycles and about the right choice of patterns. One option is to make a `COMTransaction` class the same way we did for `COMBookset`.

The overall goal is to make sure that code that works with transactions in VB is as similar as possible to the corresponding code in Python. The VB code to create and add a new transaction looks like this:

```
Dim newtran As Object

Set newtran = CreateObject("Doubletalk.Transaction")
newtran.setDateString "31/12/99"
newtran.setComment "Python on Windows Royalty Cheque"
newtran.addLine "MyCo.Assets.NCA.CurAss.Cash", 5000
newtran.addLastLine "MyCo.Capital.PL.Income.Writing"

BookServer.Add newtran
```

There is another choice, however. Adding a factory method to `BookServer` gives a new transaction (outside of the `BookSet` but otherwise fully formed). In this case there is no need to register the class at all; it's never created directly from the registry. Microsoft Office uses this model a lot. Most of the Excel objects are obtained from the application object's factory methods and are not directly creatable. If you go this way, your VB code to add a transaction looks like this:

```
Dim newtran As Object

Set newtran = BookServer.CreateTransaction
newtran.setDateString "31/3/2000"
newtran.setComment "Even more royalties"
newtran.addLine "MyCo.Assets.NCA.CurAss.Cash", 5000
newtran.addLastLine "MyCo.Capital.PL.Income.Writing"

BookServer.Add newtran
```

The benefit is that the COMTransaction class can be much smaller.

We've added a class called COMTransaction to *comservers.py* that delegates to a pure Python transaction. This provides all the methods needed to edit and create transactions in your client code. Here's an example:

```python
class COMTransaction:
    # we don't need all the _reg_ stuff, as we provide our own
    # API for creating these and don't use the registry.
    _public_methods_ = [
                    'asString',
                    'getDateString',
                    'setDateString',
                    'setCOMDate',
                    'getCOMDate',
                    'getComment',
                    'setComment',
                    'getLineCount',
                    'getAccount',
                    'getAmount',
                    'addLine',
                    'addLastLine',
                    'getOneLineDescription'
                    ]

    def __init__(self, tran=None):
        if tran is None:
            self._tran = doubletalk.transac.Transaction()
        else:
            self._tran = tran

    def asString(self):
        return self._tran.asString()

    def getDateString(self):
        return self._tran.getDateString()

    def setDateString(self, aDateString):
        self._tran.setDateString(str(aDateString))

    def setCOMDate(self, comdate):
        self._tran.date = (comdate - 25569.0) * 86400.0

    def getCOMDate(self):
        return (self._tran.date / 86400.0) + 25569.0

    def getComment(self):
        return self._tran.comment

    def setComment(self, aComment):
        self._tran.comment = str(aComment)

    def getOneLineDescription(self):
        return '%-15s %s %10.2f' % (
```

```
                    self._tran.getDateString(),
                    self._tran.comment,
                    self._tran.magnitude()
                    )

        def getLineCount(self):
            return len(self._tran.lines)

        def getAccount(self, index):
            return self._tran.lines[index][0]

        def getAmount(self, index):
            return self._tran.lines[index][1]

        def addLine(self, account, amount):
            self._tran.addLine(str(account), amount)

        def addLastLine(self, account):
            self._tran.addLastLine(str(account))
```

This example has a number of interesting features:

- Like COMBookSet, this has an instance variable called self._tran pointing to a pure Python transaction instance. You can pass in an existing transaction on initialization to wrap it up, or it creates one if none is provided.

- There's no need to register it at all, since you will create instances from a factory method provided in COMBookSet. The only special attribute needed is the list of public methods.

- Since Python dates use a different representation than Microsoft, we have provided setCOMDate and getCOMDate methods to handle the conversion. Python's date system is that of Unix, counting seconds since 1/1/1970; COM uses the Excel format of days since 31-Dec-1899. We also offer setDateString and getDateString methods to sidestep the need for a conversion routine.

- Rather than expose comment as a simple attribute, we have implemented setComment and getComment methods. These let you convert the Unicode string. As a general principle, we are not directly exposing any attributes (although the Python COM framework does allow it).

- We provided some extra methods to get the number of lines and to retrieve a specific account name or amount using an index. These let you write a VB loop to get all the lines. Alternative ways of exposing the detail rows would be to return arrays (which are covered later in this chapter) and enumerators (which appear in Chapter 12).

Now we need to look at how to get hold of these and store them in our BookServer. At this point you need to do a little more conversion and understand a little more about COM. In the previous VB example to create and add a transaction, there were actually three different **Transaction** objects involved. The raw one used by VB is an **IDispatch** object. **IDispatch** is a standard COM interface that lets you attempt to call any method or property and finds out later whether they work; the Python COM framework creates these around Python objects. Hiding within this is an instance of our **COMTransaction** class, written in Python. And because you are using a delegation mechanism, you have your own pure Python **Transaction** class as an attribute of the **COMTransaction**. When you create new transactions to use with COM or try to add ones to the **BookSet**, you have a little more conversion to do.

This method in **COMBookSet** creates a new transaction for Visual Basic to use:

```
def createTransaction(self):
        comTran = COMTransaction()
        idTran = win32com.server.util.wrap(comTran)
        return idTran
```

Before handing this out to a client language such as VB, call the **wrap** utility. This creates a **PyIDispatch** wrapper around the Python object, which is what VB actually works with. More information on wrapping Python objects for COM can be found in Chapter 12.

When you want to add a new transaction to the **BookSet**, you need to unwrap it to get at the Python object inside:

```
def add(self, idTran):
        comTran = win32com.server.util.unwrap(idTran)
        pyTran = comTran._tran
        self.__BookSet.add(pyTran)
```

Throughout this code we have prefixed the **PyIDispatch** object with *id*, the Python COM classes in *comservers.py* with *com*, and the pure Python classes in *bookset.py* and *transac.py* with *py*.

If you design your application purely to work with COM and not for general Python use, you can take another tack and store the **PyIDispatch** objects in the list.

Adding and Editing Transactions

Now we are ready to add and edit transactions. The natural thing to do is to allow a double-click on a transaction to lead to a special dialog for editing. This should perform the necessary validation to ensure that the transaction balances before the dialog is closed, and, if there is a change, it should update all of the current views. We've built a pair of dialogs in VB: one to edit transactions and the other (called from it) to edit individual line items. Figure 7-3 shows the transaction dialog.

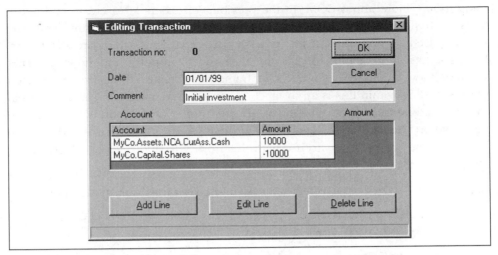

Figure 7-3. Transaction editing dialog

The code to edit the transaction is exposed as a method of the form as follows:

```
Public Function Edit(index As Integer) As Boolean
    'returns true is the transaction was successfully edited
    Dim i As Integer
    Dim linecount As Integer

    Set tran = frmMain.BookServer.getTransaction(index)

    'display the transaction details
    lblTranIndex.Caption = Str(index)
    txtDate.text = FormatDateTime(tran.getCOMDate)
    txtComment.text = tran.getComment

    linecount = tran.getLineCount
    grdItems.rows = linecount + 1
    For i = 0 To linecount - 1
        grdItems.TextMatrix(i + 1, 0) = tran.GetAccount(i)
        grdItems.TextMatrix(i + 1, 1) = tran.getAmount(i)
    Next i
    Set tran = Nothing
    UpdateFormState

    'display and allow editing
    Me.Show vbModal

      If FormExit = vbOK Then
         Set tran = frmMain.BookServer.CreateTransaction
         tran.setComment txtComment.text

         If IsDate(txtDate.text) Then tran.setCOMDate
                                         CDbl(CDate(txtDate.text))
```

```
        For i = 1 To grdItems.rows - 1
            tran.AddLine grdItems.TextMatrix(i, 0), _
                            CDbl(grdItems.TextMatrix(i, 1))
        Next i
        frmMain.BookServer.Edit index, tran
        Set tran = Nothing
        Edit = True
    Else
        Edit = False
    End If

End Function
```

This example is one of many ways to organize the code. Fetch a transaction from the `BookSet` and display its attributes in the user interface before discarding it. Then display the dialog modally: the user must finish using the dialog before the `Edit` method continues. During this period, quite a bit of validation code is running; the OK button is enabled only if the transaction is valid and in balance. If OK is clicked, the transaction is valid. Now create a new `COMTransaction` to hold the data, copy the data from the user interface into it, and tell the `BookSet` to accept this as a replacement for the its existing data in that position. An alternative might be to work with the same transaction throughout.

The dialog also exposes a method to add a new transaction; this displays an empty dialog, but behaves identically after displaying the form.

To summarize, you can now add and edit transactions from Visual Basic. The techniques used would be the same for any kind of nested or master-detail object. The VB code to do this looks extremely natural and straightforward, pretty much the same as the Python code for creating transactions. On the server side, you need to distinguish between the `PyIDispatch` objects COM is using and Python's internal representations, but this needs to be done only once per class.

Building Views with Arrays

So far we've seen examples of passing numbers, strings, and Python objects back and forth between Python and VB. Now we'll develop some more kinds of views and look at passing around arrays of data at a time. This is a real time saver and can simplify the preceding code in several places.

Many financial reports take the form of a 2D grid or spreadsheet. What's needed is a generic solution for getting a Python list of lists into such a grid. In the last chapter we showed a number of `BookSet` methods for getting a list of accounts, the details of an account and so on. For example, `getAccountDetails` returns a list of tuples of (`transaction number, date, comment, amount, runningTotal`). This is effectively a matrix with five columns but an unknown number of rows. You need to expose this the usual way in `COMBookSet`, but then access the entire matrix from VB. The Python COM framework automatically converts lists (or lists of lists, or lists of tuples) into arrays that can be accessed in VB.

We've created a new form, frmAccountView, which can be given the name of an account as a string. This has a Microsoft FlexGrid control called grdTable. Here's the UpdateView method that fetches and displays the data:

```
Public Sub UpdateView()
    Dim table As Variant
    Dim rows As Integer, cols As Integer
    Dim row As Integer, col As Integer

    table = frmMain.BookServer.getAccountDetails(AccountName)

    rows = UBound(table, 1) - LBound(table, 1) + 1
    cols = UBound(table, 2) - LBound(table, 2) + 1 'should be 5

    grdTable.rows = rows + 1   'leave room for titles
    For row = 0 To rows - 1
        For col = 0 To cols - 1
            grdTable.TextMatrix(row + 1, col) = table(row, col)
        Next col
    Next row
End Sub
```

Figure 7-4 displays the new view in action.

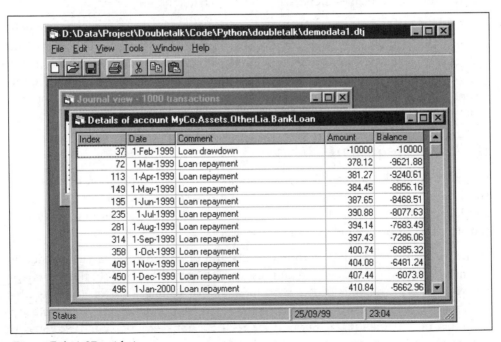

Figure 7-4. A 2D grid view

Although we've hardcoded a view, it would be easy to write a completely generic form to display any data and push the management of views back into Python itself. We'll look at this in Chapter 8, *Adding a Macro Language*.

Graphics and Callbacks

It would be convenient to look at a graphical view of an account, so let's create one. This allows you to illustrate another level of integration between Python and VB: *callbacks*. Within the framework you've just created, the VB COM client has been accessing the properties and methods of the Python COM server. But it doesn't have to be that way; the Python code can access the properties and methods of any VB object, whether built-in or user-defined.

You need to pass a VB form to Python, which then draws directly on it. You could also instead write another view that grabs the same array of data as the last one and uses VB graphics code to do the drawing. That is a better design, since it keeps a strict separation between the engine and interface; once you add drawing code on the Python side, you presume that a VB form with a certain API is provided. But this example is fun and highly instructive.

Let's start by creating a new form in our application called `frmAccountChart`, similar to the other views so far. Add a public method to the `COMBookSet` server called `drawAccountChart`, which expects a VB form as an argument. We'll start with a simple test: our drawing routine sets the caption of the form with a timestamp. On the VB side, the `UpdateView` method for `frmAccountChart` asks Python to do the work:

```
'Method of frmAccountChart
Public Sub UpdateView()
    'ask Python to scribble on me
    frmMain.BookServer.drawAccountChart Me
End Sub
```

The form passes itself (using the keyword `Me`, which is VB's equivalent of `self`) to the `BookServer`. On the Python side, here is a method that does something visible to the form:

```
def drawAccountChart(self, vbForm):
    # Make a Dispatch wrapper around the VB Form object so we can call
    # any of its methods.
    idForm = win32com.client.Dispatch(vbForm)

    # access a property of the VB form
    idForm.Caption = "Python Drew this chart at " + time.ctime(time.time())
```

The first line is critical. The actual object passed to Python in the variable `vbForm` is a raw `IDispatch` object, which is difficult to use directly. However, by creating a dynamic `Dispatch` wrapper around it, you can access any of its methods and properties as a normal COM object. Figure 7-5 shows the proof.

Figure 7-5. Python accessing VB objects

The meaning of this wrapping is discussed in greater detail in Chapter 12. For now, just remember to do it for any Visual Basic objects you want to manipulate.

Python can access the public methods and properties of any VB object, not just user-interface widgets such as forms and list boxes, but also classes you define yourself.

Exposing a graphics API to Python, a more complex example

Now let's extend what we just did and let Python do some real work. VB provides a picture control that allows drawing. However, some of the drawing methods use an esoteric syntax with hyphens, seen nowhere else in VB, and which no other language could reasonably be expected to call. You should therefore provide your own easy-to-use graphics API in VB at the form level. Add a single picture control called `picChart` to `frmAccountChart`, along with code to fill the entire form when the form is resized. Then add a few methods to the Visual Basic form to make it easier to do the graphics. Python can then call these methods. Here is the minimal graphics API defined for `frmAccountChart`:

```
'Visual Basic code to provide a minimal graphics API
Public Sub DrawLine(x1 As Integer, y1 As Integer, x2 As Integer, _
                    y2 As Integer, color As Long)
    picChart.FillStyle = vbTransparent

    picChart.Line (x1, y1)-(x2, y2), color
    ' see what we mean about the funny syntax?

End Sub
Public Sub DrawBox(x1 As Integer, y1 As Integer, x2 As Integer, _
                   y2 As Integer, lineColor As Long, _
                   isSolid As Boolean, fillColor As Long)
    If isSolid Then
        picChart.FillStyle = vbSolid
    Else
        picChart.FillStyle = vbTransparent
    End If
    picChart.fillColor = fillColor
    picChart.Line (x1, y1)-(x2, y2), lineColor, B
End Sub
```

```
Public Sub DrawText(x As Integer, y As Integer, size As Integer, _
                    text As String)
    picChart.CurrentX = x
    picChart.CurrentY = y
    picChart.FontSize = size
    picChart.Print text
End Sub

Public Function GetClientArea() As Variant
    'return a two-element variant array
    GetClientArea = Array(picChart.Width, picChart.Height)
End Function
```

This code gives one method to clear the chart, and three methods to draw lines, boxes (filled or otherwise), and place text with a choice of font size. There's also a method that says which account the form is tracking and another method to return the dimensions of the form, so you can figure out how to scale the chart.

The **drawAccountChart** method in our Python COM server now needs to do three things: first, it queries the form to find out which account to draw; then it queries it to determine its size; finally it uses the graphics methods to do some drawing.

We won't repeat all the chart code but here are a few lines:

```
def drawAccountChart(self, vbForm):
    # Make a Dispatch wrapper around the vb Form object so we can call
    # any of its methods.
    print 'Drawing chart...'
```

Note the **print** statement. In normal use this won't go anywhere. However, the Python COM framework provides a debugging mode for COM servers and a tool for collecting these traces. It took a few tries to get all of the scaling right, and we used numerous **print** statements to examine the data.

Debugging COM Servers

At this point, we need to briefly explain how to debug a COM server. The theory behind this is covered in Chapter 12. It's easy to use: just run the COM server script (*comservers.py* in our case) with the argument --**debug**: note the double hyphen. The output of any **print** statements in the server code can then be seen in the Trace Collector window on the PythonWin Tools menu.

Now it's time to work with the form passed in from Visual Basic:

```
idForm = win32com.client.Dispatch(vbForm)
```

As before, you wrap the VB object using **Dispatch**:

```
# call a method we defined on the VB form
# arrays are converted automatically to Python tuples we can access
```

```
(width, height) = idForm.GetClientArea()
account = idForm.GetAccount()
```

The previous line is interesting for two reasons. First, you called a public method of the VB form you defined. This works in exactly the same way as calling methods of built-in VB objects. Second, you received back an array. Earlier we saw that a Python list or tuple can be passed to VB, where it's interpreted as a variant array. The `GetClientArea()` method of our VB form returned a two-element variant array, which is received as a straightforward tuple. You can pass arrays easily in both directions. (Bear in mind that if VB returns an array containing strings, they are Unicode strings that must be tidied with the `str` function).

```
# access a built-in property of the VB form
idForm.Caption = "Account " + account


##############################################################
# now for the chart drawing - calling our own VB methods...
##############################################################

idForm.ClearChart()      #clear the form

# if the area is too small to do anything with, exit
if width < 1440:
    return
if height < 1440:
    return

#work out the inner drawing rectangle
plotrect = (720,720, width-720, height - 720)

# draw a blue bounding rectangle
idForm.DrawBox(plotrect[0], plotrect[1], plotrect[2], plotrect[3], 0xFF0000,
    0xFFFFFF)
```

We've omitted the rest of the charting code, but as you can see in Figure 7-6, it works rather nicely.

Writing a Delphi User Interface

Little of what we have seen is specific to Visual Basic. You can call Python COM servers from any language that supports COM, and we know of substantial programs using Visual Basic, Visual Basic for Applications, Visual C++, Delphi and PowerBuilder. We have also implemented a cut-down `BookSet` browser in Delphi, which is included in the examples for this chapter. We'll show a few edited highlights.

The authors believe that Delphi is a superior language to Visual Basic. However, in a corporate environment the choice is usually made for you. We will try to restrain our comparisons to how each language interacts with our Python COM server.

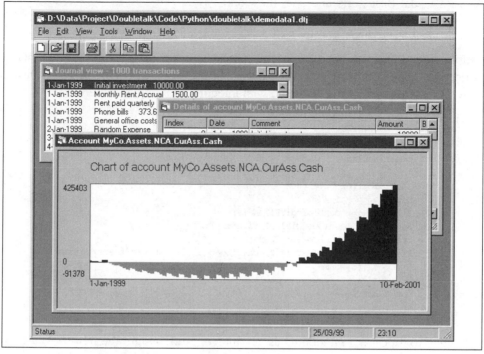

Figure 7-6. Python drawing charts on VB forms

Instantiating the Server

We declared a variable of type **Variant** in the main form to hold the COM server. Delphi supports **Variant**s purely in order to support COM, although they go somewhat against the grain in Delphi programming where the type of every variable is specified. The Delphi code to instantiate the server is as follows:

```
procedure TfrmMain.FormCreate(Sender: TObject);
begin
  try
    BookServer := CreateOleObject('Doubletalk.BookServer');
    StatusBar1.SimpleText := 'BookServer running';
  except
    MessageDlg(
      'An instance of the "Doubletalk.BookServer" COM class ' +
      'could not be created. Make sure that the BookServer application ' +
      'has been registered using a  command line.  If you have modified ' +
      'the source of the server, make very sure all public methods and '+
      'attributes are spelled correctly',
      mtError, [mbOk], 0);
    Application.Terminate;
  end;
end;
```

As with Visual Basic, one line does the work.

Calling simple methods

Delphi does exactly as good a job as VB as far as passing simple arguments is concerned. The following example, behind the File → Open menu item, shows how to call methods of the BookSet with integer and string arguments:

```
procedure TfrmMain.Open1Click(Sender: TObject);
{prompt for a filename and ask BookSet to load it}
var trancount: integer;
    filename: string;
begin
    if OpenDialog1.Execute then
      begin
      filename := OpenDialog1.FileName;
      BookServer.load(OpenDialog1.FileName);
      trancount := BookServer.Count;
      StatusBar1.SimpleText := Format('Loaded file %s, %d transactions',
            [filename, trancount]
            );
      UpdateAllViews;
      end;
end;
```

It's legal to declare `trancount` as an integer and assign the return value of `BookServer.Count` to it, even though the Delphi compiler can't know the type of the return value; the compiler knows that `BookServer` is a COM object and decides that type checking is somebody else's problem.

Unpacking Variant Arrays

Delphi's handling of variant arrays is somewhat closer to that of C or C++ than Visual Basic. It provides three functions to find the number of dimensions in a variant array and the high and low bounds of a given dimension. The first of these, `VarArrayDimCount`, is extremely useful and something VB lacks; the easiest way to find this from VB is to ask for the bounds of higher and higher dimensions until an error occurs. `VarArrayHighBound(array, dimension)` and `VarArrayHighBound(array, dimension)` are the equivalents of `UBound()` and `LBound()`. Arrays returned from Python always have a lower bound of zero.

If you want to iterate over a 1D array, you can't use a `for each` loop as in VB; instead you need to find the upper bound of the array. Here's the code to update a list box of accounts:

```
procedure TfrmMain.UpdateAccountList;
var AccountList: Variant;
    i: integer;
begin
    lstAllAccounts.Items.Clear;
```

```
    AccountList := BookServer.GetAccountList;
    for i := 0 to VarArrayHighBound(AccountList, 1) do
        lstAllAccounts.Items.Add(AccountList[i]);
end;
```

The array has one dimension, so ask for the upper bound of dimension 1.

The expression `AccountList[i]` returns a `Variant`, which Delphi coerces to a string when adding to the list box.

Delphi also offers more functions for constructing `Variant` arrays of given dimensions, which can efficiently pass data to Python.

Callbacks, or the lack thereof

Unfortunately this isn't so easy as with Visual Basic. In VB, every user interface object and class module supports automation; that is, all their properties and methods can be accessed from Python with the `Dispatch` wrapper. Delphi lets you create automation objects that can be accessed in the same way, but it isn't done by default; the compiler just won't let you do the following:

```
procedure TfrmMain.doCallbackDemo;
begin
    {this just does not work:
    BookServer.doDelphiCallbackDemo(Self);
    }
end;
```

However, Delphi does provide tools to create automation objects and a wizard to make it easier. With a bit more work, you could explicitly provide a Delphi API for your Python server to call.

As previously noted, we think the use of callbacks is generally a poor design principle; the server is much more useful if not tied to a particular GUI implementation, so this isn't much of a limitation in practice.

Conclusion

In this chapter we have learned how to build a functioning Python COM server, and a graphical client application that uses it. This approach uses each language where it's strongest: Python excels at data manipulation and object-oriented development, whereas Visual Basic allows you to build rich, commercial-quality user interfaces. From the user's viewpoint, there's no way to tell she is using Python.

In addition to building the core of an application in Python, this technique offers an easy way to add a small amount of Python functionality to existing applications. For example, if you have a large VB application and want to use a specific Python tool or library, you could wrap it with a COM server and call it from VB.

We have seen examples of the various data types that can be passed back and forth between the two languages: numbers, strings, and arrays. The ability to pass multidimensional arrays allows you to move large amounts of data between the two languages without writing a lot of conversion code. The exact rules on parameter passing are covered later in Chapter 12, but in general it all works as expected with little effort on your part.

Although we focused on VB, the client can be built in many different development tools. We've given an example in Delphi, and we know of people working in other environments such as PowerBuilder.

Although the application so far is technically interesting, it could have been written (with a bit more work) in VB without any of Python's powerful language features. In the next chapter we develop our application further to offer exciting capabilities only Python can provide.

8

Adding a Macro Language

Python made it easy to write the core of our application, but just about everything so far could have been done in one of many different languages. In this chapter, we move to one of Python's greatest strengths: making applications *extensible*. In the process, we'll learn a lot about how Python works internally.

Many popular applications (notably the Microsoft Office family) have a macro language that allows users to customize the way the application behaves. The kind of things users should be able to do are:

Write scripts

Users can write arbitrary scripts in Python that work with `BookSets` and `Transactions`. These run from within our GUI application or independently.

Handle events

Adding, editing, and deleting transactions are good candidates for events users can hook into.

Create validation rules

Validation rules can get you closer to a robust accounting system. With the right events to trap, users can produce their own rules to ensure the validity of their data.

Create user-defined queries

Some queries have been hardcoded into our system. You can generalize this concept to specify the inputs and outputs to a query and allow users to write their own. These would need some limitations, e.g., return a 2D array suitable for display in a grid.

If you start writing your application in a compiled language such as Visual Basic, Delphi, or Visual C++, you'll find it hard to add the macro capability. Writing your own macro language is not a small task, and there is little point when so many exist. Even if you decide to use Python as your macro language, you still need to write a huge amount of code to bridge between, for example, your Delphi objects and methods and your Python macros. However, we've written the core of the application in Python already. This makes it easy to create an extensible application. In the next few sections we'll run through some of the capabilities you can add to open up the application to users.

Dynamic Code Evaluation

With the right documentation, your users can already write Python scripts that create and manipulate BookSets and Transactions. However, these scripts are totally detached from your browser application. What would be smart to do is to provide a command window within the browser that works on the current BookSet. If a user creates a custom import function and runs it, he could hit an update key and see the new records on the screen immediately.

Executing Commands and Evaluating Expressions

Python has built-in functions and statements to facilitate this dynamic code evaluation: eval(*expression, [globals[, locals]]*) is a built-in function that evaluates a string, and exec *expression, [globals[, locals]]* is a statement (not a function: no parentheses needed) that executes a string. The following clarifies how it works:

```
>>> exec "print 'this expression was compiled on the fly' "
this expression was compiled on the fly
>>> exec "x = 3.14"
>>> eval("x + 1")
4.14
```

Let's pause for a moment and consider the implications of this code. You could pass a chunk of text to a running Python application, and it's parsed, compiled, and executed on the fly. In Python, the interpreter is always available. Few languages offer this capability, and it's what makes Python a good macro language.

You may not have consciously absorbed this until a few lines back, but Python distinguishes between expressions and statements. What happens if you aren't sure what the user wants and get it wrong? Here are two more examples:

```
>>> exec "x+2"          # try to execute an expression - nothing happens
>>> eval("print x+3")   # and evaluate a command - causes an exception
Traceback (innermost last):
  File "<interactive input>", line 0, in ?
  File "<string>", line 1
    print x+3
          ^
SyntaxError: invalid syntax
>>>
```

Case Study: Formula Evaluation

In 1997, one of the authors was consulting for a large packaging company building a database of its packaging designs. A cardboard box has a certain geometry, which may be thought of as a collection of flat panels joined at the edges, with a series of folding instructions. The overwhelming majority of designs were for cuboid boxes. This allowed the length of a certain edge of a panel to be expressed as a formula such as "2L + 3.5W + T," where L is the length of the product to be packed, W is the width, and T is the thickness of the board. Packaging designers all over Europe had been patiently entering formulae for each panel of a design into a database for months. An urgent need arose to verify these formulae. Using Python, it was a simple exercise to load a dictionary with the standard variables (L, W, H, T, and a few more for various flap lengths), plug in some numbers, and evaluate the expressions. Those cases that generated exceptions could be identified easily. A Python script was rapidly produced that queried the database and verified the integrity of all the strings. In addition to checking for errors, it produced a report listing standard panel sizes for a generic $400 \times 400 \times 400$mm box. Meanwhile, the main development team spent a great deal of time looking for and eventually writing a library of their own to evaluate simple numeric expressions in PL/SQL.

Executing an expression is generally safe, but evaluating a statement causes a syntax error. If the user gives a single line of input to process, and you don't know what it is, you can try to evaluate, then execute it if an exception occurs.

The **exec** function accepts not only single-line statements such as the previous example, but multiline ones as well. These can range from a two-line loop command to print the numbers 1–10, to a function definition, or even a 500-line class definition.

You may be wondering where the variable **x** was stored in the previous examples. To understand this, you need to delve into some Python internals. The previous console commands are executed in the *global namespace*, which means that **x** becomes a global variable. There is a function called **globals()** that allows you to examine this namespace directly; let's see what it returns:

```
>>> # where is the 'x' kept?
>>> for item in globals().items():
...     print item
...
('__doc__', None)
('pywin', <module 'pywin'>)
('x', 3.14)
('__name__', '__main__')
('__builtins__', <module '__builtin__'>)
>>>
```

This seems scary, but look at the third line. The global namespace is just a dictionary, and it has an entry called x with value 3.14. It also has a few other bits and pieces you don't need to worry about at this point.

At this point we touch on a significant fact about Python: almost everything is built out of dictionaries. Objects are implemented using dictionaries; their keys are the method or attribute names stored as strings, and the values are the attribute values and function objects themselves. Namespaces are dictionaries, too. And when a chunk of code is evaluated, it's internally handed two dictionaries: one containing the global variables at that point in time, the other containing the local variables to the current function or method.

This detail is interesting to language lawyers, but it also has an immediate practical payoff: you can design a namespace to suit yourself and execute the user's code in it. Specifically, you can modify the global namespace of the Python process in your browser to include a variable called TheBookSet, which refers to the currently running BookSet, or you can create an entirely new namespace in a fresh dictionary of your own.

The simplest demonstration of a COM server, which is included in PythonWin in the file *Python\win32com\servers\interp.py*, creates a COM object called Python. Interpreter. This exposes two methods to execute and evaluate expressions, which can easily be grafted onto any COM server. We want to build a console that lets the user do both and returns any output, so we'll merge them into one method called interpretString(). This either executes or evaluates the expression; if there is a return value, you hand a string representation of it back to the user.

You also need to extend the __init__() method of the BookServer to add a namespace with the needed global variable. Here's the new initialization code and the new method to interpret a string:

```
def __init__(self):
    self.__BookSet = doubletalk.bookset.BookSet()

    # create a custom namespace for the user to work with
    # with one variable name already defined
    self.userNameSpace = {'TheBookServer', self.__BookSet}

def interpretString(self, exp):
    """Makes it easier to build consoles.
    """
    if type(exp) not in [type(''), UnicodeType]:
        raise Exception(desc="Must be a string", \
                scode=winerror.DISP_E_TYPEMISMATCH)
    try:
        # first, we assume it's an expression
        result_object = eval(str(exp), self.userNameSpace)
```

```
            if result_object == None:
                return ''
            else:
                return str(result_object)
        except:
            #failing that, try to execute it
            exec str(exp) in self.userNameSpace
            return ''
```

It's necessary to add the statement **from pywintypes import UnicodeType** at the beginning of the module. Note that the code accepts normal and Unicode strings and raises helpful exceptions if the wrong kind of object is passed in. Try to evaluate the string as an expression, then try to execute it as a statement. If it causes an error, leave it unhandled so that the error message can filter through to the VB user. Note that as we discuss in Chapter 12, *Advanced Python and COM*, leaving an unhandled Python exception to propagate to the user of the object is not considered good design, but is suitable for the purposes of this demonstration.

If there is a return value, convert it as a string. You could return it raw, allowing **eval()** to potentially return numbers and arrays, but there is a risk of a user expression returning something VB doesn't expect. The intention in this example is to get back a printable string to show the user, so make sure the return type is always either a string representation of the data or an empty string.

Grabbing Python's Output

You now have the hooks to execute arbitrary strings of Python code, but you can't necessarily see the output. You need to implement one more feature first, to capture Python's standard output, so that **print** statements in your users' code show up properly. You might think this would involve low-level Windows process control, but actually, Python knows how to redirect its own output. If you enter the following statements in a Python source file or the Python DOS prompt, any subsequent output (for example, **print** statements) are redirected to a file:

```
>>> import sys
>>> mylogfile = open('c:\\temp\\mylog.txt', 'w')
>>> sys.stdout = mylogfile
>>>
```

Output can be redirected to any Python object that offers a **write()** method. The easiest way to grab the output is to add just such a **write()** method to our **COMBookSet** class, which stores the standard output internally; provide another method to grab this data from VB on demand; and start trapping the output when our instance of **COMBookSet** starts. Here are the needed extra methods:

```
def beginTrappingOutput(self):
    self.outputBuffer = []
    self.old_output = sys.stdout
    sys.stdout = self
```

```
def write(self, expr):
    """ this is an internal utility used to trap the output.
    add it to a list of strings - this is more efficient
    than adding to a possibly very long string."""
    self.outputBuffer.append(str(expr))

def getStandardOutput(self):
    "Hand over output so far, and empty the buffer"
    text = string.join(self.outputBuffer, '')
    self.outputBuffer = []
    return text

def endTrappingOutput(self):
    sys.stdout = self.old_output
    # return any more output
    return self.getStandardOutput()
```

Everything but `write()` is exposed as a COM public method. When VB creates
the server, add a line to call `TheBookServer.beginTrappingOutput()`.

A word of warning at this point: you aren't the only person interested in Python's
standard output. In Chapter 12, you'll learn about the Trace Collector debugging
tool. This is a feature of PythonWin that enables you to debug your COM server
while calling it from VB; we used it quite a bit in writing this chapter. If you've
registered your COM server for debugging, all the output that should have gone to
the Trace Collector shows up in your console window. That's why we've provided some explicit methods to start and stop trapping, rather than just to start
trapping when the `COMBookSet` initializes and leaving it on forever.

Building an Interactive Console

Now we have everything needed to create a basic interactive console. We implemented this as an extra child window with a one-line text box for input and a
multiline, uneditable text box for output. When the user inputs an expression, the
VB console form executes the commands `TheBookServer.interpretString`
(*expression*) to get the return value and `TheBookServer.getStandardOutput`
to retrieve any output that was generated. It then assembles these together into
one chunk of text and appends this to the output text box. Figure 8-1 is an example of our console in action.

Note you have full access to the data of your running server and can modify its
data. You can also create your own variables and generally do anything you can
from a regular Python console.

Industrial-Strength Consoles

The previous console is extremely simple and allows only one statement at a time.
Ideally, something like the interactive prompt in PythonWin would be preferable.

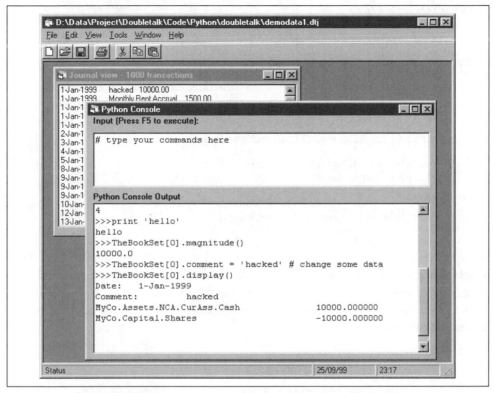

Figure 8-1. A crude Python console

There is actually quite a lot of work involved in writing such a window, and we won't go through the code to do it here. As text is entered a line at a time, your interpreter window needs to decide if it's a complete expression and when to process the input, as well as suggest indent levels for subsequent lines, and so on. The event-handling depends a great deal on the type of GUI widget used to build the console.

If you want to build such a console, look at the file *code.py* in the standard Python library. This contains a function called `interact()` that defines an interactive console written in Python. It needs adapting, but shows the general approach; as each line is entered, it tries to evaluate the current text buffer, and assumes the statement is incomplete if it gets an error. You could modify this to provide hooks for your VB console. *Code.py* is used by both IDLE and Pythonwin to emulate the Python interactive mode.

Executing Scripts

Quite often the user wants to execute simple scripts. If the user has created a simple script in a file on disk, it can be run with the built-in function `execfile` (*file[, globals[, locals]]*). This is broadly equivalent to the `exec` statement discussed earlier, except that it's a function, and it takes `filename` as an argument, processing the entire contents. To expose this, we've implemented a new method of `COMBookSet`, which takes the filename as a single argument, and calls `execfile(`*filename, self.userNameSpace*`)`:

```
def execFile(self, filename):
    if type(filename) not in [type(''), UnicodeType]:
        raise Exception(desc="Must be a string", \
                        scode=winerror.DISP_E_TYPEMISMATCH)
    execfile(str(filename), self.userNameSpace)
```

VB provides a rich-text editor component that makes it easy to create an editor, so we've added yet another form to our application called *frmScriptEditor*. This has a single editing region and a menu. We provided menu options to open and save files, and it keeps track of the filename and whether the text has changed. We won't cover those functions here. It also has a menu option to run a script, which is straightforward to implement:

```
Private Sub mnuScriptRun_Click()
    mnuScriptSave_Click
    If Saved Then
        On Error GoTo mnuScriptRun_Error
        frmMain.BookServer.execFile FileName
        On Error GoTo 0
        frmConsole.UpdateOutput
    End If
    Exit Sub

mnuScriptRun_Error:
    MsgBox "Error running script:" + vbCrLf + vbCrLf + Err.Description
End Sub
```

We handle errors, since the user is bound to make some at some stage, and ask the console window to display any new output afterwards. The user interface checks that any script is saved before running it, since we need to execute a file on disk. Figure 8-2 is a basic script in action, querying the running `BookSet` and producing some console output.

Importing a Module

The difference between importing a module and running a script is that a module object is created in memory with a name you can access. All the functions and classes defined in the module go into the newly created namespace. When executing a script, all code is executed in the global namespace. You could let the user

Figure 8-2. A script running under our control

import modules by typing **import foo** in a console, or even in a script executed in this manner. However, there are some benefits to exposing this in the user interface. For example, you could save a list of standard imports for each user in the registry as a configuration variable and import those modules every time the application starts up. To do this, let's take a look at Python's import mechanism, which gives fine-grained control of how modules are created.

The library module **imp** exposes Python's import mechanism. This includes functions to search the Python path for modules, and to load modules once located. Let's say you create a simple module in the file *c:\temp\import\temp.py* that defines one function called **func(x)**. If you want to use this from PythonWin, ensure it's on the path and type **import temp**. Within a custom application, you can often drop to a lower level of detail and customize the details of this process. For example, the text for a module might be a compiled resource in the program rather than a file on disk, and you might want to swap different source files in and out under the same module name. Let's look at what happens behind the scenes of an import by recreating the steps manually.

First, Python looks for it with the `find_module` function:

```
>>> import imp
>>> found = imp.find_module('temp', ['c:\\temp\\import'])
>>> found
(<open file 'c:\temp\import\temp.py', mode 'r' at 1078200>, 'c:\\temp\\import\\
temp.py', ('.py', 'r', 1))
>>>
```

`find_module` takes a list of locations to search as an optional second argument; if this is omitted, it searches `sys.path`. Thus, by taking control of the import mechanism, you can keep a separation between your Doubletalk code locations and your general Python code; such a separation is useful in a production application. If successful, it returns an open file handle to the module file, the full pathname, and some background information about the file.

The next step is to call `load_module`, which lets you control what the module gets called. The arguments to this are the name to give the module in your namespace, and the three return values from the previous function. This returns a module object you can manipulate further:

```
>>> mymodule = imp.load_module('temp', found[0], found[1], found[2])
>>> mymodule
<module 'temp'>
>>>
```

If the module contains errors, it raises an exception, and the file handle in `found[0]` is left open. Your code should use a `try`... `finally`... block that closes the file afterwards.

A module object is like any other Python object. Let's put this one in the global namespace as usual:

```
>>> globals()['temp'] = mymodule
>>> temp.func('blah')
'blahblah'
>>>
```

You now have a module object in memory and can call its functions.

Armed with this knowledge, you can add a menu option to your script editor to import a script and make sure it's available in the right namespace for users: the dictionary `userNameSpace` in `COMBookSet`. As usual, expose a public method in `COMBookSet`:

```
def importFile(self, fullpathname):
    #import as the filename
    import imp
    path, filename = os.path.split(str(fullpathname))
    root, ext = os.path.splitext(filename)
    found = imp.find_module(root, [path])   #takes a list of files
    if found:
```

```
            (file, pathname, description) = found
            try:
                module = imp.load_module(root, file, pathname, description)
                # ensure it's visible in our namespace
                self.userNameSpace[root] = module

                print 'loaded module', root
            finally:
                file.close()
        else:
            print 'file not found'
```

Note that this takes the name from the filename and adds it to **userNameSpace**. The VB script **import** command looks like the earlier one for **execFile**, but calls **importFile** instead. Users can now edit scripts and choose both Script → Run and Script → Import from the menu as they can in PythonWin and access the functions created from the console.

Providing a Startup Script

A useful customization is to allow an option for a startup script. The script could be a standard, hardcoded filename or a configuration variable. Users can do almost anything with this script; they can put in a series of standard import statements, go off and import commonly used data files from elsewhere, and (as we'll see) set up the **BookSet** as they want with validation rules and custom views. The script executes after the **BookSet** has been initialized, so it can't control the way **BookSet** initializes.

This feature is easy to provide with the tools we've just built. In Figure 8-3, we've gone for a user-defined script name in an Options dialog.

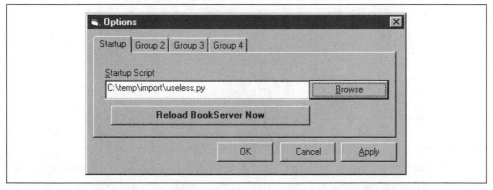

Figure 8-3. Specifying a startup script from the client

Earlier on we put two public methods in **frmMain** called **InitCOMServer** and **CloseCOMServer**, and never used the latter. Here there's a good use for it.

InitCOMServer has been expanded as follows (ignoring error trapping to save space):

```
Sub InitCOMServer()
    Dim startupScript As String

    'called when the program starts
    On Error GoTo InitCOMServer_error
    Set BookServer = CreateObject("Doubletalk.BookServer")
    On Error GoTo 0

    'tell it to capture output for the console
    BookServer.beginTrappingOutput

    'if there is an init script, run it
    If frmOptions.txtStartupScript.text <> "" Then
        On Error GoTo InitCOMServer_StartupScriptError
        BookServer.execFile frmOptions.txtStartupScript.text
        On Error GoTo 0
    End If

    'grab any standard output for the console
    frmConsole.UpdateOutput
    Exit Sub
```

Test to see if there is a startup script and run it under an error handler if there is. Then tell the console to fetch any standard output.

We've also provided a button titled Reload BookServer Now. This one just shuts down and restarts the server (losing any running data):

```
Private Sub cmdReload_Click()
    Dim Proceed As Boolean
    If frmMain.BookServer.count > 0 Then
        If MsgBox("You have data in the BookServer which will be " + _
            "lost. Proceed?", vbOKCancel, "Warning") = vbCancel Then
            Exit Sub
        End If
    End If
    frmConsole.Clear
    frmMain.CloseCOMServer
    frmMain.InitCOMServer   'this calls the script
    frmMain.UpdateAllViews
    Beep

End Sub
```

The user now has a startup script that allows almost limitless customization. We haven't implemented a place to save this script; the choices are generally the registry or an INI file.

A Reload button is extremely useful. During development, we frequently switched between Python and Visual Basic. After changing
any Python code, it was originally necessary to shut down and
restart the VB application. After implementing this button, it took just
one click to start exploring any new Python code.

Defining User and System-Code Directories

This section doesn't discuss a feature, it's just a recommendation. Your application
and documentation should define clearly where the main source package lives
(e.g., *C:\Program Files\Doubletalk\Source*) and where users' code should go (e.g.,
C:\Program Files\Doubletalk\UserSource). The application should add the latter
directory to the path when starting, and suggest it as the default location for any
user scripts if you provide a script editor.

Making an Application Extensible

We've built all the tools you need to provide the user with a macro language.
We'll now look at ways to let users extend the object model. Exactly what you
choose to make extensible depends a great deal on the application.

In the case of the Doubletalk browser, we'd like to add two new capabilities. We
want to trap certain events occurring in the BookSet and allow users to write
code to respond, and we'd like to let users write their own views.

Bear in mind that from now on we are talking about power users, who are pre-
sumed to have some programming experience or at least aptitude. With a well-
documented object model, their task should be easier in Python than in other languages; but they still have the ability to create bugs and damage data. We'll try to
structure the application in a way that keeps users away from critical code and
keeps it simple.

Changing the Delegate Class

It's useful to specify in another option what class to use in the place of the
BookSet. Imagine variations of BookSet that fetch data from a relational database
and commit each record as it's edited, or that perform some degree of caching to
answer certain queries quickly.

Changing the base class involves a lot of development and testing and is not easy
to do on the fly. However, it's possible to arrange things so that a user-written
module is consulted to determine the delegate class at startup.

If you distribute your core application as source, the users can always create a subclass to do what they want. However, subclassing involves a lot of work; users must ensure that their new `BookSet` subclass still does everything the `COMBookSet` class expects. While possible, this pattern is not really recommended for a complex class like `BookSet`.

A Delegation Framework for Responding to Events

There are four events in the `BookSet` API that allow modification: adding, editing, and deleting transactions, and renaming accounts. For each of these, you should provide a hook called before the event that gives the user a chance to modify the data or cancel the action altogether and another hook called after the event that allows the user to update other variables elsewhere.

Rather than have the user write numerous disconnected functions or subclass the entire `BookSet`, you can use a pattern known as a *delegate*. A delegate is a helper object a class informs of various events: it delegates certain responsibilities. The delegation mechanism was a cornerstone of the almost legendary NeXTStep development environment and is widely used behind the scenes in Delphi, where each component delegates the task of responding to events to its parent form. A delegate is typically much simpler than the class it's supporting. Users will find it far less work to write their own delegates to achieve a task than to rewrite or subclass the entire `BookSet`.

Views and Validators

The notifications before the event are intended to validate data, and the notifications after the event can maintain custom views. Accordingly, we define two types of delegate:

- A `Validator` is an object a `BookSet` notifies before changing data, asking for permission to proceed.

- A `View` is an object the `BookSet` notifies after changes have been made.[*] It also has a method to return a 2D array of data on demand, which contains whatever users wish.

It was traditional until recently to have just one delegate for an object. Some Java development environments allow a list of delegates that can be added and removed at runtime, and we've borrowed this pattern. We could also have built a more complex delegate that combined the functions of `Validator` and `View`, but this seemed a better fit to our goals for the users.

---

[*] Design-pattern aficionados might also argue that this is an instance of the observer pattern. Call it what you will.

For each delegate, youshould provide a base class users can subclass. You should also define a subclass of BookSet that can use them. All this code can be found in the module doubletalk.userhooks, which also includes examples of Validators and Views. Here's the definition of a View:

```
class View:
    """This delegate is informed of all changes after they occur,
    and returns a 2d array of data when asked."""
    def setBookSet(self, aBookSet):
        self.BookSet = aBookSet
        self.recalc()

    def getDescription(self):
        return 'abstract base class for Views'

    # hooks for notification after the event
    def didAdd(self, aTransaction):
        pass
    def didEdit(self, index, newTransaction):
        pass
    def didRemove(self, index):
        pass
    def didRenameAccount(self, oldname, newname):
        pass
    def didChangeDrastically(self):
        #can be used to notify of major changes such as file/open
        self.recalc()

    def recalc(self):
        #override this to work out the data
        pass

    def getData(self):
        return [()]   # simple 2D array for display
```

The View receives a SetBookset call when hooked up, triggering a recalculation. At this point it probably walks through the entire BookSet, gathering the data it needs, in the same way the existing query methods did in BookSet.

The View provides five notification methods for the BookSet to call with changes; the user won't call these directly. Define the four changes identified earlier and allow for one more (didChangeDrastically) that can be called after, for example, opening a new data file, which triggers a full recalculation. These allow the View to update its data intelligently and efficiently in response to changes.

Validators look similar, but respond to calls such as self.mayAdd (transaction). If the call returns zero (false), the action is rejected. Views are just notified of changes and don't have to return anything.

Let's look at our new UserBookSet class, which knows what to do with Views and Validators. Here's how to initialize it, add Views, and fetch their data later:

```
class UserBookSet(BookSet):
    def __init__(self):
        BookSet.__init__(self)
        self.validators = []
        self.validator_lookup = {}
        self.views = []
        self.view_lookup = {}

    def listDelegates(self):
        # utility to tell us what's hooked up
        [details omitted to save space]

    def addView(self, aView):
        #put it in both a list and a dictionary
        # join them together
        self.views.append(aView)
        self.view_lookup[aName] = aView
        aView.setBookSet(self)

    def getViewData(self, aName):
        return self.view_lookup[aName].getData()
```

Views are added with a name the user specifies. The View goes in both a list and
a dictionary, allowing you to iterate over the list of Views and to quickly access
individual Views by name. You can then ask the UserBookSet to return the data
for any of its Views. There is a broadly similar method to add a Validator.

Now we'll override the methods of BookSet that may modify data. Here's the new
method in UserBookSet to add a transaction:

```
def add(self, tran):
    for v in self.validators:
        if not v.mayAdd(tran):
            # rejected, stop
            return

    #call the inherited method
    BookSet.add(self, tran)

    # notify them all
    for v in self.views:
        v.didAdd(tran)
```

This code says, "Ask all the loaded Validators for permission before adding the
transaction to the BookSet. Then after adding it, tell each View." Similar methods
have been written for edit, remove, and renameAccount.

Finally, if you want to commit to this new architecture, change the __init__
method for COMBookSet to create a UserBookSet instead of a BookSet.

A User-Defined View: The Backend

Now we can write a new View, a simple one that keeps track of the month-end balances of an account. The array has two columns; the first entry to show year and month, and the second the month-end balance. For a two-year data file, you thus get back about 24 rows:

```
class MonthlyAccountActivity(View):
    """Keeps track of activity in an account.  Does
    smart recalculations."""

    def __init__(self, anAccount):
        self.account = anAccount
        self.balances = doubletalk.datastruct.NumDict()

    def getDescription(self):
        return 'Month end balances for ' + self.account

    def didAdd(self, tran):
        effect = tran.effectOn(self.account)
        if effect == 0:
            return
        else:
            #year and month as the key
            yymm = time.gmtime(tran.date)[0:2]
            self.balances.inc(yymm, effect)
            print 'added %s, %0.2f' % (yymm, effect)

    def didRemove(self, index):
        tran = self.BookSet[index]
        self.didAdd(-tran)    #invert and add

    def didEdit(self, index, newTran):
        oldTran = self.BookSet[index]
        self.didAdd(-oldTran)
        self.didAdd(newTran)

    def didChangeDrastically(self):
        self.recalc()

    def recalc(self):
        "Do it all quickly in one pass"
        self.balances.clear()
        for tran in self.BookSet:
            yymm = time.gmtime(tran.date)[0:2]
            for (acct, amount, etc) in tran.lines:
                if acct == self.account:
                    self.balances.inc(yymm, amount)

    def getData(self):
        # numdict returns it all sorted; just need to format
        # the date column
        formatted = []
```

```
            for (period, balance) in self.balances.items():
                (year, month) = period #unpack tuple...
                monthname = doubletalk.dates.SHORT_MONTHS[month-1]
                displayDate = monthname + '-' + str(year)
                formatted.append((displayDate,balance))
            return formatted
```

This should be fairly straightforward for users to produce. The `recalc()` method works it all out in five lines, using the `NumDict` utility class to categorize the numbers. When a single transaction is added, `recalc()` tests if the transaction affects the account; if not, no work is needed. If so, it just changes one entry in the `NumDict`.The methods for the other events are repetitive but similar. When the user requests the data from the GUI, the only work needed is to retrieve and sort a list of 24 items, which should happen almost instantaneously.

userhooks.py contains a test routine that can be called from a Python console to verify that the `UserBookSet` and `View` are working correctly.

A User-Defined View: The Front End

Now how do you look at `View` in the interface? Once again, you need to extend `COMBookSet`. First, change its initializer so that it creates a `UserBookSet` instead of a `BookSet`. Second, expose a method called `getViewData()` that calls the underlying method of `BookSet`. It's easiest to create and add the `View` with a short chunk of Python script:

```
    from doubletalk.userhooks import MonthlyAccountActivity
    view = MonthlyAccountActivity('MyCo.Assets.NCA.CurAss.Cash')
    TheBookSet.addView(v, 'CashBalances')
```

The Rolls Royce approach would be to build this on the fly after letting users select view types and parameters from a menu; however, this means having some sort of configuration dialog for each `View`. At a more basic level, power users writing their own `Views` could write this code themselves and put it in a start-up script.

Having done this, all you have to do is build a generic form with a grid. This keeps track of its name and fetches the `View` data (and a description) when asked. The next section presents a user-defined `View` of the monthly cash balances. See Figure 8-4.

User-Defined Validations

Imagine you're building a set of year-end accounts, repeatedly importing data from several sources and making manual edits. It all has to be perfect, and it's 2:00 a.m. You think you have the first half of the year sorted out and accidentally enter a transaction dated October 1998 instead of October 1999. It doesn't show up in the

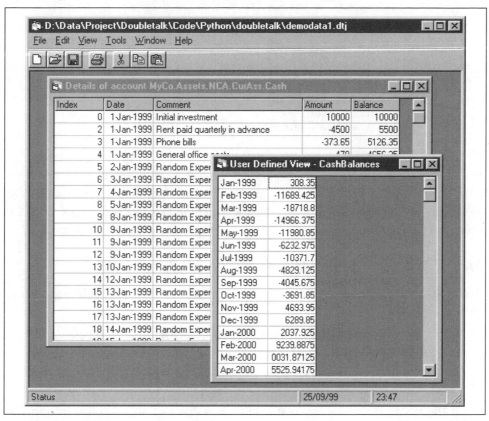

Figure 8-4. A user-defined View

View you are looking at, so you enter it again and make other corrections elsewhere based on your erroneous account balances. If you are unlucky, you could waste hours finding the error and unravelling all the dependent changes (One author knows this all too well). The *userhooks* file also defines a sample Validator that puts a time lock on the BookSet; this prevents any changes before a cutoff date. Here's the code:

```
class DateWindowValidator(Validator):
    """An example.  Prevents changes on or before a certain date
    locking the bookset"""

    def __init__(self, aDescription, aDate):
        Validator.__init__(self, aDescription)
        self.cutoff = aDate

    def mayAdd(self, aTransaction):
        return (aTransaction.date > self.cutoff)

    def mayEdit(self, index, newTransaction):
        oldtran = self.BookSet[index]
```

```
        if oldtran.date <= self.cutoff:
            return 0
        elif newTransaction.date <= self.cutoff:
            return 0
        else:
            return 1

    def mayRemove(self, index):
        tran = self.BookSet[index]
        return (tran.date > self.cutoff)


    # renameAccount will not break anything
```

More sophisticated `Validators` might have beginning and ending time windows, a list of accounts not to touch, or even a user-related permissions mechanism. All these can be implemented without the users needing to touch the core `BookSet` code.

More Ways to Extend the Application

`Views` and `Validators` can be used for other jobs as well as displaying interactive data:

- If you want to implement an error-recovery system, you could create a `View` that writes every change to a log file and then can roll backward and forward through the log (edits are reversible; renaming is not). This provides a full audit trail, invaluable when making lots of minor corrections at year-end.

- If the system were holding real data (e.g., as part of an executive information system), you could build a system of alerts to warn people or generate certain reports if accounts fell below certain levels, or if creditors were more than a certain amount of time overdue.

A Note on Performance

Extending `BookSet` to `UserBookSet` and adding in `Views` and `Validators` changes the performance characteristics enormously. If our goal is a simple, general-purpose class around which to write scripts, it may not be worth doing. The original `BookSet` can add, edit, and remove transactions quickly as it keeps them in a list, but most useful queries involve a loop over the entire set of data. A running `UserBookSet` in an interactive application might have 10,000 transactions in memory, five `Views` open, and two `Validators`. This means that any addition involves talking to seven other objects, and an edit involves 14 objects. Naturally, this dramatically slows bulk operations. However, it dramatically enhances query performance; a view on the screen displaying month-end balances of every account might need to redraw only one or two cells of the grid after an edit, rather than recalculate completely. Think of each running `View` as an extra database index, and you won't go far wrong.

Conclusion

This chapter has taken us beyond standard Windows development and into an area that is one of Python's greatest strengths: extensibility. We have taken an application that had a useful object model but a limited feature set and opened it to users. They have full access to the object model and can interact with the data. In the course of this, we've learned more about Python internals.

In addition, we have refined the object model using delegation to make it easy for users to customize. With a little training and documentation, they can build far-reaching extensions precisely tailored to the nature of their business.

This type of development would be prohibitively expensive and difficult without a dynamic environment such as Python. Python lets you create extensible applications with ease.

9

Integration with Excel

In this chapter we look at integration with Microsoft Excel using COM. This is interesting for technical and business reasons. Technically, it will give us a chance to look at both server- and client-side COM. On the business side, we've built a financial application, and a vast amount of financial data comes from and ends up going back into spreadsheets. We'll develop some simple examples that allow you to import and export data from spreadsheets, and see how to build an alternative frontend for pulling out data in Excel.

Client-Side COM and the Excel Object Model

Using Python for client-side COM basically means using Python to access an application somebody else has written. There is little to learn about client-side COM per se; what matters is learning the object model of the application or library you want to use.

Excel has a large object model—about as complex as anything you are likely to encounter. For example, just one of the objects, **Range**, has 84 properties and 72 methods. What's more, it's not particularly straightforward; the Perl community's mantra "There's more than one way to do it" probably applies even more to Excel than it does to Perl.

In Chapter 7, *Building a GUI with COM*, we stressed the importance of rerunning Office Setup to get the right help files. If you didn't do it then, do it now. The key help file is the *Microsoft Excel Visual Basic Reference*, which covers the object model.

The easiest way to learn the Excel object model is to write programs in Visual Basic for Applications. The VB editor is available with every copy of Office and is a first-rate development environment. The following key features help a great deal in learning:

Drop-down auto-completion

If you type `ActiveSheet` into the editor, a list drops down showing all the properties and methods of a `Sheet` object. This saves an enormous amount of time learning the object model (see Figure 9-1).

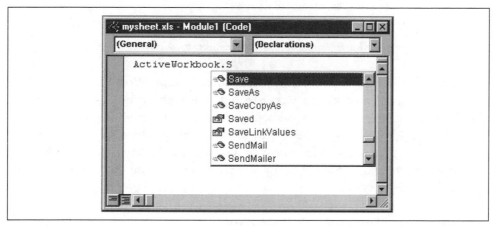

Figure 9-1. Drop-down auto-completion in VBA

Context-sensitive help

You can click on any variable, property, or method name and press F1 to get detailed help on that part of the object model. The help file also has a number of genuinely useful topic guides.

The F5 key and spreadsheet integration

You don't need to write a whole program to get started in Excel. You can write a subroutine in the editor, hit F5, and it runs. A great way to start learning about ranges and selections is to write a short routine to select some cells, and just keep running and extending it.

Having dispensed this piece of advice, we'll ignore it totally and begin by getting at Excel from Python. Within Python, you can't do any damage, but you need to know the objects and methods required.

A one-time step, which isn't required but which makes things faster and more pleasant to develop with, is to run the Python MakePy utility. What this does is explained fully in Chapter 12, *Advanced Python and COM*. On the Tools menu, choose COM Makepy utility, and select Microsoft Excel 8.0 Object Library from the list box. This may take one or two minutes to run but needs to be done only once per machine. This builds a support library of Python code for accessing the Excel object model, which allows early- rather than late-bound COM. Your code will run faster, and you'll know which Office objects you are accessing. If you don't do this, it all still works, but it uses a different technique behind the scenes.

Starting Excel

Start up PythonWin and enter the following:

```
>>> from win32com.client import Dispatch
>>> xlApp = Dispatch("Excel.Application")
>>> xlApp.Visible = 1
>>> xlApp.Workbooks.Add()
<win32com.gen_py.Microsoft Excel 8.0 Object Library.Workbook>
>>>
```

There will be a few-second pause before Excel starts. You should see Excel appear when you enter **xlApp.Visible = 1**, but with an empty main window; the final line creates a blank workbook with three sheets. Note that the return value of **Add** is informative. This is part of what Makepy does for you; if you had not run it, you'd get a less informative string back. By the way, we've made Excel visible for teaching purposes; if you just want to manipulate data, keep it hidden and save processor cycles.

Navigating Through Collections

The Excel object hierarchy basically goes **Application**, **Workbook**, **Sheet**, **Range**, **Cell**. A **Range** is an arbitrary region on a **Sheet**. You can assign variables to the various items in the hierarchy or drill down in one long statement. If you want to modify the top left cell of Sheet1 in our new workbook, you can get to it in any of the following ways:

```
>>> xlApp.ActiveSheet.Cells(1,1).Value = 'Python Rules!'
>>> xlApp.ActiveWorkbook.ActiveSheet.Cells(1,1).Value = 'Python Rules!'
>>> xlApp.Workbooks("Book1").Sheets("Sheet1").Cells(1,1).Value = "Python Rules!"
>>> xlApp.Workbooks(1).Sheets(1).Cells(1,1).Value = "Python Rules!"
>>> xlApp.Workbooks(1).Sheets(1).Cells(1,1).Value = "Python Rules!"
>>>
>>> xlBook = xlApp.Workbooks(1)
>>> xlSheet = xlApp.Sheets(1)
>>> xlSheet.Cells(1,1).Value = "Python Rules!"
>>>
```

We recommend getting a reference to the sheet you want and working with that.

The last few examples illustrate a common feature of Microsoft object models—their dependence on *collections*. A collection can be viewed as a cross between a list and a dictionary; it can be accessed by a numeric index or a named string key. Python allows you to access items via numeric indexes with both a function-call and an array syntax: in other words, with parentheses or square brackets. If you are using a string key, you must use parentheses:

```
>>> xlBook.Sheets(1)
<win32com.gen_py.Microsoft Excel 8.0 Object Library._Worksheet>
>>> xlBook.Sheets[1]
<win32com.gen_py.Microsoft Excel 8.0 Object Library._Worksheet>
>>> xlBook.Sheets["Sheet1"]
# some error details omitted
TypeError: Only integer indexes are supported for enumerators
>>>
```

However, there is a trap to watch for. Collections can be written to start indexing from one or from zero. If you are dealing with a one-based collection, you will get different answers; using square brackets gives you the true position in the collection, but parentheses gives the position according to the numbering system chosen by the author of that collection:

```
>>> xlBook.Sheets(1).Name
'Sheet1'
>>> xlBook.Sheets[1].Name
'Sheet2'
>>>
```

We recommend using parentheses throughout and relying on the object model's documentation to find how the collections work. For Microsoft Office applications, most collections start at 1.

Keyword Arguments

Both Python and Excel support keyword arguments. These are generally used when you have a long list of possible arguments to a function, most of which have default values. Excel takes this to extremes; for example, the function to save a workbook is:

WorkBook.SaveAs(*Filename, FileFormat, Password, WriteResPassword, ReadOnlyRecommended, CreateBackup, AddToMru, TextCodePage, TextVisualLayout*)

And that's a short one: some of the formatting commands have literally dozens of arguments. To call these, you supply only the arguments you want, as follows:

```
>>> xlBook.SaveAs(Filename='C:\\temp\\mysheet.xls')
>>>
```

The capitalization of the keywords must be exactly right. Microsoft generally uses mixed case for everything but **Filename**, but you'll undoubtedly have a fun time discovering more exceptions.

Passing Data In and Out

We put data into a cell with the `Value` property of a cell. We can also retrieve data the same way. This works with numbers and strings. Excel always stores numbers as floating-point values:

```
>>> xlSheet.Cells(1,1).Value = 'What shall be the number of thy counting?'
>>> xlSheet.Cells(2,1).Value = 3
>>> xlSheet.Cells(1,1).Value
'What shall be the number of thy counting?'
>>> xlSheet.Cells(2,1).Value
3.0
>>>
```

Excel users know that dates are just numbers with formatting applied. However, Excel keeps track of which cells are known to be dates and which are ordinary numbers internally. Excel (and most Windows applications, as well as COM) define a date as the number of days since 1/1/1900, while Python (and Unix) counts the number of seconds. If you want to add a date, you can work out the number yourself, but the Python COM framework provides a utility to make a COM date, which ensures that it's recognized properly but also accessible in Python format:

```
>>> import time
>>> now = time.time()
>>> now     # how many seconds since 1970?
923611182.35
>>> import pythoncom
>>> time_object = pythoncom.MakeTime(now)
>>> int(time_object)    # can get the value back...
923611182
>>> xlSheet.Cells(3,1).Value = time_object # ...or send it
>>> xlSheet.Cells(3,1).Value
<time object at 188c080>
>>>
```

When you send a date to Excel, it automatically formats the cell as well.

If you want to insert a formula, use the `formula` property and enter the formula exactly as you would in Excel:

```
>>> xlSheet.Cells(4,1).Formula = '=A2*2'
>>> xlSheet.Cells(4,1).Value
6.0
>>> xlSheet.Cells(4,1).Formula
'=A2*2'
>>>
```

Finally, empty cells are represented by the Python value **None**:

```
>>> xlSheet.Cells(1,1).Value = None  # clear a cell
>>> xlSheet.Cells(1,1).Value  # returns None
>>>
```

Accessing Ranges

We've been calling the `Value` and `Formula` methods without really knowing what they refer to. They are methods of an object called a `Range`, which refers to a range of cells. You can use `Ranges` to get hold of regions of a spreadsheet in several ways:

```
>>> myRange1 = xlSheet.Cells(4,1)        # one-cell range
>>> myRange2 = xlSheet.Range("B5:C10")   # excel notation
>>> myRange3 = xlSheet.Range(xlSheet.Cells(2,2), xlSheet.Cells(3,8))
>>>
```

A sheet has a `Range()` method that returns a `Range` object. The `Range` method can accept the usual Excel notation or a pair of one-cell `Range` objects defining the top left and bottom right. You can even perform intersections and unions to build nonrectangular ranges. Once you have a `Range` object, as mentioned earlier, you have 84 methods and 72 properties to play with. These cover all the formatting options including data.

Arrays

In Chapter 7 we built a view of an account. To do this, we fetched a 2D array of data from Python and looped over it, putting one number at a time into a grid. When we first started playing with Python and Excel, we expected to have to do something similar. Not so! Ask a range for its value, and you get an array. You can set the value of a range to an array, too. At this point we've typed a few more items into our spreadsheet to refer to (see Figure 9-2).

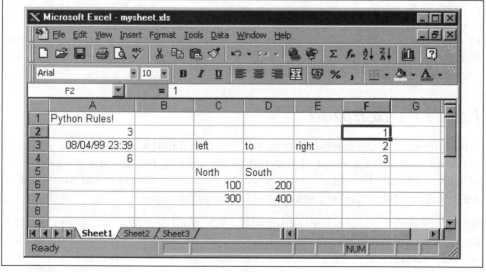

Figure 9-2. Passing arrays between Python and Excel

First, grab a horizontal array:

```
>>> xlSheet.Range('C3:E3').Value
((L'left', L'to', L'right'),)
>>>
```

Note that you get back Unicode strings, which you could convert to Python with a `str()` operation. When you asked for a single cell value earlier, the Python COM framework was smart enough to convert the Unicode string to a Python string; with a big array, you have to do the work.

Now, for a matrix with several rows and columns:

```
>>> xlSheet.Range('C5:D7').Value
((L'North', L'South'), (100.0, 200.0), (300.0, 400.0))
>>>
```

This returns a tuple of tuples, exactly the natural representation you would choose in Python. (For the rest of this section we use the term *array* to mean a Python structure of this shape—a list of lists, tuple of tuples, or list of tuples.) Finally, look at a vertical row, taking the items in column F:

```
>>> xlSheet.Range('F2:F4').Value
((1.0,), (2.0,), (3.0,))
>>>
```

As before, you get a tuple of tuples.

You may be wondering what those extra commas are inside the parentheses. They are Python's way of marking a one-element tuple. The expressions 2, (2), and `(((2)))` all evaluate to 2 in Python, as you would expect from the use of parentheses in mathematical formulae in any language. The comma tells Python it's looking at a one-element tuple rather than an expression to simplify.

Passing arrays between Excel and Python is fast. We tried passing a matrix with 100 rows and 100 columns on a Pentium 266. Sending it to Excel took 1.7 seconds; fetching back the same amount of data took just 0.07 seconds.

Excel Concluded

Having been through the mechanics, we will now build a class to make it slightly easier to get data in and out of Excel. It's easy already, but if you want to do a lot of work with Excel, you can certainly save a few lines of code in the users' scripts. An example of this can be found in the file *exceldemos.py*.

We've created a class called **easyExcel**. When an instance is created, it starts Excel. This class provides methods to open, create, and save files, and to get and set cell values and ranges. It can also deal with the Unicode strings and time objects if you wish. You could easily extend it to add new methods, but here are a selection that should be useful:

```
class easyExcel:
    """A utility to make it easier to get at Excel.  Remembering
    to save the data is your problem, as is  error handling.
    Operates on one workbook at a time."""

    def __init__(self, filename=None):
        self.xlApp = win32com.client.Dispatch('Excel.Application')
        if filename:
            self.filename = filename
            self.xlBook = self.xlApp.Workbooks.Open(filename)
        else:
            self.xlBook = self.xlApp.Workbooks.Add()
            self.filename = ''

    def save(self, newfilename=None):
        if newfilename:
            self.filename = newfilename
            self.xlBook.SaveAs(newfilename)
        else:
            self.xlBook.Save()

    def close(self):
        self.xlBook.Close(SaveChanges=0)
        del self.xlApp
```

Now put in methods to set and get cells. Users can specify a sheet name or index, row, and column:

```
def getCell(self, sheet, row, col):
    "Get value of one cell"
    sht = self.xlBook.Worksheets(sheet)
    return sht.Cells(row, col).Value

def setCell(self, sheet, row, col, value):
    "set value of one cell"
    sht = self.xlBook.Worksheets(sheet)
    sht.Cells(row, col).Value = value

def getRange(self, sheet, row1, col1, row2, col2):
    "return a 2d array (i.e. tuple of tuples)"
    sht = self.xlBook.Worksheets(sheet)
    return sht.Range(sht.Cells(row1, col1), sht.Cells(row2, col2)).Value
```

When you want to insert a block of data, just specify the first cell; there's no need for users to work out the number of rows:

```
def setRange(self, sheet, leftCol, topRow, data):
    """insert a 2d array starting at given location.
    Works out the size needed for itself"""

    bottomRow = topRow + len(data) - 1
```

```
rightCol = leftCol + len(data[0]) - 1
sht = self.xlBook.Worksheets(sheet)
sht.Range(
    sht.Cells(topRow, leftCol),
    sht.Cells(bottomRow, rightCol)
    ).Value = data
```

Sometimes you need to grab a chunk of data when you don't know how many
columns or even rows to expect. The following method scans down and right until
it hits a blank: all that is needed is the starting point:

```
def getContiguousRange(self, sheet, row, col):
    """Tracks down and across from top left cell until it
    encounters blank cells; returns the non-blank range.
    Looks at first row and column; blanks at bottom or right
    are OK and return None witin the array"""

    sht = self.xlBook.Worksheets(sheet)

    # find the bottom row
    bottom = row
    while sht.Cells(bottom + 1, col).Value not in [None, '']:
        bottom = bottom + 1

    # right column
    right = col
    while sht.Cells(row, right + 1).Value not in [None, '']:
        right = right + 1

    return sht.Range(sht.Cells(row, col), sht.Cells(bottom, right)).Value
```

Arrays coming back often contain either Unicode strings or COM dates. You could
convert these on a per-column basis as needed (sometimes there's no need to convert them), but here's a utility that returns a new array in which these have been
cleaned up:

```
def fixStringsAndDates(self, aMatrix):
    # converts all unicode strings and times
    newmatrix = []
    for row in aMatrix:
        newrow = []
        for cell in row:
            if type(cell) is UnicodeType:
                newrow.append(str(cell))
            elif type(cell) is TimeType:
                newrow.append(int(cell))
            else:
                newrow.append(cell)
        newmatrix.append(tuple(newrow))
    return newmatrix
```

The wrapper class now makes it easy to grab data out of a sheet. You can keep
extending this when you needed a new function, e.g., searching for cells.

Putting It All Together: Importing Financial Data

Now we'll write an import script using our wrapper. Excel is a good medium for entering financial data; users can enter data more quickly in Excel than in a database; Excel builds pick lists automatically; and it's easy to copy, paste, and rearrange the data quickly. However, data entered in this way isn't always properly validated. Imagine that someone in your organization is preparing a list of new invoices raised once a month and emailing the data in a standardized spreadsheet. You want to import it, validate it, get the data into double-entry format, and save it in a BookSet, as part of assembling monthly management accounts. The examples for this chapter include a spreadsheet called *invoices.xls*, which looks like Figure 9-3.

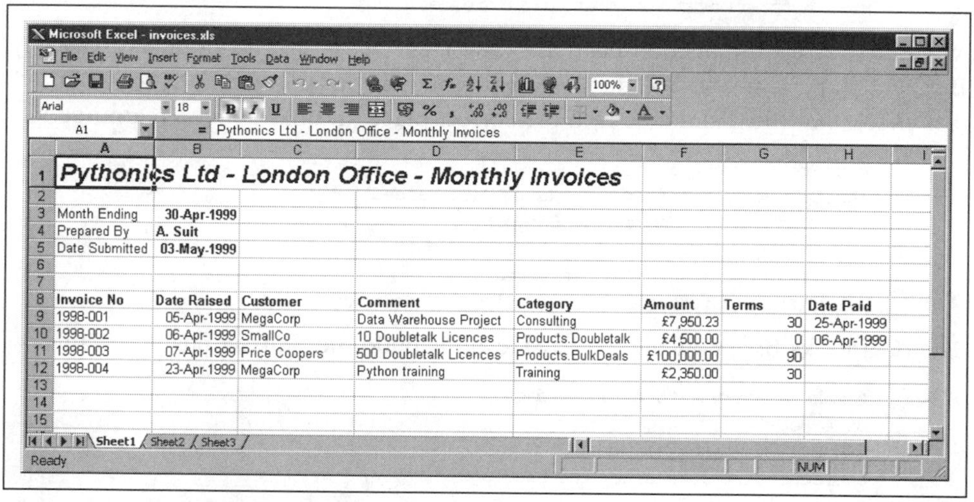

Figure 9-3. Invoices to be imported

You want to open this up, grab the three facts near the top, and import the matrix of cells describing the invoices. You're not sure how many invoices to expect, so you need to count down. If it's a cash sale (i.e., Date Raised is the same as Date Paid), create one transaction; otherwise create two: one for the bill and one for the payment. Note that some invoices are not yet paid; in this case, estimate a payment date for your forecasts and tag it as a scheduled transaction so that it can be filtered out of real accounts.

The full script to do this is in the file *exceldemos.py*, which you can find at *http://starship.python.net/crew/mhammond/ppw32/*. Using the wrapper class, it becomes easy to acquire the desired data:

```
def getInvoices():
    # the demo - get some data from a spreadsheet, parse it, make
    # transactions, save

    # step 1 - acquire the data
    spr = easyExcel('Invoices.xls')

    MonthEnd = int(spr.getCell('Sheet1', 3, 2))
    PreparedBy = spr.getCell('Sheet1', 4, 2)
    Submitted = int(spr.getCell('Sheet1', 5, 2))
    print 'Month end %s, prepared by %s, submitted %s' % (
                    time.ctime(MonthEnd),
                    PreparedBy,
                    time.ctime(Submitted)
                    )

    # do not know how many rows
    rawInvoices = spr.getContiguousRange('Sheet1',8,1)
    rows = spr.fixStringsAndDates(rawInvoices)
```

We've extracted the needed data and cleaned it up in just a few lines. Logically, the next stage is to validate the data. You could go a long way with this, but let's just check that the main table is in the correct place and hasn't been rearranged:

```
    # check correct columns
    assert rows[0] == ('Invoice No', 'Date Raised',
        'Customer', 'Comment', 'Category',
        'Amount', 'Terms', 'Date Paid'
        ), 'Column structure is wrong!'
    print '%d invoices found, processing' % len(rows)
```

The data looks fine; now all you have to do is build the transactions you want:

```
    # make a BookSet to hold the data
    bs = BookSet()

    # process the rows after the headings
    for row in rows[1:]:
        # unpack it into separate variables
        (invno, date, customer, comment,
        category, fmt_amount, terms, datepaid) = row

        # amounts formatted as currency may be returned as strings
        amount = string.atof(fmt_amount)

        if date == datepaid:
            # cash payment, only one transaction
            tran = Transaction()
            tran.date = date
            tran.comment = 'Invoiced - ' + comment
            tran.customer = customer
            tran.invoiceNo = invno
            tran.addLine('MyCo.Capital.PL.Income.' + category, - amount)
            tran.addLine('MyCo.Assets.NCA.CurAss.Cash', amount)
            bs.add(tran)
```

```
    else:
        # need to create an invoice and a (possibly future) payment
        # first the bill
        tran = Transaction()
        tran.date = date
        tran.comment = 'Invoiced - ' + comment
        tran.customer = customer
        tran.invoiceNo = invno
        tran.addLine('MyCo.Capital.PL.Income.' + category, - amount)
        tran.addLine('MyCo.Assets.NCA.CurAss.Creditors', amount)
        bs.add(tran)

        # now the payment.  If not paid, use the terms to estimate a
        # date, and flag it as a Scheduled transaction (i.e., not real)
        tran = Transaction()
        if datepaid == None:
            datepaid = date + (terms * 86400)
            tran.mode = 'Scheduled'    # tag it as not real
        tran.date = date
        tran.comment = 'Invoice Paid - ' + comment
        tran.customer = customer
        tran.invoiceNo = invno
        tran.addLine('MyCo.Assets.NCA.CurAss.Creditors', - amount)
        tran.addLine('MyCo.Assets.NCA.CurAss.Cash', amount)
        bs.add(tran)

# we're done, save and pack up
filename = 'invoices.dtj'
bs.save(filename)
print 'Saved in file', filename
spr.close()
```

Although the code is fairly lengthy, most of it is transferring a field at a time from the input to the relevant field or line of a transaction. If you define classes to represent invoices and payments, each with a standard set of attributes and the right constructors, this is simplified even further.

Server-Side COM Again: Excel as a GUI

Excel makes a wonderful frontend for financial applications. We've already built a COM server that can handle all of our data and return certain views. There's a strong case for turning things on their heads and having Excel use Python COM objects in many circumstances. We won't go through an example here, as we have covered all the necessary techniques in detail, but it's worth thinking about what's possible.

Imagine you regularly generate a set of management accounts, including results for the year to date and a forecast a year ahead, and that you extend this with various views of the data. You could easily build an Excel spreadsheet that starts a COM server when opened. Where our VB GUI had to do a double loop over the data to get it into a grid on screen, Excel can insert whole arrays into worksheets in a split second. You can configure sheets within the workbook to display arbitrary views of the data and link charts to these views. Some of these would be user-configurable; for example, selecting an account or customer from a combo box at the top of a sheet could fill the sheet with the relevant data, and a chart below it would be updated automatically.

This is the ideal format in which to deliver numbers to a user; they can immediately start doing their own calculations and building charts or comparisons of the data that interest them.

You could as easily build import applications that allow users to prepare data for import and click a submit button to save it into a **BookSet**. This involves either writing the table-processing code in VB or extending the COM server with some import functionality.

When should you use Python as the client and when as the server? There are two factors to consider:

Who's starting things off?
> If a user wants to work interactively with a spreadsheet, that implies Excel on top and a Python COM server. If a spreadsheet import/export is one step in the execution of a much larger Python script that runs over 200 files at 2:00 a.m., do it the other way around.

Does it require complex formatting or manipulation in Excel?
> If you're getting data out of Excel, you need to know only the cell references, which we've covered. If you want to build complex spreadsheets in the middle of the night, where the formatting depends on the data, consider writing the code in VBA. The spreadsheet can have an AutoOpen macro that starts up a Python COM server to deliver the data, and the fetching and formatting can be handled in Excel. The code will be the same length, but a lot easier to develop and debug in VBA.

Conclusion

In this chapter we looked at the other side of the coin, client-side COM. We learned how to control office applications from Python scripts and developed some reusable tools that allow us to easily extract data from and send data to Microsoft Excel.

References

Excel Visual Basic for Applications online help

This is not installed under the standard Office Setup; you need to rerun Office Setup, choose Custom Setup, and explicitly select the VBA help.

Your Python installation

After reading Chapter 5, *Introduction to COM*, you'll discover that Python can build a complete wrapper around Excel's object model, documenting all objects and properties. This doesn't tell you what all the methods do but provides a comprehensive and remarkably readable listing of the objects and methods.

Microsoft Office 97 Developer's Handbook, Microsoft Press

This book describes how to build custom applications using all the Office applications. There is a general overview of Excel but not enough detail on Range objects.

Microsoft Excel 97 Developer's Handbook, Microsoft Press

This book devotes 500 pages specifically to building applications in Excel. Regrettably, the majority focuses on GUI development and perhaps only 10% of the book relates to what you might use with Python. If you are developing routines in Excel VBA, this is the best reference.

10

Printed Output

We've developed an extensible package that lets power users define their own views of the data. Now they want to print it, and for people who don't use the program (i.e., senior management), the quality of the printed output is critical.

There are many different options for printing on Windows. We start by reviewing some common business needs and output formats. We then go on to look at three completely different techniques for printing: automating Word, using Windows graphics functions, and finally direct generation of Portable Document Format (PDF) files from Python.

Business Requirements

Doubletalk's obvious goal is to produce a complete set of management accounts. These will almost certainly include company logos, repeating page headers and footers, several different text styles, and charts and tables.

It would be highly desirable to view the output onscreen and keep it in files. This makes for a faster development cycle than running off to the printer and means you can email a draft to the marketing department for approval or email the output to your customers.

Most important, it should be possible for users (sophisticated ones, at least) to customize the reports. Everyone in business needs custom reports. Companies who buy large client/server systems often have to invest time and training in learning to use a report-design tool. Systems that don't allow custom reporting either fail to give their customers what they need, or (with better marketing) generate large revenues for the consulting divisions of their software houses to do things the customer could have expected for free.

If we can find a general solution that works from Python, the users are automatically in charge of the system and can write their own report scripts. This is a compelling selling point for a commercial application.

Different Document Models

There are several different document models you might wish to support. They all end up as ink on paper, but suggest different APIs and tools for the people writing the reports:

Graphics programming model
> The report designer writes programs to precisely position every element on the page.

Word-processor model
> Elements flow down the page and onto the next. There may be some sort of header and footer that can change from section to section. Tables need to be broken intelligently, with repeating page headers and footers.

Spreadsheet model
> A grid underlies the page, and this can produce sophisticated table effects. However, it starts to cause problems if you want more than one table on a page with different column structures.

Database form model
> The same form is repeated many times with varying data, possibly covering an invoice run, a mailmerge, or bank statements for customers. Forms can exceed one page and include master-detail records and group headers and footers.

Desktop-publishing model
> This is the most sophisticated document model in common use: the user specifies certain page templates and may have many pages of a given template. Within pages, there are frames within which objects can flow, and frames can be linked to successors.

You need to keep your options open; don't expect all these to be provided, but look for technologies that can be adapted to a different model for a different project.

Methodologies and Lessons from Experience

We've been involved with several different reporting systems over the last few years, and all have had their shortcomings. It is instructive to run through some of their lessons.

Project A involved a database of packaging designs, which could be understood only with diagrams showing the box designs laid out flat and semifolded. Reporting was left until the last minute because the developers were not really interested; when time and budget pressures arose, customers got something very unsatisfactory thrown together with a database reporting tool. They were told that the tools just did not support the graphics and layout they really wanted. This situation is all too common.

Project B involved extracting database data to produce 100-page medical statistical analyses; the reports were examples of a word-processor model and could include numerous multipage tables with precise formatting. A collection of scripts assembled chunks of rich text format (RTF) to build the document, inserting them into Word. It became clear that Python was the right tool to extract and organize all the data; however, RTF is complex to work with and isn't really a page-description language.

Project C was a scientific application that captured and analyzed data from a device and produced a family of reports, including charts and statistical tables. The reports needed to be viewed onscreen and printable. They were written using Windows graphics calls. Previewing accurately is a pain in the neck to implement at first, but worth it afterwards. It soon became clear that you could share subroutines to produce all the common elements; thus, one routine did the customer logo on all pages, and the same table routine could be used throughout. Changes to a common element would be applied across the whole family of reports with accuracy. It became clear that writing graphics code was a powerful approach, well suited to object-oriented development and reuse.

Project D involved a family of database reports produced using a graphic report writer (similar to the Report function in Access). A team of developers put these together. Although layout was initially easy, making a global change to all the reports was a nightmare. Furthermore, it became hard to know if calculations were done in the database or the report formulae themselves, leading to maintenance problems. Worst of all, testing involved going directly to the printer; there was no way to capture the output and email it to a colleague for scrutiny.

Project E used a dedicated scripting language that could import fixed-width and delimited text files and that output in PostScript. This was suited to high volumes of data, allowed code sharing between reports, and generally worked extremely well. The language used did not allow any kind of object-oriented programming, however, which made it hard to build higher-level abstractions.

Looking at all these experiences, the ideal solution would seem to have the following characteristics (apart from being written in Python):

- The Python script acquires the data from whatever sources it needs (databases, object servers, flat files) and validates it.

- The Python script uses a library to generate a suitable output format, preferably with all the right layout capabilities.

- The report library allows users to reuse elements of reports, building up their own reusable functions and objects over time.

Output Formats

Now let's look at some of the possible output formats and APIs:

Word documents

Most Windows desktops run Word, and a free Word viewer is available. It's easy to automate Word and pump data into it, with good control over page appearance. As we will see, you can do a lot of work with templates, separating the programming from the graphic design. Unlike all other solutions discussed, Word handles document flow for you. It isn't at all portable, but Word documents allow the user to customize the output by hand if needed.

Windows Graphical Device Interface (GDI)

Windows provides a wide range of graphics functions that can output to a screen or to a printer. Essentially the same code can be aimed at both. This needs to be initiated differently for a multipage report as opposed to a single view on screen. GDI calls involve drawing on the page at precise locations; there is no concept of document flow.

PostScript

PostScript is a page-description language with advanced capabilities. It is the language of desktop publishing and has defined an imaging model that most other graphics systems try to follow. PostScript files can be sent directly to a wide variety of printers and viewed with free software on most platforms. PostScript is quite readable and easy to generate. This is a multiplatform solution, but it isn't commonly used as an output format on Windows. PostScript can be viewed with GhostView, a popular Open Source package, or converted to PDF with Adobe's Distiller product.

Portable Document Format (PDF)

PDF is an evolution of PostScript aimed at online viewing; conceptually, it's PostScript broken into page-sized chunks, with compression and various internal optimizations for rapid viewing. Acrobat Reader is freely and widely available for Windows and other systems, and allows people to view and print PDF files. PostScript Level 3 allows PDF documents to be sent direct to Post-Script printers. PDF is much more complex than PostScript, but end users never need to look at the internals.

Excel documents

For invoices and other business forms and some financial reports, Excel offers a natural model. As we've seen, data can be pumped into it fast, and excellent charts can be generated in Excel itself. Care must be taken over the page size and zoom to get a consistent look across multipage documents, and there is little to help you with page breaking. Excel is highly useful if users want to play with the numbers themselves.

HTML

HTML is ubiquitous, and there are great tools for generating it from Python. The latest web browsers do a good job of printing it. However, it doesn't let you control page breaking or specify headers and footers, and there are no guarantees about how a web browser will print a page. As we will see later in this chapter, there are ways to incorporate HTML into your reports in other systems, which is an easy way to meet part of our requirements.

SGML and XML

SGML (Standard Generalized Markup Language) is a large and complex language used for marking up text in the publishing industry. It is well suited for the layout of a book, but not for precise graphics work. It has enormous capabilities but is quite specialized, and viewers are not widely available.

XML (Extensible Markup Language) was derived from SGML and is touted by many as the Next Big Thing on the Web—a possible successor to HTML and a foundation for electronic commerce. Python offers superb tools for working with XML data structures. It is a family of languages rather than a single one and doesn't necessarily have anything to do with page layout. The general concept is to describe the data ("this is a new customer header record") and not the appearance ("this is 18 point Helvetica Bold"). Our feeling about XML is that (like Python data structures) it's a great way to move data from place to place, but it doesn't solve the problem of how to format it.* However, once we have a useful Python printing tool, it could be put to work with some kind of style-sheet language to format and print XML data.

In general, these formats/APIs fall into three camps:

*   Windows GDI is a C-level graphics API involving precise drawing on the page.

---

* There is a web standard known as Document Style and Semantics Specification Language (DSSL) that provides a standard way to describe documents. There is also a transformation language based on Scheme that accepts arbitrary XML documents and applies formatting rules to them. However, this language is limited to a flow model, and tools are not yet widely available for working with it.

- Word and Excel are applications you can automate through COM to generate the right documents. Naturally, they have to be present to create and to view the documents.

- The others, including PostScript and PDF, are file formats. You can write pure Python class libraries to generate files in those formats. Like the Windows API (which borrowed heavily from PostScript), they offer precise page-layout control.

Let's begin by automating Microsoft Word. Later in the chapter, we discuss Windows GDI, PostScript, and PDF, with a view to a unified API for all three. We haven't done a full set of management accounts for each, but we take them far enough that you can figure it out yourself.

Automating Word

As noted previously, Word is an appealing alternative for many reasons. It has a powerful printing and formatting engine. It's on a lot of desktops; indeed it may be a standard throughout your company. A free Word viewer is also available from Microsoft. Finally, it's possible to post-process a document written in Word; you can generate a set of management accounts or a stack of letters, and users can add annotations as they wish.

As discussed with Excel, there are two options: use Python to take control of Word, or have Word VB grab data from Python and format it. In Chapter 9, *Integration with Excel*, we mentioned some guidelines for choosing which application was on top. We've shown Python automating Word for the following reasons:

- There is a good chance that report production would be an automated step in the middle of the night; people won't be using Word as an interactive query engine in the same way as Excel.

- Python excels at formatting text and getting data into the right shape.

- The Word document model is easy to automate. We'll be adding chunks to the end of a document, and the details can be wrapped easily in reusable Python code.

- Reports change and evolve rapidly. It's easier to change a generic Python script than customize a Python COM server with new special-purpose methods.

However, there's absolutely no technical barrier to doing it the other way around, and that may work for you in some circumstances.

As with Excel, make sure you have the Word VB reference installed to document the object model, and install MakePy support for the Word object model.

A Simple Example

Let's start with the simplest possible example:

```
from win32com.client import Dispatch
MYDIR = 'c:\\data\\project\\oreilly\\examples\\ch12_print'

def simple():
    myWord = Dispatch('Word.Application')
    myWord.Visible = 1   # comment out for production

    myDoc = myWord.Documents.Add()
    myRange = myDoc.Range(0,0)
    myRange.InsertBefore('Hello from Python!')

    # uncomment these for a full script
    #myDoc.SaveAs(MYDIR + '\\python01.doc')
    #myDoc.PrintOut()
    #myDoc.Close()
```

When you execute this function, Word starts, and your message is displayed. We've commented out the lines at the bottom, but you can choose to print, save, or close the document. It's fun to arrange the Python console and Word side-by-side and watch your text appearing, and a great way to learn the Word object model.

Using a Template

You could hand-build a document and automate all the formatting, but that would be tedious. Far better to use a Word template and just put in what you need from your Python code. For the next example, we've created a template called *Pythonics.dot*. This has a fancy header, page numbers, and borders. It could also contain section headings, a table of contents, standard text, or whatever you want. Using a template is a huge leap forward in productivity. Figure 10-1 shows ours.

More important, a template allows you to separate the software development from the page layout. An artistically challenged developer could provide a basic template with the required elements, and turn it over to the marketing department to define the styles and boilerplate text. If she also delivers a Python test script containing example data, the marketing person can regularly test whether the program still runs while he is modifying the template.

To create a document based on a template, you need to modify only one line:

```
>>> myDoc = myWord.Documents.Add(template=MYDIR + '\\pythonics.dot')
```

Note the use of keyword arguments. Many of the Office functions (like `Documents.Add`) take literally dozens of arguments, and entering them every time

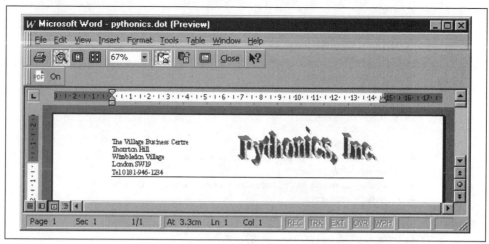

Figure 10-1. A Word template

would be tedious. Fortunately, Python also supports named arguments. However, you need to watch the case: most Word arguments have initial capitals.

A Document Wrapper

Word offers too many choices for building a document: you can loop over a document's contents, search for elements such as words or paragraphs, and select any portion of the text to work with. We'll assume you want to build a document in order from beginning to end.

Let's start with a Python class to help automate the production of documents. First we'll construct an object that has a pointer to a Word document, then add the desired methods one at a time. The class is called WordWrap and can be found in the module *easyword.py*. Here are some of its methods:

```python
class WordWrap:
    """Wrapper around Word 8 documents to make them easy to build.
    Has variables for the Applications, Document and Selection;
    most methods add things at the end of the document"""
    def __init__(self, templatefile=None):
        self.wordApp = Dispatch('Word.Application')
        if templatefile == None:
            self.wordDoc = self.wordApp.Documents.Add()
        else:
            self.wordDoc = self.wordApp.Documents.Add(Template=templatefile)

        #set up the selection
        self.wordDoc.Range(0,0).Select()
        self.wordSel = self.wordApp.Selection
        #fetch the styles in the document - see below
        self.getStyleDictionary()
```

```
def show(self):
    # convenience when developing
    self.wordApp.Visible = 1

def saveAs(self, filename):
    self.wordDoc.SaveAs(filename)

def printout(self):
    self.wordDoc.PrintOut()

def selectEnd(self):
    # ensures insertion point is at the end of the document
    self.wordSel.Collapse(0)
    # 0 is the constant wdCollapseEnd; don't want to depend
    # on makepy support.

def addText(self, text):
    self.wordSel.InsertAfter(text)
    self.selectEnd()
```

You work with the **Selection** object, which provides several methods for inserting text. When you call **Selection.InsertAfter(***text***)**, the selection expands to include whatever you add; it also provides a **Collapse** method that can take various parameters; the one you need, **wdCollapseEnd**, happens to have a value of zero, and collapses the **Selection** to an insertion point at the end of whatever you've just inserted. If you are using MakePy, you can access the constant by name; since this is the only constant we'll use in this application, we looked up the value and used it directly to produce a script that works on all PythonWin installations.

Adding Paragraphs and Styles

You can explicitly format text with precise font names and sizes by assigning them to the many properties of the **Selection** object, but it is less work and a better design to use predefined styles. It's far easier to change a style than to adjust 20 different reporting scripts.

The first thing to do is add a paragraph in a named style. Word has constants for all the standard styles. If you used MakePy to build the support for Word, you could access the built-in styles like this:

```
>>> from win32com.client import constants
>>> mySelection.Style = constants.wdStyleHeading1
>>>
```

Note that we set the **Style** property of the current **Range** to the correct style constant. This doesn't work if you use dynamic dispatch, or if you have your own custom template with styles that aren't built into Word. However, you can query a document at runtime. The following method gets and keeps a list of all styles actually present in a document:

```
def getStyleList(self):
    # returns a dictionary of the styles in a document
    self.styles = []
    stylecount = self.wordDoc.Styles.Count
    for i in range(1, stylecount + 1):
        styleObject = self.wordDoc.Styles(i)
        self.styles.append(styleObject.NameLocal)
```

The `Style` property of a `Range` or `Selection` in Word accepts either a constant or a string value, so you might as well use the names. Here's a useful method:

```
def addStyledPara(self, text, stylename):
    if text[-1] <> '\n':
        text = text + '\n'
```

Let's try:

```
>>> import easyword
>>> w = easyword.WordWrap()
>>> w.show()
>>> w.addStyledPara('What I did on Holiday', 'Heading 1')
>>> w.addStyledPara('blah ' * 50, 'Normal')
>>>
```

This should give you something that looks like Figure 10-2.

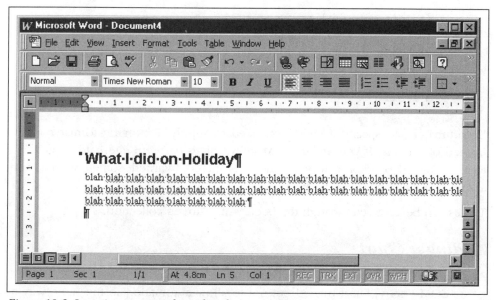

Figure 10-2. Inserting paragraphs with styles

Our wrapper class and Word's style features combine to make it easy to build a document.

Tables

Word tables are sophisticated object hierarchies in their own right, and you can manipulate them to any level of detail. However, there's also an `AutoFormat` option for tables that works in a similar way to styles. Here's the full declaration:

```
Table.AutoFormat(Format, ApplyBorders, ApplyShading, ApplyFont, ApplyColor,
ApplyHeadingRows, ApplyLastRow, ApplyFirstColumn, ApplyLastColumn, AutoFit)
```

All you have to do is insert a block of tab-delimited text with the table contents, and call the method to convert text to a table, then call the table's `AutoFormat` method. Fortunately, almost all the arguments are optional:

```
def addTable(self, table, styleid=None):
    # Takes a 'list of lists' of data.
    # first we format the text.  You might want to preformat
    # numbers with the right decimal places etc. first.
    textlines = []
    for row in table:
        textrow = map(str, row)    #convert to strings
        textline = string.join(textrow, '\t')
        textlines.append(textline)
    text = string.join(textlines, '\n')

    # add the text, which remains selected
    self.wordSel.InsertAfter(text)

    #convert to a table
    wordTable = self.wordSel.ConvertToTable(Separator='\t')
    #and format
    if styleid:
        wordTable.AutoFormat(Format=styleid)
```

Unfortunately, to specify a style, you need to supply a numeric format constant instead of a name. If you are using MakePy, this is easy; an alternate approach is to use Word's VB editor to look up the constants. Be warned: some constants vary across different language editions of Word.

Tables can be accessed through the `Document.Tables` collection.

Adding a Chart

Adding a chart proved quite a challenge. There's a promising-sounding Microsoft Chart COM library, but it turned out not to allow automation in the same way as Word and Excel. Finally we decided to just make up an Excel chart, which is probably easier for users as well. A spreadsheet and chart can be easily designed by hand, and you can update the numbers, recalculate, and save using the tools in

Chapter 9. However, the problem remained of how to add a new object and position it correctly within the document. The problem took us several hours to solve and into some dark and surprising corners of Word's object model. Since the same techniques apply to positioning any OLE object or even a bitmap from a file, it's worth going over the objects in question.

A little reading of the Word help file turned up the `Shapes` collection, which claims to represent all the nontext objects in the document: OLE objects, WordArt, graphic files, text boxes, and Word drawing objects. The collection has a number of `Add` methods, including one called `AddOLEObject`. `AddOLEObject` has a multitude of arguments, but allows you to specify a class and a file; thus `Document.Shapes.Add(ClassType='Excel.Chart',FileName='mychart.xls')` inserts the chart somewhere in the document and creates a new `Shape` object to refer to it. The `Shapes` collection lives somewhere called the *drawing layer*, which floats above each page and isn't part of the document. The `Shape` object has an `Anchor` property that should be set to a valid range in the document, and it's then constrained to stay on the same page as the first paragraph in that range. You then have to choose a coordinate system with the `RelativeHorizontalPosition` and `RelativeVerticalPosition` properties, which say whether the location is measured relative to the current page, column or paragraph. Finally, you set the `Left` and `Top` properties to define the location in the given coordinate system.

We managed to write some VBA code to position charts using these objects and properties, but found the behavior inconsistent. If you've ever struggled to position a screen shot in a document while it jumps around at random, imagine what it is like doing it in code from another application! With a large shape, Word would decide that the initial location or page was impossible before you had finished setting properties and give different behavior from Python and from VBA.[*]

Finally we discovered the `InlineShapes` collection (not a name you would look for) that filled the bill. An `InlineShape` is conceptually part of the document; put it between two paragraphs, and it stays between them forever. The arguments to its constructor didn't work as advertised; the shapes always seemed to appear at the beginning of the document, but it was possible to cut and paste them into position. The following code finally did the job:

```
def  addInlineExcelChart(self, filename, caption='',
              height=216, width=432):
   # adds a chart inline within the text, caption below.

   # add an InlineShape to the InlineShapes collection
   #- could appear anywhere
```

---

[*] We did get to the bottom of this. Word is badly behaved in its use of two COM variant types that are used to denote empty and missing arguments. This explained a number of other obscure COM bugs. The fix is complex, so we've stuck with our simple workaround.

```
shape = self.wordDoc.InlineShapes.AddOLEObject(
    ClassType='Excel.Chart',
    FileName=filename
    )
# set height and width in points
shape.Height = height
shape.Width = width

# put it where we want
shape.Range.Cut()

self.wordSel.InsertAfter('chart will replace this')
self.wordSel.Range.Paste()  # goes in selection
self.addStyledPara(caption, 'Normal')
```

The same routine can be easily adapted to place bitmaps. If you have a simpler solution, drop us a line!

Putting It Together

Now we can build a set of management accounts. The example applications include a Word template, an Excel spreadsheet with a prebuilt chart, and a test routine in *easyword.py*. Thanks to helper methods, this is simple:

```
def test():
    outfilename = MYDIR + '\\pythonics_mgt_accounts.doc'

    w = WordWrap(MYDIR + '\\pythonics.dot')
    w.show()  # leave on screen for fun
    w.addStyledPara('Accounts for April', 'Title')

    #first some text
    w.addStyledPara("Chairman's Introduction", 'Heading 1')
    w.addStyledPara(randomText(), 'Normal')

    # now a table sections
    w.addStyledPara("Sales Figures for Year To Date", 'Heading 1')
    data = randomData()
    w.addTable(data, 37) # style wdTableStyleProfessional
    w.addText('\n\n')

    # finally a chart, on the first page of a ready-made spreadsheet
    w.addStyledPara("Cash Flow Projections", 'Heading 1')
    w.addInlineExcelChart(MYDIR + '\\wordchart.xls', 'Cash Flow Forecast')

    w.saveAs(outfilename)
    print 'saved in', outfilename
```

This runs visibly for fun, but would be much faster if kept off-screen. It produces the document in Figure 10-3.

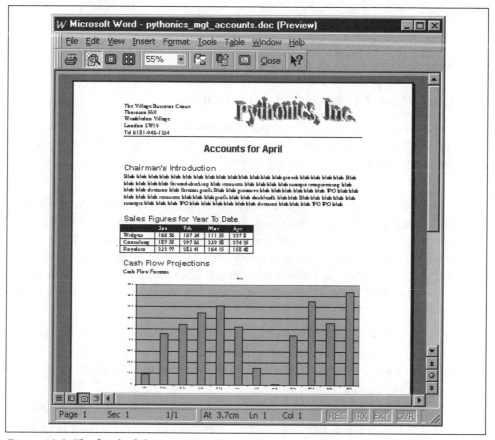

Figure 10-3. The finished document

Inserting HTML and Other Formats

Word can import and export HTML. The following line inserts an entire file into the current document:

```
>>> wordSelection.InsertFile(MYDIR + '\\tutorial.html')
>>>
```

Furthermore, some experiments revealed that you don't even need a full HTML document, just tagged text saved with the extension HTML.

So if you want an easy way to pump large amounts of text into a Word document, generate the HTML and insert it. Python has an excellent package, HTMLgen, for generating sophisticated markup from code. Word can import HTML tables with reasonable success, and all of the standard HTML styles are marked as styles in Word.

These days there is a need to produce both printed and online versions of documents. If you write code to generate the HTML, and then import it into a smart Word template with the right corporate header and footer, you have a complete solution.

Using Python COM Objects From Word

There is another approach for incorporating Word. You can use Python as the COM server and Word as the client. We discussed the pros and cons of this approach with Excel at the end of Chapter 9; the same design considerations apply.

Using Word as a client, use Visual Basic for Applications to initialize a Python server and fetch the data. The most natural way to package this is to build a Word template that includes the code and the desired document elements. When a new document is created from the template, it connects to the Doubletalk COM server we built earlier, instructs it to load the data, fetches the tables of information it needs, and uses VBA code to place the data into the document. This approach has two advantages:

- VBA offers nice editing features like drop-down auto-completion, helping you to learn the Word object model quickly. Debugging is also easier (assuming you have separately tested your Python server, and the Word object model is what is giving you trouble).

- You can safely tie functions in your template to regions of text or tables in your template without needing to be too generic. Data preparation is Python's job; formatting is Word's.

The Last Word

Please note: Word is hard to work with. Even if you plan to write a controlling program in Python, you should sort the code you need in VBA and check that it all runs first to save time. The manuals and the product itself are buggy in places. It is also somewhat unstable during development; if you make lots of COM calls that cause errors, it tends to crash frequently. Once the code is correct, it seems to keep working without problems. Some other Python users have worked with very large documents and reported stability problems in making thousands of COM calls in a row while creating large documents.

However, we do expect this situation to improve; Word 8.0 is the first version with VBA, whereas people have been automating Excel in real-time systems for years. Furthermore, we expect Word to handle XML in the future, which will allow more options for pumping in lots of data quickly.

In conclusion, you have the technology to do almost anything with Word. However, it's a heavyweight solution. Whether it's the right format for you depends on several factors:

- Word documents are the output format you want.

- Your users have Word.

- Your reports fit a word-processor flow model.

- Whether it's important to protect the integrity of a finished report or let users tweak it afterwards.

Direct Output to the Printer with Windows

The next technique to look at is Windows printing. We start off with a minimal example, then discuss the principles behind it. Start by typing the following at a Python console:

```
>>> import win32ui
>>> dc = win32ui.CreateDC()
>>> dc.CreatePrinterDC()
>>> dc.StartDoc('My Python Document')
>>>
```

At this point, you'll see a printer icon in the System Tray. Double-click, and you see Figure 10-4.

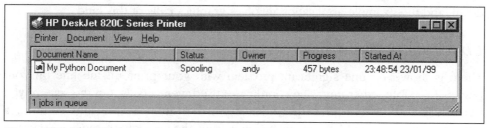

Figure 10-4. The Windows print queue

Now we'll print a few words and draw a line on the page:

```
>>> dc.StartPage()
>>> dc.TextOut(100,100, 'Python Prints!')
>>> dc.MoveTo(100, 102)
(0, 0)
>>> dc.LineTo(200, 102)
>>> dc.EndPage()
>>>
```

As soon as you type `EndPage`, your page should begin to print on your default printer. The Status column in the Printer window changes to look like Figure 10-5.

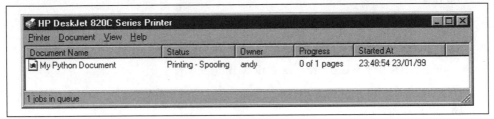

Figure 10-5. Document printing, while still being written

Finally, tell Windows you've finished printing:

```
>>> dc.EndDoc()
>>>
```

Hopefully, a few seconds later you will have a page with the words `Python Prints` near the top left and a horizontal line just above it.

If you've ever done any Windows graphics programming, this will be familiar. The variable `dc` is an instance of the Python class `PyCDC`, which is a wrapper around a Windows Device Context. The Device Context provides methods such as `MoveTo`, `LineTo`, and `TextOut`. Device Contexts are associated with windows on the screen as well as with printers; the graphics code is identical, although the way you start and finish differs: windows don't have pages, for example.

In Chapter 20, *GUI Development*, we cover PythonWin development in some detail, and the example application involves graphics calls of this kind.

Choosing a Coordinate System

There is, however, one significant problem with your printout: the line on your page is probably rather tiny. The coordinates used were pixels. On the screen, you typically get about 100 pixels per inch; if you'd written the previous code for a window, the text would be an inch down from the top left of the window and about as long as the words. On a typical HPDeskJet printer, which has a resolution of 300 dots per inch, the line is just a sixth of an inch long; yet the text is still a sensible size (it will, in fact, be in the default font for your printer, typically 10-point Courier).

For printed reports, you need precise control of text and graphics; numbers need to appear in the columns designed for them. There are several ways to get this. We will use the simplest, and choose a ready-made mapping mode, one of several coordinate systems Windows offers, based on *twips*. A twip is a twentieth of a point; thus there are 1440 twips per inch. Windows can draw only in integer units, so you need something fairly fine-grained such as twips. (Windows also provides metric and imperial scales, or lets you define your own.) In this coordinate system, the point (0, 0) represents the top left corner of the page, and y increases upwards; so to move down the page, you need negative values of y.

To set up the scale, you need just one line:

```
dc.SetMapMode(win32con.MM_TWIPS)
```

To test it, we'll write a little function to draw a six-inch ruler. If it's right, you can call this function after setting the mapping mode and take out a real ruler and check it. Here's the ruler function and a revised script:

```python
import win32ui
import win32con

INCH = 1440

def HorizontalRuler(dc, x, y):
    # draws a six-inch ruler, if we've got our scaling right!
    # horizontal line
    dc.MoveTo(x,y)
    dc.LineTo(x +  (6*INCH), y)
    for i in range(7):
        dc.MoveTo(x,y)
        dc.LineTo(x, y-INCH/2)
        x = x + INCH

def print_it():

    dc = win32ui.CreateDC()
    dc.CreatePrinterDC()    # ties it to your default printer

    dc.StartDoc('My Python Document')

    dc.StartPage()
    dc.SetMapMode(win32con.MM_TWIPS)


    # text - near the top left corner somewhere
    dc.TextOut(INCH,-INCH, 'Hello, World')  # 1 inch in, 8 up

    HorizontalRuler(dc, INCH, - INCH * 1.5)

    dc.EndPage()
    dc.EndDoc()
    print 'sent to printer'

    del dc
```

We've seen how to control precise page layout and also seen a reusable function that does something to a Windows device context. This is a first step in building your own graphics library. As everyone who's ever read a textbook on object-oriented programming knows, the natural approach is to make a class hierarchy of objects that can draw on the device context. Having shown you the basics, we'll move on, and return to the class library later.

PIDDLE: A Python Graphics API

While working on this book, we tried to create a printing system that could handle multiple formats, including Windows and PDF. At the same time, several people in the Python newsgroup felt that it was a real pity everyone was using platform-specific code to draw charts and diagrams, and that it should be possible to come up with a common API that covered several output formats. A team of four—Joe Strout, Magnus Hetland, Perry Stoll, and Andy Robinson—developed a common API during the spring of 1999, and a number of backends and a test suite are available at press time. This has produced some powerful printing solutions, which we explore here.

The API is known as Plug-In Drawing, Does Little Else (PIDDLE) and is available from *http://www.strout.net/python/piddle/*. The package includes the basic API, test patterns, and as many backends as are deemed stable. The basic API defines classes to represent fonts and colors, and a base class called **Canvas**, which exposes several drawing methods. The base canvas doesn't produce any output and exists to define an interface; specific backends implement a canvas to draw on the relevant device or file format.

Let's quickly run through the main features of the PIDDLE API.

Available Backends

At the time of writing, backends are available for PDF, the Python Imaging Library (which lets you draw into BMPs, JPEGs, and a host of other image formats—useful for web graphics), OpenGL, Macintosh QuickDraw, PostScript, Adobe Illustrator, Tkinter, wxPython, and PythonWin. Not all of these implement all features correctly, but things are evolving rapidly. When you get to Chapter 20, bear in mind that one Python graphics library can draw to all the GUI toolkits we cover.

Fonts

Each platform has a different font mechanism. PIDDLE defines a **Font** class to rise above this. A **Font** instance has attributes **face**, **size**, **bold**, **italic**, and **underline**. A standard set of font names are provided, and each backend is responsible for finding the best local equivalent.

Colors

Color class instances are created with red, green, and blue levels between zero and one. The module creates a large number of colors based on the HTML standard, so the word red may be used to refer to a ready-made Color object.

Coordinate System

The PostScript default scale of 72 units per inch is used, but with the origin at the top left of the page and y increasing downwards.

Canvas Graphics Methods

The Canvas class provides drawing methods and overall management functions. The graphics functions provided (we will skip the arguments) are drawLine, drawLines, drawString, drawCurve (which draws a Bezier curve), drawRect, drawRoundRect, drawEllipse, drawArc, drawPolygon, and drawFigure (which can manage an arbitrary sequence of line, arc, and curve segments). Each method accepts optional line and fill colors and may be used to draw an outline or a filled shape.

Canvas Attributes

At any time the Canvas has a current font, line width, line color, and fill color. Methods use the defaults unless alternatives are supplied as arguments. Thus drawLine(10,10,20,20) uses the current settings; drawLine(10,10,20,20, width=5,color=silver) does what it says but leaves the current settings unchanged.

Text Output

The drawString method is extremely versatile. It allows angled text (which forced some people to work hard at rotating bitmaps for their platforms, but they managed it), control of color, and printing of blocks of text with embedded newlines. A stringWidth method allows string widths to be measured, making it feasible to align and wrap text accurately.

Image Support

PIDDLE can use the Python Imaging Library to handle image data; bitmaps in many formats can be loaded, and either placed at their natural size or stretched to fit a desired rectangle.

Test Framework

As with all good Python packages, a test framework is provided that runs a group of standard test patterns against the bundled backends. Figure 10-6 shows a standard test pattern.

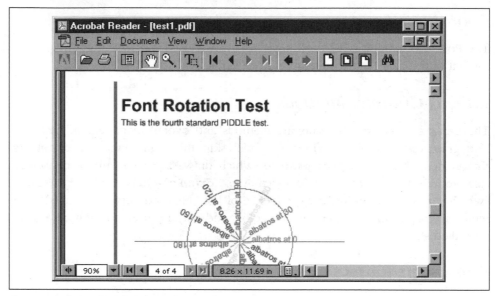

Figure 10-6. A PIDDLE test pattern

Video Recorder

A special canvas called VCRCanvas works as a recorder: when you execute graphics commands, it saves them for replay later. They are saved as text holding executable Python code. This makes it possible for a specialized graphics package to save a chart in a file, and for any other canvas to replay that file in the absence of the original package.

Having discussed the base API, we now tackle two key output formats: PostScript and PDF.

PostScript

The PostScript language is the world's most famous page description language. It was developed by Adobe Systems in 1985 as a language for printer drivers and was perhaps the key technology in the desktop publishing revolution. It consists of commands for describing the printed page, including both text and graphics. A text file of these commands is sent to a PostScript printer, which prints them. Post-

Script has some features other page description languages lack. For example, a font is a collection of subroutines to draw arbitrary curves and shapes; there's no difference in the way text and graphics are handled. This contrasts with Windows, where you can perform arbitrary scaling and translation of the lines in a chart, while watching all the labels stay right where they are in the same point size.*

This section is relevant only if you are aiming at a fairly high-end printer. However, it's worth understanding something about PostScript since it's the base for PDF, which is relevant to everyone.

PostScript printers used to be quite specialized; however, as power has increased, more printers are offering PostScript compliance, e.g., the LaserJet 5 series. Post-Script printers are the standard for high-volume/high-quality printers.

PostScript is generally produced by printer drivers or by graphics packages such as Illustrator, though masochists can do it by hand. PostScript is usually drawn on the printer. However, the public-domain package, GhostView, is available for rendering PostScript files on Windows and other platforms. GhostView lets you print to any printer, doing the best job it can with the local print technology. It also makes it possible to test Python code for generating PostScript without having a dedicated printer on hand.

Let's have a quick look at a chunk of PostScript:

```
% Example PostScript file - this is a comment
72 720 moveto
72 72 lineto
/Helvetica findfont 24 scalefont setfont
80 720 moveto
('Hello World') show
showpage
```

Comments begin with %. Lines 2 and 3 find a font and specify a size. The coordinate system uses 72 points per inch and starts at the bottom left of the screen or page; thus, the commands draw a line one inch from the left of the page, running for most of its height, and the string "Hello World" near the top left corner.

As you can see, PostScript is fairly readable; it's thus extremely easy to build a Python library to spit out chunks of PostScript. Furthermore, this can be done at very high speed; Python excels at text substitutions. That is what the `piddlePS` module does; when you make a call such as `drawLine(10,10,50,100, width=5)`, `piddlePS` does some testing to see what needs changing, then substitutes the numbers into a template string and adds them to an output queue. Here is how it was implemented:

---

* Of course, it is possible to do zoomable views in Windows, but it isn't easy. NT is beginning to approach PostScript in this regard with its World Transforms, but these are not in Windows 95 and thus have not been widely used.

```
def drawLine(self, x1, y1, x2, y2, color=None, width=None):
      self._updateLineColor(color)
      self._updateLineWidth(width)
      if self._currentColor != transparent:
         self.code.append('%s %s neg moveto %s %s neg lineto stroke' %
                           (x1, y1, x2, y2))
```

PostScript offers many capabilities beyond the scope of this chapter. Specifically, it's a full-blown language, and you can write subroutines to align text, wrap paragraphs, or even draw charts. Another key ability is coordinate transformations; you can write a routine to draw a shape, then translate, rotate, and scale space to redraw it again elsewhere. The PostScript imaging model has been used or copied in most vector graphic formats since it was developed.

Portable Document Format

PDF is a recent evolution of PostScript. Whereas PostScript was intended to be consumed by printers, PDF is designed for both online viewing and printing. It allows for features such as clickable links, clickable tables of contents, and sounds. It is intended as a final form for documents. You could possibly edit PDF if you had a few months to spare, but it isn't easy. It also remedies some basic problems with PostScript. (PostScript contains arbitrary subroutines that might generate pages in a loop or subject to conditions; so the only way to look at page 499 of a 500-page document, or even to know that there are 500 pages, is to execute the code and render it all.)

For the average developer, PDF is compelling because the Acrobat Reader is freely and widely available on almost all platforms. This means you can produce a document that can be emailed, stored on the Web, downloaded, and printed at leisure by your users, on almost any platform. Furthermore, all they get is the document, not any attached spreadsheets or data they shouldn't, and you can be confident it won't be tampered with. For this reason, many companies are looking at PDF as a format for much of their documentation.

PDF documents are generally created in two ways, both of which involve buying Adobe Acrobat. This includes PDFWriter, a printer driver that lets you print any document to a PDF file; and Distiller, which turns PostScript files into PDF files. These are excellent tools that fulfill many business needs.

PDF is a published specification, and in the last two years, a C library and a Perl library have been written to generate PDF directly. This was too much of a challenge to resist, so we have done one in Python, too.

The Structure of PDF

Technically, PDF is a complex language. The specification is 400 pages long. If you don't want to know the details, skip to the section "Putting It Together: A High-Volume Invoicing System." If you do, it'd be a good idea to open one of the sample PDF files provided with this chapter; unlike most you will find on the Web, they are uncompressed and numbered in a sensible order. We've provided a brief roadmap to the PDF format as we feel that it offers many benefits, and you might want to add your own extensions in the future.

The outer layer of the PDF format provides overall document structure, specifying pages, fonts used, and advanced features such as tables of contents, special effects, and so on. Each page is a separate object and contains a stream of page-marking operators; basically, highly abbreviated PostScript commands. The snippet of PostScript you saw earlier would end up like this:

```
72 720 m
72 72 l
/F5 24 Tf 42 TL
80 720 Td
('Hello World') Tj
```

Unfortunately this code, which can at least be decoded given time and you know where to look, can be compressed in a binary form and is buried inside an outer layer that's quite complex. The outer layer consists of a series of numbered *objects* (don't you love that word?) including pages, outlines, clickable links, font resources, and many other elements. These are delimited by the keywords `obj` and `endobj` and numbered within the file. Here's a `Catalog` object, which sits at the top of PDF's object model:

```
1 0 obj
<<
/Type /Catalog
/Pages 3 0 R
/Outlines 2 0 R
>>
```

Every object is a dictionary of keys and values. The `Catalog` is at position 1 in the file. It has a `Pages` collection, found at location 3 in the file. The `Pages` collection might contain individual `Page` objects, or perhaps other `Pages` collections with subranges of the document. These form a balanced tree, so that an application like Acrobat Reader can locate the drawing code for page 3,724 in a 5,000 page document in one second flat.

Once you get to a `Page` object, you'll find a declaration of the resources needed to draw the page, which includes a list of fonts used and might include graphics function sets to load into memory and a reference to a `Contents` object. A simple page and its associated small `Contents` object might look like this:

```
20 0 obj
<<
/Type /Page
/Parent 3 0 R
/Resources
    <<
    /Font        <<
        /F1 5 0 R    % list of font declarations
        /F2 6 0 R    % - font objects are described elsewhere
        /F3 7 0 R    % in the file
        /F4 8 0 R
        /F5 9 0 R
        >>
    /ProcSet 3 0 R       % reference to the sets of Postscript
    >>                   % drawing procedures to be loaded for page
/MediaBox [0 0 612 792]  % page in points - 8.5x11 US paper
/Contents 21 0 R         % reference to next object
>>
endobj
21 0 obj                 % beginning of contents object
<< /Length 413 >>        % predeclare the stream length
stream
% line 2 units wide from 72,72 to 72, 720
q 2 w 72 72 m 72 720 l S Q

BT                                   % begin text mode
/F6 48 Tf 80 672 Td 48 TL            % set font, position and size (48 pt)
(PDFgen) Tj T*                       % display a line of text
/F5 24 Tf24 TL                       % smaller font
80 640 Td                            % set text origin
(Automatic PDF Generation) Tj T*     % more text
ET                                   % end text mode
endstream
endobj
```

Lurking near the bottom, between the **stream** and **endstream** keywords in the Contents object, you finally get to the page-marking operators. Note also that the length of the stream of contents operators is predeclared to allow it to be read quickly.

Finally, typically at the end of the document, you find an index section that looks like this:

```
xref
0 24
0000000000 65535 f
0000000017 00000 n
0000000089 00000 n
0000000141 00000 n
<lines deleted to save space>
0000005167 00000 n
trailer
<< /Size 24 /Root 1 0 R /Info 19 0 R>>
```

```
startxref
7164
%%EOF
```

When Acrobat Reader opens a file, it looks in the last few bytes for the keyword `trailer`. The `trailer` object on the following line tells us that there are 24 objects in the file; that the root is object number 1; and that information such as the document author and date are available at object number 19. It then tells us that the cross-reference table is found starting at byte 7164 in the file. The cross-reference table itself (beginning at `xref` in the first line) shows the positions of the objects; thus object 1, the root, is at byte 17 in the file, and object 24 is at byte 5167.

This mechanism makes it possible to parse and process PDF documents quickly, but it made developing a PDF generator harder. With HTML or PostScript, you get instant gratification each time you output a well-formed chunk of code, and you can start in a small way; with PDF, you can't even look at it until you have correctly indexed the whole thing.

The *PDFgen.py* module wraps and hides most of this from the user and constructs a well-formed document. Many advanced features are missing, but the documents do open cleanly. The module does this by having Python classes that mirror the PDF ones and by building up a list of objects in memory. When it writes the file, each returns a text representation of itself for the file, and the **PDFDocument** class measures the length of this. The module is thus able to build a valid index at the end. What it doesn't do is the drawing. The module presumes that something else feeds it a complete contents stream for each page. This is where the PIDDLE interface comes in.

We won't go further into the implementation of the outer layer of the PDF library here. Instead we'll look at a few details of the current frontend.

Implementing the Frontend

Once the PIDDLE API was stable, it was fairly straightforward to implement a **PDFCanvas** object to provide a simple API. Let's take a quick look at some of the methods of the **PDFCanvas** class and how they hook up with the backend:

```python
def __init__(self, filename):
        Canvas.__init__(self)
        self.filename = filename
        self.code = []  # list of strings to join later
        self.doc = pdfgen.PDFDocument()
        self.pageNumber = 1   # keep a count
        # various settings omitted
```

When it starts up, the **PDFCanvas** instance creates a **PDFDocument** instance. This is the class that manages the overall document structure. It also creates an empty list, `self.code`, to hold strings of page-marking operators. The various drawing methods add the right operators to the list in the same way the PostScript snippets did earlier. If you compare the methods and output with the PostScript `PSCanvas`, it's easy to see the correspondence.

When you ask for a new page with the `showPage()` method, this happens:

```
def showPage(self):
      page = pdfgen.PDFPage()
      stream = string.join([self.preamble] + self.code, '\n')
      #print stream
      page.setStream(stream)
      self.doc.addPage(page)
      self.pageNumber = self.pageNumber + 1
      self.code = []      # ready for more...
```

First, create a `PDFgen` object called `PDFPage`, which is responsible for generating the output later. Then make a big string of page-marking operators by joining a standard preamble (which does some work to set up coordinate systems, default fonts, and so forth) and the list of accumulated operators. This is stored in the `PDFPage`, which is then added to the `PDFDocument`. `PDFgen` takes care of the rest when asked to save itself to disk. Finally, the page number is incremented, and the list of strings is emptied, ready for some more output.

Putting It Together: A High-Volume Invoicing System

Rather than repeating the management accounts we did in Word, we'll discuss a different situation. Imagine that Pythonics is now doing a large volume of consulting work and needs to bill customers by the hour on a weekly basis. An internal database keeps track of who works for how many hours on which project. At the end of each week, we need to raise correct invoices and simultaneously enter them into our accounts system. Although starting small, we'd like a system that will scale up in the future.

We've built a tab-delimited text file called *invoicing.dat* that contains a list of the fields for each invoice; basically, the customer details, date, invoice number, number of hours worked, hourly rate, and so on. In a real application, this data might come from database queries, flat files, or already be available as an object model in memory. The script to generate the invoices is 200 lines long and is mostly graphics code; we'll show some excerpts. First, the main loop:

```
def run():
    import os
    invoices = acquireData()    # parse the data file
    print 'loaded data'
    for invoice in invoices:
```

```
        printInvoice(invoice)
    print 'Done'
```

We'll skip the data acquisition. Note also that in a real financial application, you'd extract transaction objects from your invoice objects and save them in a **BookSet** at the point of printing.

For each invoice, construct a **PDFCanvas**, call various drawing subroutines, and save it with an appropriate filename. In this case, the filename encodes the invoice number and client name:

```
def printInvoice(inv):
    #first see what to call it

    filename = 'INVOICE_%d_%s.PDF' % (inv.InvoiceID, inv.ClientID)
    canv = pdfcanvas.PDFCanvas(filename)

    #make up the standard fonts we need and attach to the canvas
    canv.standardFont = pdfcanvas.Font(face='Helvetica',size=12)
    canv.boldFont = pdfcanvas.Font(face='Helvetica',bold=1, size=12)

    #now all the static repeated elements
    drawHeader(canv, filename)
    drawOwnAddress(canv)

    # now all the data elements
    drawGrid(canv, inv)
    drawCustomerAddress(canv, inv)
    drawInvoiceDetails(canv, inv)

    #save
    canv.flush()
```

Here's one of the drawing functions, **drawOwnAddress()**. It's passed the canvas to draw on and the invoice; it does what you'd expect:

```
def drawOwnAddress(canv):
    address = ['Village Business Centre',
            'Thornton Hill',
            'Wimbledon Village',
            'London SW19 8PY',
            'Tel +44-181-123-4567']
    fnt = Font(face='Helvetica',size=12,italic=1)
    canv.drawStrings(address, INCH, INCH * 1.5, fnt)
```

Other methods draw tables, format the numbers, and output them in the right places using methods of the **PDFCanvas**. Users don't need to worry about the details of the file format.

In practice, you'd use a standard script handler so that the script could be run with a double-click. Here it's run interactively. Running the script generates one file for each customer, at a rate of several files per second:

```
>>> invoicing.run()
loaded data
saved INVOICE_199904001_MEGAWAD.PDF
saved INVOICE_199904002_MEGAWAD.PDF
saved INVOICE_199904003_MEGAWAD.PDF
saved INVOICE_199904004_NOSHCO.PDF
Done
>>>
```

Figure 10-7 shows the output.

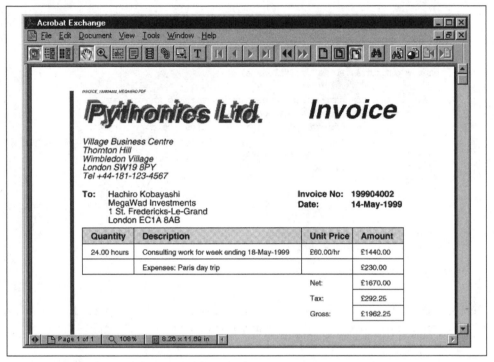

Figure 10-7. PDF invoices generated from Python

Now, let's look at the benefits of this architecture from a business perspective:

*   The report took only about two hours to assemble, including data acquisition.

*   You have a simple script that can be run with a double-click or scheduled to go off at night: no need to launch applications manually.

*   The output is filed with the correct names in an immutable format. If a dispute or problem arises in the future, you can instantly find the file and see exactly what was sent.

*   The entries have been made in the accounts system at the same time. It's easy to add further steps to the logic, such as emailing invoices to suppliers.

- The system is fast and light; it runs well with tens of thousands of pages and can be moved from a desktop PC to a Unix server with no modifications.

- It's easy to customize. You don't need a lot of Python, and there is a simple drawing API. Power users could learn to customize it or write their own reports easily.

- Data can be acquired from anything with Python: files, databases, spreadsheets, or other Python applications. You aren't tied to a database engine.

Advanced Techniques and Possibilities with PDF and PIDDLE

There are several more techniques and improvements we haven't added, but that could be easily accomplished if the need arose. This is Open Source, so if they sound useful, they probably will be done by somebody by the time you read this.

Object-oriented graphics and page layout API

The PIDDLE team is working on the "next layer up," which will hopefully be available by the time this book is printed. This consists of two ideas. First of all, frames identify regions on the page into which drawing may take place; users may specify one main frame per page, or as many as they wish. Second, we create a hierarchy of drawable objects, allowing a high level of reuse. These objects know their size and can wrap themselves to fit a frame if needed. They can be "poured into" a frame until it fills. A `Table` object might be initialized with an array of data and draw default table cells by itself; named styles allow quick and easy formatting of large tables. A `Paragraph` object, again tied to a list of styles, allows rapid formatting of text. Individual PIDDLE drawings can also constitute drawable objects and define their own coordinate systems for their contents.

Volume optimizations

The example script runs at about four pages per second, a lot faster than any printer, but nowhere near the speed limit. A large amount of processing is going into generating a text stream, which is almost the same for each page. You can generate the page once and substitute variables using Python's dictionary-substitution facility. This lets you generate documents as fast as the disk can write; however, it's applicable only for simple one-record-per-page forms.

PDF provides a similar trick: you can create something called a PDF form, which is a content stream that can be reused within a document. The reusable parts of the page can be placed in a form and stored once, and only the numbers and text that change need to print. This reduces the size of a huge invoice print run by 90% or more and leads to faster printing on the right printers.

Imported graphics

A large number of graphics packages work with PostScript. You can design pages or graphic elements in a tool such as Adobe Illustrator. These elements can be distilled and the PDF page-marking operators lifted out into a library, with some parsing tools that would be straightforward to write in Python. This library combines the freedom of visual design tools with the discipline and speed of report programs.

Onscreen views

The testing cycle was pretty fast—run a script, load the document to Acrobat in less than two seconds. However, the PIDDLE API is not platform-specific. You can use it to provide a printing engine for graphical applications; the same code that drew charts on the screen using a Windows or Tkinter back-end generates a PDF report for free.

Plotting

As discussed earlier, a key motivation for PIDDLE was to create plotting libraries that were not tied to one backend. The Graphite package (*www.strout.net/python/graphite/*) was developed alongside PIDDLE and is already capable of a wide range of plot types. Given Python's strong presence in the scientific world, we expect exciting developments here. Figure 10-8 is a sample from Graphite.

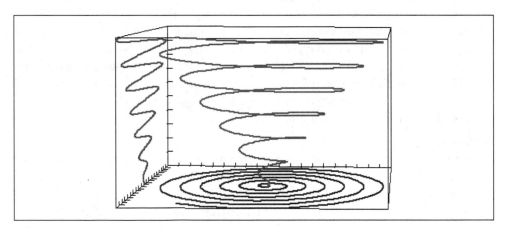

Figure 10-8. 3D plot from the Graphite library

Web and print versions

One key application area is on the Web. Python web applications can produce both bitmaps and print-ready documents on the fly from a web server.

Conclusion

Python supports many possible solutions for printing. We have looked at three: automating Word, using Windows graphics calls from PythonWin, and directly generating PDF documents. The recent evolution of a standard graphics API for Python with a variety of backends should provide more output formats in the future. The PDFgen/PIDDLE solution is lightweight (under 50 KB of code and font data), multiplatform, and scalable to large print runs; it follows the architecture of many high-volume corporate reporting systems, but with a much nicer language.

Returning to Doubletalk, our users already had an extensible application that allowed them to create their own views of the data. They are now in a position to create their own reports easily with no limits on graphical capabilities—whether as a back office job in itself, from another application, or on the Web—and to store electronic copies where they want.

References

Writing Word Macros by Steven Roman (O'Reilly) shows how to use VBA to automate many tasks in Word.

Word 97 Annoyances by Leonhard, Hudspeth, and Lee (O'Reilly) is a great guide to how Word works and how to live with it.

The Adobe PDF Specification (Version 1.3) is available from *http://partners.adobe. com/asn/developer/PDFS/TN/PDFSPEC.PDF* (5.5MB, 518 pages).

PIDDLE can be found at *http://www.strout.net/python/piddle/*. Graphite is at *http:// www.strout.net/python/graphite/*. The PDFgen package (also available in the PIDDLE distribution) is found at *http://www.robanal.demon.co.uk/pdfgen/index.html*.

11

Distributing Our Application

Now that we've written an application, let's distribute it across a network. The **BookServer** runs on one computer and the client program on another.

DCOM

Distributed COM does it all for you. You don't have to change a single line of your Python code. All you need is to enable a few settings on the server (which are not specific to this application, but to DCOM in general) and to change one line in the client code. Here are the steps:

1. DCOM needs to be enabled on the remote server. Choose Start → Run and type **dcomcnfg.exe**. A configuration dialog starts up. Select the Default Properties tab and check the box for Enable Distributed COM on this computer.

2. Python and PythonWin should be installed properly on the server, and the Doubletalk COM server should be registered.

3. In our Visual Basic program, go to the line of code where we create the **BookServer**, and add a parameter for the remote machine name. We added an extra box in the Options dialog, the contents of which are stored in the variable *RemoteMachine*. Here's the startup code:

   ```
   Set BookServer = CreateObject("Doubletalk.BookServer", RemoteMachine)
   ```

   If the string *RemoteMachine* is empty, the local server starts up. Otherwise, DCOM talks to the remote machine, and the **BookServer** starts up there. All calls to the COM object and any return values (including large arrays of data) are automatically packaged and transported across the network.

To demonstrate this, we created a data file called *remotedata.dtj* on a machine called *yosemite* and ran the client on a different machine. In the Options box input the name *yosemite* and hit the Reload button. At this point, the COM server starts on the remote machine. If you don't get an error message, it's connected. Then, in the File → Open dialog, type the path of the file on *yosemite* (you can't browse for it as it isn't on the client system), and the remote file loads. Note the window caption in Figure 11-1.

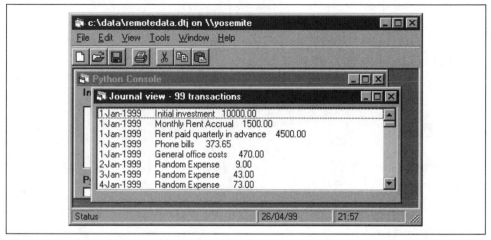

Figure 11-1. Remote server with one line of code

Conclusion

The length of this chapter speaks for itself. Distributed COM lets you build distributed network applications in Python without changing a line of code.

There is of course a great deal more to DCOM than this. More can be done, and there are also a number of caveats about machine configuration. In particular, designing a robust multiuser server architecture is a complex subject in any language; it will almost certainly involve COM singletons and either threads or an event loop for handling multiple simultaneous connections. Chapter 12, *Advanced Python and COM*, provides detailed instructions for configuring DCOM for both Python clients and servers and explains the background to the application we just distributed.

III

Python on Windows Cookbook

12

Advanced Python and COM

In Chapter 5, *Introduction to COM*, we presented some basic material about Python and COM. If you have never used Python and COM together or are unfamiliar with basic COM concepts, you should review that chapter before continuing here.

In this chapter we take a more technical look at COM and using Python from COM. We initially provide a discussion of COM itself and how it works; an understanding of which is necessary if you need to use advanced features of COM from Python. We then look at using COM objects from Python in more detail and finish with an in-depth discussion of implementing COM objects using Python.

Advanced COM

In order to fully understand Python and COM, it is necessary to understand COM itself. Although Python hides many of the implementation details, understanding these details makes working with Python and COM much easier.

If you want to see how to use Python to control COM objects such as Microsoft Word or Excel, you can jump directly to the section "Using Automation Objects from Python."

Interfaces and Objects

COM makes a clear distinction between *interfaces* and *objects*. An interface describes certain functionality, while an object implements that functionality (that is, implements the interface). An interface describes how an object is to behave, while the object itself implements the behavior. For example, COM defines an IStream interface, a generic interface for reading and writing, in a manner similar to a file. Although COM defines the IStream interface, it's the responsibility of objects to implement the interface; thus, you may have an object that implements the IStream interface writing to and from files or an object implementing the IStream interface using sockets, and so forth. This is a huge advantage to users of these interfaces, because you can code to the IStream interface, and your code works regardless of whether your data goes to a file or out over a socket. Each COM interface has a unique 128-bit GUID known as an interface ID (IID).

An interface defines a series of methods: interfaces can't have properties. An interface is defined in terms of a C++ vtable. Highly experienced C++ programmers will know that a vtable implements virtual methods in C++.

Just as with C++, COM allows one interface to derive from, or extend, another interface; in fact, COM explicitly requires it. COM defines an interface known as IUnknown, which is the root (or base) of all COM interfaces; that is, all COM interfaces explicitly support the IUnknown interface. IUnknown is a simple interface defining only three methods: AddRef(), Release(), and QueryInterface(). AddRef() and Release() manage object lifetimes; a reference counting technique is used so a particular object knows when it is no longer needed. The Python COM framework manages this behind the scenes for you, so these will not be discussed further. QueryInterface() allows an object to return a specific interface, given that interface's unique IID. Thus, regardless of the object you have, you can always call its QueryInterface() method to obtain a new interface, such as IStream.

COM also defines a standard technique for identifying and creating objects themselves. Each object class is identified by a class ID (CLSID, also a GUID) that exposes interfaces, each identified by an IID. Thus, there are a number of identifiers associated with every COM object: the CLSID identifying the class that provides the object, and a series of IIDs for each interface the object supports. Each object supports at least two interfaces, the IUnknown interface as described previously, and some useful interface (such as IStream) that allows the object to perform its task.

Objects may also register a program ID, or ProgID as well as a CLSID. A ProgID is a string describing the object, suitable for use by humans. When you need to create a particular object, it's usually more convenient to use the ProgID rather than the CLSID. There is no guarantee that ProgIDs will be unique on a given system; you should choose the names of your objects carefully to avoid conflicts with other objects. For example, the Microsoft Excel object has a ProgID of Excel.Application.

The IDispatch Interface

The COM architecture works well for languages such as C++, where the methods you need to use are known beforehand (i.e., at compile time). You create an object using the standard COM techniques, then perform a `QueryInterface()` on the object for a particular interface. Once you have the interface, you can make calls on its methods. This architecture does have some drawbacks, notably:

- There is support for methods, but no support for properties. In many cases, properties would simplify the object model you are attempting to publish.

- It doesn't work as well when using higher-level languages than C++. There may be no compile-time step involved at all. The language in use may not support using the *.IDL* or *.H* files necessary to obtain the definition of these interfaces.

COM defines the `IDispatch` interface specifically to meet the requirements of these higher-level languages. The `IDispatch` interface allows an object to expose an object model (complete with methods and properties) and allows the user of the object to determine the methods and properties available at runtime. This means the methods or properties you need to call can be determined when you need to call them, rather than requiring them to be predefined. You should note that the object model exposed using `IDispatch` is quite distinct from the `IDispatch` interface itself; `IDispatch` is a COM interface that allows an arbitrary object model to be exposed. In other words, `IDispatch` is not the object model but is the mechanism that allows an object model to be exposed.

There are two methods `IDispatch` defines for this purpose. The first is `GetIDsOfNames()`; it allows you to ask an object "do you have a method/property named foo?" If the object does have such an attribute, it returns an integer ID for the method or property. The method `Invoke()` performs the actual operation on the object—that is, either calling the method foo, or getting or setting a property named foo. The `Invoke()` method is passed the integer ID obtained from `GetIDsOfNames()`, as well as any parameters for the function or property.

In almost all languages, you don't need to use the `IDispatch` interface; your language uses `IDispatch` behind the scenes to present a natural model. For example, we'll see later that when you execute code in VB, Python, Delphi, and so forth similar to:

```
workbook = excel.Workbooks.Add()
```

behind the scenes, there is pseudo-code similar to:

```
propertyId = excel->GetIDsOfNames("Workbook")
newObject = excel->Invoke(propertyId, DISPATCH_PROPERTYGET)
methodId = newObject->GetIDsOfNames("Add")
result = newObject->Invoke(methodId, DISPATCH_METHOD)
```

The final piece of this puzzle relates to how the arguments and results are passed around. For this purpose, COM defines a VARIANT data structure. A VARIANT is defined as a self-describing C++ union and allows a wide variety of common data-types to be passed. To create a VARIANT, indicate the type of data you wish to pass and set the value. When you need to use a VARIANT passed by someone else, first query the type of data it holds and obtain the data. If the type of the data doesn't work for you, you can either attempt a conversion or reject the call returning the appropriate error code. This implies that type checking of the parameters and results can happen only at runtime (although many tools can take advantage of type information provided by the object to flag such errors at compile-time). As with the IDispatch interface itself, most high-level languages hide the details of the VARIANT and use them invisibly behind the scenes.

Objects that expose an IDispatch interface to support method calls and property references are also known as *automation objects*.

Late- Versus Early-Bound IDispatch

The process described for IDispatch has one obvious flaw: it seems highly ineffi-cient, and it is! In many cases, the inefficiency isn't important; the objects you need to call will often take longer to do their thing than it took to make the call.

Programs or languages that use IDispatch in the manner described are known as *late-bound*, because the binding of objects to methods or properties is done at the last possible moment, as the call or property reference is made.

There is, however, a technique automation objects use to publish their object model in a type library. Type libraries define a set of interfaces a program can use to determine both the methods and properties themselves, and other useful infor-mation, such as the type of the parameters or return values. Languages or environ-ments may be capable of using this information at compile-time to provide a better interface to the objects. The key benefits of knowing this information before it's used are:

- The GetIDsOfNames() step described previously can be removed, as the type information includes the integer ID of each method or property.

- Better type checking can be performed.

Languages that use the IDispatch interface after consulting type information are known as *early-bound*.

Most COM-aware languages, including Visual Basic, Delphi, and Python have tech-niques that allow the programmer to choose between the binding models. Later in this chapter we discuss the differences when using Python.

Using or Implementing Objects

There is a clear distinction between using COM objects and implementing COM objects. When you use a COM object, you make method calls on an object provided externally. When you implement a COM object, you publish an object with a number of interfaces external clients can use.

This distinction is just as true for the `IDispatch` interface; programs that use an `IDispatch` object must call the `GetIDsOfNames()` and `Invoke()` methods to perform method calls or property reference. Objects that wish to allow themselves to be called via `IDispatch` must implement the `GetIDsOfNames()` and `Invoke()` methods, providing the logic for translating between names and IDs, and so forth.

In the PythonCOM world, this distinction is known as client- and server-side COM. Python programs that need to use COM interfaces use client-side COM, while Python programs that implement COM interfaces use server-side COM.

InProc Versus LocalServer Versus RemoteServer

COM objects can be implemented either in Windows DLLs or in separate Windows processes via an EXE.

Objects implemented in DLLs are loaded into the process of the calling object. For example, if your program creates an object implemented in a DLL, that object's DLL is loaded into your process, and the object is used directly from the DLL. These objects are known as *InProc objects*.

Objects implemented in their own process, obviously, use their own process. If your program creates a COM object implemented in an EXE, COM automatically starts the process for the object (if not already running) and manages the plumbing between the two processes. Objects implemented in an EXE that run on the local machine are known as `LocalServer` objects, while objects implemented in an EXE that run on a remote machine are known as `RemoteServer` objects. We discuss `RemoteServer` objects in the later section "Python and DCOM."

These options are not mutually exclusive; any object can be registered so that it runs in either, all, or any combination of these.

In most cases, you don't need to be aware of this COM implementation detail. You can simply create an object and exactly how that object is created is managed for you. There are, however, some instances where being able to explicitly control this behavior is to your advantage.

Python and COM support `InProc`, `LocalServer`, and `RemoteServer` objects, as discussed throughout this chapter.

Python and COM

The interface between Python and COM consists of two discrete parts: the `pythoncom` Python extension module and the `win32com` Python package. Collectively, they are known as PythonCOM.

The `pythoncom` module is primarily responsible for exposing raw COM interfaces to Python. For many of the standard COM interfaces, such as `IStream` or `IDispatch`, there is an equivalent Python object that exposes the interface, in this example, a `PyIStream` and `PyIDispatch` object. These objects expose the same methods as the native COM interfaces they represent, and like COM interfaces, do not support properties. The `pythoncom` module also exposes a number of COM-related functions and constants.

The `win32com` package is a set of Python source files that use the `pythoncom` module to provide additional services to the Python programmer. As in most Python packages, `win32com` has a number of subpackages; `win32com.client` is concerned with supporting client-side COM (i.e., helping to call COM interfaces), and `win32com.server` is concerned with helping Python programs use server-side COM (i.e., implement COM interfaces). Each subpackage contains a set of Python modules that perform various tasks.

Using Automation Objects from Python

As we discussed previously, automation objects are COM objects that expose methods and properties using the `IDispatch` interface. So how do we use these objects from Python? The `win32com.client` package contains a number of modules to provide access to automation objects. This package supports both late and early bindings, as we will discuss.

To use an `IDispatch`-based COM object, use the method `win32com.client.Dispatch()`. This method takes as its first parameter the ProgID or CLSID of the object you wish to create. If you read the documentation for Microsoft Excel, you'll find the ProgID for Excel is `Excel.Application`, so to create an object that interfaces to Excel, use the following code:

```
>>> import win32com.client
>>> xl = win32com.client.Dispatch("Excel.Application")
>>>
```

`xl` is now an object representing Excel. The Excel documentation also says that a boolean property named `Visible` is available, so you can set that with this code:

```
>>> xl.Visible = 1
>>>
```

Late-Bound Automation

Late-bound automation means that the language doesn't have advance knowledge of the properties and methods available for the object. When a property or method is referenced, the object is queried for the property or the method, and if the query succeeds, the call can be made. For example, when the language sees code such as:

```
xl.Visible = 1
```

the language first queries the **xl** object to determine if there is a property named **Visible**, and if so, asks the object to set the value to 1.

By default, the **win32com.client** package uses late-bound automation when using objects. In the examples we've seen so far, the **win32com.client** package has determined the **Visible** property is available as you attempt to use it. In the parlance of PythonCOM, this is known as *dynamic dispatch*.

If you look at the object, Python responds with:

```
>>> `xl`
<COMObject Excel.Application>
```

This says there's a COM object named **Excel.Application**. Python knows the name **Excel.Application** from the ProgID that created the object.

Early-Bound Automation

The PythonCOM package can also use early binding for COM objects. This means that the information about the object model (i.e., the properties and methods available for an object) is determined in advance from type information supplied by the object.

Python uses the MakePy utility to support early-bound automation. MakePy is a utility written in Python that uses a COM type library to generate Python source code supporting the interface. Once you use the MakePy utility, early binding for the objects is automatically supported; there's no need to do anything special to take advantage of the early binding.

There are a number of good reasons to use MakePy:

- The Python interface to automation objects is faster for objects supported by a MakePy module.

- Any constants defined by the type library are made available to the Python program. We discuss COM constants in more detail later in the chapter.

- There is much better support for advanced parameter types, specifically, parameters declared by COM as BYREF can be used only with MakePy-supported objects. We discuss passing parameters later in the chapter.

And there are a few reasons to avoid MakePy:

- Using a MakePy-supported object means you must run MakePy before code that requires it can be used. Although this step can be automated (i.e., made part of your program), you may choose to avoid it.
- The MakePy-generated files can be huge. The file generated for Microsoft Excel is around 800 KB, a large Python source file by anyone's standards. The time taken to generate a file of this size, and subsequently have Python compile it, can be quite large (although it's worth noting Python can then import the final *.pyc* file quickly).

Running MakePy

MakePy is a normal Python module that lives in the *win32com\client* directory of the PythonCOM package. There are two ways to run this script:

- Start PythonWin, and from the Tools menu, select the item COM Makepy utility.
- Using Windows Explorer, locate the client subdirectory under the main *win32com* directory and double-click the file *makepy.py*.

In both cases, you are presented with a list of objects MakePy can use to support early binding.

We will try this out, continuing our example of using Microsoft Excel. Let's start PythonWin, and select the COM Makepy utility from the Tools menu. You are then presented with a list that looks similar to that shown in Figure 12-1.

The exact contents of the list depends on the software you have installed on your PC. Scroll down until you find the entry Microsoft Excel 8.0 Object Library (1.2, or the entry that represents the version of Excel you have installed) and press Enter. You should see a progress bar displayed as MakePy does its thing, and when complete, you should see a message in the PythonWin interactive window:

```
Generating to c:\Program Files\Python\win32com\gen_py\00020813-0000-0000-C000-
000000000046x0x1x2.py
```

Your first reaction may be one of horror: how are you supposed to use a filename that looks like that? The good news is that you don't need to; just use PythonCOM as normal, but from now on, all references to the Excel object model use the early binding features generated by MakePy.

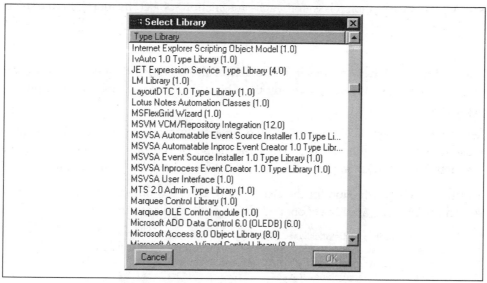

Figure 12-1. An example list of objects presented by MakePy

Now we have created MakePy support; let's see it in action. You can either use the existing PythonWin session, or start a new session and use the same code used earlier to create the **Excel.Application** object:

```
>>> import win32com.client
>>> xl=win32com.client.Dispatch("Excel.Application")
>>>
```

And you can still set the **Visible** property:

```
>>> xl.Visible=1
>>>
```

At this stage, the only difference is when you print the **xl** object:

```
>>> `xl`
<win32com.gen_py.Microsoft Excel 8.0 Object Library._Application>
>>>
```

If you compare this with the output Python presented in the previous example, note that Python knows more about the object; it has referenced the name of the type library (Microsoft Excel 8.0 Object Library) and the name of the object as defined by Excel itself (**_Application**).

How MakePy works

In most cases, you don't need to know how MakePy works, but in certain cases, particularly when tracking down problems, it is handy to know.

The **makepy** module generates Python source code into a standard *.py* source file. The items in this file may include:

- A standard Python class for each automation object included in the type library

- A set of constants exposed by the type library

The Python class has one method for each of the methods defined by the object and a list of properties supported by the object. Let's take a look at some generated code.

Let's open the source file you generated previously for Microsoft Excel. The simplest way to open this file is to copy the name of the file from the PythonWin interactive window, then paste it into the File Open dialog of your favorite editor.

To find the class definition for the Excel **_Application** object, you can perform a search for **class _Application**, and locate code similar to this:

```
class _Application(DispatchBaseClass):
  CLSID = pythoncom.MakeIID('{000208D5-0000-0000-C000-000000000046}')
  def ActivateMicrosoftApp(self, Index=defaultNamedNotOptArg):
    return self._ApplyTypes_(0x447, 1, (24, 0), ((3, 1),), \
                             'ActivateMicrosoftApp', None, Index)

  def AddChartAutoFormat(self, Chart=defaultNamedNotOptArg, \
                         Name=defaultNamedNotOptArg, \
                         Description=defaultNamedOptArg):
    return self._ApplyTypes_(0xd8, 1, (24, 0), ((12, 1), (8, 1), (12, 17)),\
                 'AddChartAutoFormat', None, Chart, Name, Description)
```

There are many more methods. Each method includes the name of each parameter (including a default value). You will notice the series of magic numbers passed to the **_ApplyTypes_**() method; these describe the types of the parameters and are used by the PythonCOM framework to correctly translate the Python objects to the required **VARIANT** type.

Each class also has a list of properties available for the object. These properties also have cryptic type information similar to the methods, so properties also benefit from the increased knowledge of the parameters.

At the end of the generated source file, there is a Python dictionary describing all the objects supported in the module. For example, our module generated for Excel has entries:

```
CLSIDToClassMap = {
  '{00024428-0000-0000-C000-000000000046}' : _QueryTable,
  '{00024423-0001-0000-C000-000000000046}' : ICustomView,
  '{00024424-0001-0000-C000-000000000046}' : IFormatConditions,
  '{00024425-0001-0000-C000-000000000046}' : IFormatCondition,
  '{00024420-0000-0000-C000-000000000046}' : CalculatedFields,
  # And many, many more removed!
}
```

This dictionary is used at runtime to convert COM objects into the actual classes defined in the module. When the PythonCOM framework receives an **IDispatch** object, it asks the object for its Class ID (CLSID), then consults the map for the class that provides the interface to the object.

Forcing Early or Late Binding

When you use the `win32com.client.Dispatch()` method, the PythonCOM framework automatically selects the best available binding method; if MakePy support for an object exists, it provides early binding; otherwise the dynamic dispatch method provides late binding. In some cases, you may wish to get explicit control over the binding method.

The `win32com.client.Dispatch()` method achieves this functionality by initially checking to see if MakePy support exists for the object. If MakePy support doesn't exist, the Python module `win32com.client.dynamic` is called to perform the late-bound functionality. To force late binding for your objects, use the `win32com.client.dynamic` module directly, bypassing any MakePy-generated objects.

The `win32com.client.dynamic` module contains only one function designed to be used by Python programmers, `win32com.client.dynamic.Dispatch()`. This function is used in the same way as `win32com.client.Dispatch()`, except that MakePy support is never used for the returned object.

To force the use of early binding to access COM objects, you must force the MakePy process in your code. Once you have ensured the MakePy support exists, use `win32com.client.Dispatch()` as usual. It always returns the MakePy-supported wrappers for your COM object.

To force the MakePy process, the `win32com.client.gencache` module is used. This module contains the code that manages the directory of MakePy-generated source files: the generated cache, or *gencache*. There are a number of useful functions in this module, and you are encouraged to browse the source file if you need to perform advanced management of these generated files.

To generate a MakePy file at runtime, you need to know the unique ID of the type library (a CLSID) and its version and language identifier. This information is usually not easy to find, so the MakePy module supports a convenient method to obtain this information.

If you run the MakePy script with a −i parameter, instead of generating the source module, it prints the information necessary to force the MakePy process at runtime. The easiest way to do this is to perform the following steps:

1. Start PythonWin and select File → Run.

2. Click on the Browse button and locate the file *makepy.py* in the *win32com\ client* directory.

3. Enter −i in the arguments control.

Your dialog should now look something like Figure 12-2.

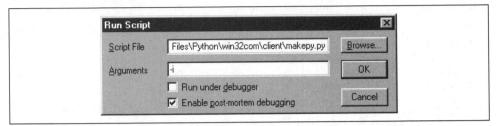

Figure 12-2. Running MakePy with the -i argument

Click on the OK button and again select the entry Microsoft Excel 8.0 Object Library (1.2). You should see the following text printed in the PythonWin interactive window:

```
{00020813-0000-0000-C000-000000000046}, lcid=0, major=1, minor=2
>>> # Use these commands in Python code to auto generate .py support
>>> from win32com.client import gencache
>>> gencache.EnsureModule('{00020813-0000-0000-C000-000000000046}', 0, 1, 2)
```

Let's tie all this together in a file that demonstrates what we've covered so far.

The following example first creates a late-bound object for Microsoft Excel, then forces MakePy to be run over the type library and create an early-bound object. You do nothing with the object; simply print the object to the output window:

```
# LateAndEarly.py - Demonstrates how to force
# late or early binding of your COM objects.

import win32com.client
import win32com.client.dynamic

print "Creating late-bound Excel object"
xl = win32com.client.dynamic.Dispatch("Excel.Application")
print "The Excel object is", `xl`


print "Running makepy for Excel"
# NOTE - these 2 lines are copied verbatim from the output
# of makepy.py when run with the -i parameter.
from win32com.client import gencache
gencache.EnsureModule('{00020813-0000-0000-C000-000000000046}', 0, 1, 2)

xl = win32com.client.Dispatch("Excel.Application")
print "The Excel object is", `xl`
```

Note that you copied the output of `makepy -i` verbatim into your source code.

Before running this code, remove the existing cache of *.py* files. If you run this code with a previously generated MakePy file for the Excel object, it won't be created again. To delete the cache of *.py* files, locate the *Python\win32com\gen_py* directory and delete it. You can delete the entire directory or just the files in the directory. Be sure to remove all files, not just the *.py* files.

If you run this code, notice that a progress bar is displayed as the *.py* file is generated, and this newly generated module is used for the early-bound object. If you then run this code a second time, notice you get the same output, but no generation process; this demonstrates you can force late-bound objects to be used, even when early-bound MakePy support exists for the object.

The output from this script should be:

```
Creating late-bound Excel object
The Excel object is <COMObject Excel.Application>
Running makepy for Excel
The Excel object is <win32com.gen_py.Microsoft Excel 8.0 Object
    Library.Application>
```

Differences Between Early and Late Binding

There are a number of differences between using early and late binding within Python. All these changes are specific to Python and not to COM itself. These differences are most significant when moving from code that uses late binding to code that uses early binding.

The key difference is the handling of parameters; in fact, these differences are so significant that we discuss them separately later in the section "Passing and Obtaining Python Objects from COM."

Another fundamental difference is case sensitivity. Late binding is generally not sensitive to the case of methods and properties, while early binding is. To see an example of this, create a late-bound Excel object and adjust its `Visible` property. As discussed in the previous section, you force a late-bound object even if MakePy support exists for the object:

```
>>> import win32com.client.dynamic
>>> xl=win32com.client.dynamic.Dispatch("Excel.Application")
>>> xl.Visible=1
>>> print xl.VISIBLE
1
>>>
```

You can use both `Visible` and `VISIBLE` in this context.

Now let's try the same example using early bindings. Assume that you have generated MakePy support for Microsoft Excel and use the same code:

```
>>> import win32com.client
>>> xl=win32com.client.Dispatch("Excel.Application")
>>> xl.Visible=1
>>> print xl.VISIBLE
Traceback (innermost last):
  File "<stdin>", line 1, in ?
  File "c:\Program Files\Python\win32com\gen_py\00020813-0000-0000-C000-
000000000046x0x1x2.py", line 1462, in __getattr__
      raise AttributeError, attr
AttributeError: VISIBLE
```

Note that using VISIBLE fails. The reason is simple; when using late binding, Python asks Excel for a Visible property and then for a VISIBLE property. Excel itself is case-insensitive, so it happily indicates both properties are OK. When using early binding, Python source code is generated, and all property and method references are handled by Python itself. Because Python is case-sensitive, it allows only the case that Excel reports for the property—in this case Visible. When the early-binding code attempts to use VISIBLE, Python raises the exception without consulting Excel.

Using COM Constants

Many COM type libraries also include enumerations, which are named constants and used with the type library. For example, the type library used with Microsoft Excel includes constants named xlAscdending, xlDescending, and so forth, and are used typically as parameters to (or return values from) methods or properties.

These are made available from the Python object win32com.client.constants, for example, win32com.client.constants.xlAscending.

It's important to note that the constants for a package don't exist until the MakePy-generated module has been imported; that is, until you create or use an object from the module. You can see this in action if you start Python and attempt to reference a constant from the Microsoft Excel type library:

```
>>> from win32com.client import constants, Dispatch
>>> constants.xlAscending
Traceback (innermost last):
  File "<stdin>", line 1, in ?
  File " win32com\client\__init__.py", line 53, in __getattr__
      raise AttributeError, a
AttributeError: xlAscending
>>>
```

You can see that attempting to use these constants results in an attribute error. However, if you first create an `Excel.Application` object, the constants become available:

```
>>> xl=Dispatch("Excel.Application")
>>> constants.xlAscending
1
```

Of course, because these constants are read from a type library, they aren't available when you use late-bound (or dynamic dispatch) objects. In this case, you must use integer literals, rather than named constants in your source code.

Passing and Obtaining Python Objects from COM

COM supports a variety of argument types, using the **VARIANT** data structure. The types that can be passed to COM functions include integers and floats of various sizes, strings, date/time values, COM objects, or arrays of any of these types.

In many cases, PythonCOM can translate between Python objects and **VARIANT** structures seamlessly. When you call a COM object and pass a Python object, PythonCOM automatically creates a **VARIANT** of the right type and passes the **VARIANT** to COM. In the absence of any hints, PythonCOM performs the translations as listed in Table 12-1 and Table 12-2. In Table 12-1, for example, you can see that a Python integer is automatically converted to a **VARIANT** type **VT_I4**.

Table 12-1. Default Python Object to VARIANT Translation

Python Object Type	VARIANT Type
Integer	VT_I4
Long Integer	VT_I4 if the value is less than 2^{32}, or VT_I8 if greater
String/Unicode	VT_BSTR
Float	VT_R8
PyTrue/PyFalse	VT_BOOL
None	VT_NULL
win32com.client.Dispatch instance	VT_DISPATCH
PyIDispatch	VT_DISPATCH
All other PyI* PythonCOM objects	VT_UNKNOWN
Pywintypes PyTIME object	VT_DATE
Any other Python sequence	An array of VARIANTs; each element of the sequence is translated using this table

Table 12-2. Default Python Object to VARIANT Translation

VARIANT Type	Python Object
VT_BOOL VT_I2 VT_I4 VT_ERROR	Integer
VT_R4 VT_R8	Float
VT_DISPATCH	PyIDispatch
VT_UNKNOWN	PyIUnknown
VT_BSTR	PyUnicode
VT_NULL VT_EMPTY	None
VT_DATE	Pywintypes PyTIME object

In some cases, these translations aren't suitable; for example, a COM object may be picky about the VARIANT types passed and accept only a VT_I2 integer, not a VT_I4 integer. This should be considered a bug in the COM object, but it does happen. In this case, you must use early-bound COM by using MakePy. The code generated by MakePy includes information about the types of parameters expected by the COM object, and the PythonCOM framework correctly coerces the Python object into the required VARIANT type. If you can't use MakePy for your COM object, you must get your hands dirty and use the PyIDispatch.InvokeTypes() method manually; this is how MakePy gets the behavior it does. The use of InvokeTypes() is beyond the scope of this book.

Just as with the C and Visual Basic languages, it's possible in COM to pass objects by value or by reference. Passing by value means the value is passed, and changes to the value aren't reflected in the calling object. Passing by reference means a pointer to the value is passed, so changes to the value are reflected in the calling object.

Python doesn't support this concept; it's not possible to pass simple parameters by reference in Python. The common pattern is for Python to return the values from the function.

Fortunately, parameters passed by reference tend to be avoided. The Microsoft Office suite doesn't use them, nor do any of the other type libraries you could reasonably assume are installed on your PC. This makes demonstrating the problem using real code somewhat difficult, but as an example, let's assume you need to call a function that in C looks like:

```
BOOL GetSize( int *left, int *right, int *top, int *bottom);
```

Your C code to call this function looks like this:

```
int left, right, top, bottom;
BOOL ok;
ok = GetSize( &left, &right, &top, &bottom);
```

Or in Visual Basic, the code looks like:

```
Declare GetSize( ByRef left as integer, ByRef right as integer, _
             ByRef top as integer, ByRef bottom as integer) as Integer
...
ok = GetSize(left, right, top, bottom);
```

In Python, the code looks something like:

```
left, right, top, bottom = GetSize() # Exception indicates error.
```

Note that the output parameters have been converted to the function result; the same style is used for PythonCOM. It's critical to note, however, that ByRef-style parameters may be detected only when using early-bound dispatch. If you haven't used MakePy for the type library, PythonCOM may not detect that the parameters are indeed marked as by reference and therefore may not work as expected.

The moral of the story is this: for anything other than simple arguments, it's highly recommended you use MakePy to force early-bound dispatch. If you have any problems with COM parameters and aren't using MakePy, try switching to it, and your problem is likely to go away.

Using Other COM Interfaces

So far, we have only discussed using IDispatch (or automation) COM objects from Python and only via Python helper classes. Although this is the most common way to use COM objects, more advanced applications often need native COM interfaces.

To illustrate this contingency, we will demonstrate the use of native interfaces with a little utility to dump statistics from a Microsoft Office application file (e.g., a Word document or Excel spreadsheet).

COM provides a technology known as *structured storage*. This is a set of functions and interfaces that allows you to store rich, hierarchical streams of data inside a single file, often referred to as a "filesystem within a file."

Part of this implementation provides for standard properties about the file—the author of the file, for example. Windows Explorer is aware of these interfaces and can display the properties without any knowledge of the application that created the file. Microsoft Office stores its documents in structured storage files, and therefore the Windows Explorer can display rich information about Office documents.

To access these properties, call a COM function to open the structured storage file. This operation results in a PyIStorage object, a Python object that wraps the

COM IStorage interface. If the document has standard properties, you get these
through the COM IPropertySetStorage interface, which means you should perform a QueryInterface() on the PyIStorage object to get the needed interface. Then open the property set you want and query for the properties.

We won't discuss the IPropertySetStorage and IPropertyStorage interfaces
in any detail; the focus for this example is how to work with COM interfaces from
Python, not what these particular interfaces do:

```
# DumpStorage.py - Dumps some user defined properties
# of a COM Structured Storage file.

import pythoncom
from win32com import storagecon # constants related to storage functions.

# These come from ObjIdl.h
FMTID_UserDefinedProperties = "{F29F85E0-4FF9-1068-AB91-08002B27B3D9}"

PIDSI_TITLE         = 0x00000002
PIDSI_SUBJECT       = 0x00000003
PIDSI_AUTHOR        = 0x00000004
PIDSI_CREATE_DTM    = 0x0000000c

def PrintStats(filename):
    if not pythoncom.StgIsStorageFile(filename):
        print "The file is not a storage file!"
        return
    # Open the file.
    flags = storagecon.STGM_READ | storagecon.STGM_SHARE_EXCLUSIVE
    stg = pythoncom.StgOpenStorage(filename, None, flags )

    # Now see if the storage object supports Property Information.
    try:
        pss = stg.QueryInterface(pythoncom.IID_IPropertySetStorage)
    except pythoncom.com_error:
        print "No summary information is available"
        return
    # Open the user defined properties.
    ps = pss.Open(FMTID_UserDefinedProperties)
    props = PIDSI_TITLE, PIDSI_SUBJECT, PIDSI_AUTHOR, PIDSI_CREATE_DTM
    data = ps.ReadMultiple( props )
    # Unpack the result into the items.
    title, subject, author, created = data
    print "Title:", title
    print "Subject:", subject
    print "Author:", author
    print "Created:", created.Format()

if __name__=='__main__':
    import sys
    if len(sys.argv)<2:
        print "Please specify a file name"
    else:
        PrintStats(sys.argv[1])
```

The first step is to check whether the file is indeed a structured storage file, then call `pythoncom.StgOpenStorage()` to obtain a Python `PyIStorage` interface object. You call the Python interface objects just like normal Python objects, as you'd expect. The `QueryInterface()` method can be used on any Python interface object, and returns a new interface object or throws an exception.

The output of running the example over the Microsoft Word document that contains this chapter is:

```
C:\Scripts>python.exe DumpStorage.py "Python and COM.doc"
Title: Python and COM
Subject:
Author: Mark Hammond
Created: 03/04/99 00:41:00

C:\Scripts>
```

A final note on native interfaces: Python can't support arbitrary COM interfaces; the `pythoncom` module (or a `pythoncom` extension) must have built-in support for the interface. Fortunately, there are tools `pythoncom` developers use that largely automate the process of supporting new interfaces.

Error Handling

COM uses three schemes to report error information to client applications:

- All COM interface methods return an integer status code (known as an HRESULT), with COM defining many common values for these HRESULTs. There is an HRESULT to indicate success and a number of HRESULTs that indicate warnings. All other HRESULT values indicate an error status.

- COM defines two special interfaces that report extended error information— `ISupportErrorInfo` and `IErrorInfo`. When any method fails, the client can perform a `QueryInterface()` to determine if the interface supports providing additional error information.

- `IDispatch` (automation) interfaces have a standard technique for reporting COM exceptions. When an `IDispatch` object encounters an error, it fills out an exception structure and returns it to the caller.

The PythonCOM framework combines all these error-reporting mechanisms into a single, Python-exception mechanism. This means you can effectively ignore the three techniques listed: PythonCOM unifies them, so you never need to know how the details of an error were obtained.

All COM errors are reported to Python programs as `pythoncom.com_error` exceptions. The exception value has the following parts:

- The HRESULT of the COM function.

- A text representation of the HRESULT. For example, if the HRESULT is E_ NOINTERFACE, the text representation is (for English users) "No such interface supported."

- Additional exception information as described later in this chapter, or None if no additional information is supported.

- If the error is due to a parameter to a function, an integer indicating the parameter in error. This may be None or −1 if no information about the argument in error can be determined.

The error codes are worthy of discussion. The COM rules state that if additional exception information is available, the HRESULT should be win32con.DISP_E_ EXCEPTION. However, not all COM objects meet this requirement, so the behavior shouldn't be relied on. If additional exception information is available, it will be a tuple of:

- An additional error code for the error (the wCode)

- The source of the error as a string, typically the application name

- A text description of the error

- The name of a Windows help file with additional information about the error

- A help context to identify the topic in the Windows help file

- Yet another error code for the error (the sCode)

As mentioned, if this exception information is available, the HRESULT should be win32con.DISP_E_EXCEPTION. In this case, either the wCode or the sCode contains the actual error. One of these must be zero, but it depends on the object implementing the error exactly which is used.

Let's see some code that catches a COM exception. For this example, we'll write a function to open an Excel spreadsheet. If this function fails, we print all the details known about the error. First, let's define the function:

```
>>> from win32com.client import Dispatch
>>> import pythoncom
>>> def OpenExcelSheet(filename):
...     try:
...         xl = Dispatch("Excel.Application")
...         xl.Workbooks.Open(filename)
...     except pythoncom.com_error, (hr, msg, exc, arg):
...         print "The Excel call failed with code %d: %s" % (hr, msg)
...         if exc is None:
...             print "There is no extended error information"
...         else:
...             wcode, source, text, helpFile, helpId, scode = exc
...             print "The source of the error is", source
```

```
...            print "The error message is", text
...            print "More info can be found in %s (id=%d)" % (helpFile, helpId)
...
>>>
```

As you can see, there's a Python **except** block to catch all COM errors. The first thing to do is print the generic information about the message, then check for extended information. If the extended information exists, decode and print that too.

To try this function, you could use the following code (assuming, of course, you don't have an Excel spreadsheet named *foo.xls* lying around):

```
>>> OpenExcelSheet("foo.xls")
The Excel call failed with code -2147352567: Exception occurred.
The source of the error is Microsoft Excel
The error message is 'foo.xls' could not be found. Check the spelling of the
file name, and verify that the file location is correct.

If you are trying to open the file from your list of most recently used
files on the File menu, make sure that the file has not been renamed,
moved, or deleted.
More info can be found in XLMAIN8.HLP (id=0)
```

The first line of output displays the raw **HRESULT** for the function. In this case, it's **winerror.DISP_E_EXCEPTION**, and we do have extended error information, so Excel is following the COM rules. The second line displays the application that generated the error. The full error text is large: in this case five lines long! The error messages have been designed to be placed directly in a message box for the user. The last line of the text tells us the name of the Windows help file that contains further information about the error.

Implementing COM Objects in Python

Implementing a COM object using Python means you expose a Python object to be used by any COM-aware environment, such as Visual Basic or Delphi.

In Chapter 5, we presented a simple example of a Python class exposed as a COM object. In this section, we provide a more detailed picture of exposing Python objects via COM.

Implementing a COM Server

In Chapter 5 we presented a sample COM server. This example recaps that code:

```
# SimpleCOMServer.py - A sample COM server - almost as small as they come!
#
# We simply expose a single method in a Python COM object.
class PythonUtilities:
    _public_methods_ = [ 'SplitString' ]
    _reg_progid_ = "PythonDemos.Utilities"
```

```
# NEVER copy the following ID
# Use "print pythoncom.CreateGuid()" to make a new one.
_reg_clsid_ = "{41E24E95-D45A-11D2-852C-204C4F4F5020}"

def SplitString(self, val, item=None):
    import string
    if item != None: item = str(item)
    return string.split(str(val), item)

# Add code so that when this script is run by
# Python.exe, it self-registers.
if __name__=='__main__':
    print "Registering COM server..."
    import win32com.server.register
    win32com.server.register.UseCommandLine(PythonUtilities)
```

The main points from the example are:

- Most COM servers are implemented as Python classes. These classes have special attribute annotations that indicate how the object is published via COM; our sample uses the minimum possible to register and expose a COM server.

- The `win32com` package automatically registers and unregisters the COM server.

The list of annotation attributes can be broken into two sets: those that expose the object via COM and those that allow the object to be registered via COM. Table 12-3 lists the annotations used at runtime; registration attributes are covered in the next section.

Table 12-3. Runtime-Related Annotations on COM Objects

Attribute	Description
_public_methods_	A list of strings that indicate the names of the public methods for the object. COM objects can use only methods listed here, the rest are considered private. This is the only required attribute; all others are optional.
_public_attrs_	A list of strings that indicate the public attributes (or properties) for the object. Any attributes not listed here are considered private. Any attributes listed here but not in _readonly_attrs_ can be read or written. It is possible to list the name of Python methods here, in which case the property is implemented by calling the Python method rather than fetching the attribute directly.
_readonly_attrs_	A list of attributes that should be considered read-only. All names in this list should also be in _public_attrs_, otherwise they shouldn't be exposed.
value	A method (not the name of a method) that provides the default value for the object. We present an example of this in the sample code. Because this is a method, the typical way to implement this is to add a method to your class named _value_.

Table 12-3. Runtime-Related Annotations on COM Objects (continued)

Attribute	Description
_NewEnum	A method (not the name of a method) that's used to when the client using this object requests an enumerator. This function must provide a function that conforms to the enumerator specification.
_Evaluate	Used when the client using this object requests to evaluate it. This appears to be a rarely used COM concept.

Registering Your COM Server

Although our sample object implements registration of the object, we haven't discussed it in detail.

Registering an object is the process of allowing the object to be independently created; once an object is registered, a language can use its standard techniques for creating COM objects to access it, e.g., `CreateObject()` in Visual Basic or `win32com.client.Dispatch()` in Python.

There are many cases where you wish to implement a COM object but don't need it registered. For example, let's assume you are designing an object model for an editor that has a root `Application` object, and inside this `Application` object there are a number of `Document` objects. In this case, you would typically want to register the `Application` object (clients need to be able to create this object directly) but not register the `Document` object (making requests on the `Application` object creates these). In this case, you don't need to specify any registration information for the `Document` object.

To prepare an object for registration, you need to provide additional attribute annotations on the object. The registration process uses these annotations to provide the correct information in the Windows registry for the object. The full list of registration related attributes can be found in Table 12-4.

Table 12-4. Registration-Related Attributes on COM Objects

Attribute	Description
_reg_progid_	The ProgID for the object. This is the name of the COM object clients use to create the object.
_reg_desc_	Optional description of the COM object. If not specified, _reg_progid_ is used as the description.
_reg_classspec_	An optional string identifying the Python module and the object in the module. The PythonCOM framework uses this string to instantiate the COM object. If neither this nor _reg_policyspec_ are provided, the COM framework determines the value from the command line.

Table 12-4. Registration-Related Attributes on COM Objects (continued)

Attribute	Description
`_reg_policyspec_`	An optional string identifying the PythonCOM policy to be used for this object. If not provided, the default policy is used. See the section "Policies" later in this chapter.
`_reg_verprogid_`	The version-dependent ProgID. This is typically the ProgID with a version number appended. For example, the second version of a particular server may have a ProgID of `Python.Object` and a VerProgId of `Python.Object.2`.
`_reg_icon_`	The default icon for the COM object.
`_reg_threading_`	The default threading model for the COM object. This must be one of the COM-defined values acceptable for the ThreadingModel key of the COM server, e.g., `Apartment`, `Free`, or `Both`. If not specified, `Both` is used. See Appendix D, *Threads*, for a discussion on COM threading models.
`_reg_catids_`	A list of category IDs for the server. See the COM documentation on categories for more information.
`_reg_options_`	A dictionary of additional keys to be written to the registry for the COM object. The PythonCOM framework doesn't define the values for this; it's up to the author to specify meaningful values.
`_reg_clsctx_`	The contexts defining how this object is to be registered. This attribute defines if the COM object is registered as an `InProc` object (i.e., implemented by a DLL) or a `LocalServer` object (i.e., implemented in an EXE). If not specified, the default of `CLSCTX_LOCAL_SERVER` | `CLSCTX_INPROC_SERVER` is used (i.e., the object is registered as both `InProc` and `LocalServer`).
`_reg_disable_pycomcat_`	A boolean flag indicating if the COM object should be associated with the list of PythonCOM servers installed on the machine. If not specified, the object is associated with the PythonCOM servers.
`_reg_dispatcher_spec_` `_reg_debug_dispatcher_spec_`	The dispatcher for the COM object. Dispatchers are largely a debugging aid, allowing you to snoop on your COM object as calls are made on it. Dispatchers are closely related to policies but aren't covered in this book.

The module `win32com.server.register` contains many utilities for registering and unregistering COM servers. The most useful of these functions is `UseCommandLine()`, which allows you to register any number of Python classes. Using this function is a no-brainer; pass to this function the class objects you wish to expose.

In the COM example, we include the following code:

```
if __name__=='__main__':
    print "Registering COM server..."
    import win32com.server.register
    win32com.server.register.UseCommandLine(PythonUtilities)
```

The `PythonUtilities` object is the class to register. Adding this functionality allows the COM object to be registered or unregistered from the command line as detailed in Table 12-5.

Table 12-5. Command-Line Options Recognized by UseCommandLine

Command-Line Option	Description
	The default is to register the COM objects.
--unregister	Unregisters the objects. This removes all references to the objects from the Windows registry.
--debug	Registers the COM servers in debug mode. We discuss debugging COM servers later in this chapter.
--quiet	Register (or unregister) the object quietly (i.e., don't report success).

Each option uses a double hyphen. For example, if your COM objects are implemented in *YourServer.py*, use the following commands.

To register objects:

```
C:\Scripts> Python.exe YourServer.py
```

To unregister the objects:

```
C:\Scripts> Python.exe YourServer.py --unregister
```

To register the objects for debugging:

```
C:\Scripts> Python.exe YourServer.py --debug
```

With a standard Python setup, double-clicking on a Python COM server script in Explorer has the same effect as the first example and registers the server.

Error Handling for COM Servers

When you implement a COM object, it's often necessary to return error information to the caller. Although Python has a powerful exception mechanism, the caller of your objects is likely to be Visual Basic or Delphi, so standard Python exceptions don't really work.

To support this, the `win32com.server.exception` module exposes the `COMException` Python object in order to raise an exception to COM. This object allows you to specify many details about the error, including the error message, the name of the application generating the error, the name of a help file in which the user can find additional information, etc. See the `win32com.server.exception` module for more details.

The PythonCOM framework makes the assumption that all Python exceptions other than `COMException` indicate a bug in your code. Thus, your object shouldn't allow normal Python exceptions to be raised when calling your methods, but should take steps to handle these Python exceptions and translate them to an appropriate `COMException`.

As an example, let's assume you want to publish a method called `sqrt()` that returns the square root of its argument. If you use the following code:

```
def sqrt(self, val):
    return math.sqrt(val)
```

you have a potential problem; in fact, a few of them. If you pass anything other than a positive number to your function, the code fails, and a Python exception is raised. This is considered a bug in your COM object. To improve this function, use the following code:

```
def sqrt(self, val):
    try:
        return math.sqrt(val)
    except (TypeError, ValueError):
        raise COMException("The argument must be a positive number", \
                           winerror.DISP_E_TYPEMISMATCH)
```

This version of the code does the right thing: it traps the exceptions that may be raised by the `math.sqrt()` function and raises a `COMException` object with a useful message and value.

Policies

PythonCOM policies are an advanced topic and typically don't need to be understood to successfully use Python and COM. However, if you need to perform advanced techniques using Python and COM, this information is valuable. You may wish to skip this section and come back to it when the need arises.

A PythonCOM policy determines how Python objects are exposed to COM; the policy dictates which attributes are exposed to COM and the IDs these attributes get. The policy actually sits between COM and your object and is responsible for responding to the `IDispatch` interface's `GetIDsOfNames()` and `Invoke()` functions. The policy dictates how these `IDispatch` calls are translated into the references to your Python object.

The default PythonCOM policy is suitable in most cases, and all the examples to date have used the default policy. The policy implemented is:

- All methods named in the _public_methods_ attribute are exposed to COM. Any method not listed in _public_methods_ is considered private.

- All properties named in the _public_attrs_ attribute are exposed to COM. If the property name also appears in the attribute _readonly_attrs_, it can be read, but not written; otherwise, users of this object can change the property.

- Other special attributes can obtain advanced behavior. You can review the full list of attributes in Table 12-4.

What this means is that the PythonCOM framework itself doesn't determine how an object is exposed via COM; it's determined by the policy.

The PythonCOM package provides two useful policies: the default policy (known as the DesignatedWrapPolicy, because the attributes exposed via COM must be explicitly designated) and the DynamicPolicy that implements a far more liberal approach to publishing objects. These policies are implemented in the win32com. server.policy module.

The DynamicPolicy requires your Python class to implement a single function named _dynamic_, and this function must implement the logic to determine if the COM call is requesting a property reference or a method call.

To demonstrate the DynamicPolicy, we present a more advanced COM server in the following example. The aim of this COM server is to expose the entire Python string module. Anyone using Visual Basic or Delphi can then use all the string-processing functions available to Python.

Before we look at the code, there are a couple of points:

- The Unicode strings bite us again! As COM passes all strings as Unicode, you need to convert them to Python strings before the string module can work with them.

- Most of the registration data is the same as discussed previously, except there is a new attribute, _reg_policy_spec_. This attribute identifies that you need to use the DynamicPolicy rather than the default DesignatedWrapPolicy.

- The handling of IDispatch.GetIDsOfNames() has been done for you (the _dynamic_ methods deal with attribute names), and the policy has dealt with the IDs for the attributes.

- There is some extra internal knowledge of COM needed to implement the _dynamic_ method. Specifically, you need to differentiate between a property reference and a method call. Also remember that VB is not case-sensitive, while Python is.

```
# DynamicPolicy.py -- A demonstration of dynamic policies in PythonCOM
import string
import pythoncom
import pywintypes
```

```python
import winerror
import types
from win32com.server.exception import COMException

def FixArgs(args):
    # Fix the arguments, so Unicode objects are
    # converted to strings.  Does this recursively,
    # to ensure sub-lists (ie, arrays) are also converted
    newArgs = []
    for arg in args:
        if type(arg)==types.TupleType:
            arg = FixArgs(arg)
        elif type(arg)==pywintypes.UnicodeType:
            arg = str(arg)
        newArgs.append(arg)
    return tuple(newArgs)

class PythonStringModule:
    _reg_progid_ = "PythonDemos.StringModule"
    _reg_clsid_ = "{CB2E1BC5-D6A5-11D2-852D-204C4F4F5020}"
    _reg_policy_spec_ = "DynamicPolicy"

    # The dynamic policy insists that we provide a method
    # named _dynamic_, and that we handle the IDispatch::Invoke logic.
    def _dynamic_(self, name, lcid, wFlags, args):
        # Get the requested attribute from the string module.
        try:
            item = getattr(string, string.lower(name))
        except AttributeError:
            raise COMException("No attribute of that name", \
                               winerror.DISP_E_MEMBERNOTFOUND)
        # Massage the arguments...
        args = FixArgs(args)
        # VB will often make calls with wFlags set to
        # DISPATCH_METHOD | DISPATCH_PROPERTYGET, as the VB
        # syntax makes the distinction impossible to make.
        # Therefore, we also check the object being referenced is
        # in fact a Python function
        if (wFlags & pythoncom.DISPATCH_METHOD) and \
           type(item) in [types.BuiltinFunctionType, types.FunctionType]:
            return apply(item, args)
        elif wFlags & pythoncom.DISPATCH_PROPERTYGET:
            return item
        else:
            raise COMException("You can not set this attribute",
                               winerror.DISP_E_BADVARTYPE)

# Add code so that when this script is run by
# Python.exe, it self-registers.
if __name__=='__main__':
    import win32com.server.register
    win32com.server.register.UseCommandLine(PythonStringModule)
```

To test the COM object, use the following VBA code:

```
Sub Test()
    ' Create the Python COM objects.
    Set stringmod = CreateObject("PythonDemos.StringModule")
    ' Call string.split
    response = stringmod.Split("Hello from VB")
    For Each Item In response
        MsgBox (Item)
    Next
    ' Call string.join
    MsgBox "The items joined are " & stringmod.join(response)
    ' Get string.uppercase
    MsgBox "The upper case character are" & stringmod.uppercase

    ' Attempt to set a property - this should fail.
    stringmod.uppercase = "Hi"

End Sub
```

When you run this code, you should see a series of message boxes, followed by an error dialog. As mentioned in the code, the attempt to set `string.uppercase` should fail, and indeed it does.

As you can see, the DynamicPolicy has given you the tools to wrap any arbitrary Python object, rather than requiring you to explicitly declare the public interface. Depending on your requirements, this may or may not serve your purpose better than the default policy, but if neither of these policies meet your requirements, just write your own! The `Python.Dictionary` sample COM object (implemented in the module `win32com.servers.dictionary`) implements its own specialized policy, so it's a good starting point if you need to go this route.

Wrapping and Unwrapping

Whenever you expose a Python object via COM, you actually expose an `IDispatch` object. As described previously, the `IDispatch` interface is used to expose automation objects. Thus, whenever a Visual Basic program is using a Python COM object, VB itself is dealing with a COM `IDispatch` object. The Python COM framework provides the `IDispatch` object that wraps your Python COM class instance. Whenever the COM framework creates a new Python COM object, the general process is:

- An instance of the selected policy for the object is created.

- The policy creates an instance of your Python class.

- An `IDispatch` object is created that wraps the Python policy (which in turn wraps your instance).

- The `IDispatch` object is returned to the client (e.g., Visual Basic).

Thus, when you need to create an `IDispatch` from a Python class instance, you should wrap the object. Unwrapping is the reverse of this process; if you have an `IDispatch` object that wraps a Python instance, you can unwrap the `IDispatch` object, returning the underlying Python instance.

In many cases you don't need to worry about this. When you expose a COM object that can be directly created via COM, the Python COM framework handles all the wrapping for you. However, there are a number of cases where the explicit wrapping of objects is necessary.

The most common scenario is when you need to expose a COM object via some sort of factory method; that is, rather than allowing the user to create your object directly using VB's `CreateObject()`, you return the object from another object. Microsoft Office provides good examples of this behavior: the object model defines `Cell` or `Paragraph` objects, but you can't create them directly. You must create the `Application` object and use it to create or reference `Cells` and `Paragraphs`.

We will use a contrived example to demonstrate the wrapping and unwrapping of objects. But before that, we take a small digression into techniques that debug the COM objects. These debugging techniques demonstrate wrapping and unwrapping and also how to use `IDispatch` objects passed as parameters.

Debugging Python COM Objects

When you use COM clients such as Excel from Python, you can employ the same debugging techniques as for any Python code; you are simply calling Python objects. However, when you implement COM objects in Python, things become more difficult. In this case, the caller of your Python code isn't Python, but another application, such as Visual Basic or Delphi. These applications obviously have no concept of a Python exception or a Python traceback, so finding bugs in your Python code can be a problem.

In a nutshell: register your COM objects using –debug on the command line. Then use the Trace Collector Debugging Tool item on the PythonWin Tools menu to see any print statements or Python exceptions. The rest of this section is devoted to how this works.

To assist with the debugging problem, the Python COM framework has the concept of a *dispatcher*. A dispatcher is similar to a policy object, but dispatches calls to the policy. The `win32com` package provides a number of useful dispatchers.

When you register the COM Server with --debug (note the double hyphen), the registration mechanism also registers a dispatcher for your object. The default dispatcher is known as `DispatcherWin32trace`, although you can specify a different dispatcher using the _reg_debug_dispatcher_spec_ attribute on your object, as described in the earlier section "Registering Your COM Server."

The default DispatcherWin32trace uses the win32trace module to display its output. To see the output of a COM server when debugging, use the Trace Collector Debugging Tool item on the PythonWin Tools menu.

The Final Sample

A final sample COM server demonstrates wrapping and unwrapping objects, how to use IDispatch objects when passed as parameters to COM functions, and also how to debug your COM servers. This example is contrived and does nothing useful other than demonstrate these concepts.

The sample exposes two COM objects, a Parent object and a Child object. The Parent object is registered with COM so VB code can use CreateObject to create it. The Child object isn't registered and can be created only by calling the CreateChild() method on the Parent. The Child object has no methods, just a Name property.

The Parent object also has a method called KissChild(), that should be called with a Child object previously created by the parent. The KissChild() method demonstrates how to use the IDispatch passed to the method and also how to unwrap the IDispatch to obtain the underlying Python object.

Finally, the code has a number of **print** statements and a lack of error handling. We use the debugging techniques to see these **print** statements and also a Python exception raised:

```
# ContrivedServer.py
#
# A contrived sample Python server that demonstrates
# wrapping, unwrapping, and passing IDispatch objects.

# Import the utilities for wrapping and unwrapping.
from win32com.server.util import wrap, unwrap

import win32com.client

# Although we are able to register our Parent object for debugging,
# our Child object is not registered, so this won't work. To get
# the debugging behavior for our wrapped objects, we must do it ourself.
debugging = 1
if debugging:
    from win32com.server.dispatcher import DefaultDebugDispatcher
    useDispatcher = DefaultDebugDispatcher
else:
    useDispatcher = None
```

```
# Our Parent object.
# This is registered, and therefore creatable
# using CreateObject etc from VB.
class Parent:
    _public_methods_ = ['CreateChild', 'KissChild']
    _reg_clsid_ = "{E8F7F001-DB69-11D2-8531-204C4F4F5020}"
    _reg_progid_ = "PythonDemos.Parent"

    def CreateChild(self):
        # We create a new Child object, and wrap
        # it using the default policy
        # If we are debugging, we also specify the default dispatcher
        child = Child()
        print "Our Python child is", child
        wrapped = wrap( child, useDispatcher=useDispatcher )
        print "Returing wrapped", wrapped
        return wrapped

    def KissChild(self, child):
        print "KissChild called with child", child
        # Our child is a PyIDispatch object, so we will attempt
        # to use it as such.  To make it into something useful,
        # we must convert it to a win32com.client.Dispatch object.
        dispatch = win32com.client.Dispatch(child)
        print "KissChild called with child named", dispatch.Name

        # Now, assuming it is a Python child object, let's
        # unwrap it to get the object back!
        child = unwrap(child)
        print "The Python child is", child

# Our Child object.
# This is not registered
class Child:
    _public_methods_ = []
    _public_attrs_ = ['Name']
    def __init__(self):
        self.Name = "Unnamed"

if __name__=='__main__':
    import win32com.server.register
    win32com.server.register.UseCommandLine(Parent, debug=debugging)
```

Before you register your class, we must mention some of the debugging-related code. Near the top of the source file, we declare a variable named debugging. If this variable is true, you then load the DefaultDebugDispatcher and assign it to a variable. In the CreateChild() method, you pass this dispatcher to the wrap function. This is due to a quirk in the debug mechanism. As mentioned previously, the registration mechanism allows you to register an object for debugging by using --debug on the command line. While this works fine for objects you register, recall that our Child object isn't registered, so it doesn't benefit from this mechanism; this code enables it for both objects. Also note that you pass this debugging variable to the `UseCommandLine()` function. This allows you to control the debugging behavior totally from your debugging variable. If set, debugging is enabled for all objects, regardless of the command line. If not set, you don't get debugging for either object.

So you can register this COM server like the other COM servers; no need for anything special on the command line. You register the server by running the script (either from within PythonWin, or using Windows Explorer). After registration, you should see the message:

```
Registered: PythonDemos.Parent (for debugging)
```

The next step is for some VB code to use your object. For this demonstration, you can use the following Visual Basic for Applications code from either Excel or Word:

```
Sub DebuggingTest()
  Set ParentObj = CreateObject("PythonDemos.Parent")

  Set child = ParentObj.CreateChild()
  MsgBox "Child's name is " & child.Name

  ParentObj.KissChild child
  MsgBox "I kissed my child"

  ' Now lets pass a non-python object!
  ' As we are using VBA (either Word or Excel)
  ' we just pass our application object.
  ' This should fail with an InternalError.
  Set app = Application
  ParentObj.KissChild (app)
End Sub
```

This code is simple: it creates a **Parent** object, then calls the **CreateChild()** method, giving a **Child** object. You fetch the name of the child, then display it in a message box. The next step is to call the **KissChild()** method and display another message box when the kiss is complete. The final step is to call the **KissChild()** method, but pass a different object, in this case the Excel (or Word) **Application** object.

Before running this code, you should open the window that displays the debugging output and select the Trace Collector Debugging Tool item on the PythonWin Tools menu.

Now, let's run the Visual Basic code and stop at the first message box. The debug window should now display:

```
Object with win32trace dispatcher created (object=None)
in _GetIDsOfNames_ with '('CreateChild',)' and '1033'
in _Invoke_ with 1000 1033L 3 ()
Our Python child is <ContrivedServer.Child instance at 2a8d5e0>
```

```
Object with win32trace dispatcher created (object=<ContrivedServer.Child instance
...
Returing wrapped <PyIDispatch at 0x2a80254 with obj at 0x2a801c0>
in _GetIDsOfNames_ with '('Name',)' and '1033'
in _Invoke_ with 1000 1033L 3 ()
```

The first thing to note is there are a number of unexpected lines; the Python COM framework has printed some extra debugging information for you. The first three lines show how internally `GetIDsOfNames()` and `Invoke()` have been translated by the Python COM framework. The fourth line is one of yours: it's the `print` statement in the `CreateChild()` method. Wrapping the `Child` object causes the Python COM framework to print the next output line, which is followed by the next `print` statement.

If you now dismiss the next couple of message boxes in the VB example, you should see an error message that looks like that in Figure 12-3.

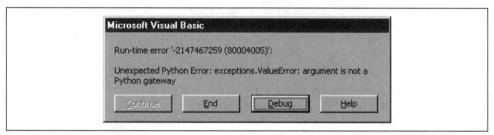

Figure 12-3. Visual Basic error dialog when running the sample

As you can see, you have the "Unexpected Python Error," discussed previously, which means you have an unhandled Python exception in the COM server. If you look in the debugging window, the last few lines are:

```
in _Invoke_ with 1001 1033L 1 (<PyIDispatch at 0x2a7bbb4 with obj at 0xcdd4f8>,)
KissChild called with child <PyIDispatch at 0x2a7bbb4 with obj at 0xcdd4f8>
KissChild called with child named Microsoft Word
Traceback (innermost last):
  File "L:\src\pythonex\com\win32com\server\dispatcher.py", line 40, in _Invoke_
    return self.policy._Invoke_(dispid, lcid, wFlags, args)
  File "L:\src\pythonex\com\win32com\server\policy.py", line 265, in _Invoke_
    return self._invoke_(dispid, lcid, wFlags, args)
  File "L:\src\pythonex\com\win32com\server\policy.py", line 486, in _invoke_
    return S_OK, -1, self._invokeex_(dispid, lcid, wFlags, args, None, None)
  File "L:\src\pythonex\com\win32com\server\policy.py", line 498, in _invokeex_
    return apply(func, args)
  File "L:\docs\Book\Python and COM\ContrivedServer.py", line 49, in KissChild
    child = unwrap(child)
  File "L:\src\pythonex\com\win32com\server\util.py", line 36, in unwrap
    ob = pythoncom.UnwrapObject(ob)
ValueError: argument is not a Python gateway
```

Here are the full details of the Python exception. This makes tracking the error much simpler: it should be obvious that the error occurs when you attempt to unwrap the Microsoft Excel application object. The unwrap fails because there is no Python object behind this interface.

One final note relates to how an `IDispatch` object is used as a parameter to a COM function. In the debugging window, locate the following messages:

```
KissChild called with child <PyIDispatch at 0x2a86624 with obj at 0x2a865b0>
KissChild called with child named in _GetIDsOfNames_ with '('Name',)' and '0'

in _Invoke_ with 1000 0L 2 ()
Unnamed
The Python child is <ContrivedServer.Child instance at 2a7aa90>
```

The raw parameter to `KissChild()` is in fact a `PyIDispatch` object. You may recall from the start of this chapter that a `PyIDispatch` object only has methods `GetIDsOfNames()` and `Invoke()`. To turn the object into something useful, you must use a `win32com.client.Dispatch()` object. Once you have the `win32com.client.Dispatch` object, use it like any other COM object; in the example, we called the `Name` property.

Python and DCOM

Microsoft has recently enhanced COM to support distributed objects. These enhancements are known as distributed COM, or DCOM. The term *distributed objects* refers to objects that operate on different machines: a COM client and COM server may be on different parts of the network.

There are a number of reasons why this may be appealing. It allows you to host your objects close to your data; for example, on a server with high-speed access to a database server. Microsoft also has a product available called the Microsoft Transaction Server (MTS) that provides additional facilities for large-scale distributed applications. Alternatively, DCOM may allow you to use specific hardware installed on a remote machine, by running on that machine and controlling it from your own workstation.

One of the key strengths of the DCOM architecture is that in many cases, the objects don't need to have special code to support distributed objects. DCOM manages all this behind the scenes, and neither the local or remote object need be aware they are not running locally.

DCOM comes with a tool that allows you to configure the DCOM characteristics of the local machine and of each specific object registered on your machine. For each individual object, you can specify the machine where that object should be executed. In addition, the code that creates a new COM object (i.e., the COM client) can specify its own settings by making slight changes to the creation process.

To demonstrate DCOM, let's use the standard `Python.Interpreter` COM object and configure it to be created on a remote machine. Here's the process:

1. Configure DCOM on the remote machine.

2. Configure DCOM and our object on the local machine.

3. Test the remote object using normal COM.

4. Test the remote object using DCOM-specific calls.

Configure DCOM on the Remote Machine

The first step is to configure DCOM on the remote machine, where the object will actually run.

To configure DCOM, start the DCOM configuration tool by selecting the Run option from the Windows start menu, and enter **dcomcnfg**. The mail display is shown in Figure 12-4.

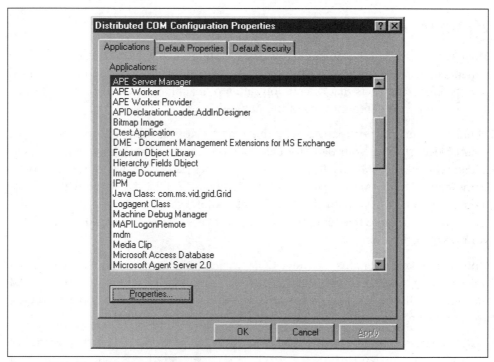

Figure 12-4. The DCOM configuration tool

Now select the Default Properties tab and ensure that DCOM is enabled for this computer, as shown in Figure 12-5.

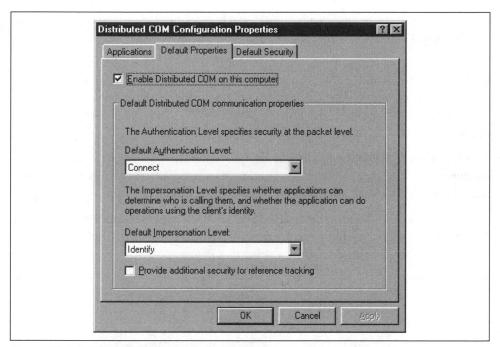

Figure 12-5. DCOM configuration tool with DCOM enabled

No additional configuration options are required on the remote machine, but you do need to ensure the COM object itself is installed on this computer. There's nothing special about registering your object for DCOM; perform a normal registration process for the object, as described in the previous section "Registering Your COM Server."

The `Python.Interpreter` object you use is part of the standard Python COM distribution, so it should have been registered when the Python COM extensions were installed. However, it can't hurt to reregister it. To register the `Python. Interpreter` object, perform the following steps on the remote machine:

1. Start PythonWin.

2. Select File → Run, select the Browse button, and locate the file *win32com\ servers\interp.py*.

3. Select OK.

The PythonWin window should report:

```
Registering COM server...
Registered: Python.Interpreter
```

Configure DCOM and the Object on the Local Machine

The next step is to configure your local machine, where you actually create and use the object running on the remote machine.

First, ensure the object is registered on the local machine; although you don't need to start the object on this local machine, the object must be registered locally so the COM and DCOM architecture know about the object and how to redirect it. To register the object locally, perform the same process you did for registering the object on the remote machine.

Now start the DCOM configuration tool to configure the object on the local machine. Use the same process you used to start the tool on the remote machine, but this time at the local machine.

The same initial dialog in Figure 12-4 is displayed. Locate the `Python.Interpreter` object in the list and select the Properties button. The default properties for the object should look something like Figure 12-6.

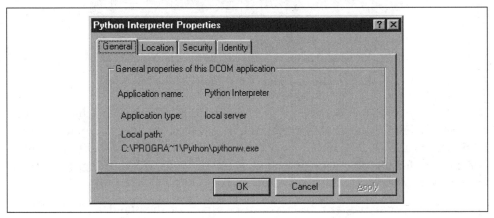

Figure 12-6. Default DCOM properties for the object

If you select the Location tab, you see the available options. The default setting should indicate that the application runs only on this computer. Disable the local computer option and enable the "Run application on the following computer" setting. The remote computer is named *SKIPPY*. Now enter the name of your remote machine. The dialog should now look something like Figure 12-7.

Select the OK button, and you're ready to go.

Testing the object using normal COM

Before testing, there is a slight complication that needs to be addressed. If you recall the discussion at the beginning of the chapter regarding `InProc`,

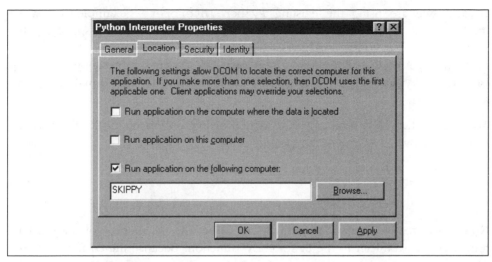

Figure 12-7. Python.Interpreter object ready for remote testing

`LocalServer`, and `RemoteServer` objects, it should come as no surprise that remote DCOM objects must be hosted by an executable. It's not possible to use an object implemented in a DLL, since the object is running on a different computer than the user of the object, so it must be in a different process. This is not a problem, since by default all Python COM objects are registered with both executable and DLL support.

The complication is on the local machine. Although you configured DCOM not to run the object on the local computer, this applies only to `LocalServer` objects. If there is an `InProc` object registered locally, this object is used regardless of the DCOM settings. As your object is registered on the local machine as an `InProc` application, you need to take action to ensure this version of the object isn't loaded.

It's worth noting that this complication is provided courtesy of COM and DCOM. There is nothing Python-specific about this problem; it exists for all COM objects regardless of their implementation language. Python is slightly unique in that the default registration for its objects are for both `LocalServer` and `InProc`; most languages force you to choose one or another quite early in the development process. There are two ways to solve this dilemma:

- Modify the COM object so it supports only `LocalServer` operations by setting the `_reg_clsctx_` attribute in the class. See the earlier section "Registering Your COM Server" for more details.

- Make a slight change to the object creation code to explicitly exclude the `InProc` version of the object from being used.

Because we are using the existing `Python.Interpreter` example, we won't modify the it, but will go for the second option. You do this by specifying the `clsctx` parameter to the `win32com.client.Dispatch()` function. If you decide to change your COM object to support only `LocalServer` operations, this step isn't necessary, and the object creation code is identical to the normal object creation process.

To execute the object remotely, start Python or PythonWin on the local computer. First, let's prove the name of the local machine:

```
>>> import win32api
>>> win32api.GetComputerName()
'BOBCAT'
>>>
```

Now, let's create a `Python.Interpreter` object. As discussed, you pass a custom `clsctx` parameter to the `Dispatch()` function. Because the `clsctx` parameter is not the second parameter, specify it by name:

```
>>> import pythoncom, win32com.client
>>> clsctx=pythoncom.CLSCTX_LOCAL_SERVER
>>> i=win32com.client.Dispatch("Python.Interpreter", clsctx=clsctx)
>>>
```

Now, let's use this object. Ask it to report what machine it is on. Then ask the remote interpreter to import the `win32api` module and print the value of `win32api.GetComputerName()`. Because the object is running remotely, expect to see the name of the remote computer:

```
>>> i.Exec("import win32api")
>>> i.Eval("win32api.GetComputerName()")
'SKIPPY'
>>>
```

If you view the Task Manager for the remote machine, notice a new process *pythonw.exe*. This is the process hosting the remote object. If you release the reference to the object, you should see the process terminate. To release the reference, execute:

```
>>> i=None
>>>
```

And within a few seconds the process on the remote server terminates.

As you can see, it worked! Setting up the machines for DCOM is quite painless, and using the remote object is as simple as if it were a local object.

Testing a Remote Object Using DCOM-Specific Calls

You may have noticed that the DCOM configuration dialog states "Client applications may override your selection." So when you configure DCOM, you really just provide default values for non-DCOM-aware programs. In fact, if you want to make your client code DCOM-aware, it isn't necessary to configure DCOM on the local machine at all; your client code provides the information needed.

To demonstrate this, let's restore the DCOM configuration on the local machine to the defaults. Restart the DCOM configuration tool and again select the **Python. Interpreter** object. Select the Location tab and restore the settings to how you first found them. The dialog should look similar to Figure 12-8.

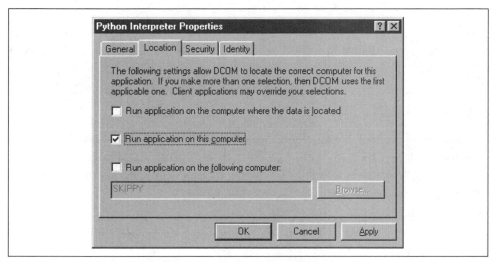

Figure 12-8. Back to the default DCOM configuration for the object

Select the OK button to apply the changes.

First, let's check that the object is indeed restored correctly. Execute the same lines of code used previously, but because the DCOM configuration has been restored, the object should be local:

```
>>> i=win32com.client.Dispatch("Python.Interpreter", clsctx=clsctx)
>>> i.Exec("import win32api")
>>> i.Eval("win32api.GetComputerName()")
'BOBCAT'
>>>
```

As expected, the local machine name is now being used, and you should be able to locate a *pythonw.exe* process running on the local computer.

The **win32com.client.DispatchEx()** function allows you to override the DCOM defaults for your object.

The first parameter to **DispatchEx()** is the ProgID for the object you wish to create, the same ProgID you would pass to **Dispatch()**. The second parameter is the name of the machine to create the object on. If the machine name isn't specified, the call operates identically to `win32com.client.Dispatch()`.

Let's test drive this function. Although the DCOM configuration for the local machine is set up to run locally, use the following code to force a remote server:

```
>>> i=win32com.client.DispatchEx("Python.Interpreter", "skippy", clsctx=clsctx)
>>> i.Exec("import win32api")
>>> i.Eval("win32api.GetComputerName()")
'SKIPPY'
>>>
```

Note that the same `clsctx` complications exist here. If the object is registered as an `InProc` server locally, all DCOM settings (including the explicit machine name) are ignored.

Conclusion

In this chapter we took a whirlwind tour of COM. We covered the important COM concepts and how they relate to Python and the Python COM package. We discussed the differences between COM interfaces and COM automation objects that expose an object model using the `IDispatch` interface.

The `pythoncom` module and the `win32com` package were introduced, and we discussed how to use COM objects from Python and how to use native COM interfaces from Python.

Implementing COM objects using Python was discussed in detail. We covered some simple examples and covered some advanced topics, such as wrapping and unwrapping your COM objects, PythonCOM policies, and how to debug your COM servers.

Finally, we showed you how you can distribute your Python COM objects across various machines on your network using DCOM.

13

Databases

Python can connect to a wide variety of databases using the various integration technologies we've studied. Once you've made a connection, Python's lists and dictionaries make data manipulation simple and compact, and its object model makes it easy to build object layers on top of databases.

We begin by surveying the various libraries available for connecting to a relational database and executing queries. In the second half of the chapter, we build some sample applications that demonstrate Python's abilities to manipulate data in sophisticated ways. We presume a knowledge of basic SQL and familiarity with the concepts of relational databases.

DAO, ADO, ODBC, OLEDB, and Other GBFLAs

Nowhere in the computing world do acronyms fly so thick and so fast as with databases (GBFLAs stands for Great Big Five-Letter Acronyms). Microsoft has produced a bewildering array of data-access APIs over the years. For most applications, these will be the primary means of getting at your data. We'll run through the common ones and try to put them in context. If you are an experienced Windows database developer, you may wish to skip ahead to the section, "Getting at Your Data," later in this chapter.

Proprietary APIs

Vendors of client/server systems such as Oracle and Sybase generally provide a CD of client software to be installed on any PC that needs to connect to one of their servers. This software often includes a tool to keep track of the various database servers on the network, a custom network protocol on top of TCP/IP, various administrative applications, command-line SQL clients, and various programming interfaces to the database.

At the lowest level, C libraries and/or preprocessors are included to allow C programs to execute queries against a database. Python modules have been written around these libraries for (at least) Oracle, Sybase, Informix, Solid, MySQL, and Interbase.

Proprietary APIs often give the fastest connections and allow access to proprietary features of a particular database. However, SQL is supposed to be a standard, and users want the freedom to switch databases without unreasonable pain, so Microsoft has been working on standard interfaces to databases for many years.

Open Database Connectivity

Open Database Connectivity (ODBC) is a standardized API that provides universal database access and is available on all Windows systems.* It consists of a DLL that exposes standard functions to connect to and query databases, and a piece of software to manage connections. Each database vendor still has to provide the necessary software to connect to their own database, as well as an ODBC driver that allows it to fit into the ODBC framework. Click Start → Settings → Control Panel → 32-bit ODBC to see the ODBC Data Source Administrator (see Figure 13-1).

Each machine provides a list of named data sources; these can be configured for a single user or available to the whole system. Clicking Add or Configure leads to a set of dialogs specific to the database vendor; for example, for a local Microsoft Access database you essentially just select the file to use. Once a data source has been defined, any of your programs can connect to that data source by name using ODBC.

This architecture has some enormous benefits. With care, it's possible to start prototyping with a data source named "Accounts" on a local Access database, and then switch to using (for example) a remote Oracle server with the same structure just by changing the configuration.

Because the capabilities of databases vary so widely, the ODBC API offers a wide range of functions at three levels of compliance. Level 1 compliance is the absolute minimum and is used for things like providing SQL access to text files; Level 2 is generally regarded as the minimum feature set for anything that is sold as a relational database.

---

* Formally speaking, it implements the ANSI SQL Part III specification for a Call Level Interface to relational databases. In other words, it's not just Microsoft; it's an approved ANSI standard.

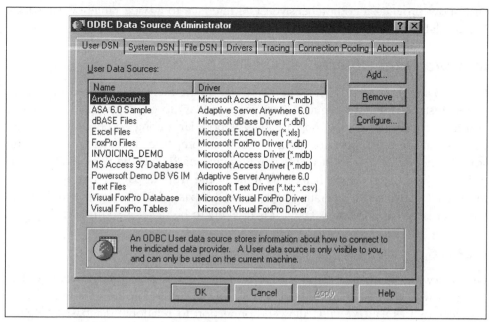

Figure 13-1. ODBC Data Source Administrator

ODBC will be our main tool for working with databases on Windows. We'll go through some examples later.

Data Access Objects, JET, and Access

Microsoft Access is the world's most popular desktop relational database, used extensively for individual and small business systems. Although it can be used on a network, it isn't a proper client/server system. If five users share a database across a network, there are five separate applications all opening and closing the same data file. Access doesn't scale up to high volumes of users.

From the beginning, Access was split into a GUI (what you see when you start Access) and an engine called Jet. The Data Access Object (DAO) hierarchy was an object hierarchy for getting at the Jet engine; it contained objects to represent databases, tables, relationships between tables, fields, and queries. It was originally accessible only from Access and Visual Basic. The ability to rapidly build database applications was one of the key factors in Visual Basic 3's huge popularity. With the arrival of Office 95, the DAO hierarchy became a full-fledged set of COM servers, allowing any COM-enabled language to open databases.

The popularity of this development model rapidly led to a demand to connect the same applications to client/server databases, and the DAO hierarchy was extended allowing it to use ODBC connections under the hood as well as Access databases.

DAO now provides a comprehensive COM interface to a wide range of databases. It is available on all Windows systems with Office 95 or 97.

Remote Data Objects

Remote Data Objects (RDO) is another COM object hierarchy, layered on top of ODBC instead of the Jet engine. When you use DAO to get at an ODBC database, you are actually using RDO objects. RDO is popular among corporate developers because it offers support for features such as prepared statements and calling stored procedures. The most visible manifestation of RDO is the Remote Data Control in Visual Basic, which helped to remedy the truly appalling performance of the Data Control when operating on remote databases.* RDO is stable and works well, but is not as popular as DAO. It is unlikely to be developed further.

OLEDB

OLEDB (which probably stands for Object Linking and Embedding Database, but as far as we can tell has never been written out in full before now) is intended as a successor to ODBC. ODBC allowed connection to relational databases; OLEDB extends this to allow querying of arbitrary data providers such as hierarchical file-systems, mailboxes in Microsoft Exchange, text files, and nonrelational main-frames. It contains functionality to let you determine the capabilities of a provider at runtime. Many database vendors have now written OLEDB providers, and it can work through ODBC for those that have not. OLEDB consists of a wide range of low-level COM interfaces, and OLEDB programming is usually done by people writing database drivers; Microsoft provides an easy-to-use layer above it, as we will see next.

ActiveX Data Objects

By now you should be sufficiently attuned to Microsoft terminology to realize that terms using *Active* are (a) invented by their marketing department and devoid of precise technical meanings and (b) probably something to do with COM. ActiveX Data Objects (ADO) is not a new technology, but simply an easy-to-use COM object hierarchy on top of OLEDB. It is bundled with Visual Basic and Visual C++ 5.0 and higher; look in the MakePy window for Microsoft ActiveX Data Objects Library 2.0. It looks superficially similar to DAO and RDO but offers vastly greater

---

* The Data Control allows you to build a database form by setting a few properties and linking text boxes to database fields. It queries the database at runtime about the kinds of fields available in the tables to which it's bound; this works fine with Jet, which has the information readily available, but generates unbelievable traffic over a client/server connection. We've watched it by logging ODBC calls, and each data control makes a separate connection; one application might have 10 or 12 database connections open.

capabilities under the hood and is thoroughly geared to the needs of client/server systems. Microsoft has stated that they will put no effort into further enhancements of RDO, DAO, and ODBC (although they are committed to supporting ODBC for the long haul), so ADO sounds like the COM interface of the future. Here are some of the enhancements offered:

- A programmer can trap events before or after commands are executed.
- A command object wraps stored procedures and simplifies setting parameters.
- ADO exposes objects that wrap up the data definition language of a data store, meaning you can write code to create and modify tables and indexes, which works against a variety of underlying databases, even nonrelational ones.
- ADO supports hierarchical recordsets, which consist of prejoined master and detail recordsets.
- Disconnected recordsets and batch updates are perhaps the most exciting features. An application for a salesman with a laptop could connect to a database before going to fetch a recordset. The recordset can be kept open after the connection to the database is closed and saved to and from files on disk. On return, it can be resynchronized with the database. ADO takes care of the persistence and of keeping track of what has changed.

The last three features will probably be exciting for Visual Basic developers, since that language doesn't let you get hold of data as directly as Python; database data generally lives in a recordset throughout the life of a program, and so, is less relevant to us. Experienced SQL developers prefer to write their own CREATE TABLE statements by hand and are quite happy without an object layer in the way. Hierarchical data shaping and persistence are simple in Python, as you will see shortly.

So What's Worth Using?

ODBC is our preferred interface technology. It is widely supported, here for the long haul, and offers all the features serious database developers require. There is an ODBC module included in the PythonWin distribution, and two enhanced ones available for download, which we examine next. As you will see, these provide the fastest and simplest ways of getting data out of a database and into Python variables. DAO is of interest because it is a standard part of Office and in such wide use; it may be relevant if you are dealing specifically with Access databases. However, ADO seems set to take over and offers significant benefits, as well as a fairly straightforward transition from DAO. We show some examples of all three in the next section, but we'll concentrate mainly on ODBC for our more advanced examples.

Python's Database API

Python has its own database API. This is intended so that people writing wrappers around ODBC and vendor-specific database drivers should expose the same database API to Python. The Database Special Interest Group (DB-SIG) maintains the database API, and has a mailing list and archives relating to it at *http://www.python.org/sigs/db-sig/*.

Version 2.0 of this standard has just been released; we include a full copy in Appendix C, *The Python Database API Version 2.0*. The various ODBC modules we demonstrate in this chapter conform closely to the standard, so we will confine ourselves here to a brief discussion of what it encompasses:

Connection objects

Connection objects manage a connection to the database. They can be opened and closed, and can commit and roll back transactions. They may offer methods or properties to set global aspects of the connection, such as transaction behavior. Everything else is done through cursor objects.

Cursor objects

These manage the context of a single statement. Users ask the connection objects to create cursors, and assign an SQL statement to the cursor. The cursor handles control of execution and of iteration through the result set. It also defines a standard format for descriptive information about the fields in the result set. Cursors provide support for parameterized queries and prepared statements.

Standard information provided

A database connection or module should be able to return information about its capabilities. These include:

— The API level to which it conforms: level 2 offers many more features than level 1. See Appendix C for details.

— The parameter style to use for arguments to prepared statements; a question mark is the most common.

— Information about how safe the module is to use with threads.

Standard errors

A standard set of exceptions is defined for database work, helping users to distinguish between SQL syntax errors, integrity warnings in the database, invalid SQL, and so on.

Standard data types

Databases have special types to represent null, dates and times, binary objects, and row IDs. Each DB-API-compliant module may create its own objects to handle these, but the constructor for them is defined. Thus, calling `mymodule.`

`Date(1999,12,31)` should return a valid `Date` object suitable for insertion in the database, even if the implementation of the `Date` object varies from one database module to another.

The Python DB-API is simple and straightforward, yet offers the features needed for high-performance database development.

Because it's just been released, adherence to the new Version 2.0 database API isn't perfect, so we'll briefly note the differences from the 1.0 specification. Version 1.0 offered the same connection and cursor objects, but defined a shared helper module named DBI (presumably short for Database Independence) that offered standard `Date` and `RAW` types. It also did not define the standard exceptions and driver information features.

As we noted earlier, there are many Python interface modules available; generally, one for each database vendor. We will concentrate exclusively on the ODBC modules, because ODBC drivers are available for virtually all database servers.

Getting at Your Data

In this section we show how to execute SQL queries and fetch data using ODBC, DAO, and ADO. First, you need a database. The examples for this chapter include an Access database called *pydbdemos.mdb*. You could as easily use any database you can access, of course modifying the SQL statements as needed. The sample database consists of a list of clients and invoices, with the structure shown in Figure 13-2.

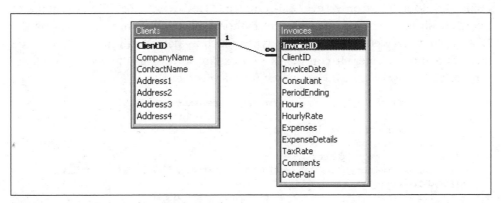

Figure 13-2. Structure of PYDBDEMOS database

If you wish to use the sample database, you need to configure an ODBC data source as follows:

1. Click on Start → Settings → Control Panel → 32-bit ODBC → User (or system) DSN → Add.

2. Select Microsoft Access Driver from the list of drivers.

3. Enter the name *PYDBDEMOS* in the box for Data Source Name.

4. Click the Select button and locate the file *pydbdemos.mdb*.

5. Click OK. The new data source should now be visible in the list.

6. Click OK to close the ODBC Data Source Administrator. Some versions of Windows contain a bug that causes an error message at this point. Ignore any messages; your data source is registered correctly.

Since Access isn't a server, we have worked with Sybase SQL Anywhere for some of the advanced examples. This is an excellent commercial database engine costing little more than Access and part of a range of products ranging from embedded database engines to enterprise servers. We've kept the Sybase examples to a minimum to illustrate the principles, and you certainly don't need a client/server system to follow this chapter. If you are working from home and want to experiment with the techniques used in large-scale database development, you'll find that most commercial database vendors are generous with extended evaluation copies and cut-down developer editions; their business model is to charge for connections to servers, and it's in their interest to encourage developers to try them.

Fetching Data with the PythonWin ODBC Module

PythonWin includes an ODBC module that is mature and stable, but no longer being developed and only Level 1.0-compliant. However, it has the advantage of being small, light, and present in every PythonWin distribution. It depends on the DBI module that defines certain data types (such as dates) and must be imported first: more on this later. It consists of two extension files in the *win32* subdirectory, *odbc.pyd* and *dbi.pyd*. Here's how we fetch some data:

```
>>> import dbi                 #database independence utilities
>>> import odbc                #the ODBC module itself
>>> from pprint import pprint  #pretty-print function
>>> myconn = odbc.odbc('PYDBDEMOS')
>>> mycursor = myconn.cursor()
>>> mycursor.execute('SELECT ClientID, CompanyName, Address1 FROM Clients')
>>> mydata = mycursor.fetchall()
>>> mycursor.close()           #close cursor when done
>>> myconn.close()             #close database when done
>>> pprint(mydata)
[('MEGAWAD', 'MegaWad Investments', '1 St. Fredericks-Le-Grand'),
 ('NOSHCO', 'NoshCo Supermarkets', '17 Merton Road'),
 ('GRQ', 'GRQ Recruitment', None)]
>>>
```

The `fetchall()` method converts the entire result set to a list of tuples of Python variables in one call.

The `connection` object is constructed with an ODBC connection string. It can be as simple as the data source name or can include a username and password; a real-world connection string might looks like this:

```
DSN=MYDATABASE;UID=MYUSER;PWD=MYPASSWORD
```

If you attempt to connect to a secure database without a password, the database driver pops up a login dialog. Access has a default user ID, Admin, and an empty password unless you enable security.

The `cursor` object manages a query. Once the query has been executed, you can use it to get information about the underlying fields. In the previous example you closed the cursor, but if it was still open, you could do this:

```
>>> pprint(mycursor.description)
[('clientid', 'STRING', 10, 10, 0, 0, 1),
 ('companyname', 'STRING', 50, 50, 0, 0, 1),
 ('address1', 'STRING', 50, 50, 0, 0, 1)]
>>>
```

The seven elements are: `name`, `type_code`, `display_size`, `internal_size`, `precision`, `scale`, and `null_ok`. Not all databases (or ODBC drivers, or Python interfaces) provide this information, but all the ones we have looked at manage the field name correctly.

Cursors also control how the information is retrieved. Some queries return large sets of data, and it is inefficient to always send all of them across a network to a client. We used the `fetchall()` method to ask for every row of data. There are also `fetchone()` and `fetchmany()` methods, which retrieve either one row or a block of rows, moving forward though the result set; they both return **None** when they reach the end. Cursors have a property **arraysize** you can set to determine the number of rows retrieved by a call to `fetchmany()`.

Update queries

Cursors can also execute **UPDATE** and **INSERT** statements or SQL Data Definition Language statements, such as **CREATE TABLE**. The call to `execute()` returns the number of rows affected:

```
>>> mycursor = myconn.cursor()
>>> mycursor.execute('UPDATE Invoices SET Hours=42 \
                WHERE InvoiceID=199904001')
1
>>>
```

However, at this point we reach a major limitation with the PythonWin ODBC module: it doesn't support prepared statements (at least not on any of the database we tested against). If you don't know what this means, rest assured, all will be revealed at considerable length in the following sections.

Working with dates

For the most part, ordinary Python variables are exactly what one needs to hold database values; they can hold integers, floating-point numbers, or strings (including strings of large binary data). The previous console session included the statement **import dbi** at the beginning. This statement must be executed prior to **import odbc**. This module defines a date type to use when working with databases, as well as the standard data types used by the ODBC API. Let's try a query that returns some dates and play with them. Assume the connection is still open:

```
>>> mycursor = myconn.cursor()
>>> mycursor.execute('SELECT ClientID, InvoiceDate, Consultant, \
                      Hours FROM Invoices')
>>> mydata = mycursor.fetchall()
>>> pprint(mydata)
[('MEGAWAD', <DbiDate object at 10f0dc0>, 'Joe Hacker', 40L),
 ('MEGAWAD', <DbiDate object at 10f0c40>, 'Arthur Suit', 24L),
 ('MEGAWAD', <DbiDate object at 10f1ed0>, 'Joe Hacker', 57L),
 ('NOSHCO', <DbiDate object at 10f1e00>, 'Tim Trainee', 18L)]
>>> dateobj = mydata[0][1]    # grab the date from the first row
>>> dateobj
<DbiDate object at 10f0dc0>
>>> int(dateobj)
924044400
>>> str(dateobj)
'Wed Apr 14 00:00:00 1999'
>>> print dateobj
Wed Apr 14 00:00:00 1999
>>>
```

Dates are returned as **DbiDate** objects. These can be treated as integers or floating point numbers, in which case you get the number of seconds since January 1, 1970 (the Python and Unix time system), or as strings, in which case you get a printable representation.

When modifying or inserting rows in a database, the syntax and format options may vary from vendor to vendor. However, there is also a standard ODBC syntax for embedding dates in SQL strings that should always work. That syntax uses the format {d 'yyyy-mm-dd'}. With Microsoft databases you can also use either a string enclosed with hashes, or a Microsoft date serial number,[*] which is based on the number of days since 1900:

```
>>> mycursor.execute('UPDATE Invoices SET InvoiceDate={d '1999-04-15' }
  WHERE InvoiceID=199904001')    # preferred
1
```

---

[*] This is the system used in COM dates as seen in Chapter 9, *Integration with Excel.*

```
>>> mycursor.execute('UPDATE Invoices SET InvoiceDate=36265 WHERE
InvoiceID=199904001')
1
>>> mycursor.execute('UPDATE Invoices SET InvoiceDate=#15-Apr-99# WHERE
InvoiceID=199904001')
1
>>>
```

The mxODBC and mxDateTime Extensions

The ODBC module distributed with PythonWin is a minimal implementation, and conforms to Version 1.0 of the Python Database API. It's stable and works well, but is unlikely to be developed further. Then again, neither is ODBC!*

If you work extensively with databases, check out Marc-André Lemburg's mxODBC extension package, available from *http://starship.python.net/crew/lemburg/*. One of its many features is an enhanced set of date and time types to save you from worrying about Microsoft and Unix date systems. These are available as a separate package, mxDateTime, which can be used in nondatabase applications. mxODBC also runs on Unix. mxODBC has some licensing restrictions; check the web site for the latest details.

mxDateTime and mxODBC are both shipped as packages that should be unzipped somewhere on the Python path.† The latter creates a directory and package named—you guessed it—ODBC. There is a naming collision with the old ODBC module, which lives in *...Python\win32\odbc.pyd*; we suggest renaming this to something else, such as *win32odbc.pyd,* so that you can still access the old module if you want to (note, however, that you need to rename the module back to the original *odbc.pyd* before it can be used again). It contains a number of subpackages aimed at other platforms; the functionality we want is in the module ODBC.Windows. Let's give it a try:

```
>>> import ODBC.Windows
>>> conn = ODBC.Windows.Connect('PYDBDEMOS')
>>> cursor = conn.cursor()
>>> cursor.execute('SELECT InvoiceID, ClientID, InvoiceDate FROM Invoices')
>>> from pprint import pprint
>>> pprint(cursor.description)
(('InvoiceID', 4, None, None, 10, 0, 1),
 ('ClientID', 12, None, None, 10, 0, 1),
 ('InvoiceDate', 11, None, None, 19, 0, 1))
>>> data = cursor.fetchall()
>>> pprint(data)
```

---

* Microsoft is committed to extending ODBC as needed to comply with developments such as SQL3, without breaking existing code.

† There are plans to merge the two into one package in the near future. At the time of this writing, the current versions are 1.1.1 for mxODBC and 1.3.0 for mxDateTime.

```
[(199904001, 'MEGAWAD', 1999-04-15 00:00:00.00),
 (199904002, 'MEGAWAD', 1999-04-14 00:00:00.00),
 (199904003, 'MEGAWAD', 1999-04-21 00:00:00.00),
 (199904004, 'NOSHCO', 1999-04-22 00:00:00.00)]
```

As can be seen, the interface is almost identical. A recent change in the Python Database API has been to use `Connect()` as the constructor for connection objects rather than `ODBC()`, but mxODBC supports both forms, as well as the lower case `connect()`.

Enhanced connection control

mxODBC offers access to a wide range of options and SQL constants that can control the behavior of a connection. The most important of these determines whether the connection commits every statement as it's executed or accumulates them in a transaction. The default behavior is to begin a transaction, so that changes to the database are permanent only when a user calls `cursor.commit()`. This can be modified two ways. First of all, when connecting, one can supply an argument as follows:

```
>>> myconn = ODBC.Windows.Connect('PYDBDEMOS',clear_auto_commit=1)
>>>
```

Second, one can set this and a wide range of other options through the `setconnectoption(option, value)` and `getconnectoption(option)` methods. The `SQL` object provides access to the full set of 636 ODBC constants that (among other things) define the options and possible values. Thus, you can achieve the same with:

```
>>> myconn.setconnectoption(SQL.AUTOCOMMIT, SQL.AUTOCOMMIT_ON)
>>> myconn.getconnectoption(SQL.AUTOCOMMIT)
1
>>>
```

This feature allows access to most of the key capabilities of ODBC drivers.

The mxDateTime package

Now we'll take a quick look at the date and time functionality. The `mxDateTime` package was developed after much discussion on the Python DB-SIG to provide a platform-independent way to move date and time data between databases and applications. Its internal epoch is the year dot, giving it a far greater range than COM dates. The first thing to note is that the date objects in the previous session were smart enough to represent themselves in a readable manner! We'll grab a date out of the row above and play with it:

```
>>> aDateTime = data[0][2]
>>> type(aDateTime)
<type 'DateTime'>
>>> int(aDateTime)
```

```
924130800
>>> str(aDateTime)
'1999-04-15 00:00:00.00'
>>>
```

`mxDateTime` also provides a large array of constants, methods, and submodules to perform date and calendar calculations, parse dates, and even work out holidays. The following snippet should give you a feel:

```
>>> import DateTime
>>> DateTime.DateTimeFromCOMDate(0) # the Microsoft system
1899-12-30 00:00:00.00
>>> aDateTime.COMDate()              # convert to Microsoft COM/Excel dates
36265.0
>>>
>>> DateTime.now() - aDateTime       # RelativeDateTime object
<DateTimeDelta object for '16:23:40:16.18' at 1106530>
>>> aDateTime + DateTime.RelativeDateTime(months=+3)
1999-07-15 00:00:00.00
>>> # first of next month...
>>> aDateTime + DateTime.RelativeDateTime(months=+1,day=1)
1999-05-01 00:00:00.00
>>> DateTime.now()
1999-05-01 23:42:20.15
>>> DateTime.Feasts.EasterSunday(2001)
2001-04-15 00:00:00.00
>>> DateTime.Parser.DateFromString('Friday 19th October 1987')
1987-10-19 00:00:00.00
>>>
```

A `DateTimeDelta` is defined for the difference between two points in time, and there are a full set of mathematical operations defined. Submodules include date parsers, holidays, and routines for ARPA and ISO dates. A large number of business applications need to handle dates and times intelligently, and these functions make it extremely easy and quick.

Support for prepared statements

One of the key advantages of `mxODBC` is that it properly supports prepared statements. While these will be familiar to database programmers who work in C, they may not be to people used to standard Visual Basic or Delphi database development tools, so we'll explain the background.

There are two stages to the execution of an SQL statement. First, the database parses the SQL, works out a plan for executing the query, and compiles it into an executable routine. Second, the database executes the statement and returns the result set. For complex queries joining several tables, the parsing is not a trivial step, and may involve some analysis of the size of tables and the best order in which to filter records. It also consumes a large amount of memory compared to the subsequent execution.

If you wish to perform the same kind of query repeatedly (for example, inserting 1,000 rows in a table), the statement could, in theory, be parsed only once, leading to substantial performance gains. To support this, it's necessary to separate the SQL statement structure from the actual parameters to go into the database.

If you are working with ODBC in C, you execute one call to get a handle to the SQL statement, then others to actually call it repeatedly with differing data. In Python it is much simpler: just parameterize the statement, using a question mark as a placeholder:

```
>>> stmt = "UPDATE Invoices SET Hours = ? WHERE InvoiceID = ?"
>>> mycursor.execute(stmt, (45, 199904001))
1
>>>
```

mxODBC and any other DBAPI-compliant interface do the right thing to pass the arguments to the database, whatever their type. Don't confuse this with Python's modulo operator for substituting into strings.

At this point you've executed only a single statement. However, the cursor object is now caching a handle to the prepared statement; so a subsequent call of the form `cursor.execute(stmt, newdata)` will be much faster on any client/server database. Later in the chapter, you'll discover how much faster, when we benchmark a range of data access methods.

If you have a large block of data to insert or update, there's a method named `executemany()`,* which takes a block or rows and saves the need to write a Python loop to insert each one. The following snippet shows the most efficient way to do a bulk insertion or update. The SQL statement is parsed only once:

```
>>> mycursor.executemany(stmt,
...      [ #begin a list of values
...       (45, 199904001),
...       (53, 199904002),
...       (52, 199904003)
...      ] )
1
>>>
```

Note that the block of data supplied is a list of tuples, the same format returned from `fetchall()` or from 2D COM arrays. Other languages let you work with one field at a time; Python lets you manipulate whole blocks of data in a single line!

The importance of prepared statements is hard to overstate. First of all, on single queries on a database that is being used lightly, there can be an increase of up to 50% in query execution. Second, if a system is designed to use only prepared

---

* `executemany()` is the new standard, but many interface modules (including mxODBC and Gadfly) allow you to pass a list of tuples to `execute()` as well.

statements, it consumes far less server memory, enabling it to support many more users and perform better under heavy loads. Third, it saves you a lot of work; there's no need to build the full SQL string yourself, leaving you free to concentrate purely on manipulating blocks of Python variables.

Calling stored procedures

One key feature offered by client/server databases (but not Microsoft Access) is the *stored procedure*. This is a named, precompiled procedure in the database that may be called from outside: conceptually, a function you can call, complete with arguments. As well as offering the same performance benefits as prepared statements, these allow the database to encapsulate business logic. For example, rather than letting developers directly execute SQL on a group of tables relating to invoices, database administrators can provide an interface allowing the users to add, edit (only where appropriate), and query interfaces. This is standard practice in many companies, and ad hoc queries by users are sometimes banned because of concerns over database integrity or performance.

Access doesn't offer this feature, so we'll switch to a demonstration version of Sybase Adaptive Server Anywhere. The example database provided includes tables of customers and products, and a stored procedure interface to them. The procedure `sp_product_info` accepts a product ID as argument and returns information on that product gathered from several tables.

The DBAPI recommends that cursors can optionally offer a method named `callproc(procname, [parameters])`. It's optional because many databases, such as mySQL and Access, don't offer stored procedures. At the time of writing this was not yet implemented in mxODBC. Nevertheless, they can be called using standard SQL without trouble, as follows:

```
>>> mycursor.execute('sp_product_info(500)')
>>> mycursor.fetchall()
[(500, 'Visor', 'Cloth Visor', 'One size fits all', 'White', 36, 7.0)]
>>> mycursor.execute('CALL sp_product_info(500)')
>>> mycursor.fetchall()
[(500, 'Visor', 'Cloth Visor', 'One size fits all', 'White', 36, 7.0)]
>>> mycursor.execute('EXEC sp_product_info(500)')
>>> mycursor.fetchall()
[(500, 'Visor', 'Cloth Visor', 'One size fits all', 'White', 36, 7.0)]
```

Sam Rushing's ODBC Module

There is a third Python module for working with ODBC that operates on different lines. Sam Rushing (*http://www.nightmare.com*) specializes in low-level work with Python and Windows and has produced a package named `calldll` that allows Python programs to dynamically load and call any function in a DLL. We discuss how this works in Chapter 22, *Extending and Embedding with Visual C++ and Delphi*. It has allowed Sam to produce an ODBC module that wraps and exposes almost every function in Microsoft's ODBC.DLL. To install this, you need to download the two files *calldll.zip* and *dynwin.zip* from his site. The latter contains a number of modules relating to ODBC. Naturally, one of these is called *odbc.py*, so you need to watch for name collisions. If you've been using the previous two modules, rename them out of the way before starting.

As with the other modules, `calldll` provides a safe, easy-to-use high-level interface for querying databases, but it bears no resemblance to the DBAPI. Here's the high-level usage:

```
>>> import odbc
>>> env = odbc.environment()
>>> conn = env.connection()
>>> conn.connect('accessdemo')
>>> import pprint
>>> pp = pprint.pprint
>>> results = conn.query('SELECT * FROM Invoices')
>>> pp(results[0])  #field information
[('InvoiceID', 4, 10, 0, 1),
 ('ClientID', 12, 10, 0, 1),
 ('InvoiceDate', 11, 19, 0, 1),
 ('Consultant', 12, 50, 0, 1),
 ('PeriodEnding', 11, 19, 0, 1),
 ('Hours', 8, 15, 0, 1),
 ('HourlyRate', 2, 19, 4, 1),
 ('Expenses', 2, 19, 4, 1),
 ('ExpenseDetails', 12, 50, 0, 1),
 ('TaxRate', 8, 15, 0, 1),
 ('Comments', 12, 50, 0, 1),
 ('DatePaid', 11, 19, 0, 1)]
>>> pp(results[1])  #first data row
['199904001',
 'MEGAWAD',
 '1999-12-31 00:00:00',
 'Joe Hacker',
 '1999-04-18 00:00:00',
 '43.0',
 '50.0000',
 '0.0000',
 None,
 '0.175',
 None,
 None]
>>>
```

The high-level interface includes classes to represent the environment, connections, and statements. Perhaps of more interest is what happens when you drop down a level. Sam has encapsulated the idea of an ODBC function call in a general way. Let's take a look at his own source code for the `connect()` method:

```
def connect (self, dsn, uid='', auth=''):
        self.dsn   = cstring (dsn)
        self.uid   = cstring (uid)
        self.auth  = cstring (auth)
        retval = odbc.SQLConnect (
            self,                          # connection handle
            self.dsn, self.dsn.strlen(),   # data source name
            self.uid, self.uid.strlen(),   # user identifier
            self.auth, self.auth.strlen(), # authentication (password)
            )
        if retval in (SQL_SUCCESS, SQL_SUCCESS_WITH_INFO):
            self.connected = 1
        else:
            raise error, 'SQLConnect failed: %d' % retval
```

If you're an experienced ODBC programmer working from C or C++, you'll recognize the call to SQLConnect and the constant values such as SQL_SUCCESS. The ODBC module in DynWin exposes the entire ODBC API to the programmer, offering the same possibilities as with programming in C.

One word of warning: while the high-level interface is reliable and quite friendly, the technologies underneath DynWin and calldll are less forgiving than most Python extensions. If you drop down to the lowest levels and call ODBC functions with the wrong arguments, it's possible to corrupt the stack and crash your program, the same as in C.

We expect this module to be of interest to experienced C and C++ programmers who know the ODBC API and wish to work with it at a low level. If this doesn't describe you, stick with the other ODBC modules; the performance is the same, but the interface operates at a much higher level of convenience.

Connecting with Data Access Objects

The Data Access Object hierarchy is installed on your system if you have Microsoft Office, Access, or Visual Basic, or if you have ever installed a VB application that works with MDB files. It doesn't need an ODBC data source configured. We recommend running MakePy over the latest version of the Microsoft DAO Library on your system, as seen in Figure 13-3.

The hierarchy starts with a database engine (class DBEngine) and allows you to open multiple Database objects. Once a database is open you can create Recordset objects that are the broad equivalent of a cursor in the Python Database API. You can navigate through a Recordset and edit its fields. A Field is an object too, with a Name, a Value, and many more properties.

Let's start by connecting to the same database as before. This time you don't need the ODBC data source, but can go straight for the file:

```
>>> import win32com.client
>>> daoEngine = win32com.client.Dispatch('DAO.DBEngine')
```

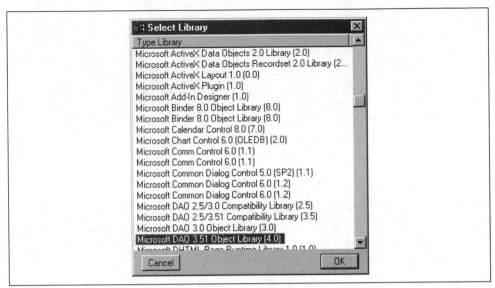

Figure 13-3. MakePy showing the DAO and ADO libraries

```
>>> daoDB = daoEngine.OpenDatabase('C:\\MYDIR\\pydbdemos.mdb')
>>> daoRS = daoDB.OpenRecordset('SELECT ClientID, InvoiceDate, \
                  Consultant, Hours FROM Invoices')
>>> daoRS.MoveLast()      # need to do this to get an accurate size
>>> daoRS.RecordCount
4
>>>
```

Opening the database and getting the result set is no harder than with the Python API and ODBC. However, instead of calling `fetchall()` to create a Python list of tuples, you have a `Recordset` object through which you must iterate. Before, you stepped to the end and got a record count. Now let's look at some data:

```
>>> daoRS.MoveLast()
>>> daoRS.Fields('ClientID').Value    # reference fields by name
'NOSHCO'
>>> daoRS.Fields(3).Value             # or by position
18.0
>>> for i in range(daoRS.Fields.Count):
...     daoField = daoRS.Fields[i]
...     print '%s = %s' % (daoField.Name, daoField.Value)
...
ClientID = NOSHCO
InvoiceDate = <time object at 1191860>
Consultant = Tim Trainee
Hours = 18.0
>>>
```

The normal mode of operations is to work a field at a time, asking for the exact values you want. However, there's a method called `Recordset.GetRows([rows_` *to_fetch]*) that can grab data in bulk. It returns the next few rows from the current position:

```
>>> daoRS.MoveFirst()
>>> data = daoRS.GetRows(4)
>>> pprint(data)
((L'MEGAWAD', L'MEGAWAD', L'MEGAWAD', L'NOSHCO'),
 (<time object at 11921f0>,
  <time object at 11921d0>,
  <time object at 11921b0>,
  <time object at 1192190>),
 (L'Joe Hacker', L'Arthur Suit', L'Joe Hacker', L'Tim Trainee'),
 (42.0, 24.0, 57.0, 18.0))
```

There are two things to notice. First, **GetRows()** returns columns, not rows. The matrix is transposed compared to the Python representation. Second, this is a COM server, so you get back Unicode strings and the date objects defined by the Python COM framework. As a reminder, let's take another look at the third date type:

```
>>> aDate = data[1][0]    # remember how these dates work?
>>> type(aDate)
<type 'time'>
>>> int(aDate)            # can coerce to a Python date...
924130800
>>> aDate.Format()        # ...and knows how to display itself
'04/15/99 00:00:00'
>>>
```

It's possible to update and insert records using DAO, but the normal technique is to use the **Edit()** and **AddNew()** methods of a **RecordSet** as follows:

```
>>> daoRS2 = daoDB.OpenRecordset('SELECT * FROM Clients')
>>> daoRS2.AddNew()
>>> daoRS2.Fields('ClientID').Value = 'WOMBLES'
>>> daoRS2.Fields('CompanyName').Value = 'Wimbledon Garbage Disposal Ltd.'
>>> daoRS2.Fields('ContactName').Value = 'Uncle Bulgaria'
>>> daoRS2.Update()       # save the record
>>> daoRS2.Close()
```

To modify an existing record, use **Edit()** rather than **AddNew()** at the beginning.

This highlights what is arguably a benefit of the DAO model: the database does type checking on individual fields as you assign them. If you try to put a string in a date field, you get an error on the relevant line of code, whereas debugging long **UPDATE** or **INSERT** statements can take a little longer. However, for large volumes of insertions, working with an ODBC module's **executemany()** method is simpler since there is no need to loop over the fields in Python and DAO.

Connecting with ADO

ADO looks almost identical to DAO at this level of detail; Microsoft simplified the object model considerably but kept the essentials the same. The big differences are that (a) data providers other than ODBC are permitted, and (b) all the Access specifics, including direct access to tables and relationships, have been dropped. The data provider can be specified either in a connection string or in a `Provider` property of the `Connection` object, before the connection is opened. Microsoft has data providers for the following applications at present:

- ODBC

- Microsoft Index Server

- Active Directory Services

- Jet engine (via DAO)

So, despite all the hype, you're still going to use either ODBC or DAO under the hood somewhere. We'll use our ODBC alias again:

```
>>> import win32com.client
>>> adoConn = win32com.client.Dispatch('ADODB.Connection')
>>> adoConn.Open('PYDBDEMOS')   # use our ODBC alias again
>>> (adoRS, success) = adoConn.Execute('SELECT * FROM Clients')
>>> adoRS.MoveFirst()
>>> adoRS.Fields("CompanyName").Value
'MegaWad Investments'
>>>
```

Adding, editing, and using `GetRows()` is identical to DAO. We won't go into the advanced capabilities of ADO here; numerous references are available.

You should use ADO if you know it's installed on client machines, because it's the COM API of the future. However, at the time of writing, you can count on DAO being present on all machines with a copy of Office, and ADO is not yet so widespread. If you stick to basic SQL statements, porting code between the two should be easy.

A Note on Speed

With database systems, performance is always important. A badly designed client/ server system can cost a great deal of money and have a shorter life than planned if attention is not paid to the way client applications interact with the server. Even with PC-based systems such as Access, database applications can often become slow, especially when multiple dynamic views of the data are used. Having discussed a wide range of data-access techniques, we now include some rough performance benchmarks. These are intended to show only the rough characteristics of different data-access APIs.

The standard task covered is to insert 1,000 rows into a simple table. The sample table, named *analysis,* can be thought of as a crude repository for financial data; it has four fields, tranid (integer), trandate (date), account (string) and amount (currency). To slow it down a bit, it's indexed uniquely on tranid and indexed with duplicates allowed on trandate and account. Thus any insertion involves updating three indexes. We created instances of this database in our sample Access database and in Sybase SQL Anywhere. It starts off empty. The tests were run on a Pentium 266, with client and server on the same machine and no other activity taking place. The source code for the test is in the module *fastinsert.py* at *http://starship.python.net/crew/mhammond/ppw32/.*

We first used mxODBC to connect to both the Access and Sybase databases and tried three different techniques, which are called Slow, Faster, and Fastest in Table 13-1.

Table 13-1. Example Database Insertion Speeds

Database	Technique	Speed (rows/second)
Access via mxODBC	Slow	136
	Faster	121
	Fastest	152
Sybase via mxODBC	Slow	292
	Faster	455
	Fastest	523
Access via JET	Raw SQL INSERT	108
	AddNew/Update	192

First, a list of tuples was prepared holding the data for the 1,000 rows. In the Slow technique, we built a literal SQL statement each time. In the Faster technique, we used prepared statements as follows:

```
mystatement = """INSERT INTO analysis (tranid, trandate, account,
                amount) VALUES(?, ?, ?, ?)"""
for row in mydata:
    mycursor.execute(mystatement, row)
```

In the technique called Fastest, we used the executemany() method. This is the same at the database end, but moves the loop over 1,000 records from interpreted Python code into compiled C code.

Finally, we connected to the same Access database using the Jet engine. The two techniques here were to build and execute INSERT statements directly or to use the AddNew() and Update() methods of the RecordSet object.

These results are highly instructive. Sybase is far and away the faster system, even on a local PC. Also, as theory suggests, using prepared statements brought about a speedup of 55%, while using executemany() to optimize out the loop gets us up to over 500 rows per second.

Access, however, shows no improvement at all; in fact, it actually gets slightly slower! The reason for this is that the Jet engine doesn't support prepared statements at all. The Access ODBC drivers do support them for compatibility purposes, but they presumably get converted back into separate calls in the driver. The final technique we tried with Access, using Recordset.AddNew(), was the fastest way to work with Access databases.

The moral of this story is simple: if you are building a client/server system in Python, or even prototyping a system in Access that might later be moved to client/server, use ODBC and parameterize your SQL statements. If you are building a (hopefully single-user) Access-based system that will never be moved to client/server, go with DAO or ADO.

Gadfly, the Pure Python Relational Database

We now step away from Microsoft APIs altogether. Gadfly is an SQL relational database written in Python by Aaron Watters. It can be found at *http://www.chordate.com*, and is distributed in a 200-KB Zip file, including documentation.

Gadfly gives Python programs relational database capabilities without relying on any external database engines. It offers the following features:

- Compliance with the Python Database API
- Total portability between platforms
- A transaction log and recovery procedure
- A built-in TCP/IP server mode, allowing it to serve clients on remote machines
- Security policies to prevent accidental deletion of data

It's not intended as a multiuser production system, and some features are missing at present, notably Null values and Date/Time variables.

Aaron previously produced both a parsing engine named kwParsing and a library of data structures, including sets, directed graphs, and dictionaries, called kjBuckets. These C extensions are part of the Gadfly package and can build an efficient and fast in-memory SQL engine. If you are interested in either how to parse SQL statements or in the low-level relational operations, Gadfly is a great package to explore. To install and set up Gadfly, perform these steps:

1. Download the 217-KB Zip file.

2. Unzip to a directory on the Python path.

3. CD to the directory in a DOS prompt.

4. Type `python gfinstall.py`.

5. Create a subdirectory for a test database with `MKDIR dbtest`.

6. Type `python gftest.py dbtest`. This creates test tables in the directory and runs a large number of queries.

Interactive Use

Gadfly can be used in almost exactly the same way as other data sources:

```
>>> from gadfly import gadfly
>>> connection = gadfly("test", "c:\\mydir\\gadfly\\dbtest")
>>> cursor = connection.cursor()
>>> cursor.execute('SELECT * FROM Frequents')
>>> from pprint import pprint
>>> cursor.description                              # only does fieldnames at present
(('PERWEEK', None, None, None, None, None, None),
('BAR', None, None, None, None, None, None),
('DRINKER', None, None, None, None, None, None))
>>> print cursor.pp()                              # it can format its own output
PERWEEK | BAR      | DRINKER
============================
1       | lolas    | adam
3       | cheers   | woody
5       | cheers   | sam
3       | cheers   | norm
2       | joes     | wilt
1       | joes     | norm
6       | lolas    | lola
2       | lolas    | norm
3       | lolas    | woody
0       | frankies | pierre
1       | pans     | peter
>>> data = cursor.fetchall()
>>>
```

Like most interactive SQL clients, it can format its own output with the `pp()` method. One immediate surprise is the speed: Gadfly operates entirely in local memory and uses highly refined logic to produce an extremely fast implementation. We won't go into how!

Gadfly offers the same ability to prepare statements as `mxODBC`; if the same statement is passed in repeated calls, the cursor parses it only once:

```
>>>insertstat = "insert into phonenumbers(name,phone) values (?, ?)"
>>>cursor.execute(insertstat, ('nan', "0356"))
>>>cursor.execute(insertstat, ('bill', "2356"))
```

```
>>>cursor.execute(insertstat, ('tom', "4356"))
>>>
```

A matrix of values can be passed to **execute()** in a single try.

Introspection

Like many SQL databases, Gadfly maintains metadata in tables, and you can query the structure of a Gadfly database:

```
>>> cursor = connection.cursor()
>>> cursor.execute('SELECT * FROM __table_names__')
>>> print cursor.pp()
IS_VIEW | TABLE_NAME
=========================
0       | EMPTY
1       | NONDRINKERS
1       | ALLDRINKERS
1       | __INDICES__
1       | DUAL
0       | LIKES
0       | FREQUENTS
0       | ACCESSES
0       | WORK
1       | __TABLE_NAMES__
0       | SERVES
1       | __DATADEFS__
1       | __COLUMNS__
1       | __INDEXCOLS__
>>>
```

Apart from the data tables, you can inspect metatables of tables, indexes, and columns in this manner.

Network Use

Gadfly incorporates a TCP/IP client and server, transforming it into a proper client/server system. To start the server on the machine we've already tested, run the following command from a DOS prompt:

```
C:\MYDIR\gadfly>python gfserve.py 2222 test dbtest admin
```

The arguments specify the port, the database name, the database directory, and the password. The server console should start up and display the message "waiting for connections."

The client machine needs only the two files, *gfclient.py* and *gfsocket.py* (as well as Python, of course). At 15 KB, this must be one of the lightest database clients around. On the client machine, start Python and run the following commands. If you don't have a second PC handy, you can run the client from a second DOS prompt (or PythonWin prompt) on the same machine provided TCP/IP is properly installed:

```
>>> # on client machine
>>> from gfclient import gfclient
>>> # connect with policy, port, password, machine name
>>> conn = gfclient("admin",2222, "admin", "tahoe")
>>> cursor = conn.cursor()
>>> cursor.execute('SELECT * FROM LIKES')
>>> pprint(cursor.fetchall())
[(2, 'bud', 'adam'),
 (1, 'rollingrock', 'wilt'),
 (2, 'bud', 'sam'),
 (3, 'rollingrock', 'norm'),
 (2, 'bud', 'norm'),
 (1, 'sierranevada', 'nan'),
 (2, 'pabst', 'woody'),
 (5, 'mickies', 'lola')]
>>>
```

As the queries execute, you should see messages on the server console.

What's It Good for?

Gadfly still lacks some features of production databases, but what is there is reputedly stable and fast. It could be useful for a local client that gathers data and occasionally downloads from or uploads to a master database elsewhere. It's an excellent tool for learning about client/server and relational concepts at zero cost. However, a major niche we see for it is in data laundering; you can develop scripts rapidly and save the output to local Gadfly tables, committing the results to a destination database only when the system is fully refined and working.

Data Laundering with Python

We have covered a wide range of database APIs and data sources, and demonstrated that Python can connect to data from any modern database. Now we will look at some areas in which Python can do useful things with the data.

The first major area of work is what we call *data laundering*. This involves writing programs to acquire data from a source database, reshape it in some way, and load it into a destination database. One major difference between database development and general application development is that databases are live; you can't just switch them off for a few months. This means that what would be a simple upgrade for a Windows application becomes a much more complex process of repeatedly migrating data and running in parallel. Here are some examples of areas where this type of work is needed:

Database upgrades and changes

When a database is replaced, the new database structure is almost always different. The new database needs to be developed with sample data available, then tested extensively, then run in parallel with the old one while all the users and client applications are moved across. Scripts are needed to migrate the data repeatedly (usually daily) from source to destination, often performing validity checks on the way in.

Connecting databases

Businesses often have databases whose areas of interest overlap. A fund manager might have a core system for processing deals in its funds, and a marketing database for tracking sales calls; marketing needs a recent copy of some of the deal information to help serve the clients, possibly simplified and pre-digested in various ways. Again, a daily process of exporting, rearranging, and loading is needed.

Data warehouses

The classic case for repeated data laundering is the data warehouse. A company has one or more transaction-processing databases, which usually have numerous highly normalized tables, optimized for insertion and lookups of small numbers of records at any one time. A data warehouse is a second, parallel database optimized for analysis. It's essentially read-only with a simple structure geared to computing averages and totals across the whole database. This is refreshed daily in a process known as the *production data load*. The production data load needs to acquire data from several databases, reshape it in ways that are often impossible for SQL, validate it in various ways, then load into the destination database. This is a perfect niche for Python.

All these tasks involve writing scripts to reshape the data.

We'll now start to build a toolkit to help with these kinds of operations. The toolkit is based on real classes and functions that have been used in a number of serious projects and have proved their utility many times over (see the case study later on), although we have simplified and cut down the code considerably for this book. All the code for the rest of this chapter can be found in the module *laundry.py* at *http://starship.python.net/crew/mhammond/ppw32/*.

Data as Rows

There are several useful ways to represent data. The most obvious is as rows. The Python format for data as rows returned from database cursors is a list of tuples.

This is such a common representation that we'll wrap it in a class called `DataSet`. The class doesn't serve to hide the data; it's just a convenient place to hang a load of data-manipulation methods (as well as to keep the field names). Here's part of its definition, showing how to construct a **DataSet** and display its contents:

```
class DataSet:
    "wrapper around a tabular set of data"
    def __init__(self):
        self.data = []
        self.fieldnames = []

    def pp(self):
        "Pretty-print a row at a time - nicked from Gadfly"
        from string import join
        stuff = [repr(self.fieldnames)] + map(repr, self.data)
        print join(stuff, "\n")

def DataSetFromCursor(cursor):
    " a handy constructor"
    ds = DataSet()
    ds.fieldnames = getFieldNames(cursor)
    ds.data = cursor.fetchall()
    return ds
```

You can use this as follows:

```
>>> import ODBC.Windows
>>> conn = ODBC.Windows.Connect('PYDBDEMOS')
>>> cursor = conn.cursor()
>>> cursor.execute('SELECT ClientID, PeriodEnding, Consultant,
    Hours FROM Invoices')
>>> import laundry
>>> ds = laundry.DataSetFromCursor(cursor)
>>> cursor.close()
>>> conn.close()
>>> ds.pp()
('ClientID', 'PeriodEnding', 'Consultant', 'Hours')
('MEGAWAD', 1999-04-18 00:00:00.00, 'Joe Hacker', 42.0)
('MEGAWAD', 1999-04-18 00:00:00.00, 'Arthur Suit', 24.0)
('MEGAWAD', 1999-04-25 00:00:00.00, 'Joe Hacker', 57.0)
('NOSHCO', 1999-04-25 00:00:00.00, 'Tim Trainee', 18.0)
('MEGAWAD', 1999-04-18 00:00:00.00, 'Joe Hacker', 42.0)
>>>
```

The ability to see the field names becomes useful when writing data-cleaning scripts at an interactive prompt.

Geometric Operations

Now that we have the data, what to do with it depends on the operation taking place. An approach that has stood the test of time is to keep adding operations to the **Dataset** class, building over time a veritable Swiss army knife. Common families of operations can include:

Field transformations

Applying functions to entire columns in order to format numbers and dates, switch encodings, or build database keys.

Row and column operations

Inserting, appending, and deleting whole columns, breaking into several separate datasets whenever a certain field changes, and sorting operations.

Filter operations

Extracting or dropping rows meeting user-defined criteria.

Geometric operations

Cross-tabulate, detabulate (see Figure 13-4), and transpose.

Storage operations

Load and save to native Python data (`marshal`, `cPickle`), delimited text files, and fixed-width text files.

Some of these operations are best understood diagrammatically. Consider the operation in Figure 13-4, which can't be performed by SQL.

						Patient	Lab	Date	Item	Value
						Patient 1	QMH	01-May-99	X	0.55
Lab	*QMH*					Patient 2	QMH	01-May-99	Y	0.54
Date	*01-May-99*					Patient 3	QMH	01-May-99	Z	0.61
	X	Y	Z			Patient 4	QMH	01-May-99	X	0.19
Patient 1	0.55	0.08	0.97			Patient 1	QMH	01-May-99	Y	0.08
Patient 2	0.54	0.11	0.07			Patient 2	QMH	01-May-99	Z	0.11
Patient 3	0.61	0.08	0.44			Patient 3	QMH	01-May-99	X	0.08
Patient 4	0.19	0.46	0.41			Patient 4	QMH	01-May-99	Y	0.46
						Patient 1	QMH	01-May-99	Z	0.97
						Patient 2	QMH	01-May-99	X	0.07
						Patient 3	QMH	01-May-99	Y	0.44
						Patient 4	QMH	01-May-99	Z	0.41

Figure 13-4. Detabulating and adding constant columns

This operation was a mainstay of the case study that follows. Once the correct operations have been created, it can be reduced to a piece of Python code:

```
>>> ds1.pp()    # presume we have the table above already
('Patient', 'X', 'Y', 'Z')
('Patient 1', 0.55, 0.08, 0.97)
('Patient 2', 0.54, 0.11, 0.07)
('Patient 3', 0.61, 0.08, 0.44)
('Patient 4', 0.19, 0.46, 0.41)
>>> ds2 = ds1.detabulate()
>>> ds2.addConstantColumn('Date',DateTime(1999,5,1),1)
>>> ds2.addConstantColumn('Lab','QMH', 1)
>>> ds2.pp()
('Row', 'Lab', 'Date', 'Column', 'Value')
('Patient 1', 'QMH', 1999-05-01 00:00:00.00, 'X', 0.55)
```

```
('Patient 2', 'QMH', 1999-05-01 00:00:00.00, 'X', 0.54)
('Patient 3', 'QMH', 1999-05-01 00:00:00.00, 'X', 0.61)
('Patient 4', 'QMH', 1999-05-01 00:00:00.00, 'X', 0.19)
('Patient 1', 'QMH', 1999-05-01 00:00:00.00, 'Y', 0.08)
('Patient 2', 'QMH', 1999-05-01 00:00:00.00, 'Y', 0.11)
('Patient 3', 'QMH', 1999-05-01 00:00:00.00, 'Y', 0.08)
('Patient 4', 'QMH', 1999-05-01 00:00:00.00, 'Y', 0.46)
('Patient 1', 'QMH', 1999-05-01 00:00:00.00, 'Z', 0.97)
('Patient 2', 'QMH', 1999-05-01 00:00:00.00, 'Z', 0.07)
('Patient 3', 'QMH', 1999-05-01 00:00:00.00, 'Z', 0.44)
('Patient 4', 'QMH', 1999-05-01 00:00:00.00, 'Z', 0.41)
>>>
```

We won't show the methods to implement this; they involve straightforward Python loops and list slicing, as do most of the things we would want to do with a `DataSet`. Their effect is to take our data-laundering scripts to a higher level of abstraction and clarity.

Data as Dictionaries

Another useful and powerful representation of data is as a dictionary of keys and values. This leads to a much easier syntax when you edit and modify records; the field names can be used rather than numeric indexes. It's also useful when putting together data about the same thing from different sources. There will be some overlap between fields, but not total agreement. Dictionaries can represent sparse data compactly. A classic example is found in the `Transaction` architecture from Part II, where there was a method to convert a transaction to a list of dictionaries. A sales transaction has different keys and values from a payroll transaction.

You'll rarely want just one dictionary, so we have added the following method to convert a `DataSet` to a list of dictionaries:

```
class DataSet:
    <continued...>
    def asDicts(self):
        "returns a list of dictionaries, each with all fieldnames"
        dicts = []
        fieldcount = len(self.fieldnames)
        for row in self.data:
            dict = {}
            for i in range(fieldcount):
                dict[self.fieldnames[i]] = row[i]
            dicts.append(dict)
        return dicts
```

This enables you to get a row from a query and modify it flexibly: let's grab our first invoice from the sample database and look at it. Assume you've just done a `'Select * FROM Invoices'` in a cursor:

```
>>> dict = ds.asDicts()[0]    # grab the first one
>>> pprint(dict)
```

Case Study: Applied Biometrics

Applied Biometrics, GmbH, in Berlin provides statistics and data quality assurance for medical studies. The company is run by Chris Tismer, the initiator and administrator of the Python Starship (*http://starship.python.net*), a web site that provides home pages to many of the most interesting Python extensions.

When drugs are being tested, case report forms are prepared on each patient in the study with literally hundreds of measurements of all kinds. Data needs to be keyboarded twice, normalized somehow, and analyzed, with the final result being a 100+ page report summarizing the data. Applied Biometrics automates the whole process with Python and Office, Access databases are built for each study, and the analysis and reporting are handled by Python scripts. The data never arrives all at once, so the whole process must be automated and repeatable.

In 1997, Applied Biometrics took on a challenge no other rival would touch: try to combine everything known about a certain drug into one comprehensive database. Studies ranged from controlled short-term lab tests (few patients, same things measured on each) to badly kept patient diaries from thousands of patients. Data sources also varied from AB's own keyboarded data to tables from statistical packages and even text files to be parsed. Andy Robinson helped to formulate an overall approach in the early stages.

It was necessary to find an approach that allowed medical and statistics graduates with little programming experience to write data-laundering scripts. We came up with the concept of a data warehouse of very general measurements (of a variable, on a patient, at a point in time). The *Dataset* concept was developed, and we wrote methods to provide common geometric operations—slicing and dicing by column or row, transposing, grouping, and detabulating. The students were able to understand these basic operations and write scripts to launder individual databases. The end product was a stream of measurements that went through a verification funnel before entering a target database.

Chris has been optimizing this system for two years, and knows more about controlling Word and Access from Python than anyone. The current system builds a database of 315,000 measurements from 29 different source databases in 50 minutes.

```
{'ClientID': 'MEGAWAD',
 'Comments': None,
 'Consultant': 'Joe Hacker',
 'DatePaid': None,
 'ExpenseDetails': None,
 'Expenses': 0.0,
 'HourlyRate': 50.0,
```

```
         'Hours': 42.0,
         'InvoiceDate': 1999-04-15 00:00:00.00,
         'InvoiceID': 199904001,
         'PeriodEnding': 1999-04-18 00:00:00.00,
         'TaxRate': 0.175}
     >>>
```

You can now modify this easily, overwriting, dropping, and adding keys as needed. It's also possible to build powerful relational joins in a few lines of code using Python dictionaries; that is part of what Gadfly does.

When you want to do the opposite, tabulate a list of dictionaries easily by specifying the keys you want. The next function creates dictionaries:

```
def DataSetFromDicts(dictlist, keylist=None):
                              # tabulates shared keys
    if not keylist:           # take all the keys
        all_key_dict = dictlist[0]
        for dict in dictlist:
            all_key_dict.update(dict)
        keylist = all_key_dict.keys()
        keylist.sort()        # better than random order
    ds = DataSet()
    ds.fieldnames = tuple(keylist)
    for dict in dictlist:     # loop over rows
        row = []
        for key in keylist:   # loop over fields
            try:
                value = dict[key]
            except:
                value = None
            row.append(value)
        ds.data.append(tuple(row))
    return ds
```

If you supply a list of the keys you want, this function builds a **Dataset** with columns to match; if you omit the keys, it shows the set of all keys found in all dictionaries. This can be used as follows:

```
>>> pc1 = {'Name':'Yosemite', 'Maker':'Carrera','Speed':266}
>>> pc2 = {'Name':'Tahoe', 'Maker':'Gateway','Memory':64}
>>> pc3 = {'Name':'Gogarth','Maker':'NeXT','Speed':25,'Elegance':'Awesome'}
>>> pc4 = {'Name':'BoxHill','Maker':'Psion','Memory':2}
>>> my_kit = [pc1,pc2,pc3,pc4]
>>> comparison = laundry.DataSetFromDicts(my_kit,
... ['Name','Model','Memory']
... )
...
>>> comparison.pp()
('Name', 'Model', 'Memory')
('BoxHill', None, 2)
('Tahoe', None, 64)
('Gogarth', None, None)
('BoxHill', None, 2)
>>>
```

You now have the ability to move back and forth from a tabular to a dictionary representation.

Inserting Data into the Destination Database

Sooner or later you need to pump data into a destination database. We've already seen how DBAPI-compliant modules allow us to insert a list of tuples at one time, and how this provides optimal performance. In a case such as a data warehouse, the number of destination tables and fields will be quite small so it's no trouble to build the SQL statements by hand for each table; and we already have the list of tuples ready to go:

```
mycursor.executemany(MyTableStatement, MyDataSet.data)
```

Where there are many destination tables, a shortcut can be taken if the field names are simple and match the underlying database well; you can write a routine that uses the field names in the `DataSet` and generates an SQL `INSERT` statement to match.

Often there are better ways to bulk-load data. The important thing is to know that you have correctly structured `DataSets` for the destination database; if that's true, you can often save them to a tab- or comma-delimited file and use the database's bulk-load facility with far greater speed.

A Three-Tier Architecture with Business Objects

For our final example of what Python can do with data, we'll look at how Python supports building a three-tier client/server architecture. This will be a fairly straightforward example, as we did a lot of the groundwork in the last section.

Simple database applications have two tiers: database and user interface. A dialog to maintain client details might perform a `SELECT` query to get all the details of a customer and store those details in the user interface; either directly in text boxes, or in variables stored in the same form or module. When the data has been changed, the system performs an `UPDATE` query to store the results.

A three-tier architecture creates a `Customer` class to hold the information, and provides functions to load customers from the database and store them back to it. The GUI layer gets data from the `Customer` objects. Objects in the middle layer are often known as *business objects*, because they model things in the business or problem domain, rather than systems objects like database connections, or GUI objects like queries. If you are writing object-oriented programs, you're already at work on the business objects.

Three-tier also describes network partitioning. With modern distributed-object technologies such as COM and CORBA (and some much lighter alternatives like Python's `RemoteCall` package), it's easy to run the database on one machine, the business objects on another, and the GUI on a third. It's highly likely that your `Customer` object will pop up in many parts of the application, so the three-tier approach is much better for all but the simplest application. There's a lot of marketing hype about this. We'll just focus on the logical aspects.

Real-life databases need lots of tables to represent a business object such as a customer or an invoice. Similarly, the objects in memory are bound to have references to other objects and lists of subobjects; a `Customer` object may provide access to a list of invoices, and a list of correspondence items received. There is a lot of work involved in building class hierarchies and tables to match each other and code to fetch and store the right records at the right time. Furthermore, every change in the database may necessitate changing and recompiling your business object code, and vice versa.

Not with Python! Python's dynamic nature makes it possible to dramatically reduce the dependencies between database and business objects.

Dynamic Attributes

We saw in Chapter 6, *A Financial Modeling Toolkit in Python,* that Python objects can hold any attributes you want, in addition to those defined for the class. Any Python object's attributes and methods are held in a hidden, internal dictionary. And we have just learned how to fetch those!

The simplest way to construct an object from a database is to use an almost-empty class. Remember you can add attributes at runtime to a Python class as follows:

```
>>> class DumbDbRecord:
...     pass
...
>>> r1 = DumbDbRecord()
>>> r1.CustomerID = 1234
>>> r1.Name = 'Pythonics Inc.'
>>>
```

It would be easy to examine a database cursor and add all attributes to an object such as this, creating a handy database record object with a clean syntax. However, this approach carries a weakness. You presumably will want to write objects that have attributes and methods important to the functioning of the program, and to keep them separate from data fetched from the database. We've therefore defined a class that can accept a dictionary of fields and values and keep them separate from its own attributes.

A helpful piece of Python magic is the ability to trap attribute access. We saw in Chapter 6 that a Python object can monitor attempts to set or get its attributes. If

you ask an instance of this next class for an attribute it can't find, it goes and
checks in the dictionary it got from the database:

```
class Record:
    #holds arbitrary database data
    def __init__(self):
        self._dbdata = {}

    def loadFromDict(self, aDict):
        "accept all attributes in the dictionary"
        self._dbdata.update(aDict)

    def getData(self):
        return self._dbdata.copy()

    def pp(self):
        "pretty-print my database data"
        pprint(self._dbdata)

    def __getattr__(self, key):
        """This is called if the object lacks the attribute.
        If the key is not found, it raises an error in the
        same way that the attribute access would were no
        __getattr__ method present.  """
        return self._dbdata[key]
```

Now you can use it to represent any kind of object you want and access the variables with the most natural syntax:

```
>>> import laundry
>>> pc_dict = {'Name':'Yosemite', 'Maker':'Carrera','Speed':266}
>>> rec = laundry.Record()
>>> rec.loadFromDict(pc_dict)
>>> rec.Maker
'Carrera'
>>> rec.Speed
266
>>>
```

It's easy to extend **DataSet** to get a list of objects rather than dictionaries, and
your data-manipulation code will be extremely readable. Furthermore, you can
derive many of the **INSERT** and **UPDATE** statements you need automatically.

If you use this class and populate it with the results of a query, whenever someone adds a database field to the Customers table, your objects acquire the new data
attribute automatically. If someone deletes a database field the program needs, your
code will need fixing (Python is powerful, but not telepathic) but your model can
be made reasonably robust against the deletion on information fields as well.*

---

* Some Python GUI libraries, such as Tkinter, make it easy to build dialogs dynamically as well, so that
  the edit boxes displayed on a customer dialog could also depend on the available data.

Lazy Fetches

The examples in this chapter used two tables, one of clients and one of invoices, with a master-detail relationship. In terms of objects, you'd say that a client has a list of related invoices. However, it might be expensive to fetch these every time when a user might want to see them only some of the time.

Let's implement a *lazy fetch* to get the data on demand. This `Customer` class inherits from our `Record` class. Given a database connection, it fetches its main attributes when explicitly asked, but the invoice list is retrieved on demand:

```python
class Customer(Record):
    def __getattr__(self, key):
        #trap attempts to fetch the list of invoices
        if key == 'Invoices':
            self.fetchInvoices()
            return self.Invoices
        else:
            #call the inherited method
            return Record.__getattr__(self, key)

    def fetch(self, conn, key):
        self.conn = conn
        cursor = self.conn.cursor()
        cursor.execute("SELECT * FROM Clients \
                    WHERE ClientID = '%s'" % key)
        dicts = DataSetFromCursor(cursor).asDicts()
        assert len(dicts) == 1, 'Error fetching data!'
        self.loadFromDict(dicts[0])

    def fetchInvoices(self):
        #presumes an attribute pointing to the database
        cursor = self.conn.cursor()
        cursor.execute("SELECT * FROM Invoices \
                    WHERE ClientID = '%s'" % self.ClientID)
        ds = DataSetFromCursor(cursor)
        self.Invoices = ds.asObjects()
```

Using this class is straightforward:

```python
>>> c = laundry.Customer()
>>> c.fetch(conn, 'MEGAWAD')     # assume an open connection
>>> c.CompanyName                # see if we got data...
'MegaWad Investments'
>>> c.pp()                       # let's see all the fields
{'Address1': '1 St. Fredericks-Le-Grand',
 'Address2': 'London EC1A 8AB',
 'Address3': None,
 'Address4': None,
 'ClientID': 'MEGAWAD',
 'CompanyName': 'MegaWad Investments',
 'ContactName': 'Hachiro Kobayashi'}
>>> len(c.Invoices)              # trigger another fetch
```

```
4
>>> c.Invoices[0].Hours        # access a child object
42.0
>>>
```

The example so far only fetches data. The __setattr__() method lets you trap attempts to set attributes in an analogous way, which you can use to update field lists, type-check arguments, and keep track of whether an object has changed and so needs updates posted back to the database.

It's possible in Python to build an even more general data-driven object framework, where you declared some mapping of objects to database rows, along with the names of classes to use and the relationships between database tables, and let Python build an entire web of objects on demand.

Conclusion

The various integration technologies in Python make it easy to acquire data from any database. ODBC is our favorite because it turns the data into Python variables with the greatest speed and least lines of code; however, we have shown you how to get connected with a wide range of tools.

Once you fetch the data, manipulating it is easy in Python. Python objects can hold numbers, strings, and dates; and sets of data can be represented in native Python lists and tuples. This means the data is right there in front of you; there's no need to loop over the properties of Recordset objects or cursors.

In this chapter, we have shown how to build the beginnings of a powerful toolkit for transforming and manipulating data in Python. This makes it easy to switch between different representations of data, as rows, dictionaries of keys and values, or objects.

Python is particularly well suited to writing data-laundering scripts and to constructing dynamic object models on top of a database.

References

There is a Python Database Topic Guide at *http://www.python.org/topics/database/* with many useful pointers.

mxODBC lives at *http://starship.python.net/crew/lemburg/mxODBC.html*.

Gadfly lives at *http://www.chordate.com/gadfly.html*.

For those interested in ODBC internals and capabilities, SolidTech include a full ODBC manual with their documentation at *http://www.solidtech.com/devzone/manuals/*.

Access Database Design and Programming by Steven Roman (O'Reilly) provides an excellent introduction to relational database concepts, SQL, and the formal operations on which it's built. It also provides a complete reference to Microsoft Access SQL (including the Data Definition Language) and to the DAO object hierarchy.

The Data Warehouse Toolkit by Ralph Kimball (John Wiley & Sons) is the definitive text on its subject and an excellent introduction to what goes on in real-world database projects.

14

Working with Email

Email is everywhere these days and is so simple, it can be used for many tasks beyond personal communications. It is not uncommon to find a program that sends an email to an administrator when it encounters some critical situation. Forms on the Web often run a simple CGI script that send the details to a specific email address. Once the volume of these emails increase, an automated script may process the mailbox and further process the messages according to some criteria based on the email contents.

For these and many other reasons, it is not a surprise to find that working with email is a common task, particularly for scripting languages. There are many email systems in use, including SMTP/POP3 facilities, Microsoft Exchange Server, and IBM's Domino (previously known as Lotus Notes) among others.

In this chapter, we look at some common techniques for working with email on Windows. For each technology, we develop short examples that send an email and then attempt to get that same mail back.

SMTP and POP3

SMTP is an acronym for Simple Mail Transfer Protocol. This is an Internet standard, specified in RFC-821, and as its name implies, is a protocol for transferring mail messages. When an SMTP server receives a piece of mail, it does one of two things: forwards the email to a host closer to the intended recipient, or if the recipient is local, places the email in the recipient's mailbox. Thus, SMTP provides a technique for putting messages in a mailbox, but it doesn't define a technique for retrieving existing messages from a mailbox. To this end, the Post Office Protocol, Version 3 (POP3) has been designed, as specified in RFC-1725. Its explicit purpose is to allow remote access to a mailbox managed on a remote computer.

In practice, this means that SMTP can send Internet email, and POP3 can retrieve Internet email.

As is common for Internet protocols, both mail protocols use a simple conversation between a client and a server. This conversation is "line-based" (meaning all commands and responses are sent as complete lines) and works exclusively with 7-bit ASCII data. Each protocol defines its own special command and response sequence to support its various options.

The mail messages handled by both these protocols must be formatted as specified in various RFCs, starting with RFC-822, to the latest, which is RFC-1521. In a nutshell, these RFCs define the format of the *message header* (a list of headers for the message, including the subject, recipient information, etc.), and the *message body*. The message body must consist of 7-bit ASCII and may optionally include a number of different sections. These sections typically encode binary attachments or alternative renderings of the message text. Messages with multiple sections are typically referred to as Multipurpose Internet Mail Extensions (MIME) messages. Unfortunately, MIME is a complex beast and beyond the scope of this chapter. Python does support various MIME standards, but using and packing everything into an email message is not for the faint hearted. If you have this requirement, and Microsoft Exchange or a slightly higher-level email system is available, you should consider using that.

Sending an SMTP Message

To begin, we'll use Python to send a simple message using the SMTP protocol. Our message will contain the minimum number of message headers, a plain ASCII message body, and no attachments.

To assist in this task, we'll use the Python module `smtplib`. This module contains a single class, `SMTP`, that manages the connection with the SMTP server and provides useful methods for interacting with the server.

Sending a simple message using SMTP is so simple it's not worth writing a sample source file for this purpose; you can do it at the interactive window. The `SMTP` class provides the following method:

```
bad_addresses = sendmail( from, to, message )
```

from
>   A string with the address of the sender.

to
>   A list of strings, one for each recipient.

message
>   A message as a string formatted as specified in the various RFCs.

So all you need is the message itself, a list of recipients, and your own email address.

As per RFC-822, the format of the message is simple. It consists of a list of message headers, followed by a blank line, followed by the message body. For this demonstration, you can set up a message with the following code:

```
>>> msg="Subject: Hi from Python\n\nHello."
```

Define the subject of the message as "Hi from Python" and the body as "Hello."

Next, define a variable with your email address and SMTP host:

```
>>> address="MHammond@skippinet.com.au"
>>> host="mail-hub"
```

And send the message to yourself:

```
>>> import smtplib
>>> s=smtplib.SMTP(host)
>>> s.sendmail(address, [address], msg)
{}
```

The result from this function is a dictionary of email addresses in the *to* list that failed; the dictionary is keyed by the email address, with the error message as the value. In this example you received an empty dictionary, so everything went OK. See the `smtplib` module documentation for more information on error handling.

Receiving via POP3

POP3 downloads messages from a remote mailbox. As we discussed previously, SMTP is used typically to send Internet email messages, and POP3 receives them.

Like most Internet protocols, POP3 uses a line-based communications protocol, and also like most Internet protocols, you will find a Python module designed to ease working with that protocol; in this case the Python module is `poplib`.

Before delving into a discussion of POP3, it is worth noting that an improved protocol known as Internet Message Access Protocol (IMAP) has been designed. Although this fixes many of the shortcomings in the POP3 protocol, it's not used as widely as POP3. Therefore, we will discuss using POP3 to ensure the code works on the widest possible range of mail servers. If you need to investigate using the IMAP protocol, you should view the module `imaplib` and its associated documentation.

There are three steps to establishing a connection to a POP3 mailbox:

1. Connect to the server by creating a `poplib.POP3()` instance, specifying the hostname.

2. Send the mailbox account name, using the `user()` method.

3. Send the mailbox password using the `pass_()` method (`pass` is a reserved word in Python, hence the trailing underscore).

You now have a valid connection, and the mailbox is locked. While the mailbox is locked, no other connections are possible, so it's important to unlock the mailbox when you're done using the `quit()` method. If you don't unlock the mailbox, other mail clients (such as your regular email client) won't be able to connect until the connection times out, which may take some time. It would be appropriate to use a Python `finally` block for this purpose, as the example will show.

POP3 messages are numbered from 1–n, where n is the number of messages currently in the mailbox. Obviously, these message numbers are not unique and are valid only for the given session. So the first step to reading the mailbox is to determine the number of messages in the mailbox using the `stat()` method. Then you can request each message by number. For the first example, don't bother looping over all the messages, but, instead, just look at the first message:

```
# DumpPop.py - Dumps the first message in a POP3 mailbox.
import sys
import poplib

def DumpAPopMessage(host, user, password):
    # Establish a connection to the POP server.
    a = poplib.POP3(host)
    # Note we print the server response, although not necessary!
    print a.user(user)
    print a.pass_(password)
    # The mailbox is now locked - ensure we unlock it!
    try:
        (numMsgs, totalSize) = a.stat()
        if numMsgs == 0:
            print "Sorry - there are no messages in the mailbox"
        else:
            (server_msg, body, octets) = a.retr(1)
            print "Server Message:", server_msg
            print "Number of Octets:", octets
            print "Message body:"
            for line in body:
                print line
    finally:
        print a.quit()

if __name__=='__main__':
    if len(sys.argv)<4:
        print "Usage:", sys.argv[0], "host username password"
    else:
        DumpAPopMessage(sys.argv[1], sys.argv[2], sys.argv[3])
```

As you can see, the example expects you to pass the hostname, the username, and password on the command line. You can test the script from the command prompt, as the following output shows:

```
C:\Scripts>DumpPop.py pop-server mhammond topsecret
+OK Password required for mhammond
+OK mhammond's maildrop has 1 messages (1730 octets)
Server Message: +OK 1730 octets
Number of Octets: 1730
Message body:
Return-Path: <MHammond@skippinet.com.au>
Received: from mr4.vic-remote.bigpond.net.au ([24.192.1.19])
          by m5.bigpond.net.au (Netscape Messaging Server 3.54)  with ESMTP
          id AAA26FD for <mhammond@vic.bigpond.net.au>;
          Thu, 15 Jul 1999 21:01:30 +1000
...
Importance: Normal
X-MimeOLE: Produced By Microsoft MimeOLE V4.72.3110.3

Hello
+OK m5.bigpond.net.au POP3 server closing connection

C:\Scripts>
```

This is the same message you sent previously. Notice all the headers this message now has; even though you specified only a few, the mail transport system has added many more. The output shown has had many headers removed for brevity.

At this point you may start to get a little worried. Looking at the code, you can see the message is returned as a list of lines, but many of those lines are headers. Worse, some of the headers are split over multiple lines (as supported by the relevant RFC). Does this mean you need to understand all this before doing anything useful?

Fortunately, Python has library support for parsing and using data of this format. The most basic support can be found in the **rfc822.Message** class, but the **mimetools** module supports an extension to this class that supports the various MIME extensions (as described earlier). Since MIME is an extension to the basic standard, you can safely use it even for non-MIME messages.

A slight complication is that the **mimetools.Message()** class expects to receive a file object from which it obtains its data, rather than a list of lines! The **StringIO** (or **cStringIO**) module can make a file object from a string, but there is a list of strings. The simplest solution is to join the list back into a huge string and feed that into **cStringIO**.

Once you create **mimetools.Message()**, all the headers are read, and the file is positioned at the start of the body. You can then use the various methods to examine the headers. Depending on the message content, you can either read the rest of the file to obtain the body or use some of the MIME-specific features to process the various sections.

You can now modify the example to take advantage of this class. Loop over all messages in the mailbox and examine the Subject header for the test message. When you find the message, print the message body and delete the message.

The significant additions to the new example are:

- A loop to examine all the messages.

- Using cStringIO to create a file object as discussed.

- Examine the Subject header of each message using the getheader() method.

- Delete the message with the dele() method of the POP3 session.

```python
# DumpPop2.py - Dumps and deletes a test message from a POP3 mailbox.
import sys
import poplib
import string
import mimetools
import cStringIO

def DumpAPopMessage(host, user, password):
    # Establish a connection to the POP server.
    a = poplib.POP3(host)
    # Note we print the server response, although not necessary!
    print a.user(user)
    print a.pass_(password)
    # The mailbox is now locked - ensure we unlock it!
    try:
        (numMsgs, totalSize) = a.stat()
        for thisNum in range(1, numMsgs+1):
            (server_msg, body, octets) = a.retr(1)
            # Create a file like object suitable for the
            # mimetools.Message class.
            pseudo_file = cStringIO.StringIO(string.join(body, '\n'))
            msg = mimetools.Message(pseudo_file)
            if msg.getheader("Subject")=="Hi from Python":
                print "Found our test message"
                print "Body is", `pseudo_file.read()`
                print a.dele(thisNum)
                print "Message deleted!"
    finally:
        print a.quit()

if __name__=='__main__':
    if len(sys.argv)<4:
        print "Usage:", sys.argv[0], "host username password"
    else:
        DumpAPopMessage(sys.argv[1], sys.argv[2], sys.argv[3])
```

You can run this example using parameters identical to the previous example:

```
C:\Scripts>DumpPop2.py pop-server mhammond topsecret
+OK Password required for mhammond
+OK mhammond's maildrop has 1 messages (1243 octets)
Found our test message
Body is 'Hello'
```

```
+OK Message 1 deleted
Message deleted!
+OK m5.bigpond.net.au POP3 server closing connection
C:\Scripts>
```

If you experiment with this code, you'll see that the **Message** class has correctly handled the continuation of long header lines. Working with the message headers is made far simpler with the **mimetools.Message** class and worth the small hoops you need to jump through to use it.

Microsoft Exchange/Outlook

The use of Microsoft messaging products is becoming quite common in larger organizations. The Microsoft Exchange Server is often used at the backend, and various versions of Microsoft Exchange or Microsoft Outlook may be used as the client.

One key feature of Microsoft Exchange is that it exposes a rich and powerful API developers can use to extend their applications. Tasks such as form processing, or processing appointments or contact lists, can all be accessed from a COM interface. Although we will only discuss sending a simple message using Microsoft Exchange, you should peruse the documentation supplied with Exchange to get a feel for its capabilities.

Collaboration Data Objects

Collaboration Data Objects (CDO) is a general-purpose COM automation interface for working with Microsoft Exchange. Because CDO is an automation interface, it's suitable for use with scripting languages, such as Visual Basic, JavaScript, and of course, Python.

CDO has gone through various name changes over its long life. Its evolution can be traced through "Simple MAPI," a set of APIs for Visual Basic 1, through a more general-purpose Visual Basic Extension (VBX), then into a general-purpose COM interface known as Active Messaging, and finally receiving even more features and being renamed CDO.

It provides a rich object model; there are objects for messages, folders, users, distribution lists, etc. The object model is "rooted" from a MAPI session object. The session object identifies the mailbox and provides a list of subfolders, each of which has its own list of messages and subfolders.

First, let's experiment with MAPI from a Python prompt. Create a MAPI session using the standard COM technique:

```
>>> from win32com.client import Dispatch
>>> s=Dispatch("Mapi.Session")
>>>
```

Then log on to the MAPI session. This presents a dialog box to authenticate the session:

```
>>> s.Logon()
>>>
```

By consulting the documentation for the MAPI session object, you can see there is an **Inbox** property, which is a **Folder** object. You can see how many messages this folder contains:

```
>>> len(s.Inbox.Messages)
304
```

And look at the first one:

```
>>> s.Inbox.Messages.Item(1).Subject
'Free WinZip Self-Extractor 2.1 Upgrade'
```

 Because the **Item()** method is the default method for a **Messages** object, you can use a shortcut to access it. It's possible to use the syntax:

```
>>> s.Inbox.Messages[1].Subject
'Free WinZip Self-Extractor 2.1 Upgrade'
```

However, since we are indirectly calling the **Item()** method and documentation is found under the method name, we'll stick to the slightly longer version.

Sending a message with CDO

The procedure to send an email with CDO is simple; create a new message in the outbox, set the message's properties, and send it. Let's do this interactively using the session object created previously. First, create a new message in the outbox using the **Add()** method. The CDO documentation states that this takes two parameters: the subject of the message and the text of the message:

```
>>> newMsg = s.Outbox.Messages.Add("Hi from Python", "Hello")
>>>
```

Now add a single recipient using the message's **Recipients** property. The **Recipients.Add()** method takes two parameters: the display name of the recipient and the email address. Note that the email address must be prefixed with the Exchange Transport to be used; in this case, use the SMTP transport for Internet email addresses:

```
>>> recip = newMsg.Recipients.Add("Mark Hammond", "SMTP:MHammond@skippinet.com.
au")
>>>
```

And send the message:

```
>>> newMsg.Send()
>>>
```

Now the message is sitting in the outbox, waiting to be delivered. Depending on the local configuration options, it may be some time before the next scheduled connection for delivery and receipt of mail. You can force this by calling the `DeliverNow()` method on the session:

```
>>> s.DeliverNow()
>>>
```

Retrieving a message with CDO

Now that we have sent out message using Microsoft Exchange, let's write a few lines to read the message back. Depending on the speed of your email server and the route the email takes before getting back, it may take some time for the mail to be returned. At any time you can force the client to connect to the server to check for new messages by calling the `DeliverNow()` method.

The first thing to do is print the subject of the last message in the inbox:

```
>>> print s.Inbox.Messages[len(s.Inbox.Messages)].Subject
Hi from Python
>>>
```

Another demonstration would be to loop over all messages in the inbox, find the test message sent previously, and delete it. CDO provides special methods for iterating over all messages, in either a forward or reverse direction. You could even allow CDO to perform additional filtering of the message, but for now, try it for yourself.

The methods we will use for iterating are `GetFirst()` and `GetNext()`. These are methods of a **Messages** collection, so the first thing to do is save the **Messages** collection to a local variable:

```
>>> messages = s.Inbox.Messages
```

You can then write a loop checking each message, and when you find one to delete, call the `Delete()` method on the message. Here's the code:

```
>>> msg = messages.GetFirst()
>>> while msg is not None:
...     if msg.Subject == "Hi from Python":
...         print "Deleting msg from", msg.Sender.Name
...         msg.Delete()
...     msg = messages.GetNext()
...
Deleting msg from Mark Hammond
>>>
```

As you can see, the code found and deleted exactly one message. CDO exposes a rich object model for folders and messages; every property imaginable about a message can be obtained. See the CDO documentation for more details.

Conclusion

In this chapter, we presented a quick overview of two common mail systems used on Windows: Internet email and Microsoft Exchange.

The protocols defined by the various standards are still the most common in use for Windows. Many Windows users use email only through an Internet service provider, and the vast majority of these provide email servers that use the POP3 and SMTP protocols. We presented enough information for you to have a basic understanding of these protocols, and how to make use of them from Python. For further information, you should consult the Python documentation on these Python modules.

In many corporate Windows environments, Microsoft Exchange is the mail server of choice. Although Microsoft Exchange generally supports the Internet protocols, it also supports a far more flexible and simple interface using COM. If you work in an Exchange environment, we've given you enough information to get started with the rich model exposed by Exchange. For more information, see the CDO documentation at *http://www.microsoft.com/exchange.*

15

Using the Basic Internet Protocols

Python grew up around the same time as the Internet. For the first few years, both Python and the Internet ran mainly on various flavors of Unix. Therefore, it's no surprise to find that Python has excellent support for most of the common Internet protocols in use today. Fortunately, this heritage has moved to the Windows platform.

This chapter shows how to use many of the common Internet protocols from Python on Windows. For information on the SMTP mail protocol, see Chapter 14, *Working with Email*.

HTTP and HTML

The Hypertext Transfer Protocol (HTTP) is one of the most widely used Internet Protocols. Anyone who has ever used a web browser has used HTTP. HTTP is a protocol for moving data across a network. Most often, the data is formatted as Hypertext Markup Language (HTML). Thus, HTTP defines how to obtain the data, and HTML defines how the data is arranged.

An HTTP server program is run on a computer set up to accept connections from client computers. The client computer connects to the HTTP server, issues a request for some content (typically a filename), and tells the server the type of data it wishes to receive. The HTTP server locates the content, and sends the data back to the client computer. The data consists of a number of headers (lines that describe the data) and the data itself. A full description of the HTTP protocol can be found on the Web at *http://www.w3.org/hypertext/WWW/Protocols/*.

Fetching Data via HTTP

The Python module `httplib` defines a class for fetching data via HTTP. As is typical with Python, only a few lines of code are needed to fetch a document via HTTP. Let's experiment with it from an interactive Python session.

First, import the Python module and instantiate the HTTP class. The HTTP class requires the name of the server you wish to connect to. Let's connect to the Python home page:

```
>>> import httplib
>>> http=httplib.HTTP('www.python.org')
>>>
```

Now you need to tell the remote server the data to retrieve and the data formats to accept. Ask the server to fetch the main index page and designate whether to accept plain text or HTML text:

```
>>> http.putrequest('GET', '/index.html')
>>> http.putheader('Accept', 'text/html')
>>> http.putheader('Accept', 'text/plain')
>>> http.endheaders()
>>>
```

All that remains is to ask for the data. The **getreply()** method does this, and returns three items: the error code, the error message, and the headers sent by the server. Make this call and print the result:

```
>>> errcode, errmsg, headers = http.getreply()
>>> print errcode, errmsg, headers
200 OK <mimetools.Message instance at 1073680>
>>>
```

HTTP defines the code 200 as success, and it's reflected in the error message. The **headers** object retrieved is an instance of another Python class. This Python class can be used in the same way as a Python dictionary, so let's see what it contains:

```
>>> len(headers)
8
```

There are eight headers from the server. You can loop and print them all, using standard Python dictionary semantics:

```
>>> for key, value in headers.items():
...     print key, "=", value
...
server = Apache/1.2.0
content-type = text/html
accept-ranges = bytes
date = Wed, 13 Jan 1999 06:41:15 GMT
connection = close
etag = "f4d6-2d66-369294d0"
content-length = 11622
```

```
last-modified = Tue, 05 Jan 1999 22:40:16 GMT
>>>
```

This reveals some interesting facts about the server, including the date the home page was last modified and the HTTP server software used. The `content-length` header says how many bytes are in the data itself. The `getfile()` method can obtain a file that can read the data:

```
>>> file=http.getfile()
>>>
```

But rather than print all 11 KB of data, you can check to see that you do indeed have all the data:

```
>>> print len(file.read())
11622
```

Reading the file gives the exact number of bytes expected. Obviously, you can do something useful with this data, such as write it to a local file.

Serving Data via HTTP

Python can also act as an HTTP server. The standard Python library contains a number of modules to act as the basis for your own HTTP server; in fact, it even comes with a basic HTTP server all ready to go.

SimpleHTTPServer.py

The Python module *SimpleHTTPServer.py* implements, as its name suggests, a simple HTTP server. For information on how to run this server, open *SimpleHTTPServer.py* in any text editor, and read the instructions.

Implementing an HTTP redirector

As an example, let's implement our own special HTTP server. Our HTTP server functions similarly to a proxy server: it accepts requests and redirects those requests to another server. For example, if you ask the server to redirect to *www. python.org*, that server appears to have the same content as *www.python.org*. Thus, people can access *www.python.org* via our server.

The implementation is straightforward. Extend the basic Python HTTP server code, but instead of searching for the file, simply open a HTTP connection to the remote server and redirect the data to your own client:

```
# HTTPRedirector.py
# An HTTP Server that redirects all requests to a named, remote server.
# BaseHTTPServer provides the basic HTTP Server functionality.

import BaseHTTPServer
```

```
# httplib establishes our connection to the remote server
import httplib

import socket # For the error!

# The server we are redirecting to.
g_RemoteServerName = "www.python.org"

class HTTPRedirector(BaseHTTPServer.BaseHTTPRequestHandler):
    # This function is called when a client makes a GET request
    # ie, it wants the headers, and the data.
    def do_GET(self):
        srcfile = self.send_headers("GET")
        if srcfile:
            # Copy the data from the remote server
            # back to the client.
            BLOCKSIZE = 8192
            while 1:
                # Read a block from the remote.
                data = srcfile.read(BLOCKSIZE)
                if not data: break
                self.wfile.write(data)

            srcfile.close()

    # This function is called when a client makes a HEAD request
    # i.e., it only wants the headers, not the data.
    def do_HEAD(self):
        srcfile = self.send_headers("HEAD")
        if srcfile:
            srcfile.close()

    # A private function which handles all the redirection logic.
    def send_headers(self, request):
        # Establish a remote connection
        try:
            http = httplib.HTTP(g_RemoteServerName)
        except socket.error, problem:
            print "Error - Cannot connect to %s: %s" \
                    % (g_RemoteServerName, problem)
            return
        # Resend all the headers we retrieved in the request.
        http.putrequest(request, self.path)
        for header, val in self.headers.items():
            http.putheader(header, val)
        http.endheaders()
        # Now get the response from the remote server
        errcode, errmsg, headers = http.getreply()
        self.send_response(errcode, errmsg)
        # Send the headers back to the client.
        for header, val in headers.items():
            self.send_header(header, val)
        self.end_headers()
        if errcode==200:
            return http.getfile()
```

```
if __name__=='__main__':
    print "Redirecting HTTP requests to", g_RemoteServerName
    BaseHTTPServer.test(HTTPRedirector)
```

To test the server, simply execute the script:

```
C:\Scripts>python HTTPRedirector.py
Redirecting HTTP requests to www.python.org
Serving HTTP on port 8000 ...
```

Now you can establish a connection to the server. Note the server is using port 8000 for requests. Since this is not the default HTTP port, you need to specify it in your URL. Open your browser and enter the following URL: *http://localhost:8000/*.

If you look at the server window, you see the following messages as the page is delivered to the browser:

```
localhost - - [13/Jan/1999 22:08:31] "GET /pics/PyBanner004.gif HTTP/1.1" 200 -
localhost - - [13/Jan/1999 22:08:47] "GET /pics/PythonPoweredSmall.gif HTTP/1.1"
200 -
localhost - - [13/Jan/1999 22:09:03] "GET /pics/pythonHi.gif HTTP/1.1" 200 -
...
```

And the Python home page appears in the browser!

FTP

The File Transfer Protocol (FTP) transfers files across a network. The Python module `ftplib` supports this protocol. An FTP server program is run on a computer client computers can connect to. The client computer sendsty5e transfer is initiated, a new connection exclusively for the data is established between the client and the server.

Fetching Data via FTP

The `ftplib` module is used in much the same way as the `httplib` module: a single class, FTP, provides all of the functionality.

The FTP protocol supports a variety of commands, which include such operations as logging in, navigating the filesystem, and retrieving directory listings. Let's create an FTP session:

```
>>> import ftplib
>>> ftp = ftplib.FTP('ftp.python.org') # connect to host, default port
>>>
```

Log on as an anonymous user:

```
>>> ftp.login('anonymous', 'your@email.address')
"230-WELCOME to python.org, the Python programming language ..."
>>>
```

Get a directory listing:

```
>>> ftp.retrlines('LIST') # list directory contents
total 38
drwxrwxr-x  11 root       4127          512 Aug 28 20:23 .
...
-r--r--r--   1 klm        1000          764 Aug 25 19:32 welcome.msg
'226 Transfer complete.'
```

Notice there's a file *welcome.msg*: let's download the file. Open a local file and indicate its **write** method should be called to store the data:

```
>>> file=open("welcome.msg", "w")
>>> ftp.retrlines("retr welcome.msg", file.write)
'226 Transfer complete.'
>>> file.close()
```

Now reopen the file and print the data:

```
>>> open("welcome.msg", "r").read()
"WELCOME to python.org, the Python programming language home site. ..."
>>>
```

To retrieve a binary file (such as an executable), you could use the method **retrbinary()**; it takes the same methods as **retrlines()**, except it also allows you to specify a block size for the transfer. In this case you should remember to open the file itself in binary mode, as discussed in Chapter 3, *Python on Windows*.

NNTP

The Network News Transfer Protocol (NNTP) exchanges news articles over a network. Whenever you run a news reader, it uses the NNTP protocol to read and post news articles.

An NNTP server program is run on a computer client computers can connect to. The NNTP protocol is text-based: all communications between the client and server use ASCII text. The NNTP protocol is similar to the SMTP mail protocol we discussed in the previous chapter. Clients send requests or news articles, and the server responds with responses and possibly a news article. News articles are structured similar to Internet mail messages; the body of the article follows a list of headers.

Fetching News Articles via NNTP

It should come as no surprise that a Python module **nntplib** supports the NNTP protocol. Following the style of the other Internet-related modules, a single class **NNTP** implements all functionality.

The NNTP protocol supports a wide variety of commands for determining which articles exist on the server computer. Information on these commands is beyond the scope of this book; you should refer to the NNTP protocol standard or the `nntplib` module itself for further information.

However, to whet your appetite, let's create a sample program that scans a newsgroup for a list of articles with a specific word in their subject. It generates an HTML file, then fires your browser with the news articles hyperlinked:

```python
# SimpleNewsViewer.py

# Finds all news articles in a news group that have a specific word
# in its subject.  Then writes the results to a HTML file for
# easy reading.

# eg, running:
# c:\> SimpleNewsViewer.py comp.lang.python python
#
# Will generate "comp.lang.python.html", and execute your
# browser on this file.

import sys, string

import nntplib

import win32api # to execute our browser.

g_newsserver = 'news-server.c3.telstra-mm.net.au'

def MakeNewsPage(groupname, subjectsearch, outfile ):
    print "Connecting..."
    nntp=nntplib.NNTP(g_newsserver)
    print "Fetching group information"
    # Most functions return the raw server response first.
    resp, numarts, first, last, name = nntp.group(groupname)
    # Get the subject line from these messages.
    print "Getting article information..."
    resp, data = nntp.xover(first, last)
    for artnum, subject, poster, time, id, references, size, numlines in data:
        # We will match on any case!
        subjectlook=string.lower(subject)
        if string.find(subjectlook, string.lower(subjectsearch))>=0:
            # Translate the "<" and ">" chars.
            subject = string.replace(subjectlook, "<", "&lt")
            poster = string.replace(poster, "<", "&lt")
            subject = string.replace(subject, ">", "&gt")
            poster = string.replace(poster, ">", "&gt")
            # Build a href
            href = "news:%s" % id[1:-1]
            # Write the HTML
            outfile.write('<P>From %s on %s<BR><a HREF="%s">%s</a>\n' \
                % (poster, time, href, subject))
    outfile.close()
```

```
if __name__=='__main__':
    if len(sys.argv)<3:
        print "usage: %s groupname, searchstring" % sys.argv[0]
        sys.exit(1)

    groupname = sys.argv[1]
    search = sys.argv[2]
    outname = groupname + ".htm"

    # Open the outfile file.
    outfile = open(outname, "w")

    MakeNewsPage(groupname, search, outfile)
    print "Done - Executing", outname
    win32api.ShellExecute(0, "open", outname, None, "", 1)
```

Now run this program using syntax such as:

```
C:\Scripts>SimpleNewsViewer comp.lang.python python
Connecting...
Fetching group information
Getting article information...
Done - Executing comp.lang.python.htm
```

You should find your browser opened with a list of news articles that match the search. Clicking on one of the links opens your news-reading software and the article.

Conclusion

In this chapter we have presented a quick look at some of the common Internet protocols and how they can be used from Python. Although we did not discuss any of the protocols in great detail, we demonstrated some of the basic concepts and provided pointers to further information on the relevant protocols.

Python is used extensively in domains that require these and similar tasks. Although we have presented a few of the common Internet protocols, you are almost certain to find that a Python module already exists to help you out regardless of your specific requirements.

16

Windows NT Administration

Administering Windows NT networks is an onerous task, requiring a combination of technical expertise to set up and maintain the machines, and also extreme patience when performing the laborious manual task of dealing with accounts, user groups, and other details. Scripting languages such as Python can help automate this process, leaving the administrator to focus on the important tasks.

This chapter shows how Python can access the Windows NT functionality often sought by an NT administrator. We show how to deal with user accounts, user groups, and information about the servers on the network, and demonstrate how a Windows NT machine can be rebooted programmatically from a remote machine. In addition to the topics discussed in this chapter, you should see Chapter 18, *Windows NT Services*, for a description of how to use the Windows NT Event Log and Performance Monitor from Python programs. Finally, if you have an existing command-line tool that provides administration functionality Python doesn't, remember that you can still execute command-line tools from within Python to help complement the tools it does have. See Chapter 17, *Processes and Files*, for more details on executing external programs.

All examples in this chapter assume you are running on a Windows NT machine. Many of these examples also will require some degree of administrator access; for example, creating a new user or initiating a server restart all require differing levels of access. If you are in doubt, please see your network administrator.

Working with Users and Groups

The Windows NT API provides a rich set of functions to control Windows NT users and groups. To cope with the large number of attributes stored for users and groups, Windows NT defines different *information levels* for these objects. Programs that require only minimal information, such as the user or group name, can specify an information level that returns only this information. Other programs may wish to view all information available for a user, and will specify a different information level when accessing user information.

The Python support for NT users, groups, shares, servers, and so forth is in the module `win32net`. This module uses dictionaries to set and obtain information about these objects. When you request information about an object, a dictionary is returned; the information level you specify determines the items in the dictionary. When you create or modify information about a user, you pass a dictionary; the information level you specify determines which dictionary elements are expected to exist.

For example, when working with users, if you specify an information level of 1, the data is in the format defined for `PyUSER_INFO_1`. If you specify an information level of 102 when dealing with servers, the data is in the format defined for `PySERVER_INFO_102`. Appendix B, *Win32 Extensions Reference*, describes the different information levels and the data.

Most of the Windows NT administration functions take as their first parameter the name of a server on which to execute the command. You can pass **None** if you want to apply the changes to the local machine, but if you are working within a Windows NT domain, you may need to specify the name of a domain controller for that domain. This obviously means you will also need the appropriate permissions on that domain. All examples in this chapter use the local machine, and hence pass **None** as the first parameter. Also be aware that in a typical Windows NT network, you may find Windows NT Primary Domain Controllers (PDCs), Backup Domain Controllers (BDCs), Windows NT servers, Windows NT workstations, and Windows 2000 machines. Although the APIs are all exposed, you may need to ensure the changes are applied as you expect. For example, as we shall see later in this chapter, working with NT users or groups differs slightly if the changes are applied to the local database, or to the domain.

All strings returned from the Windows NT API functions are Unicode, so for Python 1.5 you may need to convert them to Python strings, using the `str()` function. When you pass a dictionary to these functions, the strings can be normal Python strings or Unicode objects; Python converts them to Unicode if necessary.

Obtaining Information About a User or Group

To get a feel for this, let's start by querying information about a current user. First, obtain your username:

```
>>> import win32api
>>> userName=win32api.GetUserName()
```

And to assist working with the Python dictionaries, you can define a simple helper
function to pretty-print the data:

```
>>> def dump(dict):
...     for key, value in dict.items():
...         print key, "=", str(value)
...
>>>
```

So now you can get the user information and pass it to your function to print. Pass
None for the first parameter, so this function obtains the information from the local
machine. Pass your current username in the second parameter, and request information level 1 in the last parameter, giving the data defined in PyUSER_INFO_1:

```
>>> import win32net
>>> info=win32net.NetUserGetInfo(None, userName, 1)
>>> print info['name'] # print just the user name
skip
>>> dump(info)
priv = 2
home_dir = c:\winnt\profiles\skip\personal
password = None
script_path =
name = skip
flags = 66049
password_age = 23792806
comment =
>>>
```

By referring to Appendix B, you can determine the information returned for each
information level; however, for a thorough description, you should refer to the
Win32 documentation for these functions. Let's experiment with this a little from
the interactive prompt:

```
>>> len(info)
8
```

Level 1 (PyUSER_INFO_1) has eight items of data. You can try some other levels:

```
>>> info=win32net.NetUserGetInfo(None, userName, 2)
>>> len(info)
24
>>> info=win32net.NetUserGetInfo(None, userName, 3)
>>> len(info)
29
>>> info=win32net.NetUserGetInfo(None, userName, 4)
Traceback (innermost last):
  File "<interactive input>", line 1, in ?
ValueError: This information level is not supported
>>>
```

Level 2 provides 24 pieces of data, while level 3 provides 29. There is no information level 4, but if you refer to Appendix B, you will find other information levels
supported we don't demonstrate here.

The `win32net.NetGroupGetInfo()` function is the equivalent for obtaining the information about a group, but instead deals with `PyGROUP_INFO` structures.

You can also enumerate (i.e., loop over) all users using the `win32net.NetUserEnum()` function.

```
entries, total, resume = win32net.NetUserEnum(server, level, filter, resume, len=4096)
```

server

> The name of the server to execute on, or **None** for the current machine.

level

> An integer specifying the level of information requested.

filter

> An integer defining the type of accounts to list. A common value for this is `FILTER_NORMAL_ACCOUNT`, although Appendix B lists the valid values for Windows NT 4.

resume

> A value used to control the iteration when there is a large number of users to list. Zero should be passed the first time it is called, and while a nonzero *resume* result is returned from the function, it can be called again with the new *resume* value to obtain the next set of the users. An example of this is shown in the following code.

`len = 4096`

> A hint to the Win32 function about how much data to allocate. See the Win32 documentation for more details.

The `NetUserEnum()` function returns three items:

`entries`

> A list of dictionaries; one for each user returned.

`total`

> The total number of items left to read before making the call. Thus, `total-len(entries)` is the number of entries left to read after this call.

resume

> A resume handle, that can obtain the next set of users. When resume is zero, there are no more items to read.

The parameters and arguments to this function are probably not obvious, and all the `win32net` enumeration functions follow this pattern, so it's worth discussing at this point. The general idea is that you call this function multiple times, with each call obtaining only a portion of the total data. The `resume` parameter controls the looping and indicates when there's no more data available. These functions are designed to allow programs to process large sets of data without consuming all the memory on the local machine; however, the key drawback is that the code becomes slightly more complex.

To demonstrate the use of this function, let's write a function that loops over all users, and prints their username and the date and time they last logged on.

If you consult Appendix B, you'll notice that an information level of 2 (PyUSER_INFO_2) includes the fields **name** and **last_logon**. So you can do an enumeration at level 2. Also, you should exploit the fact that the Win32 Networking API time values are all integers holding the number of seconds since January 1, 1970, and that this is the same system the standard Python **time** module uses.

As we mentioned, the looping makes the code more complex than most code working with users and groups, but it's still small enough to type interactively:

```
>>> import win32netcon
>>> import time
>>> def ReportUsers():
...    resume = 0
...    while 1:
...        filter = win32netcon.FILTER_NORMAL_ACCOUNT
...        data, total, resume = win32net.NetUserEnum(None, 2, filter, resume)
...        for user in data:
...            lastlogon= time.strftime("%c", time.localtime(user['last_logon']))
...            print user['name'], lastlogon
...        if resume==0:
...            break
>>> ReportUsers()
Administrator 04/15/99 14:57:13
Guest 01/01/70 11:00:00
skip 04/15/99 15:07:26
VUSR_BOBCAT 10/09/98 15:33:55
>>>
```

Note the use of the **resume** parameter. Initialize this to zero before you start the loop. Each time you repeat the loop, you pass the **resume** result from the previous call. When the result returns zero, you're done.

Creating, Changing, and Deleting Users and Groups

Creating users and groups is a simple process. All you need to do is create a dictionary with the information for the user and call **win32net.NetUserAdd()** or **win32net.NetGroupAdd()**. Depending on the information you need to set for the user, the information level can be 1, 2, or 3, corresponding to PyGROUP_INFO_1, PyGROUP_INFO_2, and PyGROUP_INFO_3 respectively. Refer to Appendix B for the dictionary elements in these information levels.

```
win32net.NetUserAdd(server, level, data)
```
server

The name of the server to execute on or **None** for the current machine.

level

The level of information provided in the data parameter.

data

A dictionary with data corresponding to the level.

The simplest way to start is to create a dictionary corresponding to information level 1. Some of the attributes are optional. You can create a new user with the following code:

```
>>> d={}
>>> d['name'] = "PythonTestUser"
>>> d['password'] = "Top Secret"
>>> d['comment'] = "A user created by some Python demo code"
>>> d['flags'] = win32netcon.UF_NORMAL_ACCOUNT | win32netcon.UF_SCRIPT
>>> d['priv'] = win32netcon.USER_PRIV_USER
>>> win32net.NetUserAdd(None, 1, d)
>>>
```

Most of the attributes are self-explanatory. The **flags** attribute specifies the type of account to create. The Win32 documentation states that the use of the **UF_ SCRIPT** flag is necessary. The **priv** attribute controls the privileges of the new user; you are creating a normal user. See Appendix B for more details on these attributes.

You've now created a user. Let's see if you can read the data for the new user:

```
>>> win32net.NetUserGetInfo(None, "PythonTestUser", 0)
{'name': L'PythonTestUser'}
```

Information level 0 (**PyUSER_INFO_0**) provides only the username, so the user does exist.

To modify the details for a user, use the function **win32net.NetUserSetInfo()**.

```
win32net.NetUserSetInfo(server, userName, level, data)
```
server

The name of the server to execute on or **None** for the current machine.

userName

The username to change. The **name** element in the dictionary is ignored.

level

The level of information provided in the *data* parameter.

data

A dictionary with data corresponding to the level.

The simplest way to fill this dictionary is to call `win32net.NetUserGetInfo()`
with the appropriate information level, modify the returned dictionary, then pass it
to `win32net.NetUserSetInfo()`. This is simple to demonstrate. Let's modify the
`comment` field for the new user:

```
>>> d = win32net.NetUserGetInfo(None, "PythonTestUser", 1)
>>> d['comment']
L'A user created by some Python demo code'
>>>
```

Now you have a dictionary, and the comment is just as you created it. Now,
update the dictionary and update the user:

```
>>> d['comment'] = "The new comment for our user"
>>> d = win32net.NetUserSetInfo(None, "PythonTestUser", 1, d)
>>>
```

Finally, you can check that your data made it by rereading the user information:

```
>>> win32net.NetUserGetInfo(None, "PythonTestUser", 1)['comment']
L'The new comment for our user'
>>>
```

Working with groups

Working with groups is similar to working with users. The concepts are identical;
only the specific data that is used changes. Again, you need to refer to
Appendix B to find the exact attributes required in the dictionary for the specific
call. We will now make a slight diversion and play with some Windows NT groups
while we have a test user.

Add the new user to the standard group named *Users.* Windows NT doesn't automatically add users to this group, so you need to do it for all new users.

 Although new users are aren't added to local groups, any new users
you create in a domain are automatically added to the *Domain Users*
group.

Windows NT defines two types of groups: *local groups* are local to the machine,
while *groups* are domain groups. Rather than assume your Windows NT machine
is in a domain, you can use local groups with the function `win32net.`
`NetLocalGroupAddMembers()`. The process for using domain groups is similar,
but it employs `win32net.NetGroupAddUser()`.

`win32net.NetLocalGroupAddMembers(`*server, group, level, members_data*`)`

server
    The name of the server on which to apply the changes, or **None** for the cur-
    rent machine.

group

   The name of the local group to which the members should be added.

level

   The level of the data contained in each element of *members_data*.

members_data

   A list of dictionaries, one for each member to be added. The dictionaries must be one of the LOCALGROUP_MEMBERS_INFO structures, depending on the level parameter.

If you refer to Appendix B, notice that the LOCALGROUP_MEMBERS_INFO levels 0, 1, and 2 all require a user SID, an NT Security Identifier. Although you can work with SIDs via the win32security module, LOCALGROUP_MEMBERS_INFO_3 allows you to specify a domain and username. So the first step is to obtain the current domain name:

```
>>> import win32api
>>> domain = win32api.GetDomainName()
```

Now build a dictionary with a single element, **domainandname**, that is a string in the standard Windows NT username format, **Domain\User**. This dictionary is stored as the only item in a list:

```
>>> data = [ {"domainandname" : domain+"\\PythonTestUser"} ]
```

You can now add the member to the group. Note that you must specify information level 3, since this is the format of the data in your dictionary:

```
>>> win32net.NetLocalGroupAddMembers(None, "Users", 3, data)
```

If you wish, you could use the **win32net.NetLocalGroupGetMembers()** function to list the members in the group to prove the new member is indeed in the group.

Deleting users

Finally, you can delete the new user with the **win32net.NetUserDel()** function.

win32net.NetUserDel(*server*, *userName*)

server

   The name of the server on which to delete the user or **None** for the current machine.

userName

   The name of the user to delete.

Can't get much simpler than that. Let's delete the new user:

```
>>> win32net.NetUserDel(None, "PythonTestUser")
>>>
```

Now, check the deletion by trying to read the user's information back in:

```
>>> win32net.NetUserGetInfo(None, "PythonTestUser", 1)
Traceback (innermost last):
  File "<interactive input>", line 0, in ?
api_error: (2221, 'NetUserGetInfo', 'The user name could not be found.')
>>>
```

As you can see, the user has been deleted.

Server and Share Information

In many administrative tasks, it's handy to be able to query and change information about particular servers and the resources these servers publish. Working with server and share information is identical in concept to working with users and groups. Each function defines an information level that determines the specific data requested or being set.

Querying Information About Servers

Server information is provided by the `PySERVER_INFO_*` structures, as defined in Appendix B. `PySERVER_INFO_100` provides the lowest level of detail, so let's see what this includes.

First import the necessary modules and read the data for the server. Then print the dictionary:

```
>>> import win32net, win32netcon
>>> data=win32net.NetServerGetInfo(None, 100)
>>> data
{'name': L'BOBCAT', 'platform_id': 500}
```

Notice the `platform_id` is 500. Windows defines only two platform IDs, one for Windows NT and one for OS/2:

```
>>> win32netcon.SV_PLATFORM_ID_NT
500
>>>
```

My workstation is indeed an NT machine: what a relief!

You can also obtain a list of the Windows servers on your network with the `win32net.NetServerEnum()` function.

```
entries, total, resume = win32net.NetServerEnum(server, level, serverTypes=
win32netcon.SV_TYPE_ALL, resume = 0, len=4096)
```

server
> The name of the server to execute on or **None** for the current machine.

level
> An integer specifying the level of information requested.

serverTypes

> A bitmask of flags indicating the types of servers to list. Appendix B lists common values for this flag.

We don't discuss the **resume** or **len** parameters, or the result. Check the previous example for **win32net.NetUserEnum()** to see how to use these enumerators.

Working with Share Information

Windows NT defines the concept of a *share*. A share is a resource published by a machine designed for sharing with multiple users. Shares are usually disk-based shares or printers.

To obtain information about a share or to enumerate the shares available on a Windows NT server, the **win32net.NetShare*()** family of functions are used, with **PySHARE_INFO_*** as the corresponding data structures. The process for shares is identical to the process for working with users and servers, as we described previously.

For example, you can use the **win32net.NetShareEnum()** function to view the shares published by a server. This function is almost identical to the other enumerator functions described in this chapter, so you can use the following code to read the first few shares at your local machine at information level 0:

```
>>> data, total, resume = win32net.NetShareEnum(None, 0)
>>> for share in data:
...     print share['netname']
...
...
ADMIN$
IPC$
cdrom
C$
c_drive
l_drive
L$
>>>
```

Note that you haven't looped calling the function, so you get only the first few shares that may be available.

A new share can be created on a server using **win32net.NetShareAdd()**. This function requires data in information level 2, a **PyNET_SHARE_INFO_2** structure. By referring to Appendix B, you can find the data necessary to create a share. The following code shows how to create a share to the local *C:\TEMP* directory:

```
>>> data={}
>>> data['netname']="TEMPSHARE"
>>> data['type']=win32netcon.STYPE_DISKTREE
>>> data['path']="C:\\TEMP"
```

```
>>> data['max_uses']=-1
>>> win32net.NetShareAdd(None, 2, data)
```

The only nonobvious part may be the **max_uses** element. If you left this at zero, no users could connect to your share. The Win32 documentation states that this should be set to –1 to allow for unlimited uses.

User and Share Sample

We now present a fairly advanced sample of using some of these administrative tools in a real-world scenario.

The problem is that our company has just merged with another medium-sized company. The merger means 250 new user accounts need to be created on the network. This is clearly too many to perform manually when there is a tool such as Python available. It's not a problem to get a text file with the names of the new users, but you need a way to automate the process. The requirements for creating the new users are to:

- Create a new NT user with a default password that must be changed at first logon.

- Create a home directory for the new user with the user information reflecting this as their home directory.

- Create a new share for the user's home directory with the appropriate default permissions. Windows NT also supports connecting the user's home directory to a drive letter, so you need to set the user info to nominate *P:* to connect to this share at logon.

Of course, this is still a contrived example. Any real-world job will have additional requirements when creating many new users; for example, creating an email account for each new user. In addition, the error-handling requirements depend on the particular task at hand. To this end, and to keep the size of the sample code down, no error handling exists at all. Notwithstanding these restrictions, you should still find the sample valuable when developing your own customized scripts.

Before jumping into the code, there are a few things worth mentioning:

- The requirements state you should specify the home directory as *P:* and set the password as expired when creating the user. Looking in Appendix B, you'll see that you must use information level 3 (**PyUSER_INFO_3**) to obtain access to this information. Creating a user at this information level requires you to also set the **primary_group_id** element to a default value.

- The requirements state that the share must have special security settings. This requires the use of information level 502 (**PySHARE_INFO_502**). The directory is created without special security. If necessary, you could use `win32file.CreateDirectory()`, passing a security object similar to that used for the share.

- The handling of the NT security objects is not covered in detail in this book; for further information on Windows NT security, refer to the Windows NT documentation.

- Unlike local groups, new users are automatically added to the domain users group when they are created. Therefore, it's unnecessary to add the user to any additional groups when this code is run against a Windows NT domain.

- You should also provide some code to delete the new users. This is particularly helpful when developing and testing the script; you can delete the users created by the previous run, then re-create them with different settings.

The following code is quite large by Python standards—just over 100 lines, including comments and blank lines:

```python
# BatchUserCreate.py
#
# A sample administrative script to perform a batch
# creation of many users.

# Input to this program is a text file with one user per
# line.  Each line contains the new username and the
# user's full name.

# Creates the new user, and a new share on the server
# for the user.  The new share is secure, and can only
# be accessed by the new user.
import win32security, win32net, win32file, win32api
import win32netcon, ntsecuritycon
import os, sys, string

# The name of the server to use to create the user.
serverName = None

# The logic for naming the home_drive assumes we have
# a server name.  If we don't, get the current machine name.
if serverName is None:
    serverName = "\\\\" + win32api.GetComputerName()

# The root of each users personal directory.
# This is a local reference to the directory where each
# personal directory is created.
homeRoot = "C:\\Users"

def CreateUserAndShare(userName, fullName):
    homeDir = "%s\\%s" % (serverName, userName)
    # Create user data in information level 3 (PyUSER_INFO_3) format.
    userData = {}
    userData['name'] = userName
```

```
    userData['full_name'] = fullName
    userData['password'] = userName
    userData['flags'] = win32netcon.UF_NORMAL_ACCOUNT | win32netcon.UF_SCRIPT
    userData['priv'] = win32netcon.USER_PRIV_USER
    userData['home_dir'] = homeDir
    userData['home_dir_drive'] = "P:"
    userData['primary_group_id'] = ntsecuritycon.DOMAIN_GROUP_RID_USERS
    userData['password_expired'] = 1 # User must change password next logon.


    # Create the user
    win32net.NetUserAdd(serverName, 3, userData)


    # Create the new directory, then the share
    dirName = os.path.join(homeRoot, userName)
    os.mkdir(dirName)
    shareData = {}
    shareData['netname'] = userName
    shareData['type'] = win32netcon.STYPE_DISKTREE
    shareData['path'] = dirName
    shareData['max_uses'] = -1
    # The security setting for the share.
    sd = CreateUserSecurityDescriptor(userName)
    shareData['security_descriptor'] = sd
    # And finally create it.
    win32net.NetShareAdd(serverName, 502, shareData)

# A utility function that creates an NT security object for a user.
def CreateUserSecurityDescriptor(userName):
    sidUser = win32security.LookupAccountName(serverName, userName)[0]
    sd = win32security.SECURITY_DESCRIPTOR()

    # Create the "well known" SID for the administrators group
    subAuths = ntsecuritycon.SECURITY_BUILTIN_DOMAIN_RID, \
               ntsecuritycon.DOMAIN_ALIAS_RID_ADMINS
    sidAdmins = win32security.SID(ntsecuritycon.SECURITY_NT_AUTHORITY, subAuths)

    # Now set the ACL, giving user and admin full access.
    acl = win32security.ACL(128)
    acl.AddAccessAllowedAce(win32file.FILE_ALL_ACCESS, sidUser)
    acl.AddAccessAllowedAce(win32file.FILE_ALL_ACCESS, sidAdmins)

    sd.SetSecurityDescriptorDacl(1, acl, 0)
    return sd

# Debug helper to delete our test accounts and shares.
def DeleteUser(name):
    try:    win32net.NetUserDel(serverName, name)
    except win32net.error: pass

    try: win32net.NetShareDel(serverName, name)
    except win32net.error: pass

    try: os.rmdir(os.path.join(homeRoot, name))
    except os.error: pass
```

```
if __name__=='__main__':
    import fileinput # Helper for reading files line by line
    if len(sys.argv)<2:
        print "You must specify an options file"
        sys.exit(1)
    if sys.argv[1]=="-delete":
        for line in fileinput.input(sys.argv[2:]):
            DeleteUser(string.split(line,",")[0])
    else:
        for line in fileinput.input(sys.argv[1:]):
            userName, fullName = string.split(string.strip(line), ",")
            CreateUserAndShare(userName, fullName)
            print "Created", userName
```

To test this code, use a simple data file:

```
tu1,Test User 1
tu2,Test User 2
tu3,Test User 3
```

To run this script, start a command prompt on an NT server and change to the directory with the script and data file, and execute the command:

```
C:\Scripts>BatchUserCreate.py userdata.txt
Created tu1
Created tu2
Created tu3

C:\Scripts>
```

There are now three new users. You can remove them by executing:

```
C:\Scripts>BatchUserCreate.py -delete userdata.txt
```

Rebooting a Machine

Occasionally, it's necessary to force a Windows NT computer to reboot programmatically. You may need to perform a scheduled reboot of the current machine or force a reboot of a remote PC programmatically.

The function **win32api.InitiateSystemShutdown()** appears perfect for the job.

win32api.InitiateSystemShutdown(*machine*, *message*, *timeout*, *bForce*, *bReboot*)

machine

The name of the machine to shutdown or **None** for the current machine.

message

A message to be displayed to the user in a dialog while the **timeout** period expires.

timeout

A timeout in seconds, during which time a dialog is displayed warning the user of the pending shutdown. After the timeout expires, the shutdown process begins. If this is zero, the shutdown commences immediately.

bForce

Specifies whether applications with unsaved changes are to be forcibly closed. If this parameter is `true`, such applications are closed. If this parameter is `false`, a dialog box is displayed prompting the user to close the applications. Note that this implies the user could cancel the shutdown process by selecting Cancel in the dialog his application displays for unsaved data.

bReboot

Specifies whether the machine is rebooted after the shutdown process.

Let's try this function. Start by rebooting the current machine with a 30-second timeout (without forcing applications shut) and finally restart after shutdown:

```
>>> import win32api
>>> message = "This machine is being rebooted because it has been naughty"
>>> win32api.InitiateSystemShutdown(None, message, 30, 0, 1)
Traceback (innermost last):
  File "<interactive input>", line 0, in ?
api_error: (5, 'InitiateSystemShutdown', 'Access is denied.')
```

This will, no doubt, lead you into messing with the Windows NT User Manager, etc., to try to determine how to get permission to do so. You won't have much luck: everything will indicate you should be allowed to restart the machine. The Win32 documentation for this function briefly mentions:

> To stop the local computer from shutting down, the calling process must have the SE_SHUTDOWN_NAME privilege. To stop a remote computer from shutting down, the calling process must have the SE_REMOTE_SHUTDOWN_NAME privilege on the remote computer.

But as far as can be seen, you should have the correct privilege. The answer lies in the fact that user rights and privileges are different things. Your user rights typically allow direct access to securable resources, such as files, printers, or the registry, but access to other system resources requires privileges. Your user rights determine the privileges you hold; but by default, most privileges aren't enabled. Programs must explicitly enable the privilege before they perform an operation that requires the privilege.

Privileges are required for fairly obscure tasks, such as rebooting the local or remote machine, changing the system time, creating machine accounts on the network, or loading device drivers. Our example of rebooting a machine is the only place in this book where you encounter privileges, so we will make a slight diversion at this point. Although we discuss only the privileges required to reboot the local or remote machine, the same concept applies when you perform any operation that requires you to enable special privileges.

Obtaining the Necessary Privileges

The process of enabling new privileges is simple. We will discuss briefly the concepts and the code necessary to enable privileges, but for an in-depth discussion of privileges, refer to the Microsoft Windows NT Security documentation.

You use the `win32security` module to gain access to the necessary functions. The process for enabling a privilege is:

- Obtain the current access token using the `win32security.OpenAccess-Token()` function.

- Obtain the ID for the privilege using `win32security.Lookup-PrivilegeValue()`.

- Enable the privilege using `win32security.AdjustTokenPrivileges()`.

When you've performed the operation, you need to disable the privilege again. The same process is used: `win32security.AdjustTokenPrivileges()` supports a flag that allows you to enable or disable the privilege. An example of this code is presented in the next section.

Sample Code to Reboot the Current Machine

You now have the knowledge to successfully make a `win32api.InitiateSystemShutdown()` call.

The code obtains the necessary privileges to reboot the machine, then makes the call to `win32api.InitiateSystemShutdown()`. Unfortunately, the dialog displayed by Windows NT doesn't include any way to disable the shutdown operation. Once the shutdown has begun, the only way to stop it is programmatically.

To cater to this, the sample application, shown in the following code, initiates a shutdown with a 30-second delay. The code then sleeps for 10 seconds before programmatically aborting the shutdown using `win32api.AbortSystemShutdown()`. If you refer to the Windows NT documentation or Appendix B, you'll notice that this function requires the same privileges needed to initiate the shutdown in the first place. So before aborting the shutdown, you must jump through the same privilege hoops. To assist the process, let's move the code that manages the privileges to a helper function that should be suitable for managing any type of privilege:

```
# RebootServer.py - Reboots a remove server
import win32security
import win32api
import sys
```

```python
import time
from ntsecuritycon import *

def AdjustPrivilege(priv, enable = 1):
    # Get the process token.
    flags = TOKEN_ADJUST_PRIVILEGES | TOKEN_QUERY
    htoken = win32security.OpenProcessToken(win32api.GetCurrentProcess(), flags)
    # Get the ID for the system shutdown privilege.
    id = win32security.LookupPrivilegeValue(None, priv)
    # Now obtain the privilege for this process.
    # Create a list of the privileges to be added.
    if enable:
        newPrivileges = [(id, SE_PRIVILEGE_ENABLED)]
    else:
        newPrivileges = [(id, 0)]
    # and make the adjustment.
    win32security.AdjustTokenPrivileges(htoken, 0, newPrivileges)

def RebootServer(message="Server Rebooting", timeout=30, bForce=0, bReboot=1):
    AdjustPrivilege(SE_SHUTDOWN_NAME)
    try:
        win32api.InitiateSystemShutdown(None, message, timeout, bForce, bReboot)
    finally:
        # Now we remove the privilege we just added.
        AdjustPrivilege(SE_SHUTDOWN_NAME, 0)

def AbortReboot():
    AdjustPrivilege(SE_SHUTDOWN_NAME)
    try:
        win32api.AbortSystemShutdown(None)
    finally:
        # Now we remove the privilege we just added.
        AdjustPrivilege(SE_SHUTDOWN_NAME, 0)

if __name__=='__main__':
        message = "This server is pretending to reboot\r\n"
        message = message + "The shutdown will stop in 10 seconds"
        RebootServer(message)
        print "Sleeping for 10 seconds"
        time.sleep(10)
        print "Aborting shutdown"
        AbortReboot()
```

The function AdjustPrivilege() is where you enable the necessary privilege. Notice the specific privilege is passed as a parameter. This makes the function general purpose and so, can be used for any of the Windows NT privileges. Specifically, if you must reboot a remote machine, you should use the privilege SE_REMOTE_SHUTDOWN_NAME.

Running this script from Windows NT, you should see the dialog shown in Figure 16-1. Once the countdown timer reaches 20 seconds before shutdown, the dialog should disappear as the shutdown is aborted.

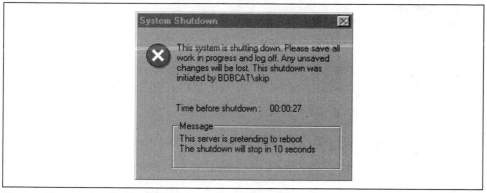

Figure 16-1. Dialog displayed when RebootServer.py runs

Conclusion

Although Windows NT comes with many GUI tools to assist with machine administration, the process is often complicated by site-specific requirements or by the sheer volume of operations that must be performed. This chapter demonstrated some techniques that help automate the administration of a Windows NT Network. We demonstrated how users, user groups, share, and server information can be perused and maintained using Python, and provided example Python programs that can be tailored by an administrator for their particular task at hand.

References

The Microsoft Developers Network (MSDN) is an excellent resource. It's available online at *http://msdn.microsoft.com.*

17

Processes and Files

This chapter covers techniques for working with files and processes. We first look at the facilities Python has for portably working with both files and processes, then we'll look at Windows-specific techniques. If you're an experienced Python developer, you may wish to skip to the later sections; if you're new to Python, this is essential groundwork.

We cover techniques for finding, moving, and rearranging files, look at file objects themselves, and then cover some of the standard Python idioms for reading and writing them. Then we look at techniques for starting, stopping, and generally working with processes.

Portable File Manipulation

Python has excellent built-in file support that works on all platforms supported by Python.

Working with Files on Disk

Most of the key file-manipulation functions live in the os module and an associated module called os.path. To provide a degree of platform independence, os loads in the right module for your platform. os provides basic file-handling functions, and os.path handles operations on paths and filenames. On Windows, these modules are called nt and ntpath respectively, although they should always be referred to as os and os.path. The functions in the os module generally accept the same arguments as their corresponding MS-DOS commands. Table 17-1 depicts the os module's file and directory functions.

Table 17-1. *File and Directory Functions*

Module and Function	Description
os.getcwd()	Gets the current working directory.
os.chdir(*newdir*)	Changes the current working directory.
os.rmdir(*dir*)	Removes a directory, if allowed.
os.mkdir(*newdir*)	Creates a directory, supplies either an absolute path or a subdirectory name to go under the current directory.
os.exists(*name*)	Says if something exists, but doesn't say if it's a file or directory.
os.isdir(*dirname*)	Says that a directory exists.
os.isfile(*filename*)	Says that a file exists. *filename* may include a path; if not, it looks in the current directory.
os.listdir(*dirname*)	Returns a list of the files and directories within the given directory.
glob.glob(*pattern*)	Returns a list of files matching the given pattern (using expressions such as dir *.doc is known as *file globbing* on Unix, hence the name). Just like the command prompt and most other Windows tools, the pattern accepts the ? character to match a single character or the * character to match any number of characters. If you need to use true regular expressions[a] to match filenames, use os.listdir() and the re module.

[a] A regular expression uses patterns to match strings. The filename-matching capabilities described are similar in concept to regular expressions, although the regular expressions provided by the Python re module provide a syntax similar to Perl and offer far more matching capabilities than the simple filename-matching patterns described here.

Here are some quick examples:

```
>>> import os
>>> os.getcwd()
'C:\\Program Files\\Python'
>>> os.chdir('C:\\temp')
>>> os.mkdir('subdirectory1')
>>> os.rmdir('subdirectory1')
>>>
```

What's with the \\? This is Python's literal string syntax. Python lets you directly enter special characters at the interactive prompt or in strings embedded in your code. For example, \n means a newline, \t is a tab, and \123 is the octal number 123. If you just want a plain old slash, you have to type \\. The only place where this feels slightly weird is in manipulating filenames. Remember to double all your slashes. An alternative is to use a forward slash (like *c:/temp*); but Python always gives backslashes when you ask for directory lists on Windows:

```
>>> mydir = 'c:\\data\\project\\oreilly\\text'
>>> os.path.exists(mydir)
1
>>> os.path.isdir(mydir)
1
```

```
>>> os.path.isfile(mydir)     #hope not
0
>>> os.listdir(mydir)
['ChapterXX.doc', '00index.txt', ...]

>>> import glob
>>> glob.glob(mydir + '\\' + '*files*.doc')
['c:\\data\\project\\oreilly\\text\\Chapter_-_Processes_and_Files1.doc', 'c:\\
data\\project\\oreilly\\text\\files.doc', 'c:\\data\\project\\oreilly\\text\\
Chapter_-_PythonFiles.doc']
>>>
```

Note that if you don't want full paths from `glob`, `chdir` into the directory first.

Working with paths and filenames

The `os.path` module provides platform-independent routines for chopping up and putting together filenames. `os.path.split(path)` separates a full path into the directory and filename components; `os.path.splitext(filename)` separates the filename (and path, if present) from the extension.

As discussed, DOS and Windows use a backslash to separate directories. We shouldn't have used the line `glob.glob(mydir + '\\' + '*files*.doc')` in the previous example; use the variable `os.sep` instead. On a Unix platform, this is a forward slash:

```
>>> os.path.split('c:\\windows\\system\\gdi.exe')
('c:\\windows\\system', 'gdi.exe')
>>> os.path.splitext('gdi.exe')
('gdi', '.exe')
>>> os.path.splitext('c:\\windows\\system\\gdi.exe')
('c:\\windows\\system\\gdi', '.exe')
>>> (root, ext) = os.path.splitext('c:\\mydata\\myfile.txt')
>>> newname = root + '.out'
>>> newname
'c:\\mydata\\myfile.out'
>>>
```

Names for temporary files

The function `tempfile.mktemp()` returns a filename suitable for temporary use; this function is available on every platform, but it's smart enough to know where your *temp* directory is on Windows:

```
>>> import tempfile
>>> tempfile.mktemp()
'C:\\WINDOWS\\TEMP\\~-304621-1'
>>>
```

When the file is closed, it's automatically deleted, assisting in the housekeeping that often goes with working with temporary files.

Getting information about files

The function `os.stat(`*`filename`*`)` returns information about files or directories without opening them. It returns a tuple of ten items. With a tuple of this size, it can be hard to recall what each element is for, so the standard Python module `stat` contains a number of constants and functions to assist in working with these entries. Table 17-2 lists the entries returned by `os.stat()`.

Table 17-2. os.stat() Return Values

Index	Constant	Description
0	stat.ST_MODE	Bit mask for file-mode information. The stat.S_IFDIR bit is set if path specifies a directory; the stat.S_IFREG bit is set if path specifies an ordinary file or a device.
1	stat.ST_INO	Not used on Windows filesystems.
2	stat.ST_DEV	Drive number of the disk containing the file.
3	stat.ST_NLINK	The Visual C++ documentation is not very helpful on this one. It simply states "Always 1 on non-NTFS filesystems."
4	stat.ST_UID	Not used on Windows.
5	stat.ST_GID	Not used on Windows.
6	stat.ST_SIZE	Size of the file in bytes. This is limited to 64 bits, so for large files you should use the **win32file.GetFileSize()** function, which returns large file sizes as a long integer.
7	stat.ST_ATIME	The time the file was last accessed or zero if the filesystem doesn't support this information.
8	stat.ST_MTIME	The time the file was last modified or zero if the filesystem doesn't support this information.
9	stat.ST_CTIME	The time the file was created or zero if the filesystem doesn't support this information.

Some of these aren't used on Windows, but contain useful information when used on other operating systems. Also, note that all dates are returned as integers compatible with the Python **time** module. Depending on the format of the disk holding the file, some of these time values may not be available.

Let's see an example of using the **stat()** function:

```
>>> os.stat('c:\\autoexec.bat')
(33279, 0, 2, 1, 0, 0, 640, 916444800, 915484932, 915484930)
>>>
```

Here's a function to decode it:

```
import os, stat, time

def getfileinfo(filename):
    stats = os.stat(filename)
```

```
size = stats[stat.ST_SIZE]
print 'File size is %d bytes' % size

accessed = stats[stat.ST_ATIME]
modified = stats[stat.ST_MTIME]

print 'Last accessed: ' + time.ctime(accessed)
print 'Last modified: ' + time.ctime(modified)
```

And the output:

```
>>> decode_stat.getfileinfo('c:\\autoexec.bat')
File size is 640 bytes
Last accessed: Sat Jan 16 00:00:00 1999
Last modified: Mon Jan 04 21:22:12 1999
>>>
```

Unfortunately, there's no portable Python module for working with file permissions. Modules exist for working with permissions on various operating systems, including Windows and Unix, but the differences between the various schemes make a simple and unified model difficult. Windows NT permissions are themselves complex and beyond the scope of this book; indeed, it would require a book of this size to cover them in detail. There is a brief example of working with permissions in Chapter 16, *Windows NT Administration.*

Walking through a directory tree

Often you need to move through a directory tree looking at all the subdirectories or files in turn. The Python library provides a powerful generic routine to do this: `os.path.walk()`.

The general idea is that you specify a directory, and `os.path.walk()` calls a function (that you write) once for each subdirectory of the main directory. Each time your function is called, it's passed a list of all filenames in that directory. Thus, your function can examine every file in every directory under the starting point you specify.

The function you write to perform the desired operation on the file is of the form `myfunc(arg, dirname, filenames)`. The first argument can be anything you want; we will see examples later. The second argument contains the name of the current directory being examined, starting with the directory you specify in the argument to `os.path.walk()`; the third is the list of filenames in the directory.

Once you have written the function, call `os.path.walk()` with three parameters: the name of the directory in which to begin the walking, your callback function, and any third parameter you choose. This third parameter is passed unchanged in your callback function's first parameter, as described previously.

This first example lists the directories examined and how many files are present in each. This makes the callback function simple: you print the **dirname** parameter, and the length of the `filenames` parameter. Then call `os.path.walk()`, passing a directory from the Python installation and the simple function as the callback:

```
>>> def walker1(arg, dirname, filenames):
...     #List directories and numbers of files
...     print dirname,' contains', len(filenames), 'files'
...
>>> os.path.walk('c:\\program files\\python\\win32', walker1, None)
c:\program files\python\win32  contains 24 files
c:\program files\python\win32\lib  contains 39 files
c:\program files\python\win32\Help  contains 3 files
c:\program files\python\win32\demos  contains 19 files
c:\program files\python\win32\demos\service  contains 8 files
c:\program files\python\win32\demos\service\install  contains 3 files
>>>
```

That was easy! Note that you don't need the extra argument and so use the value **None**. Now let's try something a bit more practical and write a program to scan for recent changes. This is useful for archiving or for trying to figure out which new application just ate your registry. The callback function becomes slightly more complex as you loop over the list of files. The example then checks the Windows system directory for all files changed in the last 30 days:

```
>>> import time
>>> def walker2(arg, dirname, filenames):
...     "Lists files modified in last ARG days"
...     cutoff = time.time() - (arg * 24 * 60 * 60)
...     for filename in filenames:
...         stats = os.stat(dirname + os.sep + filename)
...         modified = stats[8]
...         if modified >= cutoff:
...             print dirname + os.sep + filename
...
>>> os.path.walk('c:\\windows\\system', walker2, 30)
c:\windows\system\FFASTLOG.TXT
c:\windows\system\MSISYS.VXD
c:\windows\system\HwInfoD.vxd
c:\windows\system\ws552689.ocx
>>>
```

So far you haven't returned anything; indeed, if `walker2` returned a value, you'd have no easy way to grab it. This is another common use for the "extra argument." Let's imagine you want to total the size of all files in a directory. It's tempting to try this:

```
def walker3(arg, dirname, filenames):
    "Adds up total size of all files"
    for filename in filenames:
        stats = os.stat(dirname + os.sep + filename)
        size = stats[6]
        arg = arg + size

def compute_size(rootdir):
    "uses walker3 to compute the size"
```

```
total = 0
os.path.walk(rootdir, walker3, total)
return total
```

Here, a **walker** function does the work, and a controlling function sets up the arguments and returns the results. This is a common pattern when dealing with recursive functions.

Unfortunately this returns zero. You can't modify a simple numeric argument in this way, since **arg** within the function **walker3()** is a local variable. However, if **arg** was an object, you could modify its properties. One of the simplest answers is to use a list; it's passed around, and the **walker** function is free to modify its contents. Let's rewrite the function to generate a list of sizes:

```
# these two work...
def walker4(arg, dirname, filenames):
    "Adds up total size of all files"
    for filename in filenames:
        stats = os.stat(dirname + os.sep + filename)
        size = stats[6]
        arg.append(size)

def compute_size(rootdir):
    "uses walker3 to compute the size"
    sizes = []
    os.path.walk(rootdir, walker4, sizes)

    # now add them up
    total = 0
    for size in sizes:
        total = total + size
    return total
```

When run, this code behaves as desired:

```
>>> compute_size('c:\\program files\\python')
26386305
>>> # well, I do have a lot of extensions installed
```

There are numerous uses for this function, and it can save a lot of lines of code. Some possibilities include:

- Archiving all files older than a certain date

- Building a list of filenames meeting certain criteria for further processing

- Synchronizing two file trees efficiently across a network, copying only the changes

- Keeping an eye on users' storage requirements

We've started to see what makes Python so powerful for manipulating filesystems. It's not just the **walk** function: that could have been done in many languages. The key point is how **walk** interacts with Python's higher-level data structures, such as lists, to make these examples simple and straightforward.

Working with Python File Objects

Now we've had a good look at moving files around; it's time to look inside them.

Python has a built-in file object, which is available on all Python platforms. Any Python program you hope to run on platforms other than Windows should use the standard file objects. Once you have a Python file object, you can use the methods to read data from the file, write data to the file, and perform various other operations.

Opening a file

The function open(*filename*, mode="r") returns a file object. If **mode** is omitted, the file is opened read-only. **Mode** is a string, and can be **r** for reading, **w** for writing, or **a** for appending. Add the letter **b** for binary (as discussed in Chapter 3, *Python on Windows*), and **w+** opens it for updating. See the Python Library Reference (included in HTML format in the standard Python distribution) for further details.

Table 17-3 shows the most important methods for file objects. C programmers will note the similarity to the STDIO routines; this should be no surprise, as they are implemented using the C STDIO routines of the same names.

Table 17-3. Methods of File Objects

Method	Description
close()	Closes the file.
flush()	Flushes to disk. Windows caches disk activity; if you write a file, you can hear the lag between writing a file and the disk clicking. This ensures it's written immediately.
isatty()	Nonzero if the input is a terminal-type device (e.g., standard input when using Python from the console).
read([*size*])	Reads up to [*size*] bytes and returns a string. Omit [*size*], and the whole file is read into memory. When end of file is reached, returns an empty string.
readline()	Returns a string up to and including the next newline character.
readlines()	Returns a list of strings containing all lines in the file. Each string includes the trailing newline character.
seek(*offset*, [whence])	Jumps to the location *offset* in the file. whence is optional and specifies a mode: if zero, *offset* is an absolute position, if 1, relative to the current position, and if 2, relative to the end of the file.

Table 17-3. Methods of File Objects (continued)

Method	Description
`tell()`	Returns the current location in the file.
`truncate([size])`	Truncates the file at the current position or at *size* if it's provided.
`write(str)`	Writes the string to the file.
`writelines(list)`	Writes a list of strings to the file. It doesn't insert any new-lines or other delimiters.

Every language has functions, such as **read** and **write**, and many have **readline**. Python's ability to handle lists and strings is what really makes file processing a joy. Let's run through a few common idioms.

Reading a text file into a list

Here **readlines** loads the entire file into a list of strings in memory:

```
>>> f = open('c:\\config.sys','r')
>>> lines = f.readlines()
>>> f.close()
>>> from pprint import pprint
>>> pprint(lines[0:3])
['DEVICEHIGH = A:\\CDROM\\CDROM.SYS /D:CD001\012',
 'device=C:\\WINDOWS\\COMMAND\\display.sys con=(ega,,1)\012',
 'Country=044,850,C:\\WINDOWS\\COMMAND\\country.sys\012']
>>>
```

The **pprint** function (short for pretty-print) lets you display large data structures on several lines. Note also that each line still ends in a newline character (octal 012, decimal 10). Because the file is opened in text mode (by omitting the binary specification), you see a single newline character terminating each line, even if the actual file is terminated with carriage-return/linefeed pairs.

You can follow this with a call to **string.split()** to parse each line. Here's a generic function to parse tab-delimited data:

```
def read_tab_delimited_file(filename):
    "returns a list of tuples"
    # we can compress the file opening down to a one-liner -
    # the file will be closed automatically
    lines = open(filename).readlines()
    table = []
    for line in lines:
        #chop off the final newline
        line = line[:-1]
        # split up the row on tab characters
        row = string.split(line, '\t')
        table.append(row)
    return table
```

And here's what it can do:

```
>>> data = read_tab_delimited_file('c:\\temp\\sales.txt')
>>> pprint(data)
[['Sales', '1996', '1997', '1998'],
 ['North', '100', '115', '122'],
 ['South', '176', '154', '180'],
 ['East', '130', '150', '190']]
>>>
```

Note once again how useful **pprint** is! This is another of Python's key strengths: you can work at the interactive prompt, looking at your raw data, which helps you to get your code right early in the development process.

Reading a line at a time

The previous example is suitable only for files that definitely fit into memory. If they might get bigger, you should loop a line at a time. Here is the common idiom for doing this:

```
f = open(filename,'r')
s = f.readline()
while s <> '':
    # do something with string 's'
    s = f.readline()
f.close()
```

The fileinput module

A number of people have complained about having to type **readline()** twice, while Perl has a one-line construction to loop over files. The standard library now includes a module called **fileinput** to save you this minimal amount of extra typing. The module lets you do the following:

```
import fileinput
for line in fileinput.input([filename]):
    process(line)
```

If no filename is provided, the module loops over standard input, useful in script processing. Pass the **filename** parameter in single item list; **fileinput** iterates automatically over any number of files simply by including more items in this parameter. **fileinput** also lets you access the name of the file and the current line number and provides a mechanism to modify files in place (with a backup) in case something goes wrong.

Reading binary data

The **read()** command loads an entire file into memory if you don't specify a size. You often see the one liner:

```
>>> mystring = open('c:\\temp\\sales.txt').read()
>>>
```

This code uses the fact that file objects are closed just before they get garbage-collected. You didn't assign the file object to a variable, so Python closes it and deletes the object (but not the file!) after the line executes. You can slurp an entire file into a string in one line.

Python strings are eight-bit safe and are the easiest means to manipulate binary data. In addition to this, the `struct` module lets you create C-compatible structures and convert them to and from strings; and the `array` module efficiently handles arrays of data, which it can convert to and from strings and files.

More information on working with files and the other various Python modules we discussed here can be found in either of these fine O'Reilly Python books we've mentioned before: *Programming Python* and *Learning Python*.

Native File Manipulation: The win32file Module

There are times when the standard Python file objects can't meet your requirements, and you need to use the Windows API to manipulate files. This can happen in a number of situations, such as:

- You need to read or write data to or from a Windows pipe.

- You need to set custom Windows security on a file you are creating.

- You need to perform advanced techniques for performance reasons, such as "Overlapped" operations or using completion ports.

 Python file objects are integrated closely with Python. You should use the `win32file` module only when standard Python file objects can't meet your requirements. Using the `win32file` module is a good deal more complex than using native Python files.

Opening and Creating Files

The `win32file.CreateFile()` function opens or creates standard files, returning a handle to the file. Standard files come in many flavors, including synchronous files (where read or write operations don't return until the operation has completed); asynchronous (or overlapped I/O) files, where read and write operations return immediately; and temporary files that are automatically deleted when the handle is closed. Files may also be opened requesting that Windows not cache any file operations, that no buffering is performed, etc. All the variations that

CreateFile() can use are too numerous to list here. For full details, please see the Windows API documentation for CreateFile().

The CreateFile() function takes the following parameters:

- Name of the file
- Integer indicating the type of access requested on the file
- Integer-sharing options for the file
- Security attributes for the new file or None
- A flag, indicating what action to take depending on if the file exists
- A set of flags and attributes for the file itself
- Another file to act as a template or None

This function returns a PyHANDLE object. PyHANDLEs are simply objects that wrap standard Win32 HANDLEs. When a PyHANDLE object goes out of scope, it's automatically closed; thus, it's generally not necessary to close these HANDLEs as it is necessary when using these from C or C++.

Let's see how these parameters interact and test out some of the documented semantics. Here's a small script that uses the **win32file** module to work with Win32 file handles. The code creates a file, then checks that other attempts to open the file either succeed or fail, based on the flags passed to CreateFile(). You will also find that auto-delete files behave as expected; i.e., after the last handle is closed, the file no longer exists on disk:

```
# CheckFileSemantics.py
#       Demonstrate the semantics of CreateFile.

# To keep the source code small,
# we import all win32file objects.
from win32file import *

import win32api
import os

# First, lets create a normal file
h1 = CreateFile( \
        "\\file1.tst", # The file name \
        GENERIC_WRITE, # we want write access. \
        FILE_SHARE_READ, # others can open for read \
        None, # No special security requirements \
        CREATE_ALWAYS, # File to be created. \
        FILE_ATTRIBUTE_NORMAL, # Normal attributes \
        None ) # No template file.

# now we will print the handle,
# just to prove we have one!
print "The first handle is", h1
```

```
# Now attempt to open the file again,
# this time for read access
h2 = CreateFile( \
        "\\file1.tst", # The same file name. \
        GENERIC_READ, # read access \
        FILE_SHARE_WRITE | FILE_SHARE_READ, \
        None, # No special security requirements \
        OPEN_EXISTING, # expect the file to exist. \
        0, # Not creating, so attributes dont matter. \
        None ) # No template file

# Prove we have another handle
print "The second handle is", h2

# Now attempt yet again, but for write access.
# We expect this to fail.
try:
    h3 = CreateFile( \
        "\\file1.tst", # The same file name. \
        GENERIC_WRITE, # write access \
        0, # No special sharing \
        None, # No special security requirements \
        CREATE_ALWAYS, # attempting to recreate it! \
        0, # Not creating file, so no attributes  \
        None ) # No template file

except win32api.error, (code, function, message):
    print "The file could not be opened for write mode."
    print "Error", code, "with message", message

# Close the handles.
h1.Close()
h2.Close()

# Now lets check out the FILE_FLAG_DELETE_ON_CLOSE
fileAttributes = FILE_ATTRIBUTE_NORMAL | \
                    FILE_FLAG_DELETE_ON_CLOSE

h1 = CreateFile( \
        "\\file1.tst", # The file name \
        GENERIC_WRITE, # we want write access. \
        FILE_SHARE_READ, # others can open for read \
        None, # no special security requirements \
        CREATE_ALWAYS, # file to be created. \
        fileAttributes, \
        None ) # No template file.

# Do a stat of the file to ensure it exists.
print "File stats are", os.stat("\\file1.tst")

# Close the handle
h1.Close()

try:
    os.stat("\\file1.tst")
```

```
except os.error:
    print "Could not stat the file - file does not exist"
```

When you run this script, you see the following output:

```
The first handle is <PyHANDLE at 8344464 (80)>
The second handle is <PyHANDLE at 8344400 (112)>
The file could not be opened for write mode.
Error 32 with message The process cannot access the file because
it is being used by another process.
File stats are (33206, 0, 11, 1, 0, 0, 0, 916111892, 916111892, 916111892)
Could not stat the file - file does not exist
```

Thus, the semantics are what you'd expect:

- A file opened to allow reading can be opened this way.

- A file opened to disallow writing can't be opened this way.

- A file opened for automatic delete is indeed deleted when the handle is closed.

Reading and Writing Files

The win32file module has functions for reading and writing files. Not surprisingly, win32file.ReadFile() reads files, and win32file.WriteFile() writes files.

win32file.ReadFile() takes the following parameters:

- The file handle to read from

- The size of the data to read (see the reference for further details)

- Optionally, an OVERLAPPED or None

win32file.ReadFile() returns two pieces of information in a Python tuple: the error code for ReadFile and the data itself. The error code is either zero or the value winerror.ERROR_IO_PENDING if overlapped I/O is being performed. All other error codes are trapped and raises a Python exception.

win32file.WriteFile() takes the following parameters:

- A file handle opened to allow reading

- The data to write

- Optionally, an OVERLAPPED or None

win32file.WriteFile() returns the error code from the operation. This is either zero or win32error.ERROR_IO_PENDING if overlapped I/O is used. All other error codes are converted to a Python exception.

Overlapped I/O

Windows provides a number of techniques for high-performance file I/O. The most common is overlapped I/O. Using overlapped I/O, the `win32file.ReadFile()` and `win32file.WriteFile()` operations are asynchronous and return before the actual I/O operation has completed. When the I/O operation finally completes, a Windows event is signaled.

Overlapped I/O does have some requirements normal I/O operations don't:

* The operating system doesn't automatically advance the file pointer. When not using overlapped I/O, a `ReadFile` or `WriteFile` operation automatically advances the file pointer, so the next operation automatically reads the subsequent data in the file. When using overlapped I/O, you must manage the location in the file manually.

* The standard technique of returning a Python string object from `win32file.ReadFile()` doesn't work. Because the I/O operation has not completed when the call returns, a Python string can't be used.

As you can imagine, the code for performing overlapped I/O is more complex than when performing synchronous I/O. Chapter 18, *Windows NT Services*, contains some sample code that uses basic overlapped I/O on a Windows-named pipe.

Pipes

Pipes are a concept available in most modern operating systems. Typically, these are a block of shared memory set up much like a file. Typically, one process writes information to a pipe, and another process reads it. They are often used as a form of interprocess communication or as a simple queue implementation. Windows has two flavors of pipes: anonymous pipes and named pipes. Python supports both via the `win32pipe` module.

Anonymous Pipes

Anonymous pipes are simple and lightweight pipes, designed to use between the process that creates it and its child processes. Since they are unnamed, the only way to use anonymous pipes is to communicate its handle; there's no name for the pipe that processes use to obtain access to the pipe. This typically makes anonymous pipes unsuitable for interprocess communication between unrelated processes (for example, between a client and a server process).

Anonymous pipes are simple to create and use. The function `win32pipe.CreatePipe()` creates an anonymous pipe and returns two handles: one for reading from the pipe, and one for writing to the pipe. The `win32pipe.Create-Pipe()` function takes the following parameters:

- The security attributes for the pipe or **None** for the default.

- The buffer size or zero for the default.

It then returns a tuple of (`readHandle`, `writeHandle`).

A demonstration of anonymous pipes is quite simple. Let's create an anonymous pipe (obtaining the two handles), then write some data to the pipe, and read the same data back:

```
>>> import win32pipe
>>> # Create the pipe
>>> readHandle, writeHandle = win32pipe.CreatePipe(None, 0)
>>> import win32file # This module contains the ReadFile/WriteFile functions.
>>> # Write a string to the pipe
>>> win32file.WriteFile(writeHandle, "Hi from the pipe")
(0, 16)
>>> # Now read data from it
>>> win32file.ReadFile(readHandle, 16)
(0, 'Hi from the pipe')
>>>
```

Named Pipes

Named pipes are similar to anonymous pipes, except they have a unique name. Typically, a server process creates a named pipe with a known name, and other client processes connect to this pipe simply by specifying the name. The key benefit of named pipes is that unrelated processes can use them, even from over the network. All a process needs is the name of the pipe, possibly the name of the host server, and sufficient security to open it. This makes named pipes suitable for simple communication between a server and many clients.

Named pipes can be created only by Windows NT. Windows 95/98 can create a client connection to an existing named pipe, but can't create a new named pipe.

Creating and using named pipes is a complex subject and beyond the scope of this book. However, an example using named pipes can be found in Chapter 18. The `win32pipe` module supports all pipe operations supported by Windows. For further information on named pipes, please see the Windows SDK documentation or one of the pipe samples that comes with the Python for Windows Extensions.

Processes

Every program running under Windows runs in the context of a process. A process is an executing application and has a single virtual address space, a list of valid handles, and other Windows resources. A process consists of at least one thread, but may contain a large number of threads.

Python has the ability to manage processes from a fairly high level, right down to the low level defined by the Win32 API. This section discusses some of these capabilities.

Portable Process Control: The os Module

Python itself defines a few process-manipulation functions that are portable across all platforms, including Windows. As they are portable to Unix and other operating systems, they operate at a high level and don't cover the range of functionality provided natively. The Python os module provides a number of techniques for starting new processes.

os.system

`os.system` provides the most rudimentary support for new processes. It takes a single argument (the command line of the process to execute) and returns an integer "error code." For example:

```
>>> import os
>>> os.system("notepad.exe C:\\autoexec.bat")
0
>>>
```

starts an instance of *notepad*, editing your *autoexec.bat* file. The exit code from the program is zero. Unfortunately, the result of zero is often misleading; the Windows command processor responsible for executing these commands usually refuses to pass the actual error code on, always reporting a success code of zero.

The single parameter can be anything that typically works from a Windows command prompt. Thus, the system `path` is searched for the program.

There are, however, a number of other limitations to this approach. First, if you execute this code from PythonWin (or any other GUI Python environment) you will notice that an empty command prompt opens. Windows knows you are running from a GUI, but isn't smart enough to look at the program to execute to determine if it too is a GUI program; so it creates a new console for the program. This works well when executing command-line tools, but not so well for GUI programs such as *notepad*.

Second, notice that Python waits until the new process has terminated before returning. Depending on your requirements, this may or may not be appropriate.

os.execv

`os.execv` provides an interesting (although often useless) way to create new processes. The program you specify effectively replaces the calling process. Technically, the process to be created is a new process (i.e., it has a different process ID), so the new process doesn't replace the old process; the old process simply terminates immediately after the call to `os.execv`. In effect, the new process executed appears to overwrite the current process, almost as if the old process becomes the new process; therefore, it's rarely used.

`os.execv` takes two arguments: a string containing the program to execute, and a tuple containing the program arguments. For example, if you execute the following code:

```
>>> import os
>>> os.execv("c:\\Winnt\\notepad.exe", ("c:\\autoexec.bat",) )
```

Notice that your existing Python or PythonWin implementation immediately terminates (no chance to save anything!) and is replaced by an instance of *notepad*.

Also notice that `os.execv` doesn't search your system path. Therefore, you need to specify the full path to *notepad*. You will probably need to change the example to reflect your Windows installation.

Another function, `os.execve`, is similar but allows a custom environment for the new process to be defined.

os.popen

`os.popen` is also supposed to be a portable technique for creating new processes and capturing their output. `os.popen` takes three parameters: the command to execute, the default mode for the pipe, and the buffer size. Only the first parameter is required; the others have reasonable defaults (see the Python Library Reference for details). The following code shows that the function returns a Python file object, which can be read to receive the data:

```
>>> import os
>>> file = os.popen("echo Hello from Python")
>>> file.read()
'Hello from Python\012'
>>>
```

If you try this code from *Python.exe*, you will notice it works as expected. However, if you attempt to execute this code from a GUI environment, such as PythonWin, you receive this error:

```
>>> os.popen("echo Hello from Python")
Traceback (innermost last):
  File "<interactive input>", line 0, in ?
error: (0, 'No error')
>>>
```

Unfortunately, a bug in the Windows **popen** function prevents this working from a GUI environment.

Attempting to come to the rescue is the **win32pipe** module, which provides a replacement **popen** that works in a GUI environment under Windows NT; see the following code:

```
>>> import win32pipe
>>> file=win32pipe.popen("echo Hello from Python")
>>> file.read()
'Hello from Python\012'
>>>
```

Better Process Control: The win32api Module

The module **win32api** provides some additional techniques for manipulating processes. These allow you to perform many of the common requirements for starting new processes, but still don't provide the ultimate in low-level control.

win32api.WinExec

The **WinExec** function behaves similarly to the **os.system** function, as described previously, but it provides some concessions for GUI programs; namely, no console is created, and the function doesn't wait until the new process has completed. The function takes two parameters:

- The command to execute
- Optionally, the initial state for the application's window

For example, to execute *notepad*, using the default window state, you can execute the following code:

```
>>> import win32api
>>> win32api.WinExec("notepad")
>>>
```

notepad should appear in a normal window, and Python continues executing commands before you close *notepad*.

To show *notepad* maximized:

```
>>> import win32api, win32con
>>> win32api.WinExec("notepad", win32con.SW_SHOWMAXIMIZED)
>>>
```

win32api.ShellExecute

The `win32api` module also provides another useful function for creating new processes. The `ShellExecute` function is primarily used to open documents, rather than start arbitrary processes. For example, you can tell `ShellExecute` to "open *MyDocument.doc.*" Windows itself determines which process to use to open *.doc* files and start it on your behalf. This is the same function Windows Explorer uses when you click (or double-click) on a *.doc* file: it calls `ShellExecute`, and the correct program is started. The `ShellExecute` function takes these parameters:

- The handle to the parent window or zero for no parent.
- The operation to perform on the file.
- The name of the file or program to execute.
- Optional parameters for the new process.
- The initial directory for the application.
- A flag indicating if the application should be shown.

Let's try this function. Start Python or PythonWin from a directory with a *.doc* file in it, then execute the following commands:

```
>>> import win32api
>>> win32api.ShellExecute(0, "open", \
...     "MyDocument.doc", None, "", 1)
33
>>>
```

Assuming Microsoft Word is installed, this code opens the document *MyDocument.doc.* If you instead wish to print this document, execute this:

```
>>> import win32api
>>> win32api.ShellExecute(0, "print", \
...     "MyDocument.doc", None, "", 1)
33
>>>
```

Microsoft Word then opens and prints the document.

Ultimate Process Control: The win32process Module

The `win32process` module provides the ultimate in process level control; it exposes most of the native Windows API for starting, stopping, controlling, and waiting for processes. But before we delve into the `win32process` module, some definitions are in order.

Handles and IDs

Every thread and process in the system can be identified by a Windows handle, and by an integer ID. A process or thread ID is a unique number allocated for the process or thread and is valid across the entire system. An ID is invariant while the thread or process is running and serves no purpose other than to uniquely identify the thread or process. IDs are reused, so while two threads or processes will never share the same ID while running, the same ID may be reused by the system once it has terminated. Further, IDs are not secure. Any user can obtain the ID for a thread or process. This is not a security problem, as the ID is not sufficient to control the thread or process.

A handle provides additional control capabilities for the thread or handle. Using a handle, you can wait for a process to terminate, force the termination of a process, or change the characteristics of a running process.

While a process can have only a single ID, there may be many handles to it. The handle to a process determines the rights a user has to perform operations on the process or thread.

Given a process ID, the function `win32api.OpenProcess()` can obtain a handle. The ability to use this handle is determined by the security settings for both the current user and the process itself.

Creating processes

The `win32process` module contains two functions for creating new processes: `CreateProcess()` and `CreateProcessAsUser()`. These functions are identical, except `CreateProcessAsUser()` accepts an additional parameter indicating the user under which the process should be created.

`CreateProcess()` accepts a large number of arguments that allow very fine control over the new process:

- The program to execute
- Optional command-line parameters
- Security attributes for the new process or **None**
- Security attributes for the main thread of the new process or **None**
- A flag indicating if handles are inherited by the new process
- Flags indicating how the new process is to be created
- A new environment for the new process or **None** for the current environment
- The current directory for the new process
- Information indicating how the new window is to be positioned and shown

And returns a tuple with four elements:

- A handle to the new process
- A handle to the main thread of the new process
- An integer identifying the new process
- An integer identifying the main thread of the new process

Terminating processes

To terminate a process, the `win32process.TerminateProcess()` function is used. This function takes two parameters:

- A handle to the process to be terminated
- The exit code to associate with the process

If you initially created the new process, it's quite easy to get the handle to the process; you simply remember the result of the `win32process.CreateProcess()` call.

But what happens if you didn't create the process? If you know the process ID, you can use the function `win32api.OpenProcess()` to obtain a handle. But how do you find the process ID? There's no easy answer to that question. The file `killProcName.py` that comes with the Python for Windows Extensions shows one method of obtaining the process ID given the process name. It also shows how to use the `win32api.OpenProcess()` function to obtain a process handle suitable to terminate.

Controlling processes

Once a process is running, there are two process properties that can be set: the *priority* and the *affinity mask*. The priority of the process determines how the operating system schedules the threads in the process. The `win32process.SetPriorityClass()` function can set the priority.

A process's affinity mask defines which processor the process runs on, which obviously makes this useful only in a multiprocessor system. The `win32process.SetProcessAffinityMask()` function allows you to define this behavior.

Putting it all together

This section presents a simple example that demonstrates how to use the `CreateProcess` API and process handles. In the interests of allowing the salient points to come through, this example won't really do anything too useful; instead, it's restricted to the following functionality:

- Creates two instances of *notepad* with its window position carefully laid out.

- Waits 10 seconds for these instances to terminate.

- If the instances haven't terminated in that time, kills them.

This functionality demonstrates the `win32process.CreateProcess()` function, how to use `win32process.STARTUPINFO()` objects, and how to wait on process handles using the `win32event.WaitForMultipleObjects()` function.

Note that instead of waiting 10 seconds in one block, you actually wait for one second 10 times. This is so you can print a message out once per second, so it's obvious the program is working correctly:

```python
# CreateProcess.py
#
# Demo of creating two processes using the CreateProcess API,
# then waiting for the processes to terminate.

import win32process
import win32event
import win32con
import win32api


# Create a process specified by commandLine, and
# The process' window should be at position rect
# Returns the handle to the new process.
def CreateMyProcess( commandLine, rect):
    # Create a STARTUPINFO object
    si = win32process.STARTUPINFO()
    # Set the position in the startup info.
    si.dwX, si.dwY, si.dwXSize, si.dwYSize = rect
    # And indicate which of the items are valid.
    si.dwFlags = win32process.STARTF_USEPOSITION | \
                 win32process.STARTF_USESIZE
    # Rest of startup info is default, so we leave alone.
    # Create the process.
    info = win32process.CreateProcess(
                    None, # AppName
                    commandLine, # Command line
                    None, # Process Security
                    None, # ThreadSecurity
                    0, # Inherit Handles?
                    win32process.NORMAL_PRIORITY_CLASS,
                    None, # New environment
                    None, # Current directory
                    si) # startup info.
    # Return the handle to the process.
    # Recall info is a tuple of (hProcess, hThread, processId, threadId)
    return info[0]

def RunEm():
    handles = []
    # First get the screen size to calculate layout.
```

```
        screenX = win32api.GetSystemMetrics(win32con.SM_CXSCREEN)
        screenY = win32api.GetSystemMetrics(win32con.SM_CYSCREEN)
        # First instance will be on the left hand side of the screen.
        rect = 0, 0, screenX/2, screenY
        handle = CreateMyProcess("notepad", rect)
        handles.append(handle)
        # Second instance of notepad will be on the right hand side.
        rect = screenX/2+1, 0, screenX/2, screenY
        handle = CreateMyProcess("notepad", rect)
        handles.append(handle)

        # Now we have the processes, wait for them both
        # to terminate.
        # Rather than waiting the whole time, we loop 10 times,
        # waiting for one second each time, printing a message
        # each time around the loop
        countdown = range(1,10)
        countdown.reverse()
        for i in countdown:
            print "Waiting %d seconds for apps to close" % i
            rc = win32event.WaitForMultipleObjects(
                                handles, # Objects to wait for.
                                1, # Wait for them all
                                1000) # timeout in milli-seconds.
            if rc == win32event.WAIT_OBJECT_0:
                # Our processes closed!
                print "Our processes closed in time."
                break
            # else just continue around the loop.
        else:
            # We didn't break out of the for loop!
            print "Giving up waiting - killing processes"
            for handle in handles:
                try:
                    win32process.TerminateProcess(handle, 0)
                except win32process.error:
                    # This one may have already stopped.
                    pass

if __name__=='__main__':
    RunEm()
```

You should run this example from a command prompt rather than from PythonWin. Under PythonWin, the script works correctly, but due to the complications of running in a GUI environment, PythonWin appears to hang until either 10 seconds expires or the applications close. Although PythonWin is printing the messages once per second, they can't be seen until the script closes.

You run this example from a command prompt as you would any script. Running the script creates two instances of *notepad* taking up the entire screen. If you switch back to the command prompt, notice the following messages:

```
C:\Scripts>python CreateProcess.py
Waiting 9 seconds for apps to close
...
Waiting 2 seconds for apps to close
Waiting 1 seconds for apps to close
Giving up waiting - killing processes
C:\Scripts>
```

If instead of switching back to the command prompt, you simply close the new instances of *notepad*, you'll see the following:

```
C:\Scripts>python CreateProcess.py
Waiting 9 seconds for apps to close
Waiting 8 seconds for apps to close
Our processes closed in time.
C:\Scripts>
```

Conclusion

In this chapter, we have looked that the various techniques we can use in Python for working with files and processes. We discussed how Python's standard library has a number of modules for working with files and processes in a portable way, and a few of the problems you may encounter when using these modules.

We also discussed the native Windows API for dealing with these objects and the Python interface to this API. We saw how Python can be used to work with and exploit the Windows specific features of files and processes.

18

Windows NT Services

Windows NT has a special class of processes known as *services* that can execute without a user logged in to the workstation and can be controlled by the Windows Service Control Manager. Services must meet certain requirements imposed by Windows NT, primarily the ability to handle asynchronous control messages (such as Stop) from Windows. Most services also choose to use the standard Windows NT Event Log and Performance Monitor to augment their application.

Python has complete support for Windows NT Services. Python programs can run as services and meet all the Microsoft Back Office Certified requirements, including Event Log and Performance Monitor support. In addition, Python can control other services, making it suitable for many administrative tasks, such as checking the status of services, and restarting them if necessary.

Services in Brief

A Windows NT Service is a normal program with additional responsibilities and complications.

Service Control Manager

An integral part of Windows NT is the Service Control Manager (SCM). All Windows NT services must be registered with the SCM, which is responsible for starting and stopping the service process. When a process registers with the SCM, it provides attributes about the service, including:

- The username that runs the process. This may not be the same as the user currently logged in to the system; indeed, there may not be anyone logged on to the system when the service starts.

- Any other services that this service depends on. For example, if you were writing a Microsoft Exchange extension, you may specify your service is dependent on the Microsoft Exchange Information Store service. The SCM ensures that all dependent services are running before your service can start. It also ensures that when a service is stopped, all services that depend on it are also stopped.

- How the service is to start: automatically when the system boots (and all dependants have also started), or manually (i.e., when initiated by the user).

The SCM provides a user interface that allows the user to manually control services. This user interface is available from the Services applet in the control panel.

The SCM also provides an API to allow programmatic control of services. Thus it is possible for a program to control services.

Starting and Stopping

Typically, Windows NT itself is responsible for starting and stopping services via the Service Control Manager. The SCM provides a user interface to allow the user to start and stop services manually, via the Services applet in the control panel.

When a service starts, it must report its status to the SCM. Further, it must listen for control requests from the SCM. When a service is to stop, the SCM issues a control request to the service. The service itself must act on this request and report back to the SCM as it shuts down and just before it terminates.

User Interface

Services typically have no user interface associated with them. It's important to remember that services may be running while no user is logged into the system, so often there is no user with which to interact.

In some cases, it's possible for the service to display simple dialog boxes, such as a MessageBox. However, this is fraught with danger and best avoided. Communication with the user is typically done via the Windows NT Event Log.

Error Reporting and Handling

Error reporting for Windows NT Services can be viewed as very simple: use the Windows NT Event Log. Unfortunately, using the Windows NT Event Log is not as simple as it sounds! We will discuss the key concepts of the Windows NT Event Log and provide sample code that logs key events.

Performance Monitor

It's often appropriate for a Windows NT service to provide some performance statistics. These statistics can be anything that makes sense to the service: number of current connections, number of clients connected, some throughput information relevant to the service, etc.

The Windows NT Performance Monitor can provide this information. There are a number of benefits to using this instead of creating your own scheme, including:

Single common repository of performance information
> Windows NT administrators don't need to learn a new tool of interface simply for your service.

Nice user interface already provided and very general API
> The Performance Monitor has a decent user interface for performance information installed on every copy of Windows NT. As Microsoft makes enhancements to this interface, your application automatically benefits. The API used by the Performance Monitor is general and should be capable of accommodating most performance-logging requirements.

Third party tools already available
> By providing your data via the Performance Monitor, NT administrators can take advantage of third-party tools for monitoring this information. For example, tools are available that periodically check the performance information, and can take corrective action should they find any problems.

Controlling Services with Python

As a further introduction to Windows NT Services, we will discuss some of the functions available from Python to control existing services.

As is common with Python extensions, there are two Python modules that can work with services: The `win32service` module implements the Win32 service functions, while the `win32serviceutil` module provides some handy utilities that utilize the raw API. We begin with a discussion of the Win32 functions exposed by the `win32service` module before moving to some of the utilities.

Connecting to the SCM

Most of the Win32 API for working with services requires a handle to the SCM. This is obtained by the function `win32service.OpenSCManager()`.

```
handle = win32service.OpenSCManager(machineName, databaseName, access)
```

machineName
> The name of the machine on which you wish to open the SCM. This can be **None** or left empty for the current machine.

databaseName

> The name of the service database or **None** for the default. The default is almost always used.

access

> The desired access on the SCM.

The result is a handle to the SCM. Once you are finished with the handle, the function `win32service.CloseServiceHandle()` is used. See Appendix B, *Win32 Extensions Reference*, for a complete description of these functions.

To open the SCM on the current machine, we could use the following code:

```
>>> import win32service
>>> hscm=win32service.OpenSCManager(None, None, win32service.SC_MANAGER_ALL_
ACCESS)
>>> hscm
1368896
>>>
```

As you can see, service handles are implemented as integers, although this may be changed to a variation of a `PyHANDLE` object.

Connecting to a Service

Once you have a handle to the SCM, open a specific service using the function `win32service.OpenService()`, which has the following signature.

`handle = win32service.OpenService(schandle, serviceName, desiredAccess)`

schandle

> A handle to the SCM, as obtained from `win32service.OpenSCManager()`.

serviceName

> The name of the service to open.

desiredAccess

> A bitmask of flags defining the desired access. `win32service.SERVICE_ALL_ACCESS` provides all access.

Now that you're connected to the SCM, you can obtain a handle to the messenger service with the following code:

```
>>> hs=win32service.OpenService(hscm, "Messenger",
...                             win32service.SERVICE_ALL_ACCESS)
>>> hs
1375960
>>>
```

Querying the Status of a Service

Finally, we can do something useful with the service. The simplest thing is to query the current status of the service. `win32service.QueryServiceStatus()` does this:

```
>>> status=win32service.QueryServiceStatus(hs)
>>> status
(32, 4, 5, 0, 0, 0, 0)
>>>
```

So what does this say? A quick check of Appendix B gives the data returned for a service status, but briefly, the information includes:

- The type of service.

- The current state of the service, i.e., is it running, stopped, stopping, etc.

- The type of controls the service accepts, i.e., can it be stopped, paused, etc.

- A Win32 error code, as set by the service. This is typically set once the service stops.

- A service-specific error code. This is typically set once the service stops.

- The service's checkpoint. See Appendix B for details.

- The service's wait-hint. See Appendix B for details.

Armed with this information, you can create a function to print a description of the service status:

```
>>> def PrintServiceStatus(status):
...     svcType, svcState, svcControls, err, svcErr, svcCP, svcWH = status
...     if svcType & win32service.SERVICE_WIN32_OWN_PROCESS:
...         print "The service runs in its own process"
...     if svcType & win32service.SERVICE_WIN32_SHARE_PROCESS:
...         print "The service shares a process with other services"
...     if svcType & win32service.SERVICE_INTERACTIVE_PROCESS:
...         print "The service can interact with the desktop"
...     # Other svcType flags not shown.
...     if svcState==win32service.SERVICE_STOPPED:
...         print "The service is stopped"
...     elif svcState==win32service.SERVICE_START_PENDING:
...         print "The service is starting"
...     elif svcState==win32service.SERVICE_STOP_PENDING:
...         print "The service is stopping"
...     elif svcState==win32service.SERVICE_RUNNING:
...         print "The service is running"
...     # Other svcState flags not shown.
...     if svcControls & win32service.SERVICE_ACCEPT_STOP:
...         print "The service can be stopped"
...     if svcControls & win32service.SERVICE_ACCEPT_PAUSE_CONTINUE:
...         print "The service can be paused"
...     # Other svcControls flags not shown
...
```

Now let's call this function with the previously obtained status:

```
>>> PrintServiceStatus(status)
The service shares a process with other services
The service is running
The service can be stopped
>>>
```

This says that the messenger service is actually in the same process as one or more other services. It is not uncommon for many related services to be implemented in a single executable, although Python doesn't currently support hosting multiple services in this way. The service is currently running, but can be stopped. Let's give that a try.

Controlling a Service

If you haven't already guessed, to control a service you use the `win32service.ControlService()` function. This function is simple: it takes a handle to the service you wish to control and an integer identifying the control to send. The function returns the new status for the service, in the same format returned by the `win32service.QueryServiceStatus()` function.

Let's stop the messenger service:

```
>>> newStatus=win32service.ControlService(hs, win32service.SERVICE_CONTROL_STOP)
>>>
```

And use the helper function to decode the status:

```
>>> PrintServiceStatus(newStatus)
The service shares a process with other services
The service is stopping
>>>
```

The service status reports the service is stopping. If you query the service status in a few seconds, note that it finally stopped:

```
>>> PrintServiceStatus(win32service.QueryServiceStatus(hs))
The service shares a process with other services
The service is stopped
```

This is an important point. `win32service.ControlService()` returns immediately when the service has accepted the control request; it may take some time for the service to complete the request.

Let's restart the service to bring everything back to the same state in which we found it. Starting a service requires the use of the `win32service.StartService()` function. This function takes a handle to the service to start and the arguments for the service or **None** if there are no arguments.

Now restart the service:

```
>>> win32service.StartService(hs, None)
>>>
```

The service now goes through its start process. This may take some time to complete. If you need to wait until the service startup is complete, poll the `win32service.QueryServiceStatus()` function.

Closing Service Handles

You need to manually close all `win32service` handles once you no longer need them; Python doesn't automatically do so. In future, it's expected that Python will automatically close handles, but it's good practice to do it yourself.

Let's close the handles used in the examples:

```
>>> win32service.CloseServiceHandle(hs)
>>> win32service.CloseServiceHandle(hscm)
>>>
```

Utility Functions to Simplify Working with Services

While working with the SCM is not difficult, it's a little tedious dealing with the handles and the SCM. To this end, the `win32serviceutil` module attempts to make simple interactions with services quicker and easier. The module is poorly documented, so some of the functions are discussed here:

`status = StopService(`*serviceName, machine=None*`):`
  Stops the named service on the specified machine. For example, to stop the messenger service on the computer named *skippy*:

```
>>> win32serviceutil.StopService("Messenger", "skippy")
(32, 3, 0, 0, 0, 6, 20000)
>>> .
```
  The result is the same as from the `win32service.StopService()` function described previously in this chapter.

`StopServiceWithDeps (`*serviceName, machine=None, waitSecs=30*`):`
  Similar to `StopService`, but stops the named service after stopping all dependant services. This function waits *waitSecs* for each service to stop.

`StartService(`*serviceName, args=None, machine=None*`):`
  Starts the named service on the specified machine, with the specified arguments. For example, to start the messenger service on the computer named *skippy*:

```
>>> win32serviceutil.StartService("Messenger", None, "skippy")
>>>
```

RestartService(*serviceName, args=None, waitSeconds=30, machine=* **
None):**

If the service is already running, stops the service and waits *waitSeconds* for the stop process to complete. Then it starts the service with the specified arguments. This is used mainly for debugging services, where stopping then restarting a Python service is necessary for code changes to take affect.

QueryServiceStatus(*serviceName, machine=None***):**

Query the status of the named service. The result is the same as from the `win32service.QueryServiceStatus()` function as described previously in this chapter.

ControlService(*serviceName, code, machine=None***):**

Sends the specified control code to the named service on the specified machine.

Reading the Event Log

The Windows NT Event Log is a single repository applications can use to log certain types of information. The Event Log provides a number of features that make it attractive for applications to use:

- It provides a central point for an NT administrator to view all relevant messages, regardless of what application generated them.

- It is transactional and thread-safe. There's no need to protect multiple threads from writing at the same time and no need to worry about partial records being written.

- It has functionality for overwriting old records should the Event Log become full.

- The minimum amount of information possible is written to the Event Log. The Event Log message is not written to the Event Log, just the "inserts" specific to this entry. For example, a message may be defined as "Cannot open file %1." This message is not written to the log; only the event ID and its "inserts" (in this case the filename) is written. This keeps Event Log records small.

To view the Event Log, use the Event Log Viewer, which can be found under the Administrative Tools folder on the Windows NT Start menu.

Most services write information to the Event Log, but exactly what they write depends on the service. Most services write an entry when they start and stop, encounter an error, or need to report audit or access control information.

There are two Python modules that support the Event Log: `win32evtlog` supplies a Python interface to the native Win32 Event Log API, while the `win32evtlog-util` module provides utilities to make working with the Event Log simpler.

The function `win32evtlog.OpenEventLog()` obtains a handle to the Event Log. This handle can then be passed to `win32evtlog.ReadEventLog()` to obtain the raw data. When you are finished with the handle, it's closed with `win32evtlog.CloseEventLog()`. See Appendix B for more information on these functions.

`win32evtlog.OpenEventLog()` takes two parameters:

- The name of the machine whose Event Log is to be opened or **None** for the current machine
- The name of the log to open, such as Application or System

`win32evtlog.ReadEventLog()` takes three parameters:

- The handle to the Event Log
- Flags to indicate how to read the records, e.g., sequentially forward, sequentially backwards, random access, and so on
- If random access is requested, the record number to search

`win32evtlog.ReadEventLog()` returns a list of Event Log records; you never know exactly how many records you will retrieve in a single call. When you receive zero records, you've reached the end.

Python EventLogRecord Object

A record from an Event Log contains quite a bit of information. Rather than attempt to encode this information in a tuple, a `PyEventLogRecord` object is used. These objects have the attributes described in Table 18-1.

Table 18-1. Attributes of a PyEventLogRecord

Attribute	Description
`RecordNumber`	The number of the Event Log record. This number could be used to seek to the specific record.
`TimeGenerated`	A `Time` object indicating the time the record was generated.
`TimeWritten`	A `Time` object indicating the time the record was actually written to the log.
`EventID`	An integer event ID, as defined by the application writing the record.
`EventType`	An integer defining the event type. Will be one of: EVENTLOG_ERROR_TYPE EVENTLOG_WARNING_TYPE EVENTLOG_INFORMATION_TYPE EVENTLOG_AUDIT_SUCCESS EVENTLOG_AUDIT_FAILURE
`EventCategory`	An integer event category, as defined by the application writing the record.
`SourceName`	The name of the application that generated the Event Log record.

Table 18-1. Attributes of a PyEventLogRecord (continued)

Attribute	Description
ComputerName	The name of the computer that generated this message.
StringInserts	The string inserts for this message.
Sid	The security identifier of a user to be associated with this record.
Data	The raw binary data for the Event Log record.

How to Read the Event Log

This functionality is easy to demonstrate. Let's open the Event Log and read the first few records:

```
>>> import win32evtlog
>>> h=win32evtlog.OpenEventLog(None, "Application")
```

You've now opened the application Event Log. To read records sequentially backwards from the end, combine the flags using the Python bitwise-or operator (|):

```
>>> flags= win32evtlog.EVENTLOG_BACKWARDS_READ|win32evtlog.EVENTLOG_SEQUENTIAL_
READ
>>> records=win32evtlog.ReadEventLog(h, flags, 0)
>>> len(records)
7
```

This call to ReadEventLog() returned seven Event Log records. Let's look at some of the properties of the first one:

```
>>> records[0]
<PyEventLogRecord object at 187d040>
```

It's one of our objects; let's look inside:

```
>>> records[0].SourceName
L'WinSock Proxy Client'
>>> records[0].TimeWritten.Format()
'01/27/99 11:42:22'
>>>
```

This first record was written by the "Winsock Proxy Client," and you can see the date and time it was written. Note the L prefix on the returned string. All strings are returned as Unicode objects.

A Simpler Way to Read Event Log Records

The function win32evtlogutil.FeedEventLogRecords() is a helper function that makes working with Event Log records easier. To use this function, you supply your own function that takes a single parameter. As records are read, your function is called with the Event Log record. To demonstrate, let's write a function that obtains all Event Log records for the "WinSock Proxy Client" application.

First, define the "Feeder" function:

```
>>> def CheckRecord(record):
...     if str(record.SourceName)=="WinSock Proxy Client":
...         print "Have Event ID %s written at %s" % \
...             (record.EventID, record.TimeWritten.Format())
...
...
```

Then feed Event Log records to this function. Now call `FeedEventLogRecords()` specifying your function as the first parameter:

```
>>> win32evtlogutil.FeedEventLogRecords(CheckRecord)
Have Event ID -2147483645 written at 01/27/99 11:42:22
Have Event ID -2147483645 written at 01/27/99 11:42:13
Have Event ID -2147483645 written at 01/27/99 11:42:10
Have Event ID -2147483645 written at 01/21/99 21:46:43
>>>
```

Note that `win32evtlogutil.FeedEventLogRecords()` takes additional parameters allowing you to specify which Event Log to read, and the order for records to be obtained. See the *win32evtlogutil.py* module for details.

Obtaining the Message for an Event Log Record

As discussed previously, the text for a message is not written to the Event Log, just the inserts specific to this record. Obtaining the text for an Event Log record isn't a trivial matter; it requires you to look up the registry, then call a complicated Win32 function to format the message. Fortunately, the `win32evtlogutil` module comes to the rescue.

There are two functions in this module that deal with formatting messages. `win32evtlogutil.FormatMessage()` returns a formatted message, raising an exception if an error occurs (such as not being able to locate the source of the message text). `win32evtlogutil.SafeFormatMessage()` is similar, but it traps the exceptions and returns a useful value. Let's change the feeder function to print the full Event Log message:

```
>>> def CheckRecord(record):
...     if str(record.SourceName)=="WinSock Proxy Client":
...         print win32evtlogutil.SafeFormatMessage(record)
...
```

And feed Event Log records to it:

```
>>> win32evtlogutil.FeedEventLogRecords(CheckRecord)
Application [DCCMAN.EXE]. The application was started while the service manager
was locked and NtLmSsp wasn't running.
If the application will try to remote via WinSock Proxy it can cause a deadlock
with the service manager.
[and lots more boring stuff!]
```

Windows NT Performance Monitor Data

The Windows NT Performance Monitor is a tool and API that allows applications to provide performance data in a consistent way. Administrators can use the Performance Monitor tool to view this data graphically, or programs can themselves use this data for more advanced purposes, such as taking daily samples of performance data and logging to a database.

Using the Performance Monitor has a number of benefits for both the administrator and programmer. The administrator can use a single, consistent interface for monitoring performance, regardless of the application in question; indeed, the administrator can simultaneously view performance information from two unrelated applications to assist in diagnosing performance bottlenecks. For you, the programmer, the biggest advantage is that you can provide detailed performance information for your application, but don't need to deliver any tools for viewing or analyzing this data; Windows NT and third-party tools provide all the functionality anyone could need!

In the next section we discuss the concepts behind the Performance Monitor, and how you can read Performance Monitor data using Python. Later in this chapter we will present how Python can provide Performance Monitor data for our sample Windows NT Service.

Anatomy of the Performance Monitor

To use the Performance Monitor, an application must register one or more Performance Monitor *objects*. An object is a logical grouping of Performance Monitor data; it is quite common for an application to have a single object, grouping all performance-related data from the application in this single object.

For each object, the application must register one or more *counters*. A counter provides a single piece of performance data. Attributes about a counter include the units and the default scale for the final value. The units indicate how the counter values are to be transformed (for example, turned into a rate per second), while the scale defines a multiplication factor applied before the value is displayed or graphed.

For example, let's assume the application needs to keep a counter for connections per second made to it. The application is fast, so expect a hit rate in the thousands of connections per second. You would define your counter as having units of "per second" and a scale of "divide by 100." All the application needs to do is increment the counter once for each connection established, and the Performance Monitor itself will handle the transformation of the raw counter data to a value in the range 1 to 100 that represents the connections per second. The Performance

Monitor has kept track of how many counter increments were made in the last second and applied the appropriate conversions.

As you can see, from the application's point of view it's quite simple and unobtrusive; once the counters are defined, simply increment a counter whenever you do something interesting. The Performance Monitor manages the translation to useful units. For the program that wishes to view Performance Monitor information, it's also simple: the Performance Monitor itself has already translated the raw values into user-friendly values ready to display. Unfortunately, as we shall see later, the installation and definition of these counters isn't particularly easy, but once that is mastered, the actual usage of the counters in your application is simple.

In addition to objects and counters, the final Performance Monitor concept we mention is that of an *instance*. A counter can optionally have any number of instances associated with it. An instance is used where a single counter applies to multiple things. The most basic example is the Performance Monitor data for the CPU in your computer. Windows NT defines the object and a few counters for data related to a CPU. However, as there may be multiple CPUs installed in a PC, each counter can have an instance, one for each CPU. Thus, when you need to collect performance data for a specific CPU, you need to know the instance you are interested in, or you can ask to collect data for all instances. Most counters provided by applications don't have instances associated with them. In our previous example where we kept total client connections, no instance would be associated with the counter. In all the Performance Monitor examples that follow, we don't use counters with instances, but the concept is mentioned for completeness.

To see these concepts, the simplest thing is to start the Windows NT Performance Monitor (from the Administrative Tools group under the Windows NT Start menu), and select Edit → Add to chart. In the dialog that's presented, you can clearly see the list of objects, counters, and instances. As you select different objects, the available counters will change. Depending on the counter you select, instances may or may not be available. Python can also display this list, so we will move on to Python and the Performance Monitor.

Reading the Performance Monitor from Python

Python exposes the ability to read Performance Monitor information from the `win32pdh` and `win32pdhutil` modules. These modules use a Microsoft API to access the Performance Monitor known as the Performance Data Helper, or PDH, hence the name of the Python modules.

Browsing for counters

To get a feel for these Python modules, let's start with a demonstration of displaying a dialog for the user to browse and select the counters on this or any machine.

The win32pdhutil module provides a function browse() that displays such a dialog. As the user selects the Add button in the dialog, a function you provide is called with the selected counter. This callback function is supplied as a parameter to win32pdhutil.browse(). The first step is to provide the callback function, which takes a single parameter—the name of the counter. Our example simply prints this name.

Thus, the callback function can be defined as follows:

```
>>> def CounterCallback( counter ):
...     print "Counter is", counter
...
>>>
```

You can display the dialog by importing the win32pdhutil module and calling the browse() function passing the callback:

```
>>> import win32pdhutil
>>> win32pdhutil.browse(CounterCallback)
```

A dialog is presented that allows you to select all the counters available on the system and even other systems! Select the Add button and your function is called, printing the selected counter. Figure 18-1 shows the code running under Python-Win, just after selecting the Add button.

The counter definition is a simple string, with the machine, object, counter, and instance portions all embedded in the string. The win32pdh module contains functions for parsing a string of this format into the constituent parts and for building such a string from the parts; see the win32pdhutil module source code for more details.

Once you've determined the counters you want, obtaining the information is quite simple: use the win32pdhutil.GetPerformanceAttributes() function. In the simple case of a counter on the local machine without instances, you need pass only the object name and the counter name. For example, an object called Memory provides a number of counters, including one called Available Bytes. To obtain the value, use the code:

```
>>> win32pdhutil.GetPerformanceAttributes("Memory", "Available Bytes")
18358272
>>>
```

This demonstrates an interesting use of the Performance Monitor. There is some information about the system that's not easily available from the Windows API, but is available from the Performance Monitor. Statistics about processes (including its process ID) or about the memory in the system can often be obtained in far more detail by using the Performance Monitor than by using the API.

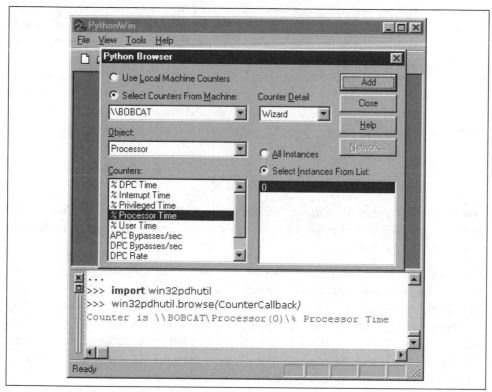

Figure 18-1. Browsing Performance Monitor counters under PythonWin

Writing Services in Python

We have already discussed how Python can control services, now let's see how to write services in Python. Services written in Python are first-class services and provide all the functionality of services written in C.

The Anatomy of a Service

Before we launch into how to write a service in Python, we must discuss some important service concepts. This will help you understand some of the design and implementation decisions made for Python services.

Windows NT starts a service by executing a process. Once this process starts, it's expected to report to the SCM that it's indeed a service and that it's starting. It also must pass to the SCM a control handler; that is, a function that responds to control messages sent by the SCM. The service process then executes. When the service is to be stopped, the SCM notifies the control handler of the stop request. The service itself is responsible for handling this request and terminating itself.

This leads to most services, regardless of the language they are written in, being structured as follows: A main thread starts. This thread initializes itself by reporting to the SCM and passing it the control handler. Once initialization is complete, the thread starts a worker loop waiting either for work to do or a notification to stop, pause, etc. The SCM calls the control handler on another thread, so once the function receives the control notification, it reports back to the SCM it's stopping, then triggers some synchronization object that the main thread will notice next time around the loop. As the main thread terminates, it continues to report its status to the SCM.

The Anatomy of a Python Service

The same executable hosts most Python services, *PythonService.exe*. This special executable is aware of the special requirements for services that make *Python.exe* unsuitable for the task.

When *PythonService.exe* is asked to start a service, it looks in the registry for the Python class that implements the service. It then creates an instance of this class, and delegates all service functionality to this instance. For example, when the service is to start, a method named SvcStart is called on the object. When the SCM makes a control request, a method named ServiceControlHandler is called. These Python methods are expected to correctly report their status to the SCM, by calling helper functions provided by *PythonService.exe*.

To make life as simple as possible for the Python programmer, a base class ServiceFramework is provided in the module win32serviceutil. The easiest way to write a service in Python is to subclass this class, then concentrate on the service functionality rather than on the interactions with the SCM.

The win32serviceutil.ServiceFramework Class

As described previously, most Python services will be a subclass of the win32serviceutil.ServiceFramework class. This has a number of default methods and helper methods to make writing services in Python easier:

__init__
> The constructor for the class. This registers the method ServiceCtrlHandler as the handler for notification messages from the SCM.

ServiceCtrlHandler
> Provides a default implementation of the service control handler. This method interrogates the class for certain named methods to determine which controls the service responds to. For example, if the service contains a SvcPause method, it's assumed the service can be paused.

SvcRun

> A default implementation of the entry point for the service. This method notifies the SCM that the service has started, calls a method SvcDoRun, then when complete notifies the SCM the service is stopping (*PythonService.exe* automatically notifies the SCM that the service has stopped). Thus, you need only provide a SvcDoRun method in the subclass that handles the functionality of your service.

The Smallest Possible Python Service

Before we move on to a more substantial service written in Python, let's write the smallest possible service in Python. This service will do no actual work other than interact with the SCM.

The key points from this example code are:

- The logic for stopping the service must be provided by your application. This sample service uses a Win32 event object and when the command to stop the service is received, it sets this event. The service itself does nothing other than wait for this event to be set.

- The name of the service and the display name of the service must be provided by the subclass.

- This code contains startup code that handles the command line when run as a script. This provides facilities for installing, debugging, and starting the service, as described in the next section.

```python
# SmallestService.py
#
# A sample demonstrating the smallest possible service written in Python.

import win32serviceutil
import win32service
import win32event

class SmallestPythonService(win32serviceutil.ServiceFramework):
    _svc_name_ = "SmallestPythonService"
    _svc_display_name_ = "The smallest possible Python Service"
    def __init__(self, args):
        win32serviceutil.ServiceFramework.__init__(self, args)
        # Create an event which we will use to wait on.
        # The "service stop" request will set this event.
        self.hWaitStop = win32event.CreateEvent(None, 0, 0, None)

    def SvcStop(self):
        # Before we do anything, tell the SCM we are starting the stop process.
        self.ReportServiceStatus(win32service.SERVICE_STOP_PENDING)
        # And set my event.
        win32event.SetEvent(self.hWaitStop)
```

```
    def SvcDoRun(self):
        # We do nothing other than wait to be stopped!
        win32event.WaitForSingleObject(self.hWaitStop, win32event.INFINITE)

if __name__=='__main__':
    win32serviceutil.HandleCommandLine(SmallestPythonService)
```

Installing, Debugging, and Running a Python Service

Now that we have a service written in Python, what to do with it? This section discusses installing the service, debugging the service, and starting and stopping the service.

Installing the service

As discussed previously, an application named *PythonService.exe* hosts all Python services. This executable must be registered before you can install the service. The registration process need only be run once per machine, regardless of how many services the program hosts. The installation package for the Python for Windows extensions automatically registers this, but the information is included here for completeness. To register *PythonService.exe*, perform the following steps:

1. Start a command prompt.

2. Change to the directory containing *PythonService.exe*, typically *Program Files* *Python\win32*.

3. Execute the command:

```
C:\Program Files\Python\win32>PythonService.exe /register
Registering the Python Service Manager...
C:\Program Files\Python\win32>
```

Now to install the service, perform the following steps:

1. Start a command prompt.

2. Change to the directory containing the Python source code that implements the service.

3. Execute the command:

```
C:\Scripts> SmallestService.py install
Installing service SmallestPythonService to Python class
    C:\Scripts\SmallestService.SmallestPythonService
Service installed
C:\Scripts>
```

The service is now installed and ready to run. To confirm the service has been correctly installed, use the control panel to start the Services applet and scroll down until you find the "The smallest possible Python Service."

Starting and stopping the service

There are a number of ways to start or stop a service. Our Python script can start and stop itself. To do this, use the following command:

```
C:\Scripts> python.exe SmallestService.py start
Starting service SmallestPythonService
C:\Scripts>
```

The service is now running. To confirm this, let's try executing the same command again:

```
C:\Scripts> python.exe SmallestService.py start
Starting service SmallestPythonService
Error starting service: An instance of the service is already running.
C:\Scripts>
```

As you can see, only one instance of a service can be running at any time. To stop the service, use the following command:

```
C:\Scripts> python.exe SmallestService.py stop
Stopping service SmallestPythonService
C:\Scripts>
```

There are two other common techniques for starting and stopping services:

- Using the Services applet in the control panel, which provides a GUI for starting, stopping, or pausing services.

- Using the *net.exe* program supplied with Windows NT. From a Windows NT command prompt, this command starts the service:

  ```
  C:\Anywhere> net start SmallestPythonService
  ```

  This command stops the service:

  ```
  C:\Anywhere> net stop SmallestPythonService
  ```

Sample Service Written in Python

Before we move to some of the advanced topics, we will develop the basis for a real Python service that actually does something useful!

The first version of our service starts by accepting connections over a named pipe and comes complete with a client that connects to the service. You then enhance the service by writing to the Event Log and by providing Performance Monitor data.

The first cut looks very much like the SmallestPythonService, except it has more meat in the SvcDoRun() method. The main thread creates a named pipe and waits for either a client to connect or a service control request.

More information on named pipes can be found in Chapter 17, *Processes and Files*. This example also shows a number of concepts important when using named pipes. It shows how to use overlapped I/O, and how to create a special security object useful for named-pipe services:

```python
# PipeService1.py
#
# A sample demonstrating a service which uses a
# named-pipe to accept client connections.

import win32serviceutil
import win32service
import win32event
import win32pipe
import win32file
import pywintypes
import winerror

class PipeService(win32serviceutil.ServiceFramework):
    _svc_name_ = "PythonPipeService"
    _svc_display_name_ = "A sample Python service using named pipes"
    def __init__(self, args):
        win32serviceutil.ServiceFramework.__init__(self, args)
        # Create an event which we will use to wait on.
        # The "service stop" request will set this event.
        self.hWaitStop = win32event.CreateEvent(None, 0, 0, None)
        # We need to use overlapped IO for this, so we don't block when
        # waiting for a client to connect.  This is the only effective way
        # to handle either a client connection, or a service stop request.
        self.overlapped = pywintypes.OVERLAPPED()
        # And create an event to be used in the OVERLAPPED object.
        self.overlapped.hEvent = win32event.CreateEvent(None,0,0,None)

    def SvcStop(self):
        # Before we do anything, tell the SCM we are starting the stop process.
        self.ReportServiceStatus(win32service.SERVICE_STOP_PENDING)
        # And set my event.
        win32event.SetEvent(self.hWaitStop)

    def SvcDoRun(self):
        # We create our named pipe.
        pipeName = "\\\\.\\pipe\\PyPipeService"
        openMode = win32pipe.PIPE_ACCESS_DUPLEX | win32file.FILE_FLAG_OVERLAPPED
        pipeMode = win32pipe.PIPE_TYPE_MESSAGE

        # When running as a service, we must use special security for the pipe
        sa = pywintypes.SECURITY_ATTRIBUTES()
        # Say we do have a DACL, and it is empty
        # (ie, allow full access!)
        sa.SetSecurityDescriptorDacl ( 1, None, 0 )
```

```
pipeHandle = win32pipe.CreateNamedPipe(pipeName,
    openMode,
    pipeMode,
    win32pipe.PIPE_UNLIMITED_INSTANCES,
    0, 0, 6000, # default buffers, and 6 second timeout.
    sa)

# Loop accepting and processing connections
while 1:
    try:
        hr = win32pipe.ConnectNamedPipe(pipeHandle, self.overlapped)
    except error, details:
        print "Error connecting pipe!", details
        pipeHandle.Close()
        break

    if hr==winerror.ERROR_PIPE_CONNECTED:
        # Client is fast, and already connected - signal event
        win32event.SetEvent(self.overlapped.hEvent)
    # Wait for either a connection, or a service stop request.
    timeout = win32event.INFINITE
    waitHandles = self.hWaitStop, self.overlapped.hEvent
    rc = win32event.WaitForMultipleObjects(waitHandles, 0, timeout)
    if rc==win32event.WAIT_OBJECT_0:
        # Stop event
        break
    else:
        # Pipe event - read the data, and write it back.
        # (We only handle a max of 255 characters for this sample)
        try:
            hr, data = win32file.ReadFile(pipeHandle, 256)
            win32file.WriteFile(pipeHandle, "You sent me:" + data)
            # And disconnect from the client.
            win32pipe.DisconnectNamedPipe(pipeHandle)
        except win32file.error:
            # Client disconnected without sending data
            # or before reading the response.
            # Thats OK - just get the next connection
            continue

if __name__=='__main__':
    win32serviceutil.HandleCommandLine(PipeService)
```

This technique for working with named pipes doesn't scale well; our version accepts only a single client connection at a time. Another alternative is to use a new thread to process each connection as it comes in, as demonstrated in *pipeTestService.py,* which comes with the Window's extensions. Even this solution doesn't scale when the number of connections starts to become large, and other techniques, such as thread pooling or NT Completion Ports should be used.

Now let's write a client program to use this service. The client program is quite simple, because the Win32 API function `CallNamedPipe()` encapsulates all of the code most clients ever need. `CallNamedPipe()` is available in the **win32pipe** module.

The client sends all the command-line parameters to the server, then prints the server's response:

```
# PipeServiceClient.py
#
# A client for testing the PipeService.
#
# Usage:
#
#   PipeServiceClient.py message

import win32pipe
import sys
import string

if __name__=='__main__':
    message = string.join(sys.argv[1:])
    pipeName = "\\\\.\\pipe\\PyPipeService"
    data = win32pipe.CallNamedPipe(pipeName, message, 512, 0)
    print "The service sent back:"
    print data
```

Now let's test the service. The first step is to register the service:

```
C:\Scripts> PipeService1 install
Installing service PythonPipeService to Python class
    C:\Scripts\PipeService1.PipeService
Service installed
C:\Scripts>
```

Now start the service:

```
C:\Scripts> PipeService1.py start
Starting service PythonPipeService
C:\Scripts>
```

And use the client to send the service some data:

```
C:\Scripts> PipeServiceClient.py Hi there, how are you
The service sent back:
You sent me:Hi there, how are you
C:>Scripts>
```

Our service seems to be working as expected!

You're now finished; you can stop the service:

```
C:\Scripts> PipeService1.py stop
Stopping service PythonPipeService
C:>Scripts>
```

And remove it from the Service database:

```
C:\Scripts> PipeService1.py remove
Removing service PythonPipeService
Service removed
C:\Scripts>
```

Writing to the Event Log

Almost all services use the Windows NT Event Log. It's quite common for services to load startup and shutdown events, and error conditions should always go to the Event Log.

We look first at the facilities provided by the **servicemanager** module for working with the Event Log. Then we will have another look at a couple of modules described previously in this chapter, **win32evtlog** and **win32evtlogutil**. We discussed how to use these modules to read the Event Log, so now let's look at how they can write to the Log.

The servicemanager Module

As mentioned previously in this chapter, *PythonService.exe* hosts all Python programs running as services. Once this host *.exe* is running, it makes a module **servicemanager** available to the Python program. Because your Python scripts are used both by *Python.exe* (when installing, starting, or debugging the service) and by *PythonService.exe* (when running as a service), you can't import this module from the top level of your Python program; the **import servicemanager** statement will fail for *Python.exe*. In practice, this means you should only import this module locally to a function.

The primary purpose of **servicemanager** is to provide facilities for interacting with the SCM at runtime. Most of this interaction is done by the base class **win32serviceutil.ServiceFramework()**, so in general this is covered for you.

There are, however, some useful utility functions you may wish to use. Among these is a set of functions for writing to the Event Log. The most general purpose is the function **LogMsg()**, which takes the following parameters:

ErrorType
> One of **EVENTLOG_INFORMATION_TYPE**, **EVENTLOG_ERROR_TYPE**, or **EVENTLOG_WARNING_TYPE**. These constants can be found in **servicemanager**.

ErrorID
> The message ID. This uniquely identifies the message text.

Inserts = None
> A list of string inserts for the message or **None**. The inserts are merged with the message text to provide the final result for the user.

There are three other Event Log-related functions in this module. `LogInfoMsg()`, `LogErrorMsg()`, and `LogWarningMessage()`. All take a single string parameter and write a generic message to the Event Log. These functions also provide an additional debugging facility. When debugging the service, these Event Log helpers write their output to the console window. This allows you to see the messages your application would log without needing to use the Event Log Viewer. When the service is running normally, these messages go to the log. We'll see this in action for our example.

The Event Log facilities of `servicemanager` use the name of the executable as the application name. This means that by default, the application name will be PythonService. The only way this can be changed is to take a copy of *PythonService.exe* and rename it to something of your liking (it's only around 20 KB!). Alternatively, you may wish to use the Event Log natively, as described later in this chapter.

Our host *.exe* also contains a number of messages related to starting and stopping the services. The `servicemanager` exposes the message ID of these through constants that include `PYS_SERVICE_STARTING`, `PYS_SERVICE_STARTED`, `PYS_SERVICE_STOPPING`, and `PYS_SERVICE_STOPPED`. These messages all have two inserts: the name of the service and an arbitrary message to be appended.

Modifying the Service to Add Messages

Finally we are ready to change our service to use the Event Log. We will change the service to write messages as it starts and stops, and also after each user has connected.

We add the code for the service starting message at the start of the service's `SvcDoRun()` method. A good place to add the service stopping message is just as this function returns.

The top of this function now looks like:

```
def SvcDoRun(self):
        # Log a "started" message to the event log.
        import servicemanager
        servicemanager.LogMsg(
                servicemanager.EVENTLOG_INFORMATION_TYPE,
                servicemanager.PYS_SERVICE_STARTED,
                (self._svc_name_, ''))
```

And the last lines are:

```
        # Now log a "service stopped" message
        servicemanager.LogMsg(
                servicemanager.EVENTLOG_INFORMATION_TYPE,
                servicemanager.PYS_SERVICE_STOPPED,
                (self._svc_name_, ''))
```

Note that you import the **servicemanager** object at the start of the function. This is because, as described previously, it's provided by the host *.exe* so it can't be imported at the top level of the program. To write a message as the user disconnects, insert this code:

```
# Log a message to the event log indicating what we did.
message = "Processed %d bytes for client connection" % len(data)
servicemanager.LogInfoMsg(message)
```

Let's see our code in action. First, let's run this service in debug mode. From a command prompt, type:

```
C:\Scripts> PipeService2.py debug
Debugging service PythonPipeService
Info 0x40001002 - The PythonPipeService service has started.
```

Now make a client connection to the pipe. It's necessary to open a new command prompt, as the service is being debugged in the other one. From this new command prompt, type:

```
C:\Scripts> PipeServiceClient.py Hi there
The service sent back:
You sent me:Hi there
```

If you look at your service's window, you see the status message:

```
Info 0x400000FF - Processed 8 bytes for client connection
```

Finally, stop the service by pressing Ctrl-Break, and the service responds:

```
Stopping debug service.
Info 0x40001004 - The PythonPipeService service has stopped.
```

As you can see, the service works as expected, and now you can run it as a real service. This forces the messages to the Event Log.

Start the service using any of the techniques described previously, then make a new client connection. If you check the Event Log Viewer, you see the messages at the top of the application log. Figure 18-2 shows the Event Log Viewer with the list of all events; Figure 18-3 shows the detail for the client connection message.

Custom Event Log Writing

There will be cases where you need better facilities than those provided by the **servicemanager** module. The primary reason is that you will require your own set of messages, tailored for your application. In this scenario, you need the message compiler from Microsoft Visual C++ to create your own custom message texts and IDs.

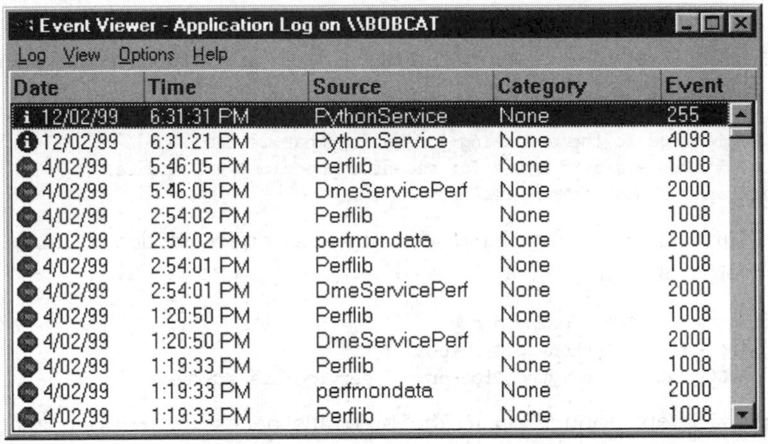

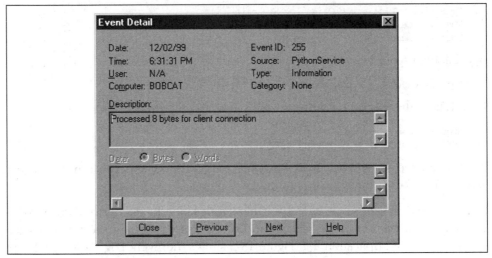

Figure 18-2. Event Log records as displayed in the Windows NT Event Viewer

Figure 18-3. Details for the client connection Event Log record

Registering with the Event Log

The Event Log doesn't store the full text of each message in the log; instead, when the text is needed, it uses the ID of the message to look it up from a DLL or EXE file nominated by the application. This means you need to tell the Event Log where your messages are located.

Applications register with the Event Log by writing an entry to the Event Log's registry. If you open the registry editor, you can view all applications providing Event Log data by looking under the key *KLM\SYSTEM\CurrentControlSet\Services\ EventLog*.

Fortunately, the `win32evtlogutil` module has a utility function for registering your application. As the registry is persistent, it's necessary to register your application only when it's installed; however, some applications choose to do this each time they start.

Any EXE or DLL can hold messages for the Event Log Viewer. The text for messages are typically created with a text editor, and the "message compiler" (supplied with Microsoft Visual C++) compiles them. When the application is linked, the compiled messages are inserted into the final executable. However, this doesn't help you use the Event Log from Python, so a number of the standard Win32 extension files have built-in generic messages for this purpose.

The files *PythonService.exe, win32evtlog.pyd,* and *win32service.pyd* each have a set of generic messages. Each file has nine messages for each of the classes Error, Informational, Warning, and Success.

To register with the Event Viewer, use the function `win32evtlogutil.Add-SourceToRegistry()`.

```
win32evtlogutil.AddSourceToRegistry(ApplicationName, MessageDll, EventLogType=
"Application")
```

ApplicationName
> The name of the application, as shown in the Event Log Viewer. This is an varbitrary name that need not match the name of the service.

MessageDll
> The name of the DLL or EXE file that contains the messages.

`EventLogType = "Application"`
> The Event Log this application writes to. Valid values are `Application` (the default), `System`, or `Security`.

Writing to the Log

Now that we are registered with the Event Log, it's time to start logging some messages. As mentioned before, you call the `win32evtlog` and `win32evtlogutil` modules to help out.

To manually insert a message in the Event Log, use the function `win32evtlogutil.ReportEvent()`.

```
win32evtlogutil.ReportEvent(ApplicationName, EventID, EventCategory, EventType,
Inserts=[], Data=None, SID=None)
```

ApplicationName
> The name of the application, as registered using the `AddSourceToRegistry()` function.

EventID
> The numeric ID of the event.

EventCategory = 0
> The event category, as defined by the message file.

EventType = win32evtlog.EVENTLOG_ERROR_TYPE
> The numeric event type. This indicates the message is an error, a warning, informational, etc.

Inserts = []
> A list of string inserts for the message. These inserts create the full text of the message and are inserted into the message text at the appropriate place holders.

Data = None
> The data for the message. This is raw binary data as a Python string and is displayed in hexadecimal by the Event Log Viewer.

SID = None
> A security identifier for the user this message relates to, if any.

Let's look at the long way we could add the startup and shutdown messages to our service. This should give you a reasonable idea of how you could implement your own custom messages in the Log.

If you use the table in Appendix B, you can see that *PythonService.exe* has messages specifically for this purpose: Informational Event IDs 1002 and 1004, respectively. The **servicemanager** module exposes these constants as **PYS_SERVICE_STARTED** and **PYS_SERVICE_STOPPED**. The table also indicates that this message requires two inserts: the first is the name of the service, and the second is arbitrary text you can append to the message. To log one of these messages, use the following code at the top of your **SvcDoRun()** method:

```
def SvcDoRun(self):
    # Log a "started" message to the event log.
    import servicemanager
    win32evtlogutil.ReportEvent(
        self._svc_name_, # Application name
        servicemanager.PYS_SERVICE_STARTED, # Event ID
        0, # Event category
        win32evtlog.EVENTLOG_INFORMATION_TYPE,
        (self._svc_name_, "")) # The inserts
```

This assumes you have already called **win32evtlogutil.Add-SourceToRegistry()**, using the service name (as defined in **_svc_name_**) as the Event Log application name.

Providing Performance Monitor Information

The next step in our service will be to generate performance information that can be used by the Windows NT Performance Monitor.

The Performance Monitor itself is a fairly complex beast with many options. We will attempt to cover only the basics, enough to install a couple of counters into our sample service. If you require more advanced techniques, you should see the Win32 SDK documentation on the Performance Monitor.

The Performance Monitor has been designed to have minimal impact on the applications providing data. Applications provide raw data (by way of counters), and the responsibility of formatting and translating that data falls to the application processing the data (e.g., the Performance Monitor application provided with Windows NT). When a counter is added to the Performance Monitor, it indicates the type of data it represents. For example, one counter may indicate a raw count, such as total connections made, or it may be a value that should be interpreted over time, such as bytes sent per second. In both cases, the application increments a counter, and the Performance Monitor itself determines how far the counter was incremented in the last second and calculates the actual value to be displayed.

Counters are grouped together to form a Performance Monitor object. These objects exist purely to group related counters together. When you use the NT Performance Monitor Application, you must first select the object you wish to obtain data on, then the counters for that object. Windows NT comes with a number of objects and counters that obtain the performance of the operating system itself. For example, there is a standard processor object, and this object has counters such as percent of processor time, percent of interrupt time, and so forth.

The Performance Monitor expects to obtain the counter and object information from a special DLL. This DLL has public entry-points specific to Performance Monitor, and this DLL is loaded whenever the Performance Monitor needs information on the specific object. In general, this DLL is not an integral part of the application itself, but is instead a custom DLL written expressly for the Performance Monitor. Memory mapped files are typically used to share the counter data between the application itself and the Performance Monitor DLL.

When the application is installed, it must provide the Performance Monitor with definitions of the objects and counters it provides. These definitions include a name for the counter, and a description for the counter. The application must also provide the name of the DLL that provides the data.

Performance Monitor Data from Python

The Python Win32 Extensions include support for providing Performance Monitor information. This support consists of the `perfmon` module that your application uses to define the counters and provide the counter data. A DLL named *perfmondata.dll* is supplied as the Performance Monitor DLL; this is the DLL that the Performance Monitor loads to acquire your performance data.

Installing Performance Monitor information

As mentioned previously, it's necessary to register with the Performance Monitor when your application is installed. To install Performance Monitor information, you must provide the following information:

- The name of a C header (*.h*) file providing information about the counters
- The name of a Windows INI file providing the definitions of the counters
- The name of the DLL providing Performance Monitor information

This information is necessary only at installation time: the *.h* and *.ini* files aren't required at runtime. The Performance Monitor APIs are very much C and C++ focussed, hence the requirement for the *.h* file. Often, this *.h* file would be included in the C/C++ project, but as we are using Python, we need to author a *.h* file that's used only for the installation process.

The header file contains `#define` statements for each counter. Each `#define` lists the offset of the specific counter in two-byte multiples. The offset zero defines the object itself.

For our sample, we provide two counters, connections per second and the bytes received per second. Thus, the header file will have three entries: the object at offset 0, the first counter at offset 2, and the last counter at offset 4.

For the sample application, use the *.h* file in the following code:

```
// PipeService2_install.h
// File used at installation time to install
// Performance Monitor Counters for our sample service.
//
// All these list the counters in order.
// Important that you add these in this order in
// the Python code.

#define SERVICE 0
#define CONNECTIONS 2 // Number of connections
#define BYTES 4 // Number of bytes received.
```

You also need a Windows INI file that defines the counters themselves. This INI file has three required sections: the `[info]` section defines the name of the application, the [languages] section defines the list of languages in which you are providing descriptions, and the [text] section that describes the counters themselves. The INI file for the sample service looks like the following code:

```
; PipeService2_install.ini
; File used at installation time to install
; Performance Monitor Counters for our sample service.
;
[info]
; drivername MUST be the same as the service name
drivername=PythonPipeService
symbolfile=PipeService2_install.h

[languages]
009=English

[text]
SERVICE_009_NAME=Python Demo Service
SERVICE_009_HELP=Shows performance statistics for the sample Python service
CONNECTIONS_009_NAME=Number of connections per second.
CONNECTIONS_009_HELP=Indicates the load on the service.
BYTES_009_NAME=Bytes read/sec
BYTES_009_HELP=Number of bytes read per second by the service.
```

Note that the text section provides the names and descriptions for both the object itself (Python Demo Service) and the counters. Also note that the **drivername** entry must be the same as the service.

The final piece of the puzzle is the name of the DLL used to provide the Performance Monitor data. As described previously, a generic DLL is provided with the Win32 Extensions for this purpose. This file can be found at *Python\Win32\ perfmondata.dll.*

Now we have all the pieces, but how do we install the data? It shouldn't be a surprise to hear that Python makes this much easier for us. As Performance Monitor information is a common requirement for services, the Python service installation procedure supports additional parameters for this purpose.

When installing a Python service, the command-line options are **--perfmonini** (names the INI file) and optionally, **--perfmondll** (names the DLL that provides the data).

Let's reinstall our service. Because the service uses the default DLL, you need to specify only the name of the *.ini* file. Use the command:

```
C:\Scripts> python.exe PipeService2.py --perfmonini=PipeService2_install.ini
install
Installing service PythonPipeService to Python class C:\Scripts\PipeService2.
PipeService
Changing service configuration
Service updated
```

The last message is "service updated" rather than "service installed." This is because the installation procedure realizes the service is already installed and simply updates the service configuration. When you remove the service later, the Performance Monitor information is automatically uninstalled.

As mentioned previously, the *.h* and *.ini* files are needed only for this one-time installation process. If you wish, you can remove these files now.

Defining the counters

Now that you've successfully registered your service with the Performance Monitor, you need to define the counters. Then you can finally update the counters while the service is running.

The process for defining the counters is:

1. Create each counter and set its attributes.

2. Create the Performance Monitor object and add the counters to it.

3. Create a Performance Monitor manager, passing the objects.

To do this, add the following two methods to your service class:

```
def InitPerfMon(self):
        # Magic numbers (2 and 4) must match header and ini file used
        # at install - could lookup ini, but then Id need it a runtime

        # A counter for number of connections per second.
        self.counterConnections=perfmon.CounterDefinition(2)
        # We arent expecting many, so we set the scale high (ie, x10)
        # Note the scale is 10^DefaultScale = ie, to get 10, we use 1!
        self.counterConnections.DefaultScale = 1

        # Now a counter for the number of bytes received per second.
        self.counterBytes=perfmon.CounterDefinition(4)
        self.counterBytes.DefaultScale = 0

        # Now register our counters with the performance monitor
        perfObjectType = perfmon.ObjectType(
                        (self.counterConnections, self.counterBytes) )

        self.perfManager = perfmon.PerfMonManager(
                        self._svc_name_,
                        (perfObjectType,),
                        "perfmondata")

    def TermPerfMon(self):
        self.perfManager.Close()
        self.perfManager = None
```

Note the magic numbers passed to the **perfmon.CounterDefinition()** calls. These must be the offsets as defined in the *.h* file used at installation. The perfmon.PerfMonManager() call also warrants some extra comments. The first parameter is the **drivername** as specified in the *.ini* file. As mentioned previously, this must be the name of the service. The last parameter is the name of the memory-mapped file that communicates the data between the service and the Performance Monitor DLL. This must be the base name of the DLL providing Performance Monitor information. The standard DLL is named *perfmondata.dll*, so you pass **perfmondata**. If you chose to rename the DLL for your own application, you must reflect the new name here and also in the installation process.

The **DefaultScale** property of the counter is not intuitive. This property specifies the power of 10 by which to scale a chart line (i.e., the base 10 log of the scale). For example, for a default scale of 1, you use 0. For a default scale of 10, use 1; to get a scale of 100, use 2, etc.

Updating the counters

Now that you've defined the counters in your code, all that remains is to update the counters with your data. This is a simple process. The counter object has a method **Increment()** taking a single optional parameter (defaulting to 1).

Change the **SvcDoRun()** method, so that just before you process the client connection, you execute the following code:

```
# But first, increment our Performance Monitor data
self.counterConnections.Increment()
```

This increments the counter by 1, which is correct for your connections counter. Then, just after you write the response to the client, execute:

```
# Update our performance monitor "bytes read" counter
self.counterBytes.Increment(len(data))
```

In this case, you increment the bytes counter by the length of the data received. And that's it: your service is now providing Performance Monitor information.

Viewing Performance Monitor data

All that remains is to view the data the service provides. The service must be running before the data is available, so let's start the new service:

```
C:\Scripts> python PipeService2.py debug
Debugging service PythonPipeService
Info 0x40001002 - The PythonPipeService service has started.
```

Now you can start the Windows NT Performance Monitor, which can be found under the Administrative Tools folder on the Start menu. You are presented with an empty Performance Monitor that looks something like Figure 18-4.

Now select Edit → Add to Chart. In the dialog displayed, select the Object dropdown and scroll to Python Demo Service, as shown in Figure 18-5. Select and add

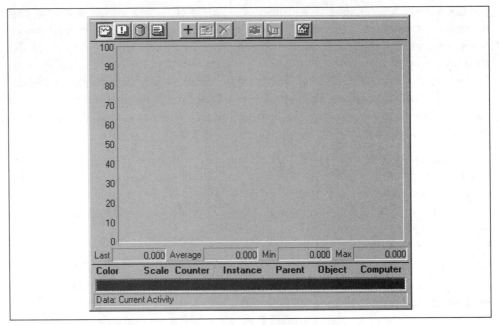

Figure 18-4. The Windows NT Performance Monitor after starting

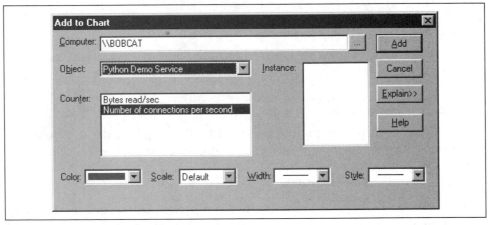

Figure 18-5. "Add to Chart" dialog showing our counters

the two counters, and you can now start your service client and repeatedly send some data. If all goes well, your Performance Monitor display should look something like Figure 18-6.

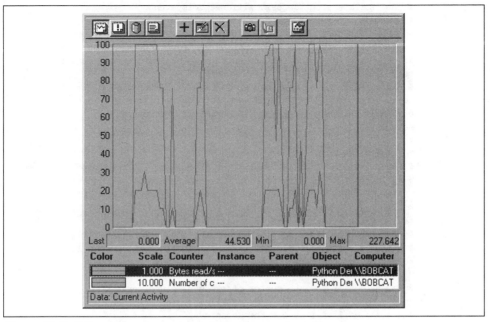

Figure 18-6. Collecting performance data for the sample service

A Final Service

We have made a number of changes to the sample service since first presented. Here's the full source code:

```
# PipeService2.py
#
# A sample demonstrating a service which uses a
# named-pipe to accept client connections,
# and writes data to the event log.

import win32serviceutil
import win32service
import win32event
import win32pipe
import win32file
import pywintypes
import winerror
import perfmon
import os

class PipeService(win32serviceutil.ServiceFramework):
    _svc_name_ = "PythonPipeService"
    _svc_display_name_ = "A sample Python service using named pipes"
    def __init__(self, args):
        win32serviceutil.ServiceFramework.__init__(self, args)
        # Create an event which we will use to wait on.
```

```python
        # The "service stop" request will set this event.
        self.hWaitStop = win32event.CreateEvent(None, 0, 0, None)
        # We need to use overlapped IO for this, so we dont block when
        # waiting for a client to connect.  This is the only effective way
        # to handle either a client connection, or a service stop request.
        self.overlapped = pywintypes.OVERLAPPED()
        # And create an event to be used in the OVERLAPPED object.
        self.overlapped.hEvent = win32event.CreateEvent(None,0,0,None)
        # Finally initialize our Performance Monitor counters
        self.InitPerfMon()

    def InitPerfMon(self):
        # Magic numbers (2 and 4) must match header and ini file used
        # at install - could lookup ini, but then Id need it a runtime

        # A counter for number of connections per second.
        self.counterConnections=perfmon.CounterDefinition(2)
        # We arent expecting many, so we set the scale high (ie, x10)
        # Note the scale is 10^DefaultScale = ie, to get 10, we use 1!
        self.counterConnections.DefaultScale = 1

        # Now a counter for the number of bytes received per second.
        self.counterBytes=perfmon.CounterDefinition(4)
        # A scale of 1 is fine for this counter.
        self.counterBytes.DefaultScale = 0

        # Now register our counters with the performance monitor
        perfObjectType = perfmon.ObjectType( (self.counterConnections,
                                              self.counterBytes) )

        self.perfManager = perfmon.PerfMonManager(
                        self._svc_name_,
                        (perfObjectType,),
                        "perfmondata")

    def TermPerfMon(self):
        self.perfManager.Close()
        self.perfManager = None

    def SvcStop(self):
        # Before we do anything, tell the SCM we are starting the stop process.
        self.ReportServiceStatus(win32service.SERVICE_STOP_PENDING)
        # And set my event.
        win32event.SetEvent(self.hWaitStop)

    def SvcDoRun(self):
        # Log a "started" message to the event log.
        import servicemanager
        servicemanager.LogMsg(
                servicemanager.EVENTLOG_INFORMATION_TYPE,
                servicemanager.PYS_SERVICE_STARTED,
                (self._svc_name_, ''))

        # We create our named pipe.
        pipeName = "\\\\.\\pipe\\PyPipeService"
```

```
openMode = win32pipe.PIPE_ACCESS_DUPLEX | win32file.FILE_FLAG_OVERLAPPED
pipeMode = win32pipe.PIPE_TYPE_MESSAGE

# When running as a service, we must use special security for the pipe
sa = pywintypes.SECURITY_ATTRIBUTES()
# Say we do have a DACL, and it is empty
# (ie, allow full access!)
sa.SetSecurityDescriptorDacl ( 1, None, 0 )

pipeHandle = win32pipe.CreateNamedPipe(pipeName,
    openMode,
    pipeMode,
    win32pipe.PIPE_UNLIMITED_INSTANCES,
    0, 0, 6000, # default buffers, and 6 second timeout.
    sa)

# Loop accepting and processing connections
while 1:
    try:
        hr = win32pipe.ConnectNamedPipe(pipeHandle, self.overlapped)
    except error, details:
        print "Error connecting pipe!", details
        pipeHandle.Close()
        break

    if hr==winerror.ERROR_PIPE_CONNECTED:
        # Client is fast, and already connected - signal event
        win32event.SetEvent(self.overlapped.hEvent)
    # Wait for either a connection, or a service stop request.
    timeout = win32event.INFINITE
    waitHandles = self.hWaitStop, self.overlapped.hEvent
    rc = win32event.WaitForMultipleObjects(waitHandles, 0, timeout)
    if rc==win32event.WAIT_OBJECT_0:
        # Stop event
        break
    else:
        # Pipe event - read the data, and write it back.
        # But first, increment our Performance Monitor data
        self.counterConnections.Increment()
        # (We only handle a max of 255 characters for this sample)
        try:
            hr, data = win32file.ReadFile(pipeHandle, 256)
            win32file.WriteFile(pipeHandle, "You sent me:" + data)
            # And disconnect from the client.
            win32pipe.DisconnectNamedPipe(pipeHandle)
            # Update our performance monitor "bytes read" counter
            self.counterBytes.Increment(len(data))

            # Log a message to the event log indicating what we did.
            message = "Processed %d bytes for client connection" % \
                    len(data)
            servicemanager.LogInfoMsg(message)
        except win32file.error:
            # Client disconnected without sending data
```

```
                    # or before reading the response.
                    # Thats OK - just get the next connection
                    continue

          # cleanup our PerfMon counters.
          self.TermPerfMon()

          # Now log a "service stopped" message
          servicemanager.LogMsg(
                  servicemanager.EVENTLOG_INFORMATION_TYPE,
                  servicemanager.PYS_SERVICE_STOPPED,
                  (self._svc_name_, ''))

if __name__=='__main__':
    win32serviceutil.HandleCommandLine(PipeService)
```

Conclusion

In this chapter, we have covered some advanced capabilities of Python and Windows NT Services. We discussed the key concepts behind:

- The Windows NT Service Control Manager
- The Windows NT Event Log
- The Windows NT Performance Monitor

We have presented three services written completely in Python, ranging from the trivial, to a complete service implementation that writes key events to the Event Log, provides core performance statistics via the Performance Monitor, and uses named pipes to communicate with clients.

## 19

Communications

This chapter surveys three completely different subjects that don't really fit together, but don't belong anywhere else either:

- Serial communications, otherwise known as your COM port
- Remote access services, a set of Windows functions for configuring, making, and breaking dial-up connections to another computer
- Sockets, the interface to the TCP/IP protocol and the layer on top of which the various Internet protocols such as FTP and HTTP are built

Each is a subject in its own right, and the techniques are not specific to Python. We'll show enough to get you started with the right Python extensions and features and try to point you at some of the right sources to learn more.

Serial Communications

The serial port has been a part of the standard PC since its inception, and a wide range of PC accessories, scientific, and medical devices use it; modems and mice are the most common. Recently, infrared ports have been gaining in popularity, and these are essentially just serial ports without wires. We will learn a little about serial ports and use that to talk to some external devices.

How COM Ports Are Accessed

Serial data is carried as a sequence of high and low voltages over a number of wires with fairly precise timing characteristics. Fortunately for the programmer, it isn't necessary to know much about how serial ports work. Under DOS, you had to work with a very low-level interface; a certain range of bytes (starting at 0x03F8 for COM1 and 0x02F8 for COM2) contained information about the serial port. Your program would loop continually checking the values of bits and bytes in this region; some of these signaled the arrival of data, others the data values itself, and others error values. It was messy and painful to program.

Windows 3.1 exposed a higher-level API, with a layer of buffering; functions such as `ReadComm` and `WriteComm` that provide insulation from the hardware and a somewhat file-like interface; and event-driven communications, which allowed you to have messages sent to a window when data arrived at the COM port. Windows NT drops the windows message concept and completes the move to a file-like interface, using the same functions to open, read and write COM ports as regular files. It also prevents programs from accessing the serial port (i.e., those previous addresses) directly.

Timing issues

Example programs give the impression of reading and writing from files, but this can be misleading. Files on the disk are all there at once, and you know when you have got to the end. Furthermore, if you open a file for reading and/or writing, you know where you are in the file, and the disk operations take place in exactly the order you specify. Serial I/O is all about timing. Consider a port running at 9600 bits per second on a Pentium 400. One byte arrives every millisecond; your computer can execute more than a hundred thousand instructions between each byte arriving. Your PC can also wander off and do something else (load a file, wait for the user, open a Word document or something) while several bytes arrive at the port unnoticed.

To resolve this, the operating system provides input and output buffers. A typical size is 1024 bytes. If your program is doing something else, up to 1024 bytes will accumulate and be saved for you, so you don't have to check the port continually. If you read from the port, it returns as many bytes as you asked for from the buffer or nothing if there is no more data. There is no way to know whether data has finished arriving, or whether more might arrive in another millisecond; each application needs to define a *protocol* so that the application knows whether to wait for more or to stop listening. Protocols can involve fixed-size transmissions, the use of delimiters such as a carriage return to say "this message has finished arriving," or time limits.

If you want to work at a low level, you can use the `CreateFile` API call exposed by the Python Win32 extensions, passing in a filename of "COM1" or "COM2." You can then read from and write to this file. Communications functions are well documented in the MSDN Library. However, for common tasks, there are easier ways to do it. We'll look at two of them, using a public domain C–level extension package and a proprietary COM interface.

The Serial Module

Our preferred route for serial I/O with Python is Roger Burnham's `Serial` package. This is free and comes with an installer and several examples.

The `Serial` package is based on a set of serial communications libraries developed by MarshallSoft (*www.marshallsoft.com*) over the last eight years. These libraries are available as a 16- and 32-bit DLL with identical interfaces, which makes it easy to migrate applications from 16- to 32-bit and back again.* The libraries are available as shareware packages for Visual Basic, C, and Delphi. MarshallSoft have kindly allowed their DLL to be used free of charge as part of the Python package provided a brief message is included with any distribution. The core DLL is not Open Source but has been heavily tested and won several awards.

The `Serial` package uses SWIG (see Chapter 22, *Extending and Embedding with Visual C++ and Delphi*) to create a Python DLL wrapper around the library, and provides easy-to-use Python wrappers and examples. The Python wrapper class is Open Source and provides a simple high-level API that simplifies many common communications tasks. The `Serial` package provides functions to open and close serial ports and to read and write from them.

The art of telephone conversation

The "Hello, World" of the communications field is to send an `AT` command to a modem and get back a response, so we will take care of this formality first. If you are not familiar with modems, they almost all speak a common command language defined by Hayes; the computer sends a line of text beginning with the letters `AT` and ending in a carriage return and linefeed, and the modem sends back a line of text with a response. In particular, the command `ATI` asks a modem to identify itself.

We tried hard to find a way of making this more interesting. Instead of using a conventional internal or external modem, we decided to make a laptop to talk to a mobile phone with a built-in modem, via its infrared port. It turned out that this didn't involve any special programming at all (IR ports are just plain old serial ports from the programmer's viewpoint) but it does far more to satisfy technolust! The console session below shows a basic conversation with the modem, which was sitting a few feet away:

```
>>> from Serial import Serial
>>> # create a 'configuration dictionary' with the port settings
>>> myconfig = Serial.PortDict()
>>> myconfig['port'] = Serial.COM4
```

---

* It would be nice to think 16-bit Windows was dead in 1999, but you would be amazed how many cash-strapped hospitals and university laboratories still have old Windows 3.1 PCs collecting data.

```
>>> # create and open a port with these settings
>>> myport = Serial.Port(myconfig)
>>> myport.open()
>>> myport.send('ATI\015') #ask modem to identify itself
>>> print myport.read() #get back any response
ATI

Ericsson SH 888 Infrared Modem
>>> # Python supports Infrared!  Cool!
```

The `Serial` package contains two classes. A `PortDict` holds the configuration information needed to begin using a serial port; this comes with a sensible set of defaults, and is smart enough to check the values you assign it. If you ask it to display itself at a command prompt, you can see all the parameters, many of which are self-explanatory:

```
>>> myconfig
<Serial Config:
   baud = 9600
   cmdTerm = ''
   cmdsEchoed = 0
   dataBits = 8
   debug = 0
   parity = None
   port = COM4
   rspFixedLen = 0
   rspTerm = ''
   rspTermPat = None
   rspType = RSP_BEST_EFFORT
   rxBufSize = 1024
   stopBits = 1
   timeOutMs = 500
   txBufSize = 1024
>

>>>
```

This is passed as an argument to the constructor of a `Port` object, which manages the conversation. You've just seen the key methods of a Port object: `open()`, `read()`, `write()`, and `close()`. We relate what they do in more detail later.

The most widely available serial devices are mice and modems; however, there is not much likelihood you will need to write a driver for either, so we'll look instead at some laboratory instruments that together illustrate some key principles. The first stage in talking to any remote device is to learn about its communications protocol and think through the timing issues involved.

Andy maintains a data-analysis package for two devices called the *Mark III* and *Mark IV GastrographH*, made by Medical Instruments Corporation of Switzerland. These are used to diagnose chronic stomach pain; patients have a probe inserted into their stomachs, and carry a small battery-powered device for 24 hours that captures the pH values, as well as user-input information about meals, sleep and pain. At the end of the 24-hour period, the data is downloaded to a PC. Fortunately it comes with a test signal generator, which removed the need to self-intubate while writing this chapter!

The Mark III: Reading large amounts of data

The Mark III GastrographH is a very simple instrument from a communication viewpoint. You press a transmit button, and it sends a fixed-size block of data (essentially dumping the contents of its RAM). It neither knows nor cares if there is a PC listening at the far end.

The port settings are 9600 baud, eight data bits, one stop bit, and no parity. One byte of data thus needs 9 bits (8 data + 1 stop), so you can expect about 1067 bytes per second (9600 / (8+1)) or one per millisecond. The device sends a header of 22 bytes, followed by 24 separate blocks of 4102 bytes each (each of these is 4 KB of RAM plus a few checksums), totaling exactly 98,470 bytes. Between each block there is a 200ms pause. The whole download takes about 97 seconds.

Let's use the `Serial` class to capture this data. The `read()` method we saw earlier is actually extremely flexible; the full header is `read(cnt=None, timed=FALSE)`. When you initialize a `Serial` class instance, you specify a timeout, which has a default value of half a second. The read method can be used in three totally different ways:

- `MySerialPort.read()` returns any data that has arrived at the serial port since you last called `read()` or since it was opened. The data is returned as a string.

- `MySerialPort.read(1024)` reads 1024 bytes from the serial port, waiting all night if necessary.

- `MySerialPort.read(1024, timed=1)` reads 1024 bytes from the serial port, or raise an error if that many bytes haven't arrived before the timeout limit. The default timeout is half a second, which is ample time to receive short responses from most devices. You can specify a timeout of up to 60 seconds when initializing a port.

The first approach that occurred to us was to change one line of *Serial.py* to allow a two-minute timeout and read the whole lot in one command. That works, but is not desperately user-friendly; if the device isn't transmitting, you still have to wait two minutes to find out. Instead, we grabbed it in a number of chunks matching the device protocol itself. Each takes about four seconds to arrive, so set a timeout of 10 seconds. This should be long enough for the user to start Python listening, then hit the Transmit button on the device. Here's the capture function:

```
from Serial import Serial
import traceback
import string

def captureMark3Data(port=Serial.COM3):

    #fill a config dictionary with the settings we want
    cfg = Serial.PortDict()
    cfg['port'] = port
    cfg['baud'] = Serial.Baud9600
    cfg['parity'] = Serial.NoParity
    cfg['stopBits'] = Serial.OneStopBit
    cfg['timeOutMs'] = 10000    # ten seconds

    # create a Port object based on these settings
    prt = Serial.Port(cfg)
    prt.open()

    print 'Port open...'

    blocks = []
    #read some data
    try:
        # first section is 22 bytes, followed by a pause
        header = prt.read(22,timed=1)
        blocks.append(header)
        print 'read header'

        # followed by 24 blocks of 4102 bytes, and pauses
        for i in range(24):
            block = prt.read(4102, timed=1)
            blocks.append(block)
            print 'read block',i,'of 24'

        prt.close()
        alldata = string.join(blocks, '')
        return alldata

    except:
        # close the port but print the error message
        prt.close()
        traceback.print_exc()
        return None
```

Note that a `try...except...` handler was used to ensure that the port is always closed. Leaving a COM port open prevents other programs (or your own) from using it for some time; on Windows 95, this can persist until a reboot.

The first thing to do is try running the function without even connecting the GastrograpH to the port. This results in a timeout error after ten seconds, which is handled gracefully:

```
>>> import commdemos
>>> data = commdemos.captureMark3Data()
Port open...
```

```
Traceback (innermost last):
  File "C:\Data\Project\OReilly\chXX_Communications\examples\
                        commdemos.py", line 30, in captureMark3Data
    header = prt.read(22,timed=1)
  File "C:\Program Files\Python\Serial\Serial.py", line 456, in read
    raise SioError, \
SioError: Timed out waiting for input chr 0 of 22, read ''.
>>>
```

Having done that, you can try it for real. Call the function; then press Transmit:

```
>>> import commdemos
>>> data = commdemos.captureMark3Data()
Port open...
read header, blocks 1 2 3 4 5 6 7 8 9 10 11 12 13 14 15 16 17 \
18 19 20 21 22 23 24 ..done!
>>> len(data)
98470
>>> data[0:10]
'\000\000\020\000HK\030\000\001\002'
>>>
```

The Mark IV and dialogs

The Mark III downloaded its whole memory. Capturing data was trivial; deciphering it was a lot of work. The Mark IV GastrograpH, which replaces the Mark III, communicates in a different way and aims to return meaningful information. The protocol is simple: you send one byte, and it replies with another in three to four milliseconds. There are about 20 separate requests you can make; one request returns start date information, another returns the next byte in a time series, and so on. This is another common serial programming paradigm; you send a short sequence and get something back promptly. This enables us to talk to the device at the command prompt. Note that you need to specify `timed=1` so that Python waits for a response; otherwise, it reads an empty string from the port long before the device has time to respond.

The `Serial.Port` class has a method to send a command and get a response that is highly configurable, but doesn't do quite what you want. Let's make a subclass that has a method to carry out the kind of dialog we want:

```
class Mark4Port(Serial.Port):
    def talk(self, byte):
        #send a byte, wait up to 500ms for one byte back
        self.write(chr(byte))
        resp = self.read(cnt=1,timed=1)
        return ord(resp[0])
```

The needed dialog requires only one three-line method. Armed with this, you can talk to the device on the command prompt in real time:

```
>>> from Serial import Serial
>>> cfg = Serial.PortDict()
>>> cfg['baud']=Serial.Baud19200
```

```
>>> cfg['port']=Serial.COM3
>>> M4 = commdemos.Mark4Port(cfg)
>>> M4.open()
>>> M4.talk(2)      # how many hours recording planned?
24
>>> M4.talk(10)     # how many hours took place?
0
>>> M4.talk(9)      # how many minutes took place?
10
>>> M4.close()
>>>
```

When you have limited documentation, the ability to interrogate a device in inter-active mode like this is a real help.

Of mice and modems

Naturally, you won't have either of these devices available, but there are two things you can play with quite easily: serial mice and modems. With a mouse, all you need is a loop that listens to the port and displays the bytes that are generated whenever you move it. Furthermore, if you look around, a growing number of peripherals and palmtop computers offer infrared ports, and it can be fun (and potentially even useful) to attempt to talk to them.

The Microsoft Communications Control (MSComm)

Microsoft has provided a COM interface to the serial port in the form of an OCX. This gives less detailed control than the Python `Serial` package, but is adequate for the kind of examples above. It's distributed with Visual Basic, Visual Studio, and most Microsoft development tools; you need one of these packages to redistribute it. In a corporate setting this isn't usually a problem. Unlike the `Serial` package, it requires the Python COM framework. Let's talk to a modem with it, this time reverting to a plain old system connected with real wires:

```
def MSCommDemo():
    #talks to a modem on COM1
    from win32com.client import Dispatch
    comm = Dispatch('MSCOMMLib.MSComm')
    comm.CommPort = 1     #COM1
    comm.PortOpen = 1
    try:
        comm.Output = "AT\015"                  # add a carriage return
        inbuf = ''
        now = time.time()
        elapsed = time.time() - now
        while (string.find(inbuf, 'OK') < 0) and (elapsed < 2):
            inbuf = inbuf + str(comm.Input)  #remember the Unicode string!
            elapsed = time.time() - now
        print inbuf
    finally:
        comm.PortOpen = 0
```

When run, you should see your command of AT echoed, followed by the response OK. Note that you don't know how long it will take to respond, so you loop until you get the desired data or until some time limit has elapsed. This behavior was wrapped for us by *Serial.py*, and you could wrap it here as well if you were going to use the MSComm control a lot.

One truly amazing thing about the MSComm control is the syntax. Microsoft loves properties; we saw that the Excel and Word object models used property assignments for lots of things, but this control takes it to new limits. MSComm has no—count 'em—no methods. One major reason for using properties is that they can be set at design time in the Visual Basic development environment, but the key properties are runtime only. You can argue that a PortOpen property has its uses; you can at least query it. Assigning a string to a write-only Input property, instead of providing a Write() method, is weird. Getting a return value from an Output property, and being able to ask for it only once, is even less natural. We can't see any design rationale behind this. Nevertheless, it works.

Remote Access Services

There is no real need to talk to modems these days, because Windows provides a standard set of dialogs and APIs for making and breaking dial-up connections. These are collectively known as Remote Access Services, or RAS for short. Users can create and save connections that specify many things, including the number to dial, usernames and passwords, and network protocols and settings.

The dialogues vary considerably between Windows 95, 98, and NT, but the principles under the hood are the same. Windows thinks in terms of a phonebook. NT can have many phonebooks, stored in files with extension PBK; on Windows 95 and 98 there is a single default phonebook. The machine in Figure 19-1 has three entries.

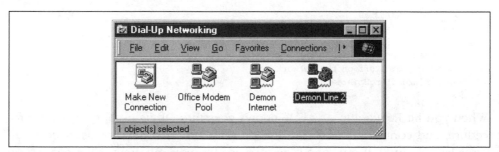

Figure 19-1. Dial-Up Networking folder in Windows 98

The `win32ras` module supplied with PythonWin provides a number of functions to manipulate these. `EnumEntries()` returns a list of tuples with the names of the entries in the phonebook:

```
>>> import win32ras
>>> win32ras.EnumEntries()    # what is in the phonebook?
[('Assi Modem Pool',), ('Demon',), ('Demon Private',)]
>>> win32ras.EnumConnections()  # show what's active now
[]
>>>
```

To make a connection, you need to specify a tuple of up to six strings. This matches the RASDIALPARAMS structure in Windows. The values are:

- Entry name

- Phone number

- Callback number (used if you are dialing an NT server configured to call you right back)

- Username for the remote network

- Password for the remote network

- Domain name for the remote network (only for NT)

You can obtain such a list from an existing phonebook entry with the `GetEntryDialParams(PhoneBook, EntryName)` function. This displays some entries but hides passwords for obvious reasons:

```
>>> params = win32ras.GetEntryDialParams(None, 'Demon Internet')
>>> params
(('Demon Internet', '', '', 'username', '', ''), None)
```

However, in most cases you just want to make a call, so you can provide the attributes you need yourself. Let's dial up an Internet provider, specifying the name of the phonebook entry to use:

```
>>> import win32ras
>>> myParams = ('Demon Internet','0845-3535666','',  \
                          'username','password','')
>>> (hras, success) = win32ras.Dial(None, None, myParams, None)
>>> # do your stuff on the network now
>>> win32ras.HangUp(hras)
>>>
```

When you hit Return after `Dial`, Windows goes through its usual connection procedure, and control is returned to Python only after a connection is made or an error has occurred. If `success` is zero or greater, you can assume the connection works.

It's also possible to supply a callback function as the fourth argument to the `Dial()` function; this is called whenever a RAS event occurs, such as a successful connection, the line being dropped, or an error. See the `win32ras` documentation in the PythonWin help file for more details.

A typical use for RAS would be writing a script to connect at various times of the day, and conversely to ensure that connections are brought down again after a certain amount of time. What you can do when you get connected depends on the type of network, which is most easily specified in the various dialogs for the phonebook entry. If dialing into a corporate NT network, you could begin mapping network drives after connecting; with a TCP/IP network, you can start using Python's many TCP/IP libraries to automate web, email and FTP operations.

Sockets

Our third and final topic under the theme of communications is the Sockets API. This is the programmer's interface to the TCP/IP protocol itself. Sockets are supported by all major operating systems, via a standard C–level interface. This interface is available in Python on all platforms, enabling you to write custom communications protocols. Chapter 15, *Using the Basic Internet Protocols*, describes a number of Python library modules that implement the standard protocols. The Python standard library contains many examples of how to write applications using sockets.

The key concepts bear some similarity to the serial communications we saw earlier: there is a file-like interface that permits reading and writing, and the same issue of not knowing when a transmission has finished. However, you can't guarantee a response in a given timeframe, and indeed responses on the Internet can vary widely from fractions of a second up to several seconds.

Sockets are great fun to experiment with, particularly in Python, where the client socket can be scripted from an interactive console session. Ideally you need two computers close to each other on the same TCP/IP network; however, one machine works fine as long as it has TCP/IP installed. Sockets can communicate between processes on the same machine.

A Simple Socket Server

The following function implements a short socket server:

```
# socketserver1.py - runs forever,
# reverse each message received.
from socket import *
import string

HOST = ''        # this means local
PORT = 8578      #arbitrary, high number
```

```
def serve():
    # this reverses each message received, lasts forever
    serversock = socket(AF_INET, SOCK_STREAM)
    serversock.bind((HOST, PORT))
    serversock.listen(1)    # max bcklog of 1-5 connections
    print 'socket listening for connections...'
    while 1:
        handlersock, addr = serversock.accept()

        # now do something with the handler socket
        print 'handler connected by', addr
        data = handlersock.recv(1024)
        print 'received', data
        handlersock.send(string.upper(data))
        handlersock.close()
        print 'handler closed'

if __name__ == '__main__':
    serve()
```

You can start this server by running it from a DOS prompt. Let's step through a line at a time:

serversock = socket(AF_INET, SOCK_STREAM)

>This creates the server socket. Don't worry about the constants; there are other types of sockets, but their use is unusual and definitely out of scope for this chapter.

serversock.bind(HOST, PORT)

>This associates the socket with a TCP/IP hostname and port number. An empty string, the hostname (if you know it), or the result of the function gethostname() all mean the local machine. PORT is a number between 0 and 65535 and can be thought of like a radio channel or telephone line. The lower port numbers are used for standard services, so pick a big one.

serversock.listen(1)

>This places the socket in a passive state and specifies a backlog of connections. We have told it that only one connection at a time is allowed; you can specify up to five. For socket applications use short-lived connections, this is usually plenty; the network buffers requests from subsequent sockets so that the server only has to deal with one at a time.

We now go into a loop. The server socket runs until you kill the process. The next line is where the action happens:

handlersock, addr = serversock.accept()

>At this point the program waits until a connection is received from a *client socket* somewhere else on the network. This could be some time. We'll look at the client side in a moment. When a client does connect, the network software creates a totally new socket, which we will call a *handler socket*. We are

also passed the address of the socket on the far end of the connection. The handler socket is a totally different beast from the server socket; in some ways it's a pity they are implemented as the same object. In fact, it's identical to the client socket we will look at in a moment. The two are welded together, with the input of one hooked up to the output of the other. They are also communicating on another network port to the one we originally specified, something assigned randomly by TCP/IP. The original server socket can continue listening on the specified port.

At this point, it doesn't really matter what the client and handler sockets do. The server socket has handled the request, the incoming port is free, and it's now free (in theory) to handle the next incoming request. A more complex server than ours might actually set up a separate thread to handle the request.

Now let's pop over to the client side and see what is going on there. We've implemented the client side of the conversation from a console session:

```
[CLIENT]
>>> from socket import *
>>> clientsock = socket(AF_INET, SOCK_STREAM)
>>> clientsock.connect('tahoe',8578)
>>>
```

The **connect method** can take the name of the machine or the IP address (represented as the usual dotted string), or **"localhost"** if you are talking to yourself on one machine. If you don't get an error message, you're connected. Now let's look back at the console for the server:

```
[SERVER]
D:\Examples\Comms>python socketserver1.py
socket listening for connections...
handler connected by ('192.42.172.3', 1029)
```

This identifies the machine from which the connection arrived, and the port on which the client socket and handler socket are now talking.

The client is in position to send requests to the handler socket and hold a conversation. We've provided a simplistic example; the client sends a short string, and the server sends it back in uppercase. After one such exchange, the two sockets close. This is dangerously simplistic (we'll discover why later). Now they can talk; it's back to the client side:

```
>>> clientsock.send('hello')    # returns bytes sent
5
>>> clientsock.recv(1024)       # max bytes to receive
'HELLO'
>>> clientsock.close()
>>>
```

The conversation is over, and the server socket is now ready to accept and process the next request. It's essential to close down sockets when finished by calling the `close()` method. This notifies the remote socket that no more data will be sent. If your program fails to close a socket cleanly, the one at the far end of the connection may hang indefinitely.

Communication Between Sockets

The previous example covered the key features of how sockets get connected, but was dangerously simple. We sent a very short string, then waited a couple of seconds while we typed the call to receive a response. We got back the expected data, but were lucky: in real life, there's more to worry about.

The `send()` call doesn't instantly send a string, however long. It tries to send the string and returns the number of bytes sent. With a big string (e.g., a file-transfer application) or in bad network conditions, the `send()` call sends only a small part on each call. It might also return zero, which indicates that the network connection has been broken. The only safe way to send a string is to do it in a loop and check the return values to see what has actually been sent. Here's a function to send an arbitrary string safely:

```
# this sends strings over sockets more safely
def safeSend(sock, message):
    msglen = len(message)
    totalsent = 0
    while totalsent < msglen:
        sent = sock.send(msg[totalsent:])
        if sent == 0:
            raise RuntimeError, 'connection broken'
        totalsent = totalsent + sent
```

At this point you've hit a fundamental problem. There is no way for the receiving socket to know how much data to expect, nor whether a message has finished arriving. You have to design your protocol so that client and handler know what to expect at every stage. There are several schemes for doing this:

- Always use fixed-size messages.

- Add a final delimiter.

- Indicate how long messages are.

- Send once and shut down. The receiving socket loops until it receives a zero and knows it's done.

One effective scheme is to make the first byte of each message a code indicating the type of message and to have a standard length for each message type, padding messages if needed. Another is to send a fixed-length message on the first exchange and include in each exchange the length of the subsequent message.

Once you've designed a protocol, you can write a `safeReceive` procedure to match it and ensure you get all of the data. Note that you can send binary data safely over sockets.

Where to Go from Here

The design here works for short-lived connections and low traffic. If you want to handle multiple simultaneous requests, there are several different strategies, but they all involve quite a bit of work. One option is to create separate threads to handle each request (look in the `thread` and `threading` modules in the Python Library Reference). Another is to use nonblocking sockets and the `select` statement, which looks at a bunch of sockets and tells you which have data ready to read or are ready to accept outgoing data.*

We won't go any further into building sockets applications here. We've gone about as far as we can simply, and it gets more complex from here on.

Fortunately the work has been done for you. The Python standard library module *socketserver.py* provides an extremely useful generic server architecture. It includes a generic server class that you might or might not need to subclass and a request-handler class you definitely want to override. This is an excellent place to go next. Several other standard library modules define web servers based on the standard socket server.

We hope we have made it clear that sockets programming is not only feasible but also straightforward on Python. It's comparatively rare to need to develop your own socket-based protocols, and if you do need to do it, you will know far more about the subject than we can cover here.

World-class networking software has been developed in Python; examples include the Infoseek search engine, Zope, and Medusa. Zope and Medusa are discussed briefly in Chapter 3, *Python on Windows.*

Other Communications Tools

Named Pipes

We ought to quickly mention named pipes again. These are a Microsoft technology similar to sockets and have been part of Windows NT since its inception. As with sockets and serial ports, you read and write to named pipes. You open them by passing a suitable network path to `CreateFile` of the form *mymachine*\

---

* Note that on Unix, `select()` can work with file descriptors as well as sockets; on Windows, it works only with sockets.

pipe\mypipe. Named pipes function over whatever network protocol NT is using; it might be TCP/IP, IPX, or NetBEUI. On Windows, they operate slightly faster than sockets and can also be secured. They are extensively used by Microsoft's networking APIs and back office products.

About the only reason to use named pipes is for their integrated security. Named pipes are fully securable by Windows NT, and you can rely on Windows reporting a valid and authenticated user at the other end of the pipe. For most communications applications that don't have a high requirement for security, sockets are often simpler to use, and have the added advantage of being cross-platform.

Remote Procedure Call (RPC)

RPC is a communications technology originally developed by the DCE consortium. It builds on top of a network protocol such as TCP/IP to provide the ability to call functions on remote machines. When you design a client/server socket application, you work hard to get to the point where you can send a request to a remote object and get a response reliably. In our case, what we wanted was a remote function to reverse strings, not a load of messages. RPC handles all this, and is supported by Windows. It lets you build tightly coupled client and server applications.

On Windows, Distributed COM (which builds on top of RPC) has made the RPC programming interface pretty much obsolete. Python supports DCOM rather than RPC. For details, see Chapter 12, *Advanced Python and COM*.

Conclusion

Python provides excellent supports for communications tasks of all kinds, including serial I/O and network programming. While the concepts and interfaces in Python are similar to those in C, Python is very successful at hiding a lot of the mess you deal with working at the C level, and lets you concentrate on the problem. Since communications channels generally run much slower than the host PCs, there is no need to work at a lower level.

References

If you want to work with serial communications at a low level on Windows NT, there is some information in MSDN Library under *Platform SDK/Windows Base Services/Files and IO/Communications.*

MarshallSoft, *http://www.marshallsoft.com/*, makes the libraries underpinning the `Serial` package; evaluation libraries are available for download, as are numerous example programs in various languages.

Gordon McMillan has written a sockets how-to guide that can be found at *www.python.org*. Much of the information in this section was based on his guide.

20

GUI Development

In this chapter, we examine the various options for developing graphical user interfaces (GUIs) in Python.

We will look in some detail at three of the GUI toolkits that operate on the Windows platform: Tkinter, PythonWin, and wxPython. Each of these GUI toolkits provide a huge range of facilities for creating user interfaces, and to completely cover any of these toolkits is beyond the scope of this single chapter. Each framework would need its own book to do it justice.

Our intent in this chapter is to give you a feel for each of these GUI frameworks, so you can understand the basic model they use and the problems they were designed to address. We take a brief tour of each of these toolkits, describing their particular model and providing sample code along the way. Armed with this information, you can make an informed decision about which toolkit to use in which situation, have a basic understanding of how your application will look, and where it will run when finished.

The authors need to express their gratitude to Gary Herron for the Tkinter section, and Robin Dunn for the wxPython section. Their information helped us complete this chapter.

Tkinter

Tkinter is the Python interface to the Tk GUI toolkit current maintained by Scriptics (*http://www.scriptics.com*). Tkinter has become the de facto standard GUI toolkit for Python due mainly to its cross-platform capabilities; it presents a powerful and adaptable GUI model across the major Python platforms, including Windows 95/98/NT, the Macintosh, and most Unix implementations and Linux distributions.

This section gives a short description of the capabilities of Tkinter, and provides a whirlwind tour of the more important aspects of the Tkinter framework. To effectively use Tkinter, you need a more thorough description than is provided for here. Fredrik Lundh has made an excellent introduction to Tkinter programming available at *http://www.pythonware.com/library.htm*, and at time of printing a Tkinter book by Fredrik has just been announced, so may be available by the time you read this. For more advanced uses of Tkinter, you may need to refer directly to the Tk reference manual, available from the Scriptics site.

Two Python applications, tkBrowser and tkDemo, accompany this section. TkBrowser is a Doubletalk application, providing several views and some small editing capabilities of Doubletalk `BookSet`s; TkDemo demonstrates a simple use of the core Tk user interface elements. Both applications are too large to include in their entirety, so where relevant, we include snippets.

Terminology

There's some new terminology with Tkinter, defined here for clarity:

Tk

A GUI toolkit provided as a library of C routines. This library manages and manipulates the windows and handles the GUI events and user interaction.

Tkinter

The Python Tk interface. A Python module that provides a collection of Python classes and methods for accessing the Tk toolkit from within Python.

Tcl

The (mostly hidden) language used by Tk and, hence, used by Tkinter to communicate with the Tk toolkit.

Widget

A user interface element, such as a text box, combo box, or top-level window. On Windows, the common terminology is *control* or *window*.

Pros and Cons of Tkinter

Before we launch into Tkinter programming, a brief discussion of the pros and cons of Tkinter will help you decide if Tkinter may be the correct GUI toolkit for your application. The following are often given as advantages of Tkinter:

Brevity

Python programs using Tkinter can be very brief, partly because of the power of Python, but also due to Tk. In particular, reasonable default values are defined for many options used in creating a widget, and packing it (i.e., placing and displaying).

Cross platform

Tk provides widgets on Windows, Macs, and most Unix implementations with very little platform-specific dependence. Some newer GUI frameworks are achieving a degree of platform independence, but it will be some time before they match Tk's in this respect.

Maturity

First released in 1990, the core is well developed and stable.

Extensibility

Many extensions of Tk exist, and more are being frequently distributed on the Web. Any extension is immediately accessible from Tkinter, if not through an extension to Tkinter, than at least through Tkinter's access to the Tcl language.

To balance things, here's a list of what's often mention as weaknesses in Tkinter:

Speed

There is some concern with the speed of Tkinter. Most calls to Tkinter are formatted as a Tcl command (a string) and interpreted by Tcl from where the actual Tk calls are made. This theoretical slowdown caused by the successive execution of two interpreted languages is rarely seen in practice and most real-world applications spend little time communicating between the various levels of Python, Tcl, and Tk.

Tcl

Python purists often balk at the need to install another (and to some, a rival) scripting language in order to perform GUI tasks. Consequently, there is periodic interest in removing the need for Tcl by using Tk's C-language API directly, although no such attempt has ever succeeded.

Tk lacks modern widgets

It's acknowledged that Tk presents a small basic set of widgets and lacks a collection of modern fancy widgets. For instance, Tk lacks paned windows, tabbed windows, progress meter widgets, and tree hierarchy widgets. However, the power and flexibility of Tk is such that you can easily construct new widgets from a collection of basic widgets. This fits in especially well with the object-oriented nature of Python.

Native look and feel

One common source of complaints is that Tkinter applications on Windows don't look like native Windows applications. As we shall see, the current version of Tkinter provides an interface that should be acceptable to almost everyone except the Microsoft marketing department, and we can expect later versions of Tkinter to be virtually indistinguishable.

Although many individuals could (and no doubt will) argue with some individual points on this list, it tends to reflects the general consensus amongst the Python community. Use this only as a guide to assist you in your decision-making process.

Running GUI Applications

Tkinter applications are normal Python scripts, but there are a couple of complications worth knowing about when running graphical applications under Windows. These were discussed in Chapter 3, *Python on Windows*, but are important enough to reiterate here; what we say in this section applies equally to wxPython later in this chapter.

The standard *Python.exe* that comes with Python is known as a *console application* (this means it has been built to interact with a Windows console, otherwise known as a DOS box or command prompt). Although you can execute your Tkinter programs using *Python.exe*, your program will always be associated with a Windows console. It works just fine, but has the following side effects:

- If you execute *Python.exe* from Windows Explorer, a new empty console window is created; then the Tkinter windows are created.

- If you execute a Tkinter application under *Python.exe* from a command prompt, the command prompt doesn't return until the Tkinter application has finished. This will be a surprise for many users, who expect that executing a GUI program returns the command prompt immediately.

To get around this problem, Python comes with a special GUI version called *Pythonw.exe*. This is almost identical to the standard *Python.exe*, except it's not a console program, so doesn't suffer the problems described previously.

There are two drawbacks to this approach. The first is that *.py* files are automatically associated with *Python.exe*. As we saw in Chapter 3, this makes it simple to execute Python programs, but does present a problem when you want to use *Pythonw.exe*. To solve this problem, Python automatically associates the *.pyw* extension with *Pythonw.exe*; thus, you can give GUI Python applications a *.pyw* extension, and automatically execute them from Windows Explorer, the command prompt, and so forth.

The second drawback is that because *Pythonw.exe* has no console, any tracebacks printed by Python aren't typically seen. Although Python prints the traceback normally, the lack of a console means it has nowhere useful to go. To get around this problem, you may like to develop your application using *Python.exe* (where the console is an advantage for debugging) but run the final version using *Pythonw.exe*.

"Hello World"

The easiest way to get a feel for Tkinter is with the ever popular "Hello World!" example. The result of this little program is shown in Figure 20-1.

```
from sys import exit
from Tkinter import *
root = Tk()
Button(root, text='Hello World!', command=exit).pack()
root.mainloop()
```

Figure 20-1. Tkinter's "Hello World"

As you can see, apart from the `import` statements, there are only three lines of interest. The `root` variable is set to the default top-level window automatically created by Tk, although applications with advanced requirements can customize the top-level frames. The code then creates a Tkinter button object, specifying the parent (the `root` variable), the text for the button, and the command to execute when clicked. We discuss the `pack()` method later in this section. Finally, turn control over to the main event-processing loop, which creates the Windows on the screen and dispatches user-interface events.

The other end of the World

From the extreme simplicity of the "Hello World" example, the other end of the scale could be considered the `tkDemo` sample included with this chapter. Although space considerations prevent us from examining this sample in detail, Figure 20-2 should give you an indication of the capabilities offered by Tkinter.

Widgets

Core widgets

Tkinter implements a fairly small set of core widgets, from which other widgets or complete applications can be based. Table 20-1 lists these core widgets with a short description of how they are used.

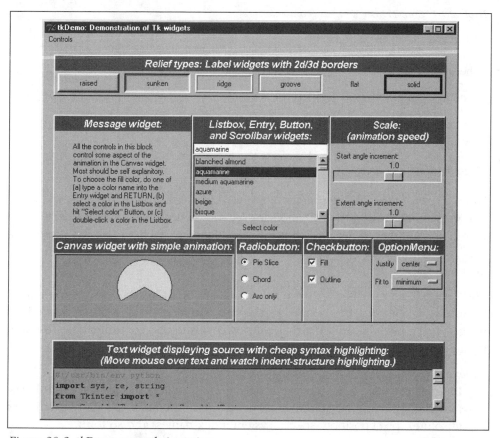

Figure 20-2. tkDemo example in action

Table 20-1. Core Tkinter Widgets

Widget Name	Description
Toplevel	Toplevel widgets are special in that they have no master widget and don't support any of the geometry-management methods (as discussed later). All other widgets are directly or indirectly associated with a Toplevel widget.
Frame	Used as a container widget for other child widgets. For instance, the tkDemo example consists of a number of frames within frames within frames to achieve its particular layout.
Label	Displays text or images.
Message	Displays text with automatic line-break and justification capabilities.
Text	Displays text with advanced formatting, editing, and highly interactive capabilities.
Canvas	Displays graphical items from a display list, with highly interactive capabilities.

Table 20-1. Core Tkinter Widgets (continued)

Widget Name	Description
Button Checkbox Entry Scale Radiobutton List box Scrollbar	Standard simple entry widgets, also known as the `control` widgets.
Menu Menubutton	Widgets for implementing and responding to menus.

Quite a few of these widgets are demonstrated in the tkBrowser sample, and every one gets an exercise in the tkDemo sample, so you are encouraged to experiment with these samples to get a feel for the capabilities of each widget. Of these widgets, we will discuss two of the most popular and powerful in more detail: the Text and Canvas widgets.

The Text widget provides for the display and editing of text, as you would expect from a text control. The Text widget is also capable of supporting embedded images and child windows, but the real power of the text control can be found in its support of *indexes*, *tags*, and *marks*:

Indexes

Indexes provide a rich model for describing positions in the text control. The position specification can be in terms of line and column position (relative or absolute), pixel position, special system index names, and so forth.

Tags

Tags are an association between a name and one or more regions of text. There is no restriction on overlapping regions, so a character may belong to any number of tags, and tags can be created and destroyed dynamically. In addition, the text associated with a tag may be given any number of display characteristics (such as font, color specifications, and so forth). When we combine these capabilities with the Tkinter event model described later, it becomes easy to build highly interactive applications (such as a web browser) around this Text widget.

Marks

A mark is a single position within the text (or more accurately, a position between two characters). Marks flow naturally with the surrounding text as characters are inserted and deleted, making them particularly suitable for implementing concepts such as bookmarks or breakpoints. Tkinter manages a number of predefined marks, such as `insert`, which defines the current insertion point.

The Canvas widget displays graphical items, such as lines, arcs, bitmaps, images, ovals, polygons, rectangles, text strings, or arbitrary Tkinter widgets. Like the Text widget, the Canvas widget implements a powerful tagging system, allowing you to associate any items on the canvas with a name.

Dialog and other noncore widgets

Many useful widgets are actually built from the core widgets. The most common example is the dialog widget, and recent versions of Tkinter provide some new sophisticated dialog widgets similar to the Windows common dialogs. In many cases when running on Windows, the standard Windows dialog is used.

Many of these dialogs come in their own module. Table 20-2 lists the common dialog box modules and their functionality.

Table 20-2. Tkinter Common Dialog Box Modules

Module Name	Description
tkMessageBox	Simple message box related dialogs, such as Yes/No, Abort/Retry/ Ignore, and so forth.
tkSimpleDialog	Contains base classes for building your own dialogs, and also includes a selection of simple input dialogs, such as asking for a string, integer, or float value.
tkFileDialog	A dialog with functionality very close to the Windows common file dialogs.
tkColorChooser	A dialog for choosing a color.

There are many other widgets available; both included with the Tkinter package, and also available externally. One interesting and popular source of Tkinter widgets can be found in the Python megawidgets (Pmw) package. This package comes with excellent documentation and sample code and can be found at *http://www. dscpl.com.au/pmw/.*

In most cases, you build your own dialogs by deriving them from the tkSimpleDialog.Dialog. Our tkBrowser sample defines an **EditTransaction** class that shows an example of this.

Widget properties and methods

Tkinter provides a flexible and powerful attribute set for all widgets. Almost all attributes can be set at either widget-creation time or once the widget has been created and displayed. Although Tkinter provides obvious attributes for items such as the color, font, or visible state of a widget, the set of enhanced attributes for widgets is usually the key to tapping the full potential of Tkinter.

Tkinter makes heavy use of Python keyword arguments when specifying widget attributes. A widget of any type (for instance a Label) is constructed with code similar to:

```
w = Label(master, option1=value1, option2=value2,...)
```

And once constructed, can be reconfigured at any time with code like:

```
w.configure(option1=value1, option2=value2, ...)
```

For a specific example, you can create a label with the following code:

```
label = Label(parent, background='white',
                      text='Hello World!',
                      relief=RAISED,
                      borderwidth=3)
```

And provide an annoying blinking effect by periodic execution of:

```
label.configure(background='red')
```

And:

```
label.configure(background='white')
```

There are dozens of options that can be specified for each widget. Table 20-3 lists a few common properties available for each widget.

Table 20-3. Common Tkinter Widget Properties

Property	Description
height width	The height and width of the widget in pixels.
background foreground	The color of the widget as a string. You can specify a color by name (for example, red or light blue), or you can specify each of the RGB components in hexadecimal notation prefixed with a # (e.g., #ffffff for white).
relief	A 3D appearance for the object (RAISED, SUNKEN, RIDGE, or GROOVE) or a 2D appearance (FLAT or SOLID).
borderwidth	Width of the border, in pixels.
text wrap justify	The Window text (i.e., the caption) for the widget and additional formatting options for multiline widgets.
font	The font that displays the text. This can be in a bewildering array of formats: some platform-independent and some platform-dependent. The most common form is a tuple containing font name, point size, and style (for example, ("Times", 10, "bold"). Tkinter guarantees that the fonts Times, Helvetica, and Courier exist on all platforms, and styles can be any combination of bold, roman, italic, underline, and overstrike, which are always available, with Tkinter substituting the closest matching font if necessary.

Table 20-3. Common Tkinter Widget Properties (continued)

Property	Description
command variable	Techniques used by control widgets to communicate back to the application. The command option allows you to specify an arbitrary Python function (or any callable Python object) to be invoked when the specified action occurs (e.g., when a Button widget is pushed). Alternatively, several widgets take the variable option and, if specified, must be an instance of one of the StringVar, IntVar, DoubleVar, or BooleanVar classes (or subclass). Once set up, changes to the widget are immediately reflected in the object, and changes in the object are immediately reflected to the widget. This is demonstrated in *tkBrowser.py* in a number of places including the EditTransaction class, which uses this technique for managing the data shown in the dialog.

There are also dozens of methods available for each widget class, and the Tkinter documentation describes these in detail, but there is one important method we mention here because it's central to the Tkinter event model.

The bind() method is simple, but provides an incredible amount of power by allowing you to bind a GUI event to a Python function. It takes two parameters, the event you wish to bind to (specified as a string) and a Python object to be called when the event fires.

The power behind this method comes from the specification of the event. Tkinter provides a rich set of events, ranging from keyboard and mouse actions to Window focus or state changes. The specification of the event is quite intuitive (for example, <Key> binds any key, <Ctrl-Alt-Key-Z> is a very specific key, <Button-1> is a the first mouse-button click, and so forth) and covers over 20 basic event types. You should consult the Tkinter reference guides for a complete set of events supported by Windows and a full description of the Tkinter event model.

Geometry Management

Tkinter provides a powerful concept typically not found in Windows GUI toolkits, and that is geometry management. Geometry management is the technique used to lay out child widgets in their parent (for example, controls in a dialog box). Most traditional Windows environments force you to specify the absolute position of each control. Although this is specified in dialog units rather than pixels and controls can be moved once created, Tkinter provides a far more powerful and flexible model.

Tkinter widgets provide three methods for geometry management, pack(), grid(), or place().

place() is the simplest mechanism and similar to what most Windows users are used to; each widget has its position explicitly specified, either in absolute or relative coordinates. The grid() mechanism, as you may expect, automatically aligns the widgets in a grid pattern, while the `pack()` method is the most powerful and the most commonly used. When widgets are packed, they are automatically positioned based on the size of the parent and the other widgets already placed. All of these techniques allow customization of the layout process, such as the padding between widgets.

These geometry-management capabilities allow you to define user interfaces that aren't tied to particular screen resolutions and can automatically resize and layout controls as the window size changes, capabilities that most experienced Windows user-interface programmers will know are otherwise difficult to achieve. Our two samples (described next) both make extensive use of the `pack()` method, while the tkDemo sample also makes limited use of `grid()`.

Tkinter Sample Code

We have included a sample Doubletalk browser written in Tkinter. This is a fully functional transaction viewer and editor application and is implemented in *tkBrowser.py*. This implements a number of features that demonstrate how to build powerful applications in Tkinter. A number of dialogs are presented, including the transaction list, and the detail for each specific transaction. To show how simple basic drawing and charting is, a graphical view of each account is also provided. Rather than labor over the details of this sample, the best thing to do is just to run it. Then once you have a feel for the functionality, peruse the source code to see the implementation. There are ample comments and documentation strings included less than 700 lines of source. Figure 20-3 shows our final application in action.

The second sample is *TkDemo.py*, which is a demonstration of all the Tkinter core widgets. It is highly animated and provides a good feel for the basic operation of these widgets.

As mentioned previously, Tkinter is the standard GUI for Python applications, therefore you can find a large number of resources both in the standard Python documentation and referenced via the Python web site.

Tkinter Conclusion

Tkinter is excellent for small, quick GUI applications, and since it runs on more platforms than any other Python GUI toolkit, it is a good choice where portability is the prime concern.

Obviously we haven't been able to give Tkinter the depth of discussion it warrants, but it's fair to say that almost anything that can be done using the C language and Tk can be done using Python and Tkinter. One example is the Python

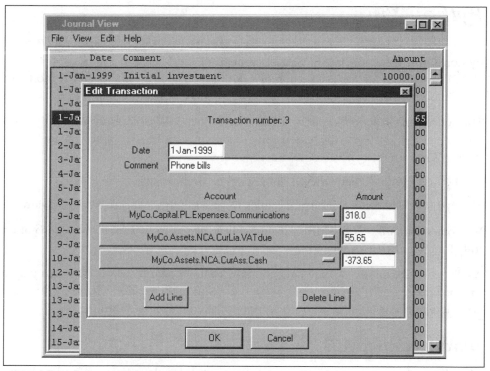

Figure 20-3. The Tkinter Doubletalk browser in action

megawidgets (PMW) package mentioned previously; this is a pure Python package that creates an excellent widget set by building on the core Tkinter widgets.

To learn more about any of the Tkinter topics discussed here, you may like to refer to the following sources:

- The standard Python documentation is optionally installed with Python on Windows and is also available online at *http://www.python.org/doc.*

- PythonWare and Fredrik Lundh provide excellent Tkinter resources, including tutorials available at *http://www.pythonware.com.*

- Tcl and Tk are developed and supported by the Scriptics Corporation, which can be found at *http://www.scriptics.com.* Tcl and Tk documentation is available from *http://www.scriptics.com/resource/doc/.* O'Reilly has an excellent book on the subject, *Tcl/Tk in a Nutshell* by Paul Raines and Jeff Trantor.

- Python megawidgets are available via *http://www.dscpl.com.au/pmw/.*

- Keep your eye out for O'Reilly's *Tkinter Programming* by Fredrik Lundh.

PythonWin

As mentioned in Chapter 4, *Integrated Development Environments for Python*, PythonWin is a framework that exposes much of the Microsoft Foundation Classes (MFC) to Python. MFC is a C++ framework that provides an object-based model of the Windows GUI API, as well as a number of services useful to applications.

The term *PythonWin* is a bit of a misnomer. PythonWin is really an application written to make use of the extensions that expose MFC to Python. This means PythonWin actually consists of two components:

- Python modules that provide the raw MFC functionality
- Python code that uses these modules to provide the PythonWin application

We focus primarily on the MFC functionality exposed to Python so we can build a fully functional GUI application.

As PythonWin mirrors MFC, it's important to understand key MFC concepts to understand how PythonWin hangs together. Although we don't have room for a complete analysis of MFC, an introduction to its concepts is in order.

Introduction to MFC

The Microsoft Foundation Classes are a framework for developing complete applications in C++. MFC provides two primary functions:

- An object-oriented wrapper for the native Windows user-interface API
- Framework facilities that remove much of the grunge work involved in making a complete, standalone Windows application

The object-oriented wrapping is straightforward. Many Windows API functions take a "handle" as their first parameter; for example, the function `SendMessage()` takes a handle to a window (an `HWND`), `DrawText()` takes a handle to a device context (an `HDC`) and so forth. MFC wraps most of these handles in objects and thus provides `CWnd` and `CDC` classes, both of which have the relevant methods.

So, instead of writing your C++ code as:

```
HWND hwnd = CreateWindow(...); // Create a handle to the window...
EnableWindow(hwnd); // and enable it.
```

You may write code similar to:

```
CWnd wnd; // Create a window object.
wnd.CreateWindow(...); // Create the Window.
wnd.EnableWindow();// And enable it.
```

There are a large number of objects, including generic window objects, frame windows, MDI child windows, property pages, fonts, dialogs, etc. It's a large object model, so a good MFC text or the MFC documentation is recommended for anything more than casual use from Python.

The framework aspects of MFC provides some useful utility classes, both for structuring your application and performing many of the mundane tasks a good Windows application should do. The mundane but useful tasks it performs include automatic creation of tool-tip text and status-bar text for menus and dockable toolbars, reading and writing preferences in the registry, maintaining the "recently used files" list, and so forth.

MFC also provides a useful *application/template/document/view* architecture. You create an application object, then add one or more document templates to the application. A document template knows how to create a specific document, meaning your application can work with many documents. A "document" is a general concept; it holds the data for the object your application manages, but doesn't provide any user interface for viewing that data. The last link in the chain is the view object that's responsible for the user interaction. Each view defines a way of looking at your data. For example, you may have a graphical view and also a tabular view. Included in all of this are many utility functions for managing these objects. For example, when a view notifies its document that data has been changed, the document automatically notifies all other views, so they can be kept up-to-date.

If your application doesn't fit this model, don't be alarmed: you can customize almost all this behavior. But there is no doubt that utilizing this framework is the simplest way to use MFC.

The PythonWin Object Model

Think of PythonWin as composed of two distinct portions. The `win32ui` module is a Python extension that provides access to the raw MFC classes. For many MFC objects, there is an equivalent `win32ui` object. For example, the functionality of the MFC `CWnd` object is provided by a `PyCWnd` Python object; an MFC `CDocument` object by a `PyCDocument` object, etc. For a full list, see the PythonWin reference (on the PythonWin help menu).

For the MFC framework to be useful, you need to be able to override default methods in the MFC object hierarchy; for example, the method `CView::OnDraw()` is generally overridden to draw the screen for a view. But the objects exposed by the `win32ui` module are technically Python types (they aren't classes) and a quirk in the Python language prevents these Python types from having their methods overridden.

To this end, the `win32ui` module provides a mechanism to "attach" a Python class instance object to a `win32ui` type. When MFC needs to call an overridden method, it then calls the method on the attached Python object.

What this means for the programmer is that you can use natural Python classes to extend the types defined in `win32ui`.

The `pywin.mfc` package provides Python base classes that interface with many of the `win32ui` objects. These base classes handle the interaction with `win32ui` and allow you to use Python subclassing to get your desired behavior.

This means that when you use a PythonWin object, there are two Python objects involved (the object of a `win32ui` type and the Python class instance), plus an underlying MFC C++ object.

Let's see what this means in practice. We will examine a few of these objects from the PythonWin interactive window and create a dialog object using one of the standard PythonWin dialogs:

```
>>> import win32ui
>>> from pywin.mfc.dialog import Dialog
>>> d=Dialog(win32ui.IDD_SIMPLE_INPUT)
```

Looking at the object, you can see it's indeed an instance of a Python class:

```
>>> d
<pywin.mfc.dialog.Dialog instance at 1083c80>
```

And you can see the underlying `win32ui` object:

```
>>> d._obj_
object 'PyCDialog' - assoc is 010820C0, vf=True, notify=0,ch/u=0/0, mh=1, kh=0
>>>
```

It says that the C++ object is at address 0x010820c0 and also some other internal, cryptic properties of the object. You can use any of the underlying `win32ui` methods automatically on this object:

```
>>> d.CreateWindow()
>>> button=d.GetDlgItem(win32ui.IDC_PROMPT1)
>>> button.SetWindowText("Hello from Python")
>>>
```

The prompt in the dialog should now read "Hello from Python."

Developing a PythonWin Sample Application

During the rest of this section, we will develop a sample application using PythonWin. This will lead us through many of the important MFC and PythonWin concepts, while also leveraging the dynamic nature of PythonWin.

MFC itself has a tutorial/sample called Scribble, which delivers a basic drawing application. We will develop a version of Scribble written in Python.

We will make use of some of the features of PythonWin to demonstrate how rapidly you can create such an application. Specifically, we will develop the Scribble framework first to run under the existing PythonWin framework, then make changes to it so it can run standalone. This is in contrast to the traditional technique of developing MFC applications, where the application object is often one of the first entities defined. A key benefit in using the PythonWin application object is that you get the full benefits of the PythonWin IDE, including error handling and reporting in the interactive window. This makes development much easier before we finally plug in our custom application object.

The general design of the Scribble application is simple. Define the document object to keep a list of strokes. A *stroke* is the start and end coordinates of a line. The document object also can load and store this list of strokes to a file. A view object is also defined that can render these strokes onto a Window.

The first step in the sample is to provide a placeholder for the document template, document, and view objects. Once this skeleton is working, we fill out these objects with a useful implementation.

Defining a Simple Framework

Our first step is to develop a simple framework with placeholders for the major objects.

We define three objects: a `ScribbleTemplate`, a `ScribbleDocument`, and a `ScribbleView`. These objects derive their implementation from objects in the `pywin.mfc.docview` module. The `ScribbleTemplate` object remains empty in this implementation. The `ScribbleDocument` object has a single method, `OnNew-Document()`, which is called as a document object is initialized; the implementation defines an empty list of strokes. The view object is based on a `PyCScrollView` (i.e., an MFC `CScrollView`) and defines a single method `OnInitialUpdate()`. As the name implies, this method is called the first time a view object is updated. This method places the view in the correct mapping mode and disables the scrollbars. For more information on mapping modes and views, see the MFC documentation.

The final part of the skeleton registers the new document template with the MFC framework. This registration process is simple, just a matter of calling `AddDocTemplate()` on the application object. In addition, this code associates some doc strings with the template. These doc strings tell the MFC framework important details about the document template, such as the file extensions for the documents, the window title for new documents, etc. For information on these

doc strings, see the PythonWin Reference for the function `PyCDocTemplate.`
`SetDocStrings()`.

 The term *doc strings* has a number of meanings. To Python, a doc
string is a special string in a Python source file that provides documentation at runtime for specific objects. In the context of an MFC
document template, a doc string is a string that describes an MFC
document object.

A final note before we look at the code. This application has no special requirement for a frame window. The standard MFC/PythonWin Frame windows are perfectly suitable for the application. Therefore, we don't define a specific Frame
window for the sample.

Let's look at the example application with the described functionality:

```python
# scribble1.py
#
# The starting framework for our scribble application.
import win32ui
import win32con
import pywin.mfc.docview

class ScribbleTemplate(pywin.mfc.docview.DocTemplate):
    pass

class ScribbleDocument(pywin.mfc.docview.Document):
    def OnNewDocument(self):
        """Called whenever the document needs initializing.
        For most MDI applications, this is only called as the document
        is created.
        """
        self.strokes = []
        return 1

class ScribbleView(pywin.mfc.docview.ScrollView):
    def OnInitialUpdate(self):
        self.SetScrollSizes(win32con.MM_TEXT, (0, 0))

# Now we do the work to create the document template, and
# register it with the framework.

# For debugging purposes, we first attempt to remove the old template.
# This is not necessary once our app becomes stable!
try:
    win32ui.GetApp().RemoveDocTemplate(template)
except NameError:
    # haven't run this before - that's ok
    pass
```

```
# Now create the template object itself...
template = ScribbleTemplate(None, ScribbleDocument, None, ScribbleView)
# Set the doc strings for the template.
docs='\nPyScribble\nPython Scribble Document\nScribble documents (*.psd)\n.psd'
template.SetDocStrings(docs)

# Then register it with MFC.
win32ui.GetApp().AddDocTemplate(template)
```

Notice there's some code specifically for debugging. If you execute this module multiple times, you'd potentially create multiple document templates, but all for the same class of documents (i.e., the ScribbleDocument). To this end, each time you execute this module, try to remove the document template added during the previous execution.

What does this sample code do? It has registered the ScribbleTemplate with MFC, and MFC is now capable of creating a new document. Let's see this in action. To register the template in PythonWin, perform the following steps:

- Start PythonWin.

- Open the sample code in PythonWin using the File menu and select Open.

- From the File menu, select Import. This action executes the module in the PythonWin environment.

To test this skeleton, select New from the File menu. You will see a list of all the document templates registered in PythonWin. The list should look something like Figure 20-4.

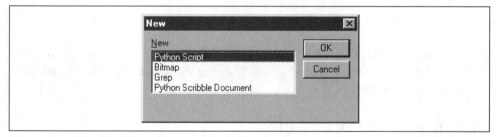

Figure 20-4. The File/New dialog in PythonWin after executing the sample application

You can now select the Python ScribbleDocument and see what happens. You should see a new Frame window, with the title PyScribble1. MFC has given the new document a default name based on the doc strings you supplied the template.

Because you haven't added any code for interacting with the user, your application won't actually do anything yet! We will now develop this skeleton into a usable Scribble application.

Enhancing the DocumentTemplate

Although MFC and PythonWin support multiple document templates, there's a slight complication that isn't immediately obvious. When MFC is asked to open a document file, it asks each registered `DocumentTemplate` in turn if it can handle this document type. The default implementation for `DocumentTemplates` is to report that it "can possibly open this document." Thus, when you're asked to open a Scribble document, one of the other `DocumentTemplate` objects (e.g., the Python editor template) may be asked to handle it, rather than your `ScribbleTemplate`. This wouldn't be a problem if this application handled only one document template, but since PythonWin already has some of its own, it could be a problem.

Therefore, it's necessary to modify the `DocumentTemplate` so that when asked, it answers "I can definitely open this document." MFC then directs the open request to the template.

You provide this functionality by overriding the MFC method `MatchDocType()`. It's necessary for this function to first check if a document of that name is already open; this prevents users from opening the document multiple times. The document template code now looks like:

```
class ScribbleTemplate(pywin.mfc.docview.DocTemplate):
    def MatchDocType(self, fileName, fileType):
        doc = self.FindOpenDocument(fileName)
        if doc: return doc
        ext = string.lower(os.path.splitext(fileName)[1])
        if ext =='.psd':
            return win32ui.CDocTemplate_Confidence_yesAttemptNative
        return win32ui.CDocTemplate_Confidence_noAttempt
```

As you can see, you check the extension of the filename, and if it matches, tell MFC that the document is indeed yours. If the extension doesn't match, tell MFC you can't open the file.

Enhancing the Document

As mentioned previously, this `ScribbleDocument` object is responsible only for working with the document data, not for interacting with the user. This makes the `ScribbleDocument` quite simple. The first step is to add some public methods for working with the strokes. These functions look like:

```
class ScribbleDocument(pywin.mfc.docview.Document):
    ...
    def AddStroke(self, start, end, fromView):
        self.strokes.append((start, end))
        self.SetModifiedFlag()
        self.UpdateAllViews( fromView, None )
```

```
def GetStrokes(self):
    return self.strokes
```

The first function appends the new stroke to the list of strokes. It also sets the document's "modified flag." This flag is used by MFC to automatically prompt the user to save the document as the program exits. It also automatically enables the File/Save option for the document.

The last thing the document must do is to load and save the data from a file. MFC itself handles displaying of the Save As, etc., dialogs, and calls Document functions to perform the actual save. The function names are OnOpenDocument() and OnSaveDocument() respectively.

As the strokes are a simple list, you can use the Python `pickle` module. The functions become quite easy:

```
def OnOpenDocument(self, filename):
    file = open(filename, "rb")
    self.strokes = pickle.load(file)
    file.close()
    win32ui.AddToRecentFileList(filename)
    return 1

def OnSaveDocument(self, filename):
    file = open(filename, "wb")
    pickle.dump(self.strokes, file)
    file.close()
    self.SetModifiedFlag(0)
    win32ui.AddToRecentFileList(filename)
    return 1
```

OnOpenDocument() loads the strokes from the named file. In addition, it places the filename to the most recently used (MRU) list. OnSaveDocument() dumps the strokes to the named file, updates the document status to indicate it's no longer modified, and adds the file to the MRU list. And that is all you need to make your document fully functional.

Defining the View

The View object is the most complex object in the sample. The View is responsible for all interactions with the user, which means the View must collect the strokes as the user draws them, and also draw the entire list of strokes whenever the window requires repainting.

The collection of the strokes is the most complex part. To collect effectively, you must trap the user pressing the mouse button in the window. Once this occurs, enter a drawing mode, and as the mouse is moved, draw a line to the current position. When the user releases the mouse button, they have completed the stroke, so add the stroke to the document. The key steps to coax this behavior are:

- The View must hook the relevant mouse messages: in this case, the LBUTTONDOWN, LBUTTONUP, and MOUSEMOVE messages.

- When a LBUTTONDOWN message is received, remember the start position and enter a drawing mode. Also capture the mouse, to ensure that you get all future mouse messages, even when the mouse leaves the window.

- If a MOUSEMOVE message occurs when you are in drawing mode, draw a line from the remembered start position to the current mouse position. In addition, erase the previous line drawn by this process. This gives a "rubber band" effect as you move the mouse.

- When a LBUTTONUP message is received, notify the document of the new, completed stroke, release the mouse capture, and leave drawing mode.

After adding this logic to the sample, it now looks like:

```python
class ScribbleView(pywin.mfc.docview.ScrollView):
    def OnInitialUpdate(self):
        self.SetScrollSizes(win32con.MM_TEXT, (0, 0))
        self.HookMessage(self.OnLButtonDown,win32con.WM_LBUTTONDOWN)
        self.HookMessage(self.OnLButtonUp,win32con.WM_LBUTTONUP)
        self.HookMessage(self.OnMouseMove,win32con.WM_MOUSEMOVE)
        self.bDrawing = 0

    def OnLButtonDown(self, params):
        assert not self.bDrawing, "Button down message while still drawing"
        startPos = params[5]
        # Convert the startpos to Client coordinates.
        self.startPos = self.ScreenToClient(startPos)
        self.lastPos = self.startPos
        # Capture all future mouse movement.
        self.SetCapture()
        self.bDrawing = 1

    def OnLButtonUp(self, params):
        assert self.bDrawing, "Button up message, but not drawing!"
        endPos = params[5]
        endPos = self.ScreenToClient(endPos)
        self.ReleaseCapture()
        self.bDrawing = 0
        # And add the stroke to the document.
        self.GetDocument().AddStroke( self.startPos, endPos, self )

    def OnMouseMove(self, params):
        # If Im not drawing at the moment, I don't care
        if not self.bDrawing:
            return
        pos = params[5]
        dc = self.GetDC()
        # Setup for an inverting draw operation.
        dc.SetROP2(win32con.R2_NOT)
```

```
              # "undraw" the old line
              dc.MoveTo(self.startPos)
              dc.LineTo(self.lastPos)

              # Now draw the new position
              self.lastPos = self.ScreenToClient(pos)
              dc.MoveTo(self.startPos)
              dc.LineTo(self.lastPos)
```

Most of this code should be quite obvious. It's worth mentioning that you tell Windows to draw the line using a NOT mode. This mode is handy; if you draw the same line twice, the second draw erases the first. Thus, to erase a line you drew previously, all you need is to draw the same line again.

Another key point is that the mouse messages all report the position in "Screen Coordinates" (i.e., relative to the top-left corner of the screen) rather than in "Client Coordinates" (i.e., relative to the top-left corner of our window). You use a member function PyCWnd.ScreenToClient() to transform these coordinates.

The final step to complete the View is to draw all your strokes whenever the window requires updating. This code is simple: you iterate over the list of strokes for the document, drawing lines between the coordinates. To obtain this behavior, use the code:

```
          def OnDraw(self, dc):
              # All we need to is get the strokes, and paint them.
              doc = self.GetDocument()
              for startPos, endPos in doc.GetStrokes():
                  dc.MoveTo(startPos)
                  dc.LineTo(endPos)
```

And that's it! You now have a fully functional drawing application, capable of loading and saving itself from disk.

Creating the Application Object

The simplest way to create an application object for Scribble is to subclass one of the standard application objects. The PythonWin application object is implemented in pywin.framework.intpyapp, and it derives from the CApp class in pywin.framework.app. This base class provides much of the functionality for an application, so we too will derive our application from CApp.

This makes the application object small and simple. You obviously may need to enhance certain aspects; in this case, you should use the pywin.framework modules as a guide. The minimal application object looks like:

```
      # scribbleApp.py
      #
      # The application object for Python.
      from pywin.framework.app import CApp
```

```
class ScribbleApplication(CApp):
    def InitInstance(self):
        # All we need do is call the base class,
        # then import our document template.
        CApp.InitInstance(self)
        import scribble2

# And create our application object.
ScribbleApplication()
```

To run this, use the following command line:

```
C:\Scripts> start pythonwin /app scribbleApp.py
```

An instance of *Pythonwin.exe* now starts, but uses the application object you defined. Therefore, there'a no Interactive Window, the application doesn't offer to open *.py* files, etc. The Scribble application should look like Figure 20-5.

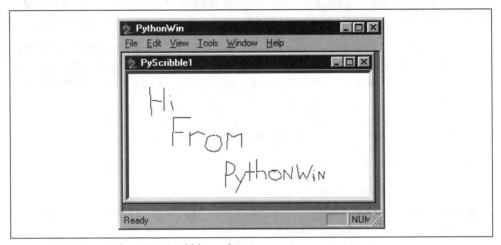

Figure 20-5. Our PythonWin Scribble application

There is also a technique to avoid this command line, but you need a copy of a resource editor (such as Microsoft Visual C++). You can take a copy of *Pythonwin. exe* (name it something suitable for your application), then open the *.exe* in the resource editor and locate an entry in the string table with the value `pywin. framework.startup`. This is the name of a module executed to boot the PythonWin application; the default script parses the "/app" off the command line and loads that application. You can change this to any value you like, and PythonWin then loads your startup script. See *startup.py* in the PythonWin distribution for an example of a startup script.

PythonWin and Resources

As we've discussed, MFC provides a framework architecture, and much of this architecture is tied together by resource IDs, integers that identify Windows resources in a DLL or executable.

For example, when you define a `DocumentTemplate`, you specify a resource ID. The previous example doesn't specify a resource ID, so the default of `win32ui.IDR_PYTHONTYPE` is used. When a document is created, MFC uses the resource ID in the following ways:

- The menu with the ID is loaded and used for the document's frame. This allows each document supported in an application to have a unique set of menus as is common in MDI applications.

- The icon with the ID is loaded and used for the document's frame.

- The accelerator with that ID is loaded, providing document-specific shortcut keys to many of the menu functions.

Another example of the reliance on resource IDs is in the processing and definition of menu and toolbar items. Each command in the application is assigned an ID. When you define menu or toolbar items, you specify the menu text (or toolbar bitmap) and the command ID. When MFC displays a menu item, it uses a string defined with the same ID and places this text automatically in the application's status bar. When the mouse hovers over a toolbar item, MFC again looks for a string with the specified ID and uses it for the tooltip-text for the button. This architecture has a number of advantages:

- Hooking the various pieces of your application together becomes simple. You define an icon, menu, accelerators, strings, and so forth with the same resource ID, and MFC automatically ties all these together for your application.

- If you are working with an existing MFC or C++ application, there's a good chance you already use resources in a similar fashion, so PythonWin often fits naturally when embedded in these applications.

- When you need to respond to a GUI command, specify the command ID. The same code then handles the command regardless of whether it was sourced from the keyboard, toolbar or menu.

- Localizing your application for other languages becomes simpler. You define new resources in the new language but use the same IDs, and the application still works regardless of the particular resources in use at the time.

However, it also has a number of disadvantages:

- Python doesn't have a technique for defining resources, such as dialogs, menus, toolbars, or strings. So while this scheme works well using MFC from

Microsoft Visual C++ (which does provide this facility), it doesn't work as well from Python.

- It's a pain to move beyond the MFC-provided framework. As soon as you begin manually defining and managing these resources, you aren't much better off than if you simply had used the raw Windows GUI API.

PythonWin can use resources from arbitrary DLLs, thus you can define your own DLL containing only resources. PythonWin makes it easy to use these resources; just load the DLL (using `win32ui.LoadLibrary()`), and PythonWin locates and uses the resources in this DLL.

If you are writing a large application, you'll probably find it worthwhile to define your own resource DLL when using PythonWin. The benefits offered by the framework make it worth the pain of initially setting everything up. On the other hand, it does make PythonWin somewhat cumbersome for defining these applications purely from Python code.

PythonWin Conclusion

For the vast majority of Python users in Windows, PythonWin will never be more than an interesting IDE environment for developing Python applications. But many other Windows developers are beginning to use PythonWin to develop Windows applications. When comparing the three GUI toolkits available in this book, you will probably come to the conclusion that PythonWin is the least suitable for simple, small GUI applications written in Python, and this would be fair. However, depending on your particular circumstances (usually either because you have an existing MFC investment or it's important to use some user-interface features offered only by PythonWin), it may be a good choice.

PythonWin suffers from a lack of decent documentation. A Windows help file is included that contains a reference guide for all of the objects and methods exposed by PythonWin, but PythonWin doesn't include a comprehensive overview of the MFC framework. There are many good MFC books available, so a specific recommendation is impossible. Information from Microsoft on MFC can be found at *http://msdn.microsoft.com/visualc/*.

wxPython

Another GUI toolkit available for Python is called wxPython. The current incarnation is fairly new to the Python scene and is rapidly gaining popularity amongst Python developers. wxPython is a Python extension module that encapsulates the wxWindows C++ class library.

wxPython is a cross-platform GUI framework for Python that is quite mature on the Windows platform. It exposes the popular wxWindows C++ framework Python to provide an attractive alternative for GUI development.

wxWindows

wxWindows is a free C++ framework designed to make cross-platform programming child's play. Well, almost. wxWindows 2.0 supports Windows 3.1/95/98/NT, Unix with GTK/Motif/Lesstif, with a Mac version underway. Other ports are under consideration.

wxWindows is a set of libraries that allows C++ applications to compile and run on several different types of computers, with minimal source-code changes. There's one library per supported GUI (such as Motif, or Windows). As well as providing a common API for GUI functionality, it provides functionality for accessing some commonly used operating-system facilities, such as copying or deleting files. wxWindows is a framework in the sense that it provides a lot of built-in functionality, which the application can use or replace as required, thus saving a great deal of coding effort. Basic data structures such as strings, linked lists, and hash tables are also supplied.

Native versions of controls, common dialogs, and other window types are used on platforms that support them. For other platforms, suitable alternatives are created using wxWindows itself. For example, on Win32 platforms the native list control is used, but on GTK, a generic list control with similar capabilities was created for use in the wxWindows class library.

Experienced Windows programmers will feel right at home with the wxWindows object model. Many of the classes and concepts will be familiar. For example, the Multiple Document Interface, drawing on Device Contexts with GDI objects such as brushes, pens, and so on.

wxWindows + Python = wxPython

wxPython is a Python extension module that provides a set of bindings from the wxWindows library to the Python language. In other words, the extension module allows Python programers to create instances of wxWindows classes and to invoke methods of those classes.

The wxPython extension module attempts to mirror the class hierarchy of wxWindows as closely as possible. This means that there is a wxFrame class in wxPython that looks, smells, tastes, and acts almost the same as the wxFrame class in the C++ version.

wxPython is close enough to the C++ version that the majority of the wxPython documentation is actually annotations to the C++ documentation that describe the places where wxPython is different. There is also a series of sample programs included, and a series of documentation pages that assist the programmer in getting started with wxPython.

Where to get wxPython

The latest version of wxPython can always be found at *http://alldunn.com/ wxPython/*. From this site you can download a self-installer for Win32 systems that includes a prebuilt extension module, documentation in HTML help format, and a set of demos.

Also available from this site is a Linux RPM, wxPython sources, documentation in raw HTML, and pointers to other sites, mail lists, the wxPython FAQ, and so forth.

If you want to build wxPython from sources yourself, you also need the wxWindows sources, available from *http://www.wxwindows.org/*.

Where to go from here

The remainder of this chapter gives a basic introduction to using wxPython, starting with a simple example teaching the basic structure of a wxPython application. We then build a more involved sample that touches on some of the more advanced features of the toolkit, using classes from the Doubletalk financial modeler you're already familiar with.

Using wxPython

We've always found that the best way to learn is by doing and then experimenting and tweaking with what's been done. So download and install wxPython, fire up your favorite text editor* and get ready to play along as you read the next few sections.

A simple example

Familiarize yourself with this little wxPython program, and refer back to it as you read through the explanations that follow:

```
from wxPython.wx import *

class MyApp(wxApp):
    def OnInit(self):
        frame = wxFrame(NULL, -1, "Hello from wxPython")
        frame.Show(true)
```

---

* When getting started, you should probably avoid using PythonWin or IDLE for running wxPython programs, because the interactions between the various toolkits may have unexpected consequences.

```
            self.SetTopWindow(frame)
            return true

app = MyApp(0)
app.MainLoop()
```

When you run this code, you should see a Window appear similar to Figure 20-6.

Figure 20-6. A basic wxPython application

The first thing to do is import the entire **wxPython** library with the **from wxPython.wx import *** statement. This is common practice for **wxPython** programs, but you can obviously perform more restrictive imports if you prefer.

Every **wxPython** application needs to derive a class from **wxApp** and provide an **OnInit** method for it. The framework calls this method as part of its initialization sequence, and the usual purpose of **OnInit** is to create the windows and essentials necessary for the program to begin operation. In the sample you created a frame with no parent, with a title of "Hello from **wxPython**" and then showed it. We could also have specified a position and size for the frame in its constructor, but since we didn't, defaults are used. The last two lines of the **OnInit** method will probably be the same for all applications; **SetTopWindow** method informs **wxWindows** that this frame is one of the main frames (in this case the only one) for the application, and you return **true** to indicate success. When all top-level windows have been closed, the application terminates.

The final two lines of the script again will probably be the same for all your **wxPython** applications. You create an instance of the application class and call its **MainLoop** method. **MainLoop** is the heart of the application: it's where events are processed and dispatched to the various windows, and it returns when the final window is closed. Fortunately, **wxWindows** insulates you from the differences in event processing in the various GUI toolkits.

Most of the time you will want to customize the main frame of the application, and so using the stock **wxFrame** isn't sufficient. As you might expect, you can derive your own class from **wxFrame** to begin customization. This next example builds on the last by defining a frame class and creating an instance in the application's **OnInit** method. Notice that except for the name of the class created in **OnInit**, the rest of the **MyApp** code is identical to the previous example. This code is displayed in Figure 20-7.

```python
from wxPython.wx import *

ID_ABOUT = 101
ID_EXIT  = 102

class MyFrame(wxFrame):
    def __init__(self, parent, ID, title):
        wxFrame.__init__(self, parent, ID, title,
                         wxDefaultPosition, wxSize(200, 150))
        self.CreateStatusBar()
        self.SetStatusText("This is the statusbar")

        menu = wxMenu()
        menu.Append(ID_ABOUT, "&About",
                    "More information about this program")
        menu.AppendSeparator()
        menu.Append(ID_EXIT, "E&xit", "Terminate the program")

        menuBar = wxMenuBar()
        menuBar.Append(menu, "&File");

        self.SetMenuBar(menuBar)


class MyApp(wxApp):
    def OnInit(self):
        frame = MyFrame(NULL, -1, "Hello from wxPython")
        frame.Show(true)
        self.SetTopWindow(frame)
        return true

app = MyApp(0)
app.MainLoop()
```

Figure 20-7. A wxPython application with menus

This example shows some of the built-in capabilities of the **wxFrame** class. For example, creating a status bar for the frame is as simple as calling a single method. The frame itself automatically manages its placement, size, and drawing. On the other hand, if you want to customize the status bar, create an instance of your own **wxStatusBar**-derived class and attach it to the frame.

Creating a simple menu bar and a drop-down menu is also demonstrated in this example. The full range of expected menu capabilities is supported: cascading submenus, checkable items, popup menus, etc.; all you have to do is create a menu object and append menu items to it. The items can be text as shown here, or other menus. With each item you can optionally specify some short help text, as we have done, which are shown in the status bar automatically when the menu item is selected.

Events in wxPython

The one thing that the last sample doesn't do is show how to make the menus actually do something. If you run the sample and select Exit from the menu, nothing happens. The next sample takes care of that little problem.

To process events in **wxPython**, any method (or standalone function for that matter) can be attached to any event using a helper function from the toolkit. **wxPython** also provides a **wxEvent** class and a whole bunch of derived classes for containing the details of the event. Each time a method is invoked due to an event, an object derived from **wxEvent** is sent as a parameter, the actual type of the event object depends on the type of the event; **wxSizeEvent** for when the window changes size, **wxCommandEvent** for menu selections and button clicks, **wxMouseEvent** for (you guessed it) mouse events, and so forth.

To solve our little problem with the last sample, all you have to do is add two lines to the **MyFrame** constructor and add some methods to handle the events. We'll also demonstrate one of the common dialogs, the **wxMessageDialog**. Here's the code, with the new parts in bold, and the running code shown in Figure 20-8:

```
from wxPython.wx import *

ID_ABOUT = 101
ID_EXIT  = 102

class MyFrame(wxFrame):
    def __init__(self, parent, ID, title):
        wxFrame.__init__(self, parent, ID, title,
                         wxDefaultPosition, wxSize(200, 150))
        self.CreateStatusBar()
        self.SetStatusText("This is the statusbar")
        menu = wxMenu()
        menu.Append(ID_ABOUT, "&About",
                    "More information about this program")
        menu.AppendSeparator()
        menu.Append(ID_EXIT, "E&xit", "Terminate the program")
        menuBar = wxMenuBar()
        menuBar.Append(menu, "&File");
        self.SetMenuBar(menuBar)
```

```
        EVT_MENU(self, ID_ABOUT, self.OnAbout)
        EVT_MENU(self, ID_EXIT,  self.TimeToQuit)

    def OnAbout(self, event):
        dlg = wxMessageDialog(self, "This sample program shows off\n"
                              "frames, menus, statusbars, and this\n"
                              "message dialog.",
                              "About Me", wxOK | wxICON_INFORMATION)
        dlg.ShowModal()
        dlg.Destroy()

    def TimeToQuit(self, event):
        self.Close(true)

class MyApp(wxApp):
    def OnInit(self):
        frame = MyFrame(NULL, -1, "Hello from wxPython")
        frame.Show(true)
        self.SetTopWindow(frame)
        return true

app = MyApp(0)
app.MainLoop()
```

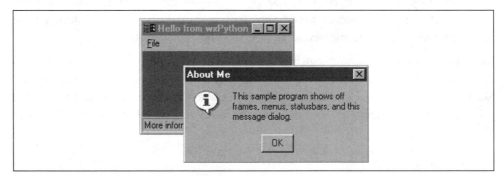

Figure 20-8. The application with an About box

The **EVT_MENU** function called here is one of the helper functions for attaching events to methods. Sometimes it helps to understand what is happening if you translate the function call to English. The first one says, "For any menu item selection event sent to the window `self` with an ID of **ID_ABOUT**, invoke the method `self.OnAbout`."

There are many of these **EVT_*** helper functions, all of which correspond to a specific type of event, or events. Some popular ones are listed in Table 20-4. See the **wxPython** documentation for details.

Table 20-4. Common wxPython Event Functions

Event Function	Event Description
EVT_SIZE	Sent to a window when its size has changed, either interactively by the user or programmatically.
EVT_MOVE	Sent to a window when it has been moved, either interactively by the user or programmatically.
EVT_CLOSE	Sent to a frame when it has been requested to close. Unless the close is being forced, it can be canceled by calling event.Veto(true).
EVT_PAINT	This event is sent whenever a portion of the window needs to be redrawn.
EVT_CHAR	Sent for each nonmodifier (Shift key, etc.) keystroke when the window has the focus.
EVT_IDLE	This event is sent periodically when the system isn't processing other events.
EVT_LEFT_DOWN	The left mouse button has been pressed down.
EVT_LEFT_UP	The left mouse button has been let up.
EVT_LEFT_DCLICK	The left mouse button has been double-clicked.
EVT_MOTION	The mouse is in motion.
EVT_SCROLL	A scrollbar has been manipulated. This one is actually a collection of events, which can be captured individually if desired.
EVT_BUTTON	A button has been clicked.
EVT_MENU	A menu item has been selected.

Building a Doubletalk Browser with wxPython

Okay, now let's build something that's actually useful and learn more about the **wxPython** framework along the way. As has been shown with the other GUI toolkits, we'll build a small application around the Doubletalk class library that allows browsing and editing of transactions.

MDI Frame

We're going to implement a Multiple Document Interface, where the child frames are different views of the transactional data, rather than separate "documents." Just as with previous samples, the first thing to do is create an application class and have it create a main frame in its **OnInit** method:

```
class DoubleTalkBrowserApp(wxApp):
    def OnInit(self):
        frame = MainFrame(NULL)
        frame.Show(true)
        self.SetTopWindow(frame)
        return true

app = DoubleTalkBrowserApp(0)
app.MainLoop()
```

Since we are using MDI, there is a special class to use for the frame's base class. Here is the code for the initialization method of the main application frame:

```
class MainFrame(wxMDIParentFrame):
    title = "Doubletalk Browser - wxPython Edition"
    def __init__(self, parent):
        wxMDIParentFrame.__init__(self, parent, -1, self.title)
        self.bookset = None
        self.views = []

        if wxPlatform == '__WXMSW__':
            self.icon = wxIcon('chart7.ico', wxBITMAP_TYPE_ICO)
            self.SetIcon(self.icon)

        # create a statusbar that shows the time and date on the right
        sb = self.CreateStatusBar(2)
        sb.SetStatusWidths([-1, 150])
        self.timer = wxPyTimer(self.Notify)
        self.timer.Start(1000)
        self.Notify()

        menu = self.MakeMenu(false)
        self.SetMenuBar(menu)
        menu.EnableTop(1, false)

        EVT_MENU(self, ID_OPEN,    self.OnMenuOpen)
        EVT_MENU(self, ID_CLOSE,   self.OnMenuClose)
        EVT_MENU(self, ID_SAVE,    self.OnMenuSave)
        EVT_MENU(self, ID_SAVEAS,  self.OnMenuSaveAs)
        EVT_MENU(self, ID_EXIT,    self.OnMenuExit)
        EVT_MENU(self, ID_ABOUT,   self.OnMenuAbout)
        EVT_MENU(self, ID_ADD,     self.OnAddTrans)
        EVT_MENU(self, ID_JRNL,    self.OnViewJournal)
        EVT_MENU(self, ID_DTAIL,   self.OnViewDetail)
        EVT_CLOSE(self, self.OnCloseWindow)
```

Figure 20-9 shows the state of the application so far.

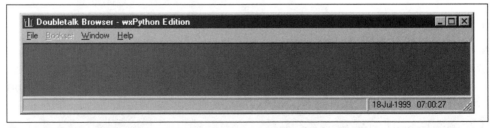

Figure 20-9. The first MDI wxPython application

Obviously, we're not showing all the code yet, but we'll get to it all eventually as we go through piece by piece.

Notice the use of **wxMDIParentFrame** as the base class of **MainFrame**. By using this class you automatically get everything needed to implement MDI for the application without having to worry about what's really happening behind the scenes. The **wxMDIParentFrame** class has the same interface as the **wxFrame** class, with only a few additional methods. Often changing a single document interface program to a MDI program is as easy as changing the base classes the application's classes are derived from. There is a corresponding **wxMDIChildFrame** to be used for the document windows, as we'll see later. If you ever need to have access to the client area (or the background area) of the MDI parent, you can use the **wxMDIClientWindow** class. You might use this for placing a background image behind all the child windows.

Icons

The next thing the previous code does is create an icon and associate it with the frame. Normally Windows applications load items such as icons from a resource file that is linked with the executable. Since **wxPython** programs have no binary executable file, you create the icon by specifying the full path to a *.ico* file. Assigning the icon to the frame only requires calling the frame's **SetIcon** method.

Timers

You may have noticed from Figure 20-9 that the status bar has two sections, with the date and time displayed in the second one. The next bit of code in the initialization method handles that functionality. The frame's **CreateStatusBar** method takes an optional parameter specifying the number of sections to create, and **SetStatusWidths** can be given a list of integers to specify how many pixels to reserve for each section. The –1 means that the first section should take all the remaining space.

In order to update the date and time, you create a **wxPyTimer** object. There are two types of timer classes in **wxPython**. The first is the **wxPyTimer** used here, which accepts a function or method to use as a callback. The other is the **wxTimer** class, which is intended to be derived from and will call a required method in the derived class when the timer expires. In the example you specify that when the timer expires, the **Notify** method should be called. Then start the timer, telling it to expire every 1000 milliseconds (i.e., every second). Here is the code for the **Notify** method:

```
# Time-out handler
def Notify(self):
    t = time.localtime(time.time())
    st = time.strftime(" %d-%b-%Y   %I:%M:%S", t)
    self.SetStatusText(st, 1)
```

You first use Python's **time** module to get the current time and format it in to a nice, human-readable formatted string. Then by calling the frame's **SetStatus-Text** method, you can put that string into the status bar, in this case in slot 1.

Main menu

As you can see in the next bit of code, we have moved the building of the menu to a separate method. This is mainly for two reasons. The first is to help reduce clutter in the __init__ method and better organize the functionality of the class. The second reason has to do with MDI. As with all MDI applications, each child frame can have its own menu bar, automatically updated as the frame is selected.

The approach taken by our sample is to either add or remove a single item from the BookSet menu based on whether a view can select transactions for editing. Here's the code for the MakeMenu method. Notice how the parameter controls whether the Edit Transaction item is added to the menu. It might have made better sense to just enable or disable this item as needed, but then you wouldn't be able to see how wxPython changes the menus automatically when the active window changes. Also notice that you don't create the Window menu. The wxMDIParentFrame takes care of that for you:

```
def MakeMenu(self, withEdit):
    fmenu = wxMenu()
    fmenu.Append(ID_OPEN,  "&Open BookSet",  "Open a BookSet file")
    fmenu.Append(ID_CLOSE, "&Close BookSet",
                "Close the current BookSet")
    fmenu.Append(ID_SAVE,  "&Save", "Save the current BookSet")
    fmenu.Append(ID_SAVEAS,  "Save &As", "Save the current BookSet")
    fmenu.AppendSeparator()
    fmenu.Append(ID_EXIT, "E&xit",   "Terminate the program")

    dtmenu = wxMenu()
    dtmenu.Append(ID_ADD, "&Add Transaction",
                "Add a new transaction")
    if withEdit:
        dtmenu.Append(ID_EDIT, "&Edit Transaction",
                    "Edit selected transaction in current view")
    dtmenu.Append(ID_JRNL, "&Journal view",
                "Open or raise the journal view")
    dtmenu.Append(ID_DTAIL,"&Detail view",
                "Open or raise the detail view")

    hmenu = wxMenu()
    hmenu.Append(ID_ABOUT, "&About",
                "More information about this program")

    main = wxMenuBar()
    main.Append(fmenu, "&File")
    main.Append(dtmenu,"&Bookset")
    main.Append(hmenu, "&Help")

    return main
```

If you skip back to the __init__ method, notice that after you create the menu and attach it to the window, the EnableTop method of the menubar is called. This is how to disable the entire `BookSet` submenu. (Since there is no `BookSet` file open, you can't really do anything with it yet.) There is also an **Enable** method that allows you to enable or disable individual menu items by ID.

The last bit of the `__init__` method attaches event handlers to the various menu items. We'll be going through them one by one as we explore the functionality behind those options. But first, here are some of the simpler ones:

```python
def OnMenuExit(self, event):
    self.Close()

def OnCloseWindow(self, event):
    self.timer.Stop()
    del self.timer
    del self.icon
    self.Destroy()

def OnMenuAbout(self, event):
    dlg = wxMessageDialog(self,
                "This program uses the doubletalk package to\n"
                "demonstrate the wxPython toolkit.\n\n"
                "by Robin Dunn",
                "About", wxOK | wxICON_INFORMATION)
    dlg.ShowModal()
    dlg.Destroy()
```

The user selects Exit from the File menu, then the `OnMenuExit` method is called, which asks the window to close itself. Whenever the window wants to close, whether it's because its `Close` method was called or because the user clicks on the Close button in the titlebar, the `OnCloseWindow` method is called. If you want to prompt the user with an "Are you sure you want to exit?" type of message, do it here. If he decides not to quit, just call the method `event.Veto(true)`.

Most programs will want to have a fancier About box than the `wxMessageDialog` provides, but for our purposes here it works out just fine. Don't forget to call the dialog's `Destroy` method, or you may leak memory.

wxFileDialog

Before doing anything with a `BookSet`, you have to have one opened. For this, use the common dialog `wxFileDialog`. This is the same File → Open dialog you see in all your other Windows applications, all wrapped in a nice `wxPython`-compatible class interface.

Here's the event handler that catches the File → Open menu event, and Figure 20-10 shows the dialog in action:

```python
def OnMenuOpen(self, event):
    # This should be checking if another is already open,
    # but is left as an exercise for the reader...
```

```
dlg = wxFileDialog(self)
dlg.SetStyle(wxOPEN)
dlg.SetWildcard("*.dtj")
if dlg.ShowModal() == wxID_OK:
    self.path = dlg.GetPath()
    self.SetTitle(self.title + ' - ' + self.path)
    self.bookset = BookSet()
    self.bookset.load(self.path)
    self.GetMenuBar().EnableTop(1, true)

    win = JournalView(self, self.bookset, ID_EDIT)
    self.views.append((win, ID_JRNL))

dlg.Destroy()
```

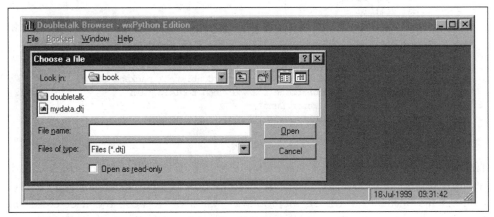

Figure 20-10. wxPython browsing for a Doubletalk transaction file

Start off by creating the file dialog and tell it how to behave. Next show the dialog and give the user a chance to select a **BookSet** file. Notice that this time you're checking the return value of the **ShowModal** method. This is how the dialog says what the result was. By default, dialogs understand the **wxID_OK** and **wxID_CANCEL** IDs assigned to buttons in the dialog and do the right thing when they are clicked. For dialogs you create, you can also specify other values to return if you wish.

The first thing to do after a successful completion of the file dialog is ask the dialog what the selected pathname was, and then use this to modify the frame's title and to open a **BookSet** file.

Take a look at the next line. It reenables the **BookSet** menu since there is now a file open. It's really two statements in one and is equivalent to these two lines:

```
menu = self.GetMenuBar()
menu.EnableTop(1, true)
```

Since it makes sense to actually let the user see something when they ask to open a file, you should create and show one of the views in the last bits of the OnMenuOpen handler above. We'll take a look at that next.

wxListCtrl

The Journal view consists of a wxListCtrl with a single-line summary for each transaction. It's placed inside a wxMDIChildFrame and since it's the only thing in the frame, don't worry about setting or maintaining the size, the frame does it automatically. (Unfortunately, since some platforms send the first resize event at different times, sometimes the window shows up without its child sized properly.) Here's a simple workaround:

```
class JournalView(wxMDIChildFrame):
    def __init__(self, parent, bookset, editID):
        wxMDIChildFrame.__init__(self, parent, -1, "")
        self.bookset = bookset
        self.parent = parent

        tID = wxNewId()
        self.lc = wxListCtrl(self, tID, wxDefaultPosition,
                             wxDefaultSize, wxLC_REPORT)
        ## Forces a resize event to get around a minor bug...
        self.SetSize(self.GetSize())

        self.lc.InsertColumn(0, "Date")
        self.lc.InsertColumn(1, "Comment")
        self.lc.InsertColumn(2, "Amount")

        self.currentItem = 0
        EVT_LIST_ITEM_SELECTED(self, tID, self.OnItemSelected)
        EVT_LEFT_DCLICK(self.lc, self.OnDoubleClick)

        menu = parent.MakeMenu(true)
        self.SetMenuBar(menu)
        EVT_MENU(self, editID, self.OnEdit)
        EVT_CLOSE(self, self.OnCloseWindow)

        self.UpdateView()
```

Figure 20-11 shows the application is progressing nicely and starting to look like a serious Windows application.

The wxListCtrl has many personalities, but they should all be familiar to you. Underneath its wxPython wrappers, it's the same control used in Windows Explorer in the right side panel. All the same options are available: large icons, small icons, list mode, and the report mode used here. You define the columns with their headers and then set some events for the list control. You want to be able to edit the transactions when they are double-clicked, so why are both event handlers needed? The list control sends an event when an item is selected, but it

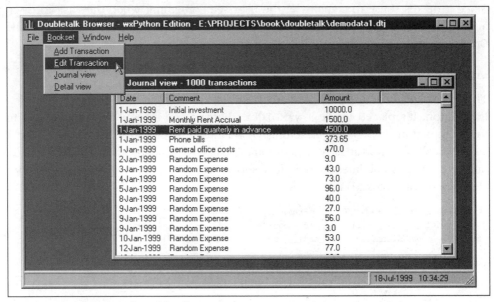

Figure 20-11. The list of Doubletalk transactions

doesn't keep track of double-clicks. The base **wxWindow** class, on the other hand, reports double-clicks, but it knows nothing about the list control. So by catching both events you can easily implement the functionality you need. Here is the code for the event handlers:

```
def OnItemSelected(self, event):
    self.currentItem = event.m_itemIndex

def OnDoubleClick(self, event):
    self.OnEdit()
```

After creating and setting up the list control, you create a menubar for this frame. Here you call the menu-making method in the parent, asking it to add the Edit Transaction menu item.

The last thing the **__init__** method does is call a method to fill the list control from the **BookSet**. We've split this into a separate method so it can be called independently whenever the **BookSet** data changes. Here's the **UpdateView** method:

```
def UpdateView(self):
    self.lc.DeleteAllItems()
    for x in range(len(self.bookset)):
        trans = self.bookset[x]
        self.lc.InsertStringItem(x, trans.getDateString())
        self.lc.SetStringItem(x, 1, trans.comment)
        self.lc.SetStringItem(x, 2, str(trans.magnitude()))
```

```
self.lc.SetColumnWidth(0, wxLIST_AUTOSIZE)
self.lc.SetColumnWidth(1, wxLIST_AUTOSIZE)
self.lc.SetColumnWidth(2, wxLIST_AUTOSIZE)

self.SetTitle("Journal view - %d transactions" %
              len(self.bookset))
```

Putting data in a list control is fairly easy; just insert each item. For the report mode, you insert an item for the first column and then set values for the remaining columns. For each column in the example, just fetch some data from the transaction and send it to the list control. If you were using icons or combination of icons and text, there are different methods to handle that.

Now that there's data in the list control, you should resize the columns. You can either specify actual pixel widths or have the list auto-size the columns based on the widths of the data.

The last thing the `JournalView` class needs to do is to enable the editing of the transactions. We saw previously that when an item is double-clicked, a method named `OnEdit` is invoked. Here it is:

```
def OnEdit(self, *event):
    if self.currentItem:
        trans = self.bookset[self.currentItem]
        dlg = EditTransDlg(self, trans,
                           self.bookset.getAccountList())
        if dlg.ShowModal() == wxID_OK:
            trans = dlg.GetTrans()
            self.bookset.edit(self.currentItem, trans)
            self.parent.UpdateViews()
        dlg.Destroy()
```

This looks like what we did with the file dialog in the main frame, and indeed you will find yourself using this pattern quite often when using dialogs. The one item to notice here is the call to `UpdateViews()` in the parent window. This is how to manage keeping all the views of the `BookSet` up to date. Whenever a transaction is updated, this method is called and then loops through all open views, telling the views to update themselves with their `UpdateView()` method.

wxDialog and friends

The next step is to build a dialog to edit a transaction. As you've seen, the transaction object is composed of a date, a comment, and a variable number of transaction lines each of which has an account name and an amount. We know that all the lines should add up to zero and that the date should be a valid date. In addition to editing the date and comment, you need to be able to add, edit, and delete lines. Figure 20-12 shows one possible layout for this dialog and the one used for this example.

wxPython Window Layout

wxPython includes a number of powerful techniques for controlling the layout of your windows and controls. There are several alternative mechanisms provided and potentially several ways to accomplish the same thing. This allows the programmer to use whichever mechanism works best in a particular situation or whichever they are most comfortable with.

Constraints

There is a class called **wxLayoutConstraints** that allows the specification of a window's position and size in relationship to its siblings and its parent. Each **wxLayoutContraints** object is composed of eight **wxIndividualLayoutConstraint** objects, which define different sorts of relationships, such as which window is above this window, what is the relative width of this window, etc. You usually have to specify four of the eight individual constraints in order for the window to be fully constrained. For example, this button will be positioned in the center of its parent and will always be 50% of the parent's width:

```
b = wxButton(self.panelA, 100, ' Panel A ')
lc = wxLayoutConstraints()
lc.centreX.SameAs    (self.panelA, wxCentreX)
lc.centreY.SameAs    (self.panelA, wxCentreY)
lc.height.AsIs       ()
lc.width.PercentOf   (self.panelA, wxWidth, 50)
b.SetConstraints(lc);
```

Layout algorithm

The class named **wxLayoutAlgorithm** implements layout of subwindows in MDI or SDI frames. It sends a **wxCalculateLayoutEvent** to children of the frame, asking them for information about their size. Because the event system is used this technique can be applied to any window, even those that aren't necessarily aware of the layout classes. However, you may wish to use **wxSashLayoutWindow** for your subwindows since this class provides handlers for the required events and accessors to specify the desired size of the window. The sash behavior in the base class can be used, optionally, to make the windows user-resizable. **wxLayoutAlgorithm** is typically used in IDE style of applications, where there are several resizable windows in addition to the MDI client window or other primary editing window. Resizable windows might include toolbars, a project window, and a window for displaying error and warning messages.

—Continued—

Sizers

In an effort to simplify the programming of simple layouts, a family of **wxSizer** classes has been added to the **wxPython** library. These are classes that are implemented in pure Python instead of wrapping C++ code from **wxWindows**. They are somewhat reminiscent of the layout managers from Java in that you select the type of sizer you want and then add windows or other sizers to it, and they all follow the same rules for layout. For example, this code fragment creates five buttons that are laid out horizontally in a box, and the last button is allowed to stretch to fill the remaining space allocated to the box:

```
box = wxBoxSizer(wxHORIZONTAL)
box.Add(wxButton(win, 1010, "one"), 0)
box.Add(wxButton(win, 1010, "two"), 0)
box.Add(wxButton(win, 1010, "three"), 0)
box.Add(wxButton(win, 1010, "four"), 0)
box.Add(wxButton(win, 1010, "five"), 1)
```

Resources

The **wxWindows** library has a simple dialog editor available that can assist with the layout of controls on a dialog and generates a portable cross-platform resource file. This file can be loaded into a program at runtime and transformed on the fly into a window with the specified controls on it. The only downfall with this approach is that you don't have the opportunity to subclass the windows that are generated, but if you can do everything you need with existing control types and event handlers, it should work out great. Eventually, there will be a **wxPython**-specific application builder tool that will generate either a resource type of file or actual Python source code for you.

Brute force

Finally, there is the brute-force mechanism of specifying the exact position of every component programmatically. Sometimes the layout needs of a window don't fit with any of the sizers or don't warrant the complexity of the constraints or the layout algorithm. For these situations, you can fall back on doing it "by hand," but you probably don't want to attempt it for anything much more complex than the Edit Transaction dialog.

Since there's quite a bit going on here, let's go through the initialization of this class step by step. Here's the first bit:

```
class EditTransDlg(wxDialog):
    def __init__(self, parent, trans, accountList):
```

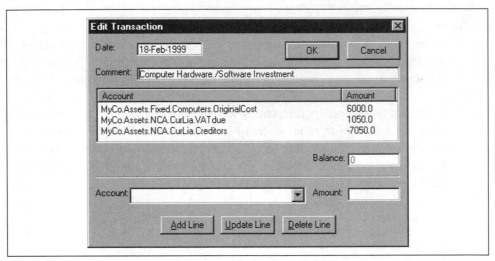

Figure 20-12. The wxPython Doubletalk transaction editor

```
wxDialog.__init__(self, parent, -1, "")
self.item = -1
if trans:
    self.trans = copy.deepcopy(trans)
    self.SetTitle("Edit Transaction")
else:
    self.trans = Transaction()
    self.trans.setDateString(dates.ddmmmyyyy(self.trans.date))
    self.SetTitle("Add Transaction")
```

This is fairly simple stuff. Just invoke the parent class's **__init__** method, do some initialization, and determine if you're editing an existing transaction or creating a new one. If editing an existing transaction, use the Python copy module to make a copy of the object. You do this because you will be editing the transaction in-place and don't want to have any partially edited transactions stuck in the **BookSet**. If the dialog is being used to add a new transaction, create one, and then fix its date by truncating the time from it. The default date in the transaction includes the current time, but this dialog is equipped to deal only with the date portion.

If you review the sidebar "wxPython Window Layout," you'll see a number of choices available, but we have chosen to use the brute-force mechanism for the Edit Transaction dialog:

```
# Create some controls
wxStaticText(self, -1, "Date:", wxDLG_PNT(self, 5,5))
self.date = wxTextCtrl(self, ID_DATE, "",
                wxDLG_PNT(self, 35,5), wxDLG_SZE(self, 50,-1))
```

```
wxStaticText(self, -1, "Comment:", wxDLG_PNT(self, 5,21))
self.comment = wxTextCtrl(self, ID_COMMENT, "",
                  wxDLG_PNT(self, 35, 21), wxDLG_SZE(self, 195,-1)
```

The code shows how to create the labels and the text fields at the top of the dialog. Notice the use of **wxDLG_PNT** and **wxDLG_SZE** to convert dialog units to a **wxPoint** and a **wxSize**, respectively. (The –1's used above mean that the default size should be used for the height.) Using dialog units instead of pixels to define the dialog means you are somewhat insulated from changes in the font used for the dialog, so you use dialog units wherever possible. The **wxPoint** and **wxSize** are always defined in terms of pixels, but these conversion functions allow the actual number of pixels used to vary automatically from machine to machine with different fonts. This makes it easy to move programs between platforms that have completely different window managers. Figure 20-13 shows this same program running on RedHat Linux 6.0, and you can see that for the most part, the controls are still spaced appropriately even though a completely different font is used on the form. It looks like the **wxTextCtrl** is a few dialog units taller on this platform, so perhaps there should be a bit more space between the rows. We leave this as an exercise for you.

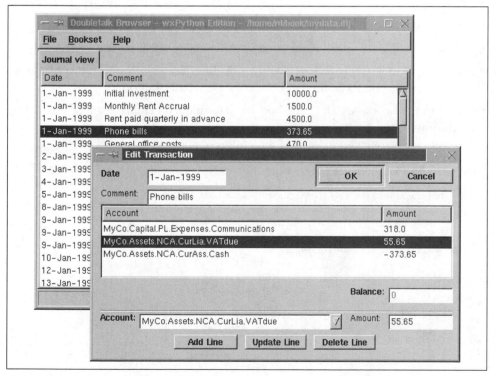

Figure 20-13. The wxPython Doubletalk editor running on Redhat Linux 6.0

The next control to be defined is the `wxListCtrl` that displays the account and amount lines:

```
self.lc = wxListCtrl(self, ID_LIST,
                     wxDLG_PNT(self, 5,34), wxDLG_SZE(self, 225,60),
                     wxLC_REPORT)

self.lc.InsertColumn(0, "Account")
self.lc.InsertColumn(1, "Amount")
self.lc.SetColumnWidth(0, wxDLG_SZE(self, 180,-1).width)
self.lc.SetColumnWidth(1, wxDLG_SZE(self,  40,-1).width)
```

It's important to note that the width of this control is 225 dialog units. Since this control spans the entire width of the dialog, you know the space you have to work with. You can use this value when deciding where to place or how to size the other controls.

Instead of auto-sizing the width of the list columns, let's now use explicit sizes. But you can still use dialog units to do it by extracting the **width** attribute from the **wxSize** object returned from **wxDLG_SZE**. We should mention the following points:

- The balance field is disabled, as you only want to use it to display a value.

- Use a **wxStaticLine** control for drawing the line across the dialog.

- A **wxComboBox** is used for selecting existing account names from a list.

- Use the standard IDs **wxID_OK** and **wxID_CANCEL** for OK and Cancel buttons, respectively, and force the OK button as the default button.

- Call the base class **Fit()** method to determine the initial size of the dialog window. This function calculates the total required size based on the size information specified in each of the children.

Here's the rest of the code for creating the controls:

```
wxStaticText(self, -1, "Balance:", wxDLG_PNT(self, 165,100))
self.balance = wxTextCtrl(self, ID_BAL, "",
                          wxDLG_PNT(self, 190,100),
                          wxDLG_SZE(self, 40, -1))
self.balance.Enable(false)

wxStaticLine(self, -1, wxDLG_PNT(self, 5,115),
                       wxDLG_SZE(self, 225,-1))

wxStaticText(self, -1, "Account:", wxDLG_PNT(self, 5,122))
self.account = wxComboBox(self, ID_ACCT, "",
                          wxDLG_PNT(self, 30,122), wxDLG_SZE(self, 130,-1),
                          accountList, wxCB_DROPDOWN | wxCB_SORT)
```

```
                wxStaticText(self, -1, "Amount:", wxDLG_PNT(self, 165,122))
                self.amount = wxTextCtrl(self, ID_AMT, "",
                                    wxDLG_PNT(self, 190,122),
                                    wxDLG_SZE(self, 40, -1))

                btnSz = wxDLG_SZE(self, 40,12)
                wxButton(self, ID_ADD, "&Add Line", wxDLG_PNT(self, 52,140), btnSz)
                wxButton(self, ID_UPDT, "&Update Line", wxDLG_PNT(self, 97,140),
                        btnSz)
                wxButton(self, ID_DEL, "&Delete Line", wxDLG_PNT(self, 142,140),
                        btnSz)

                self.ok = wxButton(self, wxID_OK, "OK", wxDLG_PNT(self, 145,5),
                                    btnSz)
                self.ok.SetDefault()
                wxButton(self, wxID_CANCEL, "Cancel", wxDLG_PNT(self, 190,5), btnSz)

                # Resize the window to fit the controls
                self.Fit()
```

The last thing to do is set up some event handlers and load the dialog controls with data. The event handling for the controls is almost identical to the menu handling discussed previously, so there shouldn't be any surprises:

```
                # Set some event handlers
                EVT_BUTTON(self, ID_ADD,  self.OnAddBtn)
                EVT_BUTTON(self, ID_UPDT, self.OnUpdtBtn)
                EVT_BUTTON(self, ID_DEL,  self.OnDelBtn)
                EVT_LIST_ITEM_SELECTED(self,  ID_LIST, self.OnListSelect)
                EVT_LIST_ITEM_DESELECTED(self, ID_LIST, self.OnListDeselect)
                EVT_TEXT(self, ID_DATE, self.Validate)

                # Initialize the controls with current values
                self.date.SetValue(self.trans.getDateString())
                self.comment.SetValue(self.trans.comment)
                for x in range(len(self.trans.lines)):
                    account, amount, dict = self.trans.lines[x]
                    self.lc.InsertStringItem(x, account)
                    self.lc.SetStringItem(x, 1, str(amount))

                self.Validate()
```

The last thing the code snippet does is call a `Validate()` method, which as you can probably guess, is responsible for validating the dialog data; in this case, validating the date and that all transaction lines sum to zero. Check the date when the field is updated (via the `EVT_TEXT()` call shown in the code) and check the balance any time a line is added or updated. If anything doesn't stack up, disable the OK button. Here is `Validate`:

```
        def Validate(self, *ignore):
            bal = self.trans.balance()
            self.balance.SetValue(str(bal))
            date = self.date.GetValue()
```

```
try:
    dateOK = (date == dates.testasc(date))
except:
    dateOK = 0

if bal == 0 and dateOK:
    self.ok.Enable(true)
else:
    self.ok.Enable(false)
```

Notice that the balance field is updated. The next thing we demonstrate is the Add Line functionality. To do this, you need to take whatever is in the account and amount fields, add them to the transaction, and also add them to the list control:

```
def OnAddBtn(self, event):
    account = self.account.GetValue()
    amount = string.atof(self.amount.GetValue())
    self.trans.addLine(account, amount)

    # update the list control
    idx = len(self.trans.lines)
    self.lc.InsertStringItem(idx-1, account)
    self.lc.SetStringItem(idx-1, 1, str(amount))

    self.Validate()
    self.account.SetValue("")
    self.amount.SetValue("")
```

You call **Validate** again to check if the transaction's lines are in balance. The event handlers for the Update and Delete buttons are similar and not shown here.

That's about all there is to it! **wxPython** takes care of the tab-traversal between fields, auto-completion on the Enter key, auto-cancel on Esc, and all the rest.

wxPython Conclusion

This small section has barely touched the surface of what **wxPython** is capable of. There are many more window and control types than what have been shown here, and the advanced features lend themselves to highly flexible and dynamic GUI applications across many platforms. Combined with the flexibility of Python, you end up with a powerful tool for quickly creating world-class applications.

For more information on **wxPython**, including extensive documentation and sample code, see the **wxPython** home page at *http://alldunn.com/wxPython/*.

For more information on the underlying **wxWindows** framework, please visit its home page at *http://www.wxwindows.org/*.

21

Active Scripting

Active Scripting is a COM-based technology from Microsoft that allows applications to plug in different languages for macros or scripting. Rather than force the application to choose a single scripting language, end users of the application can pick the language they're most comfortable with. The application need not know anything specific about the scripting language; indeed, the language may have been written (or support for Active Scripting added) after the application was written.

The best examples of this technology are Microsoft's Internet Explorer (IE) and Internet Information Server (IIS). IE supports client-side scripting; an HTML file can have script code embedded in it in any language, and when the browser displays the page, it executes the code. Hence the term client-side scripting: the script code is actually executed on the client PC, the PC with the browser. IIS includes a component called Active Server Pages (ASP) that supports active scripting. Similar to IE, the code is embedded inside HTML files, but ASP executes the code at the server before it's converted to the final HTML sent to the client.

Many Microsoft applications are starting to support Active Scripting. These applications typically come standard with VBScript and JScript* language implementations, and all documentation and sample code use one of these languages. In fact, many users of these applications (IE and IIS users included) aren't aware you can use additional languages as well as the standard ones. Using a language such as Python and its extensive library can help you take full advantage of these applications.

Each application that supports Active Scripting exposes an object model to the script code. Regardless of the language the script is using, the object model avail-

---

* VBScript is a redistributable Active Scripting implementation by Microsoft using a subset of the Visual Basic language. JScript, also implemented by Microsoft and redistributable, uses syntax somewhat like Java.

able is identical. Although this is the key strength of Active Scripting, it's also a problem when attempting to document how to use it. If we discuss how to use Active Scripting within IE, it really doesn't help you use Active Scripting within IIS. Each application supports its own object model, so the code you write is completely different. Therefore, we start this chapter with a cursory look at some of the popular Active Scripting applications from Microsoft, showing sample VBScript alongside Python code. We won't discuss any of these applications in detail, just enough for you to understand how to use Python in their environments. We then focus on how Active Scripting works and Python's implementation of Active Scripting. These will give you enough grounding so you can use Python inside any Active Scripting application armed with only the documentation for the application and its VBScript or JScript samples.

Finally, we take a look at adding Active Scripting support to your Python application. This lets your application's customers use any language they choose. You will be amazed at how simple it is to do from Python.

Further information on Active Scripting, including a number of Active Scripting-related tools can be found at *http://msdn.microsoft.com/scripting/*.

Registering the Python Active Script Support

When you install the Python Win32 extensions, the Python Active Scripting implementation is automatically registered. If for some reason you need to install it manually, you should run the Python script *python\win32comext\axscript\client\pyscript.py*. You can run this script from Windows Explorer, PythonWin, or a command prompt.

Python and Popular Microsoft Applications

The most popular and visible Active Scripting applications come from Microsoft; This isn't surprising, since Microsoft developed the Active Scripting implementation.

Here we discuss Internet Explorer, Internet Information Server, and the Windows Scripting Host (WSH). Of these, IE is probably the most fun to play with, but has the least practical use. Using Active Scripting implies that the particular language is installed along with the browser, and for the vast majority of Internet Explorer users, this will not be true of Python. IIS and WSH are more practical, as they usually run on a machine over which you have more control; for example, it's often not a problem to install Python on the same machine that runs IIS. Similarly, WSH is often used for Windows NT administration, so installing Python on the servers you are administering also shouldn't present a problem.

Internet Explorer

Internet Explorer, Version 4 and above, supports Active Scripting by embedding script code inside the HTML. As the HTML is parsed and rendered by IE, the code is detected, the particular language loaded, and the code executed. The script code is embedded in the HTML inside blocks delimited by <SCRIPT> and </SCRIPT> tags. The following is an example script that displays a message box:

```
<SCRIPT>
alert("Hello there")
</SCRIPT>
```

The default language for IE is VBScript, so this code is executed using VBScript. Because the script is so simple, the only change needed to make it use Python is to specify the language, as shown:

```
<SCRIPT Language=Python>
alert("Hello there")
</SCRIPT>
```

If you wish to experiment, you can save these three lines as a HTML file and open it in Internet Explorer. You should see a message box, followed by a blank web page.

You may be wondering where the alert() function came from, since it's not a standard Python built-in function. This is the key to how Active Scripting works. As the application (in this case IE) loads the particular language, it notifies the language of global functions and objects the language should make available; alert() is one of the functions made available by Internet Explorer. This is how the application exposes its object model to the language; the programmer uses these functions and objects to manipulate the application.

The object model exposed by Internet Explorer is similar to the Dynamic HTML object model. There is a window object, a document object, and so forth, all of which allow you to get information from the browser (for example, the current URL) or to direct the browser to perform some action (for example, open a new URL or reposition the window).

As mentioned previously, the fact that Python must be installed on each client PC is likely to be a barrier to using Python in the IE environment. It may be tempting to believe you could use Python to overcome some limitations in VBScript or JScript: for example, access the registry, open files, or create socket connections. Unfortunately, Python also restricts the capabilities available to the programmer when used with Internet Explorer. The whole concept of client-side scripting is dangerous, as you are downloading arbitrary code from a web page and running it on your computer. To avoid the potential problems with people writing malicious code, IE explicitly tells Python that it should operate in an untrusted mode, and Python complies by seriously restricting the operations the script can perform. For example, when running in Internet Explorer, it's impossible to import Python extension modules (such as `win32api`), open local files, create sockets, and so forth.

For this reason, we won't spend any time discussing the object model for Internet Explorer. Instead, we present a few examples and discuss the differences between VBScript and Python.

The following code presents an HTML file containing a form with one edit control and three buttons. A VBScript handler is added for one of the buttons and Python handlers to the remaining two. All the buttons perform the same operation: update one of the text controls with the current URL.

To keep the size of the example down, we avoided all HTML elements not absolutely necessary to demonstrate the scripts. For your own HTML, you should make all efforts to ensure your files conform to valid HTML (e.g., are enclosed in <HTML> and <BODY> tags):

```
<FORM NAME="TestForm">
    <!-- A single text control all the buttons will use -->
    <INPUT TYPE="Text"
           NAME="txtControl"
    >
    <!-- VBScript using inline event handling -->
    <INPUT NAME="butVB"
           TYPE="Button"
           VALUE="VB Script"
           OnClick="txtControl.value=document.location"
    >
    <!-- Python using inline event handling -->
    <INPUT NAME="butPy1"
           TYPE="Button"
           VALUE="Python inline"
           OnClick="TestForm.txtControl.value=document.location"
           LANGUAGE=Python
    >
    <!-- Python using an implicit event handler -->
    <INPUT NAME="butPy2"
           TYPE="Button"
           VALUE="Python implicit"
    >
    <!-- Now the code for the implicit handler -->
    <SCRIPT LANGUAGE=Python>
# Note we can not indent this block,
# as the leading whitespace will upset Python
def butPy2_onClick():
```

```
        TestForm.txtControl.value=document.location
        </SCRIPT>
    </FORM>
```

This code demonstrates a few key points relating to the Python implementation of Active Scripting. If you examine the VBScript handler for the first button, notice that it can refer to the `txtControl` object without any special prefixes or annotations; because both the script and the control are part of the same form, a concept similar to scoping is applied. Python doesn't support this degree of scoping, so the Python handlers all must name each object explicitly.

Another important point is that in all Active Scripting applications, you must be careful regarding whitespace. Although HTML is generally insensitive to whitespace, any Python code embedded still is.

The event handling in Python attempts to conform to the conventions VBScript and JScript programmers would be familiar with. Event handling can be inline, where the script code is specified directly in the definition of the object as we demonstrated in the previous example. Alternatively, you can write a function with the name `object_event()`, where `object` is the name of the object, and `event` is the name of an event this object fires. Nothing is needed to explicitly attach the event to this function: the name of the function is all that is needed to get this behavior. This is demonstrated using `PyBut2_onClick()`, which responds to the `onClick` event for the `PyBut2` object.

For more examples using Python within Internet Explorer, please see the Active Scripting samples, available from the PythonCOM *README*, installed with the Python for Windows extensions. For more information on the Internet Explorer object model, please see *http://www.microsoft.com/windows/ie/*.

Internet Information Server

The Microsoft Internet Information Server is a web server that supports the standard Unix web-server scripting technique called the Common Gateway Interface (CGI). In addition to CGI, IIS also supports Active Server Pages (ASP), which use Active Scripting to implement a richer scripting model than offered by CGI.

Active Server Pages uses a scheme to embed the script code that is similar to Internet Explorer. Code is still delimited with `<SCRIPT>` tags, but the tag has a `RunAt=Server` attribute added. For example:

```
<SCRIPT RunAt=Server Language=Python>
# This code will run at the server
</SCRIPT>
<SCRIPT Language=Python>
# This code will run at the client
</SCRIPT>
```

Although this sounds simple, the complication again is that the object model exposed by ASP is quite different to that exposed by IE. If you attempt to call the `alert()` function, your code fails as `alert()` doesn't exist in the ASP object model.

In addition to using `<SCRIPT>` tags, ASP allows alternative forms delimited by `<% %>` and `<%= %>` tags. Script code delimited by `<%` and `%>` tags are almost identical to those delimited by `<SCRIPT>` tags. The `<%= %>` tag allows you to specify arbitrary Python expressions, and the result of the expression is replaced in the output. For example, if ASP encounters HTML of the form:

```
Hello <%= name %>
```

The value of the **name** variable is printed in the output sent to the client.

The source files for Active Server Pages are stored as *.asp* files, although for all intents and purposes they are HTML files. The *.asp* extension allows IIS to determine if the page could potentially contain scripting code and hence should be executed under the control of ASP.

ASP also allows Python to run completely unrestricted. There are no limitations on the files that can be opened or the operations that can be performed. As the script code is maintained on the server, it's assumed the scripts are trusted. For a final feature that makes Python and ASP a great match, you can specify the default language for an ASP script. If an ASP page begins with the code `<%@ LANGUAGE=Python %>`, Python is used as the default language for all `<SCRIPT>`, `<%`, and `<%=` tags.

ASP exposes seven key objects, as detailed in Table 21-1. For details on the attributes and methods available on these objects, refer to the ASP documentation.

Table 21-1. Key ASP Objects

Object	Description
Application	The ASP application under which the script is running. An ASP application is a collection of ASP files that share certain state and other information.
ObjectContext	Exposes the transaction mechanisms behind ASP.
Request	Represents the values the client browser passed to the server when establishing the connection.
ASPError	Contains information about an error condition in ASP.
Response	Sends output to the client.
Server	Represents the ASP server, allowing you to query information and carry out commands.

The following example uses the **Server**, **Reponse**, and **Request** objects. It's simple and again skips the **<HTML>** and other tags your file normally has. It begins by nominating Python as the default language for the page. This means all other code in the file uses Python without explicitly specifying it for each script block. The first script block uses the **Request** object to look up the URL of the current page and save it to a local variable. You then use **<%=** tags to print the variable value and call the **Server.MapPath()** method to translate this to a local filesystem reference. The final script block loops over all variables in the **Request.Server-Variables** collection, printing the variable name and value using the **Response.Write()** method:

```
<!--
ServerSample.asp - an example of Python
and Active Scripting
-->

<%@ Language=Python %>

<%
# Save the URL into a local variable
url = Request.ServerVariables("PATH_INFO")
%>

<H2>Current Document</H2>
The URL to this file is <pre><%= url %></pre><p>
The local path to this URL is <pre><%= Server.mappath(url) %></pre>

<H2>Client Request Headers</H2>
<%
for key in Request.ServerVariables:
    Response.Write("%s=%s<br>" % (key, Request.ServerVariables(key)))
%>
```

The **Response.Write()** method sends output to the client. The string can contain any valid HTML, including tags. It's worth noting that the Python **print** statement is never redirected by the scripting engine. For example, it could be argued that when used with ASP, the **print** statement should send the output to the **Response.Write()** method, but this doesn't happen.

We are now ready to run the script, but how do we do this? At this point, we better take a slight diversion into how you configure IIS to run scripts.

Configuring IIS

The process of configuring IIS is simple. Before you do anything, you must ensure that Python is installed on the IIS server, and the Active Scripting engine is registered, as we discuss previously in this chapter. There is nothing Python-specific

that needs to be configured within IIS; all you need to do is tell IIS where to find
your scripts. Do this with the following process:

1. Start the Internet Service Manager on the machine where IIS is installed.

2. Locate and select the default web server entry under your ASP server.

3. Select Action → New → Virtual Directory. The New Virtual Directory Wizard
   begins.

4. Enter *PythonTest* as the alias that accesses the virtual directory and select Next.

5. You are then prompted to enter the physical path of the directory containing
   the content. Enter the name of the directory where your test or sample *.asp*
   files are located and select Next.

6. You are then prompted for the permissions for the new directory. The default
   options are acceptable, so you can select Finish.

The ISM should then look something like Figure 21-1.

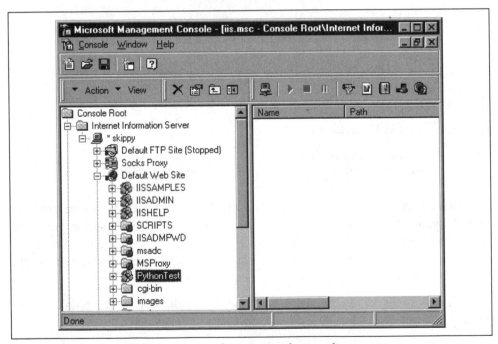

Figure 21-1. Internet Service Manager after creating the new directory

Let's now execute the sample script. The simplest thing is to test your script by
running Internet Explorer on the same machine as the server. If you enter a URL,
http://localhost/PythonTest/ServerSample.asp, it executes the *ServerSample.asp* file
from the physical path you specified for the *PythonTest* virtual directory.

Once this is done, the Explorer window should look like Figure 21-2.

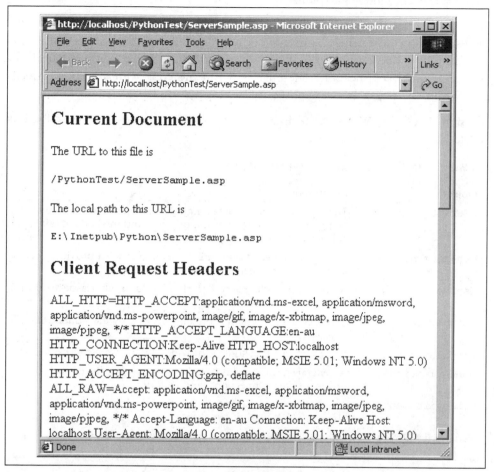

Figure 21-2. The sample ASP file running under IIS

Windows Scripting Host

Another handy Active Scripting tool is the Windows Scripting Host (WSH). WSH exposes an object model that makes it particularly suitable for tasks that are normally attempted with Windows batch files. WSH is often used for general Windows administration and can run the logon scripts as each user logs on to the network.

The Windows Scripting Host is included with Windows 98 and 2000, or can be obtained from *http://msdn.microsoft.com/scripting* for Windows 95 and NT. It's packaged as two executables: *cscript.exe*, a command-line tool, suitable for running from the Windows command prompt; and *wscript.exe*, a GUI application generally run from Windows Explorer.

WSH uses simple text files to hold the script code; Python files run under the Windows Scripting Host using the extension *.pys*. There are no tags or any other special characters needed, so WSH files that use Python are syntactically identical to a Python source file. The only difference is that if the code were executed directly by Python, the object model exposed by WSH is not available.

Version 5 of the Windows Scripting Host supports the objects described in Table 21-2.

Table 21-2. Windows Scripting Host Top-Level Objects

Object	Description
WScript	The top-level object containing information about the script being executed or the version of WSH, and methods to take specific actions, such as display a message, or create a COM object
WshArguments	An object exposed via `Wscript.Arguments` that provides access to the script arguments
WshShell	An object providing access to shortcuts and other aspects of the Windows Shell API
WshShortcut	Represents a filesystem shortcut; provided by the `WshShell` object
WshUrlShortcut	Represents a URL shortcut; provided by the `WshShell` object
WshCollection	A general-purpose collection that provides the list of shared drives, printer connections, and so forth
WshEnvironment	An object that provides access to the Windows environment variables
WshSpecialFolders	An object representing the special Windows folders, such as the location of the desktop or favorites

The following code is a simple demo of Python used by the WSH. It prints the name of the script, the first argument passed to the script on the command line, and the first network connection:

```
# wsh.pys
# A Windows Scripting Host file that uses Python.

WScript.Echo("The script name is", WScript.ScriptName)
if len(WScript.Arguments):
    WScript.Echo("The first argument is", WScript.Arguments(0))

net = WScript.CreateObject("Wscript.Network")

netInfo = net.EnumNetworkDrives()
WScript.Echo(netInfo[0], "=", netInfo[1])
```

You can run this script from a command prompt and see the output:

```
C:\Scripts>cscript wsh.pys Hello
Microsoft (R) Windows Scripting Host Version 5.0 for Windows
Copyright (C) Microsoft Corporation 1996-1997. All rights reserved.

The script name is wsh.pys
The first argument is Hello
Z: = \\SKIPPY\d_drive

C:\Scripts>
```

Alternatively, you could use the GUI version of WSH by executing the command:

```
C:\Scripts>wscript C:\Scripts\wsh.pys Hello
```

This command can be executed from a command prompt or from the Windows Start → Run menu item. It should be possible to execute a *.pys* file by double-clicking it in Windows Explorer, but Python currently doesn't support this.

When you execute the script under the GUI version, notice that all the `WScript.Echo()` calls are displayed as message boxes rather than printing a console message. This means that the example generates three message boxes. Depending on the needs of your script, either or both versions of WSH may be suitable.

Blurring the edges: WSH or straight Python

One of the questions that may come to mind is "Why bother?" Python provides much of this functionality via the Win32 Extensions, and the native Python code is often simpler than the WSH version. For example, `sys.argv` and `os.environ[]` are certainly less to type than `WScript.Arguments` and `WScript.CreateObject ("WScript.Shell").Environment`.

To further blur the distinction, it's worth noting that much of the functionality provided by WSH is exposed via the `WScript.CreateObject()` function. This function is almost identical to the Python function `win32com.client.Dispatch()`; it creates a COM object by name.

What this means is as long as WSH is installed on a machine, Python can still make use of most WSH objects, even when not running under WSH. For example, you can call `EnumNetworkDrives()` from a Python prompt as follows:

```
>>> from win32com.client import Dispatch
>>> net=Dispatch("Wscript.Network")
>>> netInfo=net.EnumNetworkDrives()
>>> print "%s=%s" % (netInfo[0], netInfo[1])
Z:=\\SKIPPY\d_drive
>>>
```

You have the best of both worlds: you can make use of all Python's features when running under WSH, and also make use of the best WSH features when running standard Python.

Active Debugging

A popular extension to Active Scripting is Active Debugging, a technology that allows you to debug your scripts. Regardless of the language your scripts are implemented in, you can debug them in a single debugging environment provided by Microsoft. Interestingly, this allows you to step through multiple languages; for example, as Python code calls VB code that calls Python code, you can step through each individual line.

Microsoft provides two Active Debugging environments. The Windows Script Debugger is a free tool available from *http://msdn.microsoft.com/scripting/*, and while a nice debugger, the Microsoft Visual Interdev provides a richer debugging environment. The only drawback with Interdev is that it comes with Microsoft Visual C++ and is not available for free download.

There is not much to say about Active Debugging when using Python. You simply use the debugger, and Python is right there, ready to be debugged.

Unfortunately, the Active Debugging specification is new and not everything works quite as expected. For example, it's impossible to debug scripts under Internet Explorer 4, as the Active Desktop enhancements cause the debugger to complain that you are attempting to debug the desktop. A solution to this particular problem is to debug your script using a different **EXE** that still uses the IE4 control, e.g., PythonWin and the *webrowser.py* sample. A further complication is that not all Active Scripting hosts support Active Debugging. The Debugging interfaces are optional, and if the host doesn't support debugging the utility of the debugger is severely limited.

How Active Scripting Works

This section discusses some internals of the Active Scripting mechanism. Although this information isn't necessary for you to use Python in an Active Scripting environment, it may help you understand some of the intricacies of the Active Scripting implementations. Understanding this section is required for the next section.

As mentioned previously, Active Scripting is a COM-based technology and works by providing an object model for the end user. It should come as no surprise that this object model is provided by COM.

To summarize a complicated specification in a few paragraphs, here's the general process an application uses when using Active Scripting:

1. Determines the language to be used for a particular script block and creates the language engine as a normal COM object. Thus, **VBScript**, **JScript**, and **Python** are the COM ProgIDs used for the languages described here.

2. Passes the language engine a series of named items. Each named item is a COM object (that is, an `IDispatch` pointer) with a name and attributes. The attributes include whether the item is considered global and whether the item fires events.

3. Each named item is placed in the namespace by the language engine. Any named items that fire events have the event-handling mechanism put in place. In addition, any object considered global should have all its methods and properties made available as global methods and properties.

4. The application then gives the language engine the script code to execute. When the code refers to an object previously placed in the namespace, the language engine makes a standard COM call on the COM `IDispatch` pointer passed for the named item.

Let's reconsider the original example in the previous section "Internet Explorer." When IE loads the Python engine, it passes a number of standard items (such as `Window`, `Document`, and so forth). In addition to the standard items, a number of additional items are passed dependent on the HTML content. In the example, an item named `TestForm` and each element in the form are added. Many of these items may source events (such as the user interface `Window` and form element objects), but only a few are considered global. Internet Explorer designates the `Window` items as global, and if you refer to the IE documentation you will note that the `Window` item has an `alert()` method; hence you can refer to the `alert()` method globally, as in that first example.

Internally, everything is achieved using normal COM concepts; all method calls and property references are done with `IDispatch`, as discussed in Chapter 12, *Advanced Python and COM*. All event handling is done using normal `IConnectionPoint` interfaces, and although beyond the scope of this book, is fully supported by the standard Python COM framework.

Active Script Hosting in Python

As a fitting finale to this section of the book, we will discuss how you can incorporate Active Scripting in your Python application. If you are working with Python, you already have a very cool extension language built right-in, but there may be good reasons for wanting to extend this to include other languages, marketing being just one!

If there is any end of the Active Scripting specification to work with, creating an application that supports Active Scripting is the one to choose over building a language engine. The COM specifications for applications using Active Scripting are not difficult to understand, and Python has additional helpers that reduce this to a small amount of code.

The sample application exposes an Active Scripting object model. It loads script code from a text file and executes it using any Active Scripting-supported language: two more examples will demonstrate VBScript and Python. The object model the application exposes is simple; there's a single `Application` object supporting a single method `Echo`, which displays a message box.

These are the steps:

1. Creates a `PyIActiveScriptSite` object. The `win32com.axscript.server.axsite` module provides an Active Scripting Site base-class that is suitable for our purposes. All you need to do is add an error handler; it's simple and prints the message to the console.

2. Defines the object model. The `win32com.axscript.server.axsite` module allows you to specify a dictionary of **string-object** pairs, where **string** is the name for the object model, and **object** is any `PyIDispatch` object. The example provides a simple Python COM object. For more information on implementing COM objects using Python, see Chapter 12.

3. Loads the code and passes it to the required language engine. This sample accepts two command-line parameters, the name of the language to use, and the name of a text file containing the code:

```
# ActiveApp.py - Demonstration of a Python Active Scripting Application.
import string, sys
from win32com.axscript import axscript
from win32com.axscript.server import axsite
import pythoncom
import win32com.server.util

class MySite(axsite.AXSite):
    # Our error handler will print to the console.
    def OnScriptError(self, activeScriptError):
        exc = activeScriptError.GetExceptionInfo()
        print "Exception:", exc[1]
        try:
            sourceText = activeScriptError.GetSourceLineText()
        except pythoncom.com_error:
            sourceText = None
        if sourceText is not None:
            context, lineNo, charNo = activeScriptError.GetSourcePosition()
            print sourceText
            indent = " " * (charNo-1)
            print indent + "^"
        return winerror.S_OK

# A named object for our namespace
# A normal Python COM object (minus registration info)
class Application:
    _public_methods_ = [ 'Echo' ]
    def Echo(self, *args):
        print string.join(map(str, args))
```

```
        # Our function that creates the site, creates the engine
        # and runs the code.
        def RunCode(engineName, code):
            app = win32com.server.util.wrap( Application() )
            # Create a dictionary holding our object model.
            model = {
              'Application' : app,
            }

            # Create the scripting site.
            site = MySite(model)
            # Create the engine and add the code.
            engine = site.AddEngine(engineName)
            engine.AddCode(code)
            # Run the code.
            engine.Start()

    if __name__ == '__main__':
        if len(sys.argv) < 3:
            print "Usage: ActiveApp.py Language ScriptFile"
        else:
            code = open(sys.argv[2]).read()
            RunCode( sys.argv[1], code )
```

The error-handling function takes up the bulk of the code as it attempts to accurately indicate the exact location of the error. The code that runs the engine is surprisingly small. You create the script site and the engine, and add the code. When you start the engine, all previously loaded code is executed.

To test this Active Scripting engine, let's use two text files: the first is for VBScript:

```
rem Sample VBScript code to be used with ActiveApp.py

sub JustForTheSakeOfIt
    Application.Echo("Hello from VBScript")
end sub

rem Now call the Sub
JustForTheSakeOfIt
```

The second is for Python:

```
# Sample Python code to be used with ActiveApp.py

def JustForTheSakeOfIt():
    Application.Echo("Hello from Python")

JustForTheSakeOfIt()
```

Testing the application is straightforward. Assuming that the Python program and both sample text files are in the same directory, use the following commands:

```
C:\Scripts>ActiveApp.py VBScript ActiveApp_VBScript.txt
Hello from VBScript

C:\Scripts>
```

And testing Python:

```
C:\Scripts>ActiveApp.py Python ActiveApp_Python.txt
Hello from Python

C:\Scripts>
```

Finally, to test the error handler, mix the filename and the language. Let's ask VBScript to execute the Python code:

```
C:\Scripts>ActiveApp.py VBScript ActiveApp_Python.txt
Exception: Microsoft VBScript compilation error
# Same Python code to be used with ActiveApp.py
  ^
Traceback (innermost last):
  File "C:\Scripts\ActiveApp.py", line 49, in ?
    RunCode( sys.argv[1], code )
  File "C:\Scripts\ActiveApp.py", line 40, in RunCode
    engine.AddCode(code)
  File "C:\Program Files\Python\win32comext\axscript\server\axsite.py", line 31,
in AddCode
    self.eParse.ParseScriptText(code, None, None, None, 0, 0, 0)
pywintypes.com_error: (-2146827264, 'OLE error 0x800a0400', (0, 'Microsoft
VBScript compilation error', 'E
xpected statement', None, 0, -2146827264), None)

C:\Scripts>
```

The error handler worked fine, but the error information was propagated back to the calling function; in this case, the `engine.AddCode()` line in the sample. Obviously you'd want to add an exception handler for this case.

Although this has not been a thorough discussion of adding Active Scripting to your application, it should whet your appetite and give you enough information to get started. To really take advantage of Active Scripting, you should consult the Active Scripting documentation, available on MSDN.

Conclusion

In this chapter, we looked at using Python in an Active Scripting environment. The most common use of Active Scripting and Python is using Python as a scripting language in another application, and we discussed some popular Microsoft applications that can work with Python.

We also showed a brief teaser how you could leverage Active Scripting in your own Python application, allowing your users to choose the specific language they use; we all know that not every Windows programmer has seen the Python light!

22

Extending and Embedding with Visual C++ and Delphi

Although there are many factors you could attribute to Python's success, one is surely the ability to extend and embed Python in other languages. If there is anything Python itself can't do, but can be done from other languages, there is a good chance you can build a Python interface to this other language.

In this chapter, we discuss how to extend Python using the C/C++ and Delphi languages. The topics we cover include:

- Writing a Python extension in C (or compiling someone else's) by hand
- Using Simplified Wrapper and Interface Generator (SWIG) to make it easy to expose C and C++ libraries for use by Python
- Embedding a Python interpreter in a C++ application
- Dynamically calling DLLs without a C compiler

Delphi is another popular programming language that can operate at a low enough level to hook into Python at the C level, and a Delphi package exists to make this easier than the equivalent steps would be in C or C++. We also cover:

- Embedding a Python interpreter in a Delphi application
- Building a Python extension DLL in Delphi

When reading this chapter, you should keep in mind some capabilities offered by the Python COM framework, as we discussed in Chapter 12, *Advanced Python and COM*. When Python is using COM objects, you could view this as extending Python, since the capabilities offered by the COM object are made available to Python. When you create a COM object using Python, it's like embedding Python in another application: you make all the facilities of Python available to any application that uses your COM object.

Python and Visual C++

Python is written in C and can be embedded in both C and C++ programs and extended with routines written in C and C++. The standard Python documentation includes a good tutorial on extending and embedding Python, which we won't repeat, and we certainly won't try to teach you C.

There are a number of reasons to use Visual C++ during your travels with Python:

- To build Python from sources. Many companies that ship Python binaries like to know they can build everything from C sources and have control over those sources (for example, checked into their source control system). The same applies to all Python extensions your application may use.

- To write a Python extensions as a DLL or if you have the sources to an interesting Python extension, but no binary for Windows for your Python version.

- To make an existing C or C++ library available to Python.

- To embed Python in a C or C++ application for one of the many good reasons for doing so!

 When you install Python in Windows, the C language header and library files are also optionally installed. These files are enough to build Python extensions on Windows without downloading the full Python sources.

Many of you are familiar with compiling C programs (and Python) on Unix, while others aren't C programmers at all. Although we attempt to make this chapter understandable for C novices, we certainly don't attempt to teach either the C++ language or the Microsoft Developers Studio environment.

One Size Doesn't Fit All

It should be noted that once you start delving into building from sources, the world takes a murkier turn. When you download different source packages and attempt to build them into a single system, things rarely work as expected first time around.

One of the biggest problems is interproject dependencies. If you download the core Python sources, they will probably build well. However, if you then download some other Python extensions (such as the Win32 or COM sources), you may strike some problems when Visual C++ tries to find the Python files (such as header or library files) it needs.

The fundamental problem is that every programmer stores his or her source code in a different directory structure than everyone else. Sometimes these directory structures are dictated by corporate policy, or sometimes they are personal taste. Even worse than this is the problem of changing between versions of Python and other extensions you use. When a new version of Python comes out, you will probably need to change every single project file to reference the new version.

To attempt to make this problem bearable, here are a couple of tricks to make working with source code easier:

- Don't specify *Python15.lib*, *PyWinTypes.lib*, or *PythonCOM.lib* in your project file. These packages employ a Visual C++ trick so that by including the necessary headers (such as *Python.h* or *PyWinTypes.h*), an implicit reference is made to the necessary *.lib* files. This automatically uses the correct release (e.g., *Python15.lib*) or debug library (*Python15_d.lib*), and is also useful when upgrading Python; for example, Python 1.6 will presumably change the names of these *.lib* files, but this scheme avoids changing your project in that case.

- Use Microsoft Visual C++ to specify the Python and other directories globally, rather than on a per-project basis. This allows you to avoid referencing the location of the Python sources directly in your project file and applies for all projects. When you wish to move to a new version of Python, you can change Visual C++ so it references the new directories and rebuild all your projects.

Configuring Visual C++ to build Python or extensions

The process of configuring Visual C++ in the manner described previously is quite simple. The first thing to do is to determine the location of the necessary Python files. If you installed the binary version of Python, these files are likely under the *C:\Program Files\Python\Include* and *C:\Program Files\Python\libs*. If you are building from the Python source archive, the directories for the headers may be something like *Python-1.5.2\include* and *Python-1.5.2\pc*, while the library files would be in *Python-1.5.2\pcbuild*. Then perform the following steps:

1. Start Microsoft Visual C++.

2. Select Tools → Options → Directories. Drop down the Show Directories For combo box, and select Include Files. Add the directory or directories where the Python headers can be located. Your screen should look something like Figure 22-1.

3. Select the combo box again, select Library files, and update the directories appropriately.

4. Select OK to close the dialog, and you're ready to go!

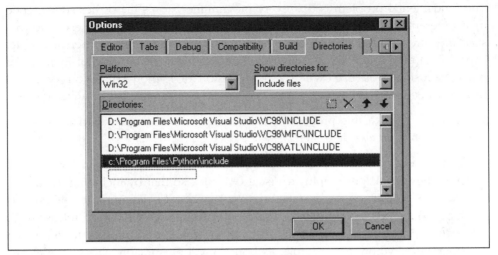

Figure 22-1. Microsoft Visual C++ configured with the Python include directories

You may also wish to perform this same process for other common Python extensions you use. For example, you may make extensive use of the Win32 or COM extensions so you could perform this same procedure and specify their directories. Indeed, if you wish to build the COM extensions from sources you may need to ensure your directories are set up so that *PyWinTypes.h* and *PyWinTypes.lib* from the Win32 extensions can be found.

Building an Extension Using Visual C++

One of Python's most powerful features is how well it integrates with extensions written in C. If you have a library or toolkit available for C or C++, it is almost certain you can expose this library to Python using an extension module.

Alternatively, you may have a program with special requirements, such as crunching huge complex datasets, and your program could benefit immensely if you could speed up one small, but important part of the application. Writing this small speed-critical part in C and calling it from your Python program is an attractive solution many people adopt.

For whatever reason you need to do this, we provide here a short discussion of extension modules and building the modules on Windows.

For this example, we use a simple extension module from the Python tutorial. This creates a module called **spam** and exposes a function called **system()**, which runs a DOS command. This is obviously a contrived example as this same functionality can be obtained from the Python function **os.system()**; indeed, you would expect to find almost identical code implementing **os.system()**. The source code is as follows:

```
/* spammodule.c - pasted from Python extending/embedding manual*/

# include "Python.h"

static PyObject *SpamError;

static PyObject *spam_system(self, args)
    PyObject *self;
    PyObject *args;
{
    char *command;
    int sts;
    if (!PyArg_ParseTuple(args, "s", &command))
        return NULL;
    sts = system(command);
    return Py_BuildValue("i", sts);
}

static PyMethodDef SpamMethods[] = {
    {"system",   spam_system, METH_VARARGS},
    {NULL,       NULL}           /* Sentinel */
};

#ifdef MS_WIN32
__declspec(dllexport)
#endif

void initspam()
{
    PyObject *m, *d;

    m = Py_InitModule("spam", SpamMethods);
    d = PyModule_GetDict(m);
    SpamError = PyErr_NewException("spam.error", NULL, NULL);
    PyDict_SetItemString(d, "error", SpamError);
}
```

The format for Python extensions is well covered in the standard Python documents and in the various books to date. Our target is simply to get it to build on
Windows. When this is done, you should end up with a file named *spam.pyd*, and
be able to use it just like the following example:

```
>>> import spam
>>> spam.system('start notepad')
0
>>>
```

And you see a *notepad* appear on the screen.

You take the high road...

Before we start on a fairly long spiel about how to create a Microsoft Visual C++
Project file by hand, we would be remiss not to make mention of a handy Python

tool that can save you lots of heartache and may let you skip the next section completely!

Python on Unix has a well-established build procedure that uses a file named *setup.in* to control the build process. Each different operating system reads the *setup.in* file and generates an appropriate *makefile* for the system.

David Ascher has developed a tool that takes one of these Unix *setup.in* files, generates a Microsoft Visual C++ project file, then invokes Visual C++ to build the project. Although this would appear to be of interest mainly for people with existing Unix source code, these *setup.in* files are so simple that creating one of these files for our project is simpler than mastering Visual C++.

The simplest possible *setup.in* file consists of two lines. The first line contains *shared* (this tells Unix systems the module is to be built as a shared module, the equivalent of a DLL on Windows). The second line consists of the name of the module we wish to build, and the source files needed to build it. The *setup.in* file contains the following two lines:

```
*shared*
spam spammodule.c
```

Here, the module is called **spam** and there is a single source file, *spammodule.c*.

The tool that creates the Visual C++ project file is a single Python source file, *compile.py*, available from *http://starship.python.net/crew/da/compile/*. You can also find it, along with this book's code samples, at *http://starship.python.net/crew/mhammond/ppw32/*.

Using this tool to build the sample is simple; create a directory with *spammodule.c* and *setup.in* files, and from this directory, run the compile tool. A Visual C++ project is generated and the project built. Let's try this out. For this example, assume that *compile.py* is in your *C:\Scripts* directory and the spam files in *C:\Scripts\spam*:

```
C:\Scripts\spam>dir
 Volume in drive C has no label.
 Volume Serial Number is B423-50BF

 Directory of C:\Scripts\spam

18/05/99  19:29         <DIR>          .
18/05/99  19:29         <DIR>          ..
07/05/99  18:59                     33 setup.in
07/05/99  14:53                    761 spammodule.c
               4 File(s)            794 bytes
                        113,135,104 bytes free

C:\Scripts\spam>..\compile.py
Attempting to start MSDev...
```

```
Building workspace (.dsw) file for workspace
   Found python15.lib in L:\src\python-1.5.2\pcbuild
   Found Python include directory in L:\src\python-1.5.2\include
Creating project (.dsp) file for spam
Building project
```

As you can see, you start with only the two files mentioned previously and run the compile tool. During this process, you should see Visual C++ start, the build process complete, then Visual C++ exit. Let's see what's in the directory now:

```
C:\Scripts\spam>dir
 Volume in drive C has no label.
 Volume Serial Number is B423-50BF

 Directory of C:\Scripts\spam

18/05/99  19:31         <DIR>          .
18/05/99  19:31         <DIR>          ..
18/05/99  19:30         <DIR>          pyds
07/05/99  18:59                    33  setup.in
18/05/99  19:30                 2,454  spam.dsp
18/05/99  19:30                 1,182  spam.plg
07/05/99  14:53                   761  spammodule.c
18/05/99  19:30         <DIR>          tmp
18/05/99  19:30                   618  workspace.dsw
18/05/99  19:31                33,792  workspace.ncb
18/05/99  19:31                49,664  workspace.opt
             11 File(s)          88,504 bytes
                           112,688,128 bytes free

C:\Scripts\spam>dir pyds\*.pyd
 Volume in drive C has no label.
 Volume Serial Number is B423-50BF

 Directory of C:\Scripts\spam\pyds

18/05/99  19:30                20,480  spam.pyd
              1 File(s)          20,480 bytes
                           113,736,704 bytes free

C:\Scripts\spam>
```

The script creates Visual C++ Project (*spam.dsp*) and Workspace (*workspace.dsw*) files (you can specify a different name for the workspace file by providing it as an argument to *compile.py*). There are some miscellaneous files created by the build process as well as two directories. The *tmp* directory is where the C object files (*.obj*) files are stored, and *pyds* is where the final Python extension is built. As you can see, the extension weighs in at around 20 KB.

All that's needed now is to copy the final *spam.pyd* to a directory on the Python-Path. *C:\Program Files\Python\Dlls* is where Python installed some standard extensions, so this may be suitable. Once *spam.pyd* is in a location where Python can find it, the sample code presented earlier should work.

...and I'll take the low road

There will be cases where you choose to use Visual C++ yourself rather than rely on the *compile.py* tool covered in the previous section. Although this takes longer to set up and doesn't provide a portable build solution, it does provide greater control over the build process. Of course, you're free to use both solutions: use the compile tool to generate your first project file and workspace, but maintain them manually after creation.

Either way, we will briefly discuss creating a project file from scratch using Visual C++ that builds our *spam* sample. Here are the three steps:

1. Create a new project file.

2. Modify the project settings.

3. Build the project.

Create a new project file. Creating a new project is fairly simple, although we're faced with a Microsoft Wizard! Complete the following steps:

1. Start Microsoft Visual C++.

2. Choose File → New → Projects → Win32 Dynamic Link Library.

3. Under Location, choose a directory. We have used *D:\MyStuff*.

4. In the Project Name box, enter *spam*. A subdirectory called *spam* is suggested in the location box. The dialog should now look like Figure 22-2.

5. Select OK to start the New Project Wizard. When asked "What kind of DLL would you like to create?" choose "An empty DLL Project."

6. After a confirmation screen, VC++ creates an empty project, and the wizard exits.

7. Place the *spammodule.c* source file into the new spam directory.

8. Locate and select the File View tab at the bottom of the Workspace Explorer window.

9. Right-click on Spam Files, and select Add Files To Project from the context menu that appears and select the *spammodule.c* source file.

10. If you expand the Source Files tree and double-click on *spammodule.c*, it's opened in Visual C++, and the screen should now look like Figure 22-3.

Modify the project settings. We now have a project file, but some of the default settings aren't suitable for Python, so your next step is to modify some of the project settings. Specifically, you need to:

- Change the C runtime library settings so the extension and Python share this library. This is a fairly obscure requirement, but it's needed to prevent the

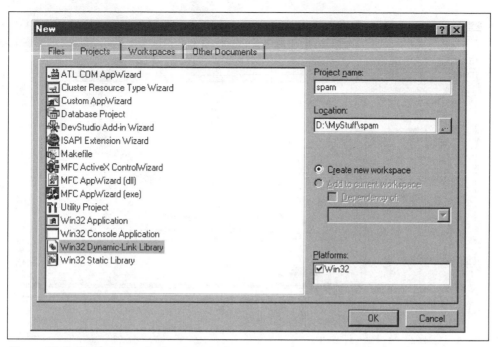

Figure 22-2. Ready to create the spam project

extension module crashing under specific circumstances (see the later section "Debug Versus Release Builds" for more information).

- Change the extension of the final DLL to *.pyd*. Although unnecessary, this is an established convention that allows easy identification of Python extensions versus normal Windows DLLs.

- If you wish to perform a debug build, you need to change the debug version of the final DLL *spam_d.pyd* (again, see the later section "Debug Versus Release Builds" for more information).

The process to perform these steps is:

1. Choose Project → Settings. In the top left combo box, select the Win32 Release configuration.

2. Select the C/C++ tab and drop down the Category combo box, stopping to admire the breathtaking lack of adherence to Microsoft's own GUI design standards. Choose Code Generation, and a new property page appears on the C/C++ tab. Change "Use runtime library" to "Multithreaded DLL." The property page should look like Figure 22-4.

3. Select the Link tab and change the name of the output file from *Release/spam. dll* to *Release/spam.pyd*, which should look like Figure 22-5.

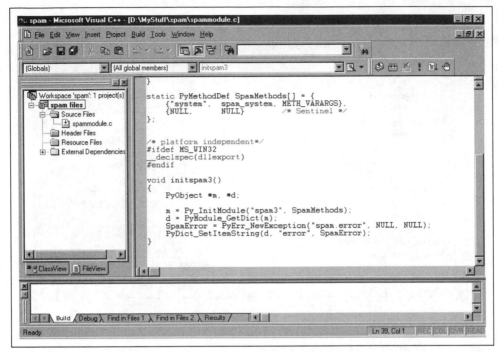

Figure 22-3. The completed project file

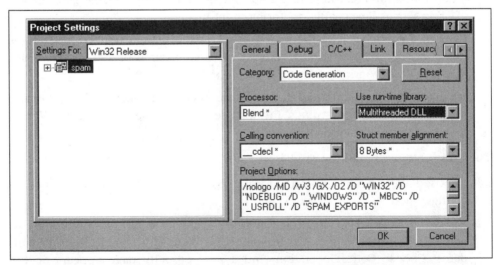

Figure 22-4. Changing the C compiler options for the Win32 Release build

If you need to perform a debug build, repeat this process for the Win32 Debug configuration, but substitute Debug Multithreaded DLL for Multithreaded DLL in the first step and change the output file to *spam_d.pyd* as discussed previously.

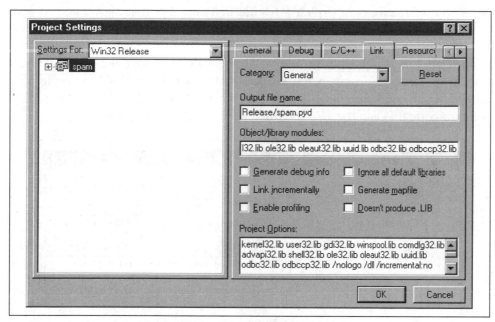

Figure 22-5. Changing the linker options for the Win32 Release build

You need the full Python sources to build a debug version of your extension, as *Python15_d.dll* isn't distributed with the Python binaries. Instead of building a full debug version, consider keeping the standard release build, but temporarily modifying the project settings to include debug information. As discussed later in this chapter, as long as you ensure that the C runtime library in use is Multithreaded DLL, everything should work correctly.

Everyone works differently, so exactly how you manage your environment depends on your circumstances, but there are a number of other tips that relate to making your built extension module available to Python.

One alternative is to modify your PythonPath to explicitly include the directory where your PYD files are built; in our example, that would be *D:\MyStuff\Spam\ Release*. Then the latest changes are available to Python as soon as the project is built, with no need to copy the extension anywhere else. A further refinement to this is to exploit the fact that release and debug builds create different files, *spam. pyd* and *spam_d.pyd*. This allows you to change your project to build our extensions into the same directory, avoiding the need to specify one directory for release builds and another for debug builds.

A second alternative is to exploit a feature in Visual C++ that allows you to execute an arbitrary command after your extension has built. It's quite common to use this feature to copy the final extension to another directory already on your PythonPath. To set this up, again go to the Visual C++ Project Settings, and you'll find, way off to the right in the available tabs, is Custom Build. Selecting this allows you to specify a simple copy command. Figure 22-6 shows the project setup to copy files into the *C:\Program Files\Python\DLLs* directory.

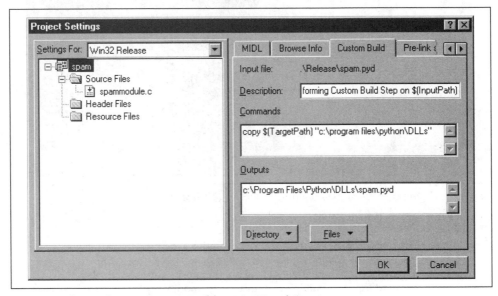

Figure 22-6. Specifying a Custom Build step in Visual C++

You're now almost ready to build, but faced with one Windows-specific complication the *compile.py* tools managed to hide. The problem is that you need to tell Windows that your module-initialization function (`initspam()`) is a public function, so Python can call it as the module is loaded. There are a number of ways to do this, the most common being: providing a module definition (*.def*) file, adding a special `/EXPORT:initspam` argument to the linker or modifying the code itself. For this demonstration let's take the last option and modify the module-initialization code from the original:

```
void initspam()
{
```

To:

```
#ifdef MS_WIN32
__declspec(dllexport)
#endif

void initspam()
{
```

Figure 22-3 shows the source code after this change.

Building our project. Finally, we're ready to build the project. Perform the following steps:

1. Choose Build → Set Active Configuration and select Win32 Release.

2. Choose Build → Build *spam.pyd*. If all goes well, you see some messages in the Visual C++ output window, finishing like this:

```
--------------Configuration: spam - Win32 Release--------------
Compiling...
spammodule.c
Linking...
   Creating library Release/spam.lib and object Release/spam.exp
Performing Custom Build Step on .\Release\spam.pyd
       1 file(s) copied


spam.pyd - 0 error(s), 0 warning(s)
```

Note that because you specified an additional copy operation after the build, you can see the `1 file(s) copied` message generated by the copy. A quick check in *C:\Program Files\Python\DLLs* shows the new *spam.pyd*.

Now, start Python (or PythonWin). Type `import spam`, followed by `spam.system ('start notepad')` or the command of your choice.

Debug Versus Release Builds

A couple of times now, we have glossed over some differences between debug and release builds for our extensions and Python. This is a symptom of the important, although somewhat technical, issue of the C runtime library.

If you don't know what a C runtime library is or don't care about the technical details, the simple rules to follow are:

- Release builds of your project must use the Multithreaded DLL and link with the standard Python *.lib* files.

- Debug builds of your project must use the Debug Multithreaded DLL C runtime library, must link with the _d version of the Python *.lib* files, and must themselves be named following the _d convention.

This is simple to set up, as we demonstrated when building the *spam* sample. The compile tool described previously automatically creates the correct settings, so in some cases you don't need to do anything. However, a deeper understanding of the issues will help you understand why the _d convention exists and how to exploit or work around it for your situation. Feel free to skip the rest of this section.

The underlying issue is that Python and its extensions are DLLs, and these DLLs need the same C runtime library. Particularly at issue are FILE objects and memory allocated via malloc(). If all Python extensions aren't using the same C runtime library, the FILE objects passed between Python and the extensions are considered invalid. The result is likely to be an access violation.

Although this problem isn't unique to Windows, Microsoft Visual C++ is one of the few compilers that provide different libraries for debug and release builds. The debug libraries are useful and contain all sorts of diagnostic and sanity checks for using these objects. As a result, it's common for a programmer to build a debug version of his module, but attempt to run it with a release version of Python or other modules. The result is a problem far worse than he was originally trying to debug, so Python invented a scheme to avoid this common pitfall.

The idea is that when Python itself is built for debug, it looks for only modules with _d appended to the name. A debug build of Python then finds only specific debug modules, and a release build of Python finds only release modules.

As you can see, the _d convention is not a true solution to the problem; the underlying issue is that Python and all the extensions must be built with the same, shared C runtime library. Python's use of _d is a convention that makes the more common errors less likely. This convention also means it's possible to have both debug and release builds of the same extension in the same directory. When you run *Python.exe*, the release extensions are automatically found. When you run *Python_d.exe*, the debug extensions are found without needing to change the PythonPath. This makes debugging quite simple: just run *Python_d.exe* under the debugger and your debug extension module can be debugged automatically.

The biggest problem with this scheme is that to debug a single extension module, you must have debug builds of every extension module your program uses. Depending on the application, this may be difficult and even impossible. You can exploit this information to make your debugging easier. Because the issue we have been discussing is the C runtime library, you can change almost every other compiler or linker option for your debug or release build except this. Thus, for your release build, you can temporarily disable optimizations and enable symbolic debugging information; just make sure the C runtime library never changes. Then step through your extension in the C debugger (but not through Python or other extensions) before restoring the default project settings.

Building Python Itself

There are occasions when it's necessary or desirable to build Python itself from its sources. As mentioned previously, reasons may include wanting to build a debug version, or simply the satisfaction or security of knowing you can build your entire project from scratch.

The process is quite simple, and Python builds easily. The sources come with Visual C++ project and workspace files, and building is as simple as opening the workspace and starting the build.

The sources are available from *http://www.python.org*, usually in a file with the name *pythxxx.tgz*, where *xxx* is the version of Python. For example, Python 1.5.2 sources are available in *pyth152.tgz*. The *.tgz* file is a gzipped *tar* file and is understood by the ubiquitous WinZip program (*http://www.winzip.com*). Once you expand this archive into a suitable directory (be careful to maintain the directory structure when expanding), you should have a Python–1.5.2 directory with a number of subdirectories including *PCBuild, Python, Modules*, and so forth.

In the *PCBuild* directory you'll find *pcbuild.dsw*; this is the Visual C++ workspace. Once opened, Visual C++ should look similar to Figure 22-7.

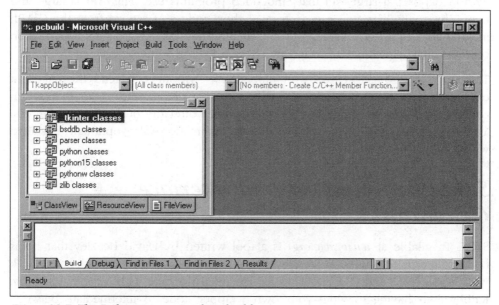

Figure 22-7. The Python sources ready to build

Depending on your requirements, you may wish to build some or all of the projects. At a minimum, you need to build the *Python15* project that builds *Python15.dll* (or *Python15_d.dll* for debug builds). All built files are placed in the *PCBuild* directory, ready to be distributed, copied to the Windows System directory, etc.

Visual C++ generates large numbers of temporary files, often totaling megabytes. When you have created a DLL or EXE you are happy with, you may choose to copy it somewhere else and choose Build → Clean. This deletes all the built files reclaiming the list disk space.

Embedding a Python Interpreter in a C++ Application

The process we described previously of building a DLL extension module for Python is known as *extending* Python; you extend its capabilities with a new module. The other common process is to put Python inside another existing application, possibly for use as a macro or extension language. This process is known as *embedding* Python.

If you look at the files Python installs, notice that the bulk of Python itself is implemented in a DLL, *Python15.dll*, for all Python 1.5.x versions. *Python.exe* itself is tiny, and simply uses the Python DLL. In fact, consider *Python.exe* as a trivial example of how to embed Python in your application.

Python exposes a large API that embedded programs use. This API is large and rich; almost anything you can do from Python code you can do from the C API, including running code, calling objects, creating new objects, pulling apart Python objects (such as getting the string value from a Python string object), and so forth.

The best way to get started with embedding Python is to read the excellent extending and embedding documentation (optionally installed with Python) in conjunction with the sample in the *Demo\Embed* directory of the Python sources. You can then peruse the *Python/C API* documentation (also optionally installed with Python).

Simplified Wrapper and Interface Generator

SWIG (available at *www.swig.org*) is a tool written by David Beazley that helps connect programs written in high-level languages such as Python, Perl, and Tcl/Tk with low-level C and C++ code. It's a substantial package with a large following. Rather than having to write your own wrapper code to intermediate between Python and C data structures, SWIG automates the process of producing a Python extension based on a description of the functions you wish to export. A large number of popular Python extensions have been built using SWIG, including parts of the Win32 extensions. You should look into SWIG before embarking on any nontrivial Python extension project.

Space doesn't permit a detailed example of SWIG, but we refer you to the excellent documentation that comes with the package. This covers all the specifics relating to building Python extensions under Visual Studio.

Python and Delphi

The Big Three development environments must be Visual Basic, Visual C++, and Borland Delphi. Delphi users feel that the language and development environment combine the ease of use of Visual Basic with the power of C++, and the Visual Component Library that comes with Delphi does a superb job of hiding the complexities of the Windows API. Delphi is particularly popular in Europe, where Pascal has often been the teaching language for computer science.

Delphi uses Object Pascal, the latest stage in the evolution of Pascal. Like C++, Delphi is a fully compiled language that allows both high-level object-oriented programming and "down-to-the-metal" manipulation of raw memory and pointers. It's a pure Windows tool that allows you to write DLLs and EXEs and to access all the Windows API calls. It also supports the C calling convention. This means that in theory Delphi can access the main Python DLL in the same way as C/C++ programs, and can compile DLLs Python can use as extensions.

During 1997 and 1998, a package called PyDelphi (included in the examples for this chapter at *http://starship.python.net/crew/mhammond/ppw32/* and also available at *www.multimania.com/marat/delphi/index.htm*) evolved through a merger of work by Morgan Martinet, Dietmar Budelsky, and Grzegorz Makarewicz. This makes integration of Python and Delphi at the C level almost effortless. PyDelphi includes a Delphi package library that can be installed in the component gallery and a comprehensive set of demos and tutorials.

The core component is a Pascal module called *PythonEngine.pas*, which declares Pascal types to match those in *Python.h* and function headers to match most of those exported by the Python DLL. This makes it possible to access Python the same way as C/C++. Going on from this, the authors provide a number of components that represent the Python engine itself, Python modules and variables, and I/O components.

Embedding Python in a Delphi Application

Figure 22-8 shows the first example from the PyDelphi tutorial.

To achieve this, you create a new project with the visual components shown in Figure 22-8. In addition, place two special Python-Delphi components on the form. These are invisible at runtime, but allow you to set up many properties from the Object Inspector rather than in code. The essential one is a `PythonEngine`, (highlighted in Figure 22-9).

The `PythonEngine` component has events that can be trapped for initialization and finalization, and—most usefully—an `InitScript` property of type `TStrings`. This is a list of strings that can be set at design time in an editor and can hold any Python code you want.

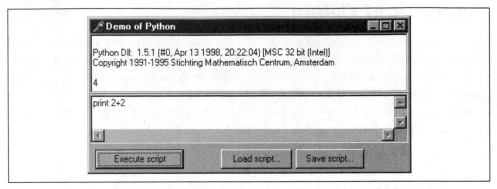

Figure 22-8. Python interpreter inside a Delphi application

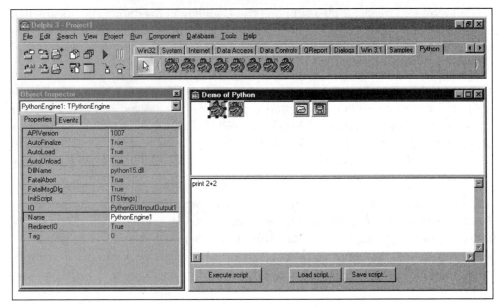

Figure 22-9. The same form at design time

In addition, you add a `PythonGUIInputOutput` component. After setting a couple of properties, this redirects the output of the Python engine to the upper Rich Edit window in the form. The user can now type Python code into the lower window and execute it with a click on a button.

In addition to the usual header, you need one line of code behind the button:

```
procedure TForm1.Button1Click(Sender: TObject);
begin
  PythonEngine1.ExecStrings( Memo1.Lines );
end;
```

PyDelphi exposes almost the entire Python C API; but Delphi also has a very useful data structure called a **StringList**, and **PythonEngine** has some higher-level functions to work with these, such as **ExecStrings**, in the previous snippet. A related and useful trick with PyDelphi is to place invisible list boxes and memos on a form and paste chunks of Python, or even whole modules, into them; these can easily be passed to Python later. To distribute an application, you need to include just the Delphi executable and the usual *python15.dll*, plus any extra Python modules required; these can be frozen inside the Delphi executable if desired.

Extending Python with a Delphi DLL

It's easy to create a DLL in Delphi and expose it as a Python module. Let's start with one of the PyDelphi tutorial examples, then extend it into something more useful. The initial example exports one function to add two numbers together. In Delphi, choose File → New → DLL to create a DLL project, and save it. Then create a new Pascal module (called just *module.pas*) containing the following code:

```
unit module;

interface
uses PythonEngine;

procedure initdemodll; cdecl;
var
  gEngine : TPythonEngine;
  gModule : TPythonModule;

implementation

function Add( Self, Args : PPyObject ) : PPyObject; far; cdecl;
var
  a, b : Integer;
begin
  with GetPythonEngine do
    begin
      if PyArg_ParseTuple( args, 'ii:Add', [@a, @b] ) <> 0 then
        begin
          Result := PyInt_FromLong( a + b );
        end
      else
        Result := nil;
    end;
end;

procedure initdemodll;
begin
  try
    gEngine := TPythonEngine.Create(nil);
    gEngine.AutoFinalize := False;
```

```
      gEngine.LoadDll;
      gModule := TPythonModule.Create(nil);
      gModule.Engine := gEngine;
      gModule.ModuleName := 'demodll';
      gModule.AddMethod( 'add', @Add, 'add(a,b) -> a+b' );
      gModule.Initialize;
    except
    end;
  end;

  initialization
  finalization
    gEngine.Free;
    gModule.Free;
    frmAbout.Free;
  end.
```

You can see the similarity between this and the minimal C extension earlier in the chapter. However, PyDelphi includes a **TPythonModule** component that slightly changes the initialization of the Python function names. Having written this, you can edit the Delphi project file (extension DPR) to export the `initdemodll` function:

```
  library DemoDll;

  uses
     SysUtils,
     Classes,
     module in 'module.pas';

  exports
     initdemodll;
  {$E pyd}

  begin
  end.
```

The project can be compiled to a DLL and saved with the extension *.PYD* somewhere on the PythonPath.

Accessing Delphi's Visual Component Library

If you are creating a Python script to be run from a command prompt, it's perfectly feasible to write GUI code in Delphi. The DLL could contain forms and dialogs, which can be launched from within a DLL function called by Python. One use for this might be to provide stock dialogs for a Python script, although you could go further and write an entire application that is launched from Python and uses a Delphi GUI.

For reasons discussed in Chapter 20, *GUI Development*, don't try to run DLLs that use a GUI within the PythonWin editor. Plain-vanilla Object Pascal extensions are safe to use in any Python IDE, but the Delphi VCL application framework and the MFC application framework in PythonWin will both assume they are running the application and so, you get an immediate error message.

The authors of the package have also written their own Python IDE in Delphi and a tool that automatically examines Pascal source code and generates Python wrappers for the entire Visual Component Library. These make it possible to write Python code that creates Delphi forms and objects and accesses their methods and properties, just as you would in Delphi. The following is valid Python code:

```
from Forms import *
from StdCtrls import *

f = TForm().CreateNew(Application)
```

Unfortunately, this incredible capability is still experimental and limited to use within Delphi applications; thus, you can write a Delphi application with an embedded Python macro language that can create and manipulate Delphi GUI elements, but you can't just write a plain Python script. The latter is technically feasible and it is a development we hope to see in the future.

Dynamic DLL Access

As we mentioned in Chapter 13, *Databases*, Sam Rushing (*http://www.nightmare. com*) has written an extension that allows Python to dynamically load and call any function in any DLL, not just special Python extensions. For the C programmers among you, these are equivalent to using the Windows API functions `LoadLibrary()` and `GetProcAddress()`.

These tools offer a great deal of power but also carry risks. When using Python extension modules such as the Win32 extensions, you can be fairly confident the worst that will happen is a Python exception. When dynamically accessing a DLL, you are responsible for ensuring the arguments you pass are the correct type; an error in doing so can corrupt the stack and lead to either seriously misleading results or a crash.

Using these tools, Sam has built a comprehensive ODBC module that allows access to every function in the ODBC API and to a GUI application framework sitting directly on top of the Windows API.

In general, the safest way to access existing C libraries is to build Python extension modules. However, there may be occasions when a C compiler isn't available or when dynamic loading and unloading are required. A case study mentioned in Chapter 1, *What Is Python?*, uses `Calldll/Windll` to interface to an encoding translation library that moves megabytes of data between operating systems each day; for political reasons, C/C++ development was not an option in this case.

Installation and Setup

Two packages are available from Sam Rushing's site. `CallDLL` consists of a Python extension module, *calldll.pyd* that exposes a low-level API for loading modules and calling functions within them. The DynWin package builds on this to offer a much easier high-level API, and includes the GUI library mentioned previously. The package includes a key module, *windll.py* that provides a higher-level wrapper around `CallDLL` making it easy to use. In fact, only two files are needed for dynamic loading: *calldll.pyd*, and *windll.py*, both of which should be installed on the PythonPath. These are included with the examples for the chapter, which can be found at *http://starship.python.net/crew/mhammond/ppw32/*.

Using WinDll

As an example we've built an extremely basic DLL called *simple.dll*. This exports two functions, `Min(a, b)` and `Max(a, b)`, which return the minimum and maximum of two numbers. All arguments and return types are integers. The following example shows how to load and use the DLL, presuming it's in *c:\temp*. You can omit a path if it's on the Windows path:

```
>>> from dynwin.windll import *
>>> mod1 = module('c:\\temp\\simple')  # loads the DLL
>>> mod1.handle         # it can report its location in memory
22806528
>>> mod1.Min(27, 28)    # loads and executes Min function
27
>>> mod1.Min           # we now have a 'callable function' object...
<callable function "Min">
>>> mod1.Min.address    #...which knows its address too
22836704
```

`WinDLL` is doing a lot of work behind the scenes here, using Python's abilities to introspect and trap attribute access. Go to *windll.py*'s source to see how it works.

`WinDLL` can transparently handle any integer or pointer arguments. The vast majority of Windows API calls have arguments that are either an integer, a pointer to a string, or some other structure, all of which require four bytes of memory. If you need to handle other types of arguments, it may be necessary to drop down a level and use the lower-level argument-formatting functions in `CallDLL`.

C Strings and Passing by Reference

`WinDLL` also includes a class `cstring` that makes it easy to pass string or character buffer arguments back and forth. This class should be initialized with a Python string (which may be empty), and an optional length. Internally, `cString` maintains a buffer with a null-terminated string and the address of the buffer it passes to the DLL when used as an argument. To test this, the DLL exports a function `StringRepeat` that repeats a string a number of times:

```
>>> inBuf = cstring('spam')          # make a buffer holding a c string
>>> outBuf = cstring('',50)          # make another big enough for output
>>> mod1.StringRepeat(inBuf, outBuf, 10)  # returns the length of out string
40
>>> outBuf
'spamspamspamspamspamspamspamspamspamspam'
```

Rather than go any further, you can refer to the documentation and examples in the `CallDLL` and `DynWin` packages.

References

Extending and Embedding the Python Interpreter, by Guido van Rossum is included in HTML format with every Python distribution. Just click Help on the PythonWin toolbar.

O'Reilly's *Programming Python* and IDG's *Internet Programming with Python*, by Watters, van Rossum and Ahlstrom, both contain sections on extending and embedding. The former is far more detailed while the latter is ideal starting point for beginning C programmers.

SWIG lives at *http://www.swig.org/* and has good manuals available for download.

PyDelphi is available from *http://www.multimania.com/marat/*. You can also find it, along with this book's examples, at *http://starship.python.net/crew/mhammond/ ppw32/*.

`CallDLL` and `WinDLL` are available in the `DynWin` package from *http://www. nightmare.com*. The key files are included with the examples at *http://starship. python.net/crew/mhammond/ppw32/*.

Conclusion

This chapter provided a brief introduction to extending Python's capabilities using Visual C++ and Delphi languages. The topics included writing Python extensions and extension DLLs, embedding a Python interpreter with a C++ or Delphi application, and exposing C and C++ libraries for use by Python.

IV

Appendixes

Key Python Modules and Functions

The Python library is huge (231 files in the latest Windows distribution), but a full library reference in HTML format is included with every Python installation. You may also download printable versions in PostScript or PDF formats from *www.python.org* and circulate copies without restriction: the document is a similar size to this book.

As a convenience to the armchair reader we have included the key functions and modules that are likely to be used by most nontrivial programs. These are nearly direct reproductions from the Python Library. The Python Library is also Open Source, but we are required to include this copyright notice:

This appendix covers:

- Methods of built-in types such as lists, dictionaries, and files
- Built-in functions
- The sys module
- The os and os.path modules
- The string module

Built-in Types

The following sections describe the standard types that are built into the interpreter. These are the numeric types, sequence types, and several others, including types themselves. There is no explicit boolean type; use integers instead.

Some operations are supported by several object types; in particular, all objects can be compared, tested for truth value, and converted to a string (with the notation ` ...`). The latter conversion is implicitly used when an object is written by the print statement.

Truth Value Testing

Any object can be tested for truth value, to use in an if or while condition or as operand of the boolean operations below. The following values are considered false:

* None
* Zero of any numeric type, e.g., 0, 0L, 0.0
* Any empty sequence, e.g., '', (), []
* Any empty mapping, e.g., {}
* Instances of user-defined classes, if the class defines a __nonzero__() or __len__() method, when that method returns zero

All other values are considered true, so objects of many types are always true.

Operations and built-in functions that have a boolean result always return 0 for false and 1 for true, unless otherwise stated. Important exceptions are the boolean operations or and and, which always return one of their operands.

Boolean Operations

The following table depicts the boolean operations, ordered by ascending priority.

Operation	Result	Notes
x or y	If x is false, then y, else x	1
x and y	If x is false, then x, else y	1
not x	If x is false, then 1, else 0	2

Notes

1. These evaluate their second argument only if needed for their outcome.
2. "Not" has a lower priority than non-boolean operators, e.g., not a == b is interpreted as not(a == b), and a == not b is a syntax error.

Comparisons

Comparison operations are supported by all objects. They have the same priority (which is higher than that of the boolean operations). Comparisons can be chained arbitrarily, e.g., x < y <= z is equivalent to x < y and y <= z, except that y is evaluated only once (but in both cases z is not evaluated at all when x < y is found to be `false`).

The following table summarizes the comparison operations.

Operation	Meaning	Notes
<	Strictly less than	
<=	Less than or equal	
>	Strictly greater than	
>=	Greater than or equal	
==	Equal	
<>	Not equal	1
!=	Not equal	1
Is	Object identity	
is not	Negated object identity	

Notes

1. <> and != are alternate spellings for the same operator. (We couldn't choose between ABC and C!)

Objects of different types, except different numeric types, never compare equal; such objects are ordered consistently but arbitrarily (so that sorting a heterogeneous array yields a consistent result). Furthermore, some types (e.g., windows) support only a degenerate notion of comparison where any two objects of that type are unequal. Again, such objects are ordered arbitrarily but consistently.

Implementation note: objects of different types except numbers are ordered by their type names; objects of the same types that don't support proper comparison are ordered by their address.

Two more operations with the same syntactic priority, `"in"` and `"not in"`, are supported only by sequence types, see the later section "Sequence Types".

Numeric Types

There are four numeric types: *plain integers, long integers, floating-point numbers, and complex numbers.* Plain integers (also just called integers) are implemented using `long` in C, which gives them at least 32 bits of precision. Long integers have unlimited precision. Floating-point numbers are implemented using `double` in C. All bets on their precision are off unless you happen to know the machine you are working with.

Complex numbers have a real and imaginary part, which are both implemented using double in C. To extract these parts from a complex number `z`, use `z.real` and `z.imag`.

Numbers are created by numeric literals or as the result of built-in functions and operators. Unadorned integer literals (including hex and octal numbers) yield plain integers. Integer literals with an `L` or `l` suffix yield long integers (`L` is preferred because `1l` looks too much like eleven!). Numeric literals containing a decimal point or an exponent sign yield floating-point numbers. Appending `j` or `J` to a numeric literal yields a complex number.

Python fully supports mixed arithmetic: when a binary arithmetic operator has operands of different numeric types, the operand with the "smaller" type is converted to that of the other, where a plain integer is smaller than a long integer is smaller than a floating point is smaller than a complex. Comparisons between numbers of mixed type use the same rule.[*] The functions `int()`, `long()`, `float()`, and `complex()` can force numbers to a specific type.

All numeric types support the operations in the following table, sorted by ascending priority (operations in the same box have the same priority; all numeric operations have a higher priority than comparison operations).

Operation	Result	Notes
`x + y`	Sum of `x` and `y`	
`x - y`	Difference of `x` and `y`	
`x * y`	Product of `x` and `y`	
`x / y`	Quotient of `x` and `y`	1
`x % y`	Remainder of `x / y`	
`-x`	`x` negated	
`+x`	`x` unchanged	
`abs(x)`	Absolute value or magnitude of `x`	
`int(x)`	`x` converted to integer	2
`long(x)`	`x` converted to long integer	2
`float(x)`	`x` converted to floating point	
`complex(re,im)`	A complex number with real part `re`, imaginary part `im`; im defaults to zero	
`c.conjugate()`	Conjugate of the complex number c	

---

[*] As a consequence, the list `[1, 2]` is considered equal to `[1.0, 2.0]` and similar for tuples.

Operation	Result	Notes
divmod(x, y)	The pair (x / y, x % y)	3
pow(x, y)	x to the power y	
x ** y	x to the power y	

Notes

1. For (plain or long) integer division, the result is an integer. The result is always rounded towards minus infinity: 1/2 is 0, (-1)/2 is -1, 1/(-2) is -1, and (-1)/(-2) is 0.

2. Conversion from floating-point to (long or plain) integer may round or truncate as in C; see functions `floor()` and `ceil()` in the `math` module for well-defined conversions.

3. See the section "Built-in Functions" for an exact definition.

Bit-String Operations on Integer Types

Plain and long integer types support additional operations that make sense only for bit strings. Negative numbers are treated as their 2's complement value (for long integers, this assumes a sufficiently large number of bits so that no overflow occurs during the operation).

The priorities of the binary bitwise operations are all lower than the numeric operations and higher than the comparisons; the unary operation ~ has the same priority as the other unary numeric operations (+ and –).

The following table lists the bit-string operations sorted in ascending priority (operations in the same box have the same priority).

Operation	Result	Notes
x | y	Bitwise or of x and y	
x ^ y	Bitwise exclusive or of x and y	
x & y	Bitwise and of x and y	
x << n	x shifted left by n bits	1, 2
x >> n	x shifted right by n bits	1, 3
~x	The bits of x inverted	

Notes

1. Negative shift counts are illegal and cause a **ValueError** to be raised.

2. A left shift by **n** bits is equivalent to multiplication by **pow(2, n)** without overflow check.

3. A right shift by n bits is equivalent to division by pow(2, n) without overflow check.

Sequence Types

There are three sequence types: *strings, lists,* and *tuples.* String literals are written in single or double quotes: 'xyzzy', "frobozz". See Chapter 2 of the Python reference manual for more about string literals. Lists are constructed with square brackets, separating items with commas: [a, b, c]. Tuples are constructed by the comma operator (not within square brackets), with or without enclosing parentheses, but an empty tuple must have the enclosing parentheses, e.g., a, b, c or (). A single item tuple must have a trailing comma, e.g., (d,).

Sequence types support the following operations. The in and not in operations have the same priorities as the comparison operations. The + and * operations have the same priority as the corresponding numeric operations.[*]

The following table lists the sequence operations sorted in ascending priority (operations in the same box have the same priority). s and t are sequences of the same type; n, i, and j are integers.

Operation	Result	Notes
x in s	1 if an item of s is equal to x, else 0	
x not in s	0 if an item of s is equal to x, else 1	
s + t	The concatenation of s and t	
s * n , n * s	n copies of s concatenated	3
s[i]	i'th item of s, origin 0	1
s[i:j]	Slice of s from i to j	1, 2
len(s)	Length of s	
min(s)	Smallest item of s	
max(s)	Largest item of s	

Notes

1. If i or j is negative, the index is relative to the end of the string; i.e., len(s) + i or len(s) + j is substituted. But note that −0 is still 0.

2. The slice of s from i to j is defined as the sequence of items with index k such that i <= k < j. If i or j is greater than len(s), use len(s). If i is omitted, use 0. If j is omitted, use len(s). If i is greater than or equal to j, the slice is empty.

---

[*] They must have since the parser can't tell the type of the operands.

3. Values of **n** less than 0 are treated as 0 (which yields an empty sequence of the same type as **s**).

More String Operations

String objects have one unique built-in operation: the **%operator** (modulo) with a string left argument interprets this string as a C **sprintf()** format string to be applied to the right argument and returns the string resulting from this formatting operation.

The right argument should be a tuple with one item for each argument required by the format string; if the string requires a single argument, the right argument may also be a single nontuple object.* The following format characters are understood: **%, c, s, i, d, u, o, x, X, e, E, f, g, G**. Width and precision may be a ***** to specify that an integer argument specifies the actual width or precision. The flag characters **-, +, blank, #**, and **0** are understood. The size specifiers **h, l**, or **L** may be present but are ignored. The **%s** conversion takes any Python object and converts it to a string using **str()** before formatting it. The ANSI features **%p** and **%n** aren't supported. Since Python strings have an explicit length, **%s** conversions don't assume that **\0** is the end of the string.

For safety reasons, floating-point precisions are clipped to 50; **%f** conversions for numbers whose absolute value is over **1e25** are replaced by **%g** conversions.† All other errors raise exceptions.

If the right argument is a dictionary (or any kind of mapping), the formats in the string must have a parenthesized key into that dictionary inserted immediately after the **%** character, and each format then formats the corresponding entry from the mapping. For example:

```
>>> count = 2
>>> language = 'Python'
>>> print'%(language)s has %(count)03d quote types.' % vars()
Python has 002 quote types.
>>>
```

In this case no ***** specifiers may occur in a format (since they require a sequential parameter list).

Additional string operations are defined in standard module **string** and in built-in module **re**.

---

* A tuple object in this case should be a singleton.

† These numbers are fairly arbitrary. They are intended to avoid printing endless strings of meaningless digits without hampering correct use and without having to know the exact precision of floating-point values on a particular machine.

Mutable Sequence Types

List objects support additional operations that allow in-place modification of the object. These operations would be supported by other mutable sequence types (when added to the language) as well. Strings and tuples are immutable sequence types, and such objects can't be modified once created. The operations in the following table are defined on mutable sequence types (where x is an arbitrary object).

Operation	Result	Notes
s[i] = x	Item i of s is replaced by x	
s[i:j] = t	Slice of s from i to j is replaced by t	
del s[i:j]	Same as s[i:j] = []	
s.append(x)	Same as s[len(s):len(s)] = [x]	
s.extend(x)	Same as s[len(s):len(s)] = x	5
s.count(x)	Return number of i's for which s[i] == x	
s.index(x)	Return smallest i such that s[i] == x	1
s.insert(i, x)	Same as s[i:i] = [x] if i >= 0	
s.pop([i])	Same as x = s[i]; del s[i]; return x	4
s.remove(x)	Same as del s[s.index(x)]	1
s.reverse()	Reverses the items of s in place	3
s.sort([cmpfunc])	Sort the items of s in place	2, 3

Notes

1. This raises an exception when x is not found in s.

2. The sort() method takes an optional argument specifying a comparison function of two arguments (list items) that should return −1, 0, or 1 depending on whether the first argument is considered smaller than, equal to, or larger than the second argument. Note that this slows the sorting process considerably; e.g., to sort a list in reverse order, it's much faster to use calls to the methods sort() and reverse() than to use the built-in function sort() with a comparison function that reverses the ordering of the elements.

3. The sort() and reverse() methods modify the list in place for economy of space when sorting or reversing a large list. They don't return the sorted or reversed list to remind you of this side effect.

4. The pop() method is experimental and not supported by other mutable sequence types than lists. The optional argument i defaults to −1, so that by default, the last item is removed and returned.

5. This raises an exception when x is not a list object. The extend() method is experimental and not supported by mutable types other than lists.

Mapping Types

A mapping object maps values of one type (the *key* type) to arbitrary objects. Mappings are mutable objects. There is currently only one standard mapping type, the *dictionary*. A dictionary's keys are almost arbitrary values. The only types of values not acceptable as keys are values containing lists or dictionaries or other mutable types that are compared by value rather than by object identity. Numeric types used for keys obey the normal rules for numeric comparison: if two numbers compare equal (e.g., 1 and 1.0) then they can be used interchangeably to index the same dictionary entry.

Dictionaries are created by placing a comma-separated list of key: value pairs within braces, for example: {'jack': 4098, 'sjoerd': 4127} or {4098: 'jack', 4127: 'sjoerd'}.

The operations in the following table are defined on mappings (where *a* is a mapping, *k* is a key and *x* is an arbitrary object).

Operation	Result	Notes
len(a)	The number of items in a	
a[k]	The item of a with key k	1
a[k] = x	Set a[k] to x	
del a[k]	Remove a[k] from a (1)	
a.clear()	Remove all items from a	
a.copy()	A (shallow) copy of a	
a.has_key(k)	1 if a has a key k, else 0	
a.items()	A copy of a's list of (key, value) pairs	2
a.keys()	A copy of a's list of keys	2
a.update(b)	For k, v in b.items(): a[k] = v	3
a.values()	A copy of a's list of values	2
a.get(k[, f])	The value of a with key k	4

Notes

1. This raises an exception if k is not in the map.

2. Keys and values are listed in random order.

3. b must be the same type as a.

4. This never raises an exception if k is not in the map, instead it returns f. f is optional; when not provided and k is not in the map, None is returned.

Other Built-in Types

The interpreter supports several other kinds of objects. Most of these support only one or two operations.

Modules

The only special operation on a module is attribute access: *m*.name, where *m* is a module and name accesses a name defined in *m*'s symbol table. The import statement is not, strictly speaking, an operation on a module object; import foo doesn't require a module object named foo to exist, rather it requires an (external) definition for a module named foo somewhere.

A special member of every module is __dict__. This is the dictionary containing the module's symbol table. Modifying this dictionary changes the module's symbol table, but direct assignment to the __dict__ attribute isn't possible (i.e., you can write m.__dict__['a'] = 1, which defines m.a to be 1, but you can't write m.__dict__ = {}.

Modules built into the interpreter are written like this: <module 'sys' (built-in)>. If loaded from a file, they are written as <module 'os' from '/usr/local/lib/python1.5/os.pyc'>.

Classes and class instances

See Chapters 3 and 7 of the Python reference manual.

Functions

Function objects are created by function definitions. The only operation on a function object is to call it: func(argument-list).

There are really two flavors of function objects, built-in functions and user-defined functions. Both support the same operation (to call the function), but the implementation is different, hence the different object types.

The implementation adds two special read-only attributes: *f*.func_code is a function's code object (see the section "Code objects"), and *f*.func_globals is the dictionary used as the function's global namespace (this is the same as *m*.__dict__ where *m* is the module in which the function *f* was defined).

Methods

Methods are functions that are called using the attribute notation. There are two flavors: built-in methods (such as append() on lists) and class instance methods. Built-in methods are described with the types that support them.

The implementation adds two special read-only attributes to class instance methods: *m.im_self* is the object on which the method operates, and *m.im_func* is the function implementing the method. Calling *m(arg-1, arg-2, ..., arg-n)* is equivalent to calling *m.im_func(m.im_self, arg-1, arg-2, ..., arg-n)*. See the Python reference manual for more information.

Code objects

Code objects are used by the implementation to represent "pseudo-compiled" executable Python code such as a function body. They differ from function objects because they don't contain a reference to their global execution environment. Code objects are returned by the built-in **compile()** function and can be extracted from function objects through their **func_code** attribute.

A code object can be executed or evaluated by passing it (instead of a source string) to the exec statement or the built-in **eval()** function. See the Python reference manual for more information.

Type objects

Type objects represent the various object types. An object's type is accessed by the built-in function **type()**. There are no special operations on types. The standard module type defines names for all standard built-in types. Types are written like this: **<type 'int'>**.

The null object

This object is returned by functions that don't explicitly return a value. It supports no special operations. There is exactly one null object, named **None** (a built-in name); it's written as **None**.

The ellipsis object

This object is used by extended slice notation (see the Python reference manual). It supports no special operations. There is one ellipsis object, named **Ellipsis** (a built-in name); it's written as **Ellipsis**.

File objects

File objects are implemented using C's **stdio** package and can be created with the built-in function **open()** (described in the section "Built-in Functions"). They are also returned by some other built-in functions and methods, e.g., **posix.popen()** and **posix.fdopen()**, and the **makefile()** method of socket objects.

When a file operation fails for an I/O-related reason, the exception **IOError** is raised. This includes situations where the operation isn't defined for some reason, such as **seek()** on a tty device or writing a file opened for reading. Files have the following methods:

`close()`

Closes the file. A closed file can't be read or written.

`flush()`

Flushes the internal buffer; like `stdio`'s `fflush()`.

`isatty()`

Returns 1 if the file is connected to a tty (-like) device, else 0.

`fileno()`

Returns the integer "file descriptor" that's used by the underlying implementation to request I/O operations from the operating system. This can be useful for other, lower-level interfaces that use file descriptors, e.g., module `fcntl` or `os.read()` and friends.

`read([size])`

Reads at most *size* bytes from the file (less if the read hits EOF or no more data is immediately available on a pipe, tty, or similar device). If the size argument is negative or omitted, read all data until EOF is reached. The bytes are returned as a string object. An empty string is returned when EOF is encountered immediately. (For certain files, like ttys, it makes sense to continue reading after an EOF is hit.)

`readline([size])`

Reads one entire line from the file. A trailing newline character is kept in the string* (but may be absent when a file ends with an incomplete line). If the size argument is present and nonnegative, it's a maximum byte count (including the trailing newline), and an incomplete line may be returned. An empty string is returned when EOF is hit immediately. Unlike `stdio`'s `fgets()`, the returned string contains null characters (`\0`) if they occurred in the input.

`readlines([sizehint])`

Reads until EOF using `readline()` and return a list containing the lines thus read. If the optional *sizehint* argument is present, instead of reading up to EOF, whole lines totaling approximately *sizehint* bytes (possibly after rounding up to an internal buffer size) are read.

`seek(offset[, whence])`

Sets the file's current position; like `stdio`'s `fseek()`. The *whence* argument is optional and defaults to 0 (absolute file positioning); other values are 1 (seek relative to the current position) and 2 (seek relative to the file's end). There's no return value.

---

* The advantage of leaving the newline on is that an empty string can be returned to mean EOF without being ambiguous. Another advantage is that (in cases where it might matter, e.g., if you want to make an exact copy of a file while scanning its lines) you can tell whether the last line of a file ended in a newline or not (yes, this happens!).

`tell()`

Returns the file's current position; like `stdio`'s `ftell()`.

`truncate([size])`

Truncates the file's size. If the optional *size* argument is present, the file is truncated to (at most) that size. The size defaults to the current position. Availability of this function depends on the operating-system version (e.g., not all Unix versions support this operation).

`write(str)`

Writes a string to the file. There is no return value. Due to buffering, the string may not actually show up in the file until the `flush()` or `close()` method is called.

`writelines(list)`

Writes a list of strings to the file. There is no return value. (The name is intended to match `readlines()`; `writelines()` doesn't add line separators.)

File objects also offer the following attributes:

`closed`

Boolean indicating the current state of the file object. This is a read-only attribute; the `close()` method changes the value.

`mode`

The I/O mode for the file. If the file is created using the `open()` built-in function, this is the value of the mode parameter. This is a read-only attribute.

`name`

If the file object was created using `open()`, this is the name of the file. Otherwise, it's some string that indicates the source of the file object, of the form `<...>`. This is a read-only attribute.

`softspace`

Boolean that indicates whether a space character needs to be printed before another value when using the print statement. Classes that are trying to simulate a file object should also have a writable `softspace` attribute, which should be initialized to zero. This is automatic for classes implemented in Python; types implemented in C have to provide a writable `softspace` attribute.

Internal objects

See the Python reference manual for this information. It describes `code` objects, `stack frame` objects, `traceback` objects, and `slice` objects.

Special attributes

The implementation adds a few special read-only attributes to several object types, where they are relevant:

__dict__
> A dictionary of some sort that stores an object's (writable) attributes

__methods__
> List of the methods of many built-in object types, e.g., [].__methods__ yields ['append', 'count', 'index', 'insert', 'pop', 'remove', 'reverse', 'sort']

__members__
> Similar to __methods__, but lists data attributes

__class__
> The class to which a class instance belongs

__bases__
> The tuple of base classes of a class object

Built-in Exceptions

Exceptions can be class or string objects. While most exceptions have traditionally been string objects, in Python 1.5 all standard exceptions have been converted to class objects, and users are encouraged to do the same. The source code for those exceptions is present in the standard library-module exceptions; this module never needs to be imported explicitly.

For backward compatibility, when Python is invoked with the –X option, most standard exceptions are strings.* This option can run code that breaks because of the different semantics of class-based exceptions. The –X option will become obsolete in future Python versions, so the recommended solution is to fix the code.

Two distinct string objects with the same value are considered different exceptions. This forces programmers to use exception names rather than their string value when specifying exception handlers. The string value of all built-in exceptions is their name, but this isn't a requirement for user-defined exceptions or exceptions defined by library modules.

For class exceptions, in a try statement with an except clause that mentions a particular class, that clause also handles any exception classes derived from that class (but not exception classes from which it is derived). Two exception classes that

---

* For forward-compatibility the new exceptions Exception, LookupError, ArithmeticError, EnvironmentError, and StandardError are tuples.

aren't related via subclassing are never equivalent, even if they have the same name.

The built-in exceptions in the following list can be generated by the interpreter or built-in functions. Except where mentioned, they have an "associated value" indicating the detailed cause of the error. This may be a string or a tuple containing several items of information (e.g., an error code and a string explaining the code). The associated value is the second argument to the raise statement. For string exceptions, the associated value itself is stored in the variable named as the second argument of the **except** clause (if any). For class exceptions, that variable receives the exception instance. If the exception class is derived from the standard root class **Exception**, the associated value is present as the exception instance's **args** attribute, and possibly on other attributes as well.

User code can raise built-in exceptions. This code can test an exception handler or report an error condition "just like" the situation in which the interpreter raises the same exception; but beware that there is nothing to prevent user code from raising an inappropriate error.

The following exceptions are used only as base classes for other exceptions. When string-based standard exceptions are used, they are tuples containing the directly derived classes:

Exception

> The root class for exceptions. All built-in exceptions are derived from this class. All user-defined exceptions should also be derived from this class, but this isn't (yet) enforced. The str() function, when applied to an instance of this class (or most derived classes) returns the string value of the argument or arguments, or an empty string if no arguments were given to the constructor. When used as a sequence, this accesses the arguments given to the constructor (handy for backward compatibility with old code). The arguments are also available on the instance's **args** attribute, as a tuple.

StandardError

> The base class for all built-in exceptions except SystemExit. StandardError itself is derived from the root class Exception.

ArithmeticError

> The base class for those built-in exceptions that are raised for various arithmetic errors: OverflowError, ZeroDivisionError, FloatingPointError.

LookupError

> The base class for the exceptions that are raised when a key or index used on a mapping or sequence is invalid: IndexError, KeyError.

EnvironmentError

The base class for exceptions that can occur outside the Python system: `IOError`, `OSError`. When exceptions of this type are created with a two-tuple, the first item is available on the instance's `errno` attribute (it's assumed to be an error number), and the second item is available on the `strerror` attribute (it's usually the associated error message). The tuple itself is also available on the `args` attribute. New in Version 1.5.2.

When an `EnvironmentError` exception is instantiated with a three-tuple, the first two items are available as above, while the third item is available on the filename attribute. However, for backward-compatibility, the `args` attribute contains only a two-tuple of the first two constructor arguments.

The filename attribute is `None` when this exception is created with other than three arguments. The `errno` and `strerror` attributes are also `None` if the instance was created with other than two or three arguments. In this last case, `args` contains the verbatim constructor arguments as a tuple.

The following exceptions are those actually raised. They are class objects, except when the `-X` option is used to revert back to string-based standard exceptions:

AssertionError

Raised when an assert statement fails.

AttributeError

Raised when an attribute reference or assignment fails. (When an object doesn't support attribute references or attribute assignments at all, `TypeError` is raised.)

EOFError

Raised when one of the built-in functions (`input()` or `raw_input()`) hits an end-of-file condition (EOF) without reading any data. (Note that the `read()` and `readline()` methods of file objects return an empty string when they hit EOF.)

FloatingPointError

Raised when a floating-point operation fails. This exception is always defined, but can be raised only when Python is configured with the `-with-fpectl` option or the `WANT_SIGFPE_HANDLER` symbol is defined in the *config.h* file.

IOError

Raised when an I/O operation (such as a print statement, the built-in `open()` function, or a method of a file object) fails for an I/O-related reason, e.g., file not found or disk full.

This class is derived from `EnvironmentError`. See its previous discussion for more information on exception-instance attributes.

ImportError

Raised when an import statement fails to find the module definition or when a `from ... import` fails to find a name that's to be imported.

IndexError

Raised when a sequence subscript is out of range. (Slice indexes are silently truncated to fall in the allowed range; if an index isn't a plain integer, `TypeError` is raised.)

KeyError

Raised when a mapping (dictionary) key is not found in the set of existing keys.

KeyboardInterrupt

Raised when the user hits the interrupt key (normally Ctrl-C or Del). During execution, a check for interrupts is made regularly. Interrupts typed when a built-in function `input()` or `raw_input()`) is waiting for input also raise this exception.

MemoryError

Raised when an operation runs out of memory but the situation may still be rescued (by deleting some objects). The associated value is a string indicating what kind of (internal) operation ran out of memory. Note that because of the underlying memory-management architecture (C's `malloc()` function), the interpreter may not always completely recover from this situation; it nevertheless raises an exception so that a stack traceback can be printed, in case a runaway program was the cause.

NameError

Raised when a local or global name is not found. Applies only to unqualified names. The associated value is the name that can't be found.

NotImplementedError

Derived from `RuntimeError`. In user-defined base classes, abstract methods should raise this exception when they require derived classes to override the method. New in Version 1.5.2.

OSError

Derived from `EnvironmentError` and is used primarily as the `os` module's `os.error` exception. See `EnvironmentError` in the first exception list for a description of the possible associated values. New in Version 1.5.2.

OverflowError

Raised when the result of an arithmetic operation is too large to be represented. This can't occur for long integers (which would rather raise `MemoryError` than give up). Because of the lack of standardization of floating-point exception handling in C, most floating-point operations also aren't checked. For plain integers, all operations that can overflow are checked except left shift, where typical applications prefer to drop bits than raise an exception.

RuntimeError

Raised when an error is detected that doesn't fall in any of the other categories. The associated value is a string indicating what precisely went wrong. (This exception is mostly a relic from a previous version of the interpreter; it isn't used much any more.)

SyntaxError

Raised when the parser encounters a syntax error. This may occur in an `import` statement, in an `exec` statement, in a call to the built-in function `eval()` or `input()`, or when reading the initial script or standard input (also interactively).

When class exceptions are used, instances of this class have attributes `filename`, `lineno`, `offset`, and `text` for easier access to the details; for string exceptions, the associated value is usually a tuple of the form *(message, (filename, lineno, offset, text)*. For class exceptions, `str()` returns only the message.

SystemError

Raised when the interpreter finds an internal error, but the situation doesn't look so serious to cause it to abandon all hope. The associated value is a string indicating what went wrong (in low-level terms). You should report this to the author or maintainer of your Python interpreter. Be sure to report the version string of the Python interpreter (`sys.version`, also printed at the start of an interactive Python session), the exact error message (the exception's associated value), and, if possible, the source of the program that triggered the error.

SystemExit

Raised by the `sys.exit()` function. When it's not handled, the Python interpreter exits; no stack traceback is printed. If the associated value is a plain integer, it specifies the system exit status (passed to C's `exit()` function); if it's `None`, the exit status is zero; if it has another type (such as a string), the object's value is printed, and the exit status is one.

When class exceptions are used, the instance has an attribute code that is set to the proposed exit status or error message (defaulting to `None`). Also, this exception derives directly from `Exception` and not `StandardError`, since it isn't technically an error. A call to `sys.exit()` is translated into an exception so that clean-up handlers (finally clauses of `try` statements) can be executed, and so that a debugger can execute a script without running the risk of losing control. The `os._exit()` function can be used if it's absolutely necessary to exit immediately (e.g., after a `fork()` in the child process).

TypeError

> Raised when a built-in operation or function is applied to an object of inappropriate type. The associated value is a string giving details about the type mismatch.

ValueError

> Raised when a built-in operation or function receives an argument that has the right type but an inappropriate value, and the situation is not described by a more precise exception such as IndexError.

ZeroDivisionError

> Raised when the second argument of a division or modulo operation is zero. The associated value is a string indicating the type of the operands and the operation.

Built-in Functions

The Python interpreter has a number of built-in functions that are always available. They are listed here in alphabetical order:

__import__(*name[*, globals[, locals[, *fromlist]]]*)

> This function is invoked by the import statement. It exists so that you can replace it with another function that has a compatible interface, in order to change the semantics of the import statement. For examples of why and how you'd do this, see the standard library modules ihooks and rexec. See also the built-in module imp that defines some useful operations from which you can build your own __import__() function.

> For example, the statement import spam results in the call __import__ ('spam', globals(), locals(), []); the statement from spam.ham import eggs results in __import__('spam.ham', globals(), locals(),['eggs']). Even though locals() and ['eggs'] are passed in as arguments, the __import__() function doesn't set the local variable named eggs; this is done by subsequent code that's generated for the import statement. (In fact, the standard implementation doesn't use its locals argument at all, and uses its globals only to determine the package context of the import statement.)

> When the name variable is of the form *package.module*, normally, the top-level package (the name up to the first dot) is returned, not the module named by name. However, when a nonempty fromlist argument is given, the module named by name is returned. This is done for compatibility with the bytecode generated for the different kinds of import statement; when using import spam.ham.eggs, the top-level package spam must be placed in the importing namespace, but when using from spam.ham import eggs, the

`spam.ham` subpackage must find the `eggs` variable. As a workaround for this behavior, use `getattr()` to extract the desired components. For example, you could define the following helper:

```
import string
def my_import(name):
    mod = __import__(name)
    components = string.split(name, '.')
    for comp in components[1:]:
        mod = getattr(mod, comp)
    return mod
```

`abs(x)`

> Returns the absolute value of a number. The argument may be a plain or long integer or a floating-point number. If the argument is a complex number, its magnitude is returned.

`apply(function, args[, keywords])`

> The *function* argument must be a callable object (a user-defined or built-in function or method, or a class object), and the *args* argument must be a sequence (if it's not a tuple, the sequence is first converted to a tuple). The function is called with *args* as the argument list; the number of arguments is the length of the tuple. (This is different from just calling `func(args)`, since in that case, there's always exactly one argument.) If the optional *keywords* argument is present, it must be a dictionary whose keys are strings. It specifies keyword arguments to be added to the end of the argument list.

`buffer(object[, offset[, size]])`

> The *object* argument must be an object that supports the buffer call interface (such as strings, arrays, and buffers). A new buffer object is created that references the *object* argument; that buffer object is a slice from the beginning of *object* (or from the specified *offset*). The slice extends to the end of *object* (or has a length given by the *size* argument).

`callable(object)`

> Returns `true` if the *object* argument appears callable, `false` if not. If it returns `true`, it's still possible that a call fails, but if it's `false`, the calling object never succeeds. Note that classes are callable (calling a class returns a new instance); class instances are callable if they have a `__call__()` method.

`chr(i)`

> Returns a string of one character whose ASCII code is the integer *i*, e.g., `chr(97)` returns the string `a`. This is the inverse of `ord()`. The argument must be in the range [0...255], inclusive.

`cmp(x, y)`

> Compares the two objects *x* and *y* and returns an integer according to the outcome. The return value is negative if $x < y$, zero if $x == y$, and strictly positive if $x > y$.

`coerce(`*x, y*`)`

> Returns a tuple consisting of the two numeric arguments converted to a common type, using the same rules used by arithmetic operations.

`compile(`*string, filename, kind*`)`

> Compiles the *string* into a code object. Code objects can be executed by an **exec** statement or evaluated by a call to **eval()**. The *filename* argument should give the file from which the code was read; pass *string* if it wasn't read from a file. The *kind* argument specifies what kind of code must be compiled; it can be **exec** if *string* consists of a sequence of statements, **eval** if it consists of a single expression, or **single** if it consists of a single interactive statement (in the latter case, expression statements that evaluate to something other than **None** will print).

`complex(`*real [, imag]*`)`

> Creates a complex number with the value *real* + *imag**j or converts a string or number to a complex number. Each argument may be any numeric type (including complex). If *imag* is omitted, it defaults to zero, and the function serves as a numeric conversion function like **int()**, **long()**, and **float()**; in this case it also accepts a string argument that should be a valid complex number.

`delattr(`*object, name*`)`

> A relative of **setattr()**. The arguments are an *object* and a string. The string must be the *name* of one of the object's attributes. The function deletes the named attribute, provided the object allows it. For example, **delattr(x, 'foobar')** is equivalent to **del x.foobar**.

`dir(`*[object]*`)`

> Without arguments, returns the list of names in the current local symbol table. With an argument, attempts to return a list of valid attribute for that object. This information is gleaned from the object's **__dict__**, **__methods__**, and **__members__** attributes, if defined. The list is not necessarily complete; e.g., for classes, attributes defined in base classes aren't included, and for class instances, methods aren't included. The resulting list is sorted alphabetically. For example:

```
>>> import sys
>>> dir()
['sys']
>>> dir(sys)
['argv', 'exit', 'modules', 'path', 'stderr', 'stdin', 'stdout']
>>>
```

`divmod(`*a, b*`)`

> Takes two numbers as arguments and returns a pair of numbers consisting of their quotient and remainder when using long division. With mixed operand

types, the rules for binary arithmetic operators apply. For plain and long integers, the result is the same as (*a / b*, *a % b*). For floating-point numbers, the result is the same as (math.floor(*a / b*), *a % b*).

eval(*expression*[, globals[, locals]])

The arguments are a string and two optional dictionaries. The *expression* argument is parsed and evaluated as a Python expression (technically speaking, a condition list) using the globals and locals dictionaries as global and local namespace. If the locals dictionary is omitted, it defaults to the globals dictionary. If both dictionaries are omitted, the expression is executed in the environment where eval is called. The return value is the result of the evaluated expression. Syntax errors are reported as exceptions. Example:

```
>>> x = 1
>>> print eval('x+1')
2
```

This function can also execute arbitrary code objects (e.g., created by compile()). In this case, it passes a code object instead of a string. The code object must have been compiled passing eval to the kind argument.

Hints: dynamic execution of statements is supported by the **exec** statement. Execution of statements from a file is supported by the **execfile()** function. The globals() and locals() functions returns the current global and local dictionary, respectively, which may be useful to pass around for use by eval() or execfile().

execfile(*file*[, globals[, locals]])

Similar to the **exec** statement, but parses a file instead of a string. It's different from the import statement in that it doesn't use the module administration; it reads the file unconditionally and doesn't create a new module.[*]

The arguments are a filename and two optional dictionaries. The file is parsed and evaluated as a sequence of Python statements (similar to a module) using the globals and locals dictionaries as global and local namespace. If the locals dictionary is omitted, it defaults to the globals dictionary. If both dictionaries are omitted, the expression is executed in the environment where execfile() is called. The return value is None.

filter(*function, list*)

Constructs a list from those elements of *list* for which *function* returns true. If *list* is a string or a tuple, the result also has that type; otherwise it's always a list. If *function* is None, the identity function is assumed, i.e., all elements of *list* that are false (zero or empty) are removed.

---

[*] It's used relatively rarely so it doesn't warrant being made into a statement.

float(*x*)

> Converts a string or a number to floating point. If the argument is a string, it must contain a possibly signed decimal or floating-point number, possibly embedded in whitespace; this behaves identically to string.atof(*x*). Otherwise, the argument may be a plain or long integer or a floating-point number, and a floating-point number with the same value (within Python's floating-point precision) is returned.
>
> When passing in a string, values for NaN and Infinity may be returned, depending on the underlying C library. The specific set of strings accepted that cause these values to be returned depends entirely on the C library and is known to vary.

getattr(*object, name*)

> The arguments are an object and a string. The string must be the name of one of the object's attributes. The result is the value of that attribute. For example, getattr(*x, 'foobar'*) is equivalent to *x*.foobar.

globals()

> Returns a dictionary representing the current global symbol table. This is always the dictionary of the current module (inside a function or method, this is the module where it is defined, not the module from which it is called).

hasattr(*object, name*)

> The arguments are an object and a string. The result is 1 if the string is the name of one of the object's attributes, 0 if not. (This is implemented by calling getattr(*object, name*) and seeing whether it raises an exception.)

hash(*object*)

> Returns the hash value of the object (if it has one). Hash values are integers. They can quickly compare dictionary keys during a dictionary lookup. Numeric values that compare equal have the same hash value (even if they are of different types, e.g., 1 and 1.0).

hex(*x*)

> Converts an integer number (of any size) to a hexadecimal string. The result is a valid Python expression. This always yields an unsigned literal, e.g., on a 32-bit machine, hex(-1) yields '0xffffffff'. When evaluated on a machine with the same word size, this literal is evaluated as –1; at a different word size, it may be a large positive number or raise an OverflowError exception.

id(*object*)

> Returns the identity of an object. This is an integer that's guaranteed to be unique and constant for this object during its lifetime. Two objects whose lifetimes don't overlap may have the same id() value. (Implementation note: this is the address of the object.)

`input([prompt])`

    Equivalent to `eval(raw_input(prompt))`.

`intern(string)`

    Enters *string* in the table of interned strings and returns the interned string, which is *string* itself or a copy. Interning strings is useful to gain a little performance on dictionary lookup; if the keys in a dictionary are interned, and the lookup key is interned, the key comparisons (after hashing) can be done by a pointer compare instead of a string compare. Normally, the names used in Python programs are automatically interned, and the dictionaries that hold module, class, or instance attributes have interned keys. Interned strings are immortal (i.e., never get garbage-collected).

`int(x)`

    Converts a string or number to a plain integer. If the argument is a string, it must contain a possibly signed decimal number representable as a Python integer, possibly embedded in whitespace; this behaves identically to `string.atoi(x)`. Otherwise, the argument may be a plain or long integer or a floating-point number. Conversion of floating-point numbers to integers is defined by the C semantics; normally the conversion truncates towards zero.[*]

`isinstance(object, class)`

    Returns `true` if the *object* argument is an instance of the *class* argument or of a (direct or indirect) subclass thereof. Also returns `true` if *class* is a type object and *object* is an object of that type. If *object* is not a class instance or an object of the given type, the function always returns `false`. If *class* is neither a class object nor a type object, a `TypeError` exception is raised.

`issubclass(class1, class2)`

    Returns `true` if *class1* is a subclass (direct or indirect) of *class2*. A class is considered a subclass of itself. If either argument isn't a class object, a `TypeError` exception is raised.

`len(s)`

    Returns the length (the number of items) of an object. The argument may be a sequence (string, tuple, or list) or a mapping (dictionary).

`list(sequence)`

    Returns a list whose items are the same and in the same order as *sequence*'s items. If *sequence* is already a list, a copy is made and returned, similar to *sequence*`[:]`. For instance, `list('abc')` returns `['a', 'b', 'c']`, and `list( (1, 2, 3) )` returns `[1, 2, 3]`.

---

[*] This is ugly: the language definition should require truncation towards zero.

`locals()`

Returns a dictionary representing the current local symbol table. Warning: the contents of this dictionary should not be modified; changes may not affect the values of local variables used by the interpreter.

`long(x)`

Converts a string or number to a long integer. If the argument is a string, it must contain a possibly signed decimal number of arbitrary size, possibly embedded in whitespace; this behaves identically to `string.atol(x)`. Otherwise, the argument may be a plain or long integer or a floating-point number, and a long integer with the same value is returned. Conversion of floating-point numbers to integers is defined by the C semantics; see the description of `int()`.

`map(function, list, ...)`

Applies *function* to every item of *list* and returns a list of the results. If additional list arguments are passed, *function* must take that many arguments and is applied to the items of all lists in parallel; if a list is shorter than another, it's assumed to be extended with None items. If *function* is None, the identity function is assumed; if there are multiple *list* arguments, `map()` returns a list consisting of tuples containing the corresponding items from all lists (i.e., a kind of transpose operation). The list arguments may be any kind of sequence; the result is always a list.

`max(s[, args...])`

With a single argument *s*, returns the largest item of a nonempty sequence (e.g., a string, tuple, or list). With more than one argument, returns the largest of the arguments.

`min(s[, args...])`

With a single argument *s*, returns the smallest item of a nonempty sequence (e.g., a string, tuple, or list). With more than one argument, returns the smallest of the arguments.

`oct(x)`

Converts an integer number (of any size) to an octal string. The result is a valid Python expression. This always yields an unsigned literal, e.g., on a 32-bit machine, `oct(-1)` yields `'037777777777'`. When evaluated on a machine with the same word size, this literal is evaluated as –1; at a different word size, it may be a large positive number or raise an `OverflowError` exception.

`open(filename[, mode[, bufsize]])`

Returns a new file object (described earlier in the section "Built-in Types"). The first two arguments are the same as for stdio's `fopen()`: *filename* is the filename to be opened, *mode* indicates how the file is to be opened: `'r'` for reading, `'w'` for writing (truncating an existing file), and `'a'` opens it for appending (which on some Unix systems means that all writes append to the end of the file, regardless of the current seek position).

Modes `'r+'`, `'w+'`, and `'a+'` open the file for updating (note that `'w+'` truncates the file). Append `'b'` to the mode to open the file in binary mode, on systems that differentiate between binary and text files (else it is ignored). If the file can't be opened, `IOError` is raised.

If *mode* is omitted, it defaults to `'r'`. When opening a binary file, you should append `'b'` to the mode value for improved portability. (It's useful even on systems that don't treat binary and text files differently, where it serves as documentation.) The optional *bufsize* argument specifies the file's desired buffer size: 0 means unbuffered, 1 means line buffered, any other positive value means use a buffer of (approximately) that size. A negative *bufsize* means to use the system default, which is usually line buffered for tty devices and fully buffered for other files. If omitted, the system default is used.*

`ord(c)`

Returns the ASCII value of a string of one character. For example, `ord('a')` returns the integer 97. This is the inverse of `chr()`.

`pow(x, y[, z])`

Returns `x` to the power `y`; if `z` is present, return `x` to the power `y`, modulo `z` (computed more efficiently than `pow(x, y) % z`). The arguments must have numeric types. With mixed operand types, the rules for binary arithmetic operators apply. The effective operand type is also the type of the result; if the result isn't expressible in this type, the function raises an exception; e.g., `pow(2, -1)` or `pow(2, 35000)` isn't allowed.

`range([start,] stop[, step])`

This is a versatile function to create lists containing arithmetic progressions. It is most often used in `for` loops. The arguments must be plain integers. If the *step* argument is omitted, it defaults to 1. If the *start* argument is omitted, it defaults to 0. The full form returns a list of plain integers [*start, start + step, start + 2 * step, ...*]. If *step* is positive, the last element is the largest *start + i * step* less than *stop*; if *step* is negative, the last element is the largest *start + i * step* greater than *stop*. *step* must not be zero (or else `ValueError` is raised). Here's an example:

```
>>> range(10)
[0, 1, 2, 3, 4, 5, 6, 7, 8, 9]
>>> range(1, 11)
```

---

* Specifying a buffer size currently has no effect on systems that don't have `setvbuf()`. The interface to specify the buffer size is not done using a method that calls `setvbuf()`, because that may dump core when called after any I/O has been performed, and there's no reliable way to determine whether this is the case.

```
[1, 2, 3, 4, 5, 6, 7, 8, 9, 10]
>>> range(0, 30, 5)
[0, 5, 10, 15, 20, 25]
>>> range(0, 10, 3)
[0, 3, 6, 9]
>>> range(0, -10, -1)
[0, -1, -2, -3, -4, -5, -6, -7, -8, -9]
>>> range(0)
[]
>>> range(1, 0)
[]
>>>
```

raw_input([prompt])

If the *prompt* argument is present, it's written to standard output without a trailing newline. The function then reads a line from input, converts it to a string (stripping a trailing newline), and returns that. When EOF is read, **EOFError** is raised. Here's an example:

```
>>> s = raw_input('--> ')
--> Monty Python's Flying Circus
>>> s
"Monty Python's Flying Circus"
>>>
```

If the **readline** module was loaded, then **raw_input()** uses it to provide elaborate line-editing and history features.

reduce(function, sequence[, initializer])

Applies *function* of two arguments cumulatively to the items of *sequence*, from left to right, so as to reduce the sequence to a single value. For example, **reduce(lambda x, y: x+y, [1, 2, 3, 4, 5])** calculates ((((1+2)+3)+4)+5). If the optional *initializer* is present, it's placed before the items of the sequence in the calculation and serves as a default when the sequence is empty.

reload(module)

Reparses and reinitializes an already imported *module*. The argument must be a module object, so it must have been successfully imported before. This is useful if you have edited the module source file using an external editor and want to try out the new version without leaving the Python interpreter. The return value is the module object (i.e., the same as the **module** argument). There are a number of caveats:

— If a module is syntactically correct but its initialization fails, the first **import** statement for it doesn't bind its name locally, but does store a (partially initialized) module object in **sys.modules**. To reload the module you must first import it again (this binds the name to the partially initialized module object) before you can **reload()** it.

— When a module is reloaded, its dictionary (containing the module's global variables) is retained. Redefinitions of names override the old definitions, so this is generally not a problem. If the new version of a module doesn't define a name that was defined by the old version, the old definition remains. This feature can be used to the module's advantage if it maintains a global table or cache of objects; with a `try` statement it can test for the table's presence and skip its initialization if desired.

— It is legal though generally not useful to reload built-in or dynamically loaded modules, except for `sys`, `__main__`, and `__builtin__`. In certain cases, however, extension modules aren't designed to be initialized more than once, and may fail in arbitrary ways when reloaded.

— If a module imports objects from another module using `from ... import ...`, calling `reload()` for the other module doesn't redefine the objects imported from it; one way around this is to reexecute the `from` statement, another is to use `import` and qualified names (*module.name*) instead.

— If a module instantiates instances of a class, reloading the module that defines the class doesn't affect the method definitions of the instances; they continue to use the old class definition. The same is true for derived classes.

`repr(`*object*`)`

Returns a string containing a printable representation of an object. This is the same value yielded by conversions (reverse quotes). It's sometimes useful to be able to access this operation as an ordinary function. For many types, this function makes an attempt to return a string that would yield an object with the same value when passed to `eval()`.

`round(`*x[, n]*`)`

Returns the floating-point value *x* rounded to *n* digits after the decimal point. If *n* is omitted, it defaults to zero. The result is a floating-point number. Values are rounded to the closest multiple of 10 to the power minus *n*; if two multiples are equally close, rounding is done away from 0 (e.g., `round(0.5)` is 1.0 and `round(-0.5)` is -1.0).

`setattr(`*object*, *name*, *value*`)`

The counterpart of `getattr()`. The arguments are an object, a string, and an arbitrary value. The string may name an existing attribute or a new attribute. The function assigns the value to the attribute, provided the object allows it. For example, `setattr(x, 'foobar', 123)` is equivalent to `x.foobar = 123`.

`slice(`*[start,] stop[, step]*`)`

Returns a slice object representing the set of indexes specified by `range(`*start, stop, step*`)`. The *start* and *step* arguments default to `None`. Slice objects have read-only data attributes *start*, *stop*, and *step*, which merely return the argument values (or their default). They have no other explicit functionality; however, they are used by Numerical Python and other third-party extensions. Slice objects are also generated when extended indexing syntax is used, e.g., for a[start:stop:step] or a[start:stop, i].

str(*object*)

Returns a string containing a nicely printable representation of an object. For strings, this returns the string itself. The difference with repr(*object*) is that str(*object*) doesn't always attempt to return a string that is acceptable to eval(); its goal is to return a printable string.

tuple(*sequence*)

Returns a tuple whose items are the same and in the same order as *sequence*'s items. If *sequence* is already a tuple, it's returned unchanged. For instance, tuple('abc') returns ('a', 'b', 'c'), and tuple([1, 2, 3]) returns (1, 2, 3).

type(*object*)

Returns the type of an object. The return value is a type object. The standard module types defines names for all built-in types. For instance:

```
>>> import types
>>> if type(x) == types.StringType: print "It's a string"
>>>
```

vars([*object*])

Without arguments, returns a dictionary corresponding to the current local symbol table. With a module, class, or class instance object as argument (or anything else that has a __dict__ attribute), returns a dictionary corresponding to the object's symbol table. The returned dictionary should not be modified: the effects on the corresponding symbol table are undefined.*

xrange([*start*,] *stop*[, *step*])

Similar to range(), but returns an xrange object instead of a list. This is an opaque sequence type that yields the same values as the corresponding list, without actually storing them all simultaneously. The advantage of xrange() over range() is minimal (since xrange() still has to create the values when asked for them) except when a large range is used on a memory-starved machine (e.g., MS-DOS) or when all of the range's elements are never used (e.g., when the loop is usually terminated with break).

---

* In the current implementation, local variable bindings can't normally be affected this way, but variables retrieved from other scopes (e.g., modules) can. This may change.

module sys: System-Specific Parameters and Functions

This module is always available and provides access to some variables used or maintained by the interpreter and to functions that interact strongly with the interpreter.

argv

The list of command-line arguments passed to a Python script. `argv[0]` is the script name (it's operating system-dependent, whether this is a full pathname or not). If the command is executed using the `-c` command-line option to the interpreter, `argv[0]` is set to the string `-c`. If no script name is passed to the Python interpreter, `argv` has zero length.

builtin_module_names

A tuple of strings giving the names of all modules that are compiled into this Python interpreter. (This information isn't available in any other way: `modules.keys()` lists only the imported modules.)

copyright

A string containing the copyright pertaining to the Python interpreter.

exc_info()

Returns a tuple of three values that give information about the exception that's currently being handled. The information returned is specific both to the current thread and to the current stack frame. If the current stack frame is not handling an exception, the information is taken from the calling stack frame, or its caller, and so on until a stack frame is found that is handling an exception. Here, handling an exception is defined as executing or having executed an except clause. For any stack frame, only information about the most recently handled exception is accessible.

If no exception is being handled anywhere on the stack, a tuple containing three **None** values is returned. Otherwise, the values returned are (*type, value, traceback*). Their meaning is: *type* gets the exception type of the exception being handled (a string or class object); *value* gets the exception parameter (its associated value or the second argument to raise, which is always a class instance if the exception type is a class object); *traceback* gets a traceback object (see the reference manual) that encapsulates the call stack at the point where the exception originally occurred.

Note that assigning the *traceback* return value to a local variable in a function that is handling an exception causes a circular reference. This prevents anything referenced by a local variable in the same function or by the traceback from being garbage-collected. Since most functions don't need access to the traceback, the best solution is to use something like `type, value = sys.exc_info()[:2]` to extract only the exception type and value. If you do need the traceback, make sure to delete it after use (best done with a `try ... finally` statement) or to call `exc_info()` in a function that doesn't itself handle an exception.

`exc_type, exc_value, exc_traceback`

Deprecated since Release 1.5. Use `exc_info()` instead. Since they are global variables, they aren't specific to the current thread, and their use is not safe in a multithreaded program. When no exception is being handled, `exc_type` is set to `None`, and the other two are undefined.

`exec_prefix`

A string giving the site-specific directory prefix where the platform-dependent Python files are installed; by default, this is also */usr/local*. This can be set at build time with the `--exec-prefix` argument to the configure script. Specifically, all configuration files (e.g., the *config.h* header file) are installed in the directory `exec_prefix + '/lib/pythonversion/config'`, and shared library modules are installed in `exec_prefix + '/lib/pythonversion/lib-dynload'`, where version is equal to *version*`[:3]`.

`executable`

A string giving the name of the executable binary for the Python interpreter, on systems that support it.

`exit([arg])`

Exits from Python. This is implemented by raising the `SystemExit` exception, so cleanup actions specified by `finally` clauses of `try` statements are honored, and it's possible to intercept the exit attempt at an outer level. The optional argument *arg* can be an integer giving the exit status (defaulting to zero) or another type of object. If it's an integer, zero is considered successful termination, and any nonzero value is considered abnormal termination by shells and the like. Most systems require it to be in the range 0–127 and produce undefined results otherwise. Some systems have a convention for assigning specific meanings to specific exit codes, but these are generally underdeveloped; Unix programs generally use 2 for command-line syntax errors and 1 for all other kind of errors. If another type of object is passed, `None` is equivalent to passing zero, and any other object is printed to `sys.stderr` and results in an exit code of 1. In particular, `sys.exit("`*some error message*`")` is a quick way to exit a program when an error occurs.

`exitfunc`

This value is not actually defined by the module but can be set by the user (or by a program) to specify a cleanup action at program exit. When set, it should be a parameterless function. This function is called when the interpreter exits.

The `exit` function is not called when the program is killed by a signal, when a Python fatal internal error is detected, or when `os._exit()` is called.

`getrefcount(object)`

Returns the reference count of the object. The count returned is generally one higher than you might expect, because it includes the (temporary) reference as an argument to `getrefcount()`.

`last_type`, `last_value`, `last_traceback`

These three variables aren't always defined; they are set when an exception is not handled, and the interpreter prints an error message and a stack traceback. Their intended use is to allow an interactive user to import a debugger module and engage in postmortem debugging without having to reexecute the command that caused the error. (Typical use is `import pdb; pdb.pm()` to enter the postmortem debugger.)

The meaning of the variables is the same as that of the return values from `exc_info()`, as seen in the previous entry. (Since there is only one interactive thread, thread-safety is not a concern for these variables, unlike for `exc_type`, etc.)

`maxint`

The largest positive integer supported by Python's regular integer type. This is at least $2^{31}-1$. The largest negative integer is `-maxint-1`: the asymmetry results from the use of 2's complement binary arithmetic.

`modules`

A dictionary that maps module names to modules that have already been loaded. This can be manipulated to force reloading of modules and other tricks. Removing a module from this dictionary is not the same as calling `reload()` on the corresponding module object.

`path`

A list of strings that specifies the search path for modules. Initialized from the environment variable \$PYTHONPATH or an installation-dependent default.

The first item of this list, `path[0]`, is the directory containing the script that invoked the Python interpreter. If the script directory isn't available (e.g., if the interpreter is invoked interactively or if the script is read from standard input), `path[0]` is the empty string, which directs Python to search modules in the current directory first. Notice that the script directory is inserted before the entries inserted as a result of \$PYTHONPATH.

`platform`

Contains a platform identifier, e.g., `sunos5` or `linux1`. This can append platform-specific components to `path`, for instance.

prefix

A string giving the site-specific directory prefix where the platform-independent Python files are installed; by default, this is the string */usr/local.* This can be set at build time with the `--prefix` argument to the configure script. The main collection of Python library modules is installed in the directory `prefix + '/lib/pythonversion'` while the platform-independent header files (all except *config.h*) are stored in `prefix + '/include/pythonversion'`, where version is equal to *version*`[:3]`.

ps1, ps2

Strings specifying the primary and secondary prompt of the interpreter. These are defined only if the interpreter is in interactive mode. Their initial values in this case are `>>>` and `...` . If a nonstring object is assigned to either variable, its `str()` is reevaluated each time the interpreter prepares to read a new interactive command; this can implement a dynamic prompt.

setcheckinterval(*interval*)

Sets the interpreter's check interval. This integer value determines how often the interpreter checks for periodic things such as thread switches and signal handlers. The default is 10, meaning the check is performed every 10 Python virtual instructions. Setting it to a larger value may increase performance for programs using threads. Setting it to a value `<= 0` checks every virtual instruction, maximizing responsiveness as well as overhead.

setprofile(*profilefunc*)

Sets the system's `profile` function, which allows you to implement a Python source code profiler in Python. The system's `profile` function is called similarly to the system's `trace` function (see `settrace()`), but it isn't called for each executed line of code (only on call and return and when an exception occurs). Also, its return value isn't used, so it can just return None.

settrace(*tracefunc*)

Sets the system's `trace` function, which allows you to implement a Python source code debugger in Python.

stdin, stdout, stderr

File objects corresponding to the interpreter's standard input, output, and error streams. `stdin` is used for all interpreter input except for scripts but including calls to `input()` and `raw_input()`. `stdout` is used for the output of `print` and `expression` statements and for the prompts of `input()` and `raw_input()`. The interpreter's own prompts and (almost all of) its error messages go to `stderr`. `stdout` and `stderr` needn't be built-in file objects: any object is acceptable as long as it has a `write()` method that takes a string argument. (Changing these objects doesn't affect the standard I/O streams of processes executed by `os.popen()`, `os.system()`, or the `exec*()` family of functions in the `os` module.)

__stdin__, __stdout__, __stderr__
> Contain the original values of stdin, stderr, and stdout at the start of the program. They are used during finalization and can restore the actual files to known working file objects in case they have been overwritten with a broken object.

tracebacklimit
> When this variable is set to an integer value, it determines the maximum number of levels of traceback information printed when an unhandled exception occurs. The default is 1000. When set to 0 or less, all traceback information is suppressed, and only the exception type and value are printed.

version
> A string containing the version number of the Python interpreter.

module string: Common String Operations

This module defines some constants that can check character classes, and some useful string functions. See the module re for string functions based on regular expressions. The constants defined in this module are:

digits
> The string '0123456789'.

hexdigits
> The string '0123456789abcdefABCDEF'.

letters
> The concatenation of the strings lowercase() and uppercase() (check their entries in this list).

lowercase
> A string containing all characters considered lowercase letters. On most systems this is the string 'abcdefghijklmnopqrstuvwxyz'. Don't change its definition: the effect on the routines upper() and swapcase() is undefined.

octdigits
> The string '01234567'.

uppercase
> A string containing all characters considered uppercase letters. On most systems this is the string 'ABCDEFGHIJKLMNOPQRSTUVWXYZ'. Don't change its definition: the effect on the routines lower() and swapcase() is undefined.

whitespace
> A string containing all characters that are considered whitespace. On most systems this includes the characters space, tab, linefeed, return, formfeed, and

vertical tab. Don't change its definition: the effect on the routines `strip()` and `split()` is undefined.

The functions defined in this module are:

`atof(s)`

> Converts a string to a floating-point number. The string must have the standard syntax for a floating-point literal in Python, optionally preceded by a sign (+ or -). Note that this behaves identically to the built-in function `float()` when passed a string.
>
> When passing in a string, values for `NaN` and `Infinity` may be returned, depending on the underlying C library. The specific set of strings accepted that cause these values to be returned depends entirely on the C library and is known to vary.

`atoi(s[, base])`

> Converts string *s* to an integer in the given *base*. The string must consist of one or more digits, optionally preceded by a sign (+ or -). The *base* defaults to 10. If it's 0, a default base is chosen depending on the leading characters of the string (after stripping the sign): 0x or 0X means 16, 0 means 8, anything else means 10. If base is 16, a leading 0x or 0X is always accepted. When invoked without base or with base set to 10, this behaves identically to the built-in function `int()` when passed a string. (Also note: for a more flexible interpretation of numeric literals, use the built-in function `eval()`.)

`atol(s[, base])`

> Converts string *s* to a long integer in the given *base*. The string must consist of one or more digits, optionally preceded by a sign (+ or -). The *base* argument has the same meaning as for `atoi()`. A trailing 1 or L isn't allowed, except if the base is 0. When invoked without base or with base set to 10, this behaves identically to the built-in function `long()` when passed a string.

`capitalize(word)`

> Capitalizes the first character of the argument.

`capwords(s)`

> Splits the argument into words using `split()`, capitalizes each word using `capitalize()`, and joins the capitalized words using `join()`. This replaces runs of whitespace characters by a single space and removes leading and trailing whitespace.

`expandtabs(s, [tabsize])`

> Expands tabs in a string, i.e., replaces them by one or more spaces, depending on the current column and the given tab size. The column number is reset to zero after each newline occurring in the string. This doesn't understand other nonprinting characters or escape sequences. The tab size defaults to 8.

`find(s, sub[, start[, end]])`

>   Returns the lowest index in *s* where the substring *sub* is found such that *sub* is wholly contained in *s[start:end]*. Returns −1 on failure. Defaults for *start* and *end*, and interpretation of negative values is the same as for slices.

`rfind(s, sub[, start[, end]])`

>   Like `find()` but finds the highest index.

`index(s, sub[, start[, end]])`

>   Like `find()` but raises `ValueError` when the substring isn't found.

`rindex(s, sub[, start[, end]])`

>   Like `rfind()` but raises `ValueError` when the substring isn't found.

`count(s, sub[, start[, end]])`

>   Returns the number of (nonoverlapping) occurrences of substring *sub* in string *s[start:end]*. Defaults for *start* and *end*, and interpretation of negative values is the same as for slices.

`lower(s)`

>   Returns a copy of *s*, but with uppercase letters converted to lowercase.

`maketrans(from, to)`

>   Returns a translation table suitable for passing to `translate()` or `regex.compile()` that maps each character in *from* into the character at the same position in *to*; *from* and *to* must have the same length.

>   Don't use strings derived from `lowercase` and `uppercase` as arguments; in some locales, these don't have the same length. For case conversions, always use `lower()` and `upper()`.

`split(s[, sep[, maxsplit]])`

>   Returns a list of the words of the string *s*. If the optional second argument *sep* is absent or `None`, the words are separated by arbitrary strings of whitespace characters (space, tab, newline, return, formfeed). If the second argument *sep* is present and not `None`, it specifies a string to be used as the word separator. The returned list then has one more item than the number of nonoverlapping occurrences of the separator in the string. The optional third argument *maxsplit* defaults to 0. If it's nonzero, at most *maxsplit* number of splits occur, and the remainder of the string is returned as the final element of the list (thus, the list has at most *maxsplit*+1 elements).

`splitfields(s[, sep[, maxsplit]])`

>   This function behaves identically to `split()`. In the past, `split()` was used with only one argument; `splitfields()` was used with two.

`join(words[, sep])`

>   Concatenates a list or tuple of words with intervening occurrences of *sep*. The default value for *sep* is a single space character. It's always true that `string.join(string.split(s, sep), sep)` equals *s*.

`joinfields(words[, sep])`

> This function behaves identically to `join()`. In the past, `join()` was used with only one argument, while `joinfields()` was used with two arguments.

`lstrip(s)`

> Returns a copy of *s* but without leading whitespace characters.

`rstrip(s)`

> Returns a copy of *s* but without trailing whitespace characters.

`strip(s)`

> Returns a copy of *s* without leading or trailing whitespace.

`swapcase(s)`

> Returns a copy of *s*, but with lowercase letters converted to uppercase and vice versa.

`translate(s, table[, deletechars])`

> Deletes all characters from *s* that are in *deletechars* (if present) and then translates the characters using *table*, which must be a 256-character string giving the translation for each character value, indexed by its ordinal.

`upper(s)`

> Returns a copy of *s*, but with lowercase letters converted to uppercase.

`ljust(s, width)`, `rjust(s, width)`, `center(s, width)`

> Respectively left justifies, right justifies, and centers a string in a field of given width. They return a string that is at least *width* characters wide, created by padding the string *s* with spaces until the given width on the right, left, or both sides. The string is never truncated.

`zfill(s, width)`

> Pads a numeric string on the left with zero digits until the given width is reached. Strings starting with a sign are handled correctly.

`replace(str, old, new[, maxsplit])`

> Returns a copy of string *str* with all occurrences of substring *old* replaced by *new*. If the optional argument *maxsplit* is given, the first *maxsplit* occurrences are replaced.

This module is implemented in Python. Much of its functionality has been reimplemented in the built-in module **strop**. However, you should never import the latter module directly. When **string** discovers that **strop** exists, it transparently replaces parts of itself with the implementation from **strop**. After initialization, there is no overhead in using **string** instead of **strop**.

module os: Miscellaneous OS Interfaces

This module provides a more portable way to use operating system-dependent functionality than importing an OS-dependent built-in module such as `posix` or `nt`.

This module searches for an OS-dependent built-in module such as `mac` or `posix` and exports the same functions and data as found there. The design of all Python's built-in OS dependent modules is such that as long as the same functionality is available, it uses the same interface; e.g., the function `os.stat(`*path*`)` returns *stat* information about `path` in the same format (which happens to have originated with the POSIX interface).

Extensions peculiar to a particular OS are also available through the `os` module, but using them is, of course, a threat to portability.

After `os` is imported for the first time, there's no performance penalty in using functions from `os` instead of directly from the OS-dependent built-in module, so there should be no reason not to use `os`.

error

> Raised when a function returns a system-related error (e.g., not for illegal argument types). This is also known as the built-in exception `OSError`. The accompanying value is a pair containing the numeric error code from `errno` and the corresponding string, as would be printed by the C function `perror()`. See the `errno` module, which contains names for the error codes defined by the underlying operating system.
>
> When exceptions are classes, this exception carries two attributes, `errno` and `strerror`. The first holds the value of the C `errno` variable, and the latter holds the corresponding error message from `strerror()`. For exceptions that involve a filesystem path (e.g., `chdir()` or `unlink()`), the exception instance contains a third attribute, `filename`, which is the filename passed to the function.
>
> When exceptions are strings, the string for the exception is `'OSError'`.

name

> The name of the OS-dependent module imported. The following names have currently been registered: `'posix'`, `'nt'`, `'dos'`, `'mac'`, `'os2'`.

path

> The corresponding OS-dependent standard module for pathname operations, e.g., `posixpath` or `macpath`. Thus, given the proper imports, `os.path.split(`*file*`)` is equivalent to but more portable than `posixpath.split(`*file*`)`. This is also a valid module: it may be imported directly as `os.path`.

Process Parameters

These functions and data items provide information and operate on the current process and user:

chdir(*path*)

> Changes the current working directory to *path*. Availability: Macintosh, Unix, Windows.

environ

> A mapping representing the string environment. For example, environ['HOME'] is the pathname of your home directory, equivalent to getenv("HOME") in C.

> If the platform supports the putenv() function, this mapping can modify the environment as well as query the environment. putenv() is called automatically when the mapping is modified.

> If putenv() isn't provided, this mapping can be passed to the appropriate process-creation functions to cause child processes to use a modified environment.

getcwd()

> Returns a string representing the current working directory. Availability: Macintosh, Unix, Windows.

getegid()

> Returns the current process's effective group ID. Availability: Unix.

geteuid()

> Returns the current process's effective user ID. Availability: Unix.

getgid()

> Returns the current process's group ID. Availability: Unix.

getpgrp()

> Returns the current process's group ID. Availability: Unix.

getpid()

> Returns the current process ID. Availability: Unix, Windows.

getppid()

> Returns the parent's process ID. Availability: Unix.

getuid()

> Returns the current process's user ID. Availability: Unix.

putenv(*varname, value*)

> Sets the environment variable, *varname*, to the string value. Such changes to the environment affect subprocesses started with os.system(), popen(), or fork() and execv(). Availability: most flavors of Unix, Windows.

When `putenv()` is supported, assignments to items in `os.environ` are automatically translated into corresponding calls to `putenv()`; however, calls to `putenv()` don't update `os.environ`, so it's actually preferable to assign to items of `os.environ`.

`setgid(gid)`

Sets the current process's group ID. Availability: Unix.

`setpgrp()`

Calls the system call `setpgrp()` or `setpgrp(0, 0)` depending on which version is implemented (if any). See the Unix manual for the semantics. Availability: Unix.

`setpgid(pid, pgrp)`

Calls the system call `setpgid()`. See the Unix manual for the semantics. Availability: Unix.

`setsid()`

Calls the system call `setsid()`. See the Unix manual for the semantics. Availability: Unix.

`setuid(uid)`

Sets the current process's user ID. Availability: Unix.

`strerror(code)`

Returns the error message corresponding to the error code in code. Availability: Unix, Windows.

`umask(mask)`

Sets the current numeric *umask* and returns the previous *umask*. Availability: Unix, Windows.

`uname()`

Returns a five-tuple containing information identifying the current operating system. The tuple contains five strings: *(sysname, nodename, release, version, machine)*. Some systems truncate the *nodename* to eight characters or to the leading component; a better way to get the hostname is `socket.gethostname()` or even `socket.gethostbyaddr(socket.gethostname())`. Availability: recent flavors of Unix.

File Object Creation

These functions create new file objects:

`fdopen(fd[, mode[, bufsize]])`

Returns an open file object connected to the file descriptor *fd*. The *mode* and *bufsize* arguments have the same meaning as the corresponding arguments to the built-in `open()` function. Availability: Macintosh, Unix, Windows.

popen(*command*[, *mode*[, *bufsize*]])

Opens a pipe to or from *command*. The return value is an open file object connected to the pipe, which can be read or written depending on whether mode is r (default) or w. The *bufsize* argument has the same meaning as the corresponding argument to the built-in open() function. The exit status of the command (encoded in the format specified for wait()) is available as the return value of the close() method of the file object, except that when the exit status is zero (termination without errors), None is returned. Availability: Unix, Windows.

File Descriptor Operations

These functions operate on I/O streams referred to with file descriptors:

close(*fd*)

Closes file descriptor *fd*. Availability: Macintosh, Unix, Windows.

This function is intended for low-level I/O and must be applied to a file descriptor as returned by open() or pipe(). To close a file object returned by the built-in function open(), by popen(), or fdopen(), use its close() method.

dup(*fd*)

Returns a duplicate of file descriptor *fd*. Availability: Macintosh, Unix, Windows.

dup2(*fd*, *fd2*)

Duplicates file descriptor *fd* to *fd2*, closing the latter first if necessary. Availability: Unix, Windows.

fstat(*fd*)

Returns status for file descriptor *fd*, like *stat()*. Availability: Unix, Windows.

fstatvfs(*fd*)

Returns information about the filesystem containing the file associated with file descriptor *fd*, like statvfs(). Availability: Unix.

ftruncate(*fd*, *length*)

Truncates the file corresponding to file descriptor *fd*, so that it is *length* bytes in size. Availability: Unix.

lseek(*fd*, *pos*, *how*)

Sets the current position of file descriptor *fd* to position *pos*, modified by *how*: 0 to set the position relative to the beginning of the file; 1 to set it relative to the current position; and 2 to set it relative to the end of the file. Availability: Macintosh, Unix, Windows.

`open(file, flags[, mode])`

Opens the file *file* and sets various flags according to *flags* and, possibly, its mode according to *mode*. The default mode is 0777 (octal), and the current umask value is first masked out. Returns the file descriptor for the newly opened file. Availability: Macintosh, Unix, Windows.

For a description of the *flag* and *mode* values, see the C runtime documentation; flag constants (such as O_RDONLY and O_WRONLY) are also defined in this module (see later in this section).

This function is intended for low-level I/O. Normally, you should use the built-in function `open()`, which returns a file object with `read()` and `write()` methods (and many more).

`pipe()`

Creates a pipe. Returns a pair of file descriptors (*r, w*) usable for reading and writing, respectively. Availability: Unix, Windows.

`read(fd, n)`

Reads at most *n* bytes from file descriptor *fd*. Returns a string containing the bytes read. Availability: Macintosh, Unix, Windows.

This function is intended for low-level I/O and must be applied to a file descriptor as returned by `open()` or `pipe()`. To read a file object returned by the built-in function `open()` or by `popen()`, `fdopen()`, or `sys.stdin`, use its `read()` or `readline()` methods.

`tcgetpgrp(fd)`

Returns the process group associated with the terminal given by *fd* (an open file descriptor as returned by *open()*). Availability: Unix.

`tcsetpgrp(fd, pg)`

Sets the process group associated with the terminal given by *fd* (an open file descriptor as returned by `open()`) to *pg*. Availability: Unix.

`ttyname(fd)`

Returns a string that specifies the terminal device associated with file-descriptor *fd*. If *fd* isn't associated with a terminal device, an exception is raised. Availability: Unix.

`write(fd, str)`

Writes the string *str* to file descriptor *fd*. Returns the number of bytes actually written. Availability: Macintosh, Unix, Windows.

This function is intended for low-level I/O and must be applied to a file descriptor as returned by `open()` or `pipe()`. To write a file object returned by the built-in function `open()` or by `popen()`, `fdopen()`, `sys.stdout`, or `sys.stderr`, use its `write()` method.

The following data items are available for constructing the flags parameter to the open() function:

O_RDONLY

O_WRONLY

O_RDWR

O_NDELAY

O_NONBLOCK

O_APPEND

O_DSYNC

O_RSYNC

O_SYNC

O_NOCTTY

O_CREAT

O_EXCL

O_TRUNC

These can be bitwise OR'd together. Availability: Macintosh, Unix, Windows.

Files and Directories

These functions operate on files and directories.

access *(path, mode)*

Checks read/write/execute permissions for this process or file *path*. Returns 1 if access is granted, 0 if not. See the Unix manual for the semantics. Availability: Unix.

chmod *(path, mode)*

Changes the mode of *path* to the numeric mode. Availability: Unix, Windows.

chown *(path, uid, gid)*

Changes the owner and group ID of *path* to the numeric *uid* and *gid*. Availability: Unix.

link *(src, dst)*

Creates a hard link pointing to *src* named *dst*. Availability: Unix.

listdir *(path)*

Returns a list containing the names of the entries in the directory. The list is in arbitrary order. It doesn't include the special entries "." and ".." even if they are present in the directory. Availability: Macintosh, Unix, Windows.

lstat *(path)*

Like stat(), but doesn't follow symbolic links. Availability: Unix.

mkfifo*(path[, mode])*

Creates a FIFO (a named pipe) named *path* with numeric mode *mode*. The default mode is 0666 (octal). The current umask value is first masked out from the mode. Availability: Unix.

FIFOs are pipes that can be accessed like regular files. FIFOs exist until they are deleted (for example with os.unlink()). Generally, FIFOs are used as rendezvous between client and server type processes: the server opens the FIFO for reading, and the client opens it for writing. Note that mkfifo() doesn't open the FIFO, it just creates the rendezvous point.

mkdir*(path[, mode])*

Creates a directory named *path* with numeric mode *mode*. The default mode is 0777 (octal). On some systems, mode is ignored. Where it's used, the current umask value is first masked out. Availability: Macintosh, Unix, Windows.

makedirs*(path[, mode])*

Recursive directory creation function. Like mkdir(), but makes all intermediate-level directories needed to contain the leaf directory. Throws an error exception if the leaf directory already exists or can't be created. The default mode is 0777 (octal). New in version 1.5.2.

readlink*(path)*

Returns a string representing the path to which the symbolic link points. Availability: Unix.

remove*(path)*

Removes the file *path*. See the entry for rmdir() to remove a directory. This is identical to the unlink() function, documented later. Availability: Macintosh, Unix, Windows.

removedirs*(path)*

Recursive directory removal function. Works like rmdir() except that, if the leaf directory is successfully removed, directories corresponding to rightmost path segments are pruned until either the whole path is consumed or an error is raised (which is ignored, because it generally means that a parent directory isn't empty). Throws an error exception if the leaf directory can't be successfully removed. New in Version 1.5.2.

rename*(src, dst)*

Renames the file or directory *src* to *dst*. Availability: Macintosh, Unix, Windows.

renames*(old, new)*

Recursive directory or file renaming function. Works like rename(), except that the creation of any intermediate directories needed to make the new pathname good is attempted first. After the rename, directories corresponding to rightmost path segments of the old name are removed using removedirs().

This function can fail after the new directory structure is created if you lack permissions needed to remove the leaf directory or file. New in Version 1.5.2.

rmdir *(path)*

> Removes the directory *path*. Availability: Macintosh, Unix, Windows.

stat *(path)*

> Performs a stat() system call on the given path. The return value is a tuple of at least 10 integers giving the most important (and portable) members of the stat structure, in the order st_mode, st_ino, st_dev, st_nlink, st_uid, st_gid, st_size, st_atime, st_mtime, st_ctime. More items may be added at the end by some implementations. (On MS Windows, some items are filled with dummy values.) Availability: Macintosh, Unix, Windows.
>
> The standard module stat defines functions and constants that are useful for extracting information from a stat structure.

statvfs *(path)*

> Performs a statvfs() system call on the given path. The return value is a tuple of 10 integers giving the most common members of the statvfs structure, in the order f_bsize, f_frsize, f_blocks, f_bfree, f_bavail, f_files, f_ffree, f_favail, f_flag, f_namemax. Availability: Unix.
>
> The standard module statvfs defines constants that are useful for extracting information from a statvfs structure.

symlink *(src, dst)*

> Creates a symbolic link pointing to *src* named *dst*. Availability: Unix.

unlink *(path)*

> Removes the file path. This is the same function as remove(); the unlink() name is its traditional Unix name. Availability: Macintosh, Unix, Windows.

utime *(path, (atime, mtime))*

> Sets the access and modified time of the file to the given values. (The second argument is a tuple of two items.) Availability: Macintosh, Unix, Windows.

Process Management

These functions can create and manage additional processes:

execl *(path, arg0, arg1, ...)*

> This is quivalent to execv(*path, (arg0, arg1, ...)*). Availability: Unix, Windows.

execle *(path, arg0, arg1, ..., env)*

> This is equivalent to execve(*path, (arg0, arg1, ...), env)*. Availability: Unix, Windows.

execlp *(path, arg0, arg1, ...)*

This is equivalent to execvp *(path, (arg0, arg1, ...))*. Availability: Unix, Windows.

execv *(path, args)*

Executes the executable *path* with argument list *args*, replacing the current process (i.e., the Python interpreter). The argument list may be a tuple or list of strings. Availability: Unix, Windows.

execve *(path, args, env)*

Executes the executable *path* with argument list *args*, and environment *env*, replacing the current process (i.e., the Python interpreter). The argument list may be a tuple or list of strings. The environment must be a dictionary mapping strings to strings. Availability: Unix, Windows.

execvp *(path, args)*

Like execv *(path, args)* but duplicates the shell's actions in searching for an executable file in a list of directories. The directory list is obtained from environ['PATH']. Availability: Unix, Windows.

execvpe *(path, args, env)*

A cross between execve() and execvp(). The directory list is obtained from env['PATH']. Availability: Unix, Windows.

_exit *(n)*

Exits to the system with status *n*, without calling cleanup handlers, flushing stdio buffers, etc. Availability: Unix, Windows.

The standard way to exit is sys.exit *(n)*. _exit() should normally be used only in the child process after a fork().

fork()

Forks a child process. Returns 0 in the child, the child's process ID in the parent. Availability: Unix.

kill *(pid, sig)*

Kills the process *pid* with signal *sig*. Availability: Unix.

nice *(increment)*

Adds increment to the process's "niceness." Returns the new niceness. Availability: Unix.

plock *(op)*

Locks program segments into memory. The value of *op* (defined in <sys/lock.h>) determines which segments are locked. Availability: Unix.

spawnv *(mode, path, args)*

Executes the program *path* in a new process, passing the arguments specified in *args* as command-line parameters. *args* may be a list or a tuple. *mode* is a magic operational constant. See the Visual C++ runtime library documentation for further information. Availability: Windows. New in Version 1.5.2.

spawnve *(mode, path, args, env)*

Executes the program *path* in a new process, passing the arguments specified in *args* as command-line parameters and the contents of the mapping *env* as the environment. *args* may be a list or a tuple. *mode* is a magic operational constant. See the Visual C++ runtime library documentation for further information. Availability: Windows. New in Version 1.5.2.

P_WAIT
P_NOWAIT
P_NOWAITO
P_OVERLAY
P_DETACH

Possible values for the mode parameter to spawnv() and spawnve(). Availability: Windows. New in Version 1.5.2.

system *(command)*

Executes the *command* (a string) in a subshell. This is implemented by calling the standard C function system() and has the same limitations. Changes to posix.environ, sys.stdin, etc., aren't reflected in the environment of the executed command. The return value is the exit status of the process encoded in the format specified for wait(). Availability: Unix, Windows.

times ()

Returns a five-tuple of floating-point numbers indicating accumulated (CPU or other) times, in seconds. The items are: user time, system time, children's user time, children's system time, and elapsed real time since a fixed point in the past, in that order. See the Unix manpage times(2) or the corresponding Windows Platform API documentation. Availability: Unix, Windows.

wait ()

Waits for completion of a child process and returns a tuple containing its process ID and exit status indication: a 16-bit number, whose low byte is the signal number that killed the process and whose high byte is the exit status (if the signal number is zero); the high bit of the low byte is set if a core file was produced. Availability: Unix.

waitpid *(pid, options)*

Waits for completion of a child process given by process ID and returns a tuple containing its process ID and exit status indication (encoded as for wait()). The semantics of the call are affected by the value of the integer options, which should be 0 for normal operation. Availability: Unix.

WNOHANG

The option for `waitpid()` to avoid hanging if no child process status is available immediately. Availability: Unix.

The following functions take a process status code as returned by `waitpid()` as a parameter. They can determine the disposition of a process.

WIFSTOPPED *(status)*

Returns `true` if the process has been stopped. Availability: Unix.

WIFSIGNALED *(status)*

Returns `true` if the process exited due to a signal. Availability: Unix.

WIFEXITED *(status)*

Returns `true` if the process exited using the `exit(2)` system call. Availability: Unix.

WEXITSTATUS *(status)*

If `WIFEXITED(`*status*`)` is `true`, returns the integer parameter to the `exit(2)` system call. Otherwise, the return value is meaningless. Availability: Unix.

WSTOPSIG *(status)*

Returns the signal that caused the process to stop. Availability: Unix.

WTERMSIG *(status)*

Returns the signal that caused the process to exit. Availability: Unix.

Miscellaneous System Data

The follow data values can support path-manipulation operations. These are defined for all platforms. Higher-level operations on pathnames are defined in the `os.path` module.

`curdir`

The constant string used by the OS to refer to the current directory, e.g., "." for POSIX or ":" for the Macintosh.

`pardir`

The constant string used by the OS to refer to the parent directory, e.g., ".." for POSIX or "::" for the Macintosh.

`sep`

The character used by the OS to separate pathname components, e.g., "/" for POSIX or ":" for the Macintosh. This character isn't sufficient to parse or concatenate pathnames (use `os.path.split()` and `os.path.join()`) but it's occasionally useful.

altsep

> An alternative character used by the OS to separate pathname components or None if only one separator character exists. This is set to "/" on DOS and Windows systems where **sep** is a backslash.

pathsep

> The character conventionally used by the OS to separate search patch components (as in $PATH), e.g., ":" for POSIX or ";" for DOS and Windows.

defpath

> The default search path used by **exec*p*()** if the environment doesn't have a 'PATH' key.

linesep

> The string that separates (or, rather, terminates) lines on the current platform. This may be a single character, e.g., \n for POSIX or \r for MacOS, or multiple characters, e.g., \r\n for MS-DOS and MS Windows.

module os.path: Common Pathname Manipulations

This module implements some useful functions on pathnames:

abspath *(path)*

> Returns a normalized, absolute version of the pathname *path*. On most platforms, this is equivalent to normpath(join(os.getcwd()), *path*). New in Version 1.5.2.

basename *(path)*

> Returns the base name of pathname *path*. This is the second half of the pair returned by split(*path*).

commonprefix *(list)*

> Returns the longest string that is a prefix of all strings in *list*. If *list* is empty, returns the empty string (' ').

dirname *(path)*

> Returns the directory name of pathname *path*. This is the first half of the pair returned by split(*path*).

exists *(path)*

> Returns **true** if *path* refers to an existing path.

expanduser *(path)*

> Returns the argument with an initial component of "~" or "~user" replaced by that user's home directory. An initial "~" is replaced by the environment variable $HOME; an initial "~user" is looked up in the password directory through the built-in module **pwd**. If the expansion fails, or if the path doesn't begin with a tilde, the path is returned unchanged. On the Macintosh, this always returns *path* unchanged.

expandvars *(path)*

Returns the argument with environment variables expanded. Substrings of the form $name or ${name} are replaced by the value of environment variable name. Malformed variable names and references to nonexisting variables are left unchanged. On the Macintosh, this always returns *path* unchanged.

getatime *(path)*

Returns the time of last access of a filename identified by *path*. The return value is an integer giving the number of seconds since the epoch (see the time module). Raise os.error if the file doesn't exist or is inaccessible. New in Version 1.5.2.

getmtime *(path)*

Returns the time of last modification of a filename identified by *path*. The return value is an integer giving the number of seconds since the epoch (see the time module). Raise os.error if the file doesn't exist or is inaccessible. New in Version 1.5.2.

getsize *(path)*

Returns the size, in bytes, of filename identified by *path*. Raise os.error if the file doesn't exist or is inaccessible. New in Version 1.5.2.

isabs *(path)*

Returns true if *path* is an absolute pathname (begins with a slash).

isfile *(path)*

Returns true if *path* is an existing regular file. This follows symbolic links, so both islink() and isfile() can be true for the same path.

isdir *(path)*

Returns true if *path* is an existing directory. This follows symbolic links, so both islink() and isdir() can be true for the same path.

islink *(path)*

Returns true if *path* refers to a directory entry that's a symbolic link. Always false if symbolic links aren't supported.

ismount *(path)*

Returns true if pathname *path* is a mount point: a point in a filesystem where a different filesystem has been mounted. The function checks whether *path*'s parent, path/.., is on a different device than *path*, or whether *path*/.. and *path* point to the same i-node on the same device; this detects mount points for all Unix and POSIX variants.

join *(path1[, path2[, ...]])*

Joins one or more *path* components intelligently. If any component is an absolute path, all previous components are thrown away, and joining continues. The return value is the concatenation of *path1*, and optionally *path2*, etc., with exactly one slash (/) inserted between components, unless *path* is empty.

normcase *(path)*

Normalizes the case of a pathname. On Unix, this returns the path unchanged; on case-insensitive filesystems, it converts the path to lowercase. On Windows, it also converts forward slashes to backward slashes.

normpath *(path)*

Normalizes a pathname. This collapses redundant separators and up-level references, e.g., A//B, A/./B and A/foo/../B all become A/B. It doesn't normalize the case (use normcase() for that). On Windows, it converts forward slashes to backward slashes.

samefile *(path1, path2)*

Returns true if both pathname arguments refer to the same file or directory (as indicated by device number and i-node number). It raises an exception if an os.stat() call on either pathname fails. Availability: Macintosh, Unix.

sameopenfile *(fp1, fp2)*

Returns true if the file objects *fp1* and *fp2* refer to the same file. The two file objects may represent different file descriptors. Availability: Macintosh, Unix.

samestat *(stat1, stat2)*

Returns true if the *stat* tuples *stat1* and *stat2* refer to the same file. These structures may have been returned by fstat(), lstat(), or stat(). This function implements the underlying comparison used by samefile() and sameopenfile(). Availability: Macintosh, Unix.

split *(path)*

Splits the pathname *path* into a pair, *(head, tail)* where *tail* is the last pathname component, and *head* is everything leading up to that. The *tail* part never contains a slash; if *path* ends in a slash, *tail* is empty. If there is no slash in *path*, *head* is empty. If *path* is empty, both *head* and *tail* are empty. Trailing slashes are stripped from *head* unless it's the root (one or more slashes only). In nearly all cases, join(*head, tail*) equals *path* (the only exception being when there were multiple slashes separating *head* from *tail*).

splitdrive *(path)*

Splits the pathname path into a pair *(drive, tail)* where *drive* is either a drive specification or the empty string. On systems that don't use drive specifications, *drive* is always the empty string. In all cases, *drive + tail* is the same as *path*.

splitext *(path)*

Splits the pathname path into a pair *(root, ext)* such that *root + ext == path*, and *ext* is empty or begins with a period and contains at most one period.

walk *(path, visit, arg)*

Calls the function *visit* with arguments *(arg, dirname, names)* for each directory in the directory tree rooted at *path* (including *path* itself, if it's a directory). The argument *dirname* specifies the visited directory, the argument *names* lists the files in the directory (from os.listdir(*dirname*)). The *visit* function may modify *names* to influence the set of directories visited below *dirname*, e.g., to avoid visiting certain parts of the tree. The object referred to by *names* must be modified in place, using del or slice assignment.

B

Win32 Extensions
Reference

Documenting the entire Windows SDK would require a number of books this size. Therefore, we limit ourselves to a brief reference to the SDK functions and objects presented in this book.

For further information, you may wish to consult the reference guides distributed with the Python for Windows Extensions, the Microsoft SDK documentation, or any other good Windows programming text.

Common Win32 Python Objects

PyHANDLE

A PyHANDLE object represents a Win32 handle. When a PyHANDLE object is no longer referenced, the Win32 handle is automatically closed. Thus, it isn't strictly necessary (although still considered good style) to explicitly close these handles.

There are a number of variations on a PyHANDLE object, such as the PyHKEY object. These handle objects are identical in operation to a standard PyHANDLE object, but the underlying implementation uses different Win32 functions to close the handle automatically. From the Python programmers point of view, these handles all share the same interface.

Handles are obtained from a number of Win32 functions, such as functions that open or create files or registry keys. When a function requires a PyHANDLE object, it usually also accepts an integer, which is expected to be the raw Win32 handle value.

Methods

`__int__()`

Returns the raw Win32 handle value for this object. Thus, you can use the code `int(myHandle)` to obtain the Win32 handle value.

`Close()`

Manually closes the Win32 handle.

`Detach()`

Returns the raw Win32 handle and detaches the handle from the `PyHANDLE` object. After making this call, the Win32 handle isn't closed automatically, and the `PyHANDLE` object has a Win32 handle value of zero (i.e., an invalid handle value).

Attributes

`handle`

The raw Win32 handle as an integer. Thus, `myhandle.handle == int(myhandle)`.

PyIID

A `PyIID` object is used whenever a COM GUID is used. `PyIID` objects can be created using the `pywintypes.IID()` function, although all functions that accept a GUID also accept a string in the standard GUID format.

Methods

`__str__`

Obtains the string representation of a GUID. Thus, `str(myiid)` returns this string value.

`__cmp__`

Used when `PyIID` objects are compared. This ignores any case differences in the string representation.

Attributes

There are no attributes.

PySTARTUPINFO

A `PySTARTUPINFO` represents a Win32 `STARTUPINFO` structure. It's created by the function `win32process.STARTUPINFO()`. Once created, you can assign values to the attributes, then pass the object to `win32process.CreateProcess()`.

Methods

There are no methods.

Attributes

dwFlags

A bit field that determines whether certain PySTARTUPINFO attributes are used when the process creates a window. To use many of the additional attributes, you set the appropriate mask in this attribute and also set the attributes themselves.

Any combination of the following values can be specified:

win32process.STARTF_FORCEONFEEDBACK

Indicates that the cursor is in feedback mode for two seconds after CreateProcess() is called. If during those two seconds the process makes the first GUI call, the system gives five more seconds to the process. If during those five seconds the process shows a window, the system gives five more seconds to the process to finish drawing the window.

win32process.STARTF_FORCEOFFFEEDBACK

Indicates that the feedback cursor is forced off while the process is starting. The normal cursor is displayed.

win32process.STARTF_RUNFULLSCREEN

Indicates that the process should be run in full-screen mode, rather than in windowed mode. This flag is valid only for console applications running on an x86 computer.

win32process.STARTF_USECOUNTCHARS

If not specified, the dwXCountChars and dwYCountChars attributes are ignored.

win32process.STARTF_USEFILLATTRIBUTE

If not specified, the dwFillAttribute attribute is ignored.

win32process.STARTF_USEPOSITION

If not specified, the dwX and dwY attributes are ignored.

win32process.STARTF_USESHOWWINDOW

If this value isn't specified, the wShowWindow attribute is ignored.

win32process.STARTF_USESIZE

If not specified, the dwXSize and dwYSize attributes are ignored.

win32process.STARTF_USESTDHANDLES

Sets the standard input, standard output, and standard error handles for the process to the handles specified in the hStdInput, hStdOutput, and hStdError attributes. The CreateProcess() function's fInherit-Handles parameter must be set to true for this to work properly.

If this value isn't specified, the hStdInput, hStdOutput, and hStdError attributes are ignored.

dwX

An integer that specifies the **x** offset, in pixels, of the upper-left corner of a window if a new window is created. The offset is from the upper-left corner of the screen.

dwY

An integer that specifies the **y** offset, in pixels, of the upper-left corner of a window if a new window is created. The offset is from the upper-left corner of the screen.

dwXSize

An integer that specifies the width, in pixels, of the window if a new window is created.

dwYSize

An integer that specifies the height, in pixels, of the window if a new window is created.

dwXCountChars

For console processes, if a new console window is created, an integer that specifies the screen buffer width in character columns. This value is ignored in a GUI process.

dwYCountChars

For console processes, if a new console window is created, an integer that specifies the screen buffer height in character rows.

dwFillAttribute

An integer that specifies the initial text and background colors if a new console window is created in a console application. These values are ignored in GUI applications

hStdInput

A PyHANDLE object that is used as the standard input handle to the process.

hStdOutput

A PyHANDLE object that is used as the standard output handle to the process.

hStdError

A PyHANDLE object that is used as the standard error handle to the process.

lpDesktop

May be None, or on Windows NT/2000, a string containing either the name of the desktop only or the name of both the desktop and window station for this process.

lpTitle

For console processes, a string that contains the title displayed in the titlebar if a new console window is created. If None, the name of the executable file is used as the window title instead. This parameter must be None for GUI or console processes that don't create a new console window.

wShowWindow

Can be any of the SW_ constants defined in win32con. For GUI processes, this specifies the default value the first time ShowWindow() is called.

pythoncom Module

The pythoncom module provides the low-level interface between COM and Python.

CoCreateInstance( )

Creates the specified COM object and returns the requested interface.

```
interface = CoCreateInstance(clsid, unkOuter , clsctx , iid)
```

Parameters

clsid

A string or PyIID object containing the class ID for the new object.

unkOuter

Typically None, or may be a Python interface object if the object is used as part of an aggregate.

clsctx

Defines the context in which the code that manages the newly created object runs. May be a combination of the following constants:

pythoncom.CLSCTX_INPROC_SERVER

The code that creates and manages objects of this class runs in the same process as the caller of the function specifying the class context.

pythoncom.CLSCTX_INPROC_HANDLER

The code that manages objects of this class is an in-process handler. This is a DLL that runs in the client process and implements client-side structures of this class when instances of the class are accessed remotely.

pythoncom.CLSCTX_LOCAL_SERVER

The EXE code that creates and manages objects of this class is loaded in a separate process space (runs on same machine but in a different process).

pythoncom.CLSCTX_REMOTE_SERVER

A remote machine context. The LocalServer32 or LocalService code that creates and manages objects of this class is run on a different machine.

pythoncom.CLSCTX_ALL

Indicates all class contexts.

pythoncom.CLSCTX_INPROC
>   Indicates all in-process contexts.

pythoncom.CLSCTX_SERVER
>   Indicates server code, whether in-process, local, or remote.

iid
>   A string or PyIID object that defines the interface ID requested from the new object.

Result

The result is a Python interface object, the exact type of which is determined by the iid parameter.

Comments

This function is for advanced use only; in most cases, you create COM objects using the win32com.client.Dispatch() function.

CoInitialize( )

Initializes COM for apartment model threading.

```
CoInitialize()
```

Parameters

No parameters.

Comments

Equivalent to CoInitializeEx(pythoncom.COINIT_APARTMENTTHREADED). See CoInitializeEx() for more details.

CoInitializeEx( )

Initializes COM for the calling thread.

```
CoIntializeEx(flags)
```

Parameters

flags
>   An integer defining the initialization options. May include:

pythoncom.COINIT_APARTMENTTHREADED
>   Initializes the thread for apartment-threaded object concurrency.

pythoncom.COINIT_MULTITHREADED
>   Initializes the thread for multithreaded object concurrency.

pythoncom.COINIT_DISABLE_OLE1DDE
> Disables DDE for OLE1 support.

pythoncom.COINIT_SPEED_OVER_MEMORY
> Trades memory for speed.

Comments

There's no need to call this function for the Python thread that first imports the pythoncom module. Please see Appendix D, *Threads*, for a detailed description of COM threading models.

CoUninitialize( )

Closes the COM library on the current thread, unloads all COM DLLs loaded by the thread, and forces all COM RPC connections on the thread to close.

```
CoUninitialize()
```

Comments

As described in Appendix D, this function is currently never called by the COM framework.

CoMarshalInterThreadInterfaceInStream( )

Marshals a Python COM interface object from one thread to another thread in the same process.

```
stream = CoMarshalInterThreadInterfaceInStream(iid, interface)
```

Parameters

iid
> A string or PyIID object that identifies the interface to be marshaled into the new stream.

interface
> A Python COM interface object or win32com.client.Dispatch() instance to be marshaled.

Result

The result is a PyIStream object; that is, a Python wrapper around a COM IStream interface. This stream is typically passed to CoGetInterface-AndReleaseStream() to obtain the marshaled object in the new thread.

Comments

When paired with `CoGetInterfaceAndReleaseStream()`, programs can easily and reliably marshal a COM interface object to another thread in the same process. See Appendix D for further details.

CoGetInterfaceAndReleaseStream( )

Unmarshals a Python interface object from a stream and releases the stream.

```
interface = CoGetInterfaceAndReleaseStream(stream, iid)
```

Parameters

stream

> A `PyIStream` object to which the object was previously marshaled.

iid

> A string or `PyIID` object that defines the interface to be unmarshaled from the stream.

Result

The result is a Python COM interface object, the exact type of which is determined by the `iid` parameter.

Comments

When paired with `CoMarshalInterThreadInterfaceInStream()`, programs can easily and reliably marshal a COM interface object to another thread in the same process. See Appendix D for further details.

win32api Module

The `win32api` module contains a mixed bag of useful Win32 API functions. This module contains general-purpose routines often required by programs with fairly light Windows-specific requirements. Other Python modules provide more complete coverage of specific Win32 API sets.

ShellExecute( )

Performs an operation on the specified file.

```
ShellExecute(Hwnd, Operation, File, Parameters, InitialDirectory, bShow)
```

Parameters

Hwnd

> A handle to the window that is to be the parent window for the new process. This is primarily used for message boxes the new application may display. It's

expressed as a Python integer, and 0 (zero) may be passed if no parent is required.

Operation

A string representing the operation to perform on the file. Typically this is open. The value it takes depends on the process being executed. For example, if you execute a Python file, supported operations are open and edit. If you execute a Microsoft Word document, supported operations include open and print.

File

The name of the file to execute. Most commonly, this is a document, but a program can also be specified.

Parameters

If the File parameter contains the name of a document file, this should be None. If a program is specified, it should be a string containing the name of the document file.

InitialDirectory

The directory in which to open the document. This directory becomes the current directory for the application.

bShow

An integer specifying if the main window for the application is to be shown. This is typically 1.

WinExec( )

Runs the specified application.

```
WinExec(CommandLine, WindowShowState)
```

Parameters

CommandLine

The command to execute. This string can contain simply the program name in which case the Windows path is searched, or it may contain the full path to the program. Parameters to the program can also be specified here, and these parameters should contain embedded quotation marks if necessary.

WindowShowState

An optional integer that defines how the main window for the program is created. If this parameter isn't specified, win32con.SW_SHOWNORMAL is used. Common values for this flag are listed here, but for a full list, please see the Microsoft documentation for the WinExec function.

win32con.SW_SHOWNORMAL

The window is created using its default. Typically, this means the window is created in a restored or overlapped state.

win32con.SW_SHOWMAXIMIZED
> The window is created maximized.

win32con.SW_SHOWMINIMIZED
> The window is created minimized.

win32con.SW_HIDE
> The window is created hidden.

OpenProcess( )

Retrieves a handle to an existing process

```
handle = OpenProcess(reqdAccess, bInherit, processId)
```

Parameters

reqdAccess

> An integer defining the access level requested on the handle. Common values are listed here, but for a full description please see the Win32 documentation for the OpenProcess() function.

win32con.PROCESS_ALL_ACCESS
> Specifies all possible access flags for the process object

win32con.PROCESS_QUERY_INFORMATION
> Enables using the process handle in the GetExitCodeProcess() and GetPriorityClass() functions to read information from the process object.

win32con.PROCESS_TERMINATE
> Enables using the process handle in the TerminateProcess() function to terminate the process.

bInherit

> Specifies whether the returned handle can be inherited by a new process created by the current process. If true, the handle is inheritable.

processId

> An integer specifying the process identifier of the process to open.

Result

The result is a PyHANDLE object containing the handle to the process.

GetSystemMetrics( )

Retrieves information, in pixels, about various display elements and system configuration settings.

```
result = GetSystemMetrics(metricType)
```

Parameter

`metricType`

> Specifies the information to retrieve. There are over 80 valid values for this function, which can be identified by constants in the `win32con` module that begin with `SM_`, such as `SM_CXSCREEN`. Please see the Win32 documentation for further details.

Result

An integer with the requested system metric.

GetDomainName( )

Retrieves the name of the domain to which the current computer belongs.

`name = GetDomainName()`

Parameters

No parameters.

Result

The result is a string with the current domain name.

GetUserName( )

Retrieves the username for the current thread.

`name = GetUserName()`

Parameters

No parameters.

Result

The result is a string with the current username. No domain information is returned, just the username.

GetComputerName( )

Retrieves the NetBIOS name of the local computer, as defined in the control panel and read at system bootup.

`name = GetComputerName()`

Parameters

No parameters.

Result

The result is a string with the computer name.

InitiateSystemShutdown( )

Initiates a shutdown and optional restart of the specified computer.

```
InitiateSystemShutdown(machineName, message, timeout, bForceAppsClosed, bReboot)
```

Parameters

machineName

> The network name of the machine to shut down or None for the current machine.

message

> A string that specifies a message to be displayed in the shut-down dialog box or None for no message.

timeout

> An integer that specifies the time in milliseconds to display the dialog. During this period, the shutdown can be aborted by calling AbortSystem-Shutdown(). If this value is zero, no dialog is shown, and the shutdown begins immediately.

bForceAppsClosed

> An integer that specifies if applications should be forced closed. If true, users aren't given an opportunity to save their work.

bReboot

> An integer that specifies if the machine should be restarted after shutdown or left in a state safe to power off the computer.

Comments

To shut down the local computer, the calling process must have the SE_ SHUTDOWN_NAME privilege. To shut down a remote computer, the calling process must have the SE_REMOTE_SHUTDOWN_NAME privilege on the remote computer.

AbortSystemShutdown( )

Stops the system shutdown of a specified computer.

```
AbortSystemShutdown(machineName)
```

Parameters

machineName

> A string that specifies the name of the computer on which to abort the shut-down or None for the local computer.

Comments

This function can programmatically abort a system shutdown initiated by `InitiateSystemShutdown()` during the specified timeout interval.

To stop the local computer from shutting down, the calling process must have the `SE_SHUTDOWN_NAME` privilege. To stop a remote computer from shutting down, the calling process must have the `SE_REMOTE_SHUTDOWN_NAME` privilege on the remote computer.

GetCurrentThreadId( )

Returns the thread identifier for the current thread.

```
threadId = GetCurrentThreadId()
```

Result

The result is an integer containing the Win32 thread ID. Until the thread terminates, this ID uniquely identifies the thread to the system.

GetCurrentProcessId( )

Returns the process identifier for the current process.

```
processId = GetCurrentProcessId()
```

Result

The result is an integer containing the Win32 process ID. Until the process terminates, this ID uniquely identifies the process to the system.

win32event Module

The `win32event` module contains functions that interface to the various synchronization functions available in the Win32 SDK.

WaitForSingleObject( )

Waits for either the specified object to become signaled or a timeout to occur.

```
result = WaitForSingleObject(handle, timeout)
```

Parameters

`handle`

A `PyHANDLE` object or integer that specifies the object to wait for. This may be a handle to one of the following objects:

— Change notification

— Console input

— Event

— Job

— Mutex

— Process

— Semaphore

— Thread

— Waitable timer

`timeout`

An integer that specifies the timeout period in milliseconds or `win32event.INFINITE` for no timeout.

Result

The result is an integer that may be one of the following values:

`win32event.WAIT_OBJECT_0`

The state of the specified object is signaled.

`win32event.WAIT_TIMEOUT`

The time-out interval has elapsed, and the object's state is nonsignaled.

`win32event.WAIT_ABANDONED`

The specified object is a mutex object that wasn't released by the thread that owned the mutex object before the owning thread terminated.

WaitForMultipleObjects( )

Waits for either one or all of the specified objects to become signaled or a time-out to occur.

```
result = WaitForMultipleObjects(handles, bWaitAll, timeout)
```

Parameters

`handles`

A sequence (e.g., list or tuple) of `PyHANDLE` or integer objects. The supported handle types are the same as for the `win32api.WaitForSingleObject()` function.

`bWaitAll`

An integer indicating if the function should return when all the objects have become signaled (`true`) or when any one of the objects becomes signaled (`false`).

`timeout`

An integer that specifies the timeout period in milliseconds or `win32event.INFINITE` for no timeout.

Result

The result is an integer that may be one of the following values:

`win32event.WAIT_OBJECT_0 to`
`win32event.WAIT_OBJECT_0+len(handles)-1`

If `bWaitAll` is `true`, indicates that all of the objects have become signaled. If `bWaitAll` is `false`, indicates which of the objects has become signaled.

`win32event.WAIT_TIMEOUT`

The timeout interval elapsed and the object's state is nonsignaled.

`win32event.WAIT_ABANDONED_0 to`
`win32event.WAIT_ABANDONED_0+len(handles)-1`

If `bWaitAll` is `true`, the return value indicates that the state of all specified objects is signaled and at least one of the objects is an abandoned mutex object. If `bWaitAll` is `false`, the return value minus `WAIT_ABANDONED_0` indicates the sequence index of an abandoned mutex object that satisfied the wait.

MsgWaitForMultipleObjects( )

Waits for either one or all the specified objects to become signaled or a timeout to occur. The specified objects can include input event objects, which are specified using the **wakeMask** parameter.

```
result = MsgWaitForMultipleObjects(handles, bWaitAll, timeout, wakeMask)
```

Parameters

`handles`

A sequence (e.g., list or tuple) of `PyHANDLE` or integer objects. The supported handle types are the same as for the `win32api.WaitForSingleObject()` function.

`bWaitAll`

An integer indicating if the function should return when all the objects have become signaled (`true`) or when any one of the objects becomes signaled (`false`).

`timeout`

An integer that specifies the timeout period in milliseconds or `win32event.INFINITE` for no timeout.

`wakeMask`

An integer that specifies input types for which an input event object handle is added to the sequence object handles. This parameter can be any combination of the following values:

`win32event.QS_ALLEVENTS`

An input, `WM_TIMER`, `WM_PAINT`, `WM_HOTKEY` or posted message is in the queue.

`win32event.QS_ALLINPUT`

Any message is in the queue.

`win32event.QS_ALLPOSTMESSAGE`

A posted message (other than those listed here) is in the queue.

`win32event.QS_HOTKEY`

A `WM_HOTKEY` message is in the queue.

`win32event.QS_INPUT`

An input message is in the queue.

`win32event.QS_KEY`

A `WM_KEYUP`, `WM_KEYDOWN`, `WM_SYSKEYUP`, or `WM_SYSKEYDOWN` message is in the queue.

`win32event.QS_MOUSE`

A `WM_MOUSEMOVE` message or mouse-button message (`WM_LBUTTONUP`, `WM_RBUTTONDOWN`, and so on) is in the queue.

`win32event.QS_MOUSEBUTTON`

A mouse-button message (`WM_LBUTTONUP`, `WM_RBUTTONDOWN`, and so on) is in the queue.

`win32event.QS_MOUSEMOVE`

A `WM_MOUSEMOVE` message is in the queue.

`win32event.QS_PAINT`

A `WM_PAINT` message is in the queue.

`win32event.QS_POSTMESSAGE`

A posted message (other than those just listed) is in the queue.

`win32event.QS_SENDMESSAGE`

A message sent by another thread or application is in the queue.

`win32event.QS_TIMER`

A `WM_TIMER` message is in the queue.

Result

The result is an integer that may be one of the following values:

`win32event.WAIT_OBJECT_0` to
`win32event.WAIT_OBJECT_0+len(handles)-1`

If `bWaitAll` is `true`, indicates that all the objects have become signaled. If `bWaitAll` is `false`, indicates which of the objects has become signaled.

WAIT_OBJECT_0 + len(handles)

> New input of the type specified in the wakeMask parameter is available in the thread's input queue.

win32event.WAIT_TIMEOUT

> The timeout interval elapsed, and the object's state is nonsignaled.

win32event.WAIT_ABANDONED_0 to
win32event.WAIT_ABANDONED_0+len(handles)-1

> If bWaitAll is true, the return value indicates the state of all specified objects is signaled and at least one of the objects is an abandoned mutex object. If bWaitAll is false, the return value minus WAIT_ABANDONED_0 indicates the sequence index of an abandoned mutex object that satisfied the wait.

CreateEvent( )

Creates or opens a named or unnamed event object.

handle = CreateEvent(securityAttributes, bManualReset, bInitialState, name)

Parameters

securityAttributes

> A PySECURITYATTRIBUTES object that determines whether the returned handle can be inherited by child processes. If None, the returned handle can't be inherited.

bManualReset

> An integer that specifies whether an auto or manual reset object is created. If true, you must use the ResetEvent() function to manually reset the event state to nonsignaled. If false, the system automatically resets the state after a waiting thread has been released.

bInitialState

> An integer that specifies if the object is to created in the signaled state. If true, the object is created signaled; otherwise it's nonsignaled.

name

> A string that specifies the name of the event object or None if an unnamed object is to be created. If this name matches an existing event object, this function requests EVENT_ALL_ACCESS on the existing object. In this case, the bManualReset and bInitialState parameters are ignored as they have already been specified when the object was initially created.

Result

The result is a PyHANDLE object referencing the requested object.

SetEvent( )

Sets the state of the specified event object to signaled.

```
SetEvent(handle)
```

Parameters

handle

> The handle to the object to signal.

ResetEvent( )

Sets the state of the specified event object to nonsignaled.

```
ResetEvent(handle)
```

Parameters

handle

> The handle to the object to reset.

win32evtlog Module

The `win32evtlog` module interfaces to the Win32 SDK functions that deal with the Windows NT Event Log. This module also contains generic message resources suitable for reference in Event Log records.

CloseEventLog( )

Closes a handle to the Event Log.

```
CloseEventLog(handle)
```

Parameters

handle

> The **handle** to close, as obtained from **win32evtlog.OpenEventLog()**.

OpenEventLog( )

Opens a handle to one of the Event Logs on the specified machine.

```
handle = OpenEventLog(machineName, logName)
```

Parameters

machineName

> The name of the machine to connect to or **None** for the current machine.

logName

> The name of the Event Log to open, such as Application, System, or Security.

Result

The return value is an integer handle to the Event Log.

ReadEventLog( )

Reads a number of records from an open Event Log.

```
records = ReadEventLog(handle, readFlags, recordOffset)
```

Parameters

handle

> An open handle to the Event Log, obtained from **win32evtlog. OpenEventLog()**.

readFlags

> Specify how the **read** operation is to proceed and may be a combination of the following flags:

> **win32evtlog.EVENTLOG_FORWARDS_READ**

>> The Log is read in forward chronological order.

> **win32evtlog.EVENTLOG_BACKWARDS_READ**

>> The Log is read in reverse chronological order.

> **win32evtlog.EVENTLOG_SEEK_READ**

>> The **read** operation proceeds from the record specified by the **recordOffset** parameter. If this flag is used, **readFlags** must also specify **EVENTLOG_FORWARDS_READ** or **EVENTLOG_BACKWARDS_READ**, which indicates the direction for successive **read** operations.

> **win32evtlog.EVENTLOG_SEQUENTIAL_READ**

>> The **read** operation proceeds sequentially from the last call to the **win32evtlog.ReadEventLog()** function using this handle.

recordOffset

> Specifies the log-entry record number at which the **read** operation should start. This parameter is ignored unless the **readFlags** parameter includes the **EVENTLOG_SEEK_READ** flag.

Result

The result is a list of **PyEVENTLOGRECORD** objects. The number of records returned by a single call can be determined only after the call has returned.

PyEVENTLOGRECORD object

A PyEVENTLOGRECORD object reads records from the Event Log or writes new records to the Log.

Methods

This object has no methods.

Properties

RecordNumber
> The number of the Event Log record. This number can be used to find the specific record.

TimeGenerated
> A Time object indicating the time the record was generated.

TimeWritten
> A Time object indicating the time the record was actually written to the Log.

EventID
> An integer event ID, as defined by the application writing the record.

EventType
> An integer defining the event type, which can be one of the following:

> EVENTLOG_ERROR_TYPE
> EVENTLOG_WARNING_TYPE
> EVENTLOG_INFORMATION_TYPE
> EVENTLOG_AUDIT_SUCCESS
> EVENTLOG_AUDIT_FAILURE

EventCategory
> An integer event category, as defined by the application writing the record.

SourceName
> The name of the application that generated the Event Log record.

ComputerName
> The name of the computer that generated this message.

StringInserts
> A list of string inserts for this message.

Sid
> The security identifier of a user to be associated with this record.

Data
> The raw binary data for the Event Log record.

Messages

The *win32evtlog.pyd* file contains embedded messages suitable for using to write to the Event Log. Only generic messages are provided.

Message ID	Event Type	Message Text
1 to 9	Error	%1
1 to 9	Information	%1
1 to 9	Success	%1
1 to 9	Warning	%1

win32file Module

The `win32file` module contains functions that interface to the `File` and other I/O-related Win32 API functions.

CreateFile( )

Opens or creates a file or a number of other objects and returns a handle that can access the object.

```
handle = CreateFile(FileName, DesiredAccess, ShareMode, SecurityAttributes,
CreationDisposition, FlagsAndAttributes, TemplateFile)
```

Parameters

FileName

The name of the file, pipe, or other resource to open.

DesiredAccess

An integer determining the access this file is opened with. This allows the file to be opened with read access, write access, read-write access, or device access. The following flags are defined:

0   Specifies the file to be opened with device query access. This allows the application to query the device attributes without accessing the device.

win32file.GENERIC_READ

Specifies read access to the file. Combine with `win32file.GENERIC_WRITE` for read-write access.

win32file.GENERIC_WRITE

Specified write access to the file. Combine with `win32file.GENERIC_WRITE` for read-write access.

ShareMode

A set of bit flags that determines how the file is to be shared. If `ShareMode` is 0, the file can't be shared, and all subsequent attempts to open the file fail until the handle is closed. This parameter can be a combination of the following values:

`win32file.FILE_SHARE_DELETE`
>   Windows NT only. Only requests to open the file for delete mode succeed.

`win32file.FILE_SHARE_READ`
>   Only requests to open the file for read mode succeed.

`win32file.FILE_SHARE_WRITE`
>   Only requests to open the file for write mode succeed.

`SecurityAttributes`
>   Determines whether the file is inherited by child processes. On Windows NT, this specifies the security descriptor for the file if the underlying filesystem supports security.

`CreationDisposition`
>   Specifies what action to take on files that already exist and what action to take on files that don't already exist. This can be one of the following values:

`win32file.CREATE_NEW`
>   A new file is to be created. An exception is thrown if the file already exists.

`win32file.CREATE_ALWAYS`
>   A new file is to be created. If an existing file exists, it's overwritten.

`win32file.OPEN_EXISTING`
>   Opens an existing file. If the file doesn't already exist, an exception is thrown.

`win32file.OPEN_ALWAYS`
>   Opens an existing file if it exists, or creates a new file if not.

`win32file.TRUNCATE_EXISTING`
>   Opens the file and truncates its length to zero. The file must have been opened with write access. If the file doesn't exist, an exception is thrown.

`FlagsAndAttributes`
>   Specifies the attributes and other flags for the file. This can be a combination of the following flags:

`win32file.FILE_ATTRIBUTE_ARCHIVE`
>   The file should be archived; that is, it has the archive attribute set.

`win32file.FILE_ATTRIBUTE_ENCRYPTED`
>   The file or directory is to be encrypted. This flag has no affect if the filesystem doesn't support encryption.

`win32file.FILE_ATTRIBUTE_HIDDEN`

> The file is hidden and not included in a normal directory listing.

`win32file.FILE_ATTRIBUTE_NORMAL`

> There are no special attributes on the file. This value is valid only when used alone.

`win32file.FILE_ATTRIBUTE_OFFLINE`

> The data of the file isn't available immediately because it has been moved to temporary offline storage.

`win32file.FILE_ATTRIBUTE_READONLY`

> The file is marked as read-only. Applications can open the file for read access but not write access.

`win32file.FILE_ATTRIBUTE_SYSTEM`

> The file is a system file and used exclusively by the operating system.

`win32file.FILE_ATTRIBUTE_TEMPORARY`

> The file is used for temporary storage, and the operating system attempts to keep the entire file in memory when possible to speed access. Applications should remove these files as soon as possible.

`win32file.FILE_FLAG_WRITETHROUGH`

> The system writes all data immediately to the disk, bypassing the lazy-write capabilities of the cache.

`win32file.FILE_FLAG_OVERLAPPED`

> All I/O on this file occurs asynchronously. When a file is opened in this mode, read and write operations may return `ERROR_IO_PENDING`, and the event in the `OVERLAPPED` object is set when the I/O operation completes. Files opened with this flag must provide an `OVERLAPPED` object.

`win32file.FILE_FLAG_NO_BUFFERING`

> The system opens the file with no buffering or caching.

`win32file.FILE_FLAG_RANDOM_ACCESS`

> Indicates the file is accessed randomly. The system uses this as a hint to optimize caching of the file.

`win32file.FILE_FLAG_SEQUENTIAL_SCAN`

> Indicates the file is accessed sequentially. The system uses this as a hint to optimize caching of the file.

`win32file.FILE_FLAG_DELETE_ON_CLOSE`

> The operating system deletes the file automatically when the last handle to it is closed. Subsequent attempts to open the file (except for delete) fail.

`win32file.FILE_FLAG_BACKUP_SEMANTICS`

> Indicates the file is being opened for a backup operation. Special NT security requirements apply.

win32file.FILE_FLAG_POSIX_SEMANTICS

Changes the semantics of the file to resemble POSIX files. Used only by the POSIX subsystem; shouldn't be used by Windows applications.

win32file.FILE_FLAG_OPEN_REPARSE_POINT

Inhibits the reparse functionality of the NTFS filesystem and is beyond the scope of this book.

win32file.FILE_FLAG_OPEN_NO_RECALL

Used by remote storage systems and is beyond the scope of this book.

TemplateFile

A handle to another file used as a template for file attributes or **None**. Under Windows 95, this parameter must be **None**.

Result

A PyHANDLE object to the file.

ReadFile( )

Reads data from an open file.

```
errCode, data = ReadFile(FileHandle, Size, Overlapped)
```

Parameters

FileHandle

The file handle identifying the file to read from. This handle typically is obtained from win32file.CreateFile().

Size or ReadBuffer

If Size is specified as a Python integer, it's the number of bytes to read from the file. When using overlapped I/O, a ReadBuffer should be used, indicating where the ReadFile operation should place the data.

Overlapped

An OVERLAPPED object or **None** if overlapped I/O isn't being performed. This parameter can be omitted, in which case **None** is used.

Result

errCode

Either 0, or ERROR_IO_PENDING.

Data

The data read from the file.

WriteFile( )

Writes data to an open file.

```
errCode = WriteFile(FileHandle, Data, Overlapped)
```

Parameters

FileHandle
> The file handle identifying the file to read from. This handle typically is obtained from `win32file.CreateFile()`.

Data
> The data to write to the file, as a Python string.

Overlapped
> An OVERLAPPED object or None if overlapped I/O isn't being performed. This parameter can be omitted, in which case None is used.

Result

errCode
> Either 0 or ERROR_IO_PENDING.

win32pipe Module

The win32pipe module contains functions that interface to the pipe-related Win32 API functions.

CallNamedPipe( )

Connects to a message-type pipe (and waits if an instance of the pipe isn't available), writes to and reads from the pipe, and then closes the pipe.

```
data = CallNamedPipe(pipeName, sendData, readSize, timeout)
```

Parameters

pipeName
> The name of the named pipe to connect to.

sendData
> The data, as a Python string, to send to the service.

readSize
> The size of the buffer to allocate for the result data.

timeout
> Specifies the number of milliseconds to wait for the named pipe to be available or one of the following values:

win32pipe.NMPWAIT_NOWAIT
> Doesn't wait for the named pipe. If the named pipe isn't available, the function throws an exception.

win32pipe.NMPWAIT_WAIT_FOREVER
> Waits indefinitely.

win32pipe.NMPWAIT_USE_DEFAULT_WAIT
> Uses the default timeout specified by the pipe in the call to the win32pipe.CreateNamedPipe() function.

Result

The result is the data read from the pipe, as a Python string.

CreatePipe( )

Creates an anonymous pipe and returns handles to the read and write ends of the pipe.

```
readHandle, writeHandle = CreatePipe(SecurityAttributes, BufferSize)
```

Parameters

SecurityAttributes
> The security to be applied to the pipe or **None** for the default security.

BufferSize
> An integer specifying the default buffer size for the pipe. This is simply a hint to the operating system. Zero can be passed, in which case the default buffer size is used.

Result

readHandle
> A handle to the read end of the pipe. This handle can be used by the win32file.ReadFile() function.

WriteHandle
> A handle to the write end of the pipe. This handle can be used by the win32file.WriteFile() function.

win32process Module

The **win32process** module interfaces to the process and thread-related Win32 API functions.

CreateProcess( )

Creates a new process and its primary thread.

```
procHandle, threadHandle, procId, threadId = CreateHandle(ApplicationName,\
                                    CommandLine,\
                                    ProcessSecurityAttributes,\
                                    ThreadSecurityAttributes,\
                                    bInheritHandles,\
                                    CreationFlags,\
                                    Environment,\
                                    CurrentDirectory,\
                                    StartupInfo)
```

Parameters

ApplicationName

The name of the executable that creates the process. This can either be a full path to the executable or just the filename portion. If no path is specified, Windows searches the system path for the process. This parameter may be None, in which case the executable must be specified in the CommandLine parameter.

CommandLine

The command line that executes the program. If the ApplicationName parameter is None, this must also include the name of the executable. If ApplicationName is specified, this contains additional arguments for the executable.

ProcessSecurityAttributes

The security attributes for the new process or None if the current attributes are to be inherited. Security attributes can be created using the win32security module.

ThreadSecurityAttributes

The security attributes for the main thread in the new process or None if the current attributes are to be inherited.

bInheritHandles

A boolean flag indicating if the new process should inherit Windows handles from the creating process. If true (that is, 1), each open handle in the creating process is valid for the new process.

CreationFlags

A set of flags that allow special options to be set for the created process. The following flags are currently defined:

win32process.CREATE_DEFAULT_ERROR_MODE

Creates the new process using a default error mode. If this flag isn't set, the error mode for the creating process is used. The error mode for a process determines how the application handles certain error conditions and can be set via `win32api.SetErrorMode()`.

`win32process.CREATE_NEW_CONSOLE`

The new process is created using a new console, rather than inheriting the current console. If the creating process is a GUI process, and the process to be created is a console process, this flag has no effect.

`win32process.CREATE_NEW_PROCESS_GROUP`

A new process group is created for this process and all subprocesses. A process group determines Ctrl-C or Ctrl-Break handling for console application.

`win32process.CREATE_SEPARATE_WOW_VDM`
`win32process.CREATE_SHARED_WOW_VDM`

Under Windows NT when executing a 16-bit program, these flags allow you to specify the Virtual DOS machine the process executes in. The Windows SDK documentation contains more information on these flags.

`win32process.CREATE_SUSPENDED`

The main thread of the new process is created in a suspended state. The function `win32process.ResumeThread()` starts the actual execution.

`win32process.DEBUG_PROCESS`
`win32process.DEBUG_ONLY_THIS_PROCESS`

These flags are typically used by Windows debuggers. The creating process is assumed to be a debugger, and the system notifies the creator of certain debug-related events.

`win32process.DETACHED_PROCESS`

If the new process is a console application, the process is created without a console. This is often used to execute console programs in the background.

In addition, these flags can determine the new process's system priority. These flags include:

`win32process.HIGH_PRIORITY_CLASS`

Used for processes that perform time-critical operations. This should be used sparingly, as a single process at this priority could cause severe disruption to the operating system itself.

`win32process.IDLE_PRIORITY_CLASS`

Indicates the process need execute only while the machine is otherwise unused. Suitable for background operations that can execute slowly, but should not disrupt the normal operations of the machine.

`win32process.NORMAL_PRIORITY_CLASS`

Indicates a normal process with no special scheduling requirements.

`win32process.REALTIME_PRIORITY_CLASS`

> The new process has the highest possible priority. Threads at this priority preempt the threads of all other processes, including critical operating-system threads, such as the mouse driver or filesystem cache.

Environment

> The environment for the new process or **None** to inherit the environment of the calling process. If specified, this parameter must be a dictionary of string key/value pairs or Unicode string/value pairs.

CurrentDirectory

> A string that specifies the current drive and directory for the process or **None** to use the current drive and directory of the calling process.

StartupInfo

> A Python **STARTUPINFO** object that specifies information about the window for the new process. A default **STARTUPINFO** structure can be created by calling `win32process.STARTUPINFO()`, and if necessary, properties of this object can be set.

Result

procHandle

> A handle to the new process.

threadHandle

> A handle to the main thread in the new process.

procId

> The ID of the new process.

threadId

> The ID of the main thread in the new process.

TerminateProcess( )

Terminates the specified process and all its threads.

`TerminateProcess(processHandle, exitCode)`

Parameters

processHandle

> A handle to the process to be terminated. This handle must have sufficient permissions to terminate the process; otherwise an "access denied" Win32 exception will be thrown.

exitCode

> The integer exit code for the process. This exit code is returned to any program that requests it (e.g., as the return code from the `os.system()` function or via the `win32process.GetExitCodeProcess()` function.

GetProcessAffinityMask( )

Retrieves the process affinity mask for a process and the system affinity mask for the system.

```
processMask, systemMask = GetProcessAffinityMask(handle)
```

Parameters

handle

> A PyHANDLE or integer that represents the handle to the process for which the affinity mask is to be retrieved.

Result

processMask

> An integer representing the affinity mask for the specified process.

systemMask

> An integer representing the affinity mask for the system.

Comments

A *process affinity mask* is a bit mask in which each bit represents the processors on which a process is allowed to run. A *system affinity mask* is a bit mask in which each bit represents the processors that are configured in a system.

A process affinity mask is a subset of a system affinity mask. A process is allowed to run only on the processors configured into a system.

Under the Windows 95/98 family, both result masks are always set to 1.

SetProcessAffinityMask( )

Sets a processor affinity mask for the threads of a specified process.

```
SetProcessAffinityMask(handle, affinityMask)
```

Parameters

handle

> A PyHANDLE or integer that represents the handle to the process for which the affinity mask is to be set.

affinityMask

> An integer defining the new affinity mask for the process.

Comments

A process affinity mask is a bit mask in which each bit represents the processor on which the threads of the process are allowed to run. The value of the process affinity mask must be a proper subset of the system affinity mask values obtained by the `GetProcessAffinityMask()` function.

This function is supported only in the Windows 2000/NT families.

SetThreadAffinityMask( )

Sets the processor affinity mask for a thread.

```
oldMask = SetThreadAffinityMask(handle, affinityMask)
```

Parameters

`handle`

A `PyHANDLE` or integer that represents the handle to the thread for which the affinity mask is to be set.

`affinityMask`

For Windows NT/2000, an integer defining the new affinity mask for the thread. For Windows 95/98, this must be 1.

Result

On Windows NT/2000, the result is the previous affinity mask for the process. On Windows 95/98, the result is always 1.

SetPriorityClass( )

Sets the priority class for the specified process.

```
SetPriorityClass(handle, priorityClass)
```

Parameters

`handle`

A `PyHANDLE` or integer that represents the handle to the thread for which the affinity mask is to be set.

`priorityClass`

Specifies the priority class for the process. Specify one of the following values:

`win32process.ABOVE_NORMAL_PRIORITY_CLASS`

Windows 2000 only: indicates a process that has priority above `NORMAL_PRIORITY_CLASS` but below `HIGH_PRIORITY_CLASS`.

`win32process.BELOW_NORMAL_PRIORITY_CLASS`

Windows 2000 only: indicates a process that has priority above `IDLE_PRIORITY_CLASS` but below `NORMAL_PRIORITY_CLASS`.

`win32process.HIGH_PRIORITY_CLASS`

A process that performs time-critical tasks that must be executed immediately. The threads of the process preempt the threads of normal or idle priority class processes. An example is the Task List, which must respond quickly when called by the user, regardless of the load on the operating system. Use extreme care when using the high-priority class, because a high-priority class application can use nearly all available CPU time.

win32process.IDLE_PRIORITY_CLASS

Threads run only when the system is idle. The threads of the process are preempted by the threads of any process running in a higher priority class. An example is a screen saver. The idle-priority class is inherited by child processes.

win32process.NORMAL_PRIORITY_CLASS

No special scheduling needs.

win32process.REALTIME_PRIORITY_CLASS

The highest possible priority. The threads of the process preempt the threads of all other processes, including operating-system processes performing important tasks. For example, a real-time process that executes for more than a brief interval can cause disk caches not to flush or cause the mouse to be unresponsive.

Service-Related Modules

There are a number of Python modules related to Windows NT Services.

win32serviceutil Module

The `win32serviceutil` module is a higher-level interface to the Win32 Service functions. It builds on the `win32service` module to provide a more convenient interface to service-related functions.

ControlService( )

Connects to the Service Control Manager on the specified machine, then attempts to control the service.

```
status = ControlService(serviceName, code, machine = None)
```

Parameters

serviceName

The name of the service from which to obtain the status information.

code

The control code to send to the service. See the `win32service.ControlService()` function for further information.

machineName = None
> The name of the machine to connect to. If not specified, the current machine is used.

Result

The result is the same as for the **win32service.ControlService()** function.

QueryServiceStatus( )

Connects to the Service Control Manager on the specified machine, then queries the service status.

```
status = QueryServiceStatus(serviceName, machineName = None)
```

Parameters

serviceName
> The name of the service from which to obtain the status information.

machineName = None
> The name of the machine to connect to. If not specified, the current machine is used.

Result

The result is the same as the **win32service.QueryServiceStatus()** function's.

StartService( )

Connects to the Service Control Manager on the specified machine, then starts the service using the specified arguments.

```
StartService(serviceName, args = None, machineName = None)
```

Parameters

serviceName
> The name of the service to start.

args
> A sequence of strings defining the arguments for the service. May be **None** for no arguments.

machineName
> The name of the machine on which to start the service.

StopService( )

Connects to the Service Control Manager on the specified machine, then sends a SERVICE_CONTROL_STOP message to the specified service.

```
StopService(serviceName, machineName = None)
```

Parameters

serviceName
> The name of the service to stop.

machineName
> The name of the machine on which to stop the service.

win32service Module

The win32service module provides an interface to the low-level Windows NT Service-related functions.

OpenSCManager( )

Establishes a connection to the Service Control Manager on the specified computer and opens the specified SCM database.

```
handle = OpenSCManager(machineName, databaseName, desiredAccess)
```

Parameters

machineName
> Names the target computer. If None or an empty string, the function connects to the local computer.

databaseName
> Names the SCM database to open. If None, the database SERVICES_ACTIVE_DATABASE is used.

desiredAccess
> Specifies the access to the SCM. Any or all of the following flags can be used. The value win32service.SC_MANAGER_CONNECT is implied.
>
> win32service.SC_MANAGER_ALL_ACCESS
> > Includes STANDARD_RIGHTS_REQUIRED, plus the access types in this list.
>
> win32service.SC_MANAGER_CONNECT
> > Enables connecting to the SCM.
>
> win32service.SC_MANAGER_CREATE_SERVICE
> > Enables calling the win32service.CreateService() function to create a service and add it to the database.

win32service.SC_MANAGER_ENUMERATE_SERVICE

> Enables calling the win32service.EnumServicesStatus() function to list the services in the database.

win32service.SC_MANAGER_LOCK

> Enables calling the win32service.LockServiceDatabase() function to acquire a lock on the database.

win32service.SC_MANAGER_QUERY_LOCK_STATUS

> Enables calling the win32service.QueryServiceLockStatus() function to retrieve the lock status information for the database.

The following access types can also be used.

win32con.GENERIC_READ

> Combines the following access types: STANDARD_RIGHTS_READ, SC_MANAGER_ENUMERATE_SERVICE, and SC_MANAGER_QUERY_LOCK_STATUS.

win32con.GENERIC_WRITE

> Combines the following access types: STANDARD_RIGHTS_WRITE and SC_MANAGER_CREATE_SERVICE.

win32con.GENERIC_EXECUTE

> Combines the following access types: STANDARD_RIGHTS_EXECUTE, SC_MANAGER_CONNECT, and SC_MANAGER_LOCK.

Result

handle

> A handle to the SCM. When no longer needed, it should be closed with win32service.CloseServiceHandle().

OpenService( )

Opens a handle to an existing service.

`handle = OpenService(scHandle, serviceName, desiredAccess)`

scHandle

> A handle to the Service Control Manager, as obtained from win32service.OpenSCManager().

serviceName

> The name of the service to open. Service-name comparisons are case-insensitive.

desiredAccess

> Specifies the access to the service. Before granting the requested access, the system checks the access token of the calling process against the service object.

`win32service.SERVICE_ALL_ACCESS`

Includes `win32con.STANDARD_RIGHTS_REQUIRED` in addition to all the access types listed here.

`win32service.SERVICE_CHANGE_CONFIG`

Enables calling the `win32service.ChangeServiceConfig()` function to change the service configuration.

`win32service.SERVICE_ENUMERATE_DEPENDENTS`

Enables calling the `win32service.EnumDependentServices()` function to enumerate all the services dependent on the service.

`win32service.SERVICE_INTERROGATE`

Enables calling the `win32service.ControlService()` function to ask the service to report its status immediately.

`win32service.SERVICE_PAUSE_CONTINUE`

Enables calling the `win32service.ControlService()` function to pause or continue the service.

`win32service.SERVICE_QUERY_CONFIG`

Enables calling the `win32service.QueryServiceConfig()` function to query the service configuration.

`win32service.SERVICE_QUERY_STATUS`

Enables calling the `win32service.QueryServiceStatus()` function to ask the SCM about the status of the service.

`win32service.SERVICE_START`

Enables calling the `win32service.StartService()` function to start the service.

`win32service.SERVICE_STOP`

Enables calling the `win32service.ControlService()` function to stop the service.

`win32service.SERVICE_USER_DEFINED_CONTROL`

Enables calling the `win32service.ControlService()` function to specify a user-defined control code.

You may also specify any of the following standard access types:

`win32con.GENERIC_READ`

Combines the following access types: `STANDARD_RIGHTS_READ`, `SERVICE_QUERY_CONFIG`, `SERVICE_QUERY_STATUS`, and `SERVICE_ENUMERATE_DEPENDENTS`.

`win32con.GENERIC_WRITE`

Combines the following access types: `STANDARD_RIGHTS_WRITE` and `SERVICE_CHANGE_CONFIG`.

win32con.GENERIC_EXECUTE

>   Combines the following access types: STANDARD_RIGHTS_EXECUTE, SERVICE_START, SERVICE_STOP, SERVICE_PAUSE_CONTINUE, SERVICE_ INTERROGATE, and SERVICE_USER_DEFINED_CONTROL.

Result

handle

>   A handle to the service. This should be closed using win32service. CloseServiceHandle().

CloseServiceHandle( )

Closes a handle to a service or the Service Control Manager.

CloseServiceHandle(handle)

Parameters

handle

>   A handle obtained from win32service.OpenSCManager(), win32service. OpenService(), or win32service.CreateService().

ControlService( )

Sends control requests to a service.

status = ControlService(handle, code)

Parameters

handle

>   Handle to the service, as obtained from win32service.OpenService().

code

>   Specifies the requested control code. May be one of the following values:

win32service.SERVICE_CONTROL_STOP

>   Requests the service to stop. The handle must have SERVICE_STOP access.

win32service.SERVICE_CONTROL_PAUSE

>   Requests the service to pause. The handle must have SERVICE_PAUSE_ CONTINUE access.

win32service.SERVICE_CONTROL_CONTINUE

>   Requests the paused service to resume. The handle must have SERVICE_ PAUSE_CONTINUE access.

win32service.SERVICE_CONTROL_INTERROGATE

>   Requests the service to update immediately its current status information to the SCM. The handle must have SERVICE_INTERROGATE access.

Result

The result is a tuple in the same format as returned by the **win32service. QueryServiceStatus()** function.

QueryServiceStatus( )

Queries a service for status.

```
status = QueryServiceStatus(handle)
```

Parameters

handle
>   Handle to the service, as obtained from **win32service.OpenService()**.

Result

The result is a tuple with the following fields:

serviceType
>   A combination of the following flags:

>   **win32service.SERVICE_WIN32_OWN_PROCESS**
>>   Indicates a service that runs in its own process.

>   **win32service.SERVICE_WIN32_SHARE_PROCESS**
>>   Indicates a service that shares a process with other services.

>   **win32service.SERVICE_KERNEL_DRIVER**
>>   Indicates a device driver.

>   **win32service.SERVICE_FILE_SYSTEM_DRIVER**
>>   Indicates a filesystem driver.

>   **win32service.SERVICE_INTERACTIVE_PROCESS**
>>   A service process that can interact with the desktop.

currentState
>   A combination of the following flags:

>   **win32service.SERVICE_STOPPED**
>>   The service isn't running.

>   **win32service.SERVICE_START_PENDING**
>>   The service is starting.

>   **win32service.SERVICE_STOP_PENDING**
>>   The service is stopping.

>   **win32service.SERVICE_RUNNING**
>>   The service is running.

win32service.SERVICE_CONTINUE_PENDING

> The service continue is pending.

win32service.SERVICE_PAUSE_PENDING

> The service pause is pending.

win32service.SERVICE_PAUSED

> The service is paused.

controlsAccepted

A set of flags indicating the controls the service accepts:

win32service.SERVICE_ACCEPT_STOP

> The service can be stopped. This enables the SERVICE_CONTROL_STOP value.

win32service.SERVICE_ACCEPT_PAUSE_CONTINUE

> The service can be paused and continued. This enables the SERVICE_ CONTROL_PAUSE and SERVICE_CONTROL_CONTINUE values.

win32service.SERVICE_ACCEPT_SHUTDOWN

> The service is notified when system shutdown occurs. This enables the system to send a SERVICE_CONTROL_SHUTDOWN value to the service. The win32service.ControlService() function can't send this control code.

Windows 2000 supports additional flags. See the Windows NT documentation for further information.

win32ExitCode

A Win32 error code the service may set while it's starting or stopping. If this value is win32service.ERROR_SERVICE_SPECIFIC_ERROR, the next tuple item contains the service-specific error code.

serviceSpecificExitCode

An error code set by the service. This should be ignored unless the previous item is win32service.ERROR_SERVICE_SPECIFIC_ERROR.

checkPoint

A value the service periodically increments to report its progress during lengthy start, stop, pause, or continue operations. It's used primarily to indicate to the SCM that meaningful initialization or termination is still happening.

waitHint

Specifies an estimate of the amount of time, in milliseconds, that the service expects a pending start, stop, pause, or continue operation to take before the service makes its next call to the win32service.SetServiceStatus() function with either an incremented checkPoint value or a change in currentState.

StartService( )

Starts the service identified by the handle.

`StartService(handle, args)`

Parameters

handle

A handle to a service, as obtained from **win32service.OpenService()**.

args

A sequence of strings (or Unicode objects) to use as arguments to the service. **None** may be specified if no arguments are required.

servicemanager Module

The **servicemanager** module is implemented by the Python service framework; thus, there is no **servicemanager** file on disk, and the module is available only when code is running under the Service Control Manager. See Chapter 18, *Windows NT Services*, for more information.

LogMsg( )

Logs a specific message to the Event Log.

`LogMsg(errorType, eventId, inserts = ())`

Parameters

errorType

An integer that identifies the class of error. May be either the EVENTLOG_ERROR_TYPE, EVENTLOG_WARNING_TYPE, EVENTLOG_INFORMATION_TYPE, EVENTLOG_AUDIT_SUCCESS, or EVENTLOG_AUDIT_FAILURE constants from the **servicemanager** module.

eventId

The event ID, which can be any of the valid IDs listed in the messages section for this module.

inserts = ()

A sequence with the inserts for the message. Each sequence item must be a string and is replaced with the specified marker in the message text.

LogInfoMsg( )
LogWarningMsg( )
LogErrorMsg( )

Logs a generic informational, warning or error message to the Event Log.

```
LogInfoMsg(message)
LogWarningMsg(message)
LogErrorMsg(message)
```

Parameters

`message`

> A string containing the message to be written.

Messages

The `servicemanager` module contains embedded messages suitable to write to the Event Log using the methods described previously.

Message ID	Event Type	Message Text
0xFF	Error	%1
0x1000–PYS_SERVICE_STARTING	Information	The %1 service is starting %2.
0x1002–PYS_SERVICE_STARTED	Information	The %1 service has started %2.
0x1003–PYS_SERVICE_STOPPING	Information	The %1 service is stopping %2.
0x1004–PYS_SERVICE_STOPPED	Information	The %1 service has stopped %2.
1 to 9	Error	%1
1 to 9	Information	%1
1 to 9	Success	%1
1 to 9	Warning	%1

win32net Module

NetGroupGetInfo

Retrieves information about a particular global group in the security database.

```
data = NetGroupGetInfo(serverName, groupName, level)
```

Parameters

`serverName`

> A string specifying the name of the remote server on which the function is to execute. If this parameter is **None**, the local computer is used.

`groupName`

> A string specifying the name of the global group.

level
> An integer that specifies the information level of the returned data. May be 0, 1, or 2.

Result

The result is a dictionary, the contents of which are defined by one of the GROUP_ INFO structures, depending on the level parameter.

NetGroupGetUsers

Enumerates the users in a global group.

```
entries, total, resume = NetGroupGetUsers(serverName, groupName, level, resume = 0,
len=4096)
```

Parameters

serverName
> A string specifying the name of the remote server on which the function is to execute. If this parameter is None, the local computer is used.

groupName
> A string specifying the name of the global group.

level
> An integer that specifies the level of data to be returned for each group. Only 0 (zero) is currently valid.

resume
> A value that controls the iteration when there are a large number of servers to list. Zero should be passed the first time it's called, and while a non-zero resume result is returned from the function, it can be called again with the new resume value to obtain the rest of the servers.

len = 4096
> A hint to the Win32 function about how much data to allocate. See the Win32 documentation for more details.

Result

The result is a tuple with the following items:

entries
> A list of dictionaries of format GROUP_USERS_INFO_0, one for each user returned.

total
> The total number of items left to read before making the call. Thus, total- len(entries) are the number of entries left to read after this call.

resume

> A resume handle that can obtain the next set of users. When **resume** is zero, there are no more items to read.

NetGroupSetUsers( )

Sets the membership for the specified global group. Each user you specify is enrolled as a member of the global group. Users you don't specify, but who are currently members of the global group, will have their membership revoked.

```
NetGroupSetUsers(serverName, groupName ,level=0 , members)
```

Parameters

serverName

> A string specifying the name of the remote server on which the function is to execute. If this parameter is **None**, the local computer is used.

groupName

> A string specifying the name of the global group.

level

> An integer that specifies the data in the **members** parameter. Only 0 (zero) is currently valid.

members

> A sequence (for example, list or tuple) of dictionaries, each of which contains data that corresponds to the GROUP_USERS_INFO_0 structure.

NetGroupSetInfo( )

Sets information about a particular group account on a server.

```
NetGroupSetInfo(serverName, groupName, level, data)
```

Parameters

serverName

> A string specifying the name of the remote server on which the function is to execute. If this parameter is **None**, the local computer is used.

groupName

> A string specifying the name of the global group.

level

> An integer that specifies the data in the **data** parameter. May be 0, 1, 2, 1002, or 1005.

data

> A dictionary with the data for the group. The data is in the format of one of the GROUP_INFO structures, depending on the **level** parameter.

NetGroupAdd( )

Creates a new global group in the security database.

```
NetGroupAdd(serverName, level, data)
```

Parameters

serverName
> A string specifying the name of the remote server on which the function is to execute. If this parameter is **None**, the local computer is used.

level
> An integer that specifies the data in the **data** parameter. May be 0, 1, or 2.

data
> A dictionary with the data for the group. The data is in the format of one of the **GROUP_INFO** structures, depending on the **level** parameter.

NetGroupAddUser( )

Gives an existing user account membership in an existing global group in the security database.

```
NetGroupAddUser(serverName, groupName, userName)
```

Parameters

serverName
> A string specifying the name of the remote server on which the function is to execute. If this parameter is **None**, the local computer is used.

groupName
> A string specifying the name of the global group to which the user is to be given membership.

userName
> A string specifying the name of the user to be added to the group.

NetGroupDel( )

Deletes a global group from the security database.

```
NetGroupDel(serverName, groupName)
```

Parameters

serverName
> A string specifying the name of the remote server on which the function is to execute. If this parameter is **None**, the local computer is used.

groupName
> A string specifying the name of the global group to be deleted.

NetGroupDelUser( )

Deletes a user from the specified global group

`NetGroupDelUser(serverName, groupName, userName)`

Parameters

serverName

A string specifying the name of the remote server on which the function is to execute. If this parameter is **None**, the local computer is used.

groupName

A string specifying the name of the global group from which the user is to be removed.

userName

A string specifying the name of the user to be removed from to the group.

NetGroupEnum

Retrieves information about each global group in the security database.

`entries, total, resume = NetGroupEnum(serverName, level, resume = 0, len=4096)`

Parameters

serverName

A string specifying the name of the remote server on which the function is to execute. If this parameter is **None**, the local computer is used.

level

An integer that specifies the level of the data to be returned. May be 0, 1, or 2.

resume

A value that controls the iteration when there are a large number of servers to list. Zero should be passed the first time it's called, and while a non-zero **resume** result is returned from the function, it can be called again with the new **resume** value to obtain the rest of the servers.

len = 4096

A hint to the Win32 function about how much data to allocate. See the Win32 documentation for more details.

Result

The result is a tuple with the following items:

entries

A list of dictionaries in the format of one of the GROUP_INFO structures, depending on the `level` parameter, one for each group returned.

`total`

The total number of items left to read before making the call. Thus, `total-len(entries)` are the number of entries left to read after this call.

`resume`

A resume handle that can obtain the next set of users. When `resume` is zero, there are no more items to read.

NetLocalGroupAddMembers( )

Adds users to a local group.

```
NetLocalGroupAddMembers(serverName, groupName, level, members)
```

Parameters

`serverName`

A string specifying the name of the remote server on which the function is to execute. If this parameter is **None**, the local computer is used.

`groupName`

A string specifying the name of the global group.

`level`

An integer that specifies the data in the **members** parameter; can be 0 or 3.

`members`

A sequence (for example, list or tuple) of dictionaries, each of which contains data that corresponds to the relevant LOCALGROUP_MEMBERS_INFO structure, depending on the `level` parameter.

NetLocalGroupDelMembers( )

Deletes one or more users from a local group.

```
NetLocalGroupDelMembers(serverName, groupName, level, members)
```

Parameters

`serverName`

A string specifying the name of the remote server on which the function is to execute. If this parameter is **None**, the local computer is used.

`groupName`

A string specifying the name of the global group.

`level`

An integer that specifies the data in the **members** parameter; can be 0 or 3.

members

> A sequence (for example, list or tuple) of dictionaries, each of which contains data that corresponds to the relevant LOCALGROUP_MEMBERS_INFO structure, depending on the level parameter.

NetLocalGroupGetMembers

Enumerates the members in a local group.

```
entries, total, resume = NetLocalGroupGetMembers(serverName, groupName, level, resume
= 0, len=4096)
```

Parameters

serverName

> A string specifying the name of the remote server on which the function is to execute. If this parameter is None, the local computer is used.

groupName

> The name of the local group from which to enumerate the members.

level

> An integer that specifies the level of data to be returned. May be 0, 1, 2, or 3.

resume

> A value that controls the iteration when there are many servers to list. Zero should be passed the first time it's called, and while a non-zero resume result is returned from the function, it can be called again with the new resume value to obtain the rest of the servers.

len = 4096

> A hint to the Win32 function about how much data to allocate. See the Win32 documentation for more details.

Result

The result is a tuple with the following items:

entries

> A list of dictionaries in the format of one of the LOCALGROUP_MEMBERS_INFO structures; depending on the level parameter, one for each user returned.

total

> The total number of items left to read before making the call. Thus, total-len(entries) are the number of entries left to read after this call.

resume

> A resume handle that can obtain the next set of users. When resume is zero, there are no more items to read.

NetLocalGroupSetMembers( )

Sets the members of a local group. Any existing members not listed are removed.

`NetLocalGroupSetMembers(serverName, groupName, level, members)`

Parameters

serverName

A string specifying the name of the remote server on which the function is to execute. If this parameter is None, the local computer is used.

groupName

A string specifying the name of the global group.

level = 0

An integer that specifies the data in the members parameter. May be 0 or 3.

members

A sequence (for example, list or tuple) of dictionaries, each of which contains data that corresponds to one of the LOCALGROUP_MEMBERS_INFO structures.

NetMessageBufferSend( )

Sends a string to a registered message alias.

`NetMessageBufferSend(domain, userName, fromName, message)`

Parameters

serverName

A string specifying the name of the remote server on which the function is to execute. If this parameter is None, the local computer is used.

userName

The username or message alias to which the message should be sent.

fromName

A string that specifies the username or message alias from whom the message is from, or None for the logged-in user.

message

A string containing the message text.

NetServerEnum

Retrieves information about all servers of a specific type

`entries, total, resume = NetServerEnum(serverName, level, serverTypes=win32netcon.SV_`
`TYPE_ALL, resume = 0, len=4096)`

Parameters

serverName

The name of the server to execute on or **None** for the current machine.

level

An integer specifying the level of information requested; can be 101 or 102.

serverTypes

A bitmask of flags indicating the types of servers to list. A list of the common flags is presented here; please refer to the Win32 documentation for more details.

SV_TYPE_WORKSTATION

All Internet workstations.

SV_TYPE_SERVER

All Internet servers.

SV_TYPE_SQLSERVER

Any server running with Microsoft SQL Server.

SV_TYPE_DOMAIN_CTRL

Primary domain controller.

SV_TYPE_DOMAIN_BAKCTRL

Backup domain controller.

SV_TYPE_TIMESOURCE

Server running the time-source service.

SV_TYPE_PRINT

Server sharing print queue.

SV_TYPE_DIALIN

Server running dial-in service.

SV_TYPE_NT

Windows NT (either workstation or server).

SV_TYPE_SERVER_NT

Windows NT nondomain controller server.

SV_TYPE_DOMAIN_MASTER

Server running the domain master browser.

SV_TYPE_DOMAIN_ENUM

Primary domain.

SV_TYPE_WINDOWS

Windows 95 or later.

SV_TYPE_ALL

All servers.

resume
> A value that controls the iteration when there are many servers to list. Zero should be passed the first time it's called, and while a non-zero **resume** result is returned from the function, it can be called again with the new **resume** value to obtain the rest of the servers.

len = 4096
> A hint to the Win32 function about how much data to allocate. See the Win32 documentation for more details.

Result

The result is a tuple with the following items:

entries
> A list of dictionaries, each of the format define in one of the SERVER_INFO structures depending on the `level` parameter, one for each server returned.

total
> The total number of items left to read before making the call. Thus, total-len(entries) are the number of entries left to read after this call.

resume
> A resume handle that can obtain the next set of users. When **resume** is zero, there are no more items to read.

NetServerGetInfo

Retrieves information about a particular server.

```
data = NetServerGetInfo(serverName, level)
```

Parameters

serverName
> A string specifying the name of the remote server on which the function is to execute. If this parameter is **None**, the local computer is used.

level
> An integer that specifies the data returned by the function. May be 100, 101, or 102 on all platforms, 1 or 50 on Windows 95/98, or 402 or 403 for Windows 2000.

Result

The result is a dictionary in the format of one of the SERVER_INFO structures, depending on the `level` parameter.

NetServerSetInfo( )

Sets information about a particular server.

```
NetServerSetInfo(serverName, level, data)
```

Parameters

serverName

> A string specifying the name of the remote server on which the function is to execute. If this parameter is **None**, the local computer is used.

level

> An integer that specifies the data in the **data** parameter. May be one of 100, 101, 102, 402, or 403.

data

> A dictionary with the data for the server. The data is in the format of one of the SERVER_INFO structures, depending on the **level** parameter.

NetShareAdd( )

Adds a server resource.

```
NetShareAdd(serverName, level, data)
```

Parameters

serverName

> A string specifying the name of the remote server on which the function is to execute. If this parameter is **None**, the local computer is used.

level

> An integer that specifies the data in the **data** parameter. May be 2 or 502.

data

> A dictionary with the data for the server resource. The data is in the format of one of the SHARE_INFO structures, depending on the **level** parameter.

NetShareDel( )

Deletes a server resource.

```
NetShareDel(serverName, networkName)
```

Parameters

serverName

> A string specifying the name of the remote server on which the function is to execute. If this parameter is **None**, the local computer is used.

networkName

> A string specifying the resource name to be deleted.

NetShareCheck

Checks if server is sharing a device.

```
result, type = NetShareCheck(serverName, deviceName)
```

Parameters

serverName
> A string specifying the name of the remote server on which the function is to execute. If this parameter is **None**, the local computer is used.

deviceName
> A string specifying the name of the device to check for shared access

Result

result
> **true** if the device is shared, otherwise **false**.

type
> If result is **true**, indicates the type of device, and may be one of the following values:

> **win32net.STYPE_DISKTREE**
>> The device is a shared disk drive.

> **win32net.STYPE_PRINTQ**
>> The device is a shared print queue.

> **win32net.STYPE_DEVICE**
>> The device is a shared communications device.

> **win32net.STYPE_IPC**
>> An interprocess communication device.

> **win32net.STYPE_SPECIAL**
>> A special device.

NetShareEnum

Retrieves information about each shared resource on a server.

```
entries, total, resume = NetShareEnum(serverName, level, resume = 0, len=4096)
```

Parameters

serverName
> A string specifying the name of the remote server on which the function is to execute. If this parameter is **None**, the local computer is used.

level

> An integer that specifies the level of the data to be returned; may be 0, 1, 2, or 502.

resume

> A value that controls the iteration when there are many servers to list. Zero should be passed the first time it's called, and while a non-zero **resume** result is returned from the function, it can be called again with the new **resume** value to obtain the rest of the servers.

len = 4096

> A hint to the Win32 function about how much data to allocate. See the Win32 documentation for more details.

Result

The result is a tuple with the following items:

entries

> A list of dictionaries in the format of one of the **SHARE_INFO** structures, depending on the level parameter, one for each resource returned.

total

> The total number of items left to read before making the call. Thus, **total-len(entries)** are the number of entries left to read after this call.

resume

> A resume handle, that can be used to obtain the next set of users. When **resume** is zero, there are no more items to read.

NetShareGetInfo

Retrieves information about a particular share on a server.

```
data = NetShareGetInfo(serverName, networkName, level)
```

Parameters

serverName

> A string specifying the name of the remote server on which the function is to execute. If this parameter is **None**, the local computer is used.

networkName

> A string specifying the network name of the share on which to return information.

level

> An integer that specifies the data returned by the function. May be 0, 1, 2, 501, 502, or 1005.

Result

The result is a dictionary in the format of one of the SHARE_INFO structures, depending on the level parameter.

NetShareSetInfo( )

Sets information about a particular share on a server.

```
NetShareSetInfo(serverName, networkName, level, data)
```

Parameters

serverName

> A string specifying the name of the remote server on which the function is to execute. If this parameter is None, the local computer is used.

networkName

> A string specifying the network name to set.

level

> An integer that specifies the data in the **data** parameter. May be 1, 2, 502, 1004, 1006, or 1501.

data

> A dictionary with the data for the server. The data is in the format of one of the SHARE_INFO structures, depending on the level parameter.

NetUserAdd( )

Creates a new user account.

```
NetUserAdd(serverName, level, data)
```

Parameters

serverName

> A string specifying the name of the remote server on which the function is to execute. If this parameter is None, the local computer is used.

level

> An integer that specifies the data in the **data** parameter. May be 1, 2, or 3.

data

> A dictionary with the data for the server resource. The data must be in the format of the relevant USER_INFO structure, depending on the level parameter.

NetUserChangePassword( )

Changes a user's password on the specified domain.

```
NetUserChangePassword(serverName, userName, oldPassword, newPassword)
```

Parameters

serverName

A string specifying the name of a remote server or domain on which the account is changed. If this parameter is **None**, the logon domain of the caller is used.

userName

The username for which the password is to be changed or **None** for the current user.

oldPassword

The user's old password.

newPassword

The user's new password.

NetUserEnum

Provides information about all user accounts on a server.

```
entries, total, resume = NetUserEnum(serverName, level, filter=win32netcon.FILTER_
ACCOUNT_NORMAL resume = 0, len=4096)
```

Parameters

serverName

The name of the server to execute on or **None** for the current machine.

level

An integer specifying the level of information requested. This can be 0, 1, 2, 3, 10, 11, or 20.

filter

Specifies the account types to enumerate, which may be one of the following values:

FILTER_TEMP_DUPLICATE_ACCOUNT

Enumerates local user account data on a domain controller.

FILTER_NORMAL_ACCOUNT

Enumerates global user account data on a computer.

FILTER_INTERDOMAIN_TRUST_ACCOUNT

Enumerates domain trust account data on a domain controller.

FILTER_WORKSTATION_TRUST_ACCOUNT

Enumerates workstation or member server account data on a domain controller.

FILTER_SERVER_TRUST_ACCOUNT

Enumerates domain-controller account data on a domain controller.

Result

The result is a tuple with the following items:

`entries`
> A list of dictionaries, one for each user returned. Each dictionary is in the format specified by the relevant `USER_INFO` structure, depending on the `level` parameter.

`total`
> The total number of items left to read before making the call. Thus, `total-len(entries)` are the number of entries left to read after this call.

`resume`
> A resume handle, that can be used to obtain the next set of users. When `resume` is zero, there are no more items to read.

NetUserGetInfo

Retrieves information about a particular user account on a server.

`data = NetUserGetInfo(serverName, userName, level)`

`serverName`
> A string specifying the name of the remote server on which the function is to execute. If this parameter is `None`, the local computer is used.

`networkName`
> A string specifying the network name of the share on which to return information.

`level`
> An integer that specifies the data returned by the function. May be 0, 1, 2, 3, 10, 11, or 20.

Result

The result is a dictionary in the format of one of the `USER_INFO` structures, depending on the `level` parameter.

NetUserSetInfo( )

Sets information about a particular user account on a server.

`NetUserSetInfo(serverName, userName, level, data)`

Parameters

`serverName`
> A string specifying the name of the remote server on which the function is to execute. If this parameter is `None`, the local computer is used.

userName

A string specifying the username for which the information is to be set.

level

An integer that specifies the data in the **data** parameter. May be any level corresponding to a USER_INFO structure.

data

A dictionary with the data for the server. The data is in the format of one of the USER_INFO structures, depending on the **level** parameter.

NetUserDel( )

Deletes a user account from a server.

```
NetUserDel(serverName, userName)
```

Parameters

serverName

A string specifying the name of the remote server on which the function is to execute. If this parameter is None, the local computer is used.

userName

A string specifying the username to be deleted.

USER_INFO Structures

USER_INFO_0

Attribute Name	Description
name	Specifies the name of the user account. For the win32net. NetUserSetInfo() function, this member specifies the new username. The number of characters in the name can't exceed the value of win32netcon.UNLEN.

USER_INFO_1

Attribute Name	Description
name	A string that specifies the name of the user account. For the win32net.NetUserSetInfo() function, this member specifies the new username. The number of characters in the name can't exceed the value of win32netcon.UNLEN.
password	A string that specifies the password of the user.
password_age	An integer that specifies the number of seconds that have elapsed since the **password** member was last changed.

Attribute Name	Description
priv	One of three integer values specifying the level of privilege assigned the name member. May be one of win32netcon.USER_PRIV_GUEST, win32netcon.USER_PRIV_USER, or win32netcon.USER_PRIV_ADMIN.
home_dir	A string specifying the path of the home directory for the user. May be None.
comment	A string with a comment for the user, or None.
flags	An integer containing values that determine several features. May be any combination of the win32netcon.UF_ flags.
script_path	A string that specifies the path for the user's logon script file. The script file can be a *.cmd* file, an *.exe* file, or a *.bat* file. May also be None.

USER_INFO_2

Attribute Name	Description
name	A string that specifies the name of the user account. For the win32net.NetUserSetInfo() function, this member specifies the new username. The number of characters in the name can't exceed the value of win32netcon.UNLEN.
password	A string that specifies the password of the user.
password_age	An integer that specifies the number of seconds that have elapsed since the password member was last changed.
priv	One of three integer values specifying the level of privilege assigned the name member. May be one of win32netcon.USER_PRIV_GUEST, win32netcon.USER_PRIV_USER, or win32netcon.USER_PRIV_ADMIN.
home_dir	A string specifying the path of the home directory for the user. May be None.
comment	A string with a comment for the user, or None.
flags	An integer containing values that determine several features. May be any combination of the win32netcon.UF_ flags.
script_path	A string that specifies the path for the user's logon script file. The script file can be a *.cmd* file, an *.exe* file, or a *.bat* file. May also be None.
auth_flags	Specifies an unsigned long integer that contains values that specify the user's operator privileges. May be one of the win32netcon.AF_ constants.
full_name	A string containing the full name of the user.
usr_comment	A string that contains a user comment, or None.
parms	A string that's set aside for use by applications, including Microsoft applications. Don't modify this.
workstations	A string containing the names of workstations from which the user can log on. As many as eight names can be specified, and each is separated by a comma. None indicates there is no restriction.

Attribute Name	Description
last_logon	The number of seconds since Jan. 1, 1970 since the last logon by the user.
last_logoff	The number of seconds since Jan. 1, 1970 since the last logoff by the user, or zero if this information isn't known.
acct_expires	Specifies when the account will expire. Stored as the number of seconds since Jan. 1, 1970, and a value of win32netcon.TIMEQ_FOREVER indicates the account never expires.
max_storage	An integer that specifies the maximum amount of disk space the user can use. Use the value specified in win32netcon.USER_MAXSTORAGE_UNLIMITED to employ all available disk space.
units_per_week	Specifies the number of equal-length time units into which the week is divided in order to compute the length of the bit string in the logon_hours member.
logon_hours	A 21-byte (168 bits) bit string that specifies the times during which the user can log on. Each bit represents a unique hour in the week in Greenwich Mean Time (GMT). The first bit (bit 0, word 0) is Sunday, 0:00 to 0:59; the second bit (bit 1, word 0) is Sunday, 1:00 to 1:59; and so on. Note that bit 0 in word 0 represents Sunday from 0:00 to 0:59 only if you are in the GMT time zone. In all other cases you must adjust the bits according to your time zone offset (for example, GMT minus eight hours for Pacific Standard Time). None if there is no restriction.
bad_pw_count	Specifies the number of times the user tried to log on to the account using an incorrect password. A value of 0xFFFFFFFF indicates the value is unknown.
num_logons	Counts the number of successful times the user tried to log on to this account. A value of 0xFFFFFFFF indicates that the value is unknown.
logon_server	A string that contains the name of the server to which logon requests are sent. Server names should be preceded by two backslashes (\\). When the server name is indicated by an asterisk (*), the logon request can be handled by any logon server. None indicates that requests are sent to the domain controller.
country_code	Specifies the country code for the user's language of choice.
code_page	Specifies the code page for the user's language of choice.

USER_INFO_3

Attribute Name	Description
name	A string that specifies the name of the user account. For the win32net.NetUserSetInfo() function, this member specifies the new username. The number of characters in the name can't exceed the value of win32netcon.UNLEN.
password	A string that specifies the password of the user.
password_age	An integer that specifies the number of seconds have elapsed since the password member was last changed.

Attribute Name	Description
priv	One of three integer values specifying the level of privilege assigned the name member. May be one of win32netcon.USER_PRIV_ GUEST, win32netcon.USER_PRIV_USER, or win32netcon.USER_ PRIV_ADMIN.
home_dir	A string specifying the path of the home directory for the user. May be None.
comment	A string with a comment for the user, or None.
flags	An integer containing values that determine several features. May be any combination of the win32netcon.UF_ flags.
script_path	A string that specifies the path for the user's logon script file. The script file can be a *.cmd* file, an *.exe* file, or a *.bat* file. May also be None.
auth_flags	Specifies an unsigned long integer that contains values that specify the user's operator privileges. May be one of the win32netcon.AF_ constants.
full_name	A string containing the full name of the user.
usr_comment	A string that contains a user comment, or None.
parms	A string that's set aside for use by applications, including Microsoft applications. Don't modify this.
workstations	A string containing the names of workstations from which the user can log on. As many as eight names can be specified, and each is separated by a comma. None indicates there is no restriction.
last_logon	The number of seconds since Jan. 1, 1970 since the last logon by the user.
last_logoff	The number of seconds since Jan. 1, 1970 since the last logoff by the user, or zero if this information isn't known.
acct_expires	Specifies when the account will expire. Stored as the number of seconds since Jan. 1, 1970, and a value of win32netcon.TIMEQ_ FOREVER indicates the account never expires.
max_storage	An integer that specifies the maximum amount of disk space the user can use. Use the value specified in win32netcon.USER_ MAXSTORAGE_UNLIMITED to employ all available disk space.
units_per_week	Specifies the number of equal-length time units into which the week is divided in order to compute the length of the bit string in the logon_hours member.
logon_hours	A 21-byte (168 bits) bit string that specifies the times during which the user can log on. Each bit represents a unique hour in the week, in Greenwich Mean Time (GMT). The first bit (bit 0, word 0) is Sunday, 0:00 to 0:59; the second bit (bit 1, word 0) is Sunday, 1:00 to 1:59; and so on. Note that bit 0 in word 0 represents Sunday from 0:00 to 0:59 only if you are in the GMT time zone. In all other cases you must adjust the bits according to your time zone offset (for example, GMT minus eight hours for Pacific Standard Time). None if there is no restriction.

Attribute Name	Description
bad_pw_count	An integer that specifies the number of times the user tried to log on to the account using an incorrect password. A value of 0xFFFFFFFF indicates the value is unknown.
num_logons	Counts the number of successful times the user tried to log on to this account. A value of 0xFFFFFFFF indicates the value is unknown.
logon_server	A string that contains the name of the server to which logon requests are sent. Server names should be preceded by two backslashes (\\). When the server name is indicated by an asterisk (*), the logon request can be handled by any logon server. None indicates that requests are sent to the domain controller.
country_code	An integer that specifies the country code for the user's language of choice.
code_page	An integer that specifies the code page for the user's language of choice.
user_id	An integer that specifies the relative ID (RID) of the user. The RID is determined by the Security Account Manager (SAM) when the user is created. It uniquely defines this user account to SAM within the domain.
primary_group_id	An integer that specifies the RID of the primary global group for this user. For win32net.NetUserAdd(), this member must be win32netcon.DOMAIN_GROUP_RID_USERS. For win32net. NetUserSetInfo(), this member must be the RID of a global group in which the user is enrolled.
profile	A string that specifies the path to the user's profile. This value can be None, a local absolute path, or a UNC path.
home_dir_drive	A string that specifies the drive letter assigned to the user's home directory for logon purposes.
password_expired	An integer that determines whether the password of the user has expired. The win32net.NetUserGetInfo() and win32net. NetUserEnum() functions return zero if the password has not expired (and nonzero if it has). For win32net.NetUserAdd() or win32net.NetUserSetInfo(), specify nonzero to indicate that the user must change password at next logon. For win32net. NetUserSetInfo(), specify zero to turn off the message indicating that the user must change password at next logon. Note that you can't specify zero to negate the expiration of a password that has already expired.

USER_INFO_10

Attribute Name	Description
name	A string that specifies the name of the user account. The number of characters in the name can't exceed the value of win32netcon.UNLEN.
comment	A string with a comment for the user, or None.
full_name	A string containing the full name of the user.
usr_comment	A string that contains a user comment, or None.

USER_INFO_11

Attribute Name	Description
name	A string that specifies the name of the user account. The number of characters in the name can't exceed the value of win32netcon.UNLEN.
full_name	A string containing the full name of the user.
comment	A string with a comment for the user, or None.
usr_comment	A string that contains a user comment, or None.
priv	One of three integer values specifying the level of privilege assigned the name member. May be one of win32netcon.USER_PRIV_GUEST, win32netcon.USER_PRIV_USER, or win32netcon.USER_PRIV_ADMIN.
auth_flags	Specifies an unsigned long integer that contains values that specify the user's operator privileges. May be one of the win32netcon.AF_ constants.
password_age	An integer that specifies the number of seconds elapsed since the password member was last changed.
home_dir	A string specifying the path of the home directory for the user. May be None.
parms	A string that's set aside for use by applications, including Microsoft applications. Don't modify this.
last_logon	The number of seconds since Jan. 1, 1970 since the last logon by the user.
last_logoff	The number of seconds since Jan. 1, 1970 since the last logoff by the user, or zero if this information isn't known.
bad_pw_count	An integer that specifies the number of times the user tried to log on to the account using an incorrect password. A value of 0xFFFFFFFF indicates the value is unknown.
num_logons	Counts the number of successful times the user tried to log on to this account. A value of 0xFFFFFFFF indicates the value is unknown.
logon_server	A string that contains the name of the server to which logon requests are sent. Server names should be preceded by two backslashes (\\). When the server name is indicated by an asterisk (*), the logon request can be handled by any logon server. None indicates that requests are sent to the domain controller.
country_code	An integer that specifies the country code for the user's language of choice.
workstations	A string containing the names of workstations from which the user can log on. As many as eight names can be specified, and each is separated by a comma. None indicates there is no restriction.
max_storage	An integer that specifies the maximum amount of disk space the user can use. Use the value specified in win32netcon.USER_MAXSTORAGE_UNLIMITED to use all available disk space.
units_per_week	Specifies the number of equal-length time units into which the week is divided in order to compute the length of the bit string in the logon_hours member.

Attribute Name	Description
logon_hours	A 21-byte (168 bits) bit string that specifies the times during which the user can log on. Each bit represents a unique hour in the week, in Greenwich Mean Time (GMT). The first bit (bit 0, word 0) is Sunday, 0: 00 to 0:59; the second bit (bit 1, word 0) is Sunday, 1:00 to 1:59; and so on. Note that bit 0 in word 0 represents Sunday from 0:00 to 0:59 only if you are in the GMT time zone. In all other cases you must adjust the bits according to your time zone offset (for example, GMT minus eight hours for Pacific Standard Time). None if there is no restriction.
code_page	An integer that specifies the code page for the user's language of choice.

USER_INFO_20

Attribute Name	Description
name	A string that specifies the name of the user account. The number of characters in the name can't exceed the value of win32netcon.UNLEN.
full_name	A string containing the full name of the user.
comment	A string with a comment for the user, or None.
flags	An integer containing values that determine several features. May be any combination of the win32netcon.UF_ flags.
user_id	An integer that specifies the relative ID (RID) of the user. The RID is determined by the Security Account Manager (SAM) when the user is created. It uniquely defines this user account to SAM within the domain.

USER_INFO_1003

Attribute Name	Description
password	A string that specifies the password for the user.

USER_INFO_1005

Attribute Name	Description
priv	One of three integer values specifying the level of privilege assigned the name member. May be one of win32netcon.USER_PRIV_GUEST, win32netcon.USER_PRIV_USER, or win32netcon.USER_PRIV_ ADMIN.

USER_INFO_1006

Attribute Name	Description
home_dir	A string specifying the path of the home directory for the user. May be None.

USER_INFO_1007

Attribute Name	Description
comment	A string with a comment for the user or None.

USER_INFO_1008

Attribute Name	Description
flags	An integer containing values that determine several features. May be any combination of the win32netcon.UF_ flags.

USER_INFO_1009

Attribute Name	Description
script_path	A string that specifies the path for the user's logon script file. The script file can be a *.cmd* file, an *.exe* file, or a *.bat* file. May also be None.

USER_INFO_1010

Attribute Name	Description
auth_flags	Specifies an unsigned long integer that contains values that specify the user's operator privileges. May be one of the win32netcon.AF_ constants.

USER_INFO_1011

Attribute Name	Description
full_name	A string containing the full name of the user.

SERVER_INFO Structures

SERVER_INFO_100

Attribute Name	Description
platform_id	An integer that indicates the server platform.
name	A string indicating the name of the server.

SERVER_INFO_101

Attribute Name	Description
platform_id	An integer that indicates the server platform.
name	A string indicating the name of the server.

Attribute Name	Description
version_major	Specifies, in the least significant four bits of the byte, the major release version number of the operating system. The most significant four bits of the byte specifies the server type. The mask win32netcon.MAJOR_VERSION_MASK should be used to ensure correct results.
version_minor	Indicates the minor release version number of the operating system.
type	Describes the type of software the computer is running. This member can be one of the win32netcon.SV_TYPE_ constants.
comment	A string containing a comment for the server, or None.

SERVER_INFO_102

Attribute Name	Description
platform_id	An integer that indicates the server platform.
name	A string indicating the name of the server.
version_major	Specifies, in the least significant four bits of the byte, the major release version number of the operating system. The most significant four bits of the byte specifies the server type. The mask win32netcon.MAJOR_VERSION_MASK should be used to ensure correct results.
version_minor	Indicates the minor release version number of the operating system.
type	Describes the type of software the computer is running. This member can be one of the win32netcon.SV_TYPE_ constants.
comment	A string containing a comment for the server or None.
users	An integer that indicates the number of users who can attempt to log on to the system server. However, it's the license server that determines how many of these users can actually log on.
disc	Indicates the auto-disconnect time, in minutes. A session is disconnected if it's idle longer than the time specified. If the value is win32netcon.SV_NODISC, auto-disconnect isn't enabled.
hidden	Determines whether the server is visible to other computers in the same network domain. This member can be either win32netcon.SV_VISIBLE or win32netcon.SV_HIDDEN.
announce	An integer that specifies the network announce rate in seconds. This rate determines how often the server is announced to other computers on the network.
anndelta	An integer that specifies the delta value or change of the announce rate, in milliseconds. This value specifies how much the announce rate can vary from the time specified in the announce member.
licenses	Specifies the number of users per license. By default, this number is win32netcon.SV_USERS_PER_LICENSE.
userpath	A string specifying the path to user directories.

SERVER_INFO_402

Attribute Name	Description
ulist_mtime	An integer that indicates the last time (in seconds from 00:00:00, January 1,1970) the user list for servers running user-level security was modified.
glist_mtime	An integer that indicates the last time (in seconds from 00:00:00, January 1,1970) the group list for servers running user-level security was modified.
alist_mtime	An integer that indicates the last time (in seconds from 00:00:00, January 1,1970) the access control list for servers running user-level security was modified.
alerts	A string holding a list of usernames. Each name is separated by a space.
security	An integer that defines the security settings of the server; may be either win32netcon.SV_SHARESECURITY or win32netcon.SV_USERSECURITY.
numadmin	An integer that specifies how many administrators a server can accommodate at the same time.
lanmask	An integer that determines the order in which the network device drivers are served.
guestacct	A string specifying the name of a reserved guest user account for a server. The constant win32netcon.UNLEN specifies the maximum number of characters in the string.
chdevs	An integer that specifies how many character-oriented devices can be shared on the server.
chdevq	An integer that specifies how many character-oriented device queues can coexist on the server.
chdevjobs	An integer that specifies how many character-oriented device jobs can be pending on a server.
connections	An integer that specifies the number of connections to share names allowed on a server.
shares	An integer that specifies the number of share names a server can accommodate.
openfiles	An integer that specifies the number of files that can be open at once.
sessopens	An integer that specifies the number of files that can be open in one session.
sessvcs	An integer that specifies the maximum number of virtual circuits per client.
sessreqs	An integer that specifies the number of simultaneous requests a client can make on any virtual circuit.
opensearch	An integer that specifies the number of searches that can be open at once.
activelocks	An integer that specifies the number of file locks that can be active at the same time.

Attribute Name	Description
numreqbuf	An integer that specifies the number of server buffers provided.
sizreqbuf	An integer that specifies the size, in bytes, of each server buffer.
sizreqbuf	An integer that specifies the size, in bytes, of each server buffer.
numbigbuf	An integer that specifies the number of 64-KB server buffers provided.
numfiletasks	An integer that specifies the number of processes that can access the operating system at one time.
alertsched	An integer that specifies the interval, in seconds, at which to notify an administrator of a network event.
erroralert	An integer that specifies how many entries can be written to the error-log file during an interval specified in the **sv402_alertsched** before notifying an administrator.
logonalert	An integer that specifies how many invalid logon attempts to allow a user before notifying an administrator.
accessalert	An integer that specifies the number of invalid attempts to access a file to allow before notifying an administrator.
diskalert	An integer that specifies the number of kilobytes of free disk space remaining on the disk before the system sends a message to notify an administrator that free space for a disk is low.
netioalert	An integer that specifies, in tenths of a percent, the network I/O error ratio allowable before notifying an administrator.
maxauditsz	An integer that specifies, in kilobytes, the maximum size of the audit file. The audit file traces activity of the user.
srvheuristics	A string of flags that control operations on a server.

SERVER_INFO_403

Attribute Name	Description
ulist_mtime	An integer that indicates the last time (in seconds from 00:00:00, January 1,1970) the user list for servers running user-level security was modified.
glist_mtime	An integer that indicates the last time (in seconds from 00:00:00, January 1,1970) the group list for servers running user-level security was modified.
alist_mtime	An integer that indicates the last time (in seconds from 00:00:00, January 1,1970) the access control list for servers running user-level security was modified.
alerts	A string holding a list of usernames. Each name is separated by a space.
security	An integer that defines the security settings of the server; may be either win32netcon.SV_SHARESECURITY or win32netcon.SV_USERSECURITY.
numadmin	An integer that specifies how many administrators a server can accommodate at the same time.

Attribute Name	Description
lanmask	An integer that determines the order in which the network device drivers are served.
guestacct	A string specifying the name of a reserved guest user account for a server. The constant win32netcon.UNLEN specifies the maximum number of characters in the string.
chdevs	An integer that specifies how many character-oriented devices can be shared on the server.
chdevq	An integer that specifies how many character-oriented device queues can coexist on the server.
chdevjobs	An integer that specifies how many character-oriented device jobs can be pending on a server.
connections	An integer that specifies the number of connections to share names allowed on a server.
shares	An integer that specifies the number of share names a server can accommodate.
openfiles	An integer that specifies the number of files that can be open at once.
sessopens	An integer that specifies the number of files that can be open in one session.
sessvcs	An integer that specifies the maximum number of virtual circuits per client.
sessreqs	An integer that specifies the number of simultaneous requests a client can make on any virtual circuit.
opensearch	An integer that specifies the number of searches that can be open at once.
activelocks	An integer that specifies the number of file locks that can be active at the same time.
numreqbuf	An integer that specifies the number of server buffers provided.
sizreqbuf	An integer that specifies the size, in bytes, of each server buffer.
sizreqbuf	An integer that specifies the size, in bytes, of each server buffer.
numbigbuf	An integer that specifies the number of 64-KB server buffers provided.
numfiletasks	An integer that specifies the number of processes that can access the operating system at one time.
alertsched	An integer that specifies the interval, in seconds, at which to notify an administrator of a network event.
erroralert	An integer that specifies how many entries can be written to the error log file during an interval specified in the sv402_alertsched before notifying an administrator.
logonalert	An integer that specifies how many invalid logon attempts to allow a user before notifying an administrator.
accessalert	An integer that specifies the number of invalid attempts to access a file to allow before notifying an administrator.

Attribute Name	Description
diskalert	An integer that specifies the number of kilobytes of free disk space remaining on the disk before the system sends a message to notify an administrator that free space for a disk is low.
netioalert	An integer that specifies, in tenths of a percent, the network I/O error ratio allowable before notifying an administrator.
maxauditsz	An integer that specifies, in kilobytes, the maximum size of the audit file. The audit file traces activity of the user.
srvheuristics	A string of flags that control operations on a server.
auditedevents	An integer that specifies the audit event control mask.
autoprofile	Controls the action of the server on the profile. May be either win32netcon.SW_AUTOPROF_LOAD_MASK or win32netcon.SW_AUTOPROF_SAVE_MASK.
autopath	A string containing the path for the profile.

SERVER_INFO_502

Attribute Name	Description
sessopens	An integer that specifies the number of files that can be open in one session.
sessvcs	An integer that specifies the maximum number of virtual circuits per client.
opensearch	An integer that specifies the number of search operations that can be carried out simultaneously.
sizreqbuf	An integer that specifies the size, in bytes, of each server buffer.
initworkitems	An integer that specifies the initial number of receive buffers, or work items, used by the server. Allocating work items costs a certain amount of memory initially, but not as much as having to allocate additional buffers later.
maxworkitems	An integer that specifies the maximum number of receive buffers, or work items, the server can allocate.
rawworkitems	An integer that specifies the number of special work items for raw I/O the server uses. A larger value for this member can increase performance but costs more memory.
irpstacksize	An integer that specifies the number of stack locations in IRPs allocated by the server.
maxrawbuflen	An integer that specifies the maximum raw mode buffer size.
sessusers	An integer that specifies the maximum number of users that can be logged on to a server using a single virtual circuit.
sessconns	An integer that specifies the maximum number of tree connections that can be made on the server with one virtual circuit.
maxpagedmemoryusage	An integer that specifies the maximum size of pageable memory the server can have allocated at any time. Adjust this member if you want to administer memory quota control.

Attribute Name	Description
maxnonpagedmemoryusage	An integer that specifies the maximum size of nonpaged memory the server can have allocated at any time. Adjust this member if you want to administer memory quota control.
enablesoftcompat	An undocumented integer member. Please see the Win32 SDK for more details.
enableforcedlogoff	An integer that specifies whether the server should force a client to disconnect, even if the client has open files, once the client's logon time has expired.
timesource	An integer that specifies whether the server is a reliable time source.
acceptdownlevelapis	An integer that specifies whether the server will accept function calls from previous generation LAN Manager clients.
lmannounce	An integer that specifies the LAN Manager server announcement interval.

SERVER_INFO_503

Attribute Name	Description
sessopens	An integer that specifies the number of files that can be open in one session.
sessvcs	An integer that specifies the maximum number of virtual circuits per client.
opensearch	An integer that specifies the number of search operations that can be carried out simultaneously.
sizreqbuf	An integer that specifies the size, in bytes, of each server buffer.
initworkitems	An integer that specifies the initial number of receive buffers, or work items, used by the server. Allocating work items costs a certain amount of memory initially, but not as much as having to allocate additional buffers later.
maxworkitems	An integer that specifies the maximum number of receive buffers, or work items, the server can allocate.
rawworkitems	An integer that specifies the number of special work items for raw I/O the server uses. A larger value for this member can increase performance but costs more memory.
irpstacksize	An integer that specifies the number of stack locations in IRPs allocated by the server.
maxrawbuflen	An integer that specifies the maximum raw mode buffer size.
sessusers	An integer that specifies the maximum number of users that can be logged on to a server using a single virtual circuit.
sessconns	An integer that specifies the maximum number of tree connections that can be made on the server using a single virtual circuit.

Attribute Name	Description
maxpagedmemoryusage	An integer that specifies the maximum size of pageable memory the server can have allocated at any time. Adjust this member if you want to administer memory quota control.
maxnonpagedmemoryusage	An integer that specifies the maximum size of nonpaged memory the server can have allocated at any time. Adjust this member if you want to administer memory quota control.
enablesoftcompat	An undocumented integer member. Please see the Win32 API documentation for more details.
enableforcedlogoff	An integer that specifies whether the server should force a client to disconnect, even if the client has open files, once the client's logon time has expired.
timesource	An integer that specifies whether the server is a reliable time source.
acceptdownlevelapis	An integer that specifies whether the server will accept function calls from previous generation LAN Manager clients.
lmannounce	An integer that specifies the LAN Manager server announcement interval.
domain	A string that specifies the name of the server's domain.
maxcopyreadlen	An undocumented integer member. Please see the Win32 API documentation for more details.
maxcopywritelen	An undocumented integer member. Please see the Win32 API documentation for more details.
minkeepsearch	An undocumented integer member. Please see the Win32 API documentation for more details.
maxkeepsearch	An integer that specifies the length of time the server retains information about directory searches that have not ended.
minkeepcomplsearch	An undocumented integer member. Please see the Win32 API documentation for more details.
maxkeepcomplsearch	An undocumented integer member. Please see the Win32 API documentation for more details.
threadcountadd	An undocumented integer member. Please see the Win32 API documentation for more details.
numblockthreads	An undocumented integer member. Please see the Win32 API documentation for more details.
scavtimeout	An integer that specifies the time the scavenger remains idle before waking up to service requests. A smaller value for this member improves the response of the server to various events but costs CPU cycles.
minrcvqueue	An integer that specifies the minimum number of free receive work items needed by the server before it begins allocating more. A larger value for this member helps ensure there are always work items available, but a value that is too large is simply inefficient.

Attribute Name	Description
minfreeworkitems	Specifies the minimum number of available receive work items needed for the server to begin processing a server message block.
xactmemsize	An integer that specifies the size of the shared memory region that processes server functions.
threadpriority	An integer that specifies the priority of all server threads in relation to the base priority of the process. Higher priority can give better server performance at the cost of local responsiveness. Lower priority balances server needs with the needs of other processes on the system.
maxmpxct	An integer that specifies the maximum number of simultaneous requests any one client can send to the server. For example, 10 means you can have 10 unanswered requests at the server. When any single client has 10 requests queued within the server, the client must wait for a server response before sending another request.
oplockbreakwait	An integer that specifies the time to wait before timing out an opportunistic lock break request.
oplockbreakresponsewait	An integer that specifies the time to wait before timing out an opportunistic lock break request.
enableoplocks	An integer that specifies whether the server allows clients to use opportunistic locks on files. Opportunistic locks are a significant performance enhancement, but have the potential to cause lost cached data on some networks, particularly wide-area networks.
enableoplockforceclose	An undocumented integer member. Please see the Win32 API documentation for more details.
enablefcbopens	An integer that specifies whether several MS-DOS file control blocks (FCBs) are placed in a single location accessible by the server. This saves resources on the server.
enableraw	An integer that specifies whether the server processes raw server message blocks (SMBs). If enabled, this allows more data to transfer per transaction and also improves performance. However, it's possible that processing raw SMBs can impede performance on certain networks. The server maintains the value of this member.
enablesharednetdrives	An integer that specifies whether the server allows redirected server drives to be shared.
minfreeconnections	An integer that specifies the minimum number of connection structures the server sets aside to handle bursts of requests by clients to connect to the server.
maxfreeconnections	An integer that specifies the maximum number of connection structures the server sets aside to handle bursts of requests by clients to connect to the server.

GROUP_INFO Structures

GROUP_INFO_0

Attribute Name	Description
name	A string containing the group name.

GROUP_INFO_1

Attribute Name	Description
name	A string containing the group name.
comment	A string containing a comment for the group.

GROUP_INFO_2

Attribute Name	Description
name	A string containing the group name.
comment	A string containing a comment for the group.
group_id	An integer value that contains the relative identifier of the global group.
attributes	An integer that holds the attributes for the group.

GROUP_INFO_1002

Attribute Name	Description
comment	A string containing a comment for the group.

GROUP_INFO_1005

Attribute Name	Description
attributes	An integer that holds the attributes for the group.

GROUP_USERS_INFO Structures

GROUP_USERS_INFO_1

Attribute Name	Description
name	A string containing the group name.

LOCALGROUP_USERS_INFO Structures

LOCALGROUP_USERS_INFO_0

Attribute Name	Description
name	A string containing the name of a local group to which the user belongs.

LOCALGROUP_INFO Structures

LOCALGROUP_INFO_0

Attribute Name	Description
name	A string containing the local group name.

LOCALGROUP_INFO_1

Attribute Name	Description
name	A string containing the local group name.
comment	A string containing a comment for the local group.

LOCALGROUP_INFO_1002

Attribute Name	Description
comment	A string containing a comment for the local group.

LOCALGROUP_MEMBERS_INFO Structures

LOCALGROUP_MEMBERS_INFO_0

Attribute Name	Description
sid	A PySID object identifying the user.

LOCALGROUP_MEMBERS_INFO_1

Attribute Name	Description
sid	A PySID object identifying the user.
sidusage	Specifies the account type associated with the sid element. May be one of ntsecuritycon.SidTypeUser, ntsecuritycon.SidTypeGroup, ntsecuritycon.SidTypeWellKnownGroup, ntsecuritycon.SidTypeDeletedAccount, or ntsecuritycon.SidTypeUnknown.
name	The account name of the local group member identified by the sid.

LOCALGROUP_MEMBERS_INFO_2

Attribute Name	Description
sid	A PySID object identifying the user.
sidusage	Specifies the account type associated with the sid element.
domainandname	The domain and account name of the local group member identified by the sid.

LOCALGROUP_MEMBERS_INFO_3

Attribute Name	Description
domainandname	The domain and account name of the local group member identified by the sid.

C

The Python Database API Version 2.0

This appendix is a direct reproduction of Version 2.0 of the Python Database API. The same information can be found at *http://www.python.org/topics/database/DatabaseAPI-2.0.html*.

Footnotes are collected as endnotes at the end of the chapter, as in the online specification.

Python Database API Specification 2.0

This API has been defined to encourage similarity between the Python modules that access databases. By doing this, we hope to achieve a consistency leading to more easily understood modules, code that is generally more portable across databases, and a broader reach of database connectivity from Python.

The interface specification consists of several sections:

- Module interface
- Connection objects
- Cursor objects
- Type objects and constructors
- Implementation hints
- Major changes from 1.0 to 2.0

Comments and questions about this specification may be directed to the SIG for Database Interfacing with Python.

For more information on database interfacing with Python and available packages see the Database Topics Guide on *www.python.org*.

This document describes the Python Database API Specification 2.0. The previous Version 1.0 version is still available as reference. Package writers are encouraged to use this version of the specification as basis for new interfaces.

Module Interface

Access to the database is made available through connection objects. The module must provide the following constructor for these:

`connect(`*`parameters...`*`)`

> Constructor for creating a connection to the database. Returns a `Connection` object. It takes a number of parameters that are database dependent.[1]

These module globals must be defined:

`apilevel`

> String constant stating the supported DB API level. Currently only the strings 1.0 and 2.0 are allowed. If not given, a Database API 1.0 level interface should be assumed.

`threadsafety`

> Integer constant stating the level of thread safety the interface supports. Possible values are:
>
> 0 = Threads may not share the module.
>
> 1 = Threads may share the module, but not connections.
>
> 2 = Threads may share the module and connections.
>
> 3 = Threads may share the module, connections, and cursors.
>
> Sharing in this context means that two threads may use a resource without wrapping it using a mutex semaphore to implement resource locking. You can't always make external resources thread-safe by managing access using a mutex: the resource may rely on global variables or other external sources that are beyond your control.

`paramstyle`

> String constant stating the type of parameter marker formatting expected by the interface. Possible values are:[2]
>
> `qmark` = Question-mark style, e.g., ...WHERE name=?
>
> `numeric` = Numeric, positional style, e.g., ...WHERE name=:1
>
> `named` = Named style, e.g., ...WHERE name=:name
>
> `format` = ANSI C `printf` format codes, e.g., ...WHERE name=%s
>
> `pyformat` = Python extended format codes, e.g., ...WHERE name=%(name)s

The module should make all error information available through these exceptions or subclasses thereof:

Warning

Exception raised for important warnings such as data truncations while inserting, etc. It must be a subclass of the Python `StandardError` (defined in the module exceptions).

Error

Exception that is the base class of all other error exceptions. You can use this to catch all errors with one single `except` statement. Warnings are not considered errors and thus you should not use this class as base. It must be a subclass of the Python `StandardError` (defined in the module exceptions).

InterfaceError

Exception raised for errors that are related to the database interface rather than the database itself. It must be a subclass of `Error`.

DatabaseError

Exception raised for errors that are related to the database. It must be a subclass of `Error`.

DataError

Exception raised for errors that are due to problems with the processed data like division by zero, numeric value out of range, etc. It must be a subclass of `DatabaseError`.

OperationalError

Exception raised for errors that are related to the database's operation and not necessarily under the control of the programmer, e.g., an unexpected disconnect occurs, the data source name is not found, a transaction can't be processed, a memory allocation error occurred during processing, etc. It must be a subclass of `DatabaseError`.

IntegrityError

Exception raised when the relational integrity of the database is affected, e.g., a foreign key check fails. It must be a subclass of `DatabaseError`.

InternalError

Exception raised when the database encounters an internal error, e.g., the cursor is not valid anymore, the transaction is out of sync, etc. It must be a subclass of `DatabaseError`.

ProgrammingError

Exception raised for programming errors, e.g., table not found or already exists, syntax error in the SQL statement, wrong number of parameters specified, etc. It must be a subclass of `DatabaseError`.

`NotSupportedError`

> Exception raised in case a method or database API was used that is not supported by the database, e.g., requesting a `.rollback()` on a connection that doesn't support transaction or has transactions turned off. It must be a subclass of `DatabaseError`.

This is the exception inheritance layout:

```
StandardError
|__Warning
|__Error
    |__InterfaceError
    |__DatabaseError
        |__DataError
        |__OperationalError
        |__IntegrityError
        |__InternalError
        |__ProgrammingError
        |__NotSupportedError
```

The values of these exceptions are not defined. They should give the user a fairly good idea of what went wrong, though.

Connection Objects

`Connection` objects should respond to the following methods:

`close()`

> Closes the connection now (rather than whenever `__del__` is called). The connection is unusable from this point forward; an `Error` (or subclass) exception is raised if any operation is attempted with the connection. The same applies to all cursor objects trying to use the connection.

`commit()`

> Commits any pending transaction to the database. Note that if the database supports an auto-commit feature, this must be initially off. An interface method may be provided to turn it back on.
>
> Database modules that don't support transactions should implement this method with void functionality.

`rollback()`

> This method is optional since not all databases provide transaction support.[3]
>
> In case a database does provide transactions, this method causes the database to roll back to the start of any pending transaction. Closing a connection without committing the changes first causes an implicit rollback to be performed.

cursor()

> Returns a new Cursor object using the connection. If the database doesn't provide a direct cursor concept, the module has to emulate cursors using other means to the extent needed by this specification.[4]

Cursor Objects

These objects represent a database cursor, which manages the context of a fetch operation.

Cursor objects should respond to the following methods and attributes:

description

> This read-only attribute is a sequence of seven-item sequences. Each of these sequences contains information describing one result column: (*name*, *type_code*, *display_size*, *internal_size*, *precision*, *scale*, *null_ok*). This attribute is None for operations that don't return rows or if the cursor has not yet had an operation invoked via the executeXXX() method.
>
> The type_code can be interpreted by comparing it to the Type objects specified in the next section.

rowcount

> This read-only attribute specifies the number of rows the last executeXXX() produced (for DQL statements such as select) or affected (for DML statements such as update or insert).
>
> The attribute is –1 if no executeXXX() has been performed on the cursor or the row count of the last operation can't be determined by the interface.[7]

callproc(*procname[,parameters]*)

> This method is optional since not all databases provide stored procedures.[3]
>
> Calls a stored database procedure with the given name. The sequence of parameters must contain one entry for each argument the procedure expects. The result of the call is returned as modified copy of the input sequence. Input parameters are left untouched, output and input/output parameters are replaced with possibly new values.
>
> The procedure may also provide a result set as output. This must then be made available through the standard fetchXXX() methods.

close()

> Closes the cursor now (rather than whenever __del__ is called). The cursor is unusable from this point forward; an Error (or subclass) exception is raised if any operation is attempted with the cursor.

execute(*operation[,parameters]*)

Prepares and executes a database operation (query or command). Parameters may be provided as sequence or mapping and will be bound to variables in the operation. Variables are specified in a database-specific notation (see the module's **paramstyle** attribute for details).[5]

A reference to the operation is retained by the cursor. If the same operation object is passed in again, the cursor can optimize its behavior. This is most effective for algorithms where the same operation is used, but different parameters are bound to it (many times).

For maximum efficiency when reusing an operation, it's best to use the **setinputsizes**() method to specify the parameter types and sizes ahead of time. It's legal for a parameter to not match the predefined information; the implementation should compensate, possibly with a loss of efficiency.

The parameters may also be specified as a list of tuples to, for example, insert multiple rows in a single operation, but this kind of use is depreciated: executemany() should be used instead. Return values are not defined.

executemany(*operation,seq_of_parameters*)

Prepares a database operation (query or command) and then executes it against all parameter sequences or mappings found in the sequence *seq_of_parameters*.

Modules are free to implement this method using multiple calls to the execute() method or by using array operations to have the database process the sequence as a whole in one call. The same comments as for **execute**() also apply accordingly to this method. Return values aren't defined.

fetchone()

Fetches the next row of a query result set, returning a single sequence, or **None** when no more data is available.[6]

An **Error** (or subclass) exception is raised if the previous call to executeXXX() doesn't produce any result set or no call was issued.

fetchmany(*[size=cursor.arraysize]*)

Fetches the next set of rows of a query result, returning a sequence of sequences (e.g., a list of tuples). An empty sequence is returned when no more rows are available.

The number of rows to fetch per call is specified by the parameter. If it isn't given, the cursor's **arraysize** determines the number of rows to be fetched. The method should try to fetch as many rows as indicated by the size parameter. If this isn't possible due to the specified number of rows not being available, fewer rows may be returned.

An `Error` (or subclass) exception is raised if the previous call to `executeXXX()` doesn't produce any result set or no call was issued.

Note there are performance considerations involved with the `size` parameter. For optimal performance, it's usually best to use the `arraysize` attribute. If the size parameter is used, then it's best for it to retain the same value from one `fetchmany()` call to the next.

fetchall()

Fetches all (remaining) rows of a query result, returning them as a sequence of sequences (e.g., a list of tuples). The cursor's `arraysize` attribute can affect the performance of this operation.

An `Error` (or subclass) exception is raised if the previous call to `executeXXX()` doesn't produce any result set or no call was issued.

nextset()

This method is optional since not all databases support multiple result sets.[3] It makes the cursor skip to the next available set, discarding any remaining rows from the current set. If there are no more sets, the method returns `None`. Otherwise, it returns a `true` value and subsequent calls to the `fetch` methods return rows from the next result set.

An `Error` (or subclass) exception is raised if the previous call to `executeXXX()` doesn't produce any result set or no call was issued.

arraysize

This read/write attribute specifies the number of rows at a time to fetch with `fetchmany()`. It defaults to 1, meaning to fetch a single row at a time.

Implementations must observe this value with respect to the `fetchmany()` method but are free to interact with the database a single row at a time. It may also be used in the implementation of `executemany()`.

setinputsizes(sizes)

This can be used before a call to `executeXXX()` to predefine memory areas for the operation's parameters.

`sizes` is specified as a sequence: one item for each input parameter. The item should be a `Type` object that corresponds to the input used, or it should be an integer specifying the maximum length of a string parameter. If the item is `None`, no predefined memory area is reserved for that column (this is useful to avoid predefined areas for large inputs).

This method is used before the `executeXXX()` method is invoked. Implementations are free to have this method do nothing, and users are free to not use it.

```
setoutputsize(size[,column])
```
> Sets a column buffer size for fetches of large columns (e.g., LONGs, BLOBs, and so on). The column is specified as an index into the result sequence. Not specifying the column sets the default size for all large columns in the cursor.

> This method is used before the executeXXX() method is invoked. Implementations are free to have this method do nothing, and users are free to not use it.

Type Objects and Constructors

Many databases need to have the input in a particular format in order to bind to an operation's input parameters. For example, if an input is destined for a DATE column, it must be bound to the database in a particular string format. Similar problems exist for "Row ID" columns or large binary items (e.g., BLOBs or RAW columns). This presents problems for Python since the parameters to the executeXXX() method are untyped. When the database module sees a Python string object, it doesn't know if it should be bound as a simple CHAR column, as a raw BINARY item, or as a DATE.

To overcome this problem, a module must provide the constructors defined here to create objects that can hold special values. When passed to the cursor methods, the module can then detect the proper type of the input parameter and bind it accordingly.

A cursor object's description attribute returns information about each of the result columns of a query. The type_code must compare equal to one of type objects defined here. Type objects may be equal to more than one type code (e.g., DATETIME could be equal to the type codes for date, time, and timestamp columns; see the implementation hints later in this appendix for details).

The module exports the following constructors and singletons:

```
Date(year,month,day)
```
> This function constructs an object holding a date value.

```
Time(hour,minute,second)
```
> This function constructs an object holding a time value.

```
Timestamp(year,month,day,hour,minute,second)
```
> This function constructs an object holding a timestamp value.

```
DateFromTicks(ticks)
```
> This function constructs an object holding a date value from the given *ticks* value (number of seconds since the epoch; see the documentation of the standard Python time module for details).

TimeFromTicks(*ticks*)

This function constructs an object holding a time value from the given *ticks* value (number of seconds since the epoch; see the documentation of the standard Python time module for details).

TimestampFromTicks(*ticks*)

This function constructs an object holding a timestamp value from the given *ticks* value (number of seconds since the epoch; see the documentation of the standard Python time module for details).

Binary(*string*)

This function constructs an object capable of holding a binary (long) string value.

STRING

This type object describes columns in a database that are string-based (e.g., CHAR).

BINARY

This type object describes (long) binary columns in a database (e.g., LONG, RAW, BLOBs).

NUMBER

This type object describes numeric columns in a database.

DATETIME

This type object describes date/time columns in a database.

ROWID

This type object describes the "Row ID" column in a database.

SQL NULL values are represented by the Python None singleton on input and output.

Using Unix ticks for database interfacing can cause troubles because of the limited date range they cover.

Implementation Hints

The preferred object types for the date/time objects are those defined in the mxDateTime package. It provides all necessary constructors and methods both at Python and C level.

The preferred object type for binary objects are the buffer types available in standard Python starting with Version 1.5.2. Please see the Python documentation for details. For information about the C interface have a look at *Include/bufferobject.h* and *Objects/bufferobject.c* in the Python source distribution.

Here is a sample implementation of the Unix ticks based constructors for date/time delegating work to the generic constructors:

```
import time
def DateFromTicks(ticks):
    return apply(Date,time.localtime(ticks)[:3])
def TimeFromTicks(ticks):
    return apply(Time,time.localtime(ticks)[3:6])
def TimestampFromTicks(ticks):
    return apply(Timestamp,time.localtime(ticks)[:6])
```

This Python class allows implementing the above **type** objects even though the description type code field yields multiple values for on **type** object:

```
class DBAPITypeObject:
    def __init__(self,*values):
        self.values = values
    def __cmp__(self,other):
        if other in self.values:
            return 0
        if other < self.values:
            return 1
        else:
            return -1
```

The resulting **type** object compares equal to all values passed to the constructor.

Here is a snippet of Python code that implements the exception hierarchy defined previously:

```
import exceptions

class Error(exceptions.StandardError):
    pass

class Warning(exceptions.StandardError):
    pass

class InterfaceError(Error):
    pass

class DatabaseError(Error):
    pass

class InternalError(DatabaseError):
    pass

class OperationalError(DatabaseError):
    pass

class ProgrammingError(DatabaseError):
    pass

class IntegrityError(DatabaseError):
    pass
```

```
class DataError(DatabaseError):
    pass

class NotSupportedError(DatabaseError):
    pass
```

In C you can use the `PyErr_NewException(`*fullname*, *base*, *NULL*`)` API to create the exception objects.

Major Changes from Version 1.0 to Version 2.0

The Python Database API 2.0 introduces a few major changes compared to the 1.0 version. Because some of these changes will cause existing DB API 1.0-based scripts to break, the major version number was adjusted to reflect this change. These are the most important changes from 1.0 to 2.0:

- The need for a separate `dbi` module was dropped, and the functionality merged into the module interface itself.

- New constructors and `type` objects were added for date/time values, the `RAW` `type` object was renamed to `BINARY`. The resulting set should cover all basic data types commonly found in modern SQL databases.

- New constants (`apilevel`, `threadlevel`, `paramstyle`) and methods (`executemany`, `nextset`) were added to provide better database bindings.

- The semantics of `.callproc()` needed to call stored procedures are now clearly defined.

- The definition of the `.execute()` return value changed. Previously, the return value was based on the SQL statement type (which was hard to correctly implement); it's undefined now. Use the more flexible `.rowcount` attribute instead. Modules are free to return the old-style return values, but these are no longer mandated by the specification and should be considered database interface dependent.

- Class-based exceptions were incorporated into the specification. Module implementors are free to extend the exception layout defined in this specification by subclassing the defined exception classes.

Open Issues

Although the Version 2.0 specification clarifies a lot of questions that were left open in the 1.0 version, there are still some remaining issues:

- Define a useful return value for `.nextset()` for the case where a new result set is available.

- Create a fixed point numeric type for use as loss-less monetary and decimal interchange format.

Endnotes

1. As a guideline, the connection constructor parameters should be implemented as keyword parameters for more intuitive use and follow this order of parameters:

   dsn = Data source name as string
   user = User name as string (optional)
   password = Password as string (optional)
   host = Hostname (optional)
   database = Database name (optional)

   For example, a connect could look like this:

   ```
   connect(dsn='myhost:MYDB',user='guido',password='234$¶')
   ```

2. Module implementors should prefer `'numeric'`, `'named'` or `'pyformat'` over the other formats because these offer more clarity and flexibility.

3. If the database doesn't support the functionality required by the method, the interface should throw an exception in case the method is used.

   The preferred approach is to not implement the method and thus have Python generate an `AttributeError` in case the method is requested. This allows the programmer to check for database capabilities using the standard `hasattr()` function.

   For some dynamically configured interfaces, it may not be appropriate to require dynamically making the method available. These interfaces should then raise a `NotSupportedError` to indicate the inability to perform the rollback when the method is invoked.

4. A database interface may choose to support named cursors by allowing a string argument to the method. This feature is not part of the specification, since it complicates semantics of the `.fetchXXX()` methods.

5. The module uses the `__getitem__` method of the `parameters` object to map either positions (integers) or names (strings) to parameter values. This allows for both sequences and mappings to be used as input.

   The term "bound" refers to the process of binding an input value to a database execution buffer. In practical terms, this means that the input value is used directly as a value in the operation. The client should not be required to "escape" the value so that it can be used; the value should be equal to the actual database value.

6. Note that the interface may implement row fetching using arrays and other optimizations. It's not guaranteed that a call to this method will move only the associated cursor forward by one row.

7. The `rowcount` attribute may be coded in a way that updates its value dynamically. This can be useful for databases that return usable `rowcount` values only after the first call to a `.fetchXXX()` method.

D

Threads

Ahh, threads—those little things that seem so simple to understand and to use, but are so hard to use correctly. The less you have used threads, the simpler they appear, but speak to any experienced thread programmer, and they can regale you with tales of all-night sessions tracking down threading-related bugs nearly impossible to reproduce.

So why an appendix instead of a chapter? Indeed, the question should be why an appendix instead of a complete book! Threads are deceptively complex, usually due to the synchronization required between the different threads to help coordinate their activity. These considerations aren't specific to Windows, and there are plenty of excellent references available on threaded programming independent of the operating system or programming language available.

We make no attempt to cover the basics of thread programming. Instead, this appendix attempts to cover only some of the Windows specific threading-related issues. We don't attempt to teach thread programming, and certainly won't present any complex or real-world threaded examples. We simply restrict ourselves to discussions of threading-specific issues that may affect you when using Python on the Windows platform.

Python Thread Support

Python supports threads through a number of built-in modules. For many threading-related tasks, you are likely to find these modules more than adequate, your code is portable across all platforms that support threading, and you have access to the copious documentation and examples available.

The most general-purpose of these modules is the `threading` module, which provides an interface modeled after Java's threading support. This module provides a

`Thread` class to manage your threads and also a number of synchronization objects necessary in any nontrivial threading application.

Here's a trivial example using the `threading` module. Let's create a new thread as a subclass of the `threading.Thread` class and override the `run()` method that implements the thread. Each thread loops five times, printing a message each time. It should be noted that subclassing the `Thread` class is just one way to implement this thread; it's also possible to implement the new thread in a normal function.

The main thread creates three worker threads, then waits for them all to complete, using the `join()` method provided by the base class:

```
# SimpleThreads.py
#
# Trivial example of using the Python threading module.

import Threading
import time
import random

class SimpleThread(Threading.Thread):
    def run(self):
        for i in range(5):
            print self, i
            time.sleep(random.random())

if __name__=='__main__':
    threads = []
    for i in range(3):
        thread = SimpleThread()
        thread.start()
        threads.append(thread)
    # Now we wait for them to finish.
    for thread in threads:
        thread.join()
    print "All threads finished"
```

Running this script should produce output similar to:

```
<SimpleThread(Thread-8, started)> 0
<SimpleThread(Thread-9, started)> 0
<SimpleThread(Thread-10, started)> 0
<SimpleThread(Thread-8, started)> 1
<SimpleThread(Thread-10, started)> 1
<SimpleThread(Thread-8, started)> 2
<SimpleThread(Thread-9, started)> 1
<SimpleThread(Thread-9, started)> 2
<SimpleThread(Thread-10, started)> 2
<SimpleThread(Thread-8, started)> 3
<SimpleThread(Thread-10, started)> 3
<SimpleThread(Thread-9, started)> 3
<SimpleThread(Thread-8, started)> 4
```

```
<SimpleThread(Thread-10, started)> 4
<SimpleThread(Thread-9, started)> 4
All threads finished
```

As you can see, implementing, starting, and waiting for completion of threads is quite simple. Please see the Python documentation for more information on the `threading` module, including the various synchronization objects supported by the module.

Win32 Thread Support

As Python runs on many operating systems, the Python thread support is limited to a reasonable subset of what a platform can be expected to provide in the way of threading. Windows provides a number of additional features that relate to threads and synchronization, and we discuss some of these here.

Native Win32 Threads

The `win32process` module provides access to the `beginthreadex()` function provided by the Microsoft Visual C++ runtime library. This function allows you to specify a function as the thread, as well as some custom Win32 setting for the thread.

There are only a small number of situations when it's necessary to use this function in preference to the standard `threading` module. The first is when you need access to the Win32-specific features, such as the security for the object or flags that indicate the thread should be created in a suspended mode. Another common situation is when the main thread requires the Win32 `HANDLE` of the new thread; this is not easy using the other Python threading modules (where only the new thread itself has easy access to this information).

win32event Module

Each application has different synchronization requirements. Some programs may need to wait for threads to complete, while some threads may need to wait for a file operation to complete or mutexes to become available. To cater to these various requirements, Windows bases all its synchronization primitives around Windows `HANDLES`. When you wish to wait for something of significance, you usually pass a handle. For example, you can wait for a thread or process to complete by specifying its handle; you can wait for a file operation to complete by waiting on the handle in the `OVERLAPPED` object you specified. You can wait for the mutex, semaphore, event, or other objects by passing the handle you obtained when opening or creating the object. Thus, regardless of the type of object or event you are waiting for, you always use handles and can use the same Win32 functions.

There are three functions exposed by `win32event` that wait for Win32 objects: `WaitForSingleObject()`, `WaitForMultipleObjects()`, and `MsgWaitFor-MultipleObjects()`. Each of these functions allow you to wait for one or more handles to become *signaled*, but exactly what signaled means depends on the object. For example, a signaled synchronization object typically means you have acquired the object, a signaled thread or process handles mean the thread has terminated, and so forth.

Here are the three functions.

`WaitForSingleObject()`

> As the name implies, this function allows you to wait for a single object to become signaled. It takes two parameters; the handle to the object you wish to wait for, and a timeout in milliseconds (or `win32event.INFINITE` for no timeout). The return value from the function is `win32event.WAIT_OBJECT_0` if the object becomes signaled, `win32event.WAIT_TIMEOUT` if the timeout interval expired, or `win32event.WAIT_ABANDONED` in certain situations for mutexes (see the Win32 documentation).

`WaitForMultipleObjects()`

> Allows you wait for one or all of a number of objects. The first parameter is a sequence (e.g., list or tuple) of handles, while the second is a boolean flag indicating if you wish the function to return when all objects are signaled (`true`) or when any one of the objects becomes signaled (`false`). The third parameter is a timeout interval, as for `WaitForSingleObject()`. The return code from this function is similar to `WaitForSingleObject()`, except the result may range from `win32event.WAIT_OBJECT_0` to `win32event.WAIT_OBJECT_0 + len(handles)-1`. If you indicate you wish to wait for only one of the objects, this tells which object became signaled. Chapter 18, *Windows NT Services*, contains examples of using `WaitForMultipleObjects()` to wait for either a service control request or a client connection and demonstrates how to decode the return values.

`MsgWaitForMultipleObjects()`

> Almost identical to `WaitForMultipleObjects()` but also allows you to detect that a Windows message is ready to be processed by the thread. This information is particularly relevant for both GUI programs that make use of threading, and objects that use apartment-threaded COM objects, as described later in this appendix. Please see Appendix C, *The Python Database API Version 2.0*, for a description of these functions or the final sample in this appendix for an example of this function's usage.

The Python Thread Lock

Although Python fully supports threads, Python itself is not fully free-threaded. Python maintains an internal lock that prevents more than one thread from being inside the interpreter at one time. Although this initially sounds restricting, there are a number of reasons why it is less of a burden in practice.

Most real-world programs spend their time waiting on the external world (such as data to be read from a disk or input to arrive from the keyboard). Most Python functions (even in extension modules) that take significant time to execute, release the Python lock. This leaves other Python threads free to run while this thread is waiting for the call to complete.

On single-processor machines, there is only one thread on the system executing anyway; the operating system provides the illusion that the threads are running at the same time. For these machines, the Python thread lock typically doesn't impede threading performance.

For some applications, where multiple Python threads are waiting on some external relatively slow process that can take advantage of multiple processors (such as SQL database engines) you may still find that Python's threading model provides all the performance you need. However, if you are writing performance-critical applications that will run on multiprocessor computers, you should keep these threading restrictions in mind.

It should also be noted that Guido et al. are considering how to remove this threading restriction. Greg Stein made some experimental free-threaded patches for Python 1.4 that were the inspiration for some threading changes in Python 1.5, but at time of writing, debate is still continuing about exactly how to incorporate free-threading changes without severely impacting performance for single-threaded programs or on single-processor machines.

COM Threading Models

For various, and mainly historic, reasons, COM has the concept of threading models. Most often it's an implementation detail of little importance, so can safely be skipped by the casual COM user. A full discussion of COM's threading models is beyond the scope of this book (and seemingly beyond the scope of the COM documentation!), however some detailed information about this esoteric part of COM may help explain odd behavior you may encounter.

Apartment Living

Each object lives in what COM terms a threading apartment, of which there are two types, free-threaded and single-threaded. A process can have zero or one free-threaded apartments and any number of single-threaded apartments (one for each thread with a single-threaded object).

The apartment is nothing more than a conceptual framework invented by COM to explain the rules and other nuances of using threading with COM. An *apartment* is a grouping of objects by their threading characteristics. Before a thread can use COM, it must indicate its threading model (that is, if a new single-threaded apartment should be created, or if this thread should live in the free-threaded apartment). The apartment an object lives in is determined either by the implementation of the object or the thread that created the object, as we discuss later.

The point of the COM-threading models is to allow simple objects that aren't written with threads in mind to be used by another object that is thread-aware. If an object is written with the assumption that concurrent access to the object isn't possible, then using such an object from multiple threads is likely to be disastrous. Therefore, threads that reside in the same apartment can make unrestricted use of all objects in that apartment, but whenever threads from different apartments (that is, two threads that are not both in the free-threaded apartment) need to use an object, COM steps in. COM uses what is known as a *proxy* to automatically synchronize the threads so the object is correctly called from a thread in that object's apartment. COM also imposes rules to allow this mechanism to work.

What Apartment Do I Live in?

The obvious question to arise from this is "How do I control the apartment for my threads or objects?" There is no simple answer.

Fortunately, the rules for threads are quite simple. Before a thread can use COM, it must call one of the `CoInitialize()` or `CoInitializeEx()` functions and when it's done with COM, it must call `CoUninitialize()`; these functions are exposed to Python by the `pythoncom` module. `CoInitialize()` predates the COM threading models, so it initializes a new single-threaded apartment for the thread. `CoInitializeEx()` takes an additional parameter that allows you to specify the threading model; thus, you must use this function to have your thread in the free-threading apartment. The first single-threaded apartment created (that is, the first thread that calls either `CoInitialize()` or `CoInitializeEx()` with the `COINIT_APARTMENTTHREADED` flag) is given special significance as we discuss later, and is known as the main single-threaded apartment.

To hide some of this complexity, Python calls `CoInitializeEx()` automatically as soon as the **pythoncom** module is imported, and this is significant for the following reasons:

- The threading apartment for the first Python thread that imports the **pythoncom** module is controlled by this automatic process. By default, this thread is initialized in a single-threaded apartment, but this can be controlled by adding a `co_initflags` attribute to the **sys** module before importing **pythoncom** (see the final sample in this appendix). If this attribute exists, it's passed unchanged to the `CoInitializeEx()` function by the PythonCOM framework. For example, you could execute the following code to ensure the main thread is initialized in the multithreaded apartment:

```
import sys
sys.coinit_flags = 0 # pythoncom.COINIT_MULTITHREADED = 0
import pythoncom
```

- As the default behavior is to initialize a single-threaded apartment, this Python thread may also become the main single-threaded apartment, as discussed previously. The implications for the main single-threaded apartment are discussed later in this appendix.

- Only this main thread has `CoInitializeEx()` called automatically.[*] Any other threads you create need to call **pythoncom.CoInitializeEx()** explicitly before using COM and **pythoncom.CoUninitialize()** when complete.

The rules for which object an apartment lives in are slightly more complex. If the COM object in question is implemented in any way other than an `InProc` DLL (for example, a LocalServer or RemoteServer EXE-based object), the question becomes moot, as the object is running in a separate process, and therefore can not be in the same apartment. For DLL-implemented objects, the apartment is determined both by the apartment of the thread creating the object and the threading models actually supported by the object.

When an `InProc` object is registered, part of the information written to the registry is the threading models supported by the object. This can be either **Apartment**, to indicate the object must live in a single-threaded apartment, **Free** to indicate the object must live in the multithreaded apartment, or **Both** if the object supports either technique. As discussed in Chapter 12, *Advanced Python and COM*, this is controlled for Python objects via the **_reg_threading_** attribute, with the default for Python objects being **Both**.

If the thread creating the object and the object itself have compatible threading models, the object is created in the thread's apartment. If the object is an old COM

---

[*] `CoUninitialize()` isn't called for the main Python thread automatically, as doing so can often cause more problems than it solves. This function can still be called manually from the main thread.

object (indicated by the lack of threading information in the object's registration information) the object may be created in the main single-threaded apartment. If a multithreaded apartment needs to create a single-threaded object, COM automatically creates a new single-threaded apartment for the new object.

What Are the Apartment Rules?

For all this complicated machinery to work, there are a number of rules COM imposes on programs that use COM.

The synchronization of calls between different threads is achieved using Windows messages. This means that all threads in a single-threaded apartment must run a message loop to allow this mechanism to work. If the program is a GUI (such as PythonWin) this is no problem, but for most other applications, including Windows Services, this may not be an existing requirement. In practice, this means if any of your threads that exist in a single-threaded COM apartment need to wait on some synchronization object, you may need to use either the `win32event.MsgWaitForSingleObject()` or `win32event.MsgWaitForMultipleObjects()` calls so you can still process messages at the appropriate time. If you have no other message requirements, calling `pythoncom.PumpWaitingMessages()` processes all messages currently in the thread's queue. This technique is demonstrated in the example in the next section.

The other major rule imposed by the COM threading models is that it's illegal to pass COM interface pointers (and therefore the Python wrappers) between threads. As you may be passing the pointer from the same apartment to a different apartment, you may be avoiding or violating the synchronization mechanisms (and other optimizations) provided by COM. To pass interface objects between threads, you must use the `pythoncom.CoMarshalInterThreadInterface-InStream()` and `pythoncom.CoGetInterfaceAndReleaseStream()` functions to transfer objects between threads. These functions are demonstrated next.

Apartments Open for Inspection

It's time to demonstrate some of these concepts. To do this, we develop three COM objects, each of which support one of the various threading models discussed previously. These COM objects are quite simple and expose only two methods: `GetCreatedThreadId()` to return the thread ID of the thread that created the object, and `GetCurrentThreadId()` to return the thread ID of the current thread (that is, the thread receiving the call). If you have read Chapter 12, there will be nothing new in this example. The only points worth mentioning are that we use `win32api.GetCurrentThreadId()` to obtain the Win32 Thread ID,

and that we use a Python base class for the raw COM functionality, and subclasses for the object-specific registration information. The COM objects are implemented in *ThreadingModelsServer.py*:

```
# ThreadingModelsServer.py
# Python COM objects that demonstrate COM threading models.
#
# Exposes 3 Python objects, all of which have identical functionality,
# but each indicate they support different threading models.

import win32api
# A Base class for our 2 trivial objects.
class ThreadDemoObject:
    _public_methods_ = [ 'GetCurrentThreadId', 'GetCreatedThreadId' ]
    def __init__(self):
        self.created_id = win32api.GetCurrentThreadId()
    def GetCreatedThreadId(self):
        return self.created_id
    def GetCurrentThreadId(self):
        # Simply return an integer with the Win32 thread ID.
        return win32api.GetCurrentThreadId()

class ThreadApartmentObject(ThreadDemoObject):
    _reg_threading_ = "Apartment" # Tell COM to synchronize
    _reg_progid_ = "PythonThreadDemo.Apartment"
    _reg_clsid_ = "{511BB541-4625-11D3-855B-204C4F4F5020}"

class ThreadFreeObject(ThreadDemoObject):
    _reg_threading_ = "Free"
    _reg_progid_ = "PythonThreadDemo.Free"
    _reg_clsid_ = "{511BB542-4625-11D3-855B-204C4F4F5020}"

class ThreadBothObject(ThreadDemoObject):
    _reg_threading_ = "Both"
    _reg_progid_ = "PythonThreadDemo.Both"
    _reg_clsid_ = "{511BB543-4625-11D3-855B-204C4F4F5020}"

if __name__=='__main__':
    import win32com.server.register
    win32com.server.register.UseCommandLine(
                    ThreadApartmentObject,
                    ThreadFreeObject,
                    ThreadBothObject)
```

Before moving to the client sample code, these objects must be registered in the
normal way.

The code that uses these COM objects is considerably more complex because it's
here the COM object, and the threads that use it, are created. The general intent of
the code is to create the single-threaded object we defined and then create three
threads that use this object. The code confirms that so long as you follow the COM
rules, COM ensures that regardless of the thread actually calling the object, the

object will see the call on its single thread (i.e., the thread that created it.) You then execute the same code but create the free-threaded version of the object, and observe the differences.

Before launching into the code, there are some points to discuss:

- The main thread needs to wait for the subthreads to complete, but as you will be running single-threaded objects in the apartment, you need to process Windows messages. Therefore use the `win32process.beginthreadex()` function to create the thread, so that you can use the thread handles with `win32event.MsgWaitForMultipleObjects()`.

- All the threads exist in separate single-threaded apartments; the main thread because we haven't overridden the default Python initialization by setting `sys.coinit_flags`, and each worker thread because each calls `pythoncom.CoInitialize()` rather than `pythoncom.CoInitializeEx()`. Because all the threads are in different apartments, you must use the `CoMarshalInterThreadInterfaceInStream()` and `CoGetInterfaceAndReleaseStream()` functions to transfer the COM object between threads.

- `MsgWaitForMultipleObjects()` has a quirk that usually prevents effective use of the `bWaitAll` parameter. If set to `true`, the function waits until all objects have been signaled, and input is available. Generally, you need to know when all objects are signaled, or input is available. You can avoid this restriction by setting `bWaitAll` to `false`, and each time a thread completes remove its handle from the list before waiting again.

- The main body of the sample code accepts the name of the COM object as a parameter. This lets you run the same code with both the single-threaded and free-threaded versions of the COM object.

The code is presented in *SingleThreadedApartment.py*:

```
# SingleThreadedApartment.py
# Demonstrate the use of multiple threads, each in their own
# single-threaded apartment.

# As we do not set sys.coinit_flags=0
# before the Pythoncom import, Python
# initializes the main thread for single threading.
from pythoncom import \
     CoInitialize, CoUninitialize, IID_IDispatch,\
     CoMarshalInterThreadInterfaceInStream, \
     CoGetInterfaceAndReleaseStream, \
     PumpWaitingMessages

from win32event import \
     MsgWaitForMultipleObjects, \
     QS_ALLINPUT, WAIT_TIMEOUT, WAIT_OBJECT_0
```

```
from win32com.client import Dispatch
from win32process import beginthreadex
from win32api import GetCurrentThreadId

def Demo( prog_id ):
    # First create the object
    object = Dispatch(prog_id)
    print "Thread", GetCurrentThreadId(), "creating object"
    created_id = object.GetCreatedThreadId()
    print "Object reports it was created on thread", created_id
    # Now create the threads, remembering the handles.
    handles = []
    for i in range(3):
        # As we are not allowed to pass the object directly between
        # apartments, we need to marshal it.
        object_stream = CoMarshalInterThreadInterfaceInStream(
                        IID_IDispatch, object )
        # Build an argument tuple for the thread.
        args = (object_stream,)
        handle, id = beginthreadex(None, 0, WorkerThread, args, 0)
        handles.append(handle)
    # Now we have all the threads running, wait for them to terminate.
    # also remember how many times we are asked to pump messages.
    num_pumps = 0
    while handles:
        # A quirk in MsgWaitForMultipleObjects means we must wait
# for each event one at a time
        rc = MsgWaitForMultipleObjects(handles, 0, 5000, QS_ALLINPUT)
        if rc >= WAIT_OBJECT_0 and rc < WAIT_OBJECT_0+len(handles):
            # A thread finished - remove its handle.
            del handles[rc-WAIT_OBJECT_0]
        elif rc==WAIT_OBJECT_0 + len(handles):
            # Waiting message
            num_pumps = num_pumps + 1
            PumpWaitingMessages()
        else:
            print "Nothing seems to be happening",
            print "but I will keep waiting anyway..."
    print "Pumped messages", num_pumps, "times"
    print "Demo of", prog_id, "finished."


def WorkerThread(object_stream):
    # First step - initialize COM
    CoInitialize() # Single-threaded.
    # Unmarshal the IDispatch object.
    object = CoGetInterfaceAndReleaseStream(
        object_stream, IID_IDispatch)
    # The object we get back is a PyIDispatch, rather
    # than a friendly Dispatch instance, so we convert
    # to a usable object.
    object = Dispatch(object)
    this_id = GetCurrentThreadId()
    that_id = object.GetCurrentThreadId()
```

```
        message = "Thread is %d, and object is on thread %d" % \
                                     (this_id, that_id)
        print message
        # Be a good citizen and finalize COM, but
        # first remove our object references.
        object = None
        CoUninitialize()

if __name__=='__main__':
    print "Running with Apartment Threaded object"
    Demo("PythonThreadDemo.Apartment")
    print
    print "Running with Free Threaded object"
    Demo("PythonThreadDemo.Free")
```

You should run this code from a command prompt rather than PythonWin or IDLE, just to ensure that the threading doesn't interfere with these applications. When run, the output from this script should be similar to:

```
Running with Apartment Threaded object
Thread 355 creating object
Object reports it was created on thread 355
Thread is 354, and object is on thread 355
Thread is 314, and object is on thread 355
Thread is 306, and object is on thread 355
Pumped messages 9 times
Demo of PythonThreadDemo.Apartment finished.

Running with Free Threaded object
Thread 355 creating object
Object reports it was created on thread 318
Thread is 326, and object is on thread 433
Thread is 399, and object is on thread 433
Thread is 362, and object is on thread 318
Pumped messages 0 times
Demo of PythonThreadDemo.Free finished.
```

The output before the blank line represents the single-threaded object, so let's examine that first. The main Python thread reports itself as thread 355, and the object itself was also created on thread 355, as expected. Each of the three threads that started to use the object does indeed get a unique thread ID, but regardless of the thread making the call, the object always sees the call on thread 355, the thread that created the object. You can also see that while this simple test was running, and the main thread was waiting for the threads to terminate, you were called upon nine times to process Windows messages.

The output after the blank line represents the same test code, but uses the free-threaded object. As you can see, the same main thread is creating the COM object, but this time the object reports it was created on thread 318. As this thread is in a single-threaded apartment, and the COM object insists on a free-threading apartment, COM has spun up a new thread to host the object. As each thread calls the object, the object itself isn't restricted to receiving the call on a single thread. Because you're in different apartments the threads are still different, but the same single-threaded restrictions don't apply. Also notice that in this scenario, it's not strictly necessary to run a message pump, as there are no single-threaded COM objects being hosted on the main thread.

To help complete the picture, we now present a fully multithreaded example. It's almost identical to the one just presented, with the following changes:

- The main thread is forced into the free-threaded apartment by setting **sys. coinit_flags** to zero before importing **pythoncom**. Each worker thread is forced by calling **pythoncom.CoInitializeEx()**.

- Since all the threads are in the free-threading apartment, you can freely pass COM objects between threads and avoid those functions with the huge names!

- Since you don't need to process messages, replace the convoluted **MsgWaitForMultipleObjects()** call with a single **WaitForMultiple-Objects()** call. Ideally this code would use the Python threading model, but we've kept the basic code layout so it's easy to compare the differences.

The code is presented in *FreeThreadedApartment.py*:

```
# FreeThreadedApartment.py
# Demonstrate the use of multiple threads all in the same
# multithreading apartment.

# before the Pythoncom import, we specify free-threading.
import sys
sys.coinit_flags=0

from pythoncom import \
     CoInitializeEx, CoUninitialize, \
     COINIT_MULTITHREADED

from win32event import \
     WaitForMultipleObjects, \
     WAIT_ABANDONED

from win32com.client import Dispatch
from win32process import beginthreadex
from win32api import GetCurrentThreadId

def Demo( prog_id ):
    # First create the object
    object = Dispatch(prog_id)
    print "Thread", GetCurrentThreadId(), "creating object"
    created_id = object.GetCreatedThreadId()
    print "Object reports it was created on thread", created_id
    # Now create the threads, remembering the handles.
    handles = []
    for i in range(3):
```

```
                # Multi-threaded - just pass the objects directly to the thread.
                args = (object,)
                handle, id = beginthreadex(None, 0, WorkerThread, args, 0)
                handles.append(handle)
        # Now we have all the threads running, wait for them to terminate.
        # No need for message pump, so we can simply wait for all objects
        # in one call.
        rc = WaitForMultipleObjects(handles, 1, 5000)
        if rc == WAIT_ABANDONED:
            print "Gave up waiting for the threads to finish!"
        print "Demo of", prog_id, "finished."


    def WorkerThread(object):
        # First step - initialize COM
        CoInitializeEx(COINIT_MULTITHREADED)
        this_id = GetCurrentThreadId()
        that_id = object.GetCurrentThreadId()
        message = "Thread is %d, and object is on thread %d" % \
                                    (this_id, that_id)
        print message
        # Be a good citizen and finalize COM, but
        # first remove our object references.
        object = None
        CoUninitialize()


    if __name__=='__main__':
        print "Running Free threaded with Free Threaded object"
        Demo("PythonThreadDemo.Free")
```

When you run this script, the output should be similar to:

```
Running Free threaded with Free Threaded object
Thread 329 creating object
Object reports it was created on thread 329
Thread is 340, and object is on thread 340
Thread is 324, and object is on thread 324
Thread is 444, and object is on thread 444
Demo of PythonThreadDemo.Free finished.
```

This is exactly as expected: each call to the object is completely transparent, just like a regular function call, and always occurs on the thread that initiated the call. If you wish to get your hands even dirtier, you may wish to modify these examples to demonstrate every other possible combination of threads, objects, and threading apartments!

More Information on COM Threading

There are a number of technical articles and snippets from books available from Microsoft, from MSDN, or online at *http://msdn.microsoft.com/*. A good starting point for more information is Knowledge Base Article Q150777 (online at *http://support.microsoft.com/support/kb/articles/q150/7/77.asp*).

Threads and the User Interface

Windows has a fairly flexible threading interface when it comes to the windows and other parts of the user interface, but there are still a number of restrictions.

Almost any thread in the system can create a window, but only the thread that created the window can process messages for it. In addition, it's generally not a good idea to call window functions from threads other than the thread that created the window. Using the `PostMessage` functions is fine, but be careful using any function that either directly or indirectly causes a message to be sent a window bypassing the message queue. As this is a Win32 restriction rather than a Python one, the restriction applies whether you use PythonWin, Tkinter, wxPython or some other GUI framework on Win32.

Microsoft provide some excellent articles on threading considerations when using windows from the Win32 API, which you should review for further information.

Conclusion

This appendix has discussed some of the major threading issues you will encounter using Python on Win32. We have made absolutely no attempt to explain either thread programming in general, or the many threading and synchronization functions available on the Win32 platforms. We simply tried to explain the Python-specific issues when using these functions.

For further information on Python's standard threading capabilities, please see the Python documentation optionally installed with the Python binaries. For more information on the Win32 threading and synchronization capabilities, please see the Microsoft Win32 documentation.

Index

About the Authors

Mark Hammond is an independent Microsoft Windows consultant working out of Melbourne, Australia. He studied computer science at the South Australian Institute of Technology (now the University of South Australia), and then worked with several large financial institutions in Australia. He started his consulting operation in 1995.

Mark has produced many of the Windows extensions for Python, including PythonWin, Active Scripting, and Active Debugging support, and coauthored the COM framework and extensions. He is also a leading authority on Active Scripting and related technologies and has spoken on this subject at Microsoft's three most recent Professional Developers conferences.

Apart from being a father to his teenage daughter, having an interest in live music, and providing way-too-many free Python extensions, Mark has no life!

Andy Robinson is a London-based consultant specializing in business analysis, object-oriented design, and Windows development. He studied physics and philosophy, then Japanese studies at Oxford. He spent a year in advertising in Tokyo, two more in investment banking, and a long spell as the finance director of a startup in the sports industry. Observing that in all these positions he always ended up having to rewrite software, he moved to full-time computer consulting four years ago. He is currently helping one of the world's largest fund managers to internationalize their systems to handle Asian languages, developing Python systems for financial analysis, and reporting.

Back when Andy had spare time, his passions were track and field, and rock climbing. Right now his two sons Tim (2) and Harry (just arrived) are taking up all of his time.

Colophon

Our look is the result of reader comments, our own experimentation, and feedback from distribution channels. Distinctive covers complement our distinctive approach to technical topics, breathing personality and life into potentially dry subjects.

The animal on the cover of *Python Programming on Win32* is a caiman (caiman crocodilus). One of 23 species of crocodiles, the caiman lives primarily in the wetlands, flood plains, and river areas of Mexico and South America. They prefer less-traveled, low waters. Their diet consists of insects, fish, and small mammals.

A female builds a nest in the ground or in covered vegetation, and lays around 20 to 25 eggs in the late summer. Several females may share a nest, to help their young survive. After 90 days' gestation, the young hatch. They reach full maturity at around four to seven years of age. A caiman grows to be about four to six feet long.

Caiman young are yellow in color, while adults have a more olive-green color. In the past, caimans have been in danger due to habitat destruction, hunting, and pet trade, but some conservation efforts have helped bring their numbers up in recent years.

Mary Anne Weeks Mayo was the production editor for *Python Programming on Win32*. Colleen Gorman copyedited the book, and Jeff Holcomb and Jane Ellin provided quality control. Judy Hoer provided production assistance. Robert Romano and Rhon Porter created the illustrations using Adobe Photoshop 4 and Macromedia FreeHand 7. Brenda Miller wrote the index.

Edie Freedman designed the cover of this book, using a 19th-century engraving from the Dover Pictorial Archive. The cover layout was produced with Quark XPress 3.32 using the ITC Garamond font. Whenever possible, our books use RepKover™, a durable and flexible lay-flat binding. If the page count exceeds RepKover's limit, perfect binding is used.

Kathleen Wilson produced the cover layout with Quark XPress 3.3 using Adobe's ITC Garamond font. The interior layouts were designed by Edie Freedman and Nancy Priest, with modifications by Alicia Cech, and implemented in FrameMaker 5.5 by Mike Sierra. The text and heading fonts are ITC Garamond Light and Garamond Book. This colophon was written by Nicole Arigo.

O'REILLY™

O'Reilly & Associates, Inc.
101 Morris Street
Sebastopol, CA 95472-9902
1-800-998-9938

Visit us online at:
http://www.ora.com/
orders@ora.com

O'REILLY WOULD LIKE TO HEAR FROM YOU

Which book did this card come from?

Where did you buy this book?
- ❏ Bookstore
- ❏ Direct from O'Reilly
- ❏ Bundled with hardware/software
- ❏ Other _____
- ❏ Computer Store
- ❏ Class/seminar

What operating system do you use?
- ❏ UNIX
- ❏ Windows NT
- ❏ Other _____
- ❏ Macintosh
- ❏ PC(Windows/DOS)

What is your job description?
- ❏ System Administrator
- ❏ Network Administrator
- ❏ Web Developer
- ❏ Other _____
- ❏ Programmer
- ❏ Educator/Teacher

❏ Please send me O'Reilly's catalog, containing a complete listing of O'Reilly books and software.

Name _____   Company/Organization _____

Address _____

City _____   State _____   Zip/Postal Code _____   Country _____

Telephone _____   Internet or other email address (specify network) _____

Nineteenth century wood engraving
of a bear from the O'Reilly &
Associates Nutshell Handbook®
Using & Managing UUCP.

BUSINESS REPLY MAIL
FIRST CLASS MAIL   PERMIT NO. 80   SEBASTOPOL, CA

Postage will be paid by addressee

O'Reilly & Associates, Inc.
101 Morris Street
Sebastopol, CA 95472-9902